# COMPOSING PICTURES
## Donald W. Graham

SILMAN-JAMES PRESS　　LOS ANGELES

**For Jeanne**



First Silman-James Edition

10 9 8 7 6 5 4 3 2 1


Library of Congress Cataloging-in-Publication Data

Graham, Donald W.
  Composing pictures / Donald W. Graham. -- 1st Silman-James ed.
     p. cm.
  Originally published: New York : Van Nostrand Reinhold Co., c1970.
  ISBN 978-1-935247-00-5 (alk. paper)
  1. Composition (Art) I. Title.
  N7430.G67 2009
  701'.8--dc22
                              2009050803


Bound and printed in the United States of America.
Design Consultant: Marvin Rubin
Design by Donald W. Graham

Silman-James Press
1181 Angelo Drive
Beverly Hills, CA 90210
www.silmanjamespress.com

# COMPOSING PICTURES

# CONTENTS

# PREFACE

To compose is to bring order to the various graphic elements which make up a picture. This act is dynamic, alive. Because composing pictures is an art, it resists analysis or categorization. Pictures usually reflect an accumulation of information and experience impossible to document. How, then, can we attack a problem which cannot be formalized?

There seem to be two broad approaches to composition. First, an intuitive approach, which often is used by primitive artists and some children creating within their respective limits. This approach often is followed by young artists not yet fully aware of the subtle influences exerted upon them by all the pictures they see. Also certain highly skilled artists, steeped in a widely accumulated knowledge of pictures, may use the intuitive approach. This last group has reached the point where conscious knowledge has truly become subconscious. A statement by Picasso or Klee often may be termed intuitive, but this approach precludes direction from anyone, or any conscious conclusions drawn from observing the works of others.

The second approach may be said to be the conscious study of pictures. From such study may evolve a subconscious sense of order which becomes the foundation of the individual artist's personal creative statement. There is danger in such study, for to try to simulate the exact methods of another artist is in itself stifling, and always results in a sterile picture. Yet much as an artist prides himself upon his originality, he must admit that he has seen other pictures and has been influenced by them. Every artist has a cultural heritage, even if he attempts to reject it.

How we see pictures is the subject of this book. The way in which we interpret what we have seen and are stimulated to create original works is the personal responsibility of each of us, as artists, or as audience.

How can the young artist or the serious student of pictures profit from the extraordinary number of examples of graphic order available for study in galleries and in reproductions, yet still develop his own philosophy of picture making? During my forty-five years as an art instructor I have tried to cope with this problem.

In class, wall criticisms and individual criticism of work are constant aids to study. Individuals grasp ideas at different rates and puzzled students can ask questions or request review. But material in book form must stand alone. Although this book generally follows the sequence of material covered in class, the reader should study chapters and subjects in whatever order will best clarify the problem for him.

It should be noted that this book is not a history of art. Many fine artists are not represented, but this is not intended as a denial of their worth. Illustrations have been selected to show as clearly as possible the point discussed in the accompanying text, but other pictures by other fine artists might have served as well. Although many pictures shown are familiar to the professional artist, the young artist often has a limited picture vocabulary. The illustrations in this book should help to supplement this vocabulary.

I believe an indirect approach to composition is most sound. A picture cannot be weighed, measured, appraised, as we might a sack of potatoes. By seeing the picture in many ways, by seeing what the artist has done, we begin to develop an awareness, conscious as well as subconscious, of how a picture is made.

By studying and comparing many pictures we begin to find remarkable similarities. For this reason a point discussed in relation to one picture may often be apparent in a number of other illustrations in the book. Sometimes the apparent avoidance by an artist of certain graphic devices in a picture will open our eyes to other concepts. Only by making many comparisons do we learn to see.

Unlike many other treatises on composition, this book only rarely analyzes pictures in detail. Rather than demonstrating by dissection, I have tried to outline principles which, though not often apparent, have been understood by artists for centuries. It is startling to find that the better we understand pictures the more we find there is a common graphic language. No matter how complex pictures may be, they still reflect this common language even in totally different cultures.

This book is designed not only for the professional, but also for the young artist who has as yet not developed drawing to a high degree. Composition, like chess, depends upon the way the game is played rather than upon the elegance of the individual pieces, although these may contribute to our pleasure in the game. Very simple graphic symbols, even stick figures, when ordered compositionally can be quite adequate. In fact, very involved drawings often become so interesting in themselves that their relation to other symbols or to the picture structure often may be lost.

Therefore the diagrams in these notes are intentionally rough. By this means I have tried to demonstrate a principle in its simplest terms. Once understood the principle may be stated in more complex graphic terms. Often, of course, the more mature the artist the more simple and subtle his statement becomes.

I have included a short section on designing for film. In the limited space of a book on composing all types of pictures, only a small part can be devoted to the vast subject of motion pictures. Chapter 33 includes a short non-technical section outlining some problems characteristic of film graphics. But it must be emphasized that the study of film graphics should properly be explored not in book form, but on film. To attempt to demonstrate aspects of motion pictures in still pictures, or even a series of continuity drawings, is a paradox. The illustrations in this section should be studied with this limitation in mind.

Color in the book has been strictly limited to chapters in which its use is vital to discussion. It is hoped that the many fine art works reproduced here in black and white will be further studied in color, in books if not in the original pictures.

My gratitude to Jean Charlot who years ago opened my eyes to the many wonders of painting, and to whom I am indebted for many ideas incorporated in these notes; to Nelbert M. Chouinard my friend and employer who provided challenging work in her school with thousands of students; to Dean Albert F. Cruse for arranging time from teaching for me to make this book; and to Walt Disney who in his lifetime made possible years of independent research in all phases of drawing.

I wish to thank Marvin Rubin for designing the format of the book and for his innumerable suggestions on typography; Richard Barlow for many of the fine photographs, and Alexander Hovsepian for his generosity in putting his photographic services at my disposal.

I am indebted to Zachary Schwartz and T. Hee for their help in criticizing material devoted to the storyboard and film graphics, and to my many friends in the animation studios who have given so generously of their time and graphic material.

I also wish to thank those friends in the various fields of art who have contributed to my education, to Emerson Woelffer in helping me obtain reproductions, and especially Edward Reep for his interest, advice, and encouragement in bringing these notes to publication. And finally to Pamela Jeglinski and Roger Downing my gratitude for skillful and patient assistance, and to my wife, Phyllis, for devotion to myriad duties in creating this book.

Donald W. Graham
Topanga, California

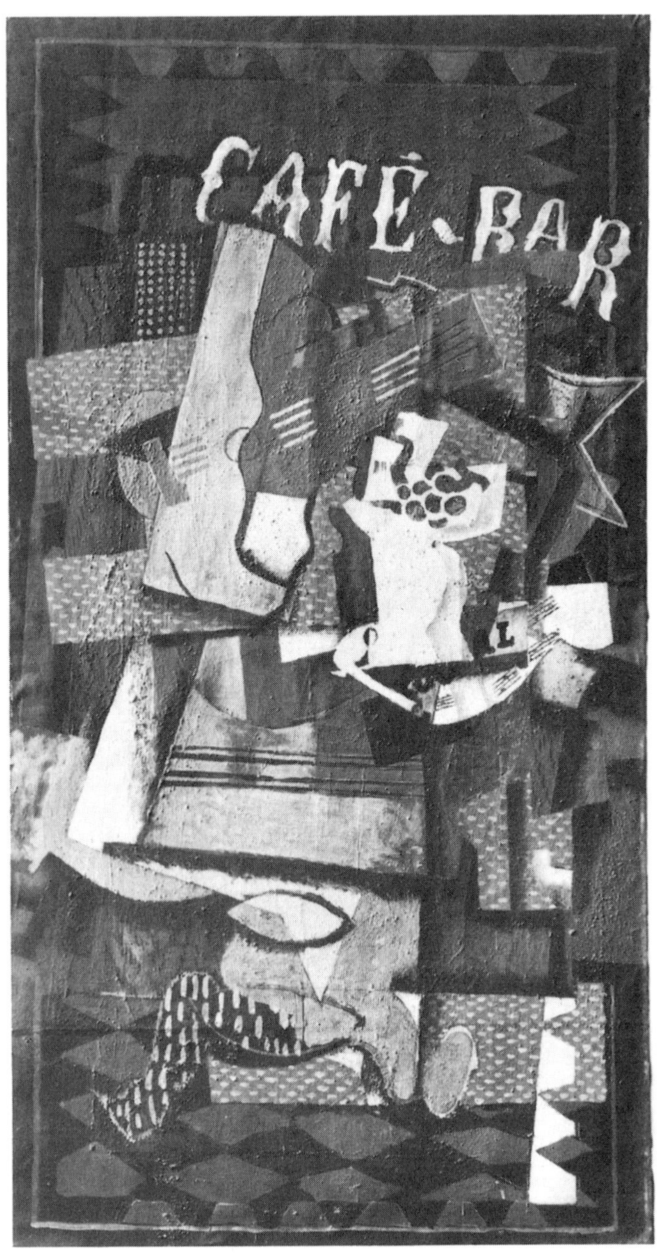

Georges Braque (French, 1882-1963)
CAFE-BAR, 1919; 62⅛″ x 31½″
oil on canvas
Kunstsammlung, Basel



# 1 The Subject

# I

# THE PICTURE

## The Two Parts of a Picture

Most of us take for granted that the world we see is three-dimensional. We seldom question our ability to judge depth or distance. If for no other reason than self-preservation we have learned to look both ways, then cross the street safely. We can distinguish threatening factors from friendly ones. For instance, we avoid touching a flame yet eagerly reach out to warm our hands at a fire. We live in a three-dimensional world and find it difficult to visualize any other kind.

Yet there is such another world for the graphic artist. Of course as a person he lives in a three-dimensional world as everyone does, but the world in which the artist really functions is his picture surface. And this world has only two dimensions. It is flat.

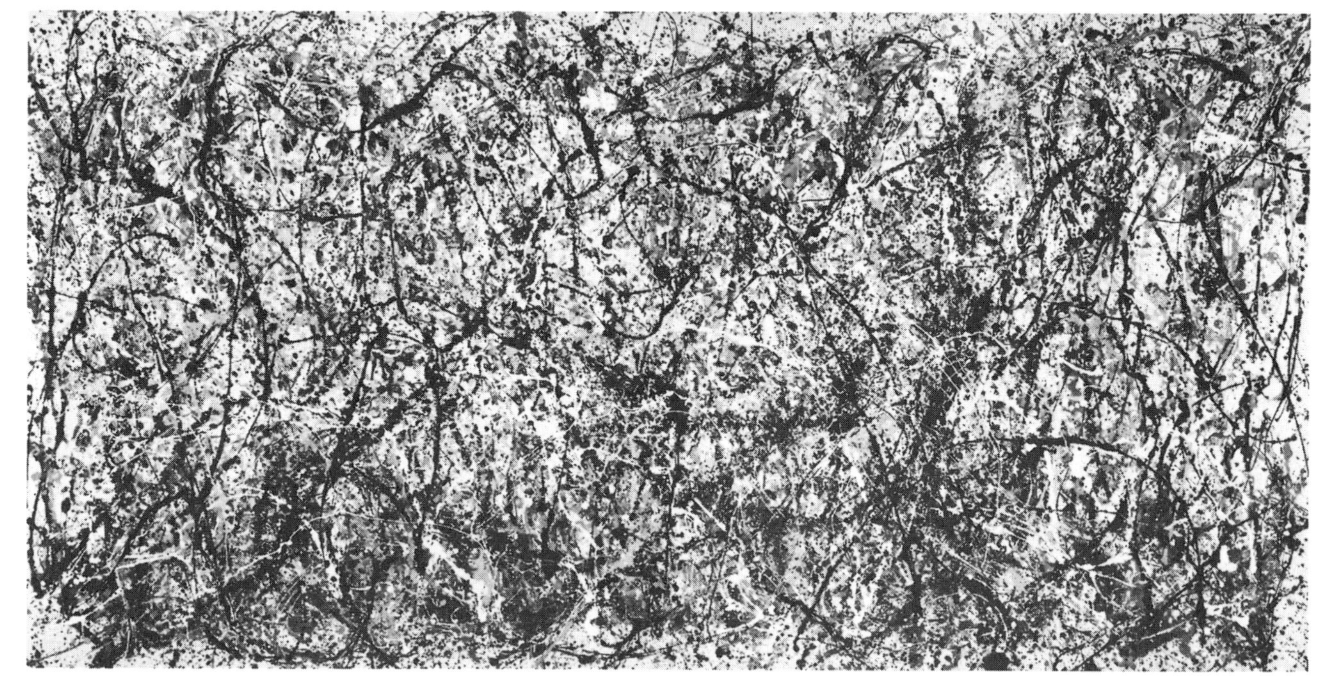

Jackson Pollock (American, 1912-1956)
ONE, 1950; 8' 9⅞" x 17' 5½"
oil and enamel paint on canvas
Collection The Museum of Modern Art, New York
Gift of Sidney Janis
(Photograph: Soichi Sunami)

The moment the artist begins to work on a picture he steps from three-dimensional reality into two-dimensional reality. His world is now made up of lines and areas, of colors, textures, and patterns. These elements lie upon the flat surface of his picture. They may be made to suggest depth and distance, such as a cloud-filled sky, yet at all times he can touch the painted clouds, or smear them with his finger.

This two-dimensional world of the artist, the picture, may be said to consist of two definite parts: the subject and the surface. The way he interprets these picture factors and the way he controls them graphically determine the basic structure of his picture.

## The Picture as Communication

We speak of a religious picture, a social statement, a portrait, a landscape—in each case suggesting the general content of the story told. Many representational pictures are allegorical, many are almost literary. Many such illustrative pictures may be simply dramatizations of a text.

Some pictures, like Braque's *Café-Bar*, though motivated by forms and events in nature, are not pictures of the forms or events, but are comments about them. They are abstract.

Other pictures stem from emotions aroused in the artist by real or imaginary occurrences. He often utilizes purely imaginary non-representational graphic elements in his picture and may even abandon reference to any visual experience we have ever had. Such pictures as Pollock's *One* arouse us emotionally in completely new ways.

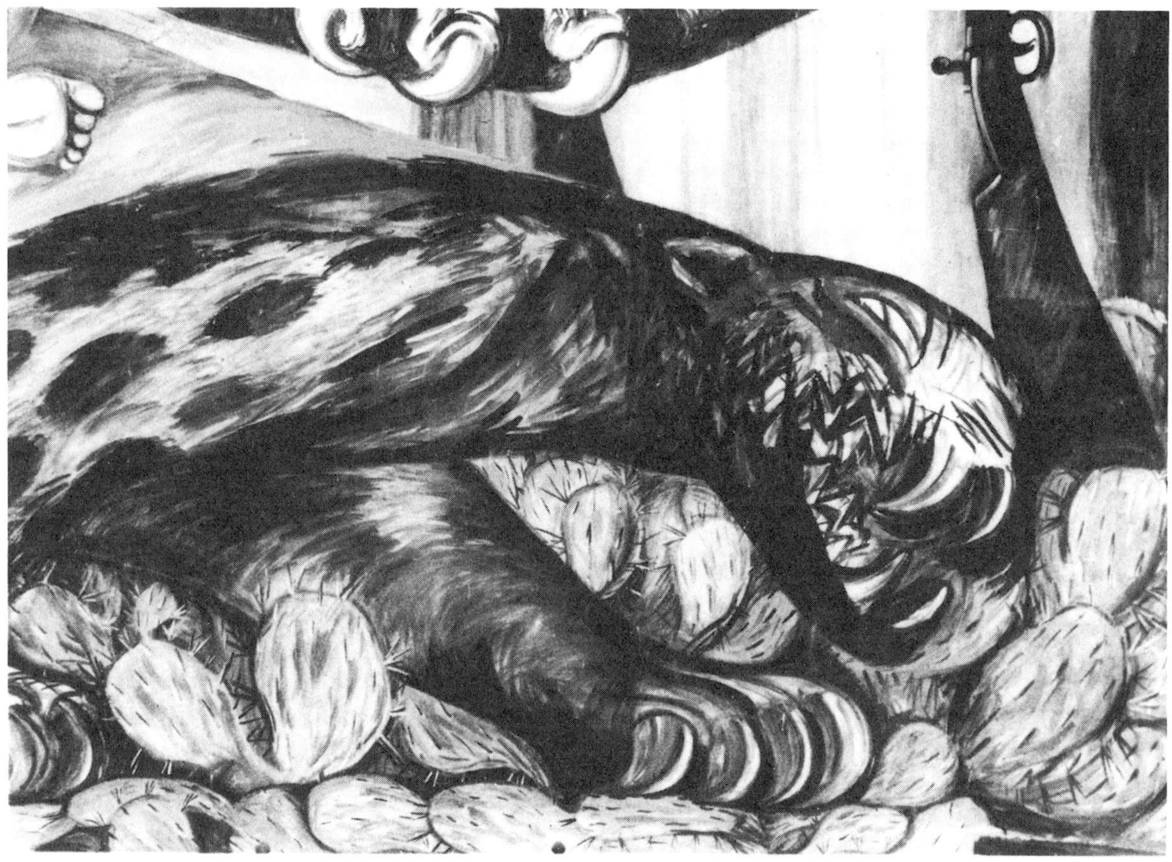

José Clemente Orozco (Mexican, 1883-1949)
Detail of Tiger, ALEGORIA DE LA MEXICANIDAD
fresco; mural in library, Jiquilpan
Courtesy Sr. Jorge Hernandez Campos
Instituto Nacional de Bellas Artes, Mexico, D. F.

(Photograph: Courtesy Manuel Alvarez Bravo, the Editorial
Fund for Mexican Plastic Arts, from the book *Mural Painting
of the Mexican Revolution 1921-1960*)

Whatever the story to be told, illustrative, abstract, or non-representational, there is always a message. Someone has gone to a lot of trouble to communicate with us. A picture is a story, a message. Sometimes the message is difficult to understand, for the picture may be completely non-representational, yet it is always there. Sometimes the message is for a limited audience. But even if the artist makes pictures only for himself and God, the message remains.

## Subject Matter

By subject matter we mean the factors, real or imaginary, which motivate the artist to make a picture. An artist may be impelled to make a picture of a dream, a bunch of grapes, a sunset, or marching soldiers. Sometimes a rock formation, a patch of grass, a disordered array of strewn newspapers may suggest picture forms that have little or no direct relation to what the artist actually sees. Or the motivation may be a sensation, a mood, an emotional need within the artist himself. Whatever the motivation, the subject matter is first recorded in the artist's mind, then translated into picture terms.

## Graphic Subject Matter

The artist must find ways to disturb his picture surface so that subject matter may be stated graphically. This organization of graphic elements, points, lines, and areas on or projected on the picture surface constitutes graphic subject matter.

We should note that subject matter usually refers to a thing or event in nature which moves the artist to make a picture. Graphic subject

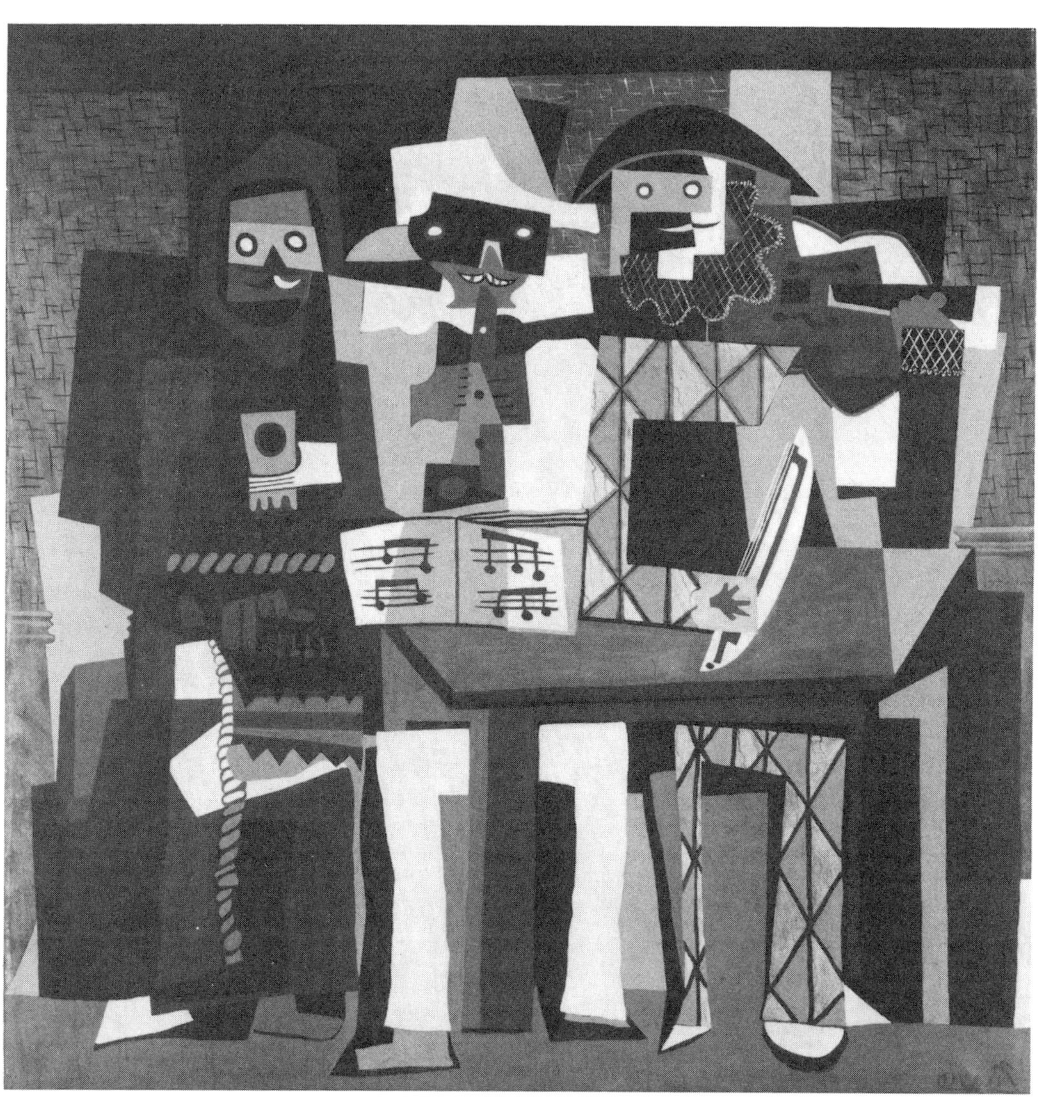

Pablo Picasso (Spanish, 1881- )
THE THREE MUSICIANS, 1921; 80″ x 74″
oil on canvas
Philadelphia Museum of Art; A. E. Gallatin Coll.
(Photograph: A. J. Wyatt)

matter encompasses the total graphic content of the picture, anything the artist paints, draws, or projects on the surface.

Graphic subject matter may give only a suggestion of a recognizable subject in nature, as we find in the Orozco above. In the case of non-representational pictures there may be no reference to nature at all.

Graphic subject matter may consist of but a single element on a surface, or it may be complex, made up of hundreds of elements involving intricate graphic organizations, that result in the illusion of great depth.

Most artists have found that a suggestion of something familiar in the picture reassures the viewer, although this is by no means the rule, as the many successful non-representational pictures prove. It is remarkable that in

the work of Picasso, who has explored so many facets of graphics, there are few examples that do not contain at least a subtle reference to something familiar to us.

However, when graphic subject matter becomes too realistic, too representational, as in some illustrations or film, there is danger of losing our interest in the picture. There is little graphic organization to hold our attention or to stir us emotionally beyond the likeness of the subject matter.

If the purpose of the picture is to inform or instruct, as in catalog illustrations, text diagrams or educational film, then subject matter may be more important than graphic organizations that arouse us emotionally. If, however, the picture should excite and not merely inform, then strong subject matter appeal may stand in the way.

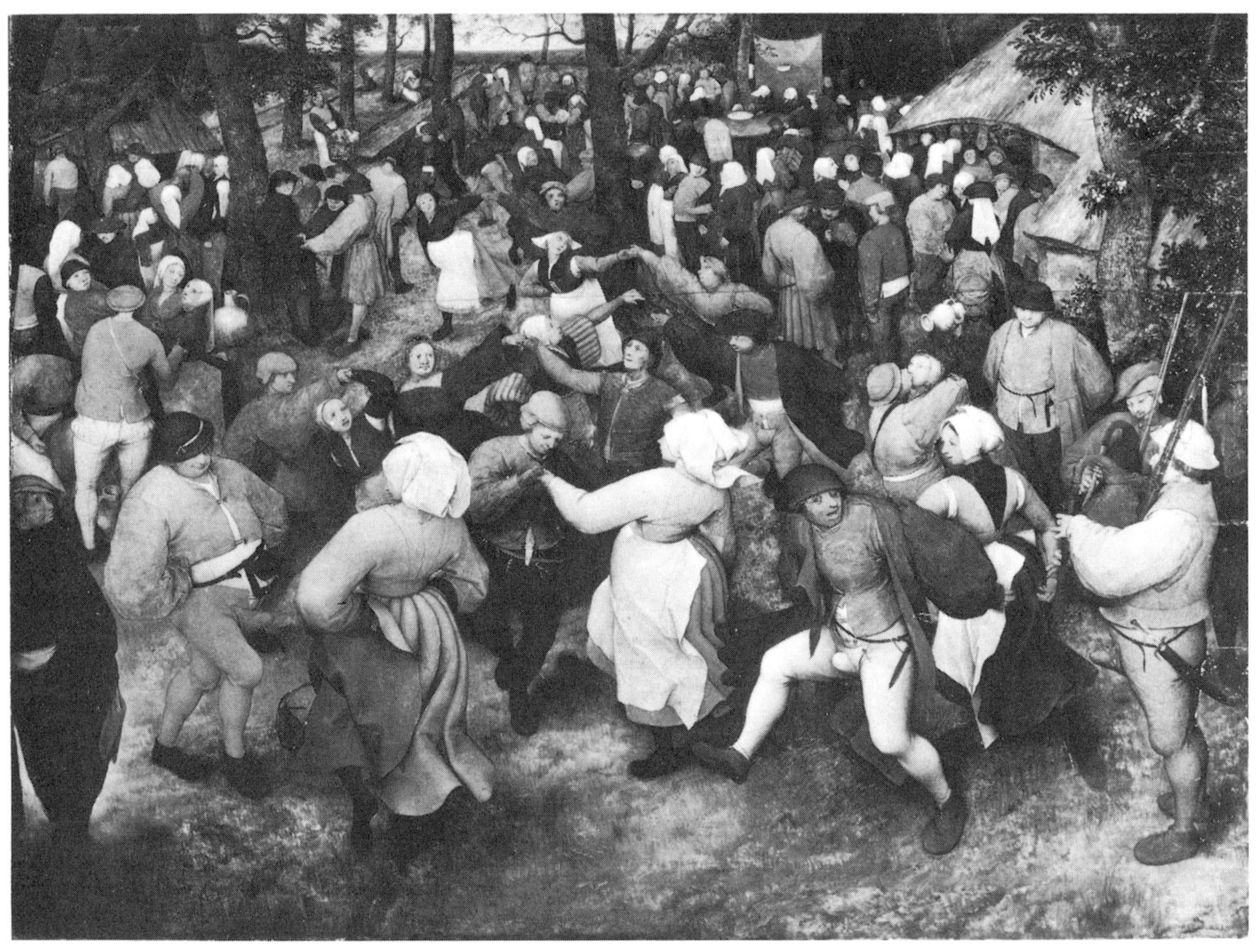

Pieter Bruegel the Elder (Flemish, 1523-30 - 1569)
THE WEDDING DANCE (after restr.), 1566; 47″ x 62″
oil on canvas
Courtesy The Detroit Institute of Arts

14     The artist has found that his organization of lines, shapes, and colors is usually a more powerful way to arouse emotional responses in his viewers than by the introduction of almost any representational subject matter.

One of the great difficulties for the artist in working with subject matter is distinguishing between attributes of a thing in nature and the same attributes in relation to the picture itself. How prettily does he paint a pretty girl? How darkly can he paint a storm? How ugly can he make a villain? If subject matter appeal were the ultimate aim of the artist, then, carried to absurdity, the first painting should be a pretty picture; the second, a gloomy picture; while the third should be an ugly picture. Fortunately, few artists have been so misled.

Factual or realistic subject matter becomes insistent if for no other reason than that pictures are viewed by people who delight in the act of recognition. In looking at Pieter Bruegel's *The Wedding Dance* it is much easier to see a picture of a white apron as a white apron than as a white shape vital to the whole space structure of the picture. No matter how skillful the artist, he is always at the mercy of his viewers. What he intends they should see and what they choose to see may be entirely different.

Time and place have much to do with the acceptance or rejection of subject matter. For one audience a picture may be obscene, for another it may be perfectly acceptable. Many of the fourteenth-century French scenes of couples

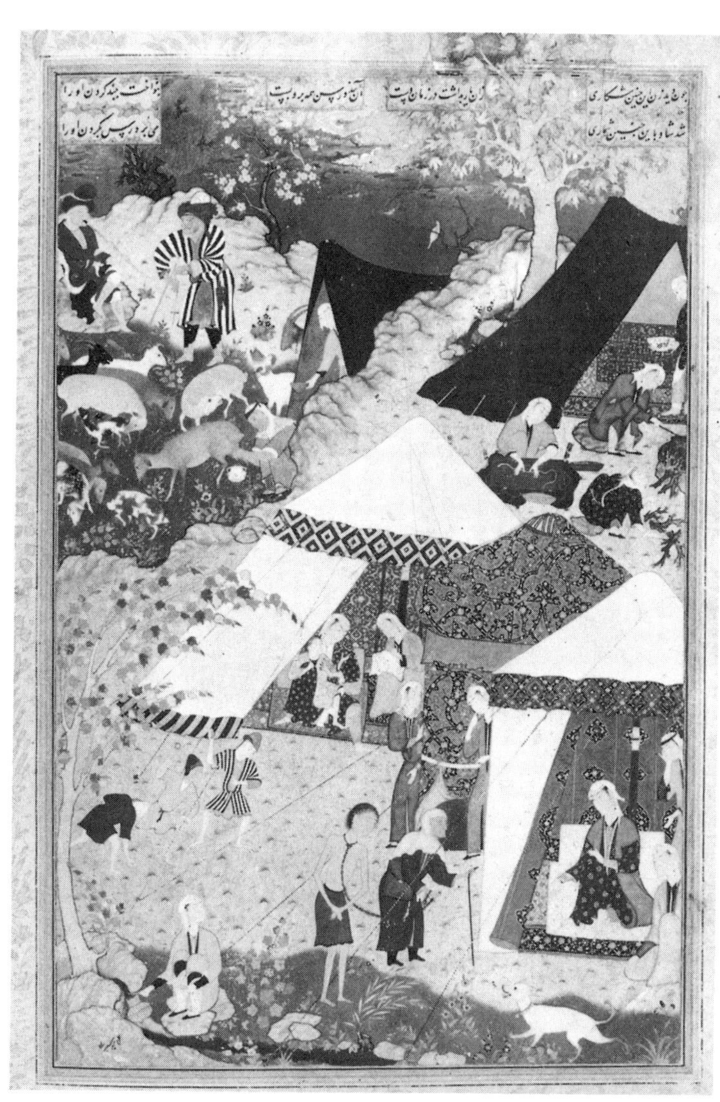

Manuscript for Shah Tahmasp by royal scribes
and artists, 1539-1543 A.D. at Tabriz
MAJNUN IN CHAINS; 11%10″ x 77⁄10″
Courtesy of the Trustees of the British Museum
(Photo: Edward Telesford Photographic Service)

bathing nude would probably have been banned later in the American colonies. Many of Pieter Bruegel's earthy pictures raise eyebrows even today.

Once we have learned to see pictures not merely as subject matter but primarily as graphic organizations, we open up entirely new categories of emotional experiences often previously hidden by subject matter appeal. With an understanding of the graphics of a picture we are better able to appreciate the works of alien artists in spite of our inability to comprehend their exact meaning. The whole of ancient art, exemplified by this Persian painting, is open to us graphically; the whole of contemporary art becomes more enjoyable.

When we wish to make pictures ourselves, there seems to be two ways to begin: the first evolves from the picture itself; the second, from an idea. Let us explore the first method, which is rather unusual in the history of painting and drawing.

It is possible to begin a picture by placing on a surface an area of color, or a line which then suggests more areas, colors, or lines, each dictated by the position, direction, size, shape, intensity of the previous accumulation of graphic disturbances on the picture surface. We might say such a picture grows, or develops. It is directed by the artist but motivated by the graphic elements themselves. At some point a concept of the picture as a whole may be formulated, but not necessarily so. Such pictures are, of necessity, non-representational.

More often a picture is based on an idea. Is the picture to be informative, illustrative, abstract, non-representational? Does the idea involve a representation of figures, nature forms, or invented or imaginary shapes or forms? With whom are we trying to communicate and on what level—informative, emotional, or both?

Our investigation will be confined to the making of pictures based on an idea, but in no way should this be construed as denying the merits of the first method of beginning a picture.

## The Image

All our lives we have trained ourselves to give meaning to, or identify with, things we see. At times this identification may be most general. We may look at a page printed in a foreign language, and though we cannot derive meaning from the letters, we accept the fact that they constitute some kind of words. And so when we look at a picture our training usually impels us to search for meaning.

Any graphic disturbance such as a point, line, or area that is arranged or projected on a picture surface creates an illusion of depth, of space. When we organize such elements in our picture to give the viewer an illusion of an object or an occurrence, real or imaginary, we usually refer to this arrangement as an *image.*

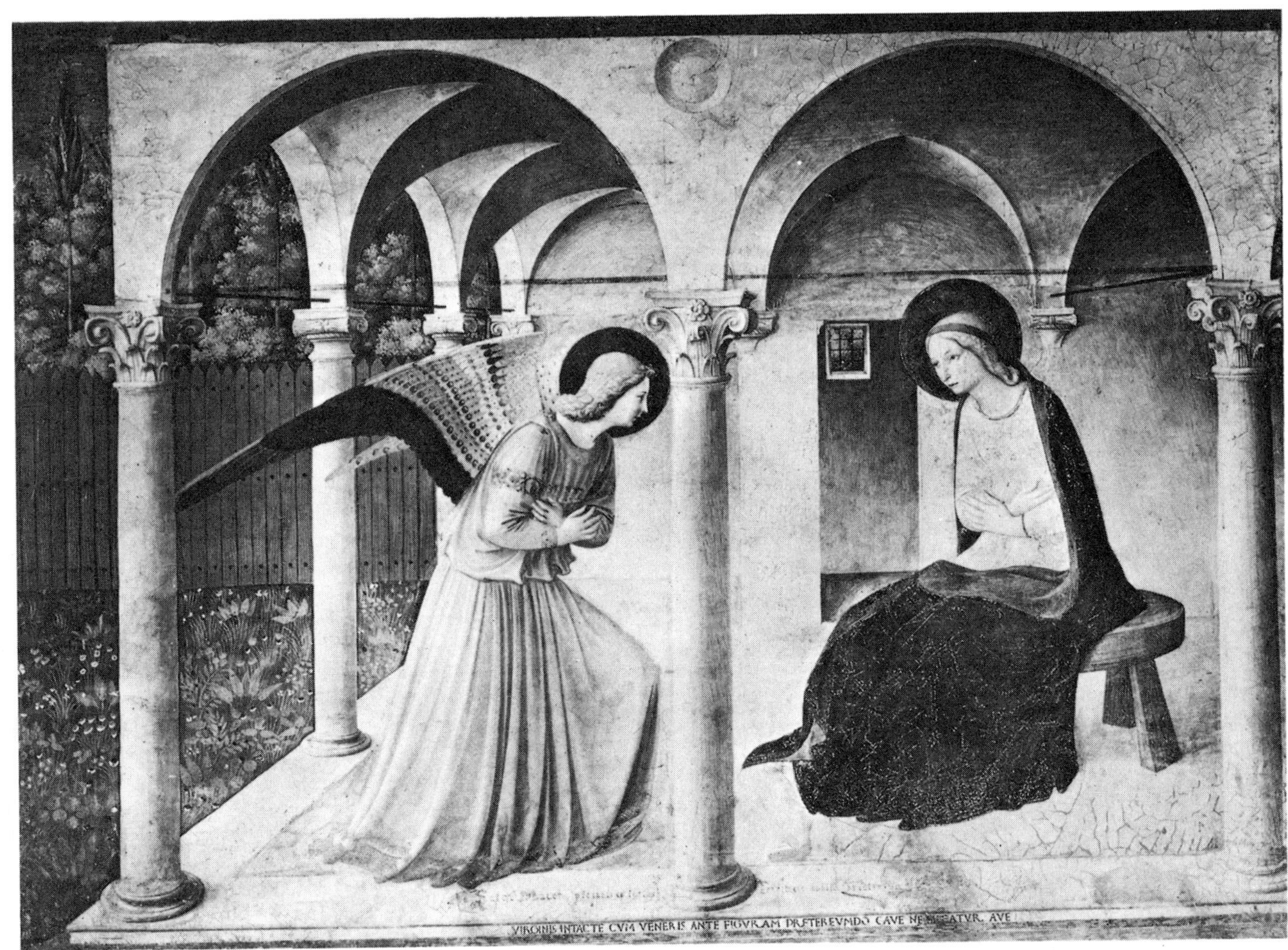

Fra Angelico (Italian, 1387-1455)
THE ANNUNCIATION, ca. 1437; fresco
Museo di San Marco, Florence
(Photo: Alinari—Art Reference Bureau
and Fototeca Unione, Rome)

The more realistic or lifelike the image, the more it seems to resemble an occurrence or object in nature, the easier it is to identify. Yet such an image, a portrait for instance, can only suggest a real head, for it is only a drawing or painting executed on a surface. Consider our reaction upon looking at a small black and white photograph of the same subject. Actually the photograph in many respects is not at all like the real head, for it suggests only certain aspects of nature. It lacks color, space, three dimensions, warmth, action, yet we often remark that the photograph "looks exactly like" the subject.

Within such limitations we accept the term "realistic" as adequate to describe our reactions to a type of abstraction or convention suggesting certain actual occurrences of objects in nature. Yet like all definitions there seem to be exceptions. Can we say that a painting of an angel, an imaginary concept, is realistic? The body of Fra Angelico's painted angel may closely resemble a real person, the wings may closely resemble those of a real bird. But are there angels?

Because we are so easily able to identify the realistic image we might believe that a picture built upon realistic imagery should be the ultimate goal of the artist. Yet this is seldom the case except if the intent of the artist is primarily to give information. As we have noted, a picture based solely upon subject matter appeal rarely arouses in us emotional responses of much intensity. We seldom become ecstatic over a realistic image of a spark-plug or a golf-ball.

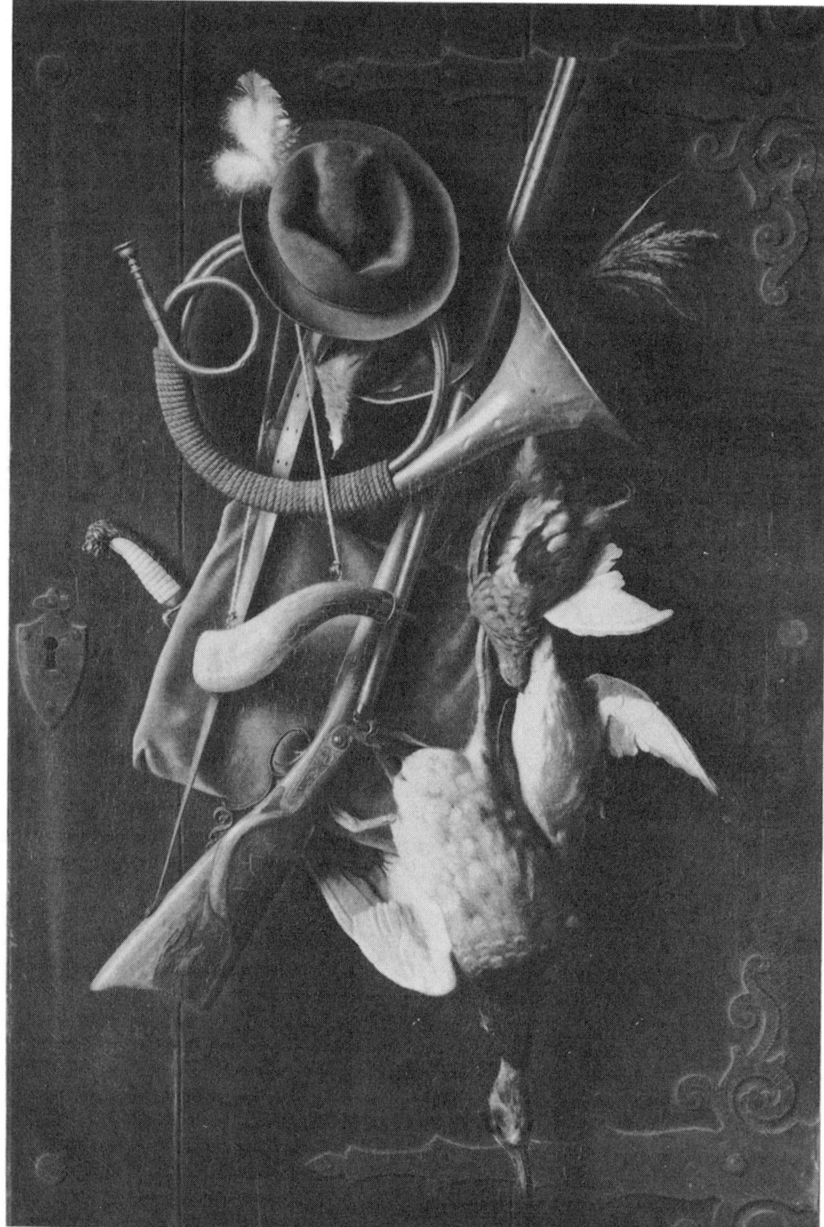

William Harnett (American, 1848-1892)
AFTER THE HUNT, 1883; 52½″ x 36″
oil on canvas
Collection the Columbus Gallery of Fine Arts
Columbus, Ohio; Gift of Francis G. Sessions

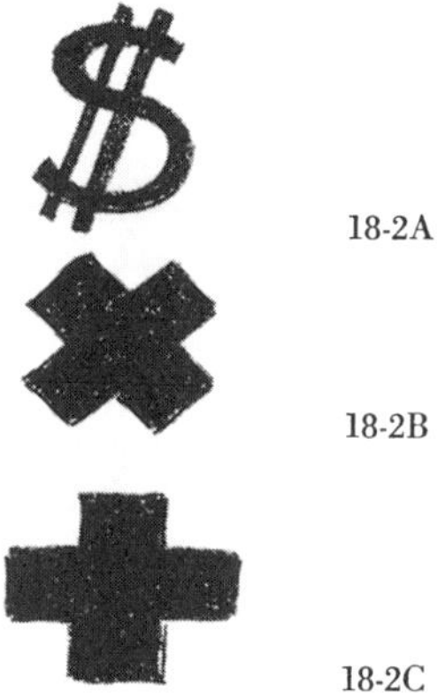

18-2A

18-2B

18-2C



At times, however, a realistic image may be made so "real" that we are forced to consider the subject in a new way. Aspects of the subject may be shown that have previously escaped us. Colors, textures, minute details may be revealed to our delight or horror; a *magic realism* results, as in Harnett's *After the Hunt*. In fact the artist may create a super-real or *surrealistic* image. The illusion of space may be intensified far beyond anything ever experienced in nature.

An artist may also organize realistic images so that new associations or meanings result that are not implicit in the natural object from which they are derived. An unexpected combination of familiar images, a human face on an animal body, or a painting of a wilted watch may affect us in surprising ways.

But to achieve such "reality" the artist invariably is extremely selective of his material and also employs many compositional structures commonly used throughout the history of picture making.

## The Symbol

A drawing of a horse, a head, a forest, each implies some kind of imagery. A picture of a centaur, an angel, a cartoon character, a castle in the sky, fanciful constructions of the artist, have become accepted as familiar images. A form or shape in a picture may be unidentifiable yet be capable of arousing in us an emotional response: a ghost-like image, for instance. Sometimes the meaning of an element in a picture has little or no direct visual relation to recognizable things. Such elements are often referred to as *symbols*.

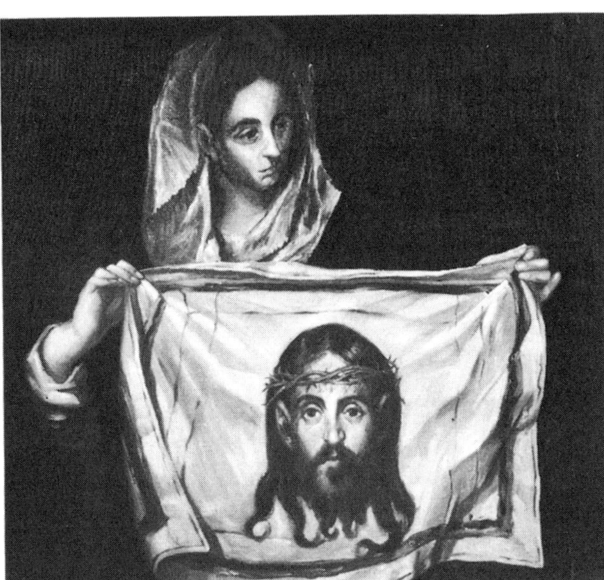

El Greco (Spanish, b. Crete 1541-1614)
THE VERONICA, ca. 1580; 27½″ x 31½″
Museo de Santa Crux, Toledo, Spain

Franz Kline (American, 1910-1962)
PAINTING #7, 1952; 57½″ x 81¾″
oil on canvas
The Solomon R. Guggenheim Museum, New York City

Usually a symbol is an image given a specific meaning which may have little to do with the actual visual source from which it is derived. For example, a dollar sign does not look like a dollar bill (*18-2A*).

A picture showing two crossed sticks may signify a railroad crossing (*18-2B*) or a grave marker (*18-2C*).

A street map is an ordered arrangement of lines giving specific information about a city but in no way resembles a city. It is a symbol.

A picture of a man's head may be simply a portrait of an individual; it also may be a representation of Christ. As a religious symbol the head in El Greco's *The Veronica* takes on entirely new meaning.

So we see that a symbol may or may not be an image, although an image is always a symbol.

An artist may create an organization of lines and areas which in no way represents an actual or imaginary occurrence, yet it may profoundly disturb us. A painting by Franz Kline depicts nothing we have seen before, yet it captures our attention. It moves us emotionally. It is not an image in the usual sense, nor does it directly symbolize anything. Yet it is a picture. The graphic elements utilized in making the picture are strong, dramatic, creating a whole which has emotional impact. We have now not an image in the true sense, not a symbol pertaining to an accepted idea, but a graphic symbol arousing in us strong emotional responses, perhaps never experienced before.

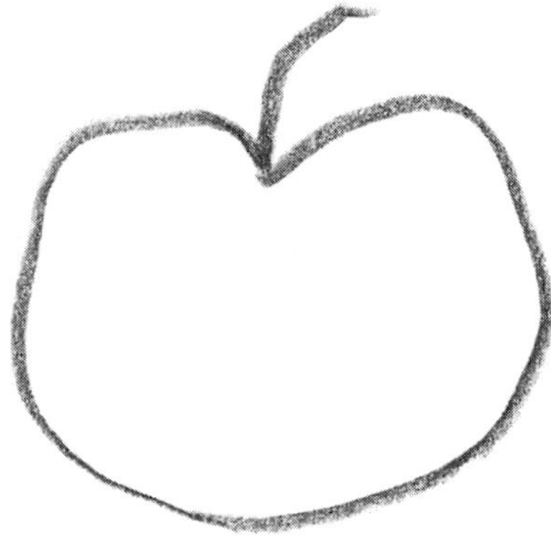

20-1A

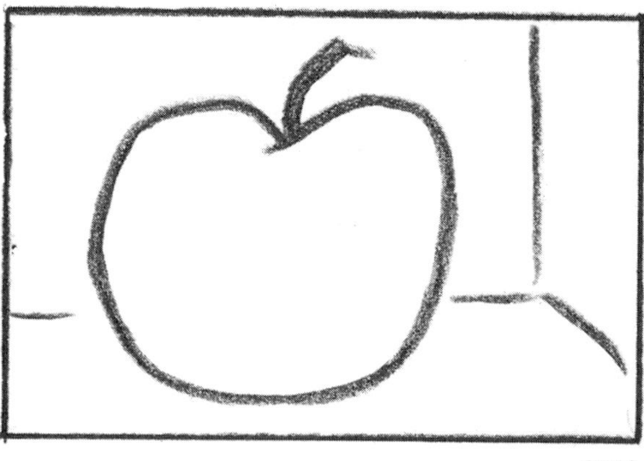

20-2A

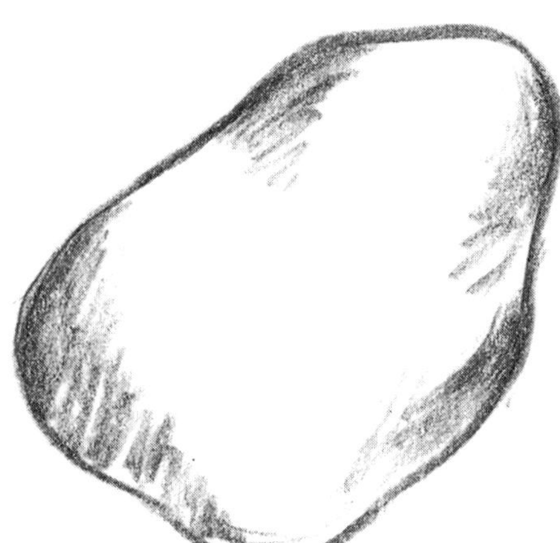

20-1B

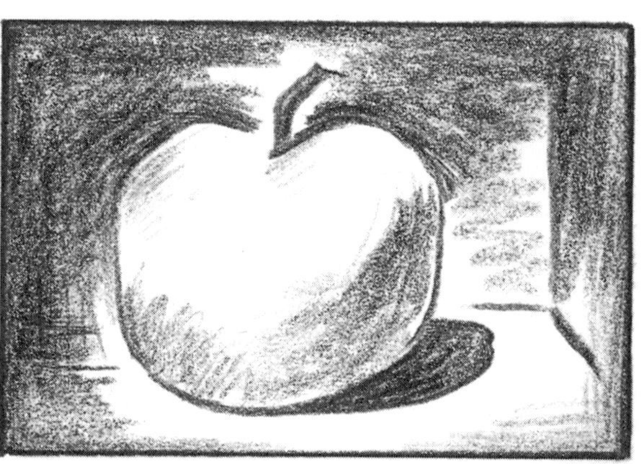

20-2B

## 20  The Volume

To avoid confusion we have tried to distinguish between subject matter in nature and the graphic subject matter of a picture. We must also distinguish clearly between a three-dimensional form in nature and the graphic image of this same form. So we use the term *volume* to indicate such an image.

An apple is a piece of fruit, a form in nature, the graphic image suggesting the apple is a volume (*20-1A*).

At times an imaginary three-dimensional form may be translated into graphic terms. It, too, is a volume (*20-1B*).

The volume as an image of a three-dimensional form, real or imaginary, introduces a new series of picture factors. It opens the door to the graphic exploitation of many of the physical attributes of a form: size, shape, color, texture, weight, etc.

If the apple depicted in line is shown in a simple environment of enclosing walls and a horizontal surface, we experience a new sense of depth (*20-2A*). The volume seems more sculptural, the surrounding space between the surfaces implied seems more convincing. We achieve an even more apparent depth, a more convincing image of the real apple by adding grays and darks organized to simulate a light source, shade, and shadow (*20-2B*).

In the last two examples not only are the apples volumes, but the drawn walls and the horizontal surfaces represent actual solid forms, and thus also are volumes. When only part of such a volume is shown, and when its surface is flat, it often is referred to as a *plane*.

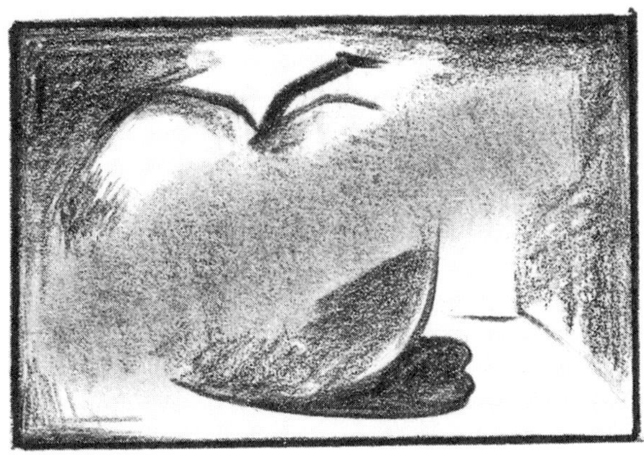

21-1

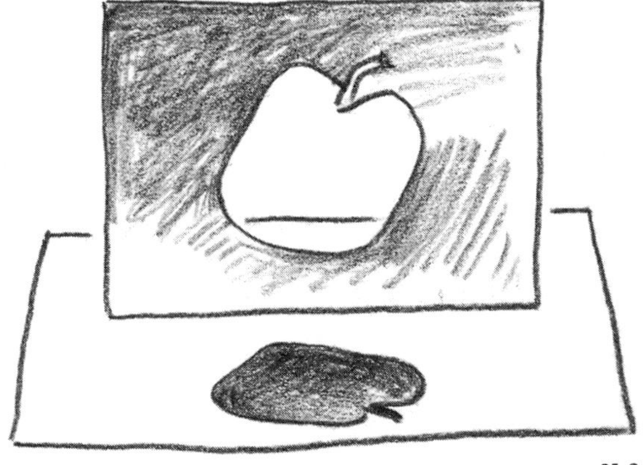

21-2

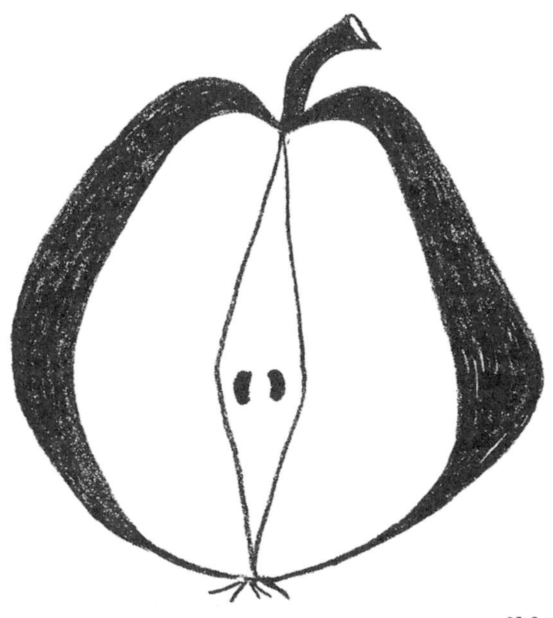

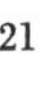

21-3

## Shape

No matter how realistic the image, no matter how lifelike the volume, no matter if it is enveloped in light and shade and shadow, it is still flat and occupies a certain amount of the flat picture surface.

We may demonstrate this phenomenon by painting a volume and background with oil paint (*21-1*). Now while the canvas is still wet, let us rub our thumb across the surface. The background colors and those representing the form are blurred and smeared. Our thumb is covered with paint from both background and painted volume. Our thumb actually glides on the surfaces of the canvas and notices no difference between background and image; only our eyes are deceived by the illusion of the image.

Let us cut the image of the form out of the canvas. We now have a hole in the canvas instead of a volume. We now have a *shape*, the cut-out. The hole is the same shape (*21-2*).

A shape is usually that part of the surface on which the form is depicted. It is always flat, for it is part of the picture surface.

We find, also, that it is possible to symbolize a three-dimensional form as a two-dimensional design. In such case the image is a shape, not a volume (*21-3*).

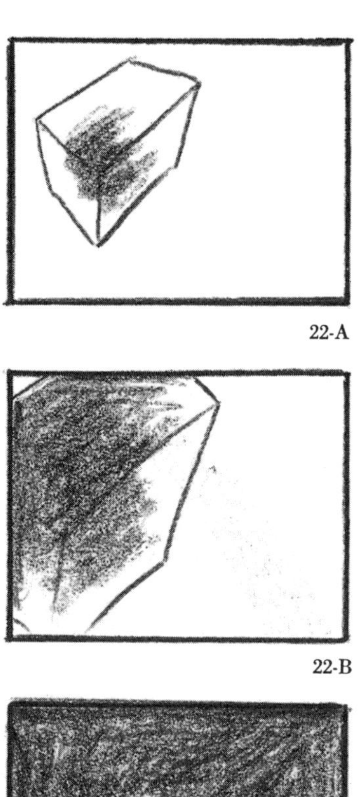

22-A

22-B

22-C

22 At times the identity of a volume or shape becomes questionable. An undefined fragment of the picture surface is called an *area*. For instance, in *22-A* we see a volume clearly in its surrounding environment. This environment is both an area and a graphic space. The volume is also a shape. In *22-B* we see enough of the volume to identify both it and the space. We still may read the volume as a shape. But in *22-C* we see so little of the volume that it loses its identity. We can read it neither as a volume nor a shape.

We see now that both the volume and shape must be identifiable. To adapt a term that is used extensively in design, the shape to read as a shape must have "integrity." If we lose the integrity of a shape we generate either an area or a space.

As we have seen, an imaginary form may be represented as a volume and, as such, is also a shape. At times a flat disturbance on the picture surface may be abstract, non-representational, or amorphous, yet be a true shape. It is apparent that although almost all volumes are shapes, many shapes are not volumes.

It should be noted that most shapes are defined by either edges or lines. But this is not always true, for some shapes are defined by diffused edges, broken lines, or points (*23-1A, -1B*).

Of all the factors in composition, that of shape is undoubtedly one of the most difficult to master. It is easy to understand the construction of a shape; it is relatively easy to describe a shape. Yet to arrive at a shape which has integrity, meaning, gesture, and true originality has been a challenge to the artist since pictures began. A shape is seldom copied directly from

23-1A

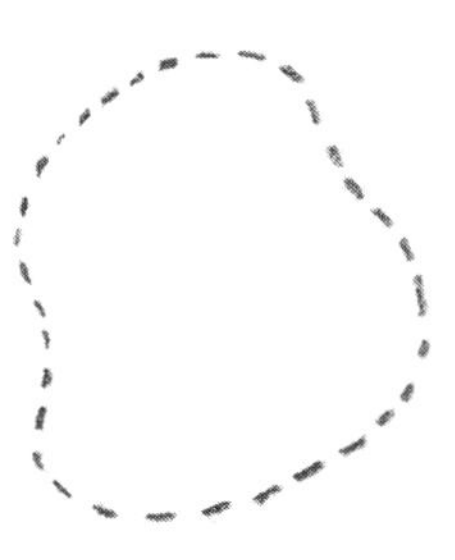

23-1B

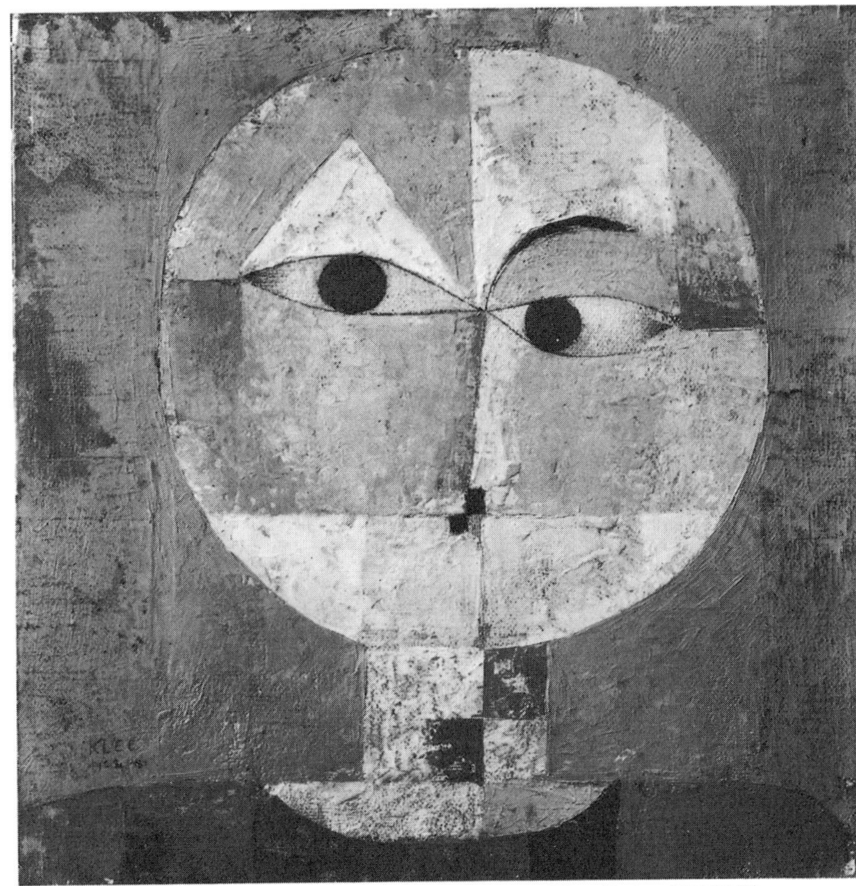

Paul Klee (Swiss, 1879-1940)
SENECIO, 1922; 16″ x 15″; oil on linen
Kunstmuseum, Basel
French Reproduction Rights, Inc., N. Y.



things in nature; it is always in some way
abstract. It is always a personal statement of
the artist.

As we study the reproductions in this book
it should be apparent that no two artists represent a subject, a human head for instance,
in the same manner. An El Greco cannot be
confused with a Bruegel, or a Fra Angelico with
a Picasso. This Klee in no way resembles any
of them. Let us call it individual graphic style
or what we may. Shape is the great enigma
of picture making.

After discussing aspects of the first picture
factor, the subject, we now turn to the second
picture factor to which shape is so closely
related, the surface.

Kurt Schwitters (German, 1887-1948)
CONSTRUCTION FOR NOBLE LADIES, 1919
40½″ x 33″ mixed media
Los Angeles County Museum of Art
Museum Purchase Fund



# 2 The Surface

### The Physical Surface

When we begin a picture we usually consider its physical construction first. Will the picture itself be seen or touched by the spectator? Will it be an easel painting, or a decoration on ceramic or other sculptured or manipulated material? Will it be a mural? Is the picture to be reproduced by any of the many methods of printing? Is it to be an etching, a lithograph, a serigraph, each a form of printing? Is it to be projected upon a screen, like an animated film?

Each technique has its particular problems and potential, but each, even the motion picture film, is founded on control of a picture surface.

The surface of the picture is real. It usually is made of paper, canvas, wood, metal, or plaster, but it can be of anything upon which lines or areas can be indicated or projected.

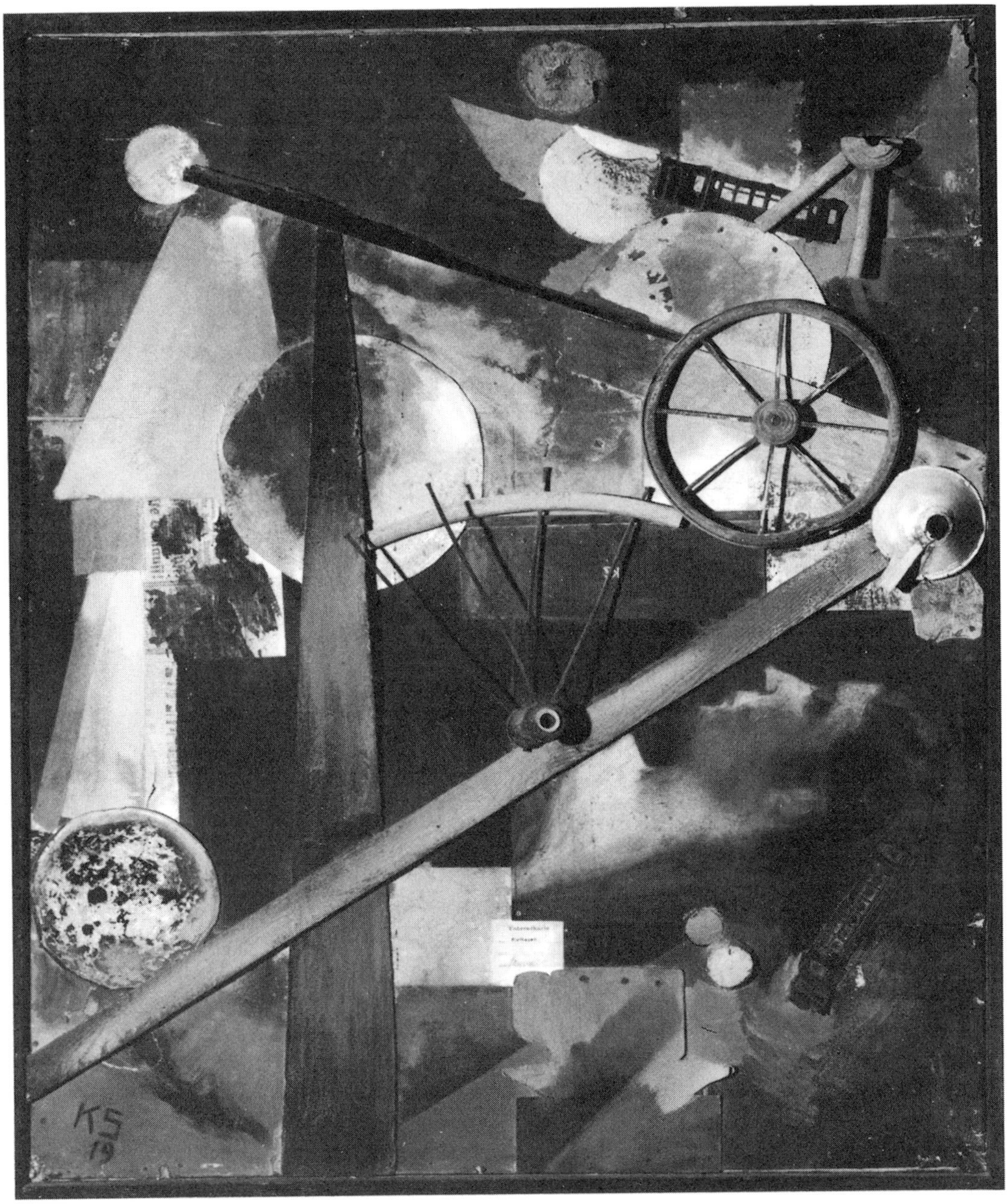

Upon such a surface any number of marking materials may be applied. This material may be of a staining or discoloring nature: charcoal, carbon, lead, silver, which in convenient forms such as chalks, pencils, and inks become our drawing tools. Earth, metals, stains or dye become pigments with which we paint. In fact anything that will stain or discolor or disturb a surface can be used to make a picture statement—even toothpaste, smoke, or blood.

Some materials may not necessarily discolor the surface. Colored lights or images projected on screens or clouds are also means of making pictures. Various materials may be applied or stuck on a surface with various adhesives and still maintain their original character. Paper. cloth, string, sand, sugar, and even biscuits have been used to activate the surface in a form of picture making usually termed *collage;* one of Kurt Schwitters' collages is shown above.

The surface itself may be manipulated. If of plaster, it may be troweled to change its texture. Many surfaces may be scratched, incised, scumbled, or scored. In every case a surface of a certain texture and color is visually altered.

Yet at no time should we overlook the fact that a picture, even if projected or printed, begins as a physical construction made on a physical surface with physical materials. Such a picture no matter what its subject, no matter how it is designed, scratched, scrubbed, burned, or torn, is as physical as a piece of pie. But it is physical in only one way, its material components.

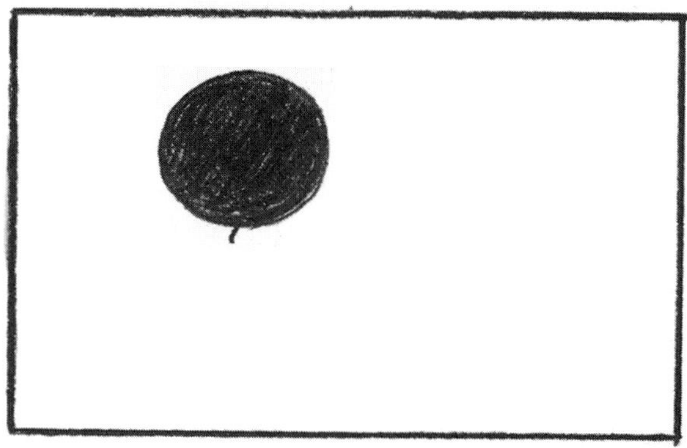

26-A

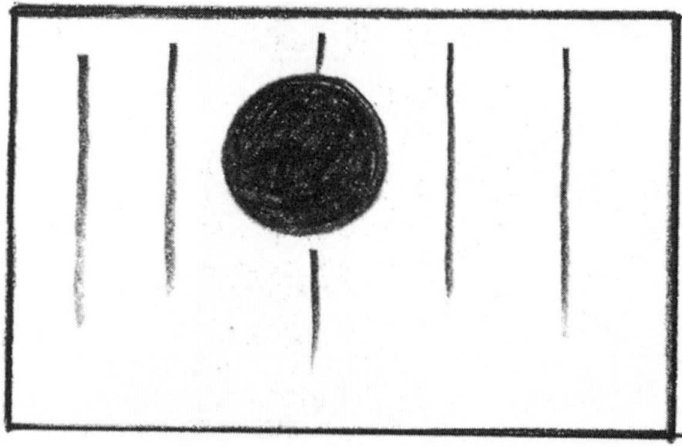

26-B

## 26 The Surface as Illusion

Suppose now that on a chosen surface we make a spot of dark with one of our marking materials. Our eyes are immediately attracted to the spot. Our natural inclination is to try to identify it. Does the spot represent a balloon floating in space (*26-A*)? Or does it represent a hole in a board fence (*26-B*)? In either case we give the spot meaning. We also have introduced a new factor, that of illusion. The spot is not a real balloon, nor is it a real hole in a real fence. It merely makes us imagine such occurrences.

Having identified the spot, we also have identified the surrounding area. If we visualize the spot as a balloon, we visualize its environment as space; if as a hole, we visualize its surroundings as solid.

Now this is truly a graphic enigma. Our solid, flat picture surface at one moment seems to be open, spacious, suggesting great depth and space in which a balloon floats; but at another moment it suggests a solid fence with a hole in it.

The picture surface has a dual character; it is always a physical reality, and when disturbed it is also an illusion which may suggest great depth.

As a general rule it may be said that the more realistic the image, the more we sense the illusion of depth, and the less we are aware of the physical reality of the actual picture surface. This effect has often been compared to looking through a window to a scene beyond.

For example, suppose one morning we get into our car and see to our irritation that the windshield is fogged over (*27-A*). We look *at*

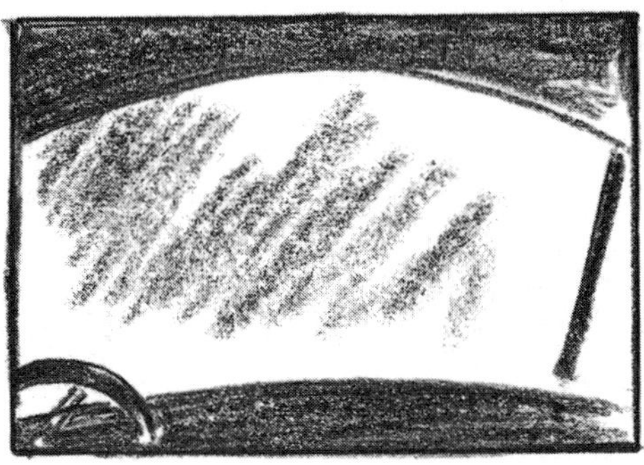

27-A

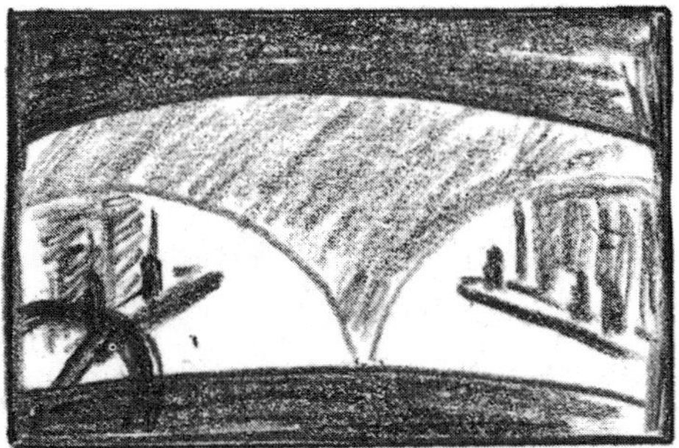

27-B

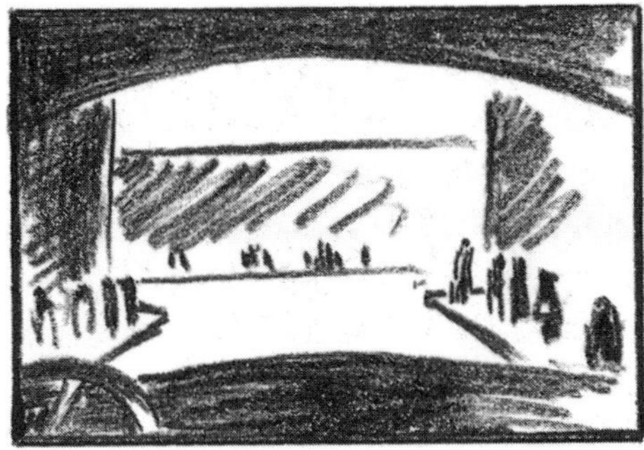

27-C

it. We cannot see *through* it. The surface has become an event. Then we turn on the windshield wipers and partially clear the glass (*27-B*). Now we see parts of the street in front of the car, but we are still aware of the unwiped areas of the windshield. As we drive, the whole glass clears, then we are no longer conscious of its existence, for our total interest is in the scene in front of us (*27-C*).

Through the whole history of picture making the enigma of surface has faced every artist. How is he to resolve it? Should he stress the importance of the image and its existence in deep space so convincingly that the picture surface seems to disappear like the clean windshield? Or should he strive as much as possible to eliminate any suggestion of depth, and merely decorate the surface with arbitrary arrangements of lines and areas which seem to lie completely on the picture surface?

This problem, which at first may seem of little consequence, is actually of tremendous importance to every artist. How he resolves this problem is reflected in every color or line he puts on his surface. His picture concepts are always conditioned by his interpretation of this problem. His solution determines the basic form of his picture, its very nature.

The study of picture composition is in large measure an investigation of this problem and an attempt to find positive ways to control the two factors: the surface as a physical event, and the surface as an illusion of space, whether limited or deep.

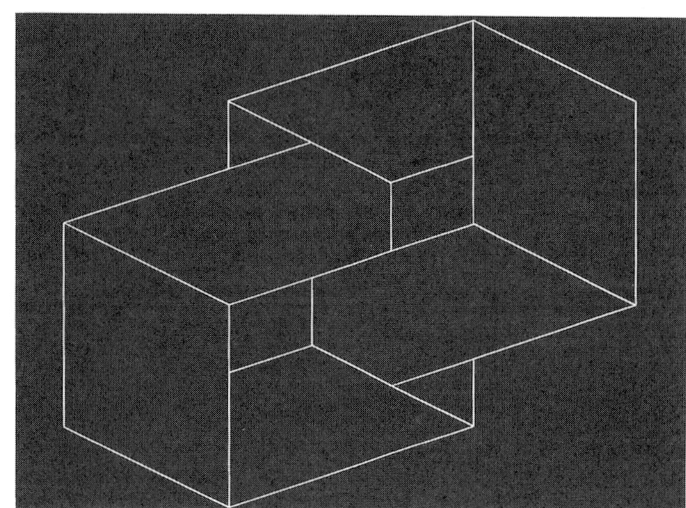

Josef Albers (b. Bottrop, Germany, 1888- )
NHb, 1957; 19¾″ x 26″
structural constellation, black & white plastic
Courtesy of the artist
(Photograph from *Josef Albers, The American Years*, Washington Gallery of Modern Art)

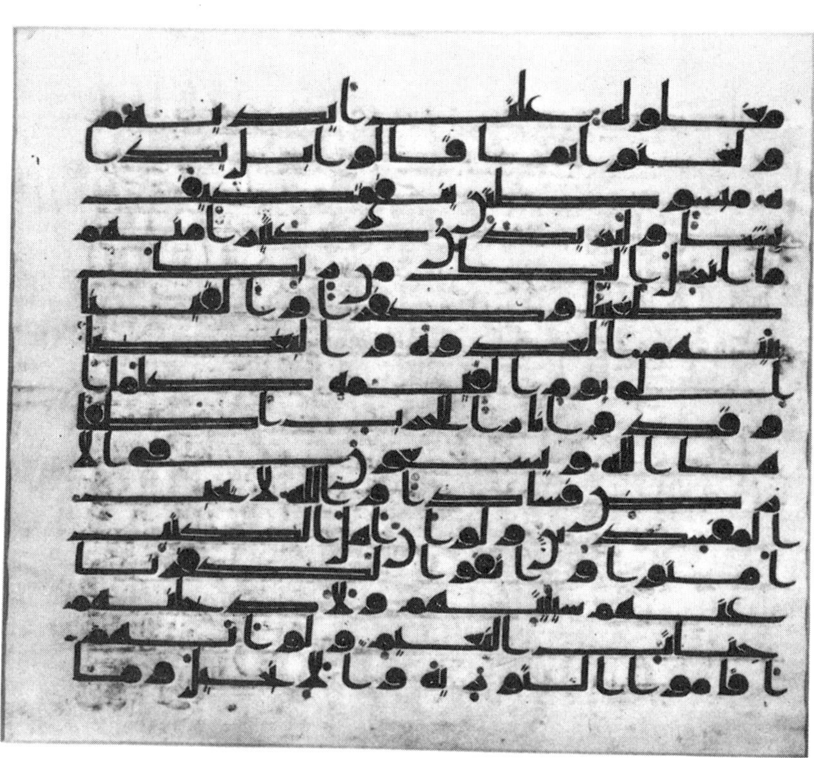

Artist unknown
KORAN PAGE, Kufic script; Iran
Seljuk Dynasty ca. 9th-10th cent.
12″ x 13½″; vellum, ink and color
Seattle Art Museum
Eugene Fuller Memorial Collection

28    Most artists have found that to create the illusion of the open window in itself presents a great contradiction. This contradiction is emphasized if the picture is a night scene. The picture, after all, is usually flat, usually has a specific shape and size, and must be illuminated in some way in order that the spectator may see it. To see the picture, which we may assume is hanging on a wall in a home, the room must be lighted. The brighter the light, the more easily the picture can be read; the less light, the more difficult it will be to see. If the picture is well lighted, its presence as a dark shape on the wall will be accentuated. Its very physical characteristics tend to destroy the illusion of its being a window opening on the night.

This contradiction, of course, is true to a certain extent of any picture no matter what its subject or construction. But if the physical nature of the picture is accepted from the start as part of the graphic problem, its size, or shape, or color becomes an asset rather than a drawback. It becomes a reminder that the picture is a picture, not an illusionary hole through which we peer into illusionary depth.

Now there are times when people enjoy being fooled by the artist, just as they enjoy a magician's tricks. In fact, symbols that reverse may be a delight, as we see in this Josef Albers. Trompe l'oeil, the art of fooling the eye in pictures, also intrigues many artists. But there is a difference between fooling the eye as to graphic subject matter within a picture, and pretending that the picture is not a picture at all.

John McLaughlin (American, 1898-   )
No. 1, 1965; 60″ x 48″; oil on canvas
Courtesy of Felix Landau Gallery
Los Angeles
(Photograph: Frank Thomas)

In contrast to illusions of deep space, pictures can be made with a suggestion of space so limited that for all practical considerations we say that they are flat. For example, the page of Arabic lettering shown here is so designed as to be of great interest and beauty, and in this sense it is a picture. Rarely is an impression of deep space experienced, although we may be aware of the elegant distribution of areas around the letters. Similarly, the flat patterns often seen in decorative designs and borders, printed surfaces such as polka-dots, stripes, etc., abstract patterns on linoleum, rugs, and wallpaper are seldom designed to give a sense of deep space.

But a painter who purposely avoids symbols in any way suggesting three dimensions—John McLaughlin, for instance—is still confronted with the almost inevitable generation of graphic space. A field of color divided by a stripe may make us sense unlimited space.

The moment we activate the surface with a spot or line we generate space. How then is it possible so to control the picture that we also are aware of its physical nature? In solving this problem most artists have tried to steer a course somewhere between the extremes of complete illusion and complete flatness. A true balance, the dream of many artists, is not easily achieved. Personal preference, the environment of the artist, his time in history, the influences on him of various schools of thought, technical knowledge, and his very materials are factors which influence his decision to create more or less space in the picture, more or less emphasis of the physical reality of surface.

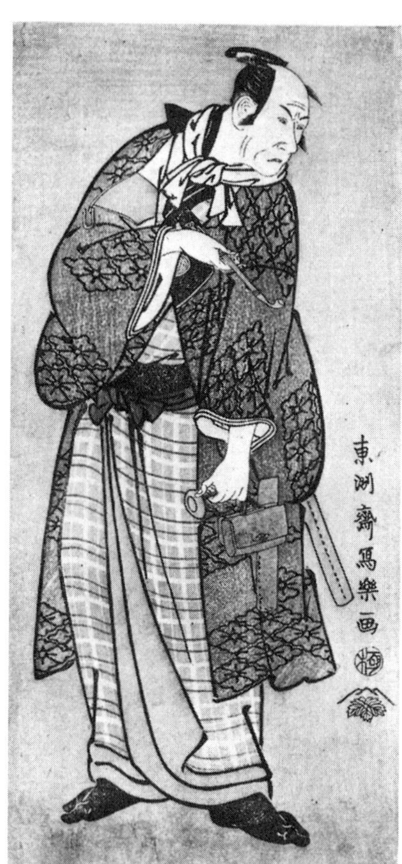

Jean Baptiste Simeone Chardin
(French, 1699-1779)
THE GOVERNESS, 1738; 18¾″ x 14¾″
oil on canvas
The National Gallery of Canada, Ottawa

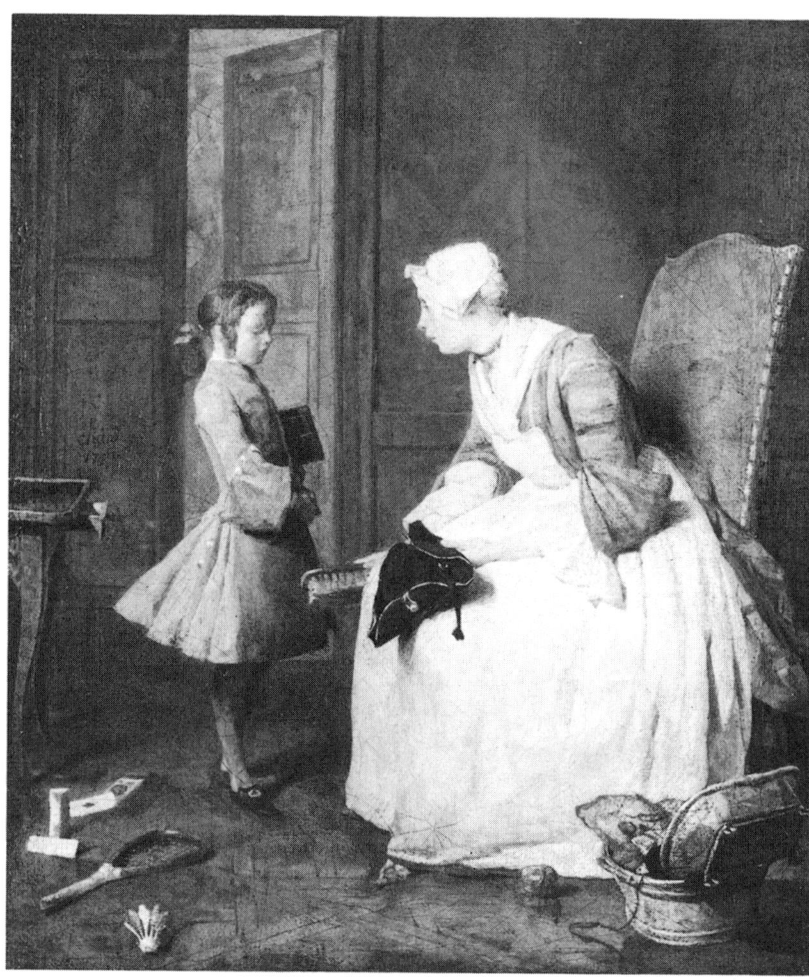

Tashusai Sharaku (Japanese, 18th cent.)
PORTRAIT OF THE ACTOR MATSUMOTO KOSHIRO IV
1794; 12¼″ x 5¾″; woodblock print
Courtesy of the Art Institute of Chicago
Clarence Buckingham Collection
of Japanese Prints

30 If we compare a Chardin and a Sharaku, we immediately are aware of profound differences in the inner space structure of the pictures. Each picture is the work of a great artist. Each is a carefully constructed picture. Yet they represent attitudes about the control of space which are diametrically opposed. The degree to which the surface factor is stressed in each case represents cultural heritages which have profoundly influenced the artist's statement. For example, the Chardin is enveloped in a deep space environment employing the illusion of a light source and shade and shadow. The Sharaku, on the other hand, avoids the use of a simulated light source, depending upon the impact of shape generated primarily by line which is supplemented by strong patterns, also generated by line. The space enveloping the Sharaku is implied rather than defined.

In our search for picture control one of our first experiments should be to learn to see a spot on a surface not as a symbol of something in nature, but as a disturbance in theoretical space, in a depth environment not associated with an actual space as experienced in nature (31-1). If successful, we may say that we truly have begun to see graphic space. Careful study of this drawing and performance of the exercises in Part VIII will eventually result in an awareness of true graphic space. Incredible as it may seem, this nothingness, emptiness, or void is an essential factor in picture structure which must be grasped before a successful deep space picture can be made. As long as we see the spot as a geometric occurrence in a geometric shape the true meaning of picture structure must remain a mystery.

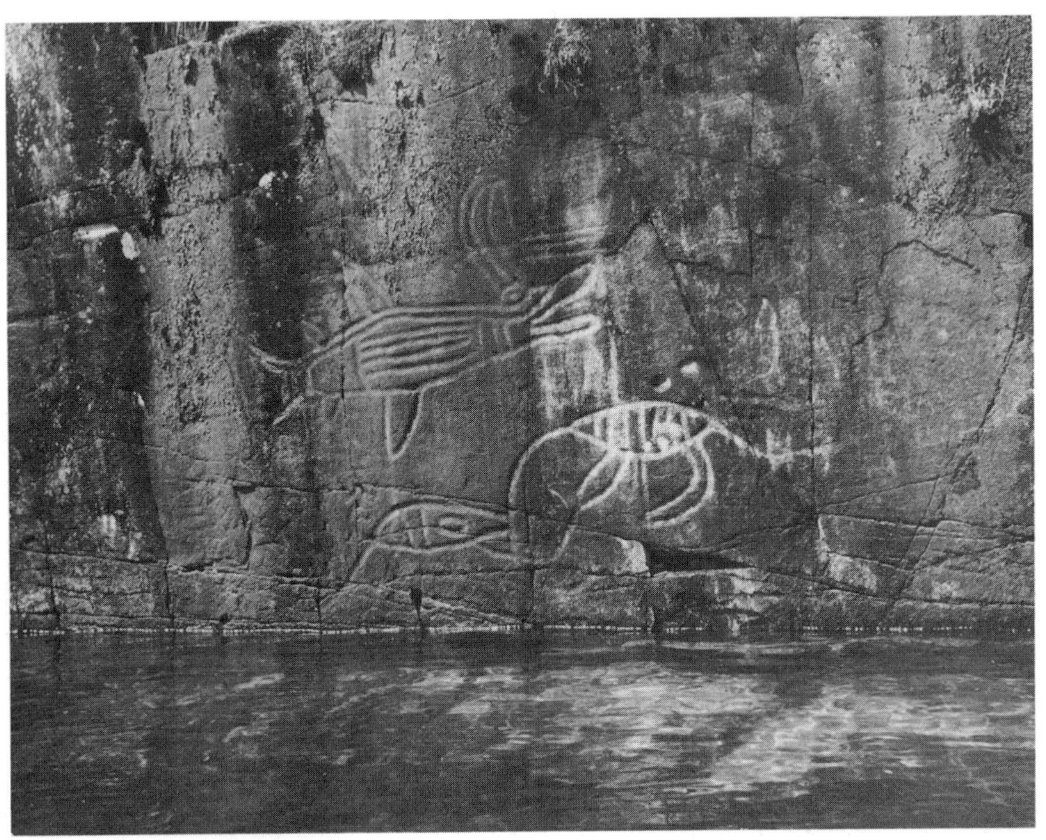

INDIAN PETROGLYPHS; Sproat Lake
Vancouver Island, B. C.
British Columbia Provincial Museum
Victoria, B. C.
(British Columbia Government photograph)

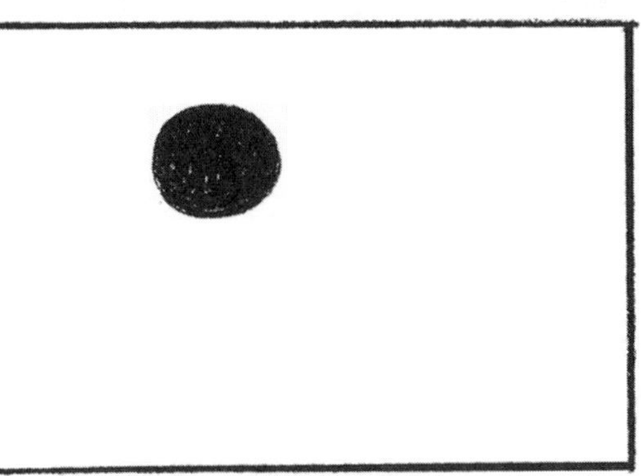

## Closed and Open Pictures

If the picture surface is limited in size and shape by the use of borders, it is usually referred to as a closed picture. If the size and shape of the surface is of little or no importance in the construction of the picture it is usually called an open picture. For instance, a small picture made on a huge wall is little influenced by the size or shape of the surface. Such open pictures also are called spot drawings, spots, or vignettes. Rock pictures such as these, graffiti, as well as small decorative drawings and designs in books and magazines fall into this category.

A picture often is made on a surface limited in size and shape, a printed page for instance. If the edges of the surface act as borders which are incorporated in the structure, in technical terms a *bleed*, the result is a closed picture. If the edges of the surface are not too directly involved in the construction of the picture it may also be a spot or vignette.

Both the open and closed picture may be equally successful, but in the study of composition usually better understanding is gained by working with the closed picture. For this reason, and this reason alone, the construction of closed pictures will be implied throughout these notes unless specifically excepted. Many of the principles discussed can be applied to the open picture, too.

32 The closed picture is characterized by a specific shape. It most often is one easily recorded by the eye: rectangular, round, oval, etc. However, concave, convex, or modifications of the more simple geometric shapes are often found in architecture and pottery and must be dealt with by the mural painter and ceramist. A picture shape that is too complex repeatedly attracts the spectator's eye and becomes a distraction which weakens the impact of the picture itself. The more involved the borders of a picture, the more difficult it is to relate elements within the picture to them.

The size of a picture also has a profound effect upon its structure. Whether it is a miniature or a huge mural, the artist must weigh and balance the effect of the size of his picture upon the viewpoint of the spectator.

## The Borders

In designing the closed picture there are great advantages in using graphic borders instead of merely the edges of the surface. As an actual graphic element, a graphic border can be directly related to other graphic elements in the picture. An edge, although a limit, is not graphic. Often an edge may be transformed into a graphic element simply by ruling a line on the picture surface just inside the turning edge. A mat or frame can substitute for such border lines when the picture is finished. As we shall see, these borders at times have the visual impact of a volume, and will exert varying and deceptive influences upon the entire picture.

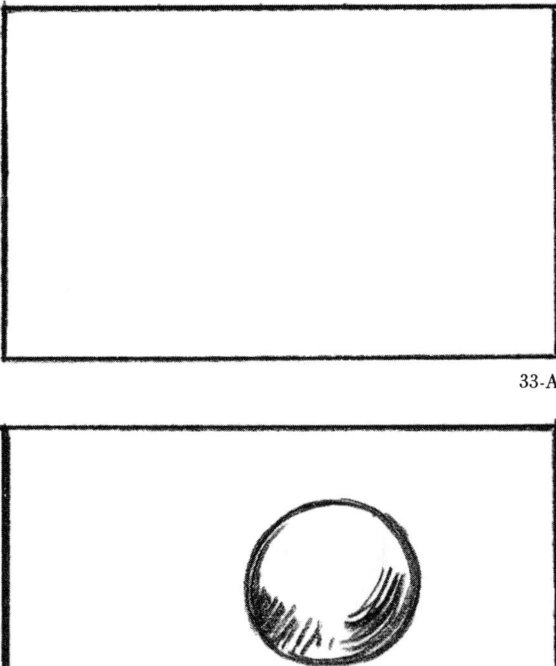

33-A

33-B

## The Field

The borders of a closed picture, a rectangle for instance, generate not just a geometric area but a field.

The field is that part of the surface to which the picture is related. It is a zone of potential visual activity in which a picture is generated by an arrangement of graphic or physical constructions. The field is a stage on which a drama is to be performed.

The way a field is conceived affects the type of picture to be made. If we look closely at a small rectangular picture area occupying only a portion of a large surface, we see that it seems to be of a different quality than the surrounding area (*33-A*). We might compare it to the illuminated area on a motion picture screen an instant after the film has broken. The image is gone, but the blank white screen seems alive, pulsing, although actually we see nothing on it. The picture field is like this illuminated area before a picture is generated within its borders. It is no longer just a flat geometric area bounded by line. It is now spacious.

Now if a graphic element, a sphere for instance, is introduced into this field, the field is immediately activated (*33-B*). We sense that something is happening, that forces are being exerted between the borders of the field and the sphere, that they have an affinity for each other. It is our awareness of this affinity of the borders to an element, of this *tension*, that generates in us a sense of space, also.

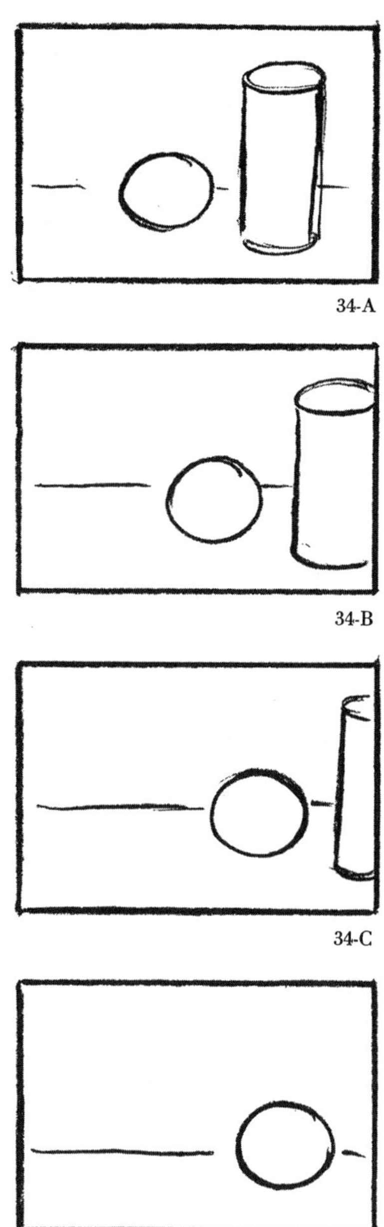

34-A

34-B

34-C

34-D

## 34  The Borders as Symbols of Force

To demonstrate how a border symbolizes a force, suppose we introduce into our picture another element, a cylinder. Between the sphere and the cylinder an affinity, a tension is generated. We become aware of a space between the two. Our eye moves easily between the two (*34-A*).

Now let us move the cylinder closer and closer to the border until finally it touches. The affinity between sphere and cylinder has not changed. We are still aware of space between them (*34-B*).

Let us decrease the width of the cylinder. The space between the narrower cylinder and the sphere is still preserved (*34-C*). As we continue to make the cylinder narrower and narrower, it finally approaches the border as a limit. Let us make them identical. The space between the border and the sphere still exists.

The border, a line, now has become a substitute for the volume (*34-D*). It has the same attractive force as a volume and generates the same space when related to a volume. So we see that for all practical purposes a border may be considered the equal of a volume. Now let us see how such borders affect the field.

Any carpenter or dressmaker can tell us how to find the center of a rectangle: establish the two diagonals of the rectangle, and the point at which they cross will be the center. A circle described around this point will also be the geometric center (*35-1*). Its circumference is equidistant from *AB* and *CD* and is also equidistant from *DA* and *BC*. But could this center be the only one? The carpenter will assure us that diagonals don't lie. But to the artist there is not only great doubt as to the validity of some geometric precepts, but also a belief that there are other "truths" as valid

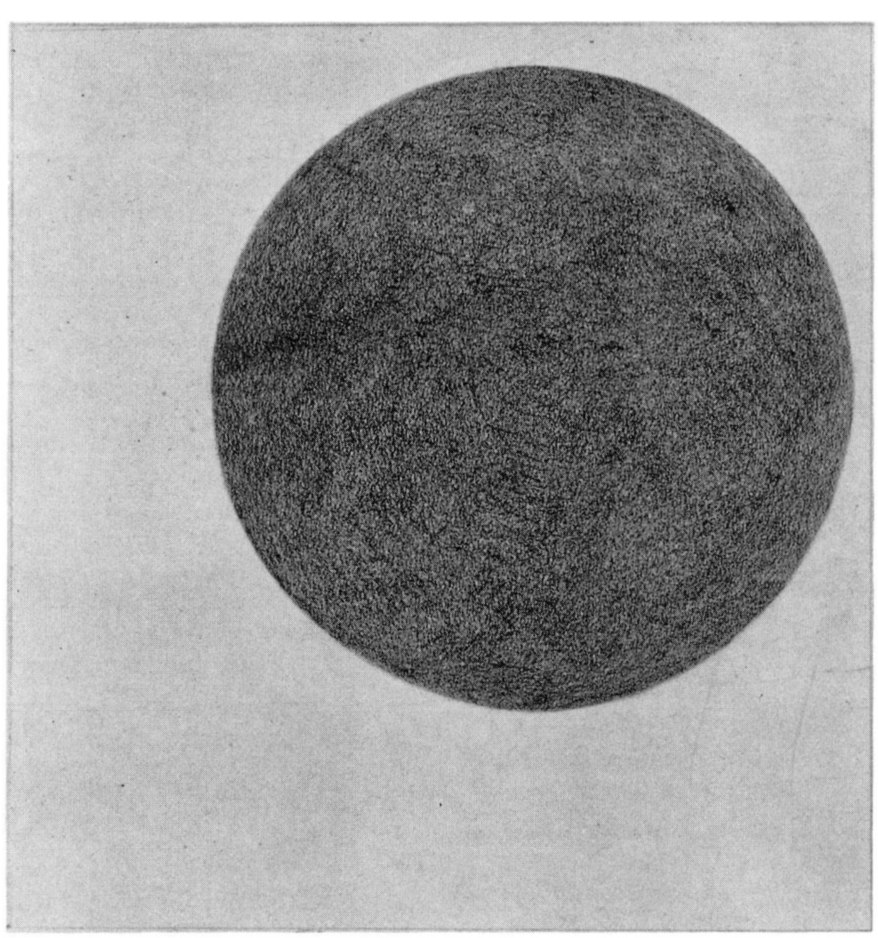

Kasimir Malevich (Russian, 1878-1935)
SUPREMATIST ELEMENT: CIRCLE, 1913
11½″ x 11⅛; pencil
Collection The Museum of Modern Art, N. Y.

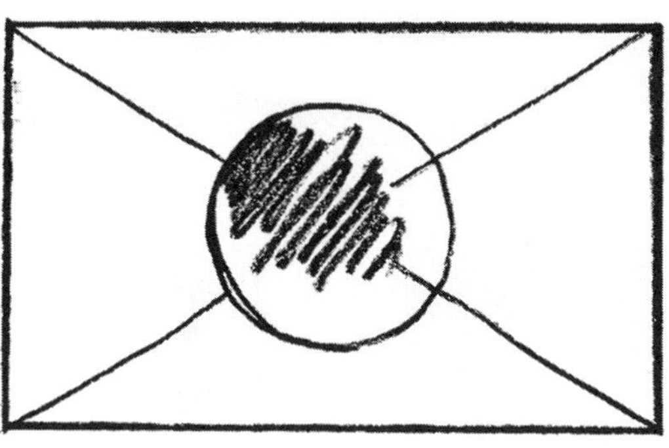

35-1

for the artist as the "truths" of geometry are for the carpenter.

In 1913 a Russian artist named Kasimir Malevich made a picture proving conclusively that what is right for geometry may not be right for painting. His picture, a circle in a rectangle, refutes the idea that a rectangle has only one center. It demonstrates that there are at least two centers, the geometric center and the visual center (*35-2*).

To make this distinction Malevich brought to our attention a fact that many artists have known and utilized for centuries, that the picture field is not a dead rectangle bounded by geometric lines, but a zone, a field, of potential activity. This zone is activated by the borders which in themselves are but symbols of forces which affect anything disturbing the field. Malevich, in this picture, synthesized or isolated a graphic premise. Like a mathematician reducing a fraction to its lowest common denominator, Malevich reduced a great problem of picture structure to its simplest graphic terms.

To understand this tremendous concept, let us examine Malevich's picture in more detail. If we look at the circle critically, we see that it seems suspended in space. Its proximity to the top and right border seems to hold it in the picture. It seems to want to fall into the picture, but in a mysterious way is prevented from doing so by its affinity for these two borders.

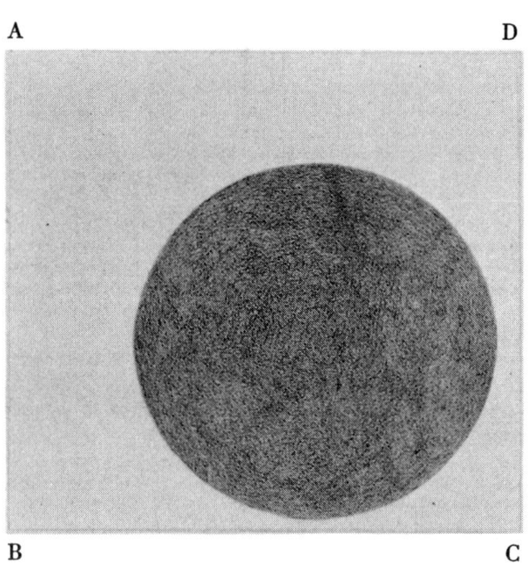


36-1

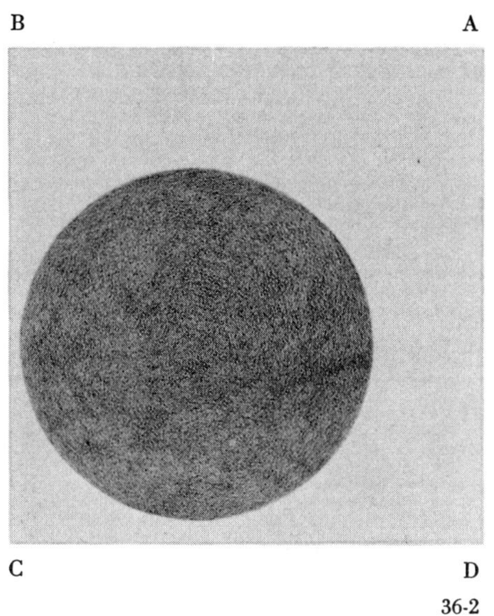


36-2



Now let us turn the picture a quarter turn so that *BC* becomes the bottom of the picture (*36-1*). Instead of being suspended in the picture, the circle now seems to be jammed into the corner *BC-CD*. The circle seems to crowd *CD* and fall out of the picture. A tightness exists between the circle and *BC* as well as *CD*.

Let us continue to rotate the picture. Now with *CD* as a base, we feel that the circle is pulling out of the picture (*36-2*). Its affinity for *BCD* seems overpowering. The attraction of the circle for this corner is stronger than for any other border or combination of borders of the picture.

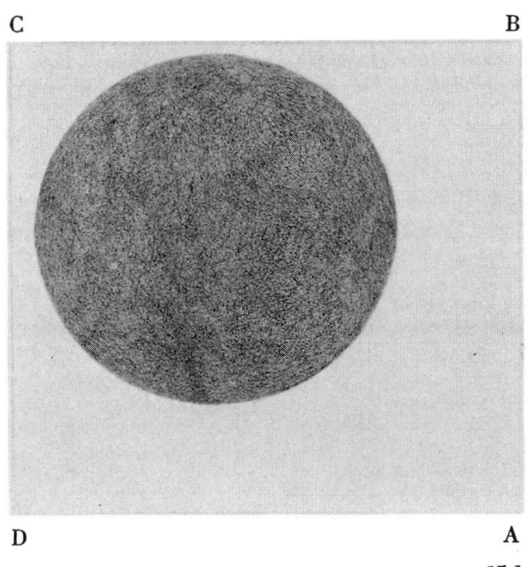



37-1

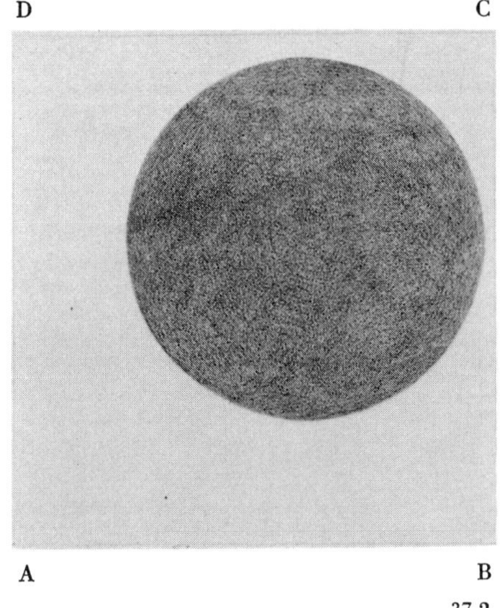



37-2

One more turn with *DA* as a base, and we feel that the circle is crowding *CD*, that it is moving out of the picture to the left (*37-1*).

Returning the picture now to its original position, we feel that the circle is suspended between *AB* and *CD* and between *DA* and *BC*, that it is in a state of equilibrium in relation to the whole picture (*37-2*).

It is evident that the lower border *AB* has much more attracting force than the upper border *DC*. In the same way, although much more difficult to see, the border *DA* seems to have more attracting force than *CB*. Although there seems to be no proof of this phenomenon many painters seem to be aware of it, judging by their pictures.

We can express these forces proportionally, but only in a relative way. A change of proportion of the picture, a change of shape, introduces variations in the relative degree of attracting force of each border which can only be estimated by the artist as he creates his picture.

Summing up, we can say that the borders of a picture are not just inert geometric boundaries but symbols of actual attracting forces. Such forces vary as to the shape and size of the field and have a profound effect upon what is placed upon the picture surface. We next examine how the picture surface relates to the surfaces of volumes.

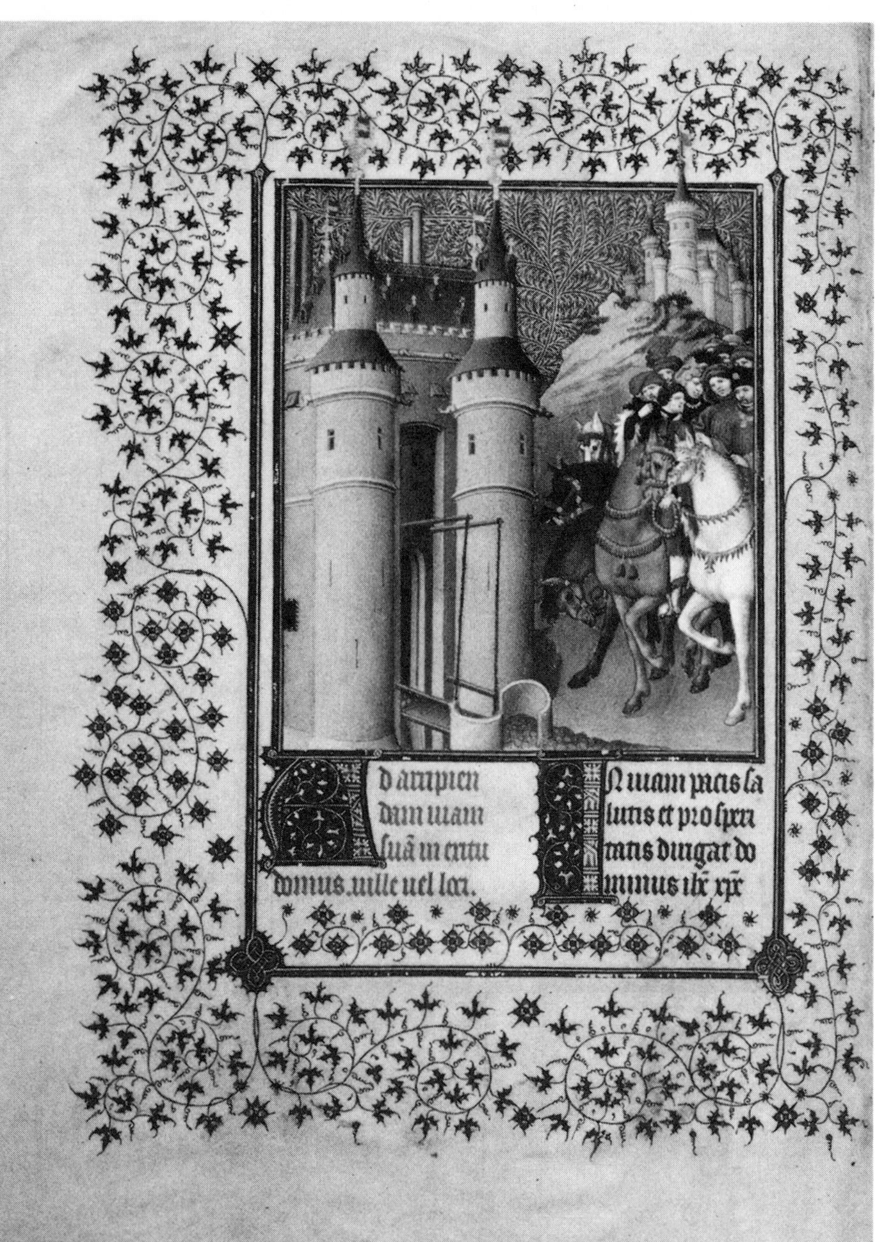



## 3 Perspective Planes and Picture Sections

**Depth Through Convergence**

We see almost everything in nature in terms of perspective. A form's size, shape, and color are seemingly modified by the distance separating us from the form itself. Except for an occasional surface which is parallel to us, almost everything else we see is made of surfaces receding into depth.

In the very early Renaissance, a period of great artistic investigation, we find that strenuous efforts were made to develop a method of indicating depth in a drawing, as we see in the illuminated manuscript above. From these efforts came a system of drawing now referred to as scientific perspective or Italian perspective. Many subtle improvements have been introduced, but basically Italian perspective has changed little since the Renaissance.

As a device to make informative drawings which simulate a linear translation of a photograph, it has wide use. As a discipline of recording some of the phenomena of vision, something of what we see and understand of nature, it is part of the artist's vocabulary. But as a method of drawing or picture making Italian perspective has grievous shortcomings.

This particular treatise on picture structure seems to be a denial of much of Italian perspective, yet much of picture making is premised upon a thorough knowledge of Italian perspective if for no other reason than as a base from which to depart. The subject has been extensively covered and material is available in any library. It is the responsibility of the individual artist to master this subject in order to be equipped as a craftsman. How or whether he chooses to use this knowledge will be his decision.

In few words, Italian perspective is a fixed, mechanical method of drawing, usually with T-square, triangle, compass, and French curves. With these tools, the length of any line or the true shape of any angle can be determined in any graphic plane, within certain fixed picture limits. All this supposes the additional limitation of seeing the form from a fixed point in space with one eye. This has often been called "the keyhole view." In a strange way Italian perspective anticipated the still camera by about five hundred years. When we transpose a photograph into line, the ensuing drawing in many respects conforms to the tenets of Italian perspective. The fact that we seldom look at either a photograph or an Italian perspective drawing from its true station point merely emphasizes how casually we look at a picture.

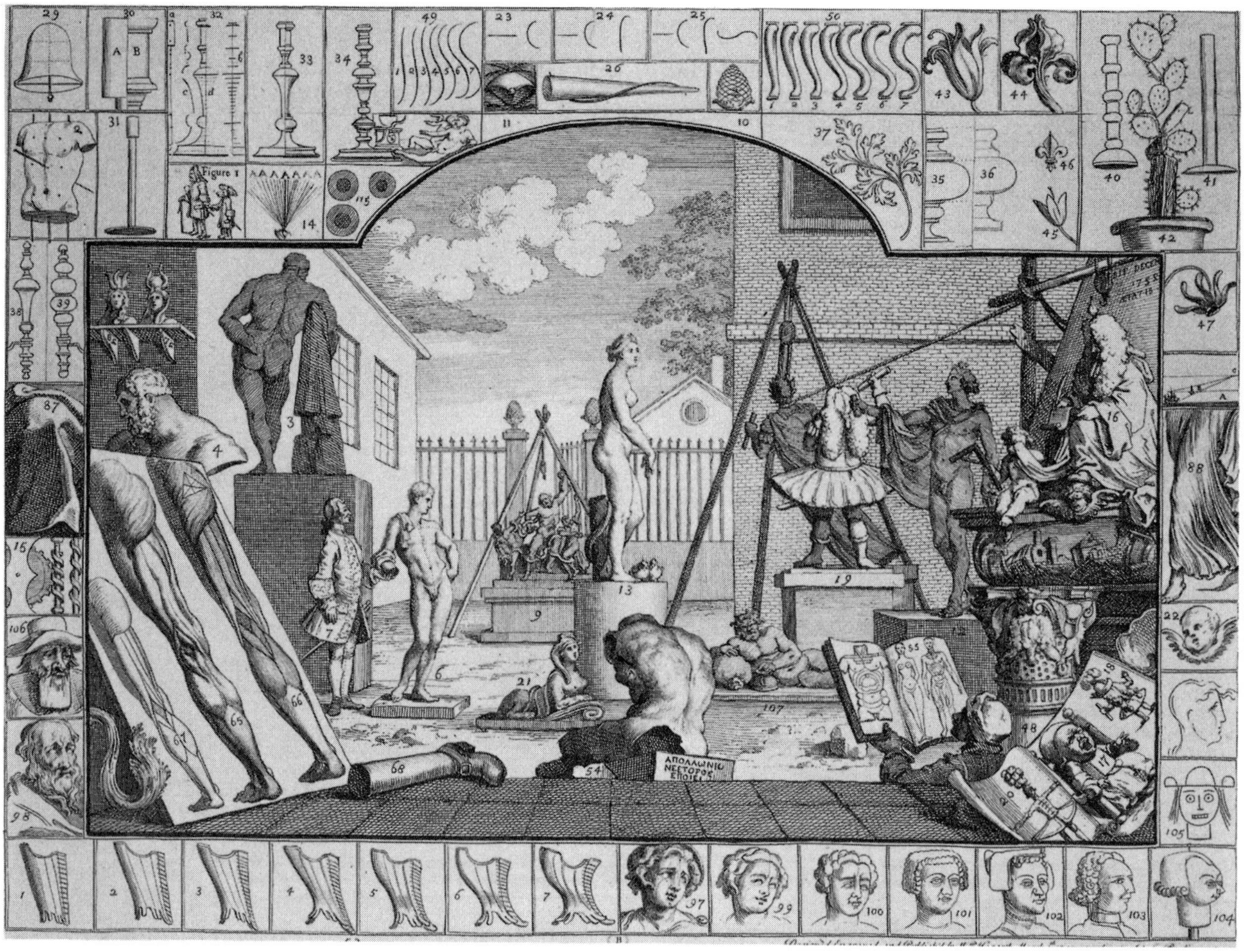

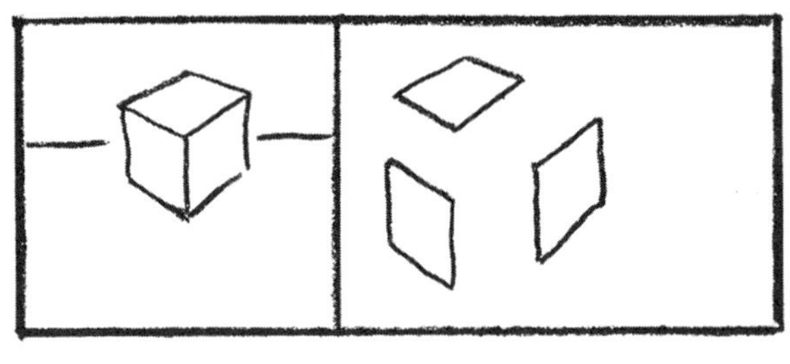

William Hogarth (British, 1697-1764)
THE ANALYSIS OF BEAUTY, Plate 1, 1753
15⅜″ x 19⅞″; engraving
National Gallery of Art, Washington, D. C.
Rosenwald Collection

40-1A       40-1B

40    When translated into graphic terms flat surfaces of forms in nature become planes, the edges become lines. The lines may define a shape, the plane may be a shape. To achieve an illusion of a cube in perspective each plane must be drawn to simulate a receding surface (*40-1A*), and each will be drawn as a distorted square (*40-1B*).

Perspective drawing may be said to consist of a series of false views so arranged that the spectator sums up these false views simultaneously and accepts the composite as a true image in depth.

In the same way, a rounded form may be conceived as made up of any number of planes or facets, each in perspective. William Hogarth in his *The Analysis of Beauty* has aptly likened this effect to that produced by wrapping wire mesh around the form.

In essence, scientific or Italian perspective is symbolized as a triangle converging into a distant horizon or vanishing line (*41-1*). A perspective triangle may be symbolized as a diagonal receding into depth. A perspective line is like an arrow piercing the picture surface at any angle except that of ninety degrees, in which case it would appear as a point (*41-2*). Through such convergences of line and plane, and with diminution of sizes of volumes, it is possible to simulate deep space.

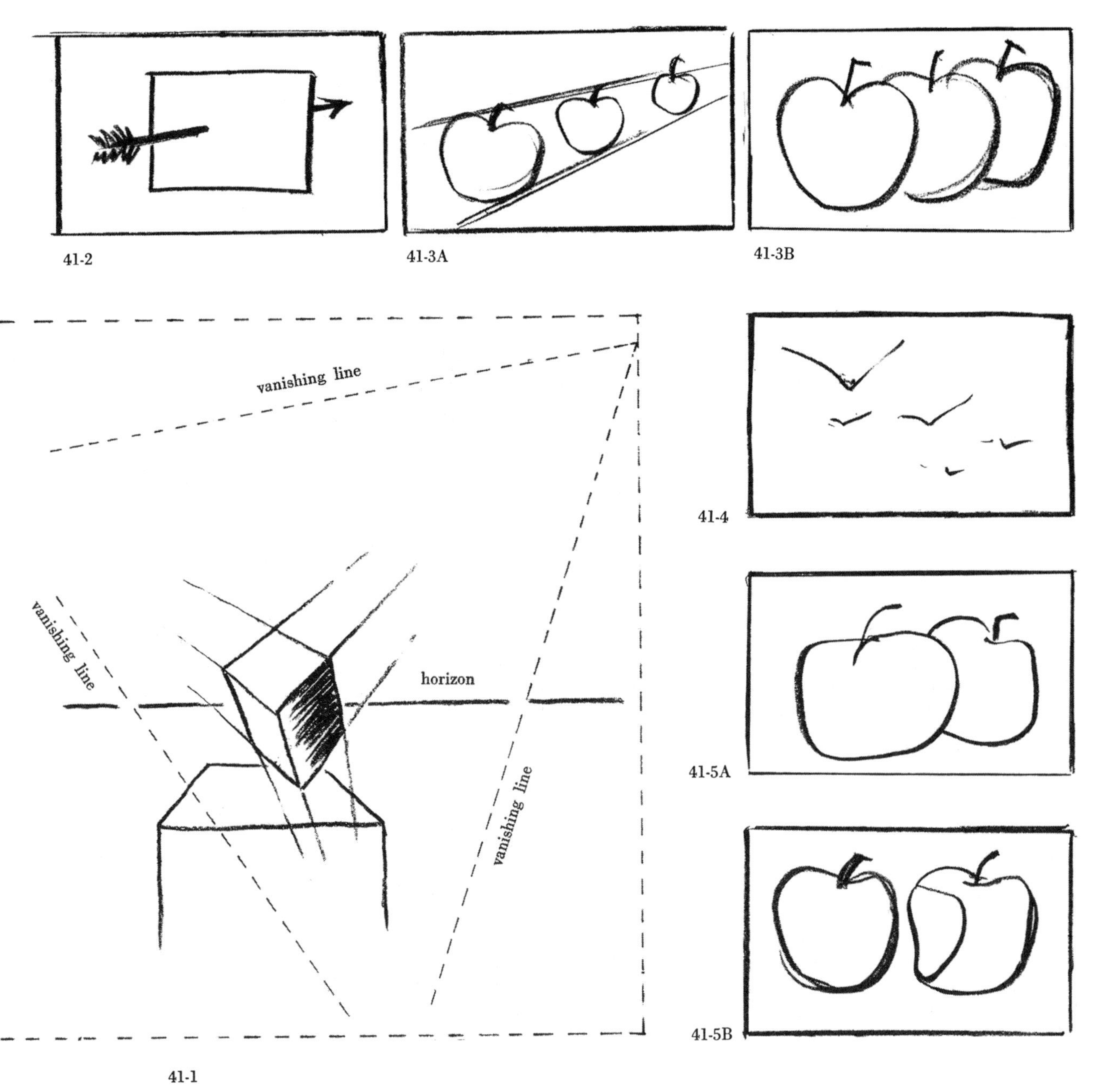



## Depth Through Overlay

In addition to perspective convergences, another effective way to suggest depth is by the use of overlays. For example, three related volumes diminishing rapidly in size as they recede constitute a triangle, a perspective (*41-3A*). The same three volumes drawn almost the same size, but overlayed, also suggest depth, but not violent convergency (*41-3B*).

Some overlay is usually involved in any perspective drawing. If we draw a flock of birds flying, some small, some large, we generally imply that all birds are the same size and in perspective. Though we may think no overlay is involved, in fact all the volumes are overlayed against the sky (*41-4*).

Depth through overlay in nature is an accepted visual phenomenon. If one apple overlays the other, we never doubt that one is in front of the other (*41-5A*). We do not believe a bite has been taken out of one to make it fit the other (*41-5B*).

The logic of overlay is of great help to the artist in simulating depth in pictures. A picture constructed upon perspective convergence, with little emphasis upon overlay, tends to result in weak surface control. Although only one way to suggest depth, an understanding of overlay is imperative in the designing of all pictures.

42-A

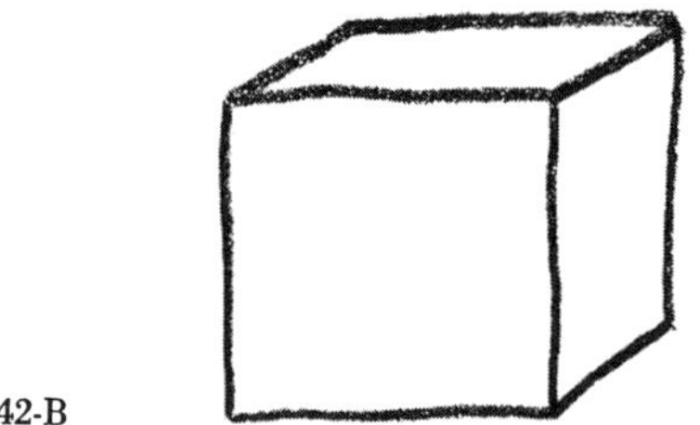

42-B

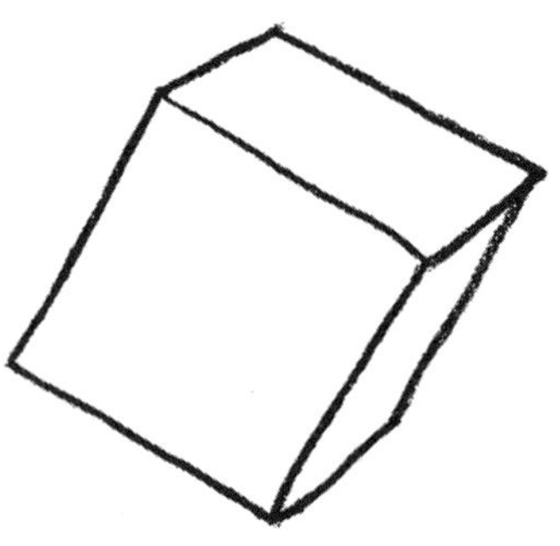

42-C

## 42 The Picture Section

We have noted that almost all forms viewed in nature consist of surfaces receding into perspective depth. Of all these myriad surfaces, one especially has particular value for us in the control of picture depth. It is the surface or facet which lies parallel to us. Such a surface when translated graphically is called a *picture section*. It has unique characteristics.

To demonstrate, if a four-inch cube is viewed so that its face is directly in front of our eyes, it will seem to be a square with no suggestion of depth (42-A). When moved slightly to either side, or up, or down, or rotated, the sides of the cube will be revealed (*42-B*). Although the converging sides of the cube seem to recede into depth and no longer appear square, the face and back of the cube retain their true shape. The front may be a little larger than the back, but both will always remain square. Both are picture sections (*42-C*).

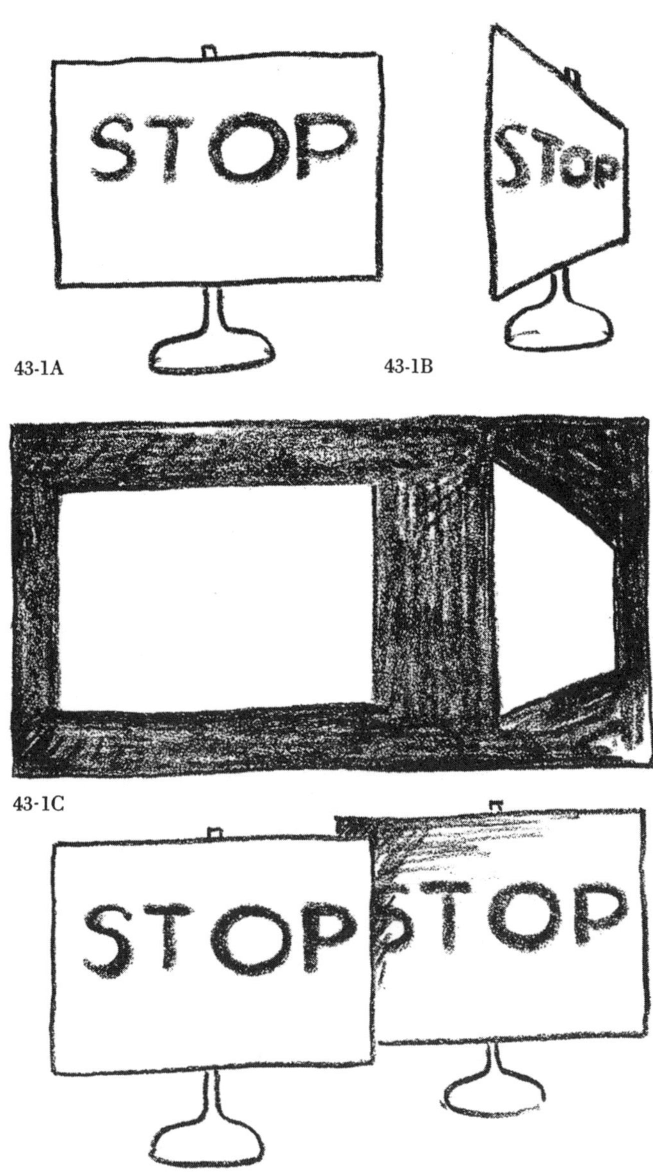


43-1A      43-1B

43-1C

43-2

As another example we may draw a true shape, a road sign, lying in the picture surface (*43-1A*). The same sign in perspective is a distorted or false shape also lying in the picture surface (*43-1B*). Both shapes are actually in the same plane, the picture surface.

We can cut out either shape with a pair of scissors. Each will be a small flat fragment of our paper, regardless of shape. Visually the false shape will wheel into perspective depth unless it is purposely accented in special ways. This wheeling effect dominates our awareness of the false shape as part of the picture surface, and we immediately sense the illusion of depth rather than the physical reality of a shape on a flat surface (*43-1C*).

By comparison, if a true shape overlays a similar or related true shape, we are still well aware of depth but are conscious of the true shapes having an intimate relation to the picture surface (*43-2*).

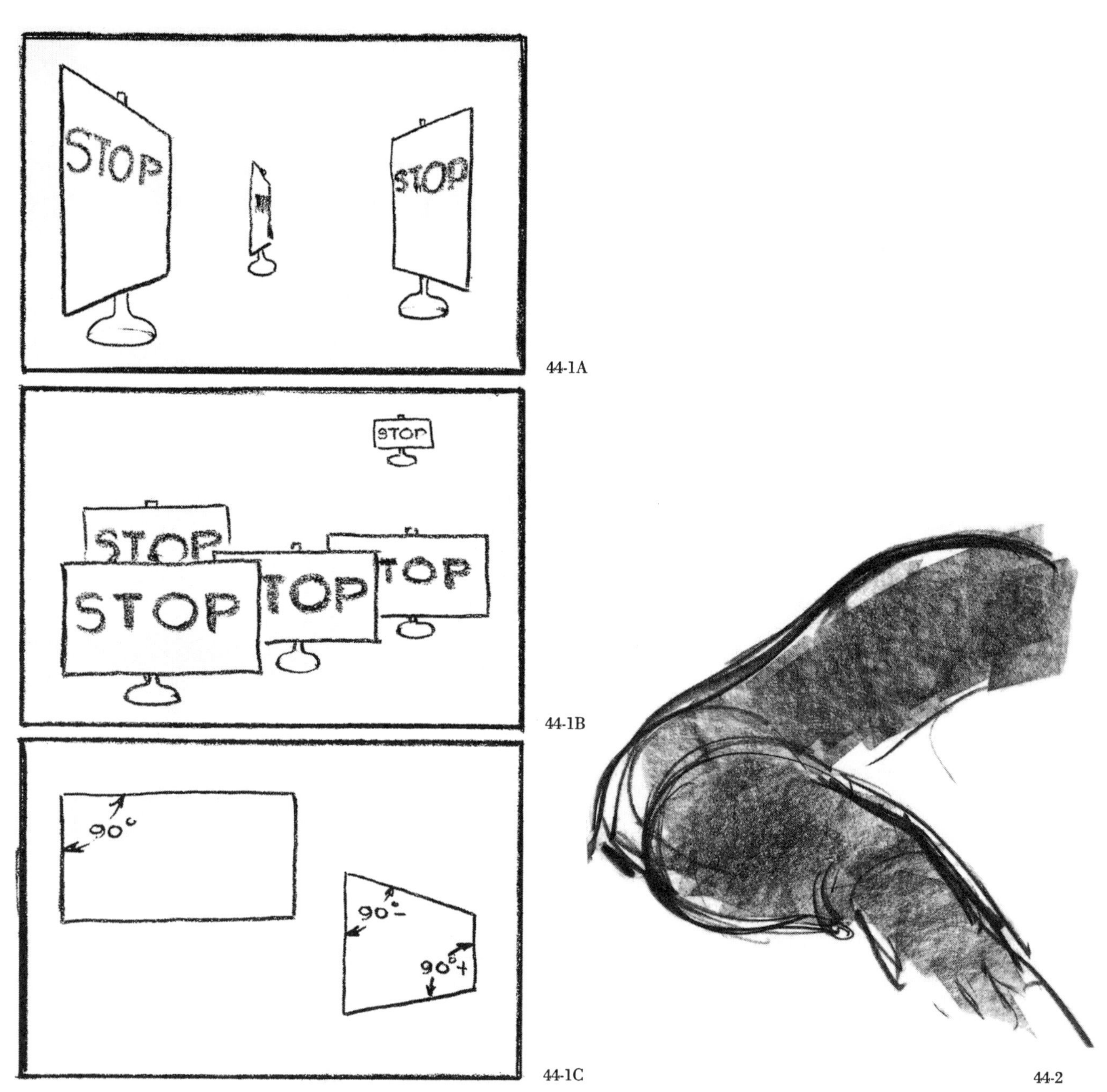



44-1A

44-1B

44-1C

44-2

 So we see there are two types of shapes, the distorted perspective shape, or false shape (*44-1A*), and the true shape (*44-1B*). Visually a perspective shape lies in an imaginary plane on edge, a graphic plane suggesting an angle to the picture surface. The true shape lies in the picture surface. The false perspective shape implies a convergence into depth. The true shape may suggest a position in space, in depth, but always lies in the picture surface or suggests a plane parallel to the picture surface. A true shape may change size as it is moved back and forth from the picture surface, but *it never changes shape*. The perspective plane, on the other hand, changes both size and shape as it assumes new positions (*44-1C*).

Most three-dimensional growth forms are rather easily drawn by the manipulation of perspective planes. However, overemphasis of convergences, or over-modeling, almost always results in weakening of the structure of the picture surface.

To transpose from a perspective drawing of such forms to the expression of these forms in terms of true shapes, we may use ordered sections or slices parallel to the picture surface. In the accompanying drawing (*44-2*), the upper arm is parallel to us and so can be resolved into a true shape parallel to the picture surface. Sections through the forearm and wrist also are in or parallel to the picture surface, so these parts can be emphasized to retain surface control. Much of contemporary composition is contingent upon exploiting the potential of symbols which lend themselves to various devices to maintain surface control. One of these devices is the picture section.

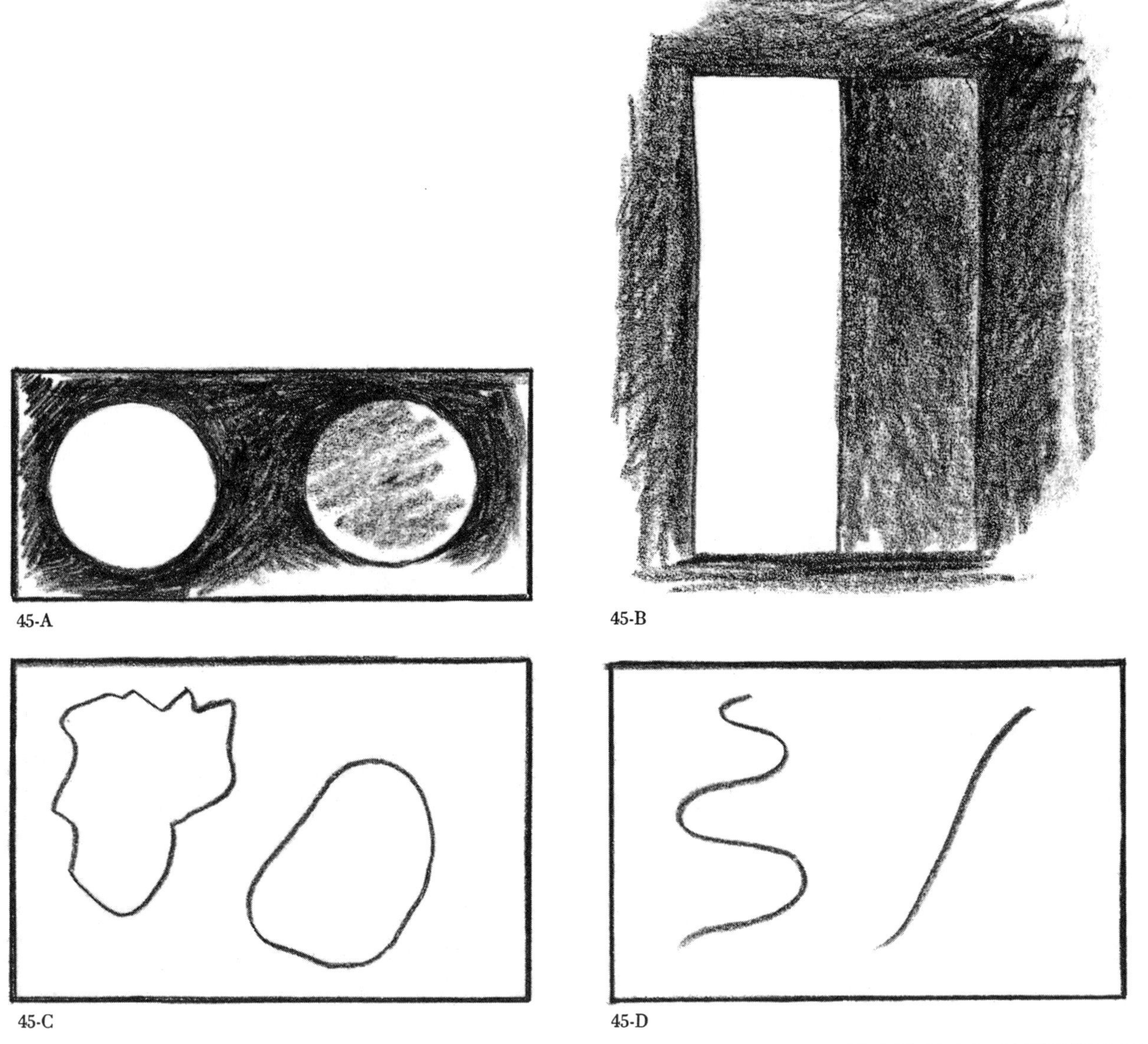

45-A

45-B

45-C

45-D

## Depth Through Contrast

The illusion of depth in a picture achieved by use of perspective convergences and by the use of overlaying shapes or volumes are only two controls of picture depth. Of even greater importance is the control of depth through the graphic or visual activity of elements making up the picture. For instance, two circles drawn with a compass are the same size, but if one circle remains the white of the paper and the other is made a middle gray against a dark background, the circles will no longer seem the same size. Not only does the white circle appear larger than the gray circle, but it also will seem closer to the viewer (*45-A*).

A panel divided geometrically in half in no way assures us that the two parts will appear visually equal, for differences of color, or dark or light, or texture will alter the balance (*45-B*). Very active shapes often seem closer than more simple shapes (*45-C*); very active lines usually seem closer than simple lines (*45-D*). Colors, textures, patterns, contrasts of all kinds affect our eyes differently and result in a movement of the various elements in or out in relation to the picture surface. This constant in or out movement has profound effect on the structure of any picture, as we will see in Chapter 20. It also results in another graphic enigma.

45

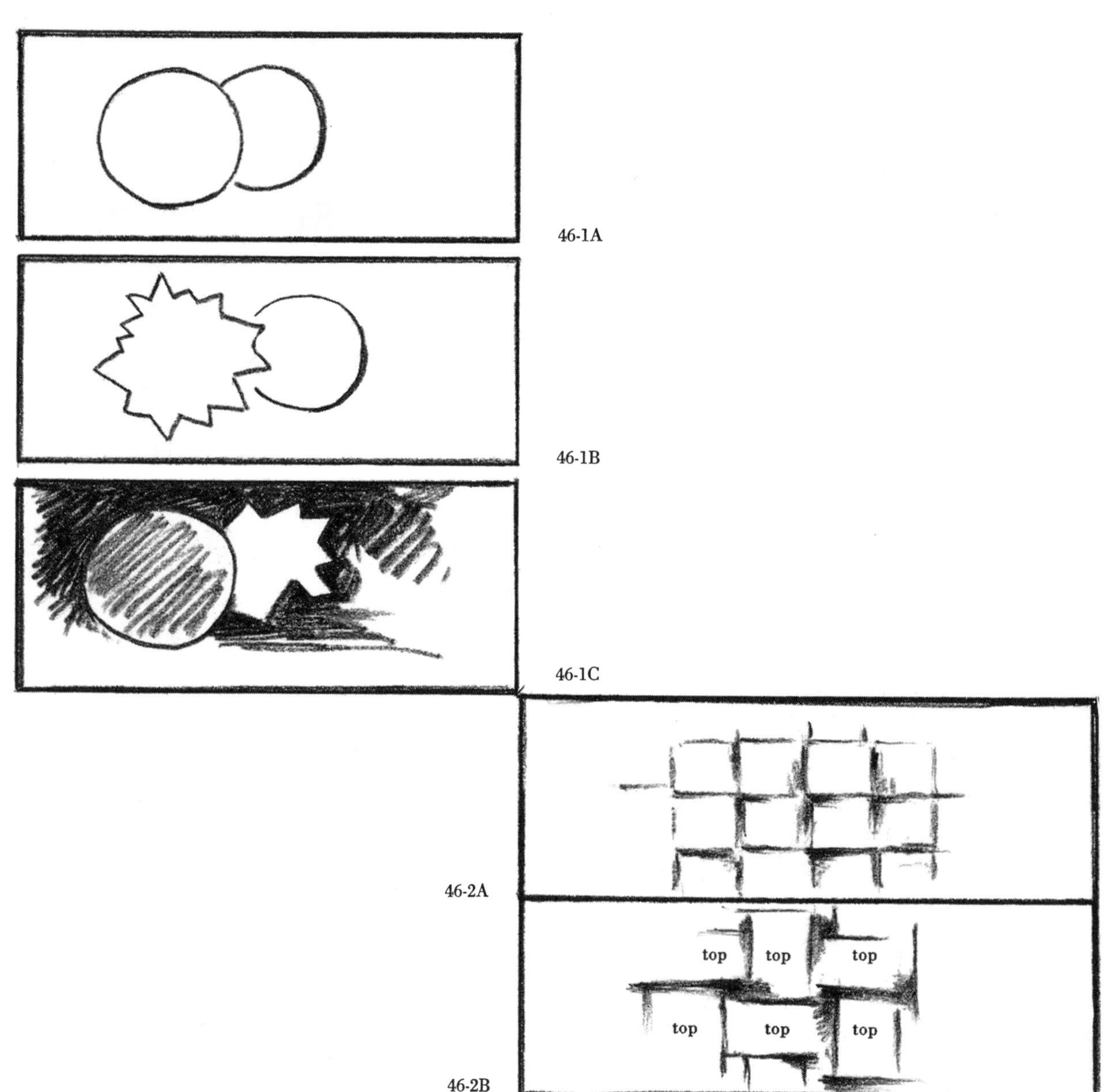




We will recall that through overlay we can create the illusion of depth (*46-1A*). By overlaying a simple shape with an active shape this sense of depth is enhanced (*46-1B*). If, however, a simple shape overlays a very active shape, the active shape may appear closer to us than the simple shape because of its graphic activity (*46-1C*). It is strange that two overlayed shapes, one in front of the other, may at the same time appear in reversed position. This is one of the great enigmas of pictures and a factor which can often be used to control the surface. Through the exploitation of contrast it is possible visually to bring a shape seemingly far in the distance into the picture surface. In fact, if care is not taken, a shape in the distance may be overemphasized so that it seems to jump out of the picture surface.

How strongly the surface factor of a picture should be emphasized depends upon the personal choice of each artist. As we noted in the last chapter, the less the surface factor is stressed the more we become conscious of the effect of looking through a window at a scene beyond the picture frame. The more the surface factor is stressed, the more we are conscious of a surface pattern achieved through an interlocking of shapes which, although seemingly in depth, occur on the picture surface. In this latter case we have a stronger balance of both the physical and visual reality of the picture. Yet too much emphasis on surface pattern at the expense of depth may result in an undesirably flat, decorative picture.

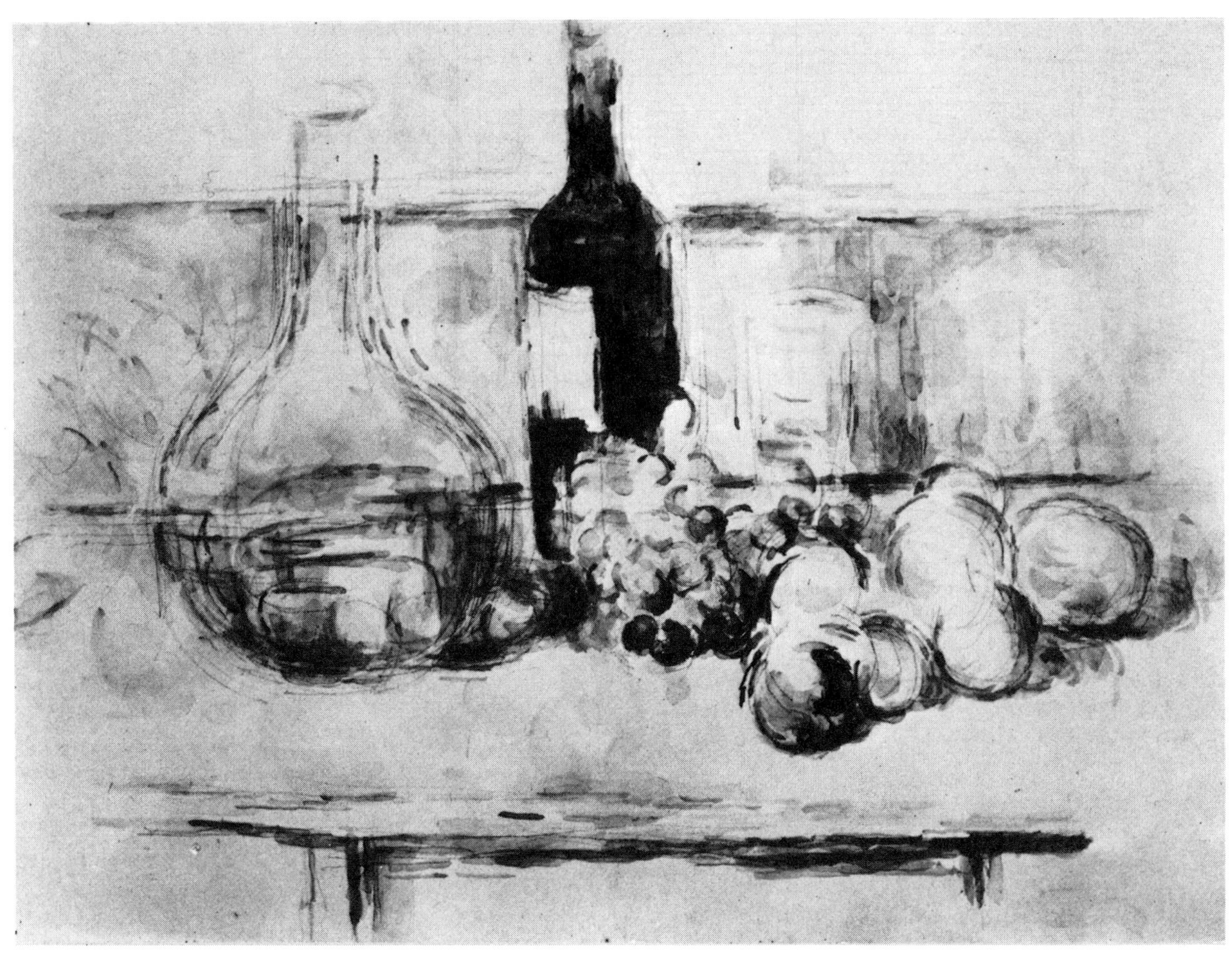

Paul Cézanne (French, 1839-1906)
STILL LIFE, 1906; 18½" x 24⅜"; watercolor
(Photo: Courtesy Prof. Dr. Kurt Badt, Uberlingen)
Cosmopress, Geneva



Although in nature the phenomenon of depth through perspective is dominant, there is one construction in nature which curiously simulates a strong surface structure in a picture. It involves both surface and depth, yet it is truly a three-dimensional arrangement of three-dimensional forms. It is a mat, or web, constructed of overlapping and woven strands or strips of material (*46-2A*). The mat is a three-dimensional construction, yet it is flat for we can sit on it comfortably. But is it flat? Each strip goes under or over an adjacent strip, and thus depth is present. Each strip, however, returns to a common surface. The web involves actual depth in nature, but bears an intriguing resemblance to an effect which can be achieved graphically (*46-2B*).

A careful relation of graphic activity of every element in this Cézanne still life results in a constant in and out balance to the picture surface. The sum of these relations is equilibrium. Elements in the background lie visually in the same plane as those in the foreground, yet at the same time they assume relative positions in depth. It is similar in construction to the diagram of the web, although infinitely more exciting.

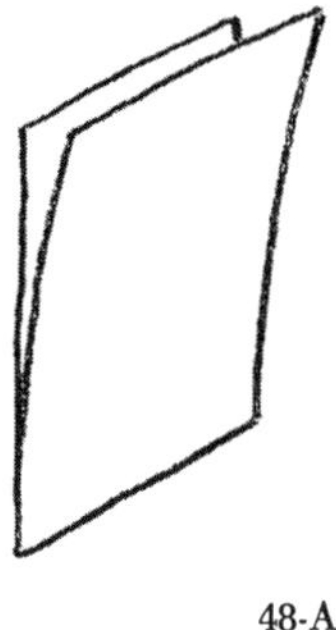

48-A

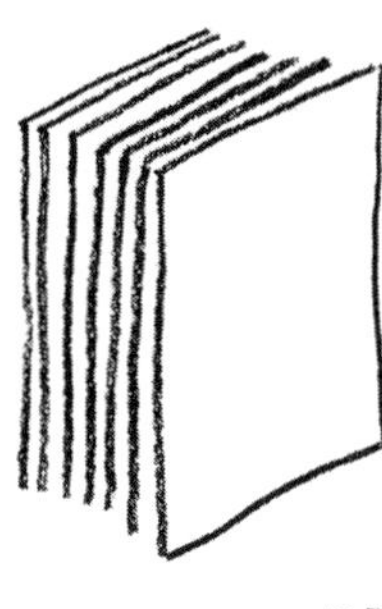

48-B

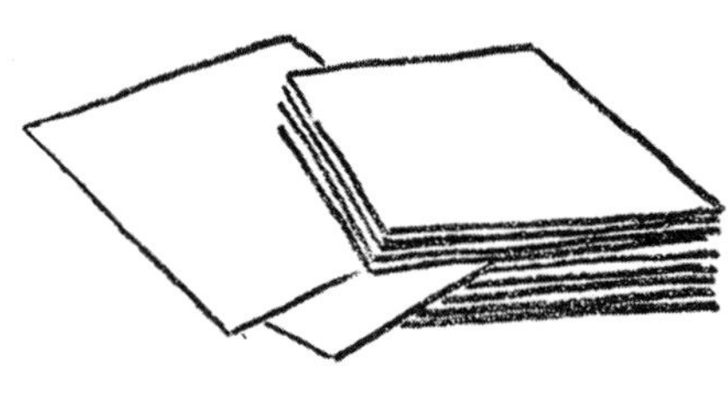

48-C



# 4 Sectional Perspective

**Planal Structure of a Form**

To better understand the difference between Italian and sectional perspective, let us examine a cubic form, in this case an ordinary deck of playing cards. Although there are usually fifty-two individual cards in a deck, it is not difficult to imagine each card split laterally into two (*48-A*), giving us over one hundred cards, or to continue splitting the cards until we have one thousand or one million cards. In other words, we may visualize a cubic structure as made up of an infinite number of parallel slices or planes (*48-B*).

When we draw a deck on corner in perspective, each separate card vanishes in a common horizon or vanishing line (*48-C*). Since each card is in perspective, each card makes an

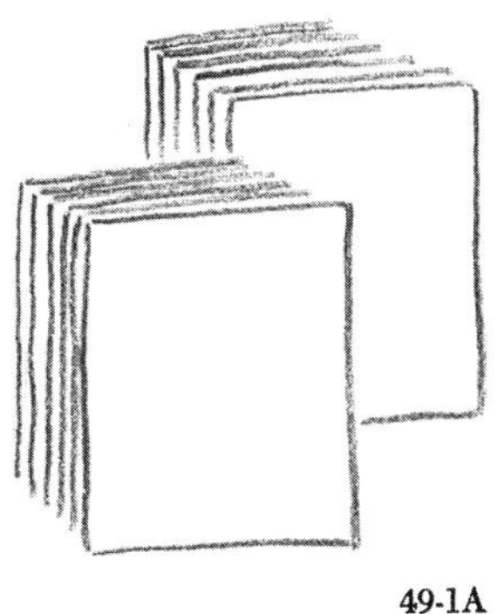

49-1A

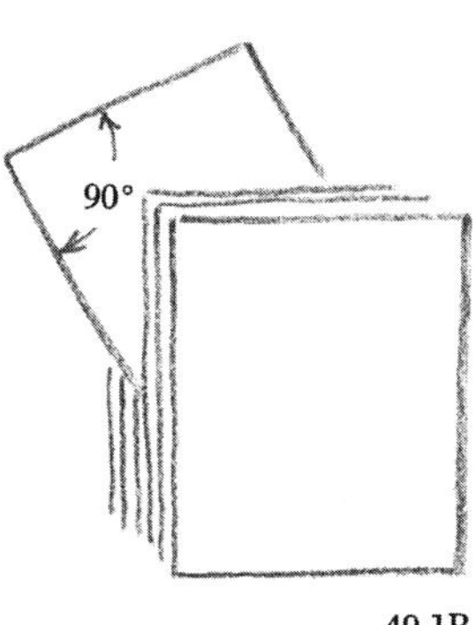



49-1B

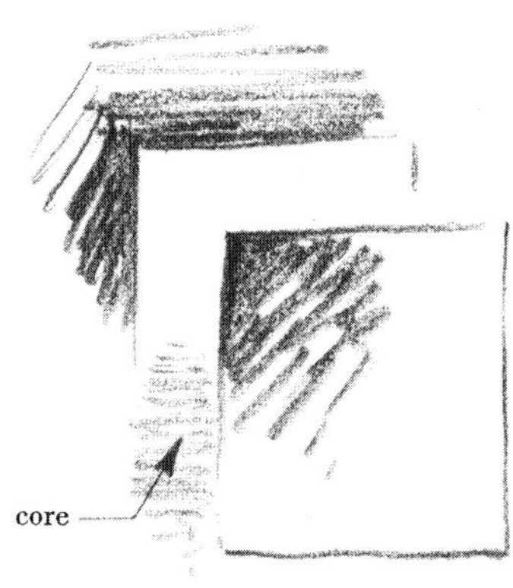



49-2

angle to the picture surface; each card, except if seen on edge, will be a distorted rectangle.

Suppose now, we draw the deck so that all the cards are parallel to us (*49-1A*). We see that a card may be drawn larger or smaller as it approaches or recedes from the picture surface, but that no matter what its position in the picture its shape remains constant. It always will be a true rectangle (*49-1B*).

## Sectional Perspective and Italian Perspective

In drawing the deck with all the cards parallel to us we introduce a new system of drawing, often called *sectional perspective* to distinguish it from Italian perspective.

We found in Chapter 3 that the dominant feature of a perspective drawing is a diagonal driving into the distance. Each plane in perspective growing out of such diagonals generates a false shape.

In sectional perspective, however, the back and front cards of our deck are parallel, often about the same size, and exactly the same shape. Between these two planes, the intervening planes, which may be imagined as infinite in number, may now be visualized as reduced to only one plane. This plane is known as the *core* of the volume (*49-2*).

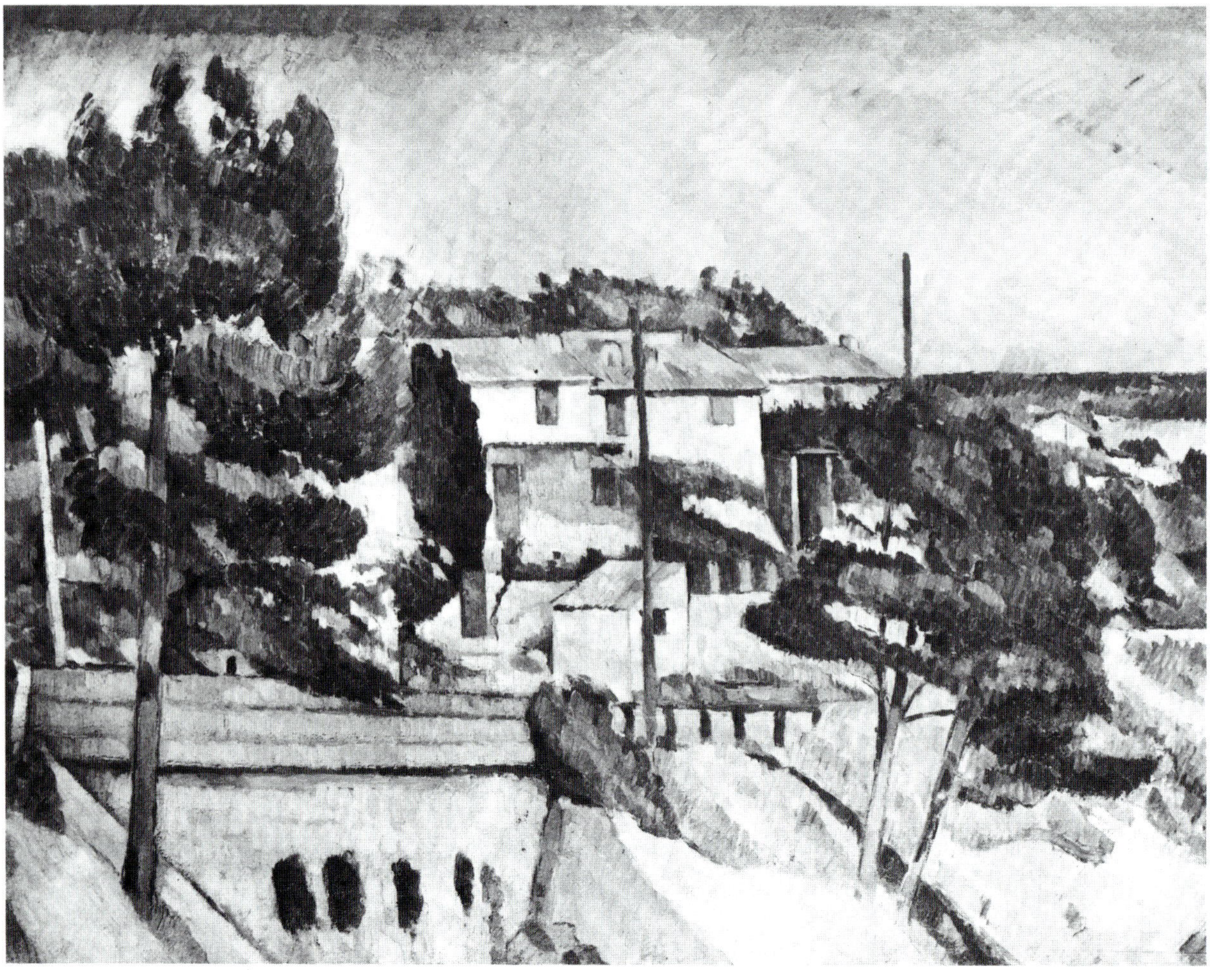

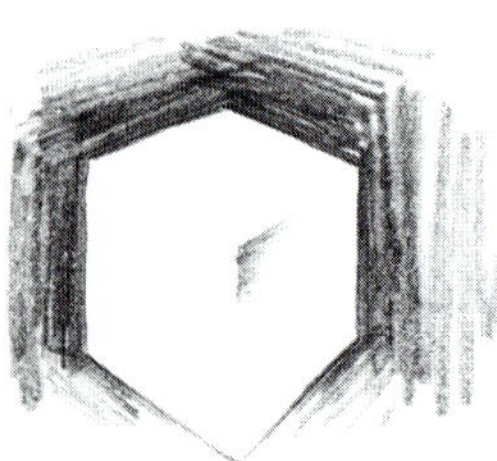

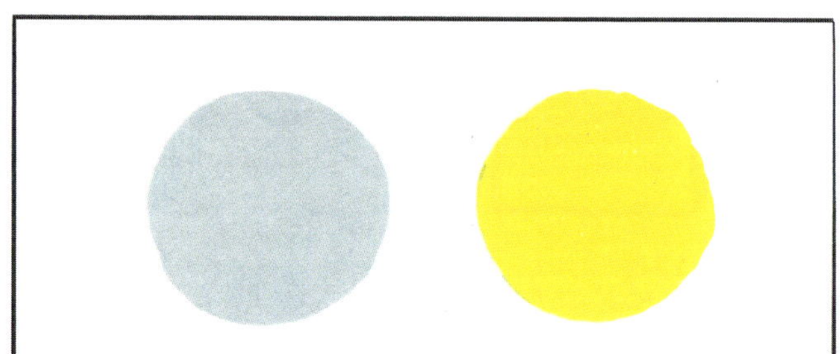

50-1       50-3



In drawing three-dimensional symbols, either in Italian or sectional perspective, diagonals are often unavoidable. But in Italian perspective they are dramatized, while in sectional perspective they usually are subordinated or almost eliminated. At times the overall shape impact of a volume may be stressed and the internal diagonals reduced in importance, as in this cube (*50-1*).

In sectional perspective a long important diagonal often may be interrupted by overlapping forms, as in Cézanne's painting above. The effect of the diagonal is preserved, yet the picture can still be controlled sectionally.

## The Development of Sectional Perspective

In drawing, painting, and composition conventions develop because of graphic necessity. The development of sectional perspective as we know it today also came about because of a necessity. This necessity arose from a need to relate drawing to color. The importance of color as an independent force in painting developed in the nineteenth century. Methods of relating drawing to color had to be developed, for they had not been exploited by the Renaissance painters or, for that matter, by most painters before Cézanne.

This is not to say that Cézanne suddenly invented contemporary painting. Many before him also realized that free color was important in painting. But it was he who opened the door to admit color as a moving, vital force in painting. With Cézanne came a new concept of painting.

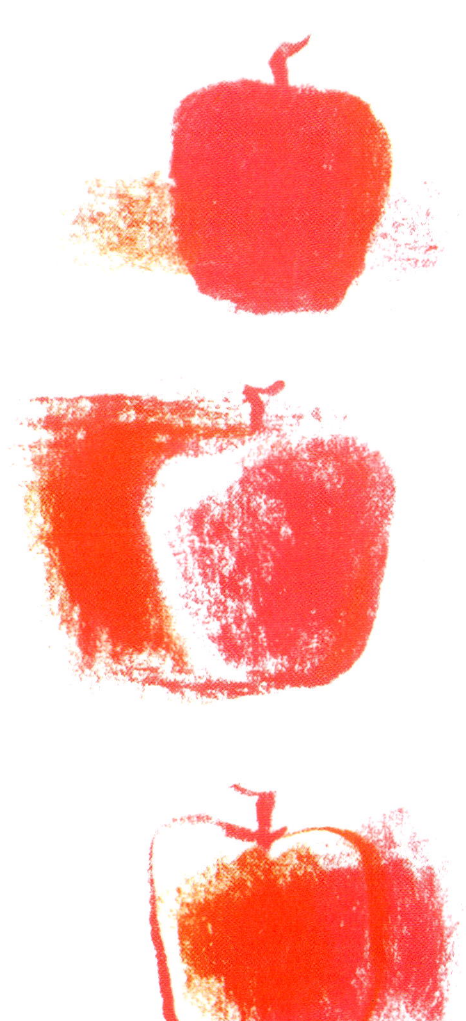

51

To emphasize this all-important concept, let us again draw with a compass two circles exactly the same size, as we did in Chapter 3. If one is now painted a bright, light yellow and the other a neutral gray, they no longer seem the same size nor in the same plane (50-3). What we have done is to demonstrate that color is not merely an adjunct of drawing, but that it has a life of its own. It expands and contracts; it moves forward and recedes.

Cézanne realized that it is impossible to paint two circles of the same size utterly different in color and brightness and expect them to maintain equal positions in the picture surface. He, and many painters since, saw that some adjustment was needed if color were to function as a moving, expanding-contracting, advancing-receding element in a picture. So the sacrifice had to be in the delineation.

Realistic projection and modeling had to go. And Italian perspective, which emphasized atmospheric space, had to be modified.

In sectional perspective, volumes are indicated with flat color and shape, rather than through modeling. And the use of a confining linear structure is avoided (51).

The result is a liberation of color. The color is allowed to expand if that is its tendency and the shape of the symbol may accommodate this. Or color may contract or recede, and its shapes may be activated or reinforced with line, often colored line, to bring the symbol back to the surface.

We see now that by transposing from Italian perspective to sectional perspective, a new type of drawing can be realized which lends itself directly to the dynamic use of color. With this concept of picture making built on sectional perspective, the movements that are potential in color become possible. The picture becomes pliable. Sectional perspective allows for the use of open or free-flowing color outside the silhouette. It permits color to expand or contract, to approach or recede. Yet it preserves the option of explaining volumes in deep space.

This is a very different concept of color than that of the Renaissance painter. The Renaissance painter exploited the use of three-dimensional symbols in deep perspective. Such volumes depended upon careful delineation. A painted symbol of an arm first had to satisfy the dictates of a believable anatomy, resulting in shapes and proportions closely derived from an actual arm. Although there were ingenious methods developed to make such volumes exciting graphic shapes, still the painter was bound by convention to utilize almost sculptural or realistic symbols.

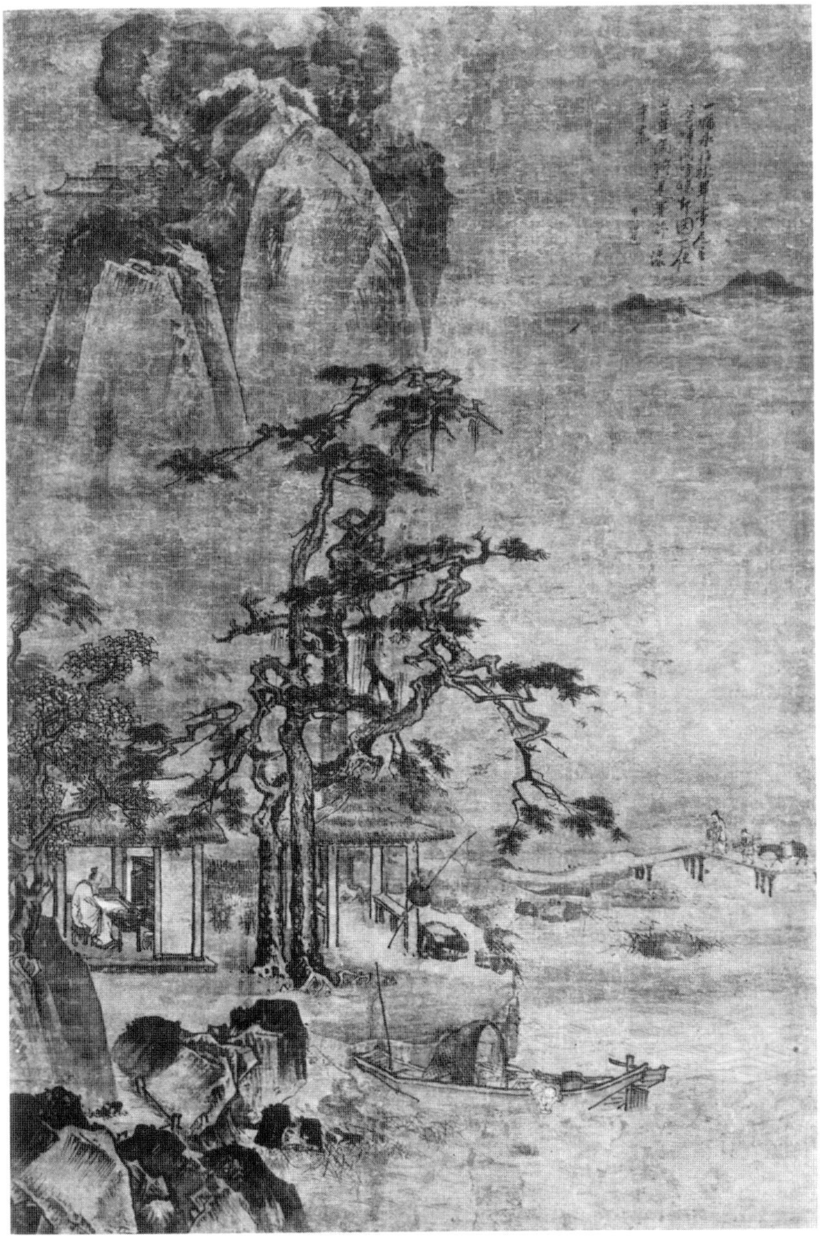

Artist unknown (Chinese, Ming Dynasty)
LANDSCAPE: A MOUNTAIN RETREAT
UNDER PINES BY A RIVER
15th century; 74¾" x 48⅜"
silk panel, ink and color
Courtesy of the Smithsonian Institution
Freer Gallery of Art; Washington, D. C.

To do so he first established his symbol as a careful drawing. Only when these volumes faithfully represented his model did he proceed to paint. And here he reached an impasse. To preserve the fidelity of the drawn symbol he could modify his color so that it was confined or subordinated to the drawing, or he could distort his drawing to accommodate his color. Because of his time in history he had little choice. The delineation of the symbols in pictures always took precedence over color.

To complicate matters, the Renaissance painter introduced devices of modeling to generate depth and often simulated light sources. It became more and more difficult to release color from these bonds. Painting, in effect, became primarily a method of tinting a drawing.

Sectional perspective was carried to a high point in Oriental art, especially by the Chinese, as demonstrated in this landscape. But they did not develop the possibilities of sectional perspective in terms of color. Oriental paintings are predominantly masterpieces of drawing, including black, gray, and white, but not using color as a vital factor in the structure of the picture. Again, color is used as an adjunct of drawing, as a tint.

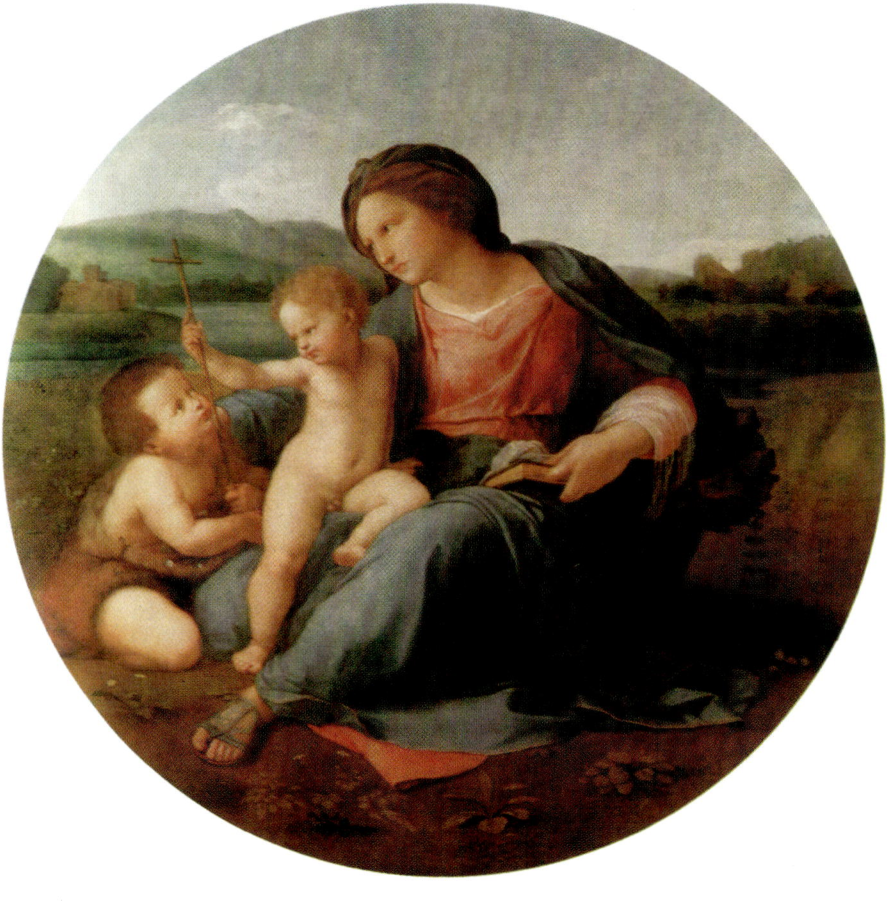

Raphael (Italian, 1483-1520)
THE ALBA MADONNA; ca. 1509-1510; diam. 37¾″
canvas transferred from wood
National Art Gallery of Art, Washington, D.C.
Andrew Mellon Collection

Even in the application of paint the difference between the approaches to Italian perspective and to sectional perspective is as night and day. The Renaissance painter mentally "painted around" his volumes as if stroking a cat. Although his brush was always on the the actual picture surface, the goal of visual roundness in the painted image dominated his every move. As a result, there always was a danger that the highly modeled volumes in deep atmospheric space would so overwhelm the audience that it would lose the impact of the picture as a construction on a surface. Thus, as the illusion of sculptured volume became more nearly perfect, color became more and more confined, as we note in Raphael's *Alba Madonna.*

The painter employing sectional perspective, on the other hand, applies paint to his picture surface as he would butter to bread. He applies his color flat to accommodate the flat surface of his picture. These flat areas of applied color on the picture surface relate directly to the image, which is also delineated with flat planes in or parallel to the picture surface. There is a logical, harmonious melding of the paint, the surface, and the image, which Matisse demonstrates here.

To implement the use of color in terms of sectional perspective, all modeling and strong perspective diagonals driving into deep space are avoided when possible.

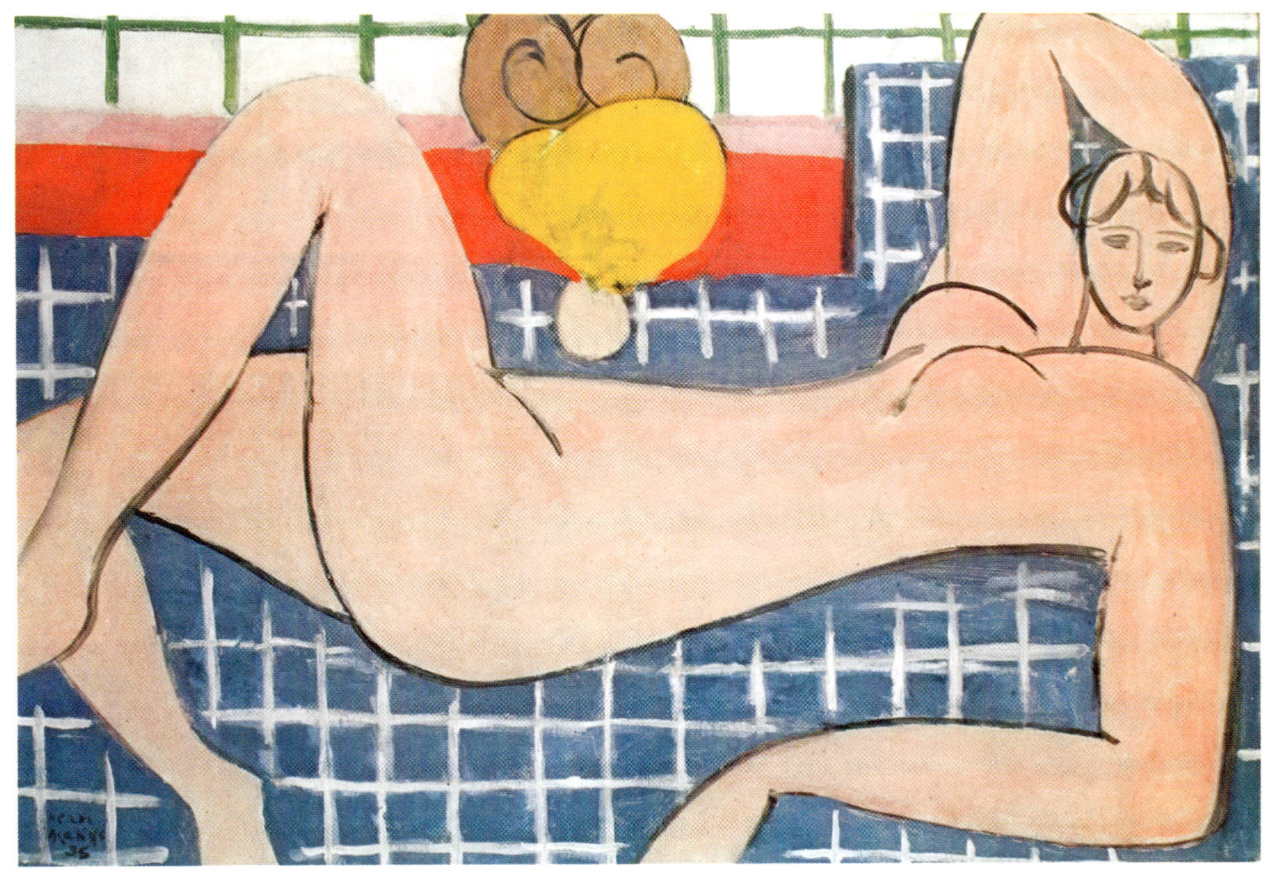

Henri Matisse (French, 1869-1954)
PINK NUDE, 1935; 26″ x 36½″
oil on canvas
The Baltimore Museum of Art

The movement of color in and out from the picture surface has always been of concern to the painter, for the way a color modifies a shape, or vice versa, is of tremendous importance. But when color is confined by a fixed delineated volume in deep space, color movement is truly a problem. Pieter Breugel was able to hold a bright color far back in a picture and at the same time relate it to his surface pattern. Since Bruegel's volumes were so vigorously three-dimensional this was a remarkable feat.

Of the later painters, Henri Matisse, who spent a lifetime studying the properties of color in relation to shape, is but one to whom we may turn for ideas.

The advent of a new painting concept does not mean that the Renaissance painting concept is faulty, however. It simply is not adequate to satisfy the demands of a newer understanding of color. Nor should we feel that all pictures before our time are dull because today paintings have a brilliance and excitement of color that was not achieved in the past. But tastes change, our demands change, and the contemporary artist is finding new ways to meet the new demands.

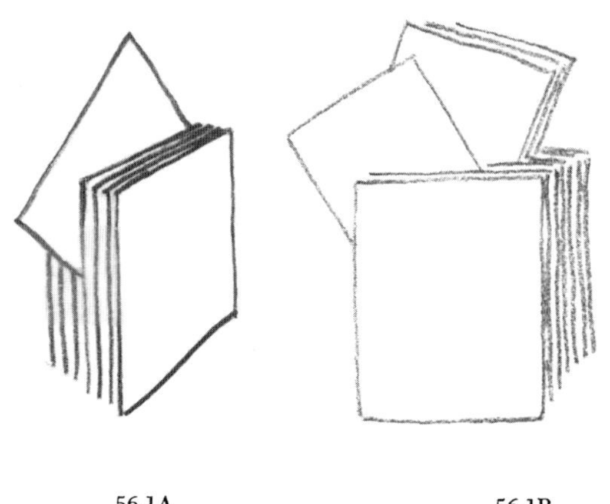

56-1A          56-1B

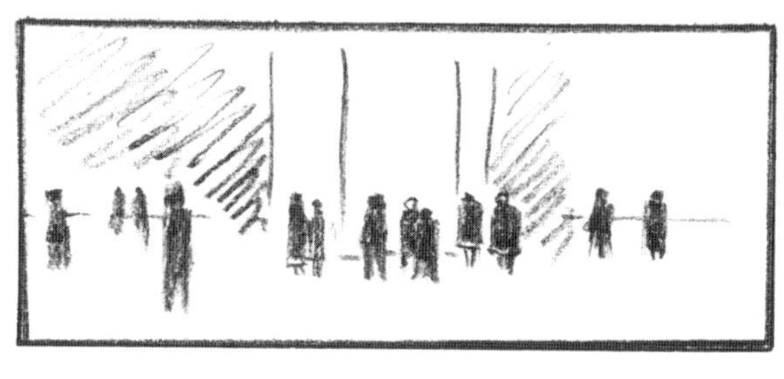

56-2

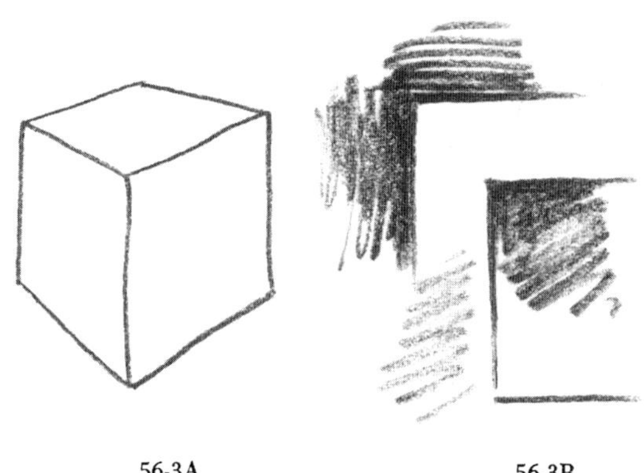

56-3A          56-3B

## 56  Planal Structure of the Picture

Returning now to our deck of cards, we see that the segmented form contains clues to the structure of a picture. If the deck is in perspective to us in nature, the displacement of any single card results in a new perspective of this card (*56-1A*). When delineated, such a card is seldom a visually integrated part of the picture surface. Although occupying part of the picture surface, it makes an angle visually to the surface. It is a false shape which belies the picture surface.

If we draw the deck so that it is parallel to the picture surface, any card in any position while still in the deck will be in or parallel to the picture surface. Its shape will remain constant and will seem visually integrated with the picture surface (*56-1B*).

As we have seen, not all views of volumes resolve themselves easily into sectional perspective. Corner views, which may be of a cube or a street corner, so overwhelm us with their perspective impact that great care must be exerted to overcome this insistence (*56-2*). Usually the artist must dramatize the visual activity of a shape and its color in relation to its position in the picture surface in order to overcome the perspective drive into depth. Insistent close corners may be reduced in visual impact; distant shapes may be intensified. Architectural forms and mechanical forms, by their very emphasis on geometric correctness, present great compositional difficulty when viewed on corner. However, emphasis upon the silhouette of the whole volume is helpful, as we saw in diagram *50-1*. Growth forms and drapery usually may be adjusted with relative ease.

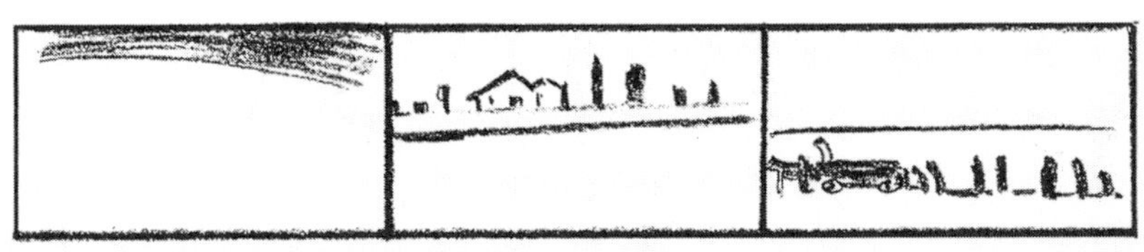
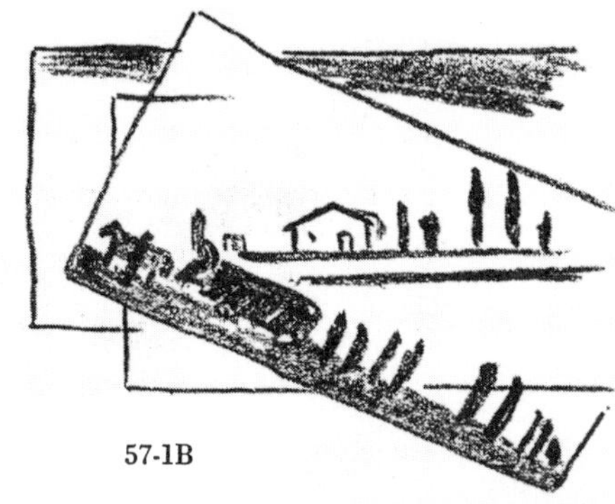

57-1A         57-1B

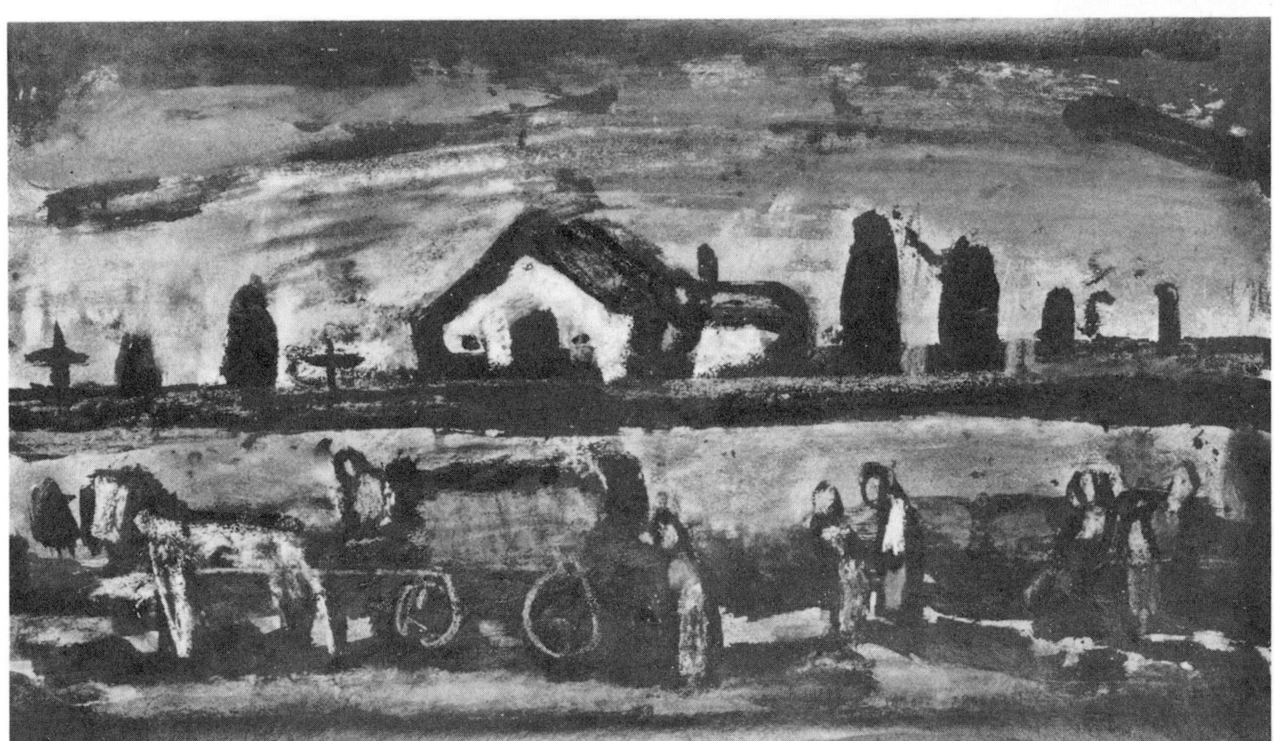

Georges Rouault (French, 1871-1958)
THE OLD WALL (THE FUNERAL), 1930
11½″ x 19¾″; gouache, pastel, on paper
The Metropolitan Museum of Art
Maria DeWitt Jesup Fund, 1951
from the Museum of Modern Art, Anonymous Gift

We might say that a cube viewed on corner typifies Renaissance picture structure (*56-3A*), while a cube facing us typifies contemporary picture structure (*56-3B*).

If, now, we visualize the whole picture as a deck of cards lying flat to us, any card displaced remains flat to us. Such a card may be visualized as representing the distant background, or the subject, or an overlay (*57-1A*). A series of such cards each represents a different symbol or group of symbols occupying different "levels" or positions in space (*57-1B*). Although each on its surface may represent a three-dimensional volume, each is conceived in terms of sectional perspective which, in turn, relates to the whole picture which is sectional in concept. We see this clearly demonstrated in Rouault's *The Old Wall*.

The basic ingredients of a picture are a surface of some kind and some way of creating on it points, areas, and lines, which with few exceptions are the only graphic elements the artist uses. Let us now examine these ingredients: points, areas, and lines.

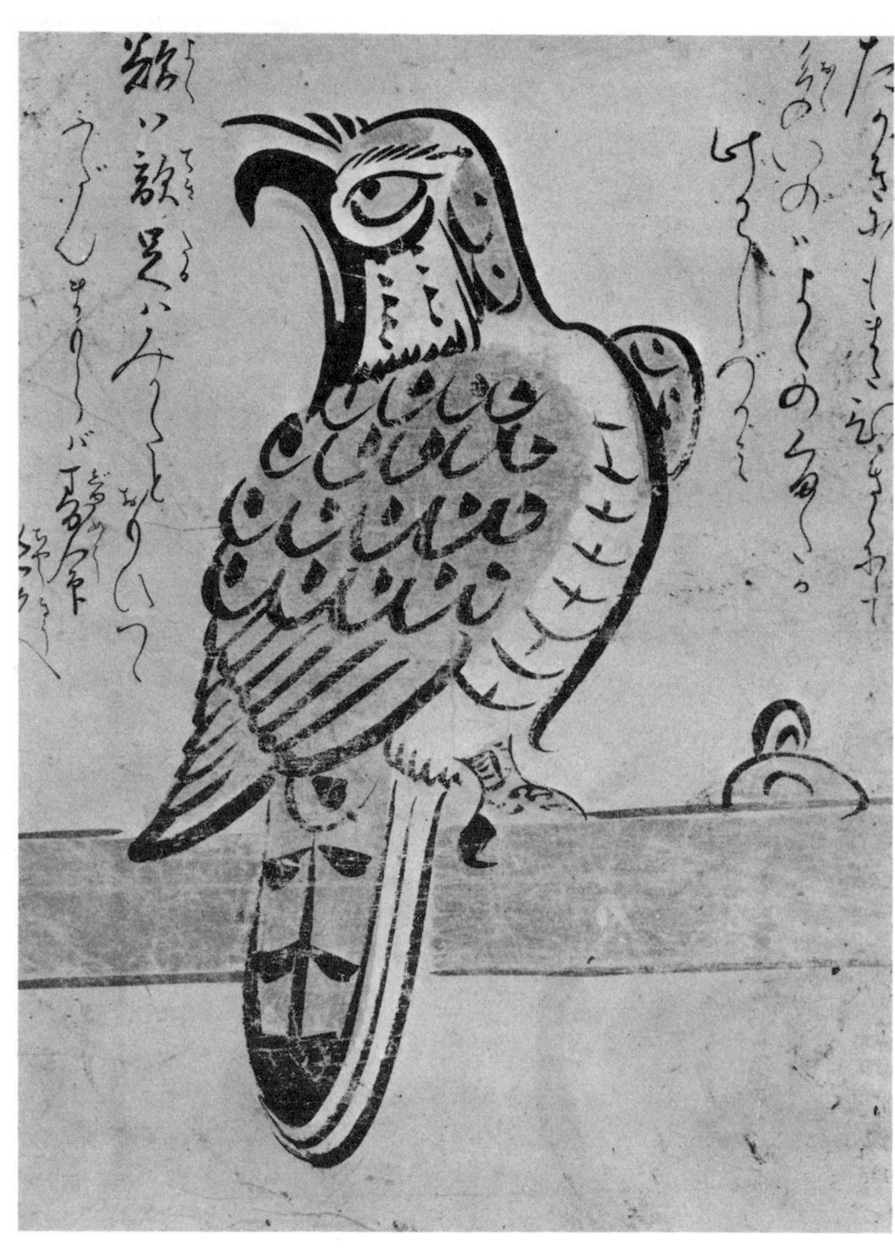

Artist unknown, Japanese folk art from Otsu
HUNTING FALCON, one of a set of 31 Otsu-e
Edo period, 17th cent.; 13″ x 9½″
color on paper; painting
Seattle Art Museum
Eugene Fuller Memorial Collection



# 5  Point-Area-Line

# II GRAPHIC ELEMENTS

## The Elements

Because all of us are familiar with points, areas, and lines we might suppose these subjects hardly justify investigation. Anyone can make a dot on a surface, mark or scratch a line, or disturb a surface by scrubbing across it with a coloring material. So, too, anyone can strike a key on a piano and make a sound; yet few can control a number of sounds to produce music as a concert pianist does.

The concert pianist and the artist have one thing in common—both are severely limited by the number of elements with which they work. The pianist uses only black and white keys; the artist, only points, areas, and lines. Yet an extraordinary variety is possible both in the pianist's music and an artist's pictures. This Japanese painting demonstrates the richness inherent in such few graphic elements.

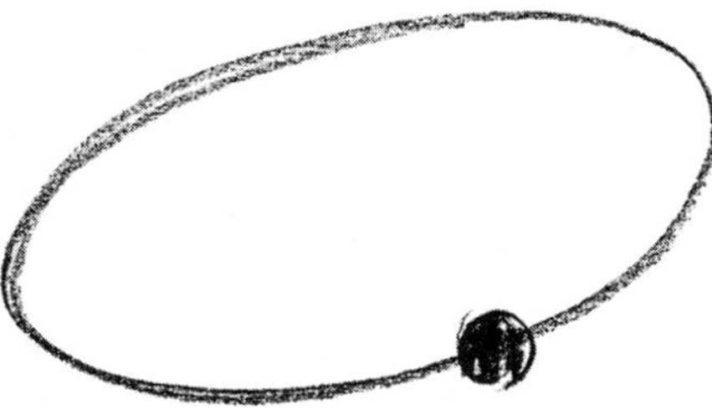

59

The pianist exploits and extends his keyboard by the ordered control and manipulation of sounds. The artist exploits his palette by the ordered arrangement of graphic elements, especially by the introduction of color. However, the ordered sound the musician produces, although a necessary part of music, in itself does not guarantee music unless we are moved in an emotional way. So, too, the ordered arrangement of points, areas, and lines in a picture in no way assures that we shall be aroused emotionally. It is *how* we disturb a surface with a point, or area, or line which is so important.

Before we can order and execute these elements we must consider a factor even more important—our concept of them. The way we understand a point, area, or line not only has great bearing upon the way any drawing or painting is made, but also dictates the limits within which we must work. For instance, a line to a child may mean a squiggle made by his finger in the sand. To an engineer or architect, a line may be a symbol of a physical limit, a dimension, the location of a wall. To a geometrician, a line may represent the locus of a moving point (*59*). To an artist, a line may mean all of these and more.

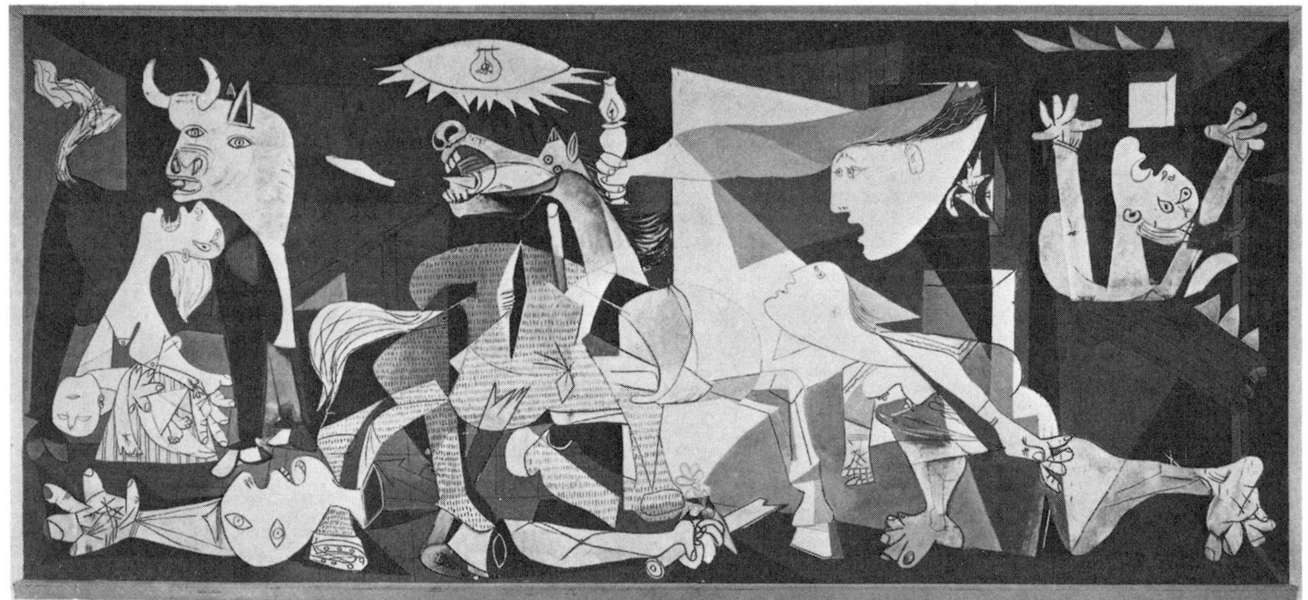

Pablo Picasso (Spanish, 1881-    )
GUERNICA; 1937; 11′ 6″ x 25′ 8″; oil on canvas
On extended loan to the Museum of Modern Art, N.Y.
from the artist

 **The Graphic Elements as Manifestations of Force**

A picture, as we noted, is made up of only a few elements on a surface. But these elements may be interpreted as more than physical disturbances of the picture surface. For instance, if we look at the line as simply a mark on a surface it is like examining a skeleton of a human being and saying "This is a man." Both are lifeless, both have ceased to function in a dynamic way. If, however, we learn to see the line as a special symbol, as a manifestation of forces, we introduce a new factor, which seems to radiate from the picture —that of vitality or energy.

We may carry our comparison further: all living human beings manifest a certain life quality. However, some almost overwhelm us with this hidden vitality. Great artists, great scientists, great leaders have a charisma that is dynamic and unmistakable, and so with pictures. All pictures generate some energy; great pictures abound with energy which is transmitted to us visually, as it is from Picasso's famous *Guernica*.

Of course, energy or force cannot be seen. It must be evidenced or manifested in some manner. We cannot see the force of wind, but a boat with full sails indicates that a wind is blowing. A falling leaf demonstrates the pull of gravity and that the leaf has weight, yet we can see neither gravity nor weight.

And so with the point, the area, the line. Through the way they are conceived, through the way they are used in a picture, they

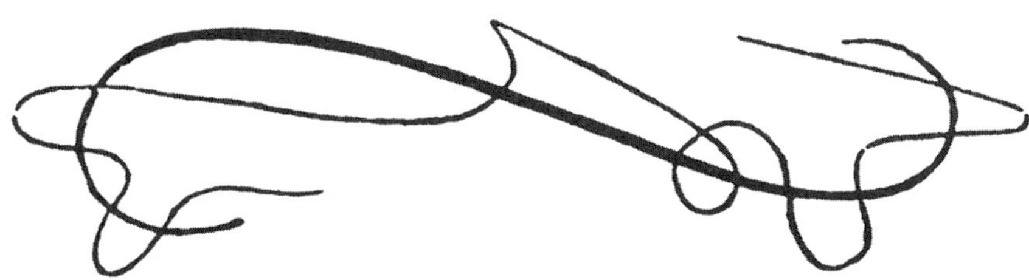

Paul Klee (Swiss, 1879-1940)
DIAGRAM No. 2, from *Pedagogical Sketchbook*
Permission SPADEM, 1969
French Reproduction Rights, Inc., N.Y.

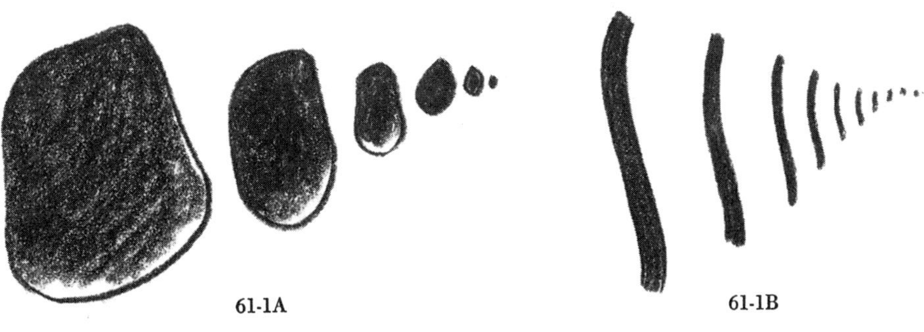

61-1A

61-1B

become visual symbols manifesting forces of various kinds: direction, action, movement, weight, speed, life. Through the manipulation of such symbols of forces the artist is able to generate emotional responses in the spectator which are impossible to achieve through subject matter appeal alone. To understand a picture we must first become aware of forces inherent in these graphic elements and then learn how to control these forces in picture construction.

## The Point

So now let us examine a point. Like the line, it can have various meanings. To some it may be seen as a dot, a small disturbance on a surface, having little significance—a fly speck. To a geometrician a point may be an intersection of two lines, or a symbol of a position, either fixed or moving, within given limits. A point also may be considered as an extreme limit of an area diminishing in size (*61-1A*) or the limit of a line diminishing in length (*61-1B*).

In his admirable syllabus *Pedagogical Sketchbook*, Paul Klee develops the idea of a point as moving freely in space, rather than being confined as in the case of the locus. From this idea he evolves a concept of a graphic line which he likens to the trace or path of a man walking (the moving point). This main line can be embellished by other lines generated in the same way. This concept is limited, for it does not encompass the weighted or graduated line and certain complex aspects of linear movement. Yet it is a provocative idea and opens up new fields of inquiry.

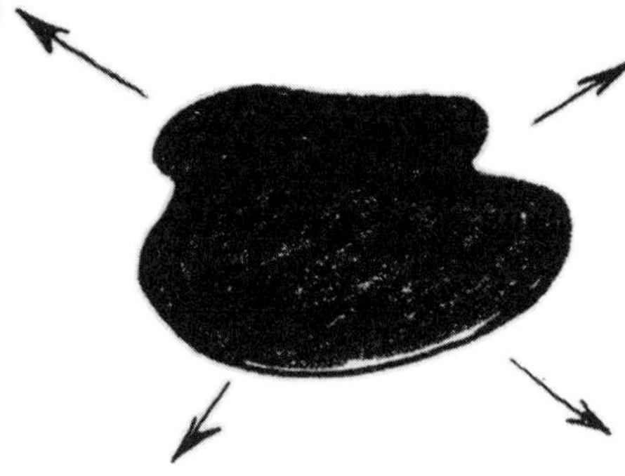




Another concept of a point is that it is a symbol of a concentration of energy. It is a symbol of a force experienced but not actually seen. As a parallel, let us imagine a spring welling up from a rock formation. If it bubbles up in a hollow, it forms a pool or lake, or if it emerges on a slope, it trickles away as a rivulet which eventually grows into a river. The spring represents a concentration of energy which we may symbolize graphically as a point.

**The Area**

As the water rises in the hollow, sometimes slowly, sometimes rapidly, its surface changes shape constantly as it reflects the contour of the enclosure. As it changes shape it also changes size. Symbolizing this surface of the pool on our paper, we generate an element subject to change of shape and change of size, whose rate of change is a variable (*62*). It is the graphic area. Its characteristic movement is dispersive. The graphic area is a symbol of dispersive force.

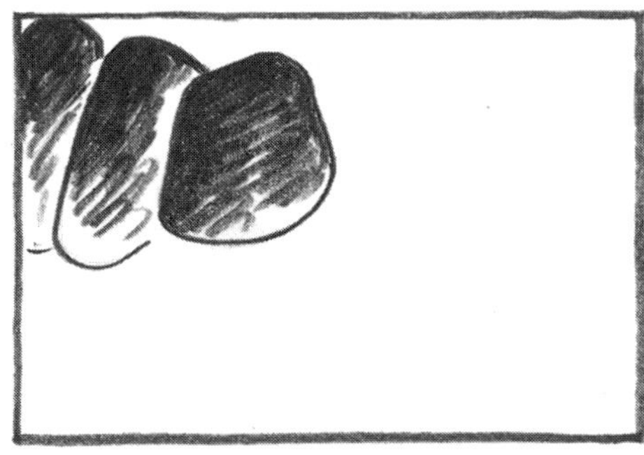

63-A

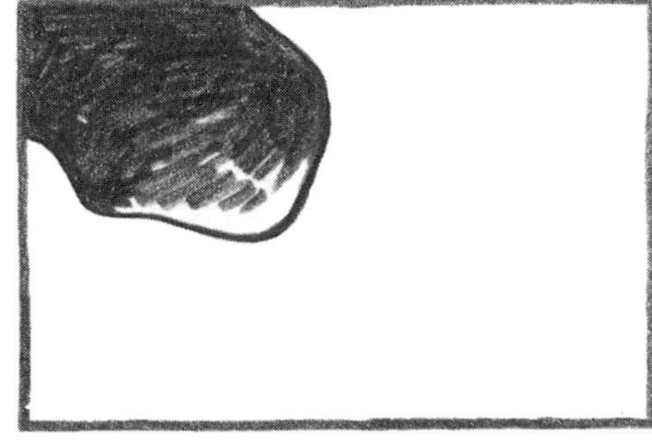

63-B

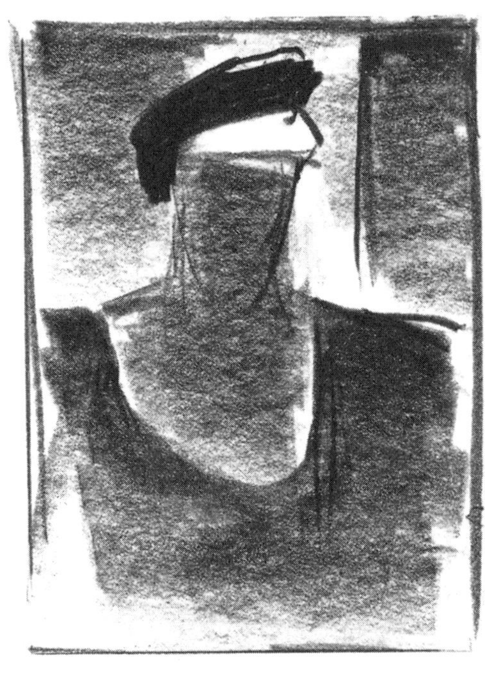

63-C

## Area and Shape

As the pool disperses it takes on various configurations which are defined by edges, either hard or diffused. In a drawing the area also is in a flowing, spreading condition and generates a constantly changing shape.

At some instant the pool reaches its maximum extension and is no longer subject to change. In graphic terms the representation of the pool is both an area and a shape. A state of balance has been reached between the two factors. The area has ceased to spread or disperse; the shape has assumed its final configuration.

This shape, when indicated on a picture surface, is fixed, not subject to actual change. Yet as our drawing medium is applied to the picture surface it arrives at this particular area, this shape, through dispersion of the medium itself.

In a closed picture it often happens that an area disperses itself until interrupted by one or more borders (*63-A*). In doing so it generates a fixed shape partly defined by the border or borders involved (*63-B*).

In the same way, an area also may be partially defined by other shapes, as we see the background limited here by the symbol of the figure (*63-C*). In this instance the background generated by the area is a shape, but lacks identity or impact. We read the background as an area, or as a space, rather than as a positive shape.

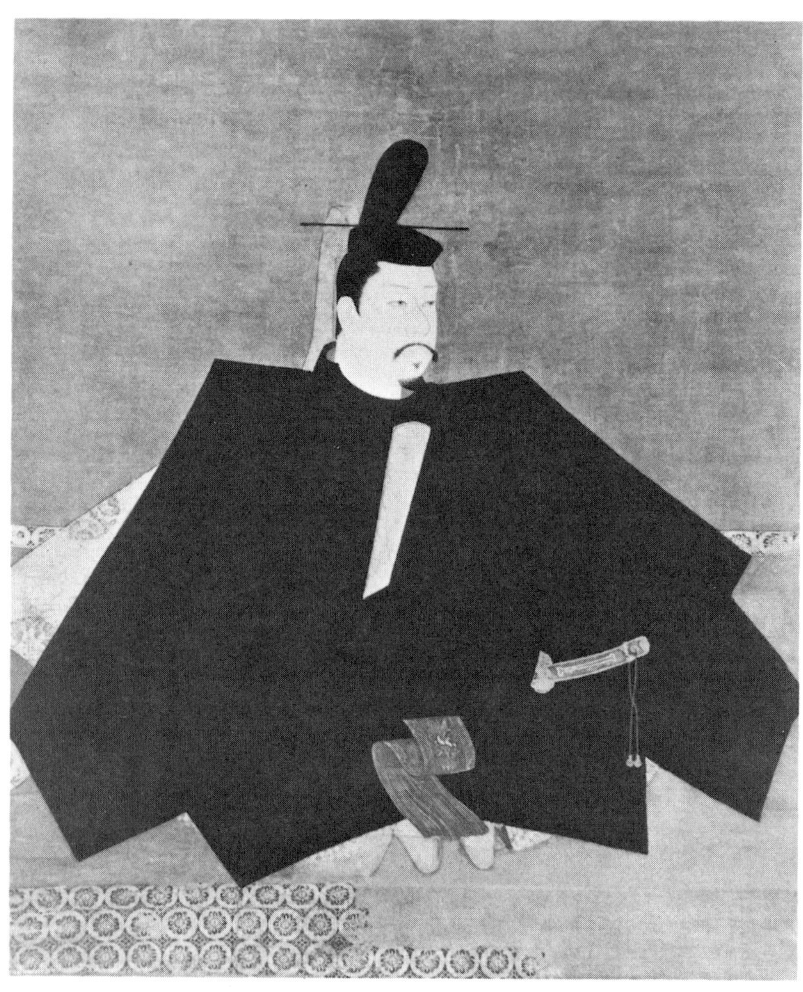

Fujiwara no Takanobu
(Japanese, 1142-1205)
MINAMOTO NO YORITOMO,
Founder of the military
government of Kamakura
Kamakura Period, 12th century
colors on silk
Courtesy Jingo-ji, Kyoto
through the Japanese National
Commission for UNESCO
(Photograph: print plate XXIV, *Japan*
UNESCO World Art Series
New York Graphic Society)

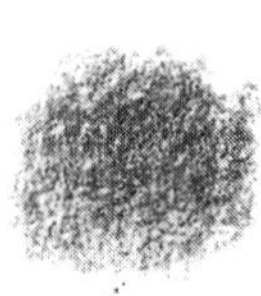

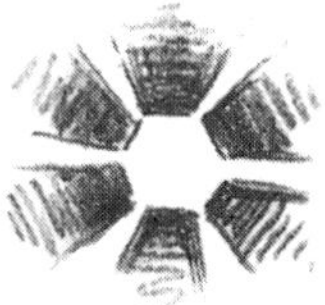

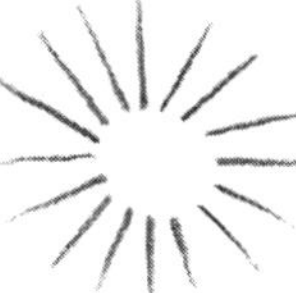

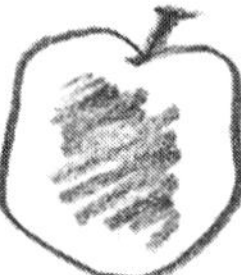

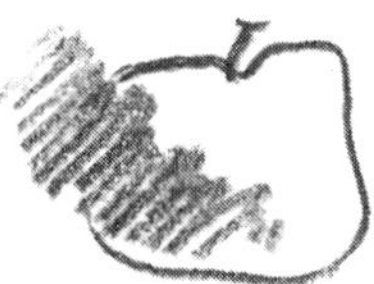

| 64-1A | 64-1B | 64-1C | 64-2A | 64-2B |

64 A graphic area is not always a well-defined shape characterized by hard edges. At times it is diffused, and the separation between an adjacent area is almost impossible to see (*64-1A*). We might liken it to the pond seeping into grasses which surround it. An area may also be indicated by other separated lines or areas (*64-1B*). The center of this ring (*64-1C*) is actually the same white as the field, but optically it is an area of a different degree of whiteness. We read its characteristic shape easily, although it is only partially defined by adjacent shapes or lines.

A colored area, especially in conjunction with line, often fails to generate a definite shape (*64-2A*). In many cases, particularly when an area of color is used as a core of a volume or when it bridges from background to volume, an identifiable shape may be inappropriate (*64-2B*).

In looking at pictures from art history, we become aware of a strange effect—that of lateral extension. Probably because the picture surface is flat, possibly because of the horizontal alignment of our eyes, but whatever the cause, this phenomenon of a shape seeming to spread laterally is found in most great pictures. Now by understanding the origin of a shape as a dispersive area, we find it easy and effective to dramatize a shape in our own picture by allowing it to continue past the limits usually imposed on a drawing based on a static concept of area. We discover that the generous proportions of a Fujiwara portrait or one by Holbein came not from a careful projection or copy of characters in nature, but from a concept of a shape having lateral extension.

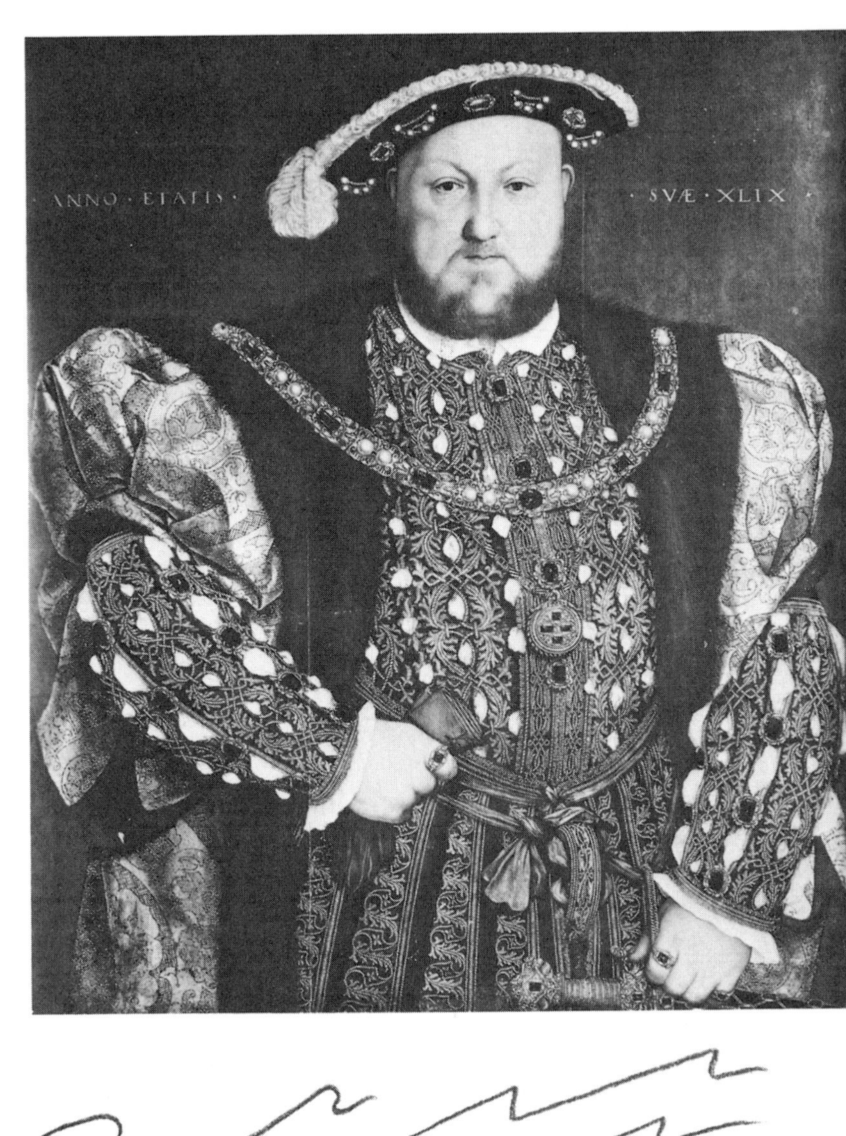



65-2A                    65-2B                    65-2C

## The Line

As water streams away from our spring, it
follows the contour of the countryside. At
times it flows rapidly, at times slowly. At times
it follows a straight course; at others, a
meandering one; sometimes it narrows, sometimes it broadens (*65-2A*). Always, however, it
strains at its banks, always it flows forward.
Symbolizing the surface of the water on our
paper, we produce an element subject to
change of size, change of shape, and whose
rate of change is a variable. It is the graphic
line. Its characteristic movement is progressive.
The graphic line is a symbol of a progressive
force.

Like the area, line structures can be simple
or complex, too. As we draw a single line,
either curved or straight, we see quite easily
how it symbolizes a progressive force, for the
line exactly portrays the force and direction
of our scribing tool (*65-2B*). But now let us
draw two parallel lines. Each line is a progressive unit, yet the dominant progressive
movement takes place between the lines
(*65-2C*). In this case, although each line
does symbolize progression, the function of
each line becomes secondary to the overpowering progressive or primary movement occurring
between them. This change from primary to
secondary interest is characteristic of graphics.
We will encounter it many times.

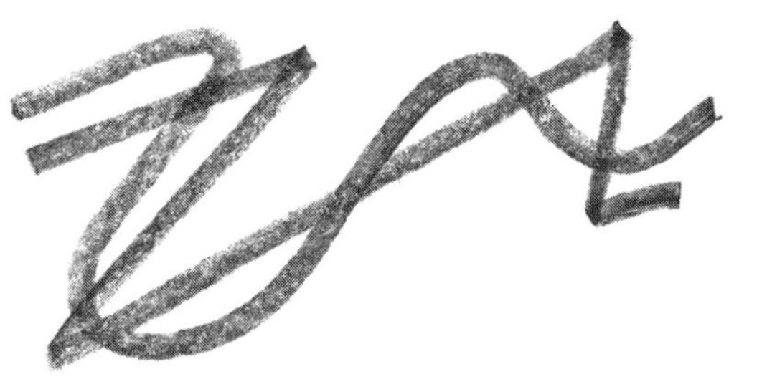

66-1A

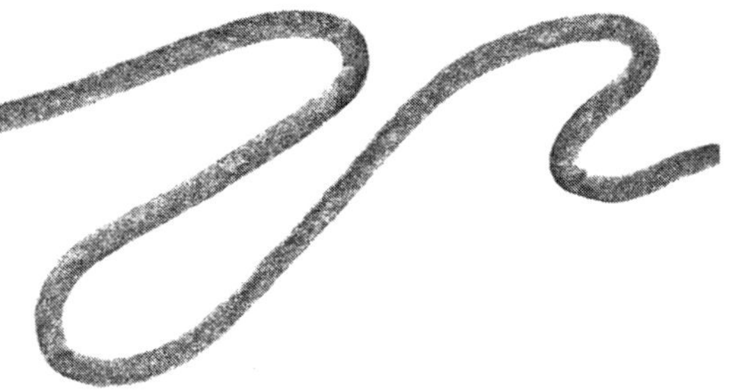

66-1B

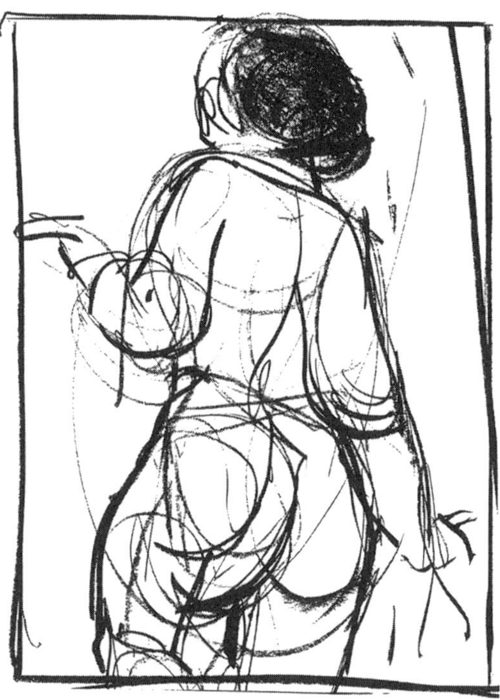

66-2A

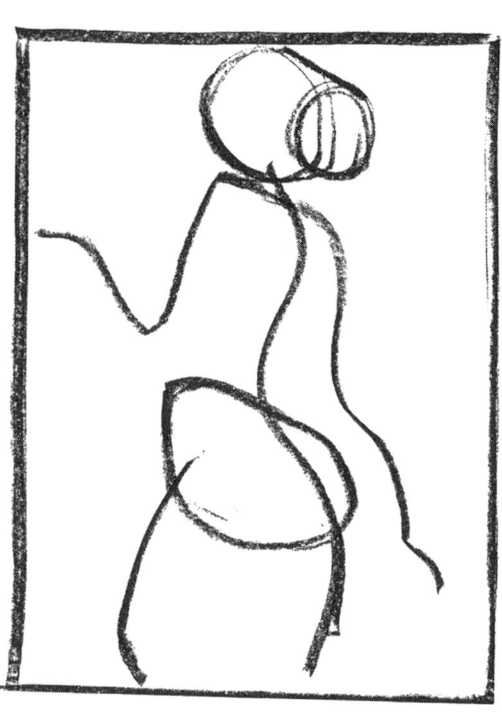

66-2B

66

By experimenting with various combinations of straight and curved lines we soon find that although the elements may be complex, the resulting primary movement is simple. In such linear organizations our eye does not follow each line consciously but responds to the composite structure as one dominant movement. (*66-1A*).

If we symbolize this dominant movement with one line, we see that at no time does it correspond to any single line in any of the complex organizations (*66-1B*).

When we make a line drawing of a figure, for example, we may employ a great many lines which simultaneously generate volumes, shape, and space. At the same time, we also generate a linear pattern which may be very complex (*66-2A*). Yet this complex pattern can be symbolized with a few simple lines, as we often find in a stick figure (*66-2B*).

An organization of points which individually have little or no perceptible direction may be so related and organized in series as to indicate a progressive force (*67-1A*). Although at no time do we actually employ a drawn line, we generate a true graphic line—a symbol of progressive force.

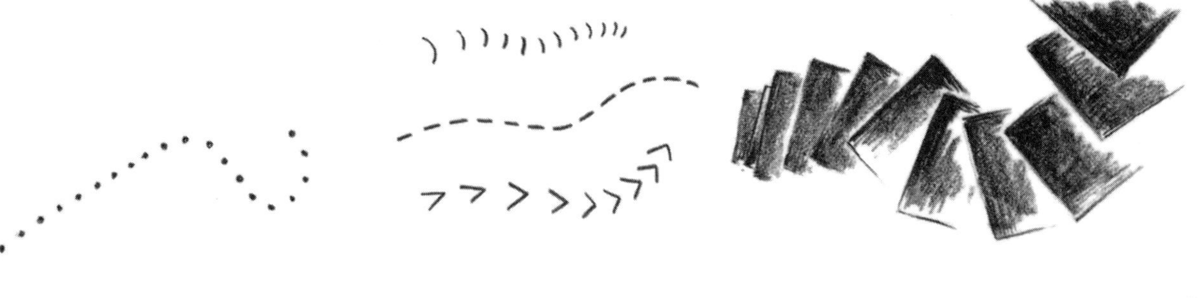



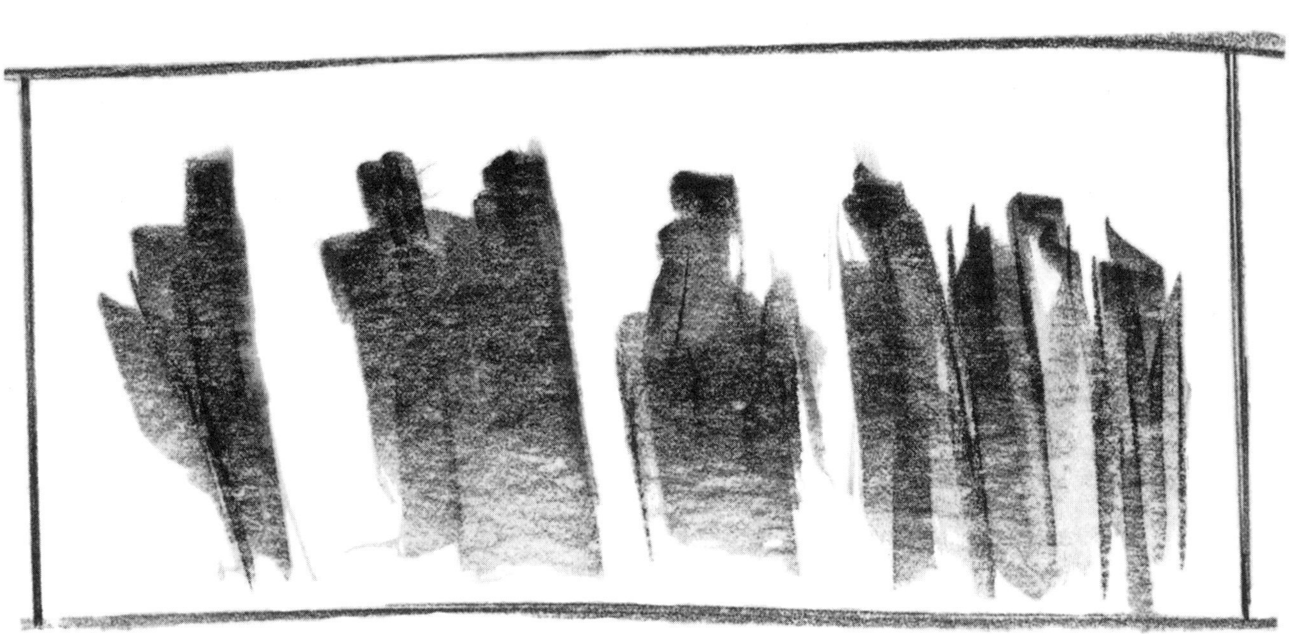

67-2

In the same way, we may indicate a progressive force by relating a series of fragmented curved or straight linear elements which often counter the direction of the dominant movement. Again we generate a graphic line progressing across the page (*67-1B*).

So, too, a series of shapes can be organized to indicate a force which is progressive in character (*67-1C*). If color is introduced it can be used to intensify this progression.

## The Elements and Picture Structure

We have examined the concept and structure of a point, a line, and an area as simple drawing elements. Yet the linear and areal composition of an entire picture also is dependent upon our concept of the meaning and structure of these elements. In particular we must distinguish between a drawn line and a graphic line which may or may not be drawn. The linear structure of a picture depends upon a control of progressive forces which, in many cases, are dependent upon the organization and relation of separate and distinct shapes (*67-2*).

We look next at what happens to line and area as they change identities in a picture.

68-A

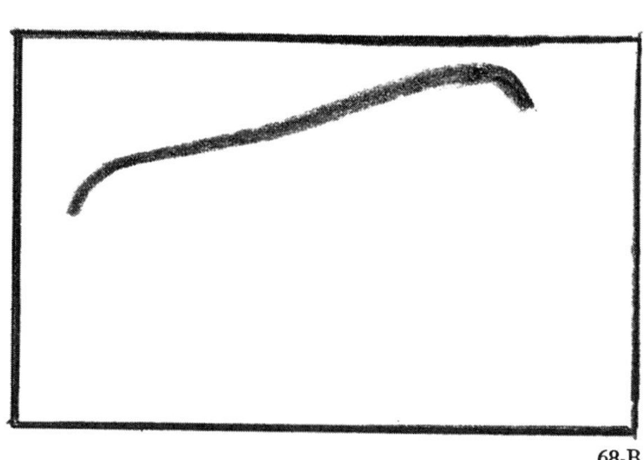

68-B



# 6 Changing Function of Line and Area

**Change of Function**

All of us have drawn aimlessly on a surface, creating the subconscious scribbling we usually call a "doodle." We consider our behavior ordinary yet, as we idly make such a drawing, truly astonishing graphic events are taking place. Let us observe what happens when we draw a line. The place where our pencil first touches the paper becomes a point (*68-A*). As we begin to draw we generate a line which reflects the pencil's action much as a contrail indicates the flight path of an airplane (*68-B*). The movement of the line, like the movement of the pencil, is progressive by nature.

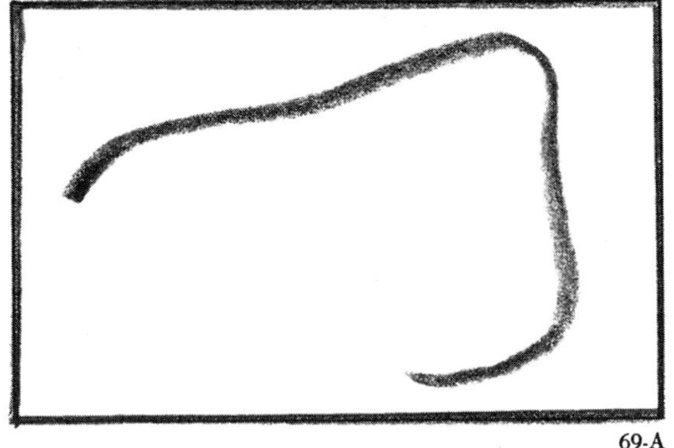

69-A

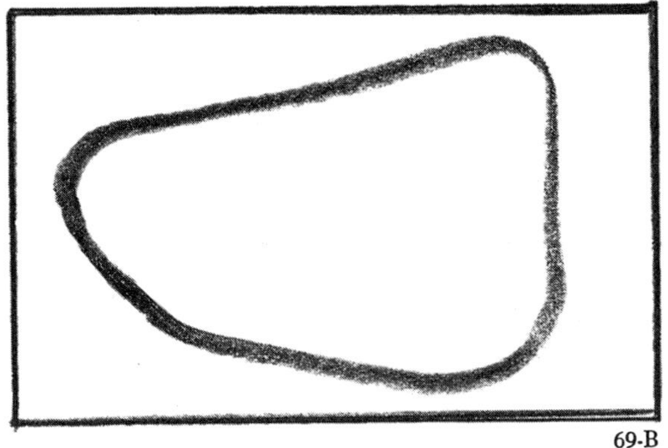

69-B

As we continue to let our pencil meander, we notice a strange and wonderful occurrence. As the line begins to return to its starting point the surface which is being enclosed by the line becomes more intense, different, more interesting than the surface generally (*69-A*). When we reach our point of departure, the pencil stops (*69-B*). The line ceases to absorb our entire interest, while the enclosure generated by the line becomes the more important event. We now have a defined area—a shape.

But how did this happen? How can a line suddenly change its character to the extent that we almost cease to see it?



We might compare this change to our reactions upon looking first at a piece of rope lying in a slack pile, then at the same rope supporting the struggling figure of a workman who has slipped from a roof. The rope has changed in our eyes from a tangled, inert mass of no importance to a taut lifeline whose strength may save the man.

Suddenly the rope has changed its character. A dress completely changes character when taken from a hanger and worn by a beautiful woman. A knife may be either a utensil or a weapon, depending upon its use. Such a change of use, or significance, or interest, we refer to as a change of function.

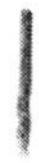

70-A

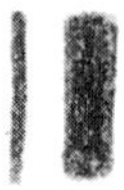

70-B

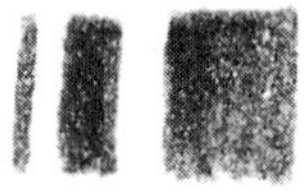

70-C

70-D

70-E

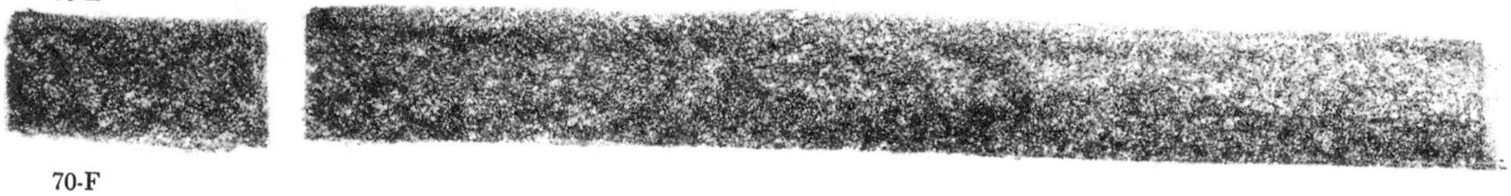

70-F

70 **Line Into Area**

Suppose now that as we doodle we draw a thin straight line (*70-A*). Then next to it we draw a thicker line (*70-B*). Each line has direction; each is progressive in character. But as we make a third, thicker line, we begin to wonder (*70-C*). Is it a thick line progressing, or does its width become obvious, does it seem to spread, thus changing its function from line to area? By increasing the width of our next line we generate a square (*70-D*). No longer are we in doubt. Our line *has* become an area, a symbol of a dispersive force.

**Area Into Line**

By making the square wider and wider, we generate a horizontal rectangle which still retains its character as an area (*70-E*). Then somewhere, as the rectangle continues to become wider, it changes and becomes a line, a thick line (*70-F*). The area has changed its function from a symbol of a dispersive force to a symbol of a progressive force—a line.

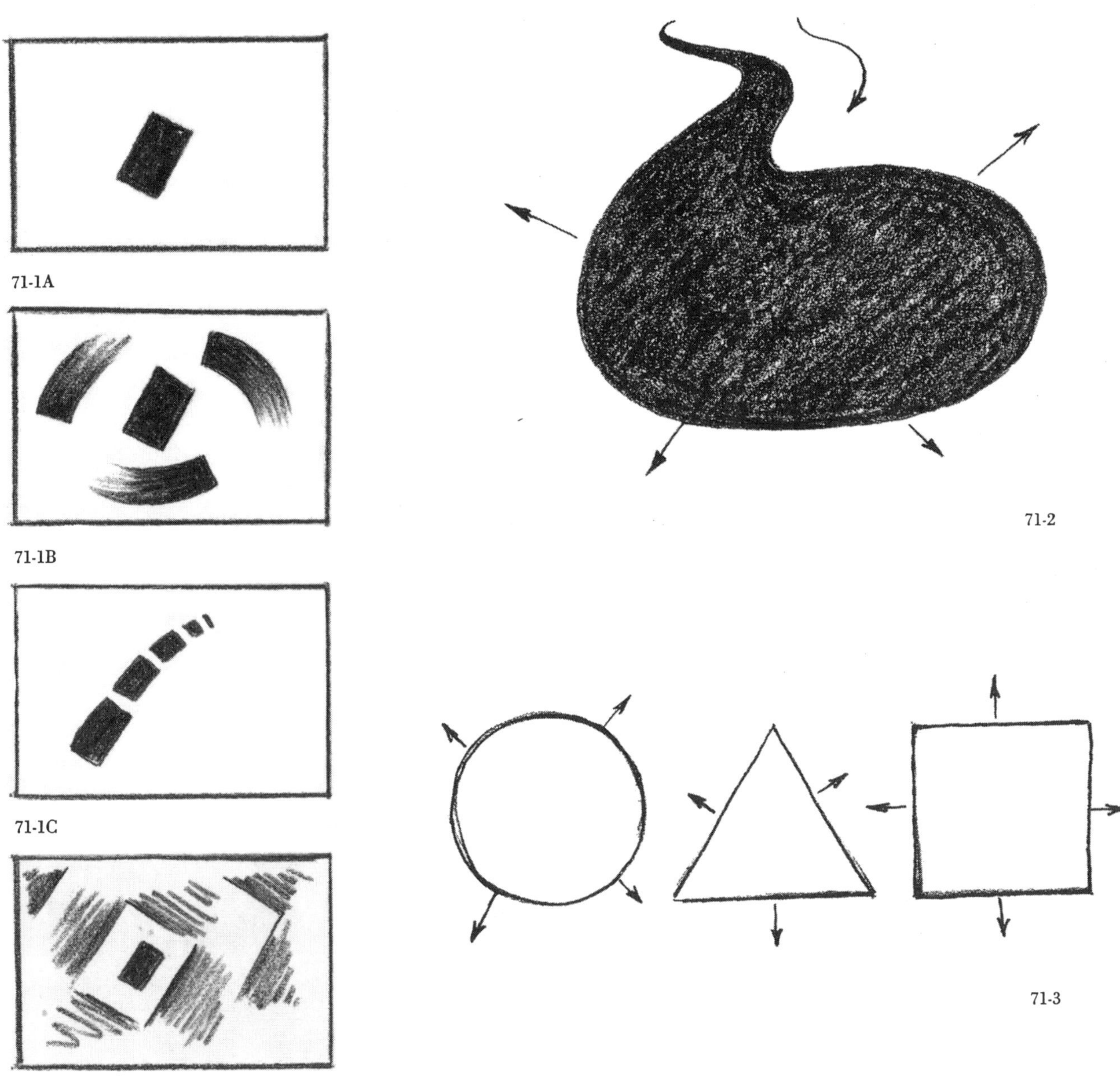

71-1A

71-1B

71-1C

71-1D

71-2

71-3

## The Medial Zone

As we have seen, the direction of the transition from line to area or area to line is ambiguous (*71-1A*). Is it progressive? Is it dispersive? This never-never land where the movement seems to die is static and becomes a medial zone.

We find that the medial zone represents a rest and in this sense may be used constructively. By its very inertness, elements surrounding it may be made to seem to move more rapidly (*71-1B*).

By relating a medial element to a series of progressing symbols we emphasize its potential linear direction (*71-1C*).

By relating such an element to other area symbols we emphasize its potential dispersive nature (*71-1D*).

## Dispersive and Progressive Shapes

In Chapter 5 we compared a line to a river, for each is a manifestation of a progressive force. We compared an area to a lake, for each is a manifestation of a dispersive force. Now by drawing a meandering river dissipating itself in a lake, we see clearly the effect of these changes of forces upon the resulting symbol (*71-2*).

We have so far consistently described an area as a symbol of dispersive forces. In so doing we run the risk of visualizing an area as something spreading from a fixed center. This is always true in certain geometric figures: the square, the circle, the equilateral triangle, etc. These are truly dispersive areas resolving themselves in dispersive shapes and do evolve from a fixed center (*71-3*).

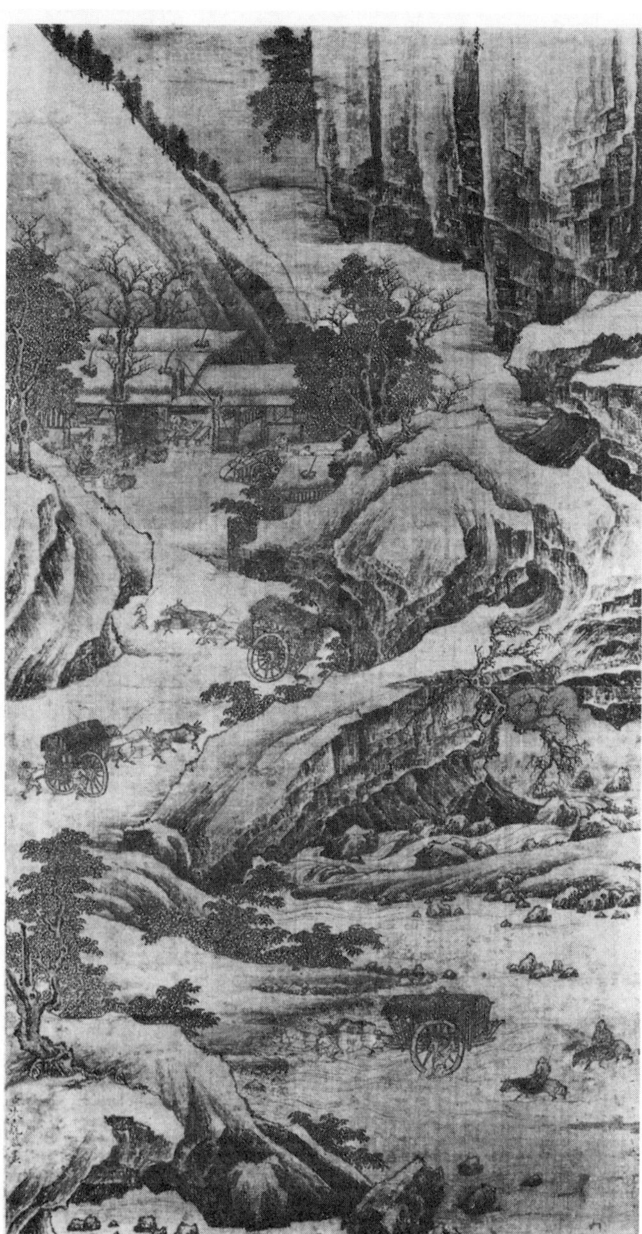



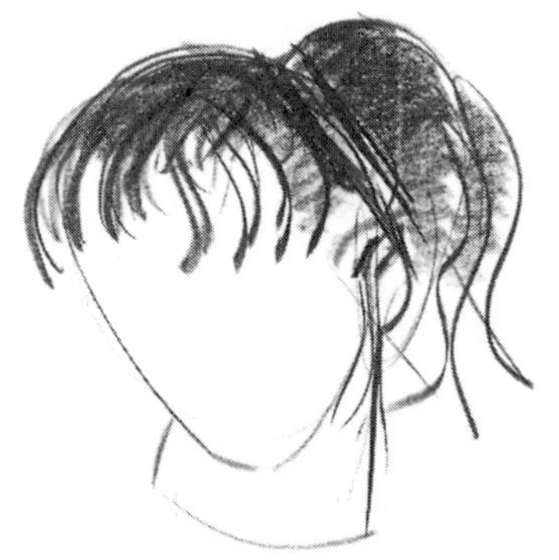

72-1

72-3A          72-3B          72-3C

72    In many other cases, however, an area will be dispersive by nature yet still generate a certain directional movement, resulting in a progressive shape. This is characteristic of most shapes derived from growth forms and also of many non-representational shapes. In fact, it is the progressive movement of shapes or volumes that keeps the picture dynamic, in a state of flux (*72-1*).

If we carefully study the Chu Jui above, we see the magnificent control he has exerted in exploiting the line-area relation. With line, he leads our eye from shape to shape. These shapes, in turn, are constantly varied in value and texture. The line ranges from dramatic verticals in the upper corner to subtle curves depicting the animals.

## Line-Area Changes

The concept of the changing function of line into area, or area into line, stimulates vigorous use of both line and area in the same picture. Unless it has strong shape impact, a picture which is predominantly tonal often runs the risk of becoming atmospheric or "soft." A picture based entirely on line usually does not have the shape impact of a picture using strong light and dark contrasts. By comparing two identical shapes, one in line on white (*72-3A*) and one solid black on white (*72-3B*), this difference is apparent. But by integrating line and area in the same picture we gain a new graphic strength (*72-3C*). Line emphasizes and contrasts the spreading, dispersive nature of area; strong dark and light contrasts of area reinforce the inherent weaker shape impact of symbols generated entirely in line.

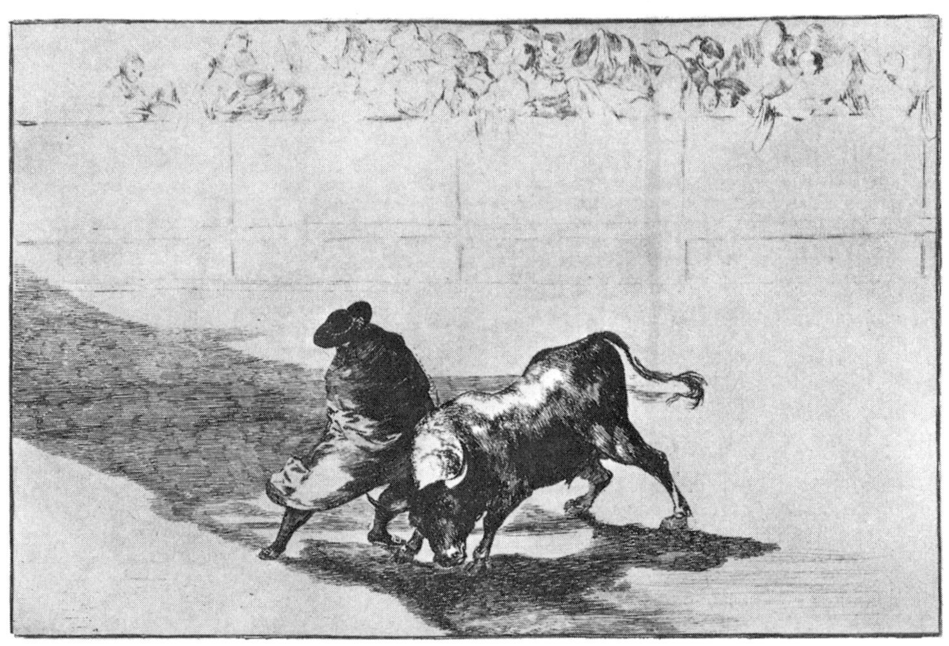

Francisco de Goya (Spanish, 1746-1828)
THE CLEVER "STUDENT OF FALCES" INFURIATES THE
BULL BY MOVING ABOUT WRAPPED IN HIS CLOAK
Plate 14, *Tauromaquia*; 1st ed., 1816
7⅛" x 11⅞"; etching and aquatint
Achenbach Foundation for Graphic Arts
San Francisco
(Photograph: Schopplein Studios)

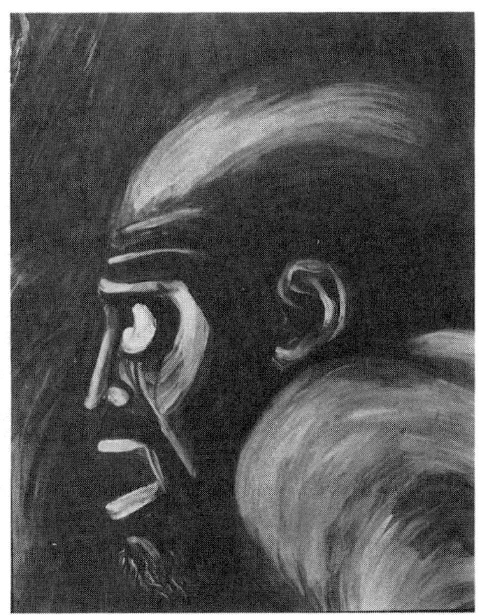

José Clemente Orozco (Mexican, 1883-1949)
Detail of man's head, THE TOWN AND THE LEADERS,
Governor's Palace, Guadalajara,; fresco
Courtesy Sr. Jorge Hernandez Campos
Instituto Nacional de Bellas Artes, Mexico, D. F.

In Goya's etching above, the impact of the dramatic black and white shapes of both bull and matador would have been seriously weakened if the picture had been executed with atmospheric modeling or close transitional grays. In the same way, if the whole picture had been executed in line alone it still might have been dramatic, but without the strong dark and light contrasts it would also lack impact.

A dramatic detail from an Orozco fresco again shows us how black lines and black shapes are used as manifestations of violent forces both in subject matter and graphics. In this picture there is a constant change from line to area, from progressive force to dispersive force.

In both pictures a factual subject has been transposed into strong graphic terms. In each case the subject is merely a vehicle. The exploitation of the lines and areas as symbols of forces is one of the chief concerns of every artist. When these forces are successfully conveyed to us, as they are here, we sense the radiant energy characteristic of most great pictures.

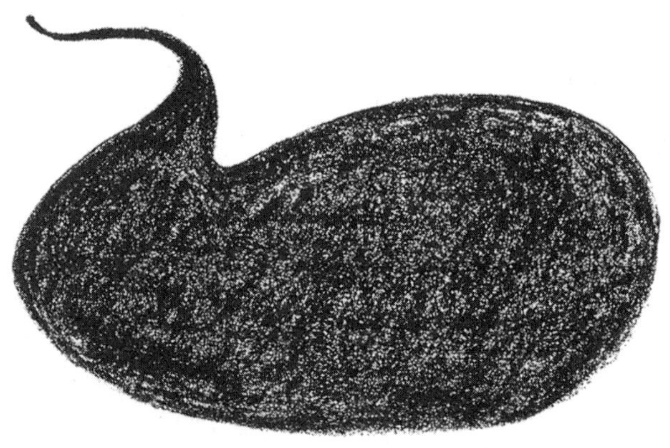





# 7 Active and Passive Line and Area

**Graphic Disturbance versus Direction of Forces**

In the preceding chapter we discussed at so length the subject of the changing functions of line and area. This was primarily a study of how the direction of forces are symbolize in a drawing. Now, however, we are concern with how a symbol, which expresses the direction of forces, affects us visually. In that the symbol itself is common to both studies, it is important that we clearly separate the two problems. Let us say that the change of function of line and area has primarily to d with the factor of direction. Our present stu has to do with visual reception, the way we respond visually to a drawn symbol.

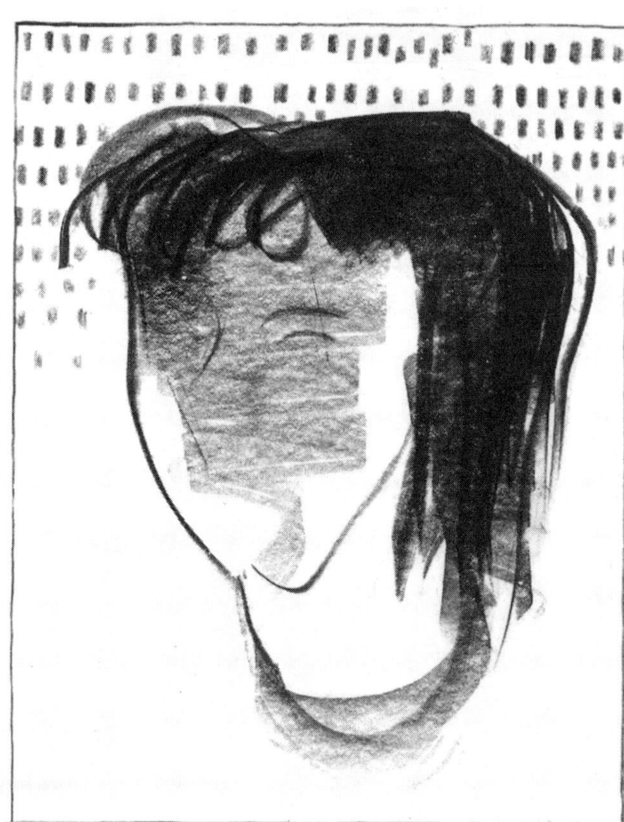

75-2

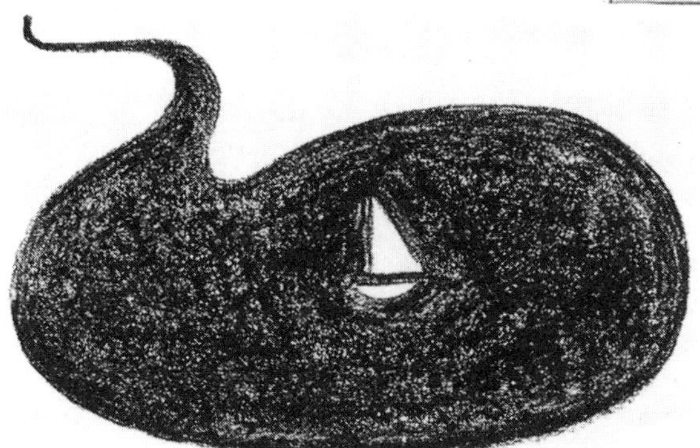

75-1

Now let us reexamine our symbol of a river emptying into a lake. We are very much aware of its distinctive shape as it progresses across the page (*74*). We observe the graphic symbol, a shape; also the blank page, the field. The graphic symbol is visually arresting, the field hardly noticeable. This is true no matter what meaning is conveyed by the symbol, or even if no specific meaning is intended.

We say, then, that the symbol is active; the background, or field, is passive. Note that we are now considering the graphic disturbance of the symbol rather than its movement structure.



Now let us draw a sailboat on the lake (*75-1*). The symbol of the lake now becomes a passive shape in relation to the activity of the symbol of the sailboat. But the lake also is an active shape against the surrounding passive field. The lake now may be said to be medial, for at one instant it is active, at another it is passive. It also acts as a secondary field to the sailboat.

Any shape may be passive, but only to a certain degree. A shape must be insistent enough to maintain its identity. If its identity is lost, the shape becomes an area.

An area is usually passive, but at times it may be activated by color, texture, or pattern and then becomes insistent, as in this head (*75-2*). However, if an area becomes so active that it dominates other shapes or lines, it violates the overall picture structure.

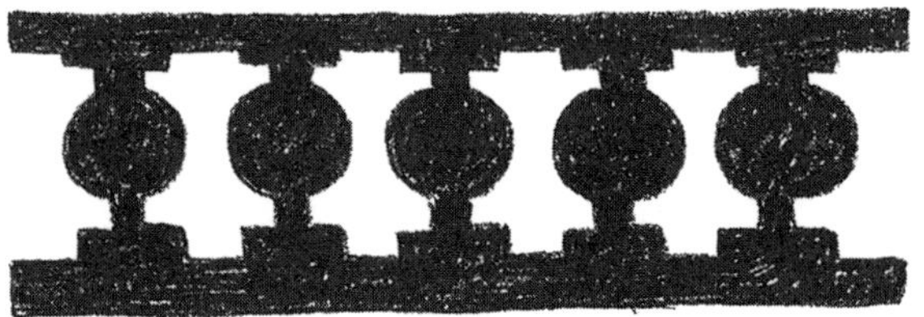

76-1

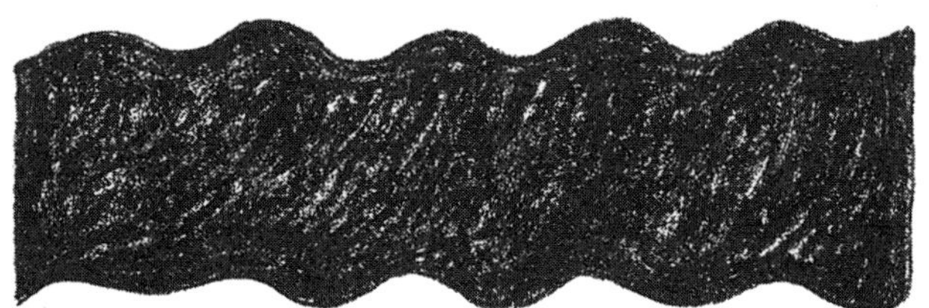

76-2

76-3

76-4

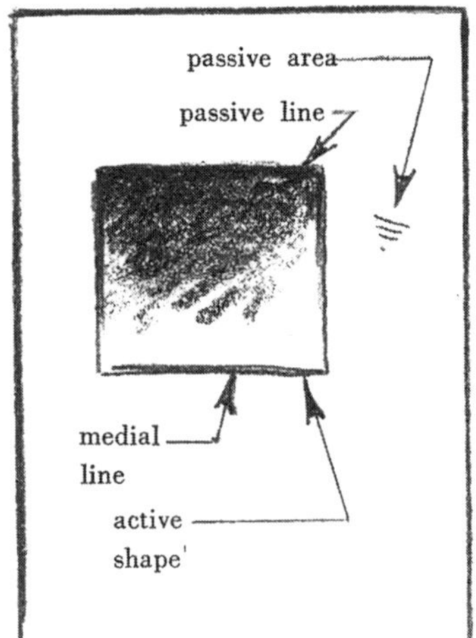



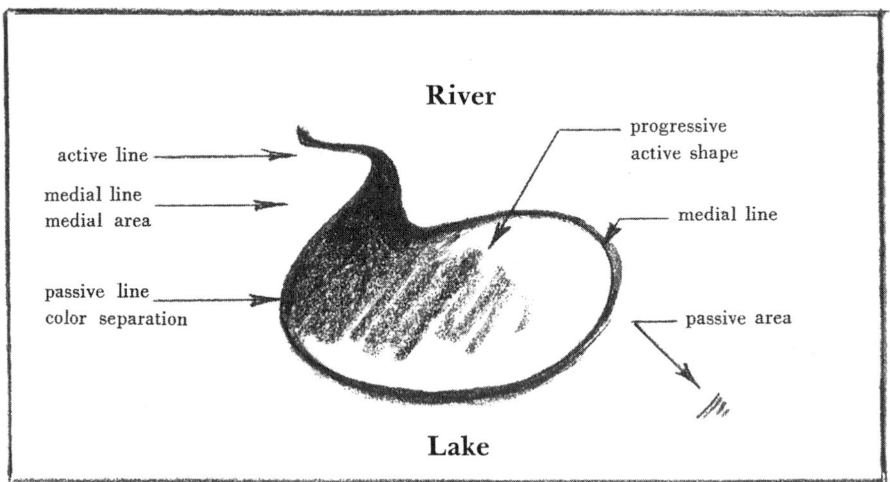





When our interest between two shapes is equal, again we have a medial condition. We see this when two shapes tend to reverse visually. There is confusion as to which shape suggests form, and which shape is space or area *(76-1)*.

A line also may be passive. When an area of one degree of light, or dark, or color impinges on another of a different gray or color, it creates what is known as a color separation. As long as this areal relationship is respected, no active line is involved *(76-2)*.

There is, however, a sense of linear direction in this separation, for our eyes sooner or later begin to follow at least part of the contour of the shape. When we first look at a shape our eyes seem to play over its entire surface rather than to fasten on its contours. But at some time the contour is examined, and at that time we begin to sense its directional character, which is progressive. Although it is actually a line its progressive movement is so weak that it is dominated by the dispersive movement of shape. The color separation is a passive line.

Not all shapes are indicated with one flat gray or color *(76-3)*. This square is an insistent shape, an active shape. Part of the shape is built upon a color separation, which is a passive line. Parts of it are expressed linearly, and since we are still strongly aware of the square as a shape these lines become medial.

In certain decorative types of pictures the progressive nature of a line may be sacrificed for the sake of the impact of the line as a texture or shape *(76-4)*.

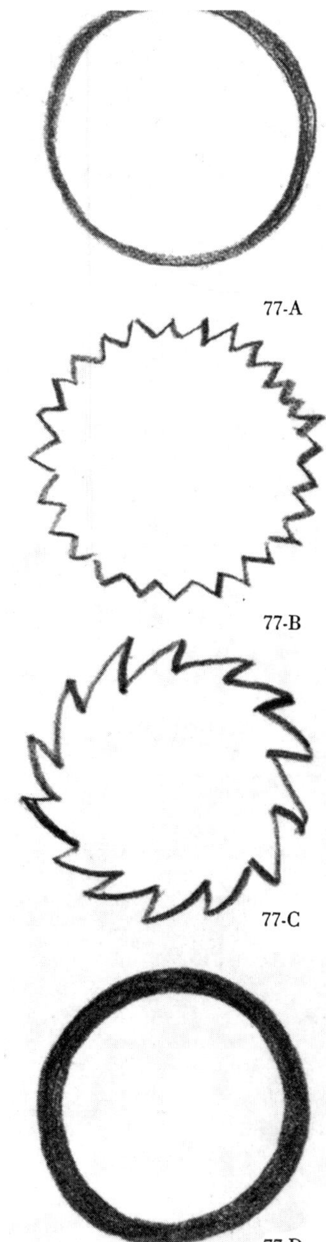



A simple line generating a circle is usually medial in interest (*77-A*). However, if this line is made increasingly more active through local disturbances it may read as a shape (*77-B*). This becomes particularly noticeable, for instance, when local bumps and hollows observed on a human figure are introduced in a drawing, not because they are essential to the structure of the drawing, but simply because they happen to be there.

At times violent activity in a line may be used constructively. For example, by using the activity of a line in a directional way we can generate a pin-wheel effect. Yet, at the same time, it is an active circular shape *(77-C)*. We now see the phenomenon of an active shape generated by an extremely active line, but the visual activity of line and shape are medial because of the powerful progressive circular direction, a spin.

## Line and the Progressive Shape

Lines generating geometric shapes, circles, squares, etc., usually become subordinated visually to the strong impact of the shape. Consequently such lines are often medial. An overstatement of the line may result in equality of interest between the line and the shape. Skillfully organized in relation to space, such equalities of line and area usually result in flat pattern units. These can be strong decorative elements in a shallow space picture, but in a deep space picture they tend to overemphasize surface (*77-D*).

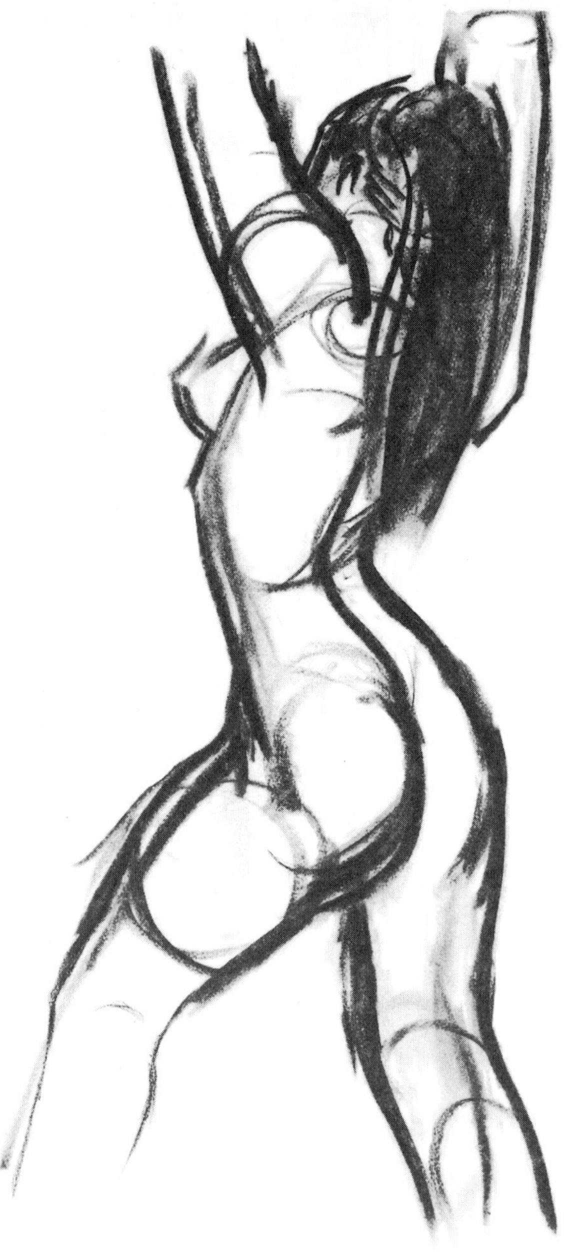

78

 We find that in a drawing of growth forms and drapery made mostly or entirely in line, one line may serve many uses (*78*). The lines and shapes generated are constantly changing functions. In this drawing, a few lines define the volumes depicting the legs. The lines delineating the right leg sustain the main line of movement of the whole body. The lines of the left leg form a counter-movement (Chapter 21). These same lines also exert tensions between each other which generate lateral movements, dramatizing the space separating the knees. The line is multi-purpose.

The volumes generated by these few lines also develop shapes. The volumes are progressive by nature, as are most volumes indicating growth forms. The shapes also are progressive.

Usually if a progressive volume is indicated in line, the progressive shape generated at the same time is active, and the line is medial. An old admonition that we should not be aware of a line in a line drawing upon first view implies that only as we study the drawing should its linear nature be apparent. This rule is easily tested, for one false line in a drawing immediately attracts attention. We see the line is in some way isolated from the rest of the drawing, and it will persist in annoying us.

Our first reaction to a line drawing is usually not to the line structure itself but to the shapes or volumes generated by the line. In a few instances, especially in pictures built on highly modeled volumes, our reaction to the three-dimensional nature of the volumes may take precedence over their shape impact. Except in

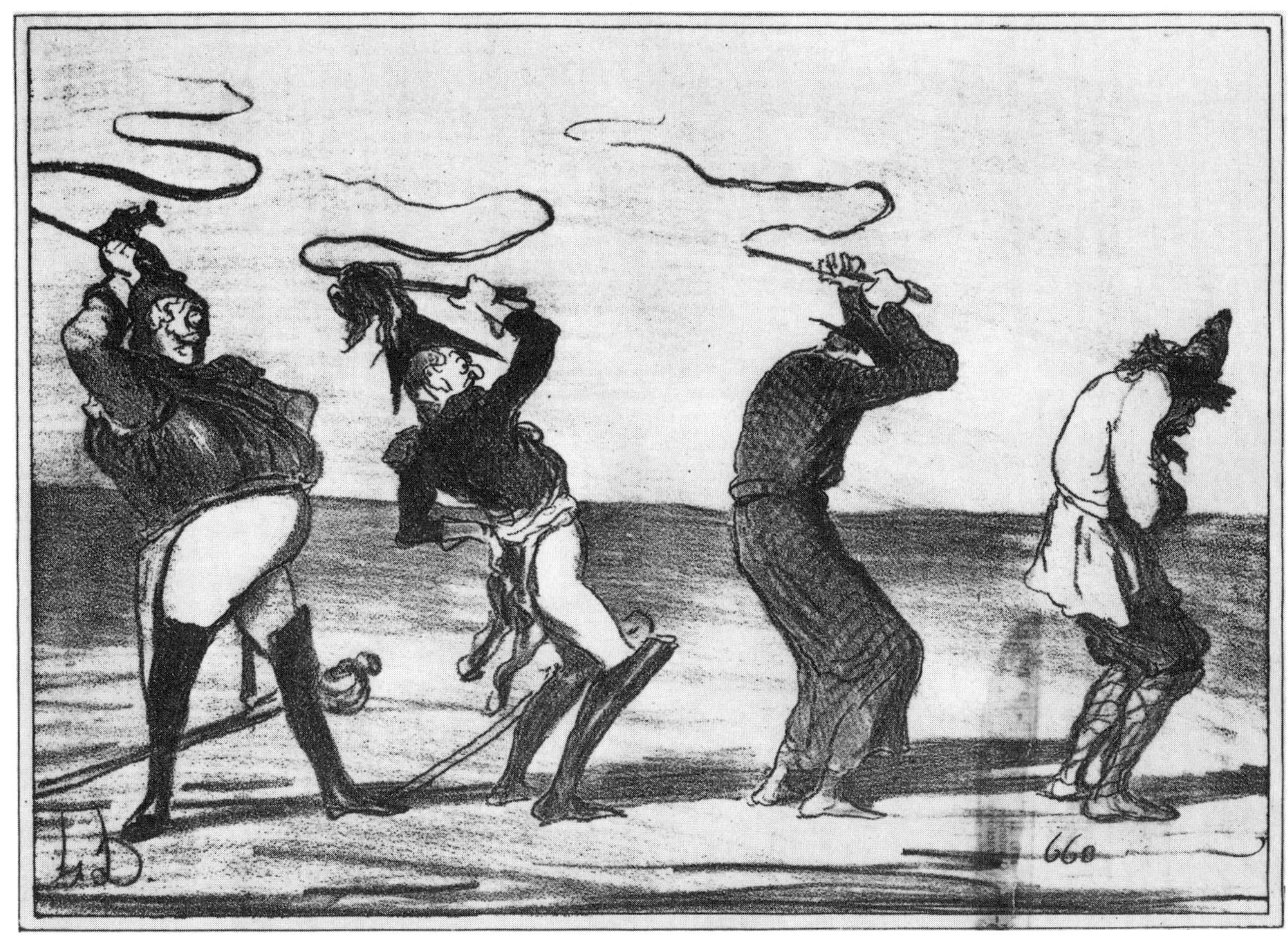

Honoré Daumier (French, 1808-1879)
SOCIAL AND POLITICAL PICTURE OF
RUSSIAN EMPIRE; lithograph in *Charivari*, July 31, 1854
The Metropolitan Museum of Art
Harris Brisbane Dick Fund, 1936

rare instances, a line arabesque for example,
line is a secondary design factor in a line
drawing.

However, the line has its importance. Most
often it is the involved interrelation of the lines
themselves that eventually becomes the dominant interest of the drawing. We see, then,
that when we first look at a drawing, the line
is medial. As we continue to study the drawing,
the line changes its visual function and
becomes active.

In Daumier's lithograph we see clearly both
a directional and a visual change of function
of line and area. The whips are linear volumes
which, expressed as line, give both strong
linear progression and an active linear pattern.
These change into the big body shapes which
are active. As our eyes move from the whips
to the bodies of the two figures on the left, the
active lines (the whips) change into active

shapes (the dark jackets) and then change to
medial lines (the trousers) and finally into
active shapes again (the boots). In the third
figure, the active line (the whip) changes to
active shape (the robe) and then into passive
lines which indicate the feet.

The ingenious reversal of dark and light
from the dark jackets in the first two figures
to the light jacket in the fourth figure, and from
the white trousers to the dark trousers, permits
a dramatic use of line which complements
the linear structure of the rest of the picture.
The medial lines delineating the white trousers
and the white jacket soon become apparent once
the impact of the big shapes has been experienced. They then become active as their
importance is felt.

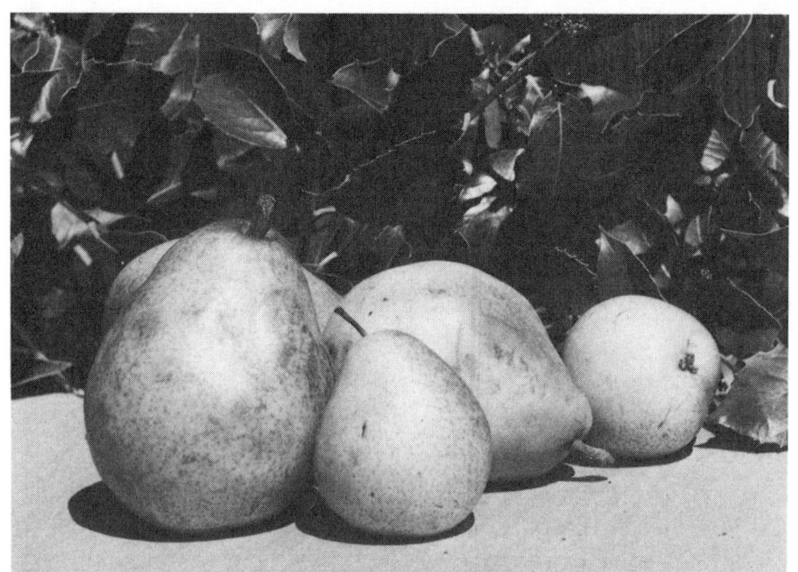

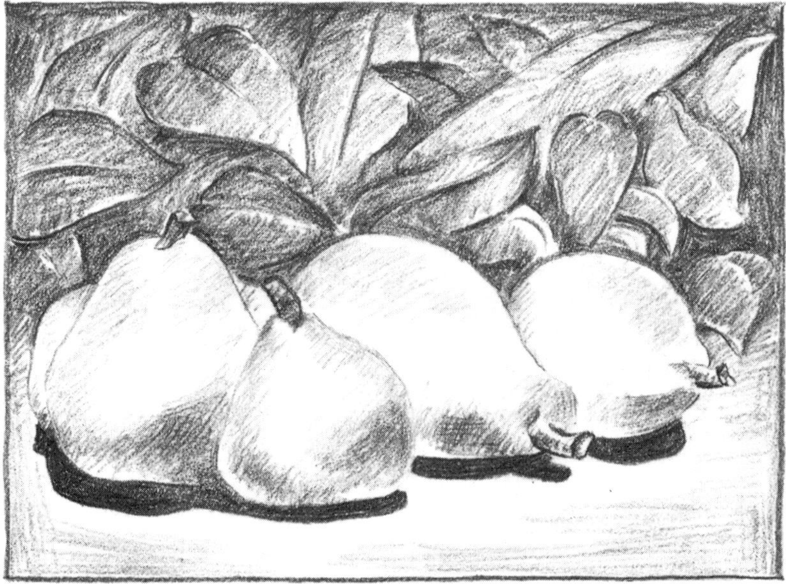

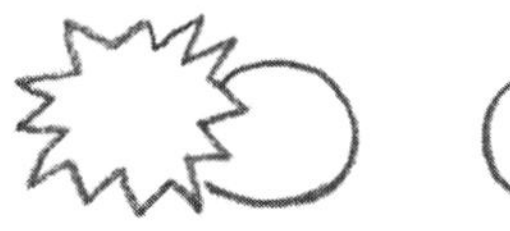
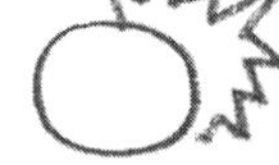

80-1A          80-1B          80-3

## 80 Line-Area Activity and Surface Control

At this time let us recall the section on contrast noted in Chapter 3. We found that graphic depth is easily achieved by using overlay and also graphic contrast (*80-1A*). At times these two devices may seem contradictory, but when utilized in preserving a strong surface control the balance of one to the other is critical (*80-1B*). In a similar way the changing function of line and area may be used to control picture depth.

To demonstrate, let us construct a picture involving very shallow depth—six or eight inches at most. On a table top let us place a number of pears, some in front of others, but in a cluster. Now let us place this arrangement in front of a hedge or plant in such a way that the leaves form a backdrop or vertical screen just behind our arrangement of fruit. As we study our subject, we notice that all the leaves are closely related as to color and grayness and that the pears seem truly sculptural, revealing strong light surfaces and shadows.

If we draw this arrangement much as we see it, the overlaying pears seem to become more and more sculptural and the leaves seem to recede as a rather dull sequence of grays. The more sculptural our drawing of the fruit, the more they seem to come forward. Soon we feel

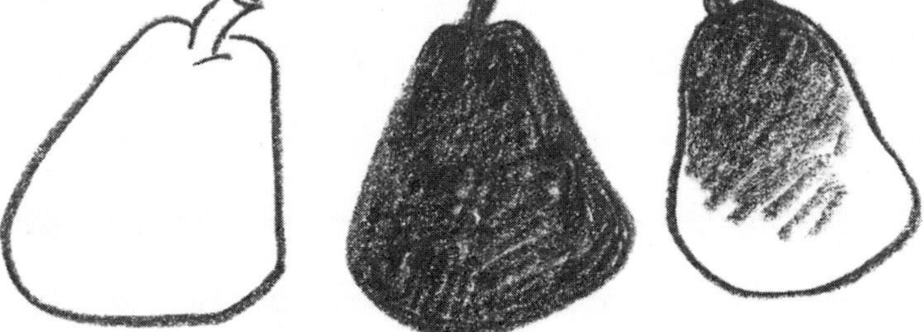



that we are looking not at the picture but through it, much as if we were looking through a window at a scene beyond (*80-3*).

Now let us make a picture approaching the problem as one of surface control. We can use the same subject but will try to maintain a strong feeling of the picture surface as a necessary part of the picture.

This time let us exploit the changing functions of line and area in relation to the picture as a whole. Let us also try to arrive at a balance between the receding and approaching elements in depth through control of their graphic activity.

There are many ways to express the sculptural aspects of the leaves and fruit. A pear can be symbolized with a line. It also may be symbolized by an almost flat shape which still says "pear." Further, the pear may be symbolized by an organization of both line and area which change their functions directionally as well as visually (*81*).

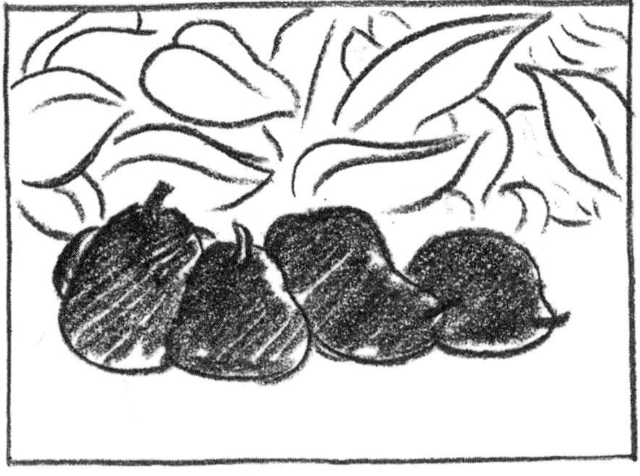

82-1

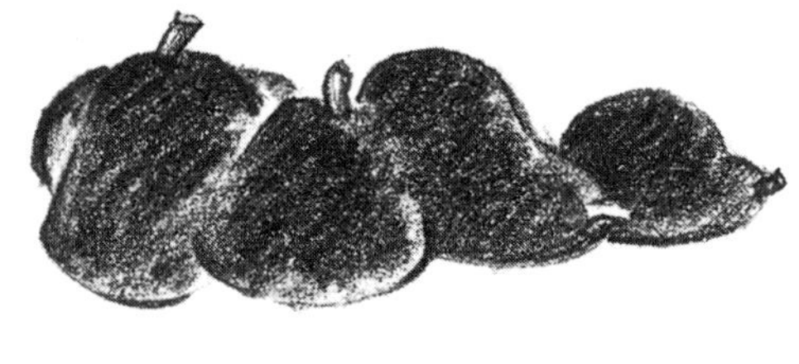

82-2

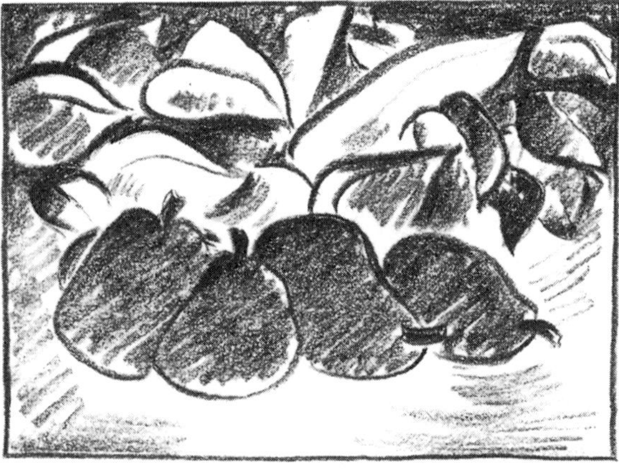

82-3

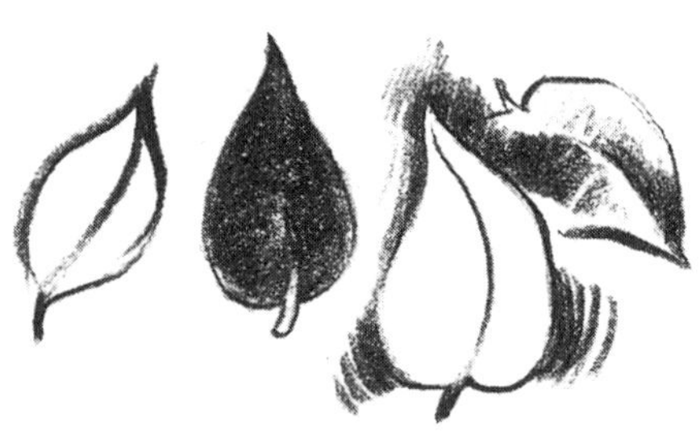

82-4

 Let us divide our picture visually into two parts, leaves and fruit *(82-1)*. In our previous drawing the leaves receded and the sculptural fruit seemed to leap forward. Now let us reverse this order by making the leaves more active graphically, subduing the fruit by transposing into area with some line *(82-2)*. The leaves are now more insistent and come forward visually, the fruit recedes *(82-3)*. If now we balance these two activities, we will still maintain depth in the picture but will bring all of the elements forward into the surface.

In developing the leaf structure let us transpose from a given gray, modified slightly by direct light, to line-area relations which continually change their functions. A leaf may now be expressed entirely with line; or entirely as a flat shape, dark, light, or gray; or by an almost infinite variety of line-into-area relations *(82-4)*.

Since both the background and the table top are areas, they too should be considered in making the picture. By holding the background back of the leaves to a minimum depth, surface control is more easily maintained. The more simply the background and table top are indicated, the more successful our picture will be.

We should note in our investigation of line and area that at no time have we been concerned with realistic effects, shadows, or light sources. By eliminating such effects we transpose from merely copying nature to the world of graphics. We will discuss the problem of illumination in our next chapter.

### Line Combined with Color Separation

In design terms the word "economy" means that the simplest devices are used to resolve a process or procedure or to arrive at a desired

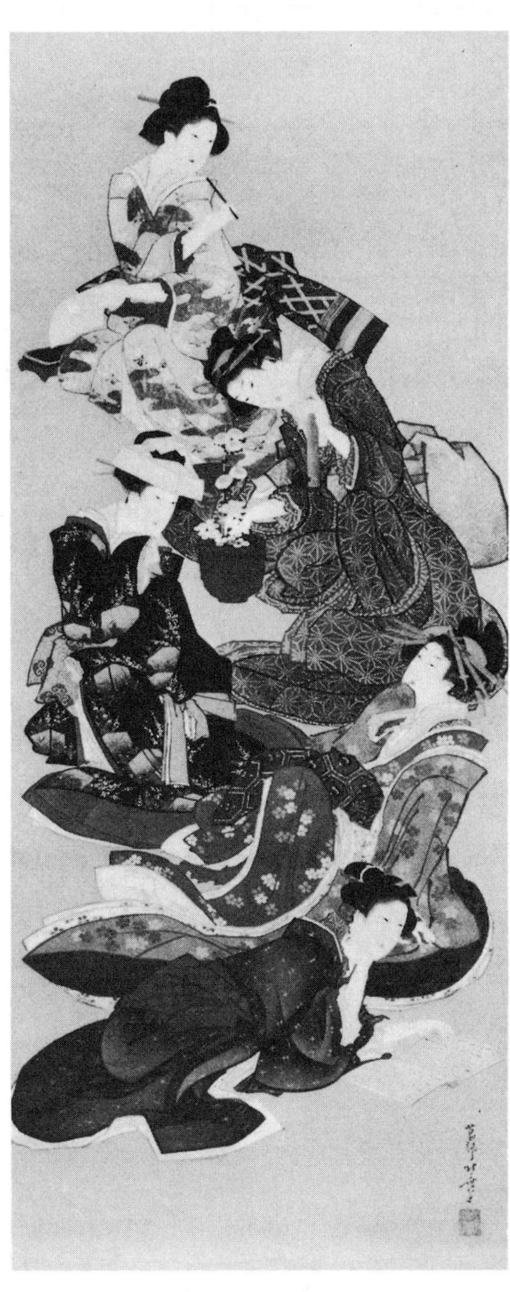

Katsushika Hokusai (Japanese, 1760-1849)
THE FIVE FEMININE VIRTUES; late Edo period
34″ x 13½″; painting, color on silk
Seattle Art Museum
Margaret E. Fuller Purchase Fund

effect, shape, color, volume, etc. If one line will explain a form, we must question the wisdom of using two. If a shape will explain a volume, we should question the use of modeling. In other words, we should avoid saying the same thing twice.

So if a shape can be identified by a color separation, there is usually no need for a line around the shape. As a way of strengthening many drawings or compositions, attention to this principle of economy of statement will often bring impressive results.

Line on a color separation is frequently used, of course, sometimes with tremendous success. We need only examine the Hokusai above, for example, to see how positively such line-area relation can be brought into play. This is equally true in much so-called "hard edge" painting, where representational symbols are seldom employed.

But if a line is used on a color separation where a representational symbol is used, it is imperative that the shapes themselves be stylized in some manner. The Hokusai is successful, not because the line is superimposed upon the color separation, but because stylized shapes add strength to the design. This principle is found frequently in art history, from Egyptian murals to contemporary cartoons. When realistic colored shapes are surrounded by line, especially an unweighted line, we can expect graphic chaos, for nothing else so quickly results in a tight, hard drawing.

In making a picture utilizing fluctuating line-area relations there is always danger of spottiness caused by the equality of dark and light areas. We shall explore this subject of light and dark in some detail in Part III.

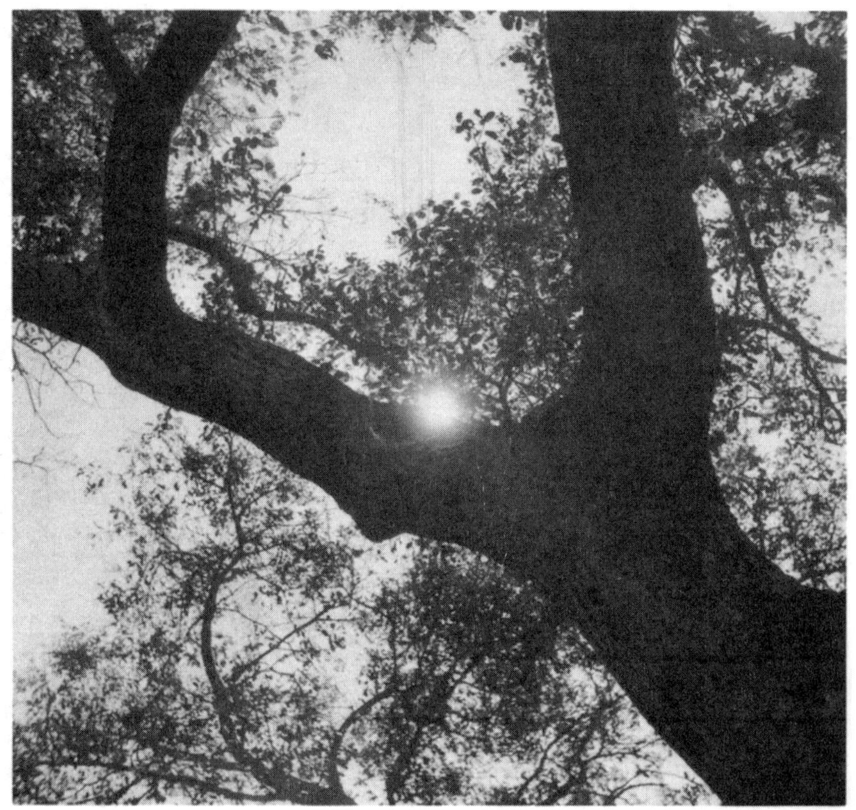

LIGHT SOURCE
(Photograph: Kenneth Graham)



# 8 Illumination and Contrast

**Light in Nature**
All things around us in nature are illuminated either by an external or internal light source. Usually things are made visible because of direct light such as sunlight, moonlight, or candle light, as in this photograph. At times we see forms illuminated from within, a street lamp at night, for instance. Many sources of light acting simultaneously, often reflected, give us diffused light with little or no emphasis on any one light source. Twilight, rainy days, the indirect lighting in buildings are but a few examples of diffused light.

# III LIGHT AND DARK

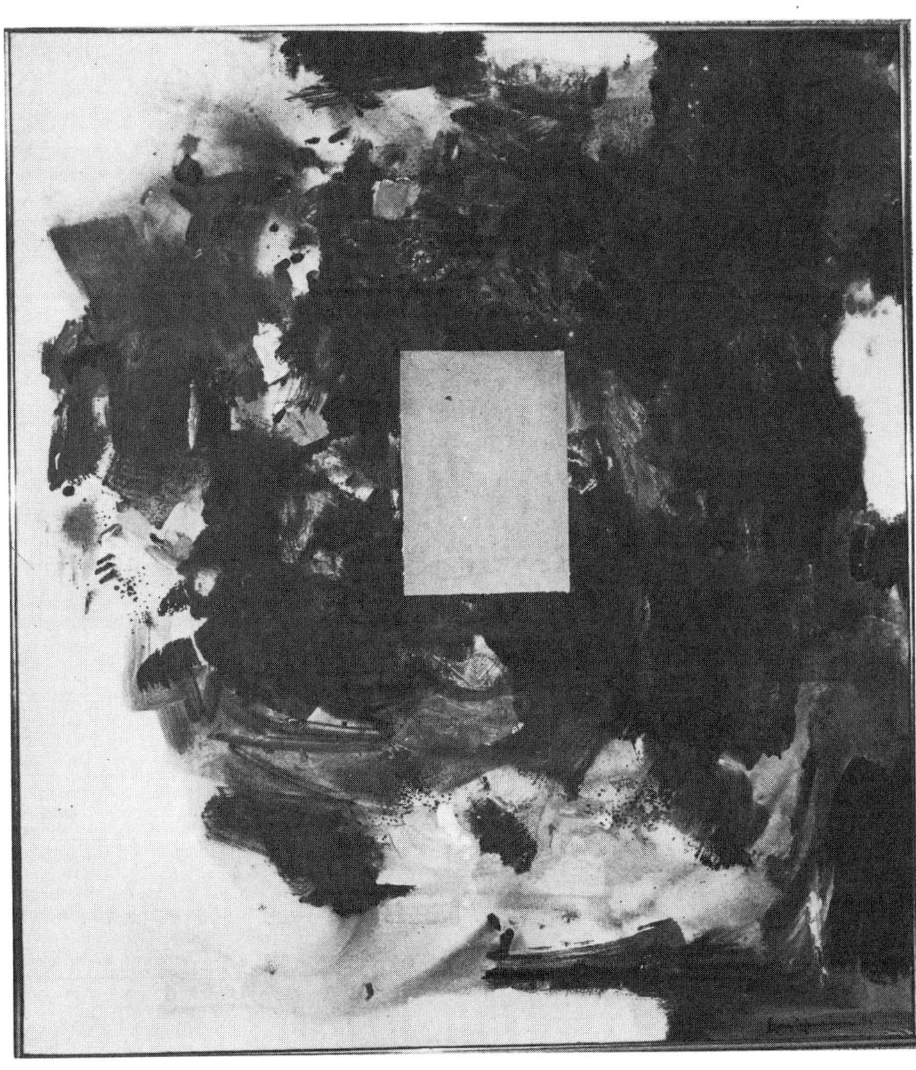

Hans Hofmann (American, b. Germany, 1880-1966)
SUN IN THE FOLIAGE; 1964; 84″ x 72″; oil
Collection of the American Republic Insurance Co.
Des Moines, Iowa

## A Similarity of Terms

In describing such effects in nature we seldom
doubt that we understand our own language.
We speak of white moonlight, or a gray day,
or a black night. In each case we refer to an
atmospheric effect. But common words often
have several meanings. We also refer to white
paper, a gray dress, or black shoes, meaning
the physical properties of the things. The first
category is concerned with effects due to
illumination; the second, with pigmentation.
Although identical terms (white, gray, black)
are used in both categories, they refer to different phenomena. In one instance we mean
atmospheric effects; in the other, the degree of
contrast of pigments.

The word "light," in particular, causes confusion. In everyday life it is used not only to
identify a source of illumination, such as
sunlight, electric light, etc., but also as a
descriptive term, such as a "light" dress,
meaning either weight or color. To the artist,
however, "light" means white pigment. Even
when he speaks of the "light and dark" of a
picture, he means the contrast between dark
lines, areas, or shapes and those which are
white or pale grays.

As graphic artists we deal only with pigments of one kind or another on a surface. With
these pigments we create contrasts which range
in shadings of colors or grays, from white
through grays, to black, as Hofmann does here.
By skillful manipulation of pigments we also
can create an illusion of illumination effects,
seen or imagined. But it must be emphasized
that all such "light" in pictures begins with
pigment. Now let us see how such illumination
effects are achieved.

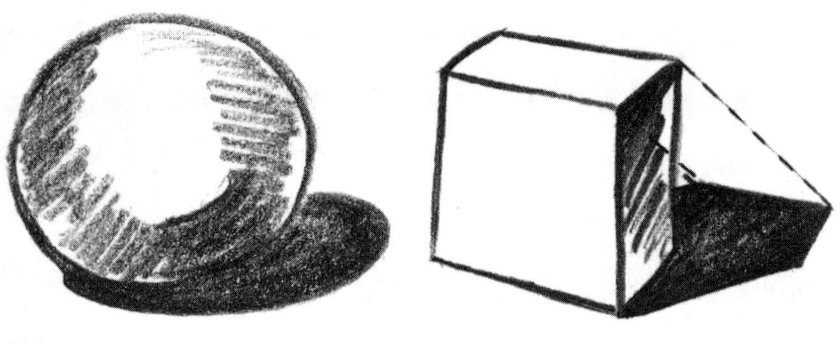

86-A

86-B

## 86  Modeling and Rendering

To create illumination effects in pictures, we must first note the effects of light, shade, and shadow in nature. When illuminated, three-dimensional forms usually are seen as surfaces which reflect more or less light as they turn toward or away from a dominant light source. At times such forms interrupt the light rays falling upon them in such a way that we observe cast shadows, either upon the forms themselves or upon adjacent surfaces of other forms (*86-A*). A nose may cast a shadow upon a cheek. The head casts a shadow upon an adjacent wall. A shade is that part of a form not in direct light yet not in a shadow. It is partly illuminated by lighting from other sources and consequently appears as a gray, somewhere between light and dark, which is called a halftone (*86-B*).

To simulate the effect of light falling upon an object, the artist usually assumes a fixed direction from which the light in the picture seems to originate. He then proceeds to explain the position of this light source, utilizing varying degrees of light and dark pigment in a skillful arrangement of simulated shades and shadows. Such an image may become so life-like that it seems to leave the picture surface. By modifying the degree of direct light, atmospheric effects may be achieved which challenge the realism of the photograph. Such drawings or paintings are usually referred to as *renderings*.

Often the three-dimensional aspects of a form are more important than an atmospheric effect suggesting a certain time of day. For instance, in an anatomical chart we are more interested in the physical characteristics of a femur than in how it might appear at sunset (87). Usually

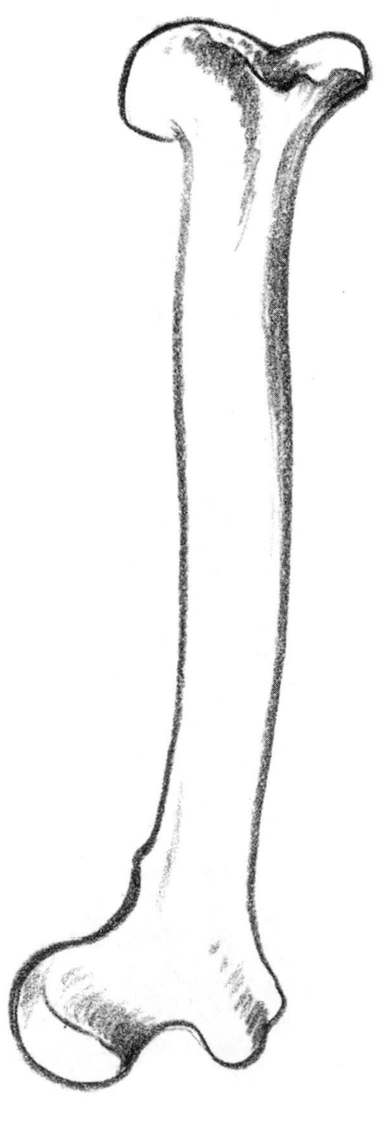

in such pictures dark and light effects are determined by the structure of the form itself rather than by a source of illumination. A system of dark and light contrast is devised, often predicated upon the use of light pigment (or the white of the paper) on the planes closest to us, turning into halftones as the planes recede from us. Any technique of drawing or painting used to achieve such sculpture-like symbols is usually referred to as *modeling*.

Such systems may give us great information and a convincing three-dimensional image of the form without indicating a light source. These informative drawings, with many variations of method, are used extensively in making anatomical charts, catalog illustrations, etc. Only rarely are they works of art.

## The Interpretation of Light Effects in Nature 

Since we see almost everything by means of some type of illumination, it seems logical to assume that our goal would be to simulate such effects in our pictures. But, because of the complexity of forms and the almost infinite number of reflecting surfaces making up these forms, this becomes an almost impossible assignment. Painting or drawing an exact reproduction of just one large tree in full foliage, or a meadow of grass, or pebbles on the beach might take years. Then the degree to which we succeeded in duplicating nature in no way guarantees that our picture would be interesting or exciting or would in any way qualify as a work of art.

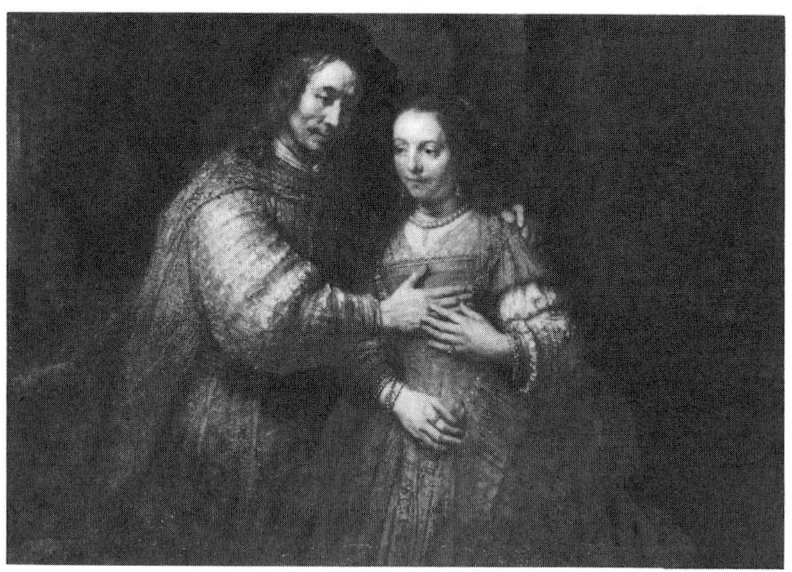

Rembrandt (Dutch, 1606-1669)
THE JEWISH BRIDE, 1665; 47$\frac{13}{16}$″ x 65$\frac{9}{16}$″
oil on canvas
Rijksmuseum, Amsterdam

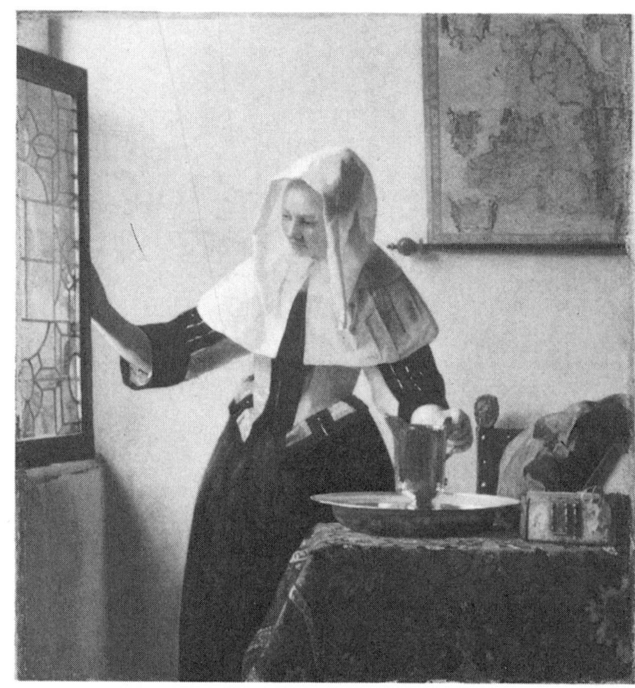

Jan Vermeer (Dutch, 1632-1675)
YOUNG WOMAN WITH A WATER JUG; 18″ x 16½″
oil on canvas
The Metropolitan Museum of Art, New York
Gift of Henry G. Marquand, 1889

 Great artists have continually explored the possibility of simulating nature's light effects without actually trying to duplicate them. Invariably they have resorted to great simplifications, both in the arrangement of the elements suggested by the subject matter in nature and in the graphic devices used. These devices are determined by adapting certain fixed methods. In plain terms, some "system" must be accepted to create order.

In his pictures, Rembrandt suggests a certain illumination effect which, though believable, is hardly characteristic of that which most of us experience in nature. Vermeer, who painted at the same time, also suggests a believable illumination effect, as we see here. Yet it is unlikely that we would ever confuse the work of the two artists. Seen separately, each artist's painting is a convincing statement of a light source. But in comparing them we wonder if Holland in the middle of the seventeenth century was dark, mysterious, and steeped in shadows like Rembrandt's pictures, or was it luminous, silvery and glowing like Vermeer's? Both artists adapted different systems of interpretation of light effects in nature, as well as the means to explain such effects graphically.

Modeling and rendering, although employed successfully by many artists in the construction of fine pictures, such as this de La Tour, are devices which may present grave dangers. When expressed in graphic terms, atmospheric effects and sculptural forms tend to overstate the subject matter and overemphasize the sculptural aspects of the picture, with potential weakening of the surface factor.

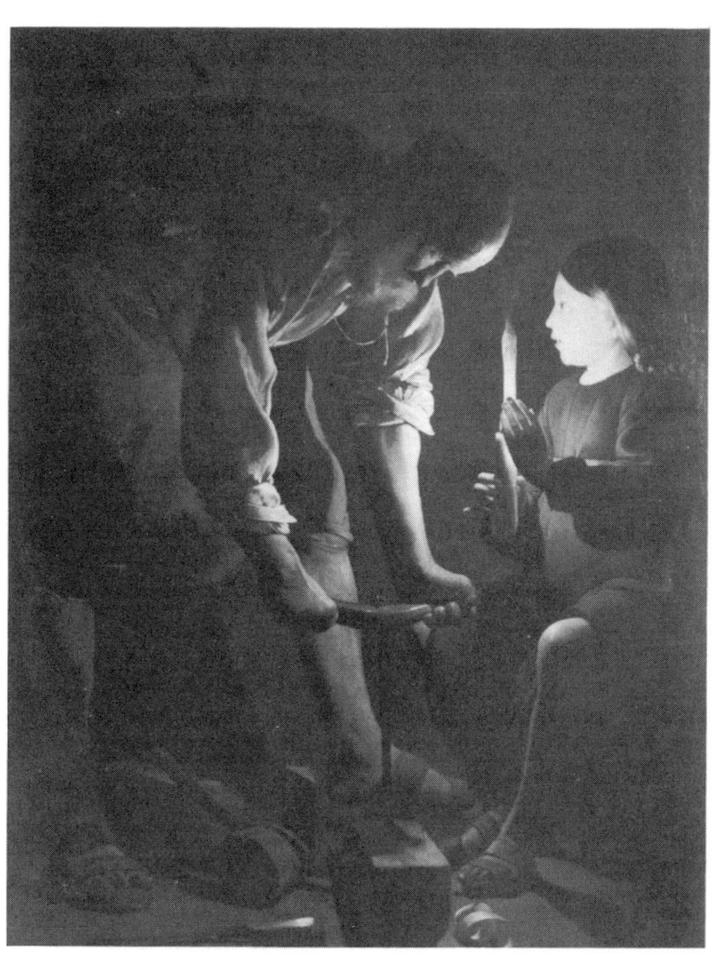

Georges de La Tour (French, 1593-1652)
ST. JOSEPH, THE CARPENTER, 1640-1650
53⅞″ x 41¾″; oil on canvas
The Louvre, Paris

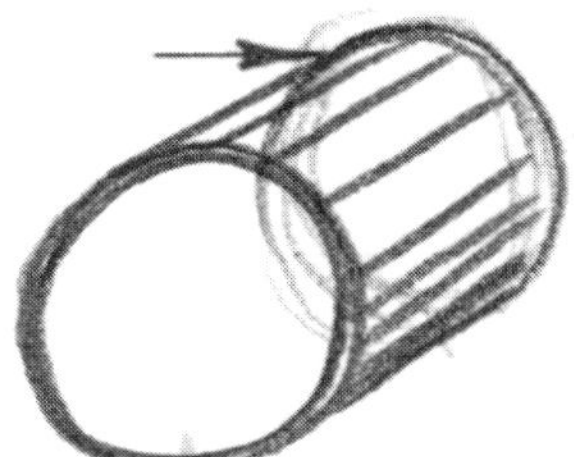

89-2A

89-2B

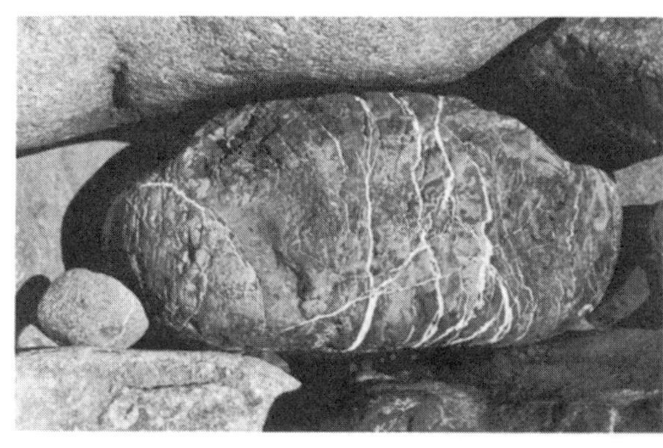

ROCK, PT. MUGU, 1969
(Photograph: Richard Barlow)

But we are not limited to employing only modeling or rendering in our pictures. We can use line and area contrasts which in no way suggest illumination or highly sculptured effects—a line drawing, for instance.

## The Absence of Line in Nature

Now when we begin a line drawing suggested by a form in nature, we find ourselves faced with a problem. In nature we rarely see a true line. Most linear structures such as telephone wires, television antennas, or reed-like growths such as grasses, twigs, and straw, are actually thin three-dimensional forms, not lines. The edge of a surface, although often linear in character, is a separation of two or more planes, not a true line (*89-2A*). The turning edge of a rounded form is a plane on edge and is determined by its association with other planes (*89-2B*). It is dependent upon planal structures, and hence it is not truly a line. Growth circles revealed in a section of a tree, patterns seen in rocks, as shown here, may be considered true linear structures, and veins in certain leaves approach linear structures. But we find that nature is generally characterized as being non-linear; nature appears to us as predominantly tonal or planal.

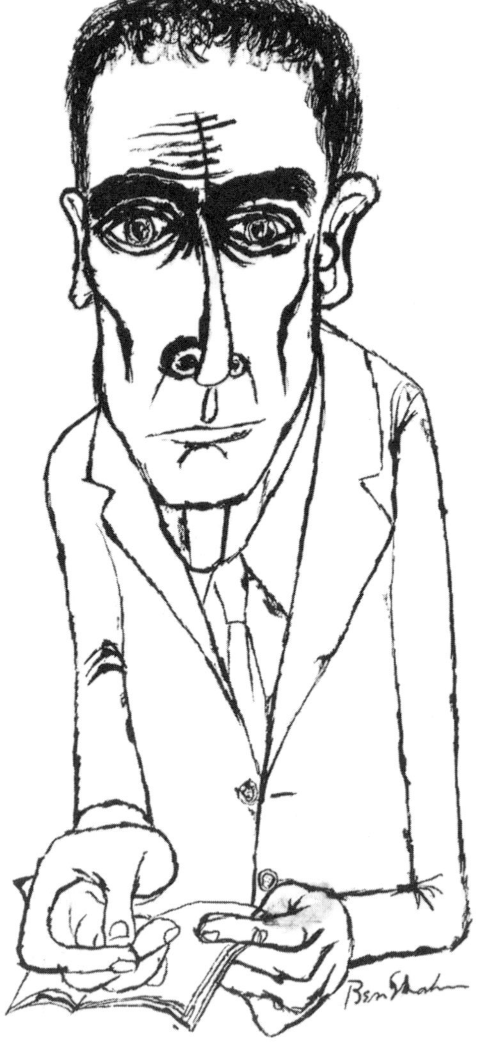

Ben Shahn (American, b. Lithuania, 1898-1969)
DR. J. ROBERT OPPENHEIMER, 1954
19½″ x 12¼″; brush and ink
Collection, The Museum of Modern Art, New York
Purchase Fund

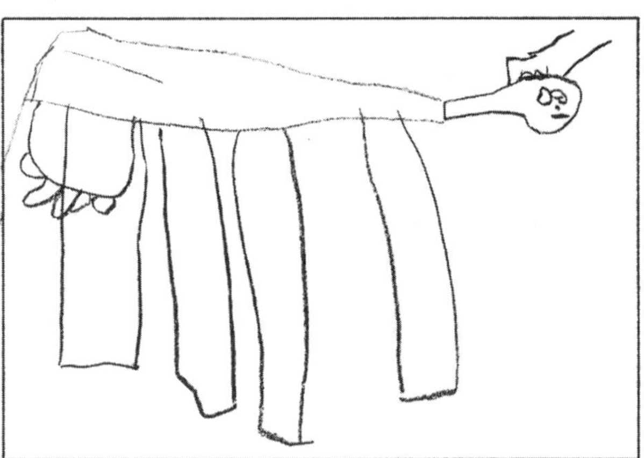

Pablo Graham (American, 1947-    )
COW, 1953; 6½″ x 9½″
charcoal pencil on paper
Courtesy of the artist
(Photograph: Alexander Hovsepian)

## Contrast

Now if there is no line in nature, where does
our concept of line come from? It comes from
the marks made with pigment on our surface by
our scribing tool or brush. Lines, and other
marks, points, and areas, in no way suggest
illumination effects, they simply contrast with
the surface. This factor of contrast inherent in
line and area can be exploited in many ways. If
we examine children's art, such as this drawing, and that of primitive people, we find that
the factor of contrast seems to evolve naturally
from the manipulation of drawing and painting
tools. Illumination effects, based on contrived
and learned techniques, are rarely seen in
such pictures.

If we examine a line drawing derived from a
form in nature, like Ben Shahn's *Dr. J.
Robert Oppenheimer*, we find that it may
suggest the three-dimensional character of the
form yet employ little or no tone. It does not
give us the same information as a modeled or
rendered drawing but can suggest the form in
new terms. Such a line drawing is known as
an *abstraction*.

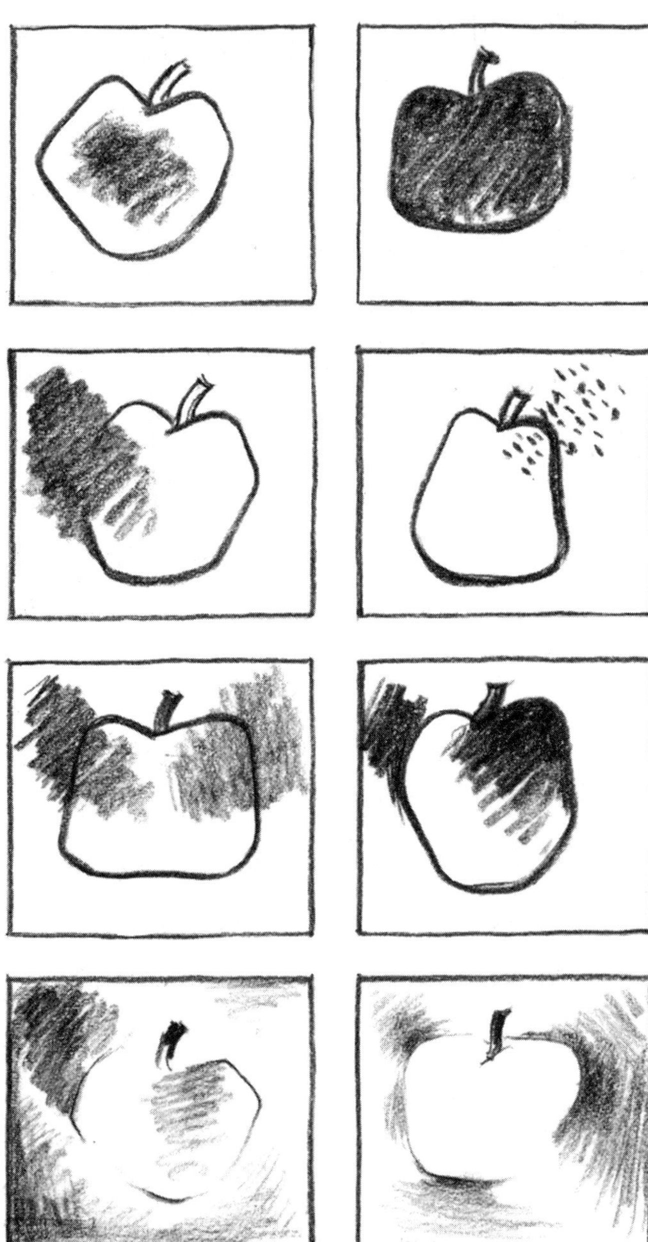



Not only may we suggest a three-dimensional form with line alone, but also we may express color or light and dark of such a form by the use of flat areas of color, or black, white, and grays. Or we may combine line with such flat areas. Often, in such a picture, the flat areas of color, or light and dark, are also abstract, having little or no reference to the color of the subject in nature. As we see in the accompanying figure, many variations of the use of line and area suggest a form, but none employ modeling or rendering (*91*).

So we see that a painting or drawing is dependent upon light only to the extent that it enables us to see the picture. Although the color or degree of light and dark we experience from a picture is the result of light reflecting from the pigment, the structure of a picture is not the study of light, or illumination, but the study of the application of pigment. Only by the skillful use of contrast of pigment, used as color, or line, or area, are we able to design graphically. But we must find ways to control the various degrees of contrast.

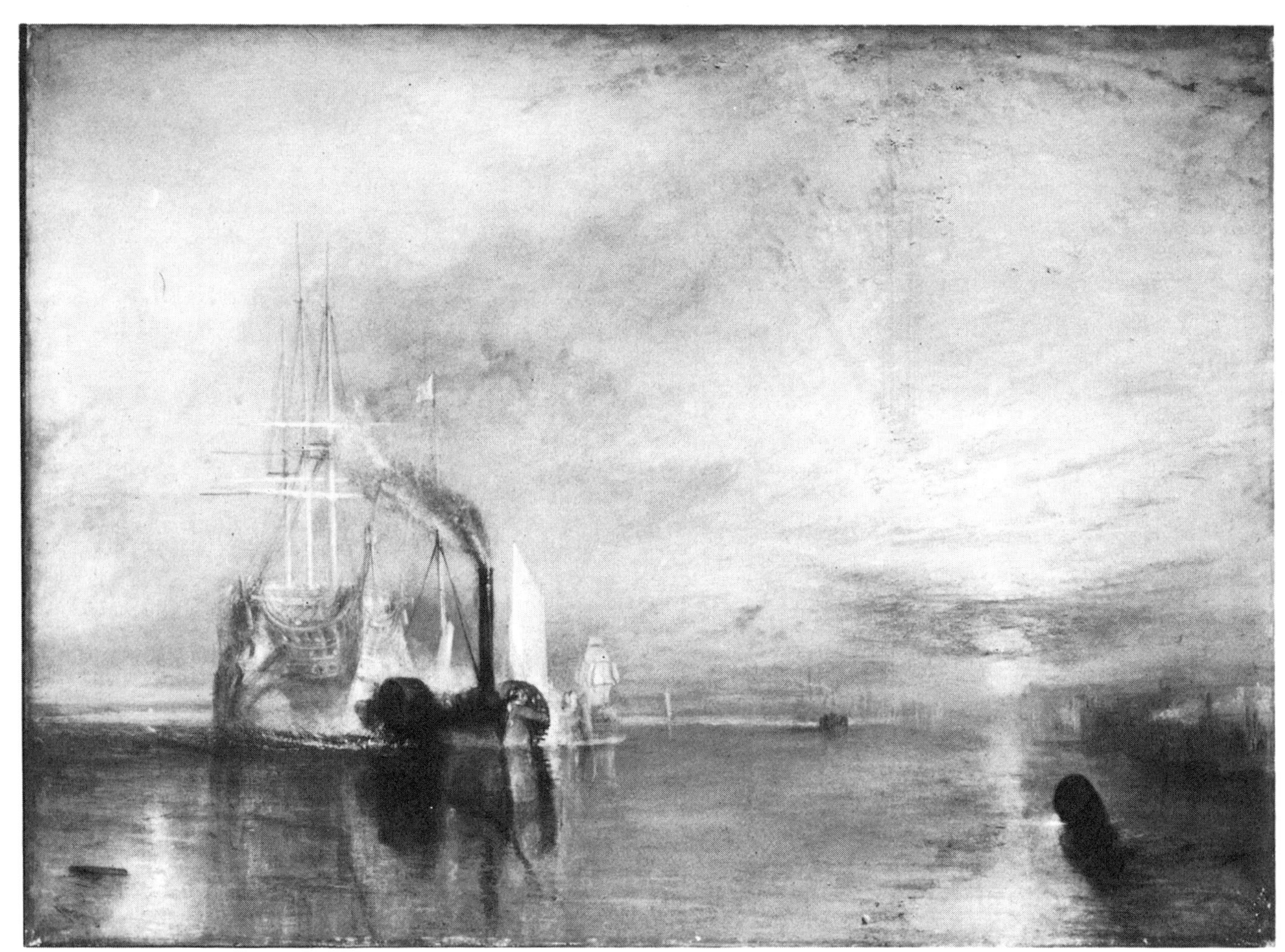

William Turner (English, 1775-1851)
THE FIGHTING "TEMERAIRE" TOWED TO HER
LAST BERTH
exhibited 1839, not dated; 35¾" x 48"
oil on canvas
Reproduced by courtesy of the Trustees
The National Gallery, London



# 9 Value

## Limits of Light and Dark

In nature we usually have little difficulty in distinguishing one object from another. Thus we usually see tables, chairs, trees, or houses as rather simple separations of shapes and colors. We tend to ignore the incredible number of closely related shadings of colors or grays ranging from black to white revealed in the objects. This degree of lightness or darkness of color, or grays, is called *value*.

When we look critically at this printed page, for instance, it is astonishing to see how many degrees of white to black we experience. Multiplying such variations of value thousands of times, we realize how complex the light and dark relationships of objects in nature really are. We should note that many adjacent shapes may be easily identified because of differences in color, but may be extremely difficult to distinguish from one another if transposed into black, white, and grays.

A great many things we see in nature are relatively gray or muted in value although sometimes bright in color. But the artist faced with creating dark and light patterns suggestive of this gray world must avoid producing a dull gray picture. Even if his picture is in no way motivated by elements in nature, as in non-representational work, the artist still must avoid dullness.

In looking at things in nature our eyes adjust to a broad range of light and dark, limited at one extreme by the physically damaging brilliance of an arc light or the sun, and at the other by the smothering darkness of a vault. Yet in looking at a picture our eyes never exert themselves to this extent, for paper is only relatively white and the blackest pigment only relatively black. It has been estimated that the clouds and sky in nature may be hundreds of thousands of times brighter than shadows or dark hollows on the ground. Yet the artist must depict this vast range of dark to brilliant using a palette whose white may be only thirty times brighter than black.

So even if we wish to duplicate a light and dark effect in nature, we are limited by our medium to an extremely narrow range of possible contrasts. Yet there are dark pictures which seem bright, as the Turner above, or in which effects of sunlight, candlelight, or firelight have been skillfully simulated, such as those we saw in the previous chapter. How do artists create illusions of such brilliance?

San Francisco     94-1

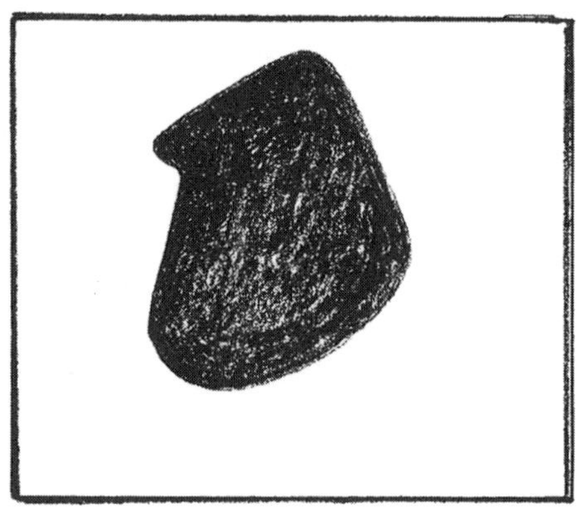

94-2A

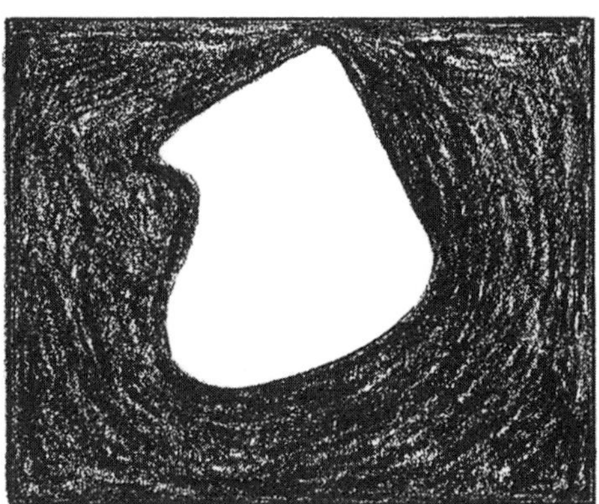

94-2B

## 94  Relative Contrasts

We all know that contrasts are relative. A warm
bowl of soup may seem hot on a cold day or
cool on a sizzling hot day. A moderately loud
sound, disturbing on a quiet night, may go
unnoticed in the din of a crowd. And so with
graphic light and dark contrasts. To simulate
brightness we must arrange our pigments in
relation to the picture surface and to each other
so that we depend upon relative contrasts of
light and dark rather than direct duplication of
natural effects. Whether our picture is illustrative, abstract, or non-representational, our
choice of values must be equally selective.

The maximum physical contrast possible on
white paper is black pigment. Yet we find that
if we surround a small area of black pigment
with a large area of white paper, the black
area will seem even blacker (*94-2A*). The
reverse is also true, for if a small white area is
surrounded by a large black area, the white
will seem whiter (*94-2B*). These are examples
of maximum contrast. But such arrangements
in no way assure maximum brightness. As we
shall see in the following chapter, decreasing
the size and number of the extremes of white
and black may increase the intensity and brilliance of the same structures.

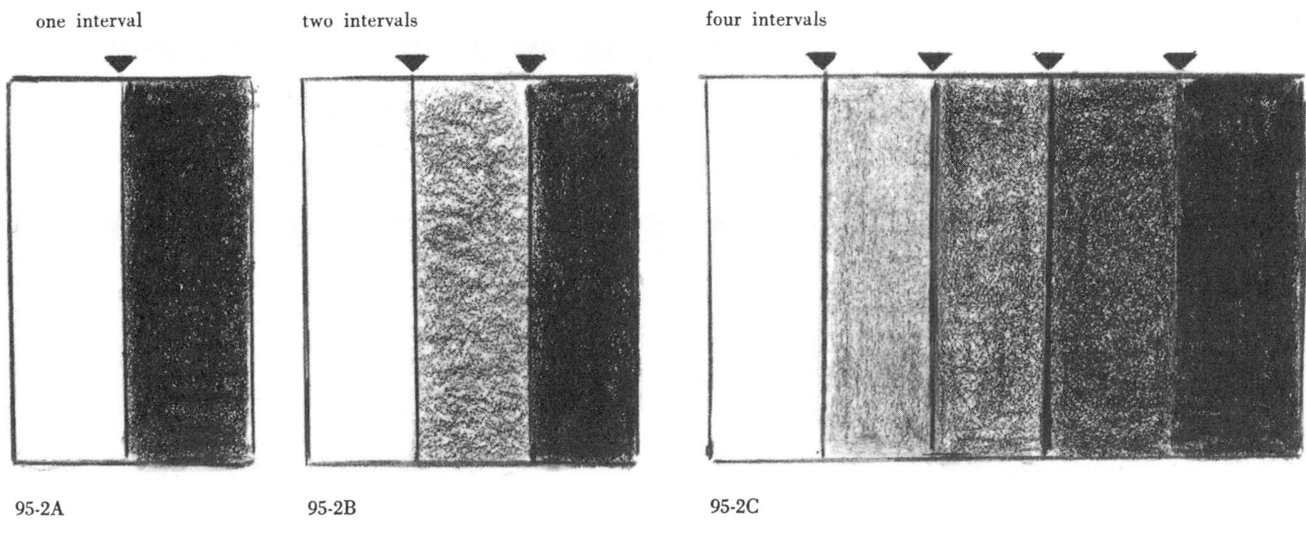

one interval

two intervals

four intervals

95-2A

95-2B

95-2C

## The Value Scale

To emphasize the almost infinite number of values at our disposal imagine placing one drop of ink into a ten-thousand-gallon tank full of clear water. Stir well. With a small brush make a swatch of this mixture on white paper. Now repeat; one more drop of ink, stir, then another swatch placed beside the first. Continue on and on. It is conceivable that such a series of tiny swatches might stretch from San Francisco to New York (*94-1, 95-1*). Yet such an extensive series would be useless in helping us control light and dark in a picture because our eyes would not be able to distinguish the difference between the values of adjacent swatches.

For us to distinguish between adjacent values in our picture there must be a perceptible difference between them. This difference is referred to as the *interval (95-2A)*. Between black and white any number of perceptible intervals may be introduced, but if the interval is too close the adjacent values will seem to slur or slide into each other and appear as one.

One helpful work rule is: never use too many values in a picture, limit the number of intervals. The number ranges from one interval between black and white, to two intervals—black, one gray, and white—to as many intervals as can be controlled by the artist (*95-2B*). An indication of the number of intervals and the difference in values can be established on a separate sheet of paper as a series of small rectangles, each representing a value to be used in the picture. Such a chart is called a *value scale (95-2C)*.

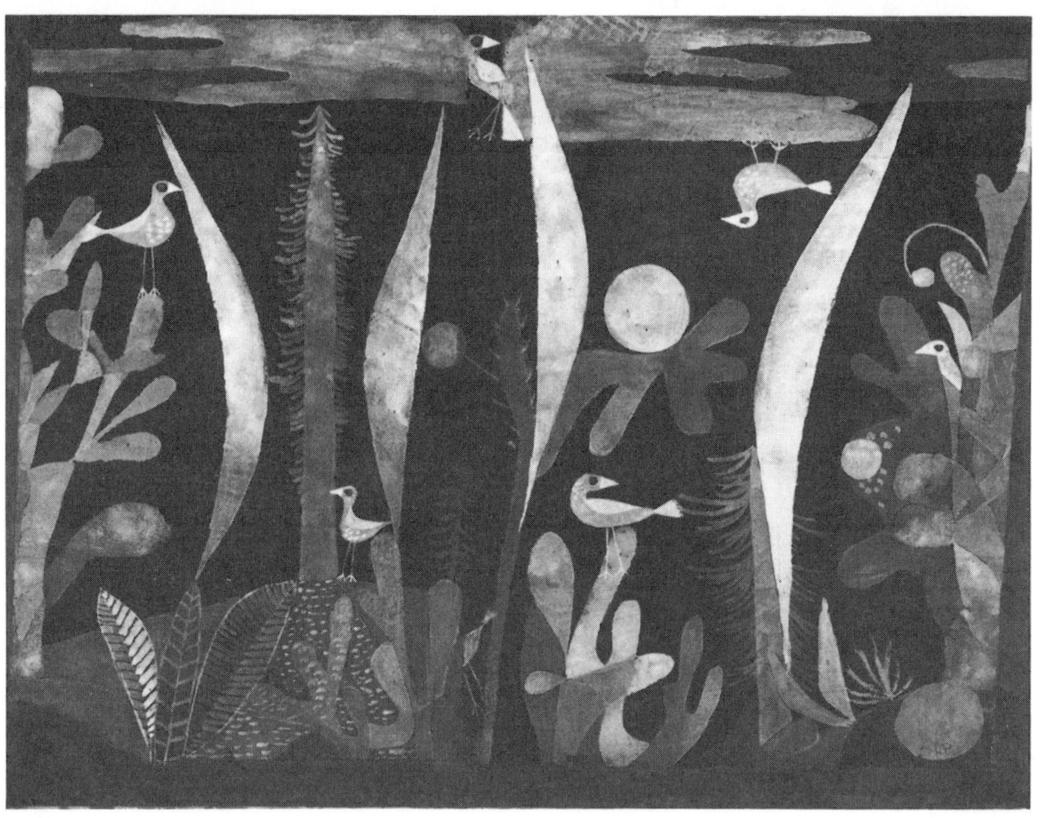

96-1

even

light

dark

split

limited

Paul Klee (Swiss, 1879-1940)
LANDSCAPE WITH YELLOW BIRDS; 1923
14″ x 17⅜″; watercolor and gouache
French Reproduction Rights, N. Y.
(Photograph: Colorphoto Hans Hinz SWB)

96     A value scale is to the artist what a score is to the musician. Each gives the artist opportunity to coordinate his respective activities to a predetermined order—the artist to color value, the musician to sound value. By limiting the choice of values in a picture to a value scale, order is preserved. Usually the subject of the picture will suggest a simple value scale. Once the value scale is established, the values of the large areas of the picture should be made to conform to it. Unless the values indicated in the scale are matched in the picture, the scale is worthless.

A value scale can be of inestimable help to the artist, especially until his control of values in a picture becomes automatic. The time taken to make a value scale and to adjust the values in the picture to this scale is not wasted.

It may be surprising to realize that black, five or six grays, and white are usually adequate for the major construction of most pictures. Limiting the values to this small number is a good work rule. By limiting the number of intervals, we learn to exploit the use of a few grays, and so we better control the contrasts of our picture.

For example, if we reserve the white of our paper and our blackest black for accents, which we will explore in the next chapter, five values are usually sufficient for most work. If large white symbols, such as white dresses or white houses, are involved, an additional value very close to white may be necessary. By adding more and more values we almost always weaken our structure. Let us not forget that a poker hand consists of only five cards. Ten cards would not improve the game.

The ordered steps in a simple scale of values may be equal from light to dark (96-1), or the value scale may favor light values or dark

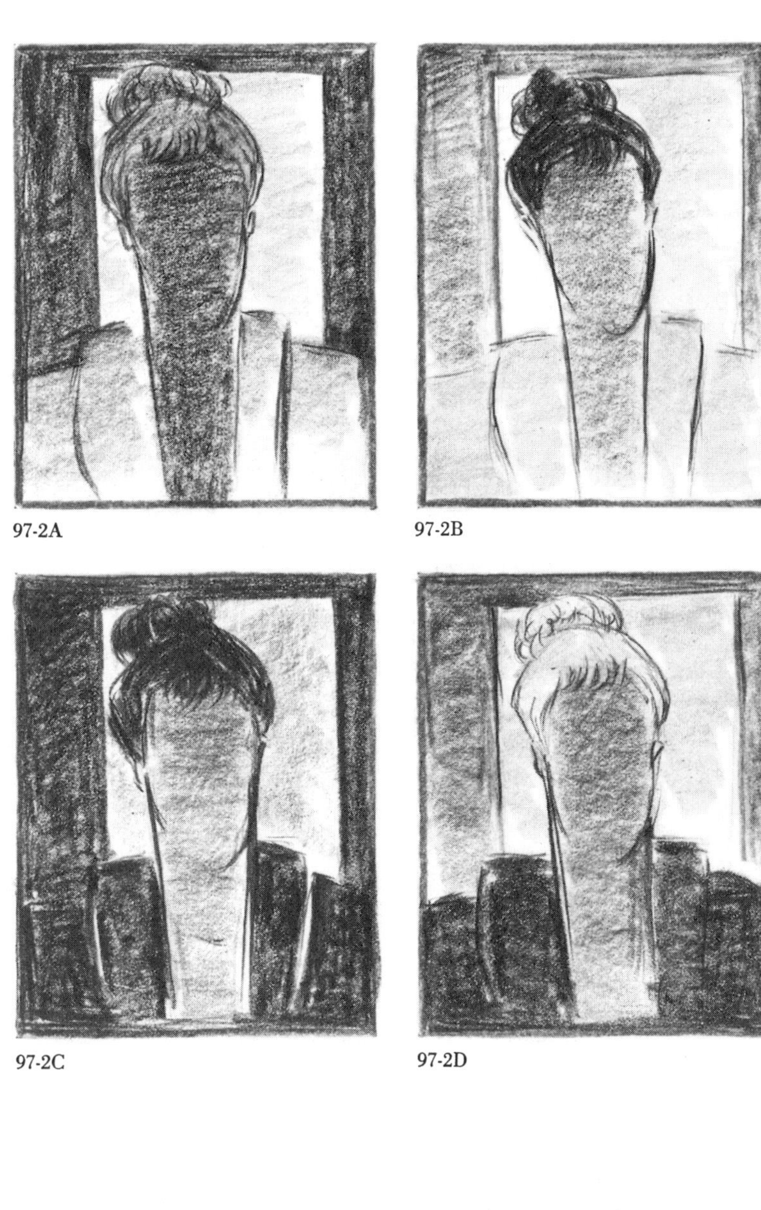

97-2A

97-2B

97-2C

97-2D

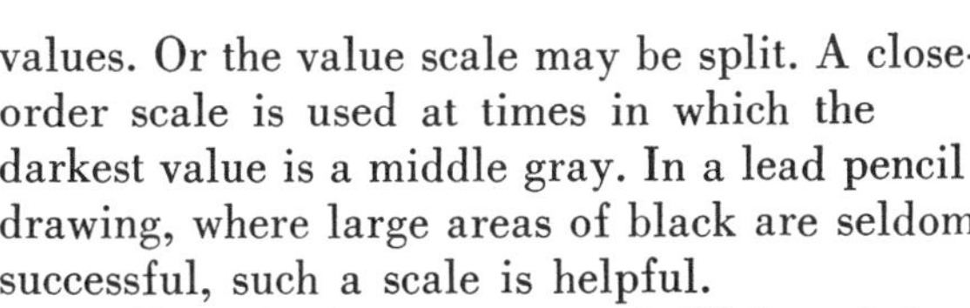

97-1

values. Or the value scale may be split. A close-order scale is used at times in which the darkest value is a middle gray. In a lead pencil drawing, where large areas of black are seldom successful, such a scale is helpful.

In Klee's landscape we see skillful exploitation of a limited number of values. The shapes are easily read yet active and full of detail. It should also be noted that although the picture is luminous there is little true white. The shape contrasts are strong yet remarkably close in value.

We may repeat a given value in the foreground, background, and subject. In relation to different environments in the picture a value completely changes impact. All the accompanying rectangles are of identical value, yet we see that each seems lighter or darker in relation to a different accompanying value (*97-1*). A picture containing few values may seem to contain a great number when such relationships are exploited.

To illustrate the flexibility of the limited scale, let us first reserve white white and black black for accents. At this time neither value should be employed in our picture. Between these two extremes let us indicate three values with a noticeable interval between each (*97-2A*). Now by making the flesh and part of the background correspond to our darkest value, the hair and dress correspond to our middle value, and a very light gray activating the light panel our lightest value, we set a basic order for our light and dark structure. If we examine the accompanying diagrams we begin to sense the incredible amount of graphic control potential in the use of a limited number of values, especially in relation to the large shapes on which the impact of the picture depends (*97-2B, -2C, -2D*).

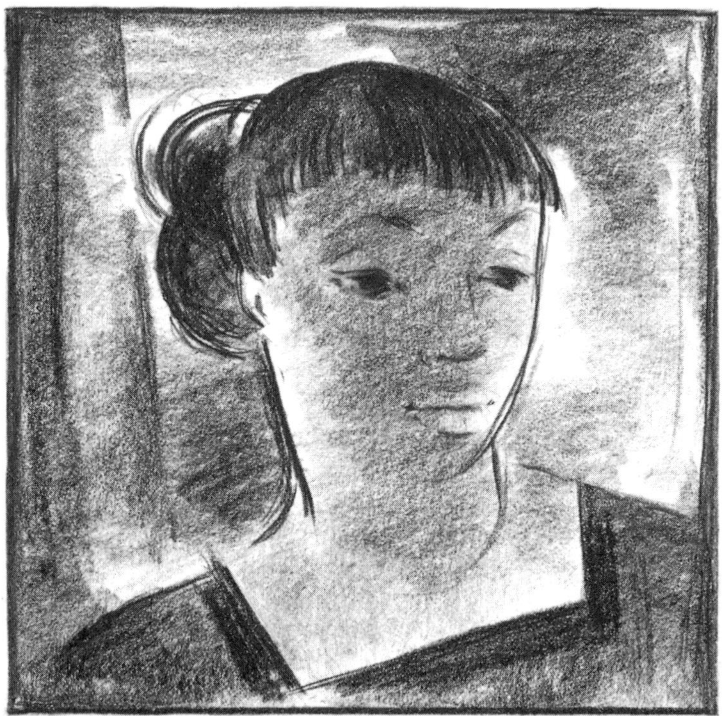

98-B

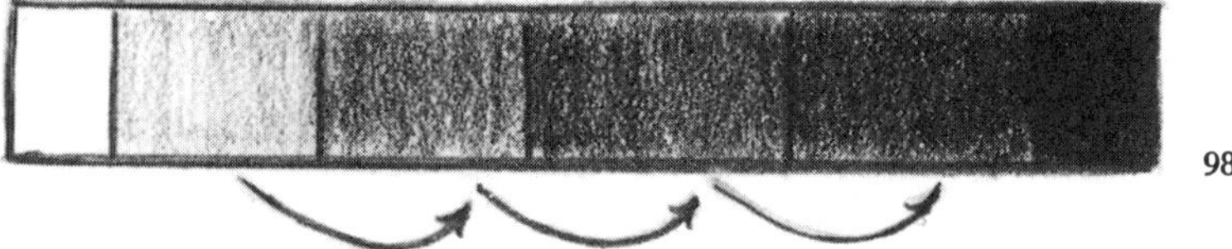

98-A



As we begin to compose pictures we are tempted to break up large shapes simply for the sake of minor details, especially if we insist upon introducing shade and shadow effects, or modeling or rendering within a shape. Fragmentation of big shapes by minor details, or shade and shadow effects, has been successfully employed in many pictures, but for the young artist this fragmentation is a real hazard. Such internal activity often weakens the impact of the shape and contributes to chaos in the picture structure.

Contrasts within a shape are useful, however, to give information and as a means of separating planes in space. To control such contrasts, first limit the number of values in the large areas, such as the face, hair, or a drape.

Now by dropping down one value toward dark in our scale, two rather closely related values may be utilized in any one large shape without destroying its impact (*98-A*). In doing so we are also establishing value bridges between adjacent areas (*98-B*). Thus the darkest value of the face will be the same as the lightest hair value, which also will be the lightest background value. Now by dropping down one value in the hair, and also in the background, we find that only three values on our scale have been used. The darkest value in the hair may become the lightest value in the drape. As yet we have used only three values. By dropping down one value in the drape, a fourth value is finally brought into play. As we noted, we shall discover in the next chapter how the first and last values, black and white on the scale, can be used as accents to gain brilliance.

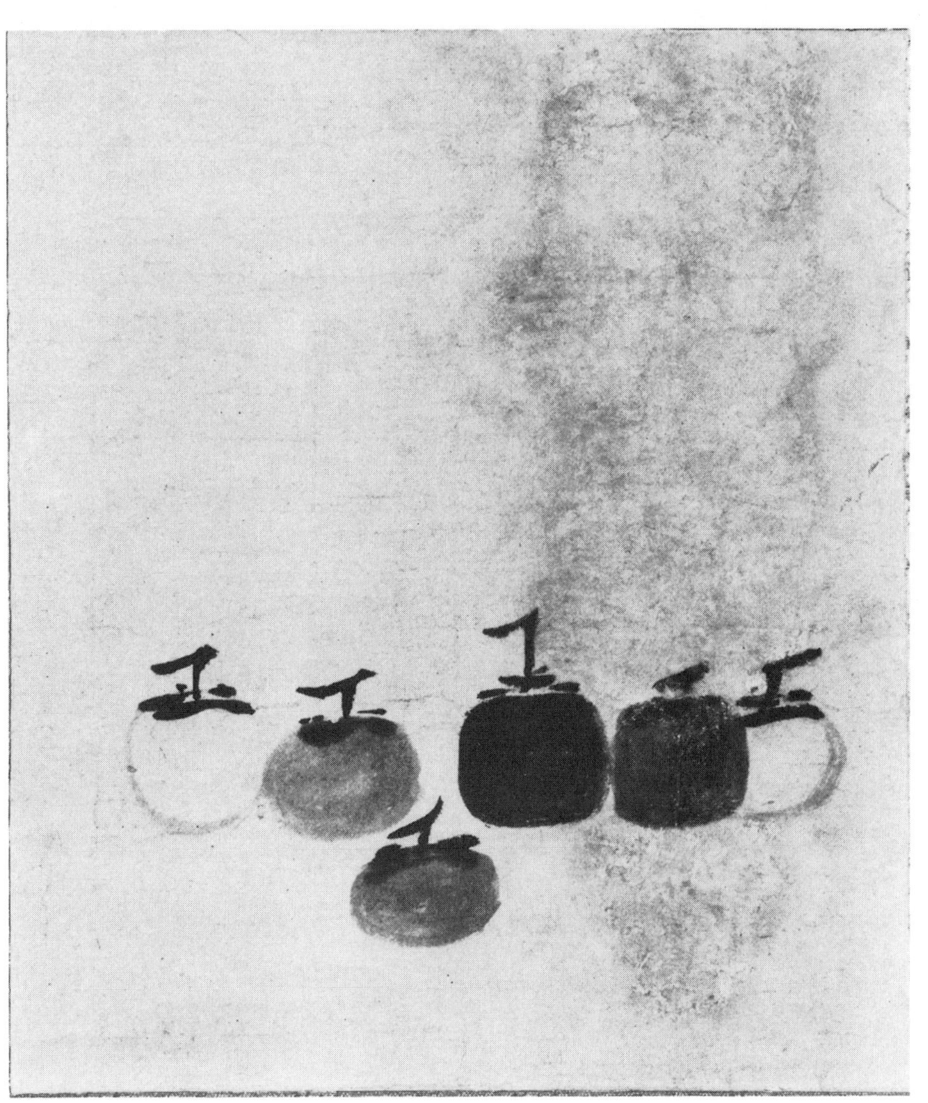

Fa-ch'ang (Mu Ch'i) (Chinese, 12th century)
PERSIMMONS; Sung Dynasty 1181-1239; ink on paper
Daikotuji Monastery, Kyoto
(Photograph: *Art News*)

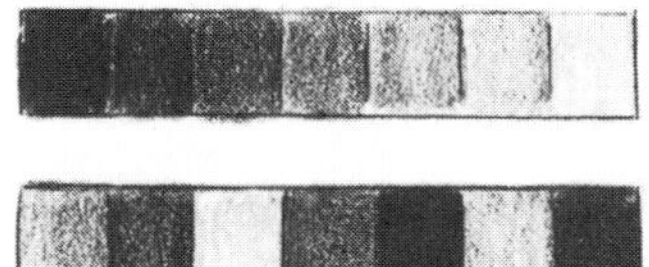

99-1A

99-1B

## The Value Series

When we relate numbers in the order 1-2-3-4
we expect 5, and then 6. Such a series is
usually dull, particularly in an expected order
of different values adjacent to one another:
light light, light, gray, gray gray, etc. Not only
is the series dull, but the order almost eliminates
possibility of strong value and shape contrasts
(*99-1A*).

To overcome this deadening effect, the values
of a series of adjacent shades may be altered
in a number of ways. A series 2-5-1-4-7-3-6,
etc., gives both variety and contrast. When
translated into value terms we find that this
is especially true (*99-1B*). By simple adjustments in the values of adjacent shapes we may
generate contrasts which can make an exciting
picture of only a few elements, such as
Fa-ch'ang's painting of persimmons.

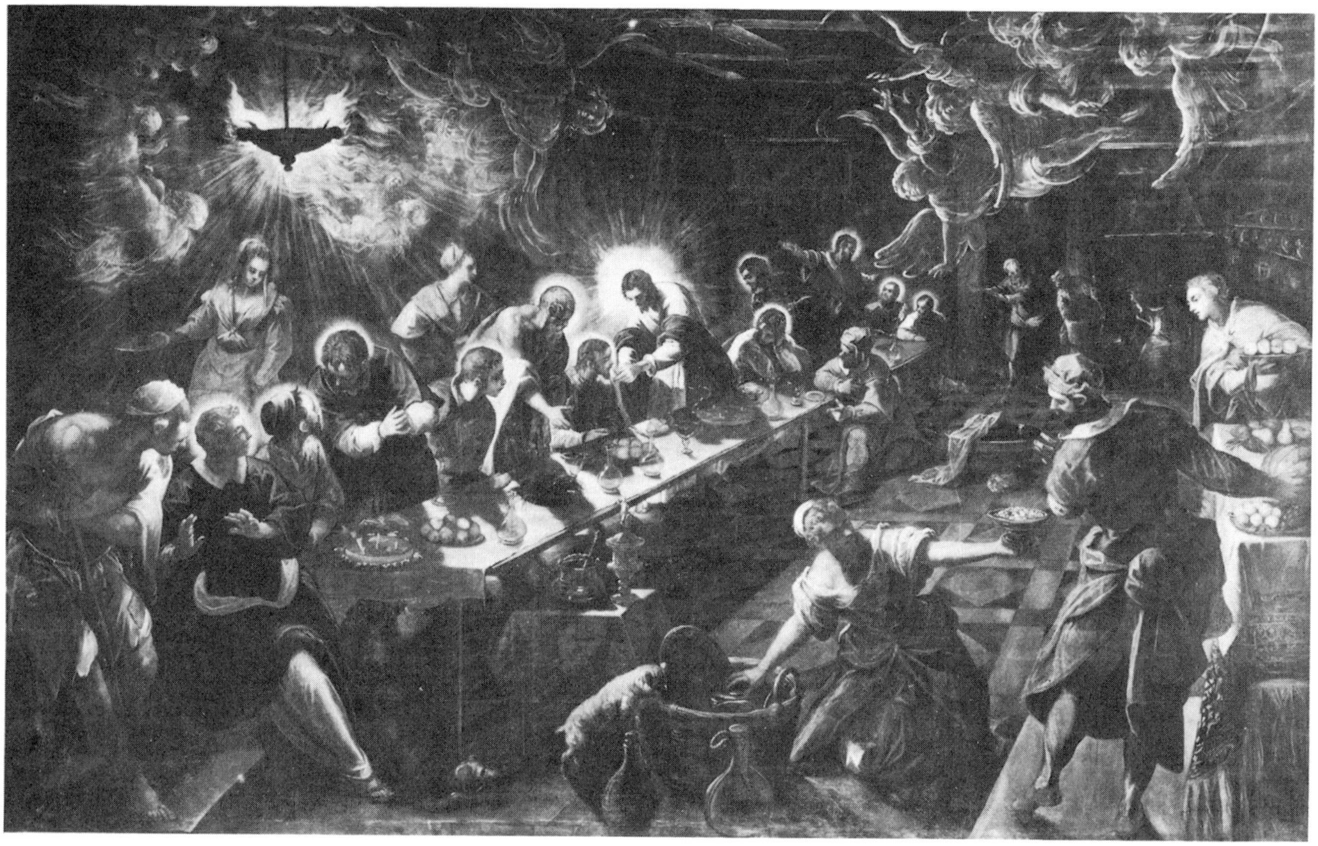

Jacopo Tintoretto (Italian, 1518-1594)
THE LAST SUPPER, ca. 1594; 12′ x 18′8″
oil on canvas
Basilica di San Giorgio Maggiore, Venice



# 10 The Graphic Accent

### Three Types of Accent

Most graphic accents are like the salt and pepper used in cooking. If we use too much, we ruin the dish; if too little, the food tastes insipid. A graphic accent is of the same nature. It must be used with great discretion, but it must be used.

Accenting consists primarily of introducing lights and darks so skillfully into a picture that we are not aware of their presence, yet we feel their effect through a brightening of the picture. Tintoretto's *The Last Supper* is bright not merely from obvious illumination effects but also from his use of accents.

There are three types of accents which we use constantly: first, the *general accent*, like salt, is used most frequently but must not be apparent; second, the *linear accent*; and third, the *shape accent*, which is used sparingly and which must be seen as a shape.

## The General Accent

Before investigating the general accent, let us try to find a reason for its use. When two areas of color come together as a color separation, the difference in color intensities, or value, or hue often is sufficient to generate a strong contrast. This may be true even when the two contrasting colors are of identical value.

In transposing color into terms of light and dark, some difference of value of adjacent areas must be indicated, or they must be differentiated by means of line or graphic accents (an exception is the passage, which is discussed in Chapter 12). Otherwise, the two areas may seem as one. Now, if we examine impinging areas of two values that are closely related but different enough to be distinguishable, we may note contrast but we almost always sense a lack of brilliance. Except in cases of extreme contrast, a lack of brightness is characteristic of most areas that abut each other. Usually a dark and light picture based upon such contrasting areas of close grays will be extremely dull. Yet, in color, the same picture, utilizing the same value organization, may well be exciting. To overcome this almost assured dullness in a light and dark picture, the general accent is introduced.

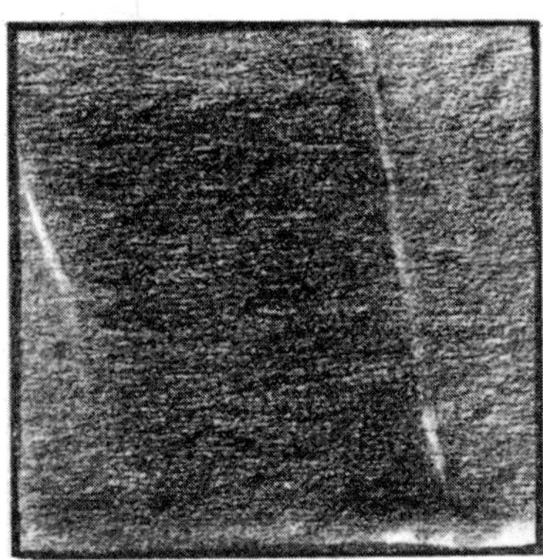

102-1

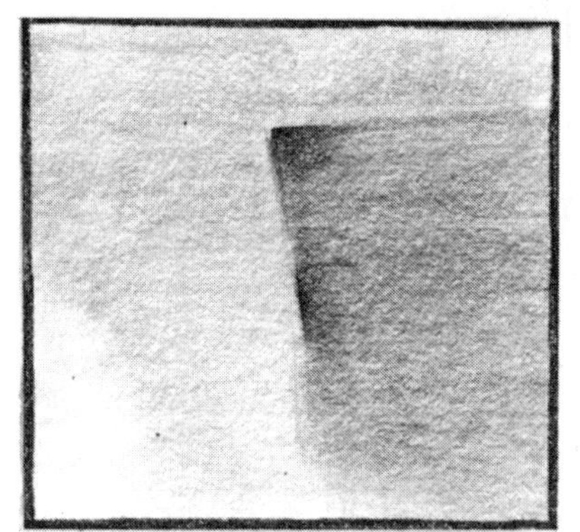

102-2

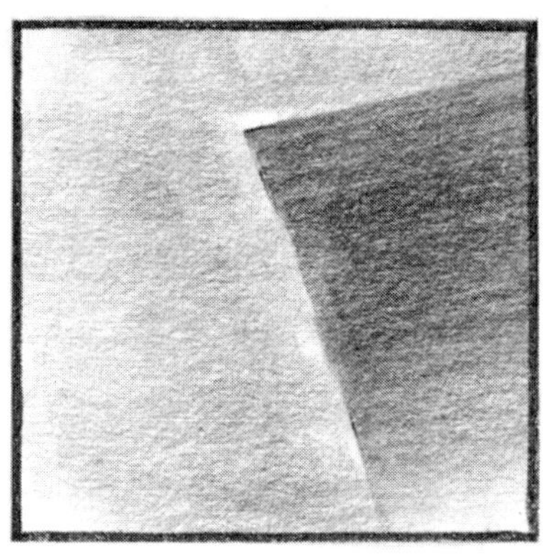

102-3



In a tonal picture we find that there are many possible ways of accenting with black and white. Between two closely related dark gray areas we may introduce a little pure white, not large enough or spreading enough to be a shape, nor progressive enough to be experienced as a line. This is the white accent which should be felt, not seen (*102-1*).

Similarly, we may place a sharp black between two closely related light grays or between a light gray and white in such a way that it does not appear as a shape or a line. But the grays and the white will seem brighter. The black acts as an accent (*102-2*).

Both black and white accents may be used in the same picture. Frequently we may introduce a black accent and a white accent side by side (*102-3*). The combination can produce great brilliance. By experimenting, various arrangements of accents with different values of grays will reveal the great range of possibilities of black and white accents.

In a picture containing many light values with a preponderance of white and light grays, we find that a dark gray may seem black by contrast. In such a case, a dark gray may occasionally be used as an accent.

When using color, effective accents may also be achieved which are less dark than black. We know that many dark colors never can be as dark as black. Yet because of their color properties they lend themselves well to accenting. A rich, dark, warm color, when contrasted against a light, cool color, becomes an accent having great strength. Similarly, a pure color on the silhouette of a dark shape may enhance the brilliance of the shape immeasurably.

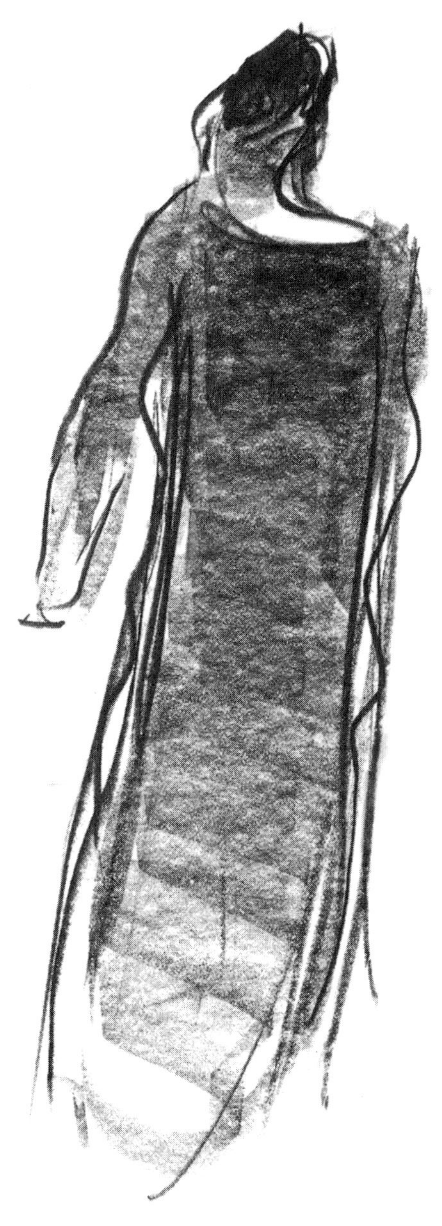

103

We find that any black point, line, or area, when correctly used, may become an accent. Usually we add the element to the picture surface in some opaque form such as lead pencil, chalk, ink, paint, etc. (*103*). If a black ground is used, parts of it may be revealed or allowed to show through the pigmented areas which are applied over most of this black ground.

In a dark picture a light gray is seldom very effective as an accent. The darks seem to overwhelm it. Yet, as we shall see, sometimes it can be used successfully. In such structures a white accent usually gives more brilliance to the picture.

The construction of the white accent is a little more involved. In some cases we may add white in some opaque form, especially when the picture is executed with an opaque medium such as tempera or oil. If the working surface, or ground, of the picture is gray or black, we usually are forced to add a white opaque accent. In most drawings or watercolors, however, areas of the white ground of the surface are preserved to act as accents.

A white ground has the property of reflecting a maximum amount of light. When exploited in a picture this reflective property may be used to advantage in accenting or in giving luminosity to applied pigments or chalks which possess some transparency. This may be accomplished in a watercolor or fresco by keeping the washes of pigment transparent.

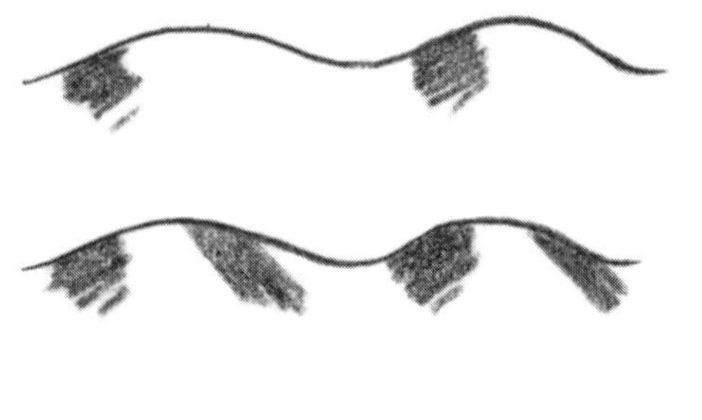
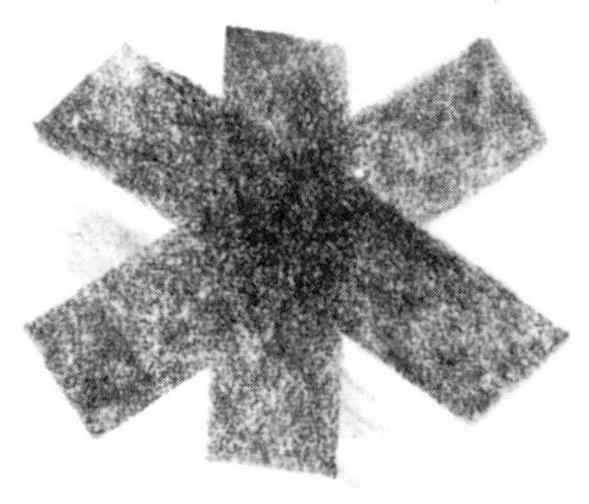
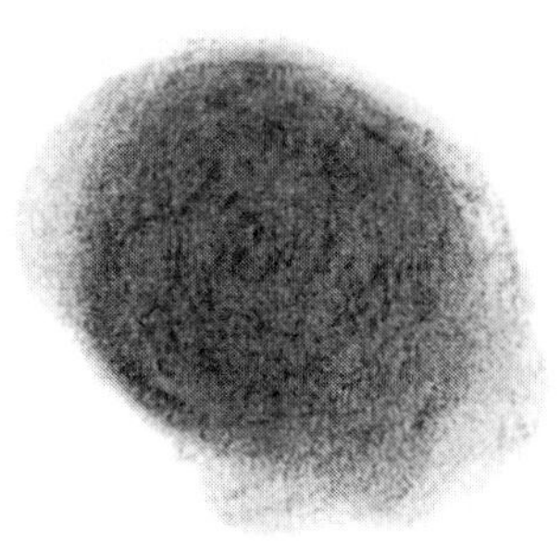

104-A          104-B          104-C

104      In pencil or chalk drawings we may use the special qualities of the surface such as the paper or lithograph stone to help us. Most paper and all stones are textured or granular. As we draw our chalk across this granular surface some pigment is deposited on one side of each protuberance in its path (*104-A*). Some part of one such little mountain, however, is not disturbed and remains white. If now we change the direction of our stroke, the pigment is deposited on another side of the mountain, but still some white remains. In this way a dark dark may be created which yet contains some flecks of white and, thus, the area will have a certain luminosity (*104-B*). Of course there are times when an intense opaque black may be desired. Usually, however, when we scrub the white out of a gray or black area dullness results (*104-C*).

With slight modification the small areas of white paper we inadvertently leave in making a tonal drawing may be developed into white accents, especially the white areas found between adjacent areas of grays or blacks.

We find that, when working into flat gray areas or on a light-colored ground, the area may be disturbed slightly allowing the light gray to come through as a light accent. Often this can be accomplished by the introduction of hatch, stipple, or texture. Accents generated in this way may make an otherwise dull area quite brilliant.

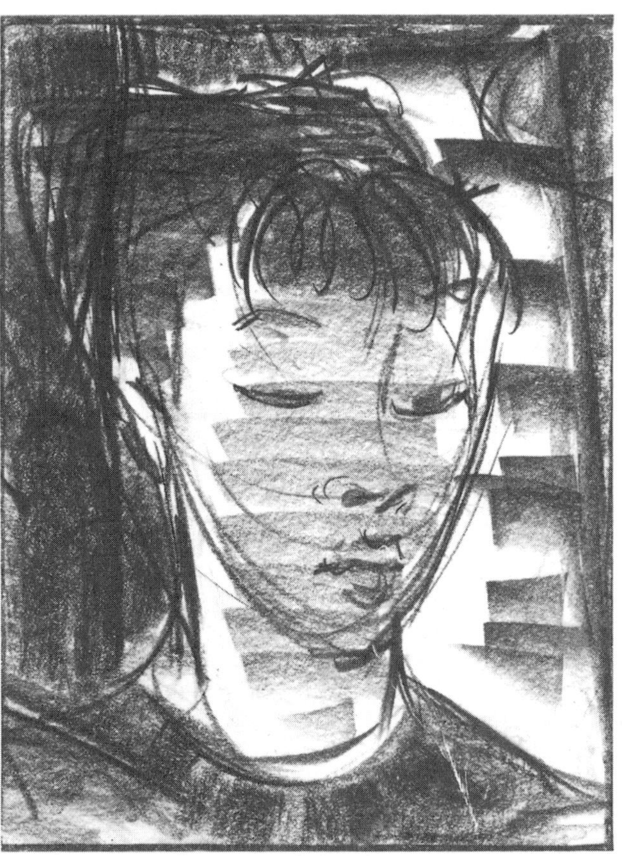

105-1

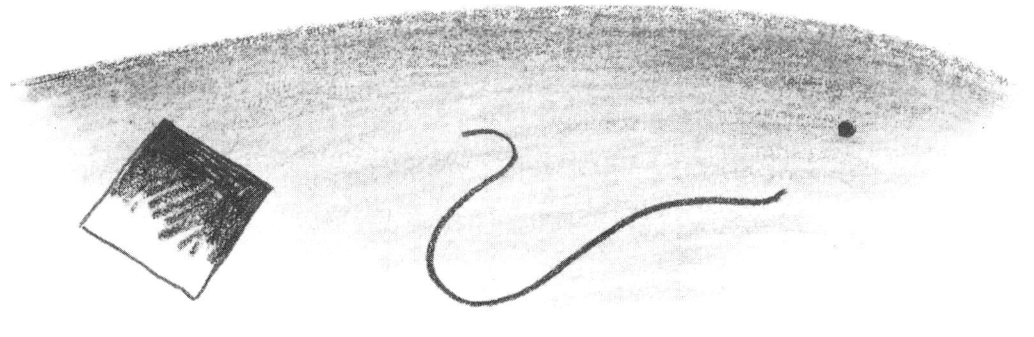

105-2

Often a black shape, black hair, for instance, will seem blacker and more brilliant if rendered not with black but with a very dark gray. Both white and black accents may still be used effectively in such a shape (*105-1*). If the hair shape is made completely black, the use of the black accent in the internal structures of the shape of the head is negated.

In Chapter 9 we remarked upon the danger of losing the interval between adjacent grays. A *slur* results. This effect and the similar *scumble* may produce an objectionable softness, yet, with accenting, each can be used to advantage. One of the most successful design contrasts is that of a sharp, crisp, or hard element played against a soft element. Here, now, we see a use for the slur or scumble. Into an indeterminate area of changing grays, a sharp point, line, or crisp shape may be introduced which accents the soft area, giving great contrast (*105-2*).

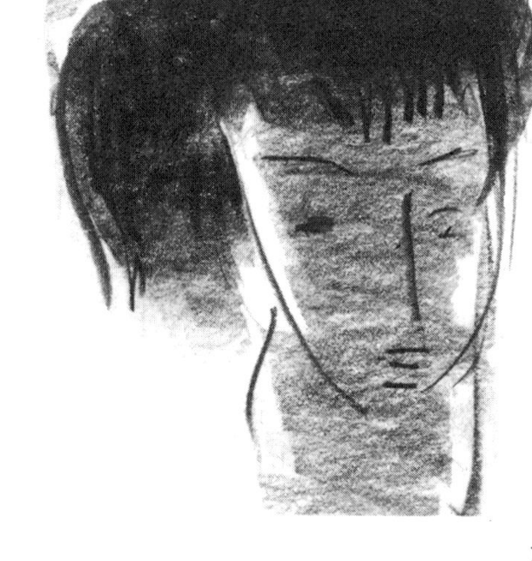

106



## The Linear Accent

As we saw in Chapter 8, a true line in nature
is rarely experienced. Usually linear effects
such as telephone lines or fine strands of hair
are actually very thin forms. At times in a
picture we may carry a symbol of such a form,
a strand of black hair, for instance, into a
white area. It creates a graphic accent which
for all working purposes may be described
as a linear accent.

Often a flat black or very dark colored
shape silhouetted against a white or very light
area may seem dull or lifeless. To give life
to the shape we may resort to *over-drawing*.
By allowing a black line or dark colored line
to escape in places from the shape and then
return to it, we introduce a small white or light
colored accent between the line and the shape.

This accent activates line and shape, giving a
brilliance to both. The line becomes a linear
accent (*106*).

Generally such over-drawing does not change
the proportional relations of the black shape.
It gives an extension of the shape, a feeling
of generosity to it. It helps to give gesture
to the shape and the drawing seems less tight
or hard. Since the line is dominated by the
impact of the shape, its presence is sensed
rather than actually seen.

Since we are making symbols, not factual
reproductions of things in nature, we are free
to introduce lines, as in over-drawing, which
may or may not be related to actual occurrences
in nature. In other words, a line may be truly
graphic, a disturbance independent of any
physical reference. Speed lines in cartooning,
lines of force in certain pictures, those of the

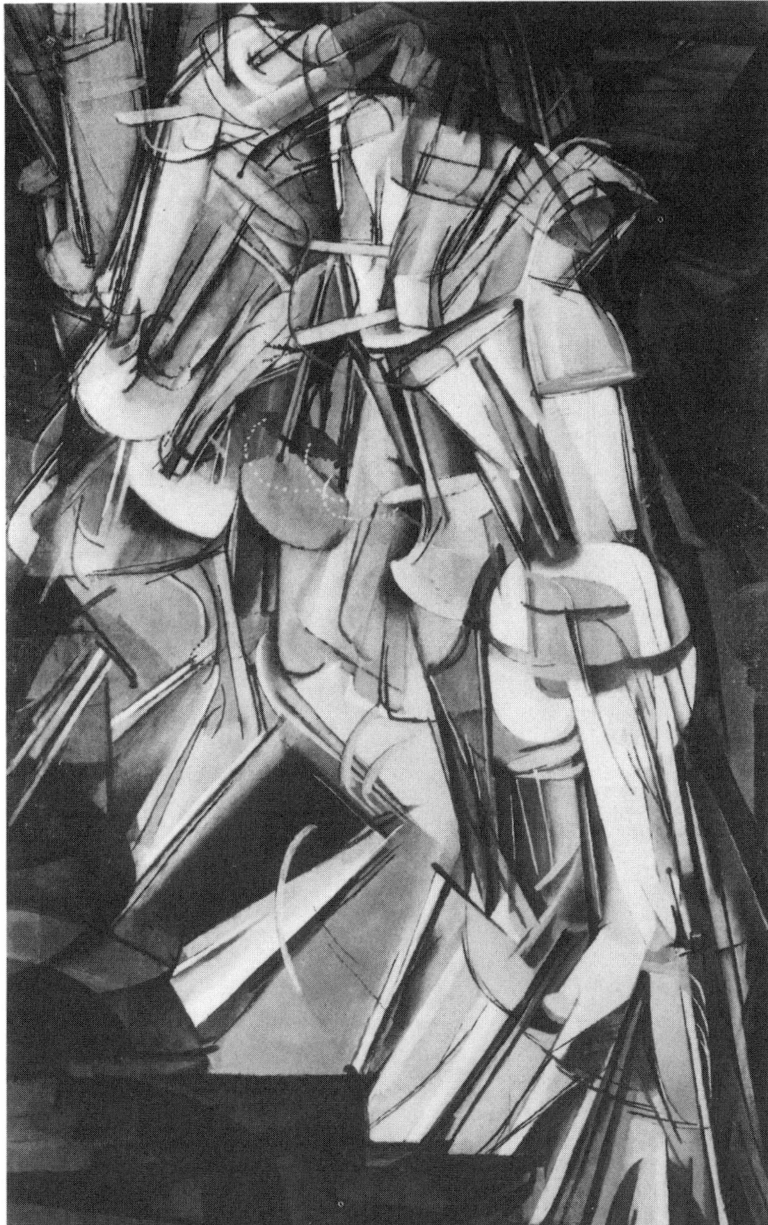



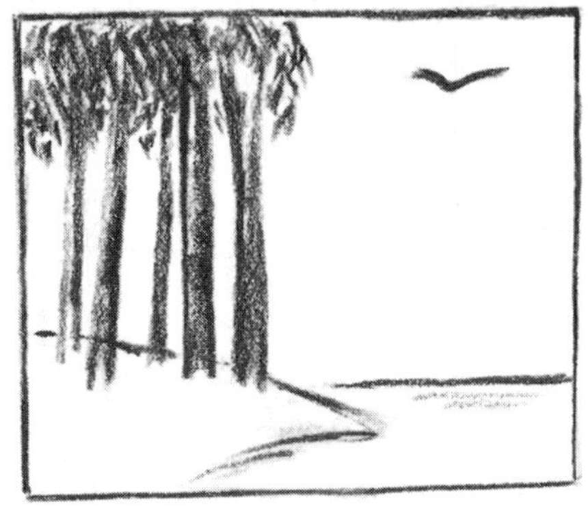

107-2

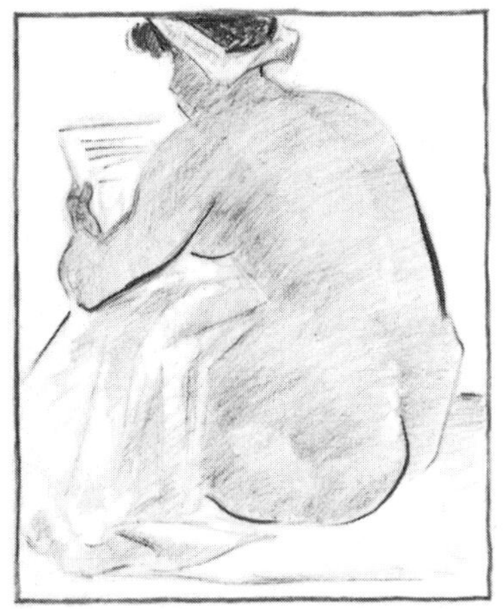

107-3

Marcel Duchamp (French, 1887-1968)
NUDE DESCENDING A STAIRCASE, No. 2
1912; 58″ x 35″; oil on canvas
Philadelphia Museum of Art
The Louise and Walter Arensberg Collection

Futurists especially, after-images of moving forms, as we see in Duchamp's *Nude Descending a Staircase,* are examples of the use of line independent of volumes or shapes. At times such lines become linear accents.

One of the most effective ways to use lines or points as accents is in activating a large area. Such accents introduced as cores become concentrations of energy or attention, as we saw in Chapter 5. A disturbance in an area, such as a point or a line, changes a certain amount of this flat area into space. The core thus becomes an accent and gives brilliance to the space (*107-2*).

At times a series of lines is introduced to give emphasis or contrast to a tonal arrangement of either shapes or volumes. Since in many cases no attempt is made to relate the line to the tone, such drawings run the risk of becoming spotty. Often such constructions give the impression of two types of drawing, one superimposed upon the other, a line drawing over a tonal drawing (*107-3*). Although such a use of line may accent the drawing, care must be taken that the line constitutes a pattern, an entity in itself. If the lines are used as indiscriminate accents they immediately become noticeable and will appear as floating elements in the picture.

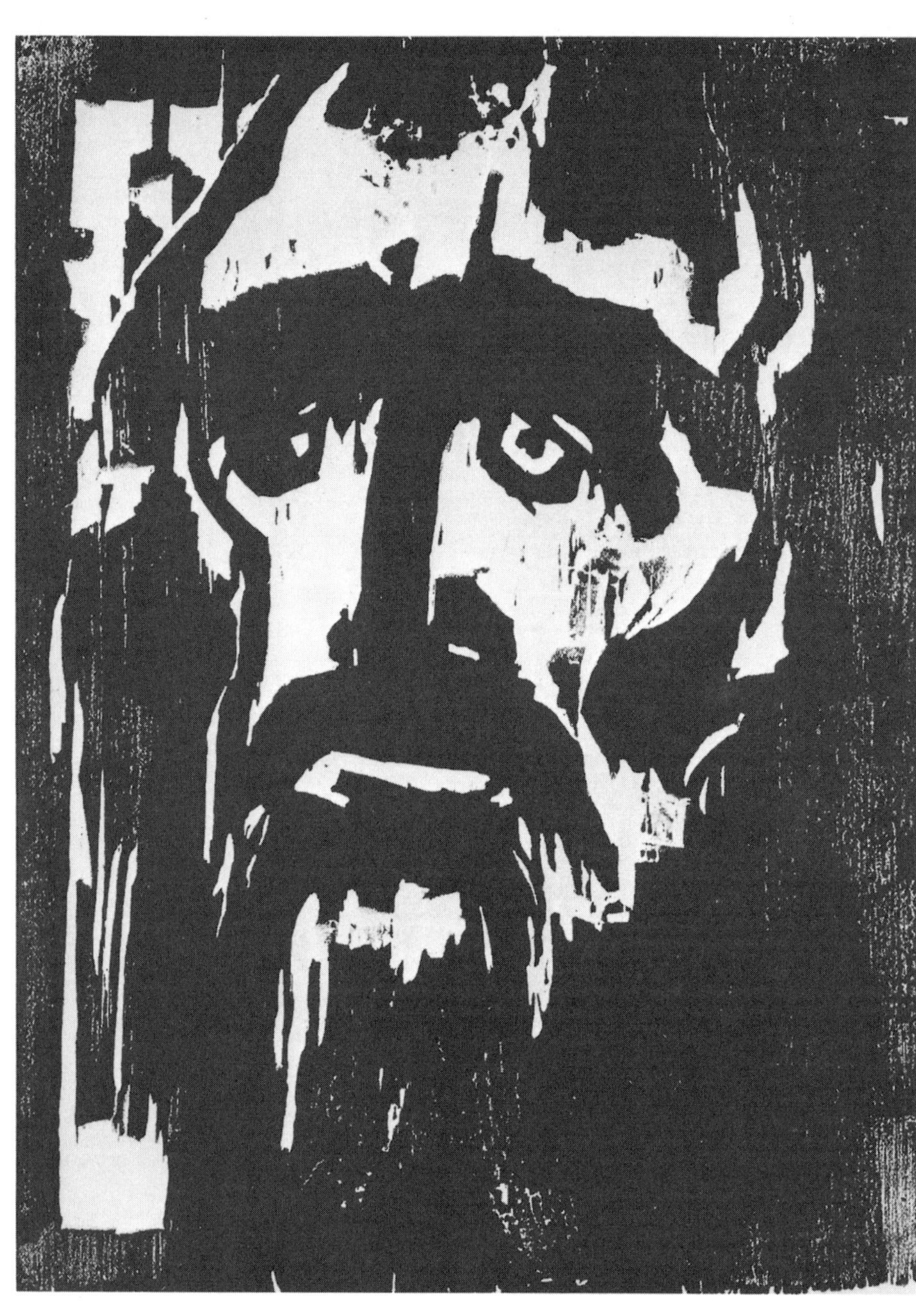

Emil Nolde (German, 1867-1956)
THE PROPHET, 1912
12¾″ x 8⅞″; woodcut
National Gallery of Art, Wash., D.C.
Rosenwald Collection

 **The Shape Accent**

Unlike the general accent which is never
seen as a shape, the shape accent must be
experienced as a shape, usually as a dramatic
shape. Since it is an accent it must be used
sparingly. The shape accent is generally
employed in three categories: in a black and
white picture, in a tonal picture based upon a
generous use of darks and black, and in a
picture dominated by white and very light grays.

In making a picture executed entirely with
black and white using no grays, we are faced
with a special problem. Such a picture as
Nolde's *The Prophet* is made entirely of
maximum contrasts. Everywhere in the picture
black is thrown against white. Naturally such
contrasts do not all seem of equal interest,
yet each truly is an accent. To make any one
of these accents dominant we must in some
way dramatize certain parts of our picture
and subordinate many others.

To do so we usually reinforce the accent by
bringing to it the added interest inherent in
a shape. By drawing attention to a specific
area of our picture, by attracting our eye with
an unusual, interesting, or dramatic shape,
we momentarily cease to be aware of
other black-white contrasts of lesser shape
importance. The shape contrast will seem
brighter; the less interesting contrasts duller.
The shape now serves as an accent dominating
its surroundings.

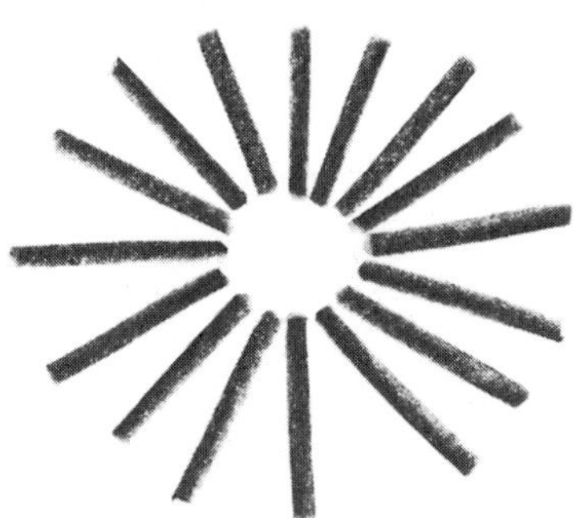

109-1A

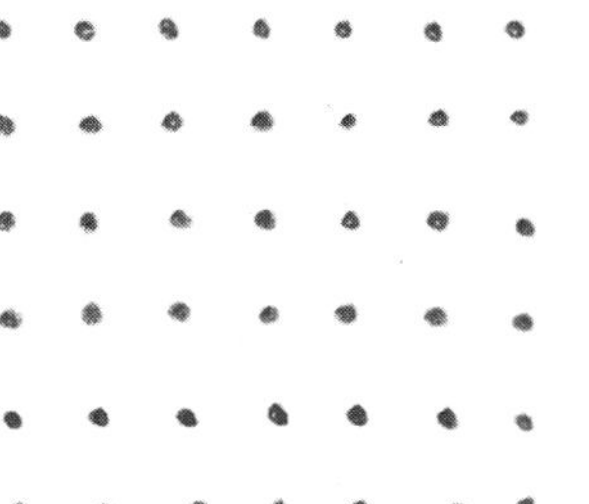

109-1B

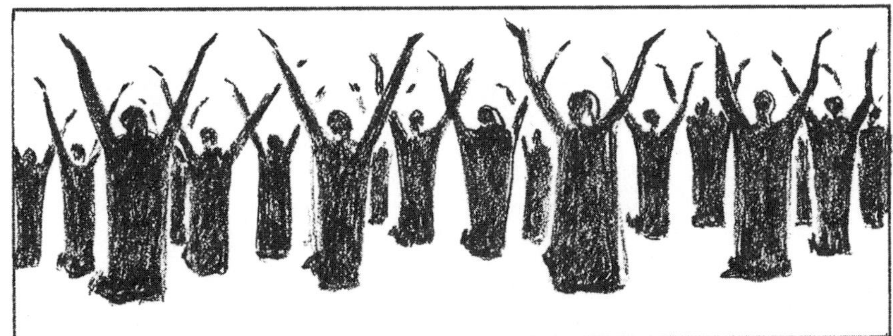

109-2

A shape may be built up from a number of black lines on a white ground (*109-1A*), or the opposite, or from a number of points (*109-1B*). In either case, though constructed upon a number of black-white contrasts, the impact of the total configuration may act as a shape accent.

Usually, however, in most black-white drawings, the shape accent is predominantly black or predominantly white, depending upon the type of contrast demanded. Its interest is determined by its shape activity, its size, its movement. Its meaning or gesture is of great importance, especially in representational pictures.

The dramatic use of two or three shape accents, either black or white, is usually sufficient in most black and white pictures. Since such accents must supersede any number of secondary black and white accents, they must be used sparingly to be effective. This is not to say that all black and white pictures employ only a few shape accents. Certain statements call for just such multiple use of accents. But as accents are added, individual accents suffer as a device to create local brilliance. Their sum total, however, may create a pattern or a shape, as in the sun-burst (*109-1A*) or in the accompanying rough which has some brilliance (*109-2*).

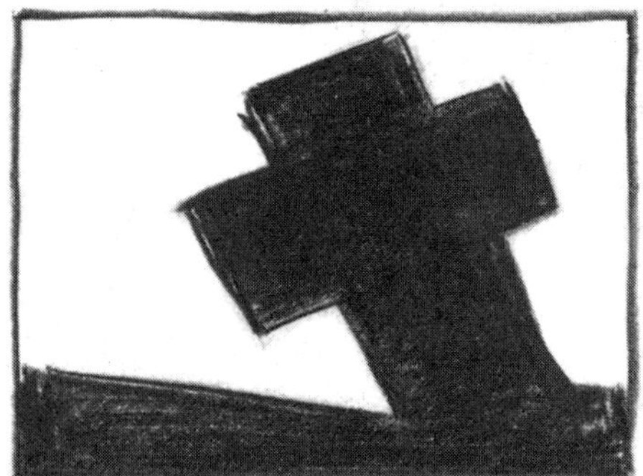

110-1A

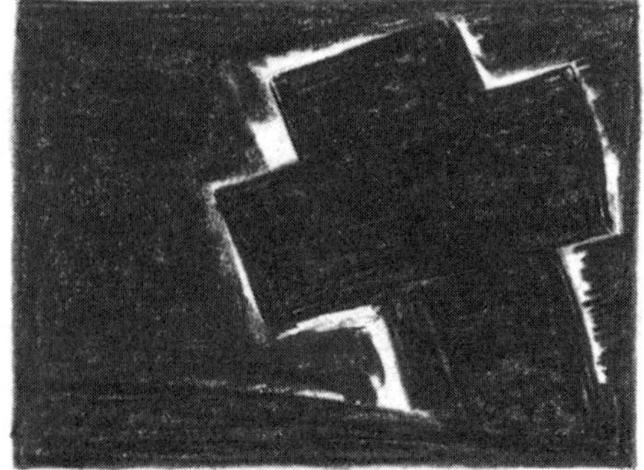

110-1B

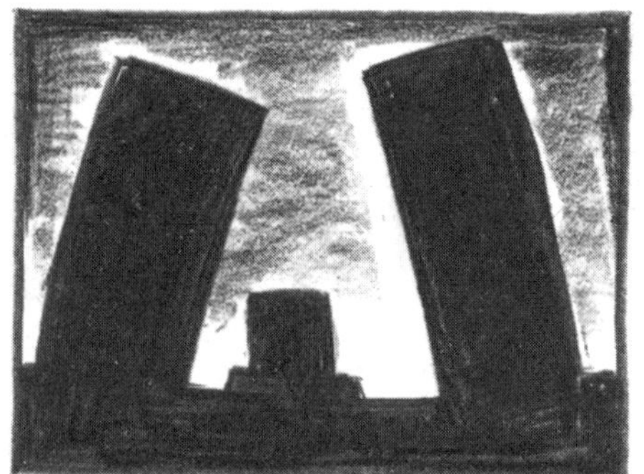

110-1C

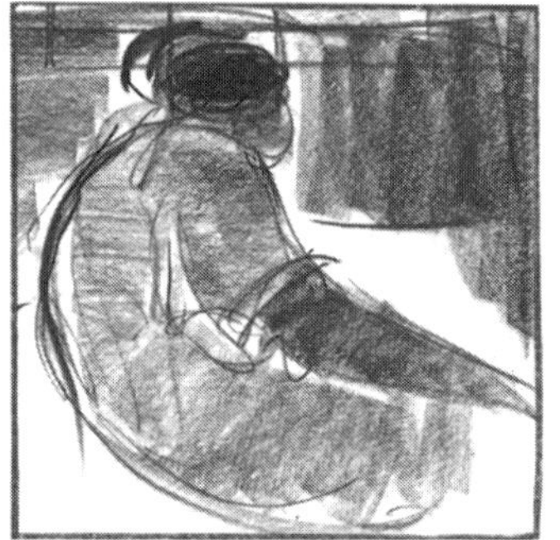

110-2

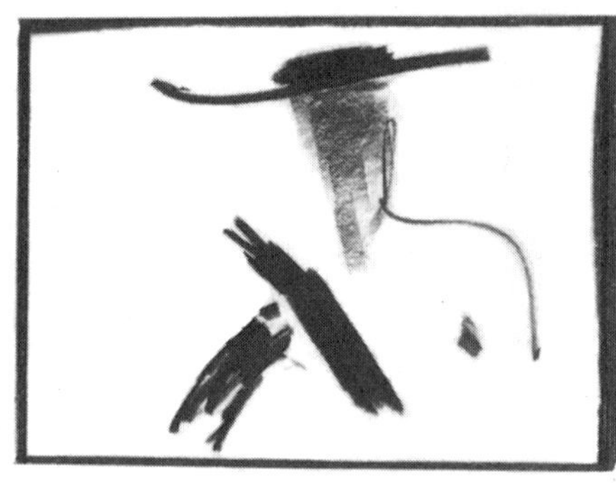

110-3



Too many accents tend to cancel each other both as to shape impact and brilliance. So in black and white pictures made up of maximum contrasts we should not expect to create the luminosity or brilliance possible in a picture constructed upon black, white, and grays.

By reducing the number of secondary black-white contrasts, the impact of the shape accent is enhanced (*110-1A*). This usually leads to a dramatic intensification of the shape, especially if the amount of white is kept to a minimum (*110-1B*).

In effect, such a structure is a bridge between the pure black-white picture and the dark picture in which blacks and dark grays usually predominate. The introduction of grays makes the modification of secondary black-white accents relatively simple. White accents are more easily controlled (*110-1C*). Quite often in black and white pictures, grays are simulated by the introduction of textures, hatch, points, etc. Such modifications are again bridges between the black-white picture and the tonal picture.

By introducing dark grays we can adjust a shape by emphasizing only part of it without losing its identity. By so doing, dramatic aspects of a shape may be exploited while other parts of it may be employed to satisfy other requirements of the picture. A profile may have dramatic shape impact and serve as a shape accent, while the hair structure may be related to the background or to overlays to contribute to the surface pattern of the whole picture (*110-2*). Almost always in such a picture the general accent is used to relieve the blacks and grays.

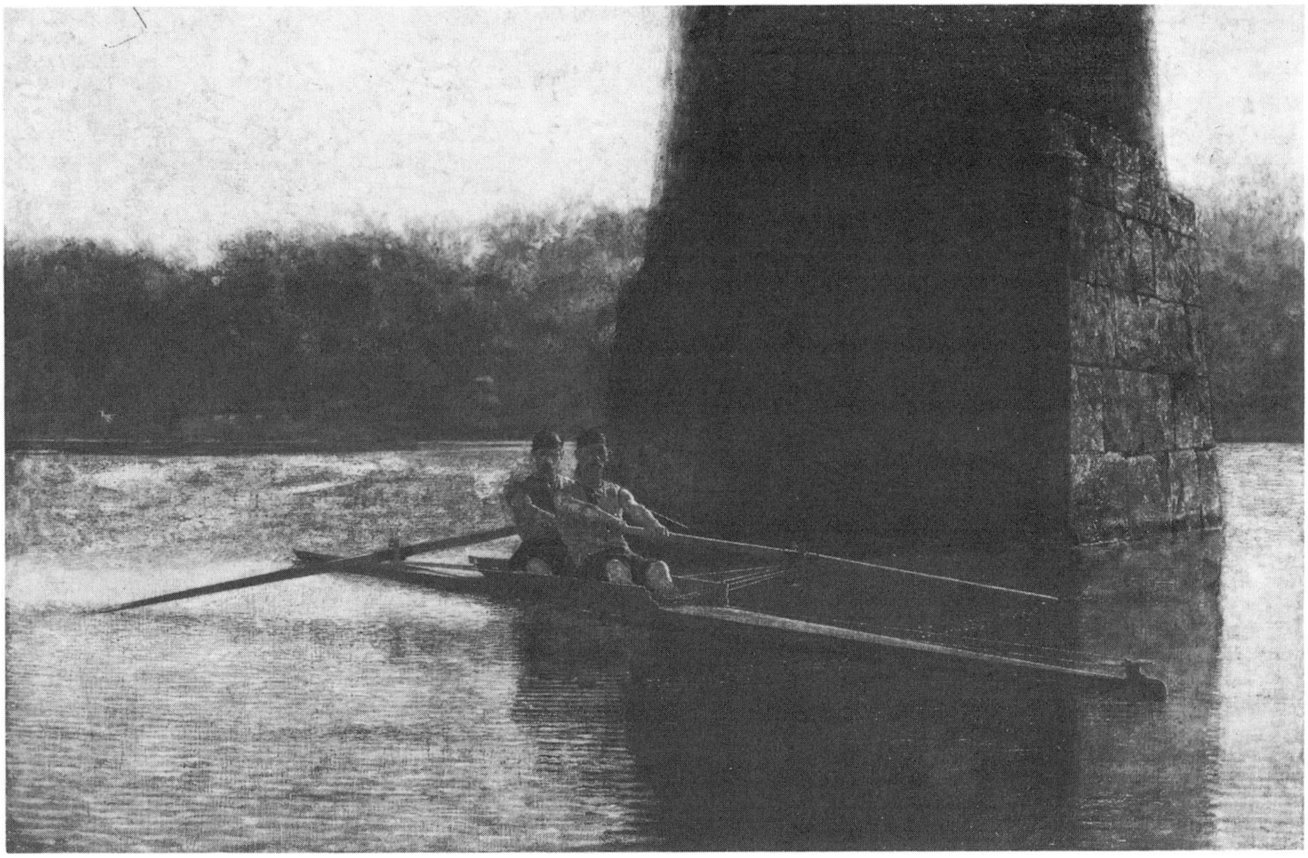

Thomas Eakins (American, 1884-1916)
THE PAIRED-OARED SHELL (THE OARSMEN), 1872
24″ x 36½″; oil on canvas
Collection of the Philadelphia Museum of Art
(Photograph: A. J. Wyatt)

In a picture constructed primarily upon whites and light grays, the dark shape accent may be used with great effectiveness (*110-3*). The use of light grays brightens the whites, and thus we achieve greater contrast with the shape accents.

A shape accent usually dominates the whole picture. Because it is so noticeable, its position in the picture field is critical to the structure of the entire picture. A general accent, on the other hand, although contributing to the brightness of the picture, may fall in rather unimportant areas of the picture. Not so the shape accent. It must be skillfully related to the surface pattern and the space implied in the picture, as Eakins uses the pier shape here.

Since the shape accent contributes so strongly to the pattern of the picture surface, we must account for the *relative* sizes of such accents. Should they all be the same size? Should one be large and the others small and of the same size? Quite often they are proportionally related in some kind of ratio ranging from large to small.

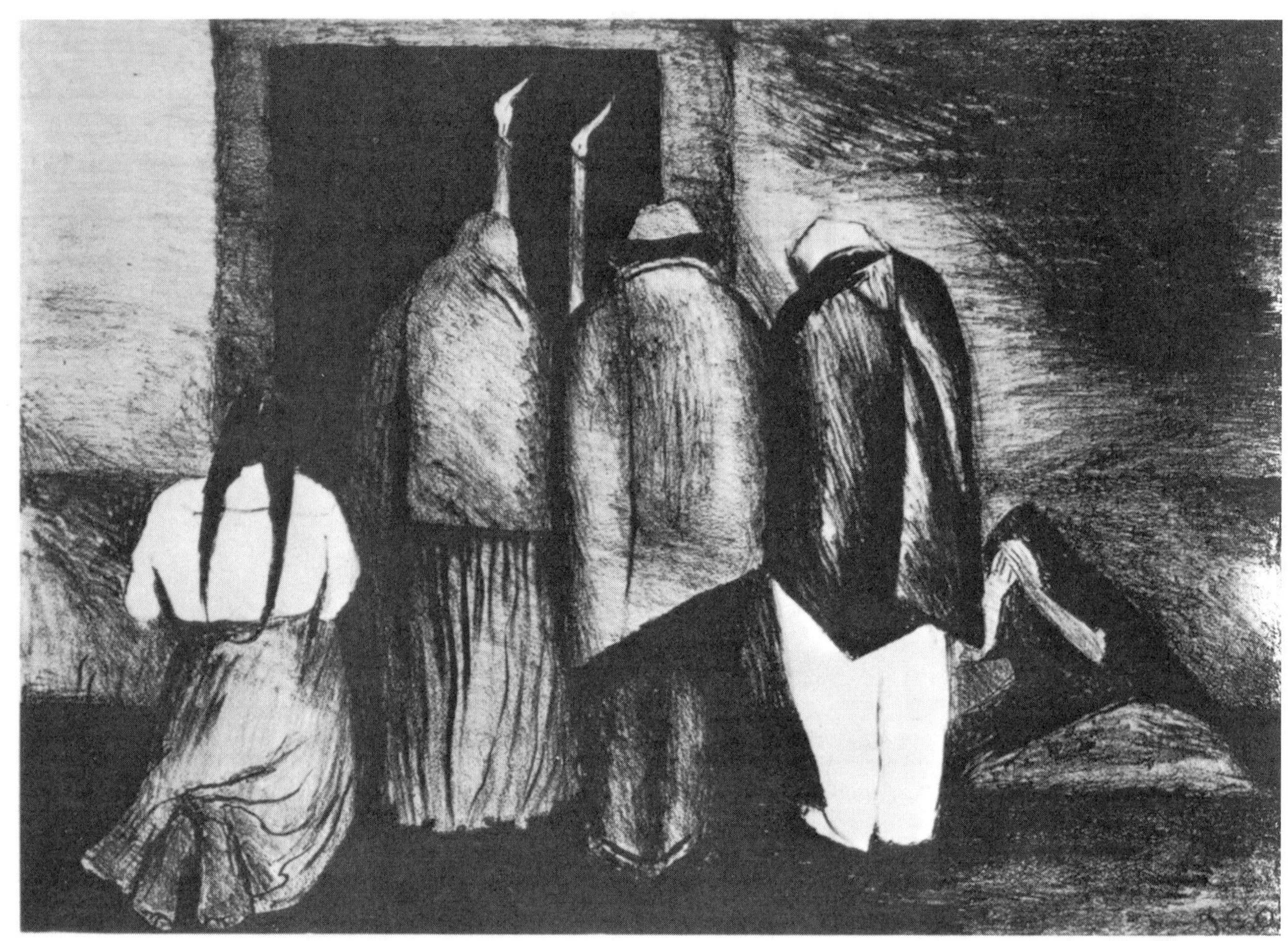

José Clemente Orozco (Mexican, 1883-1949)
REQUIEM, 1928; 11⅞″ x 15⅞″; lithograph
Collection of the Philadelphia Museum of Art

## 112    The Bright Tonal Picture

It is conceivable that we may be called upon to construct a somber or gray picture. The subject may even be funereal. Yet such a picture may be graphically exciting, as Orozco's *Requiem*. Although somber it is not dull. A picture usually becomes dull not because of subject matter but through misuse of our graphic elements.

In the same sense, a picture involving many maximum contrasts of black and white shapes may be exciting and dramatic yet not seem luminous. We may purposely sacrifice brightness for dramatic impact. A subject may suggest a certain starkness, a prize fight, a murder scene, a non-representational arrangement of shapes that manifest great forces being exerted. Though exciting, such pictures may have a certain graphic dullness. On the other hand, a picture constructed with few or no large maximum contrasts may be luminous or bright and give us a feeling of greater excitement than if large areas of black and white had been employed.

113-A

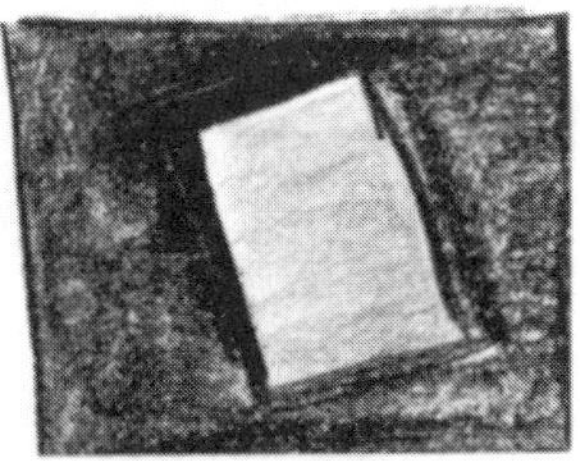

113-B

113-C

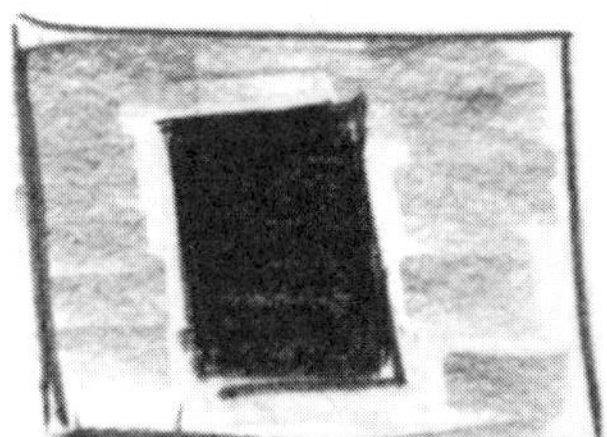

113-D

To demonstrate this phenomenon let us surround a pure white shape with a solid black area (*113-A*). We now have maximum physical contrast. Yet every part of the white shape, each edge, each corner is impacting against a large area of black. We now have a number of maximum contrasts. Yet through repetition we begin to lose the impact of any one. Our senses become dulled. We soon run the risk of seeing the arrangement of shapes merely as two pigments or values rather than responding to their actual impact upon each other.

If now we reduce the black to dark grays and introduce into our white shape a light gray just darker than white, with the addition of a second supporting gray a bit darker, we still have in reserve the black black and the white white of our paper (*113-B*). Next, by forcing a small amount of white against our darkest value, reinforced by the addition of some black black, we create a maximum contrast. But this contrast is concentrated in one small area of our picture. Secondary accents, either black or white, are used to support lesser contrasts.

We no longer are distracted by a great number of maximum contrasts which negate each other. We respond to this limited maximum contrast as a maximum shock. Our dark gray area will still seem black; our white area, which is no longer truly white, will still seem white. The resulting picture will seem luminous or bright. Of course, brightness can be achieved by a reversal of the order of the shapes (*113-C, -D*).

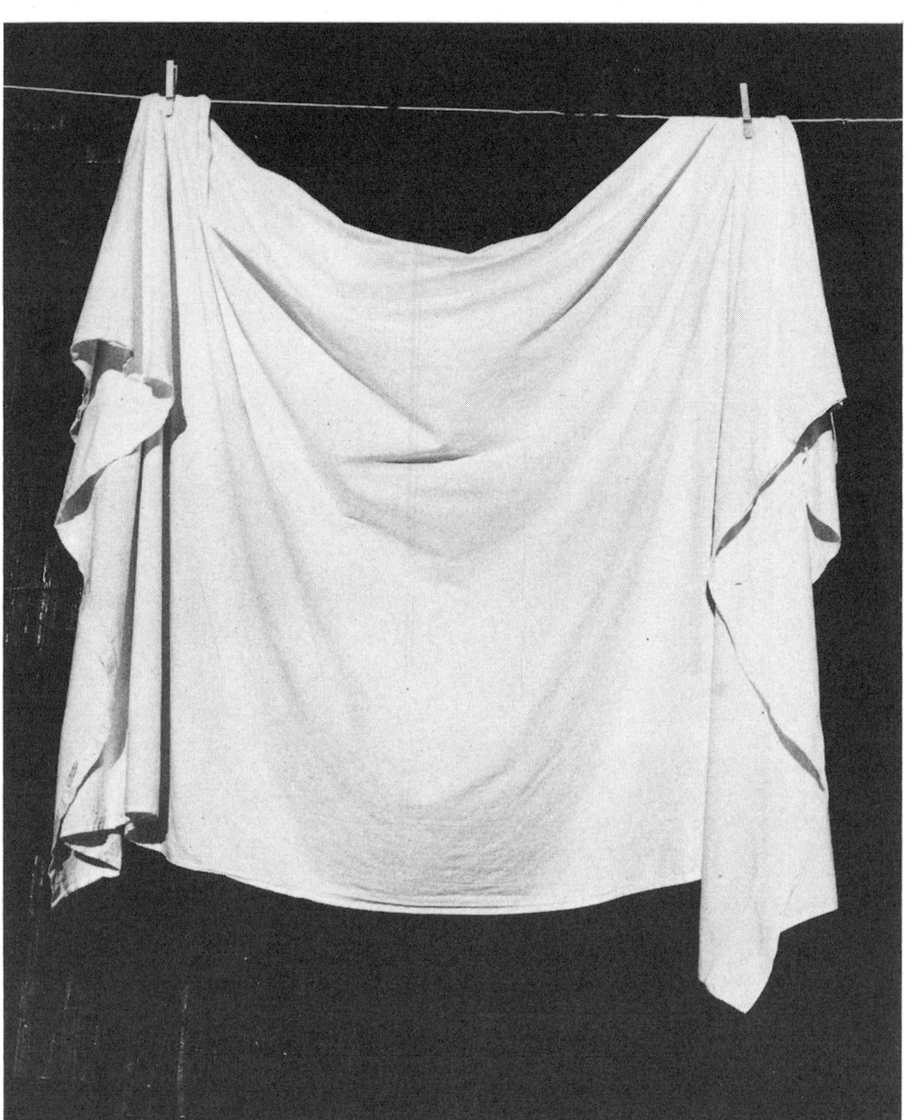

SHEET ON CLOTHESLINE
(Photograph: Kenneth Graham)

To demonstrate how brilliance may be generated in a picture, let us draw a piece of white drapery, a white sheet, for instance, hanging from a clothesline. In nature it is flooded with light. Playing over it is a changing pattern of shades and shadows, for there are folds involved which at times will be quite dark, as in the photograph.

To attack this problem graphically, first let us eliminate all these local internal disturbances in order to arrive at a simple white shape that will be satisfactory in relation to our picture requirements. This we can indicate in a simple rough (*115-A*).

A scale of values can now be made against which the finished picture can be keyed. Let us use a maximum of six values, two of which will be light grays and one of these just darker than white. Our white white is reserved for accenting purposes, as is our black black. Now by reducing the white shape to the lightest gray, but allowing for the introduction of the white accent, we still feel the impact of the white shape. The second light gray can be introduced to give added information while still preserving the character of the white shape.

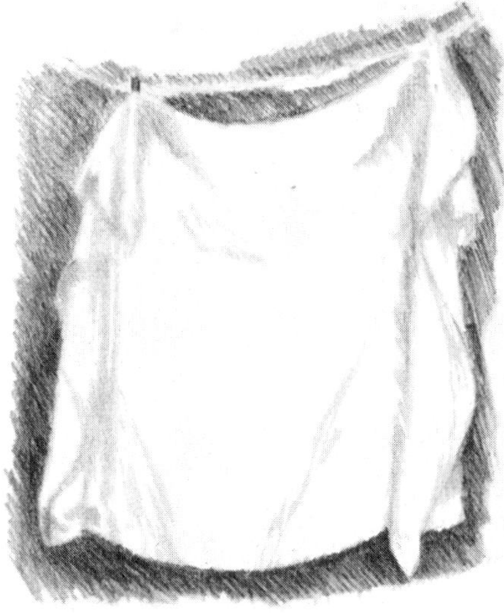

115-A

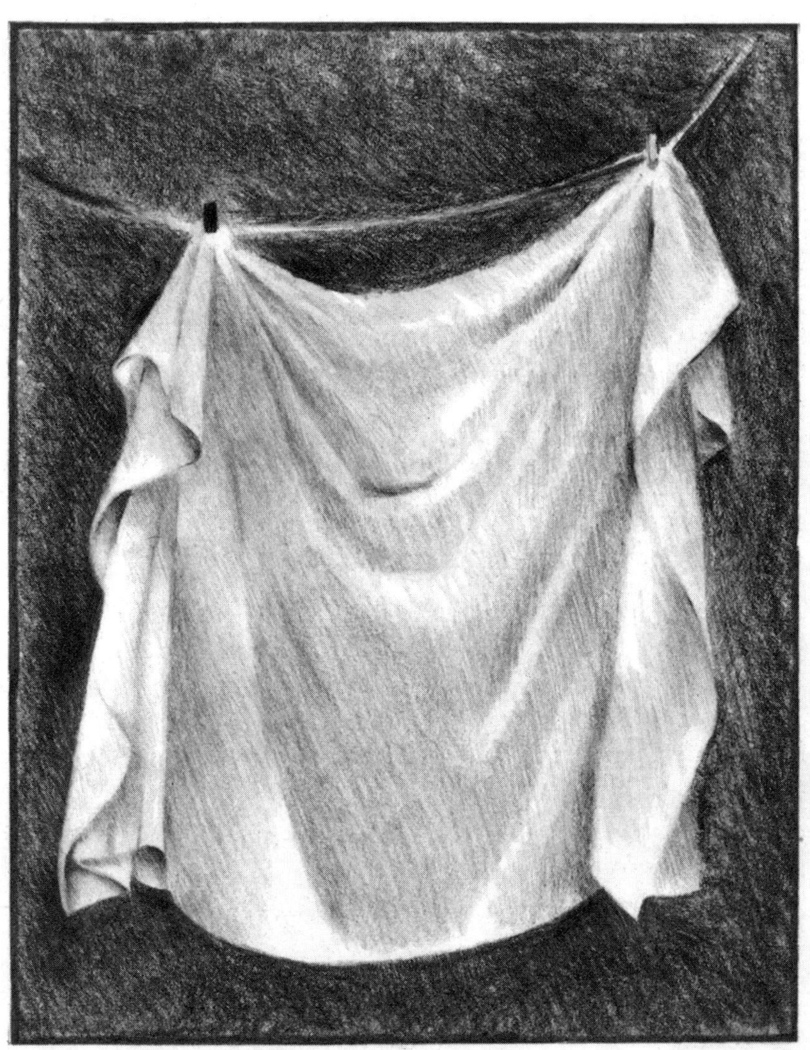

115-B

When dark accents are brought into play against the off-white shape and the white accents, the picture should begin to seem bright. Further accenting of the remainder of the picture will help preserve the brightness throughout.

**The Division of Work Time**
Inadvertent loss of value control usually may be traced to three factors: lack of planning, failure to exploit the accent, and failure to carry the picture to completion. Much of the trouble can be traced to failure to accept the time factor involved in planning and accenting a picture (*115-B*).

Following a progress chart helps correct this weakness. The chart, of course, will vary with the individual and also with the nature of each picture. A division of time which has proved valuable to many is to allow one third of the total time to planning; one third to execution; one third to accenting. Since each accent involves a judgment in relation to the almost finished picture, it must be considered with great care. This takes time. It is the final step in finishing a picture.

As we shall see in the following chapter, value and accents combine in a picture to produce the factor known as the matrix. The matrix has great bearing on the failure or success of the accent.

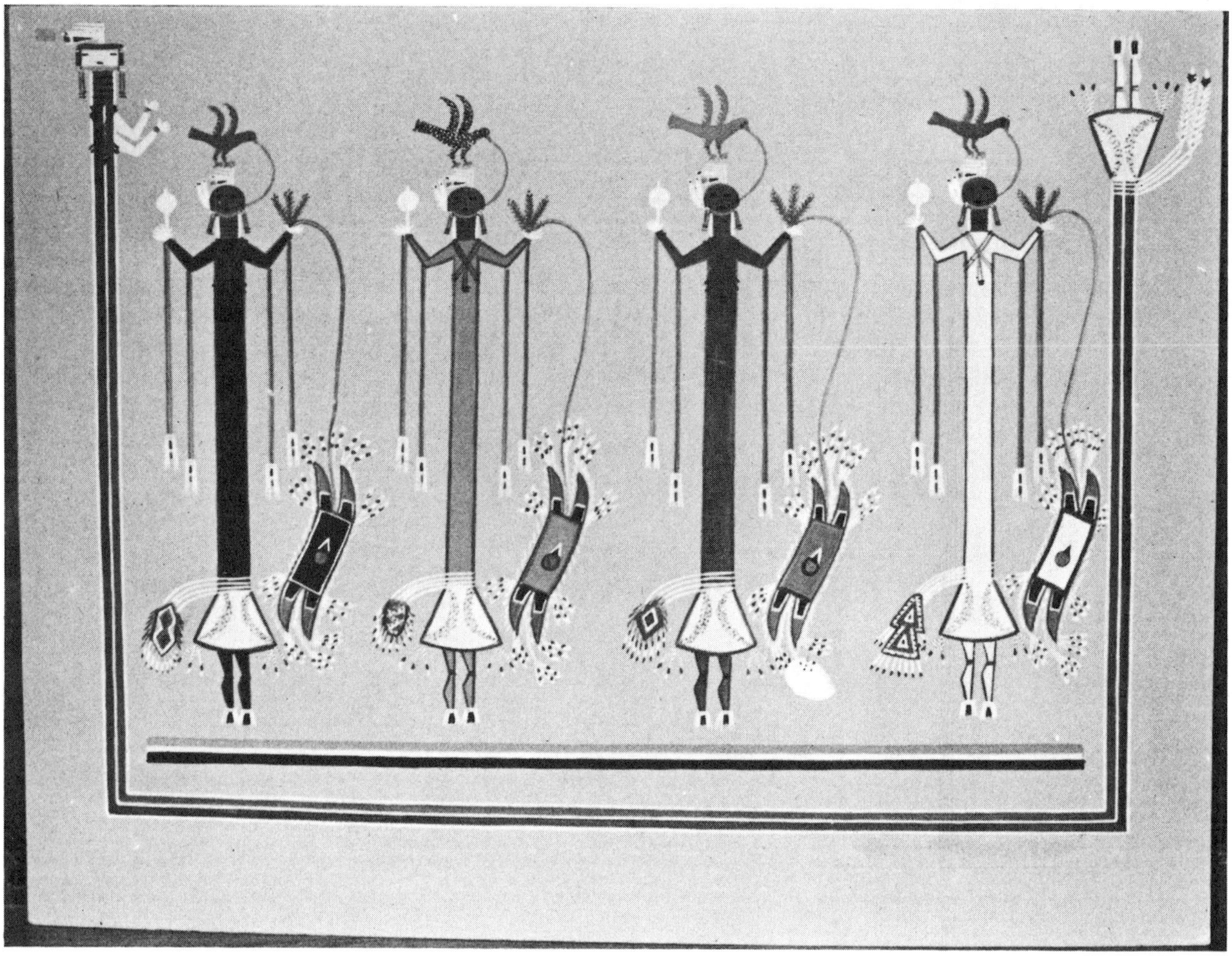

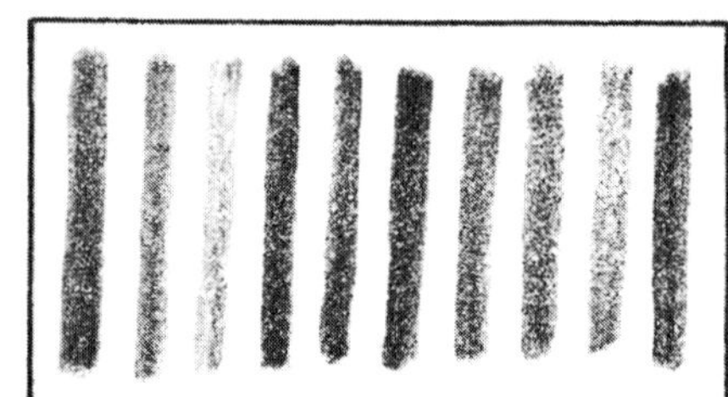

Hosteen Klah (Navaho,    ?-1937)
DANCERS WITH RAINBOW GIRL
from Big God Way chant; 1933
copy of drypainting by Mrs. Franc J.
Newcomb; size of sand original not known
copy, 22″ x 28″; colored sand and pollen
Museum of Navaho Ceremonial Art
Santa Fe, New Mexico
(Photograph: Diane Oppenheimer)

116-2



# 11 The Matrix

## Determining the Pattern

As we have noted, a picture is an ordered disturbance of the picture surface which may be achieved by utilizing various elements ranging from a beam of light projected upon a surface, as in motion pictures, to a sprinkling of sand upon the ground, as practiced by certain Southwest Indians. Elements such as paper, photographs, or leaves may be made to adhere to the picture surface, or more conventional media—paint, chalk, carbon, etc. —may be used. Whatever the nature of the disturbance, however we apply it to the surface, we create a pattern which must be controlled to achieve a successful picture. This pattern will have impact, weak or strong, upon our viewer.

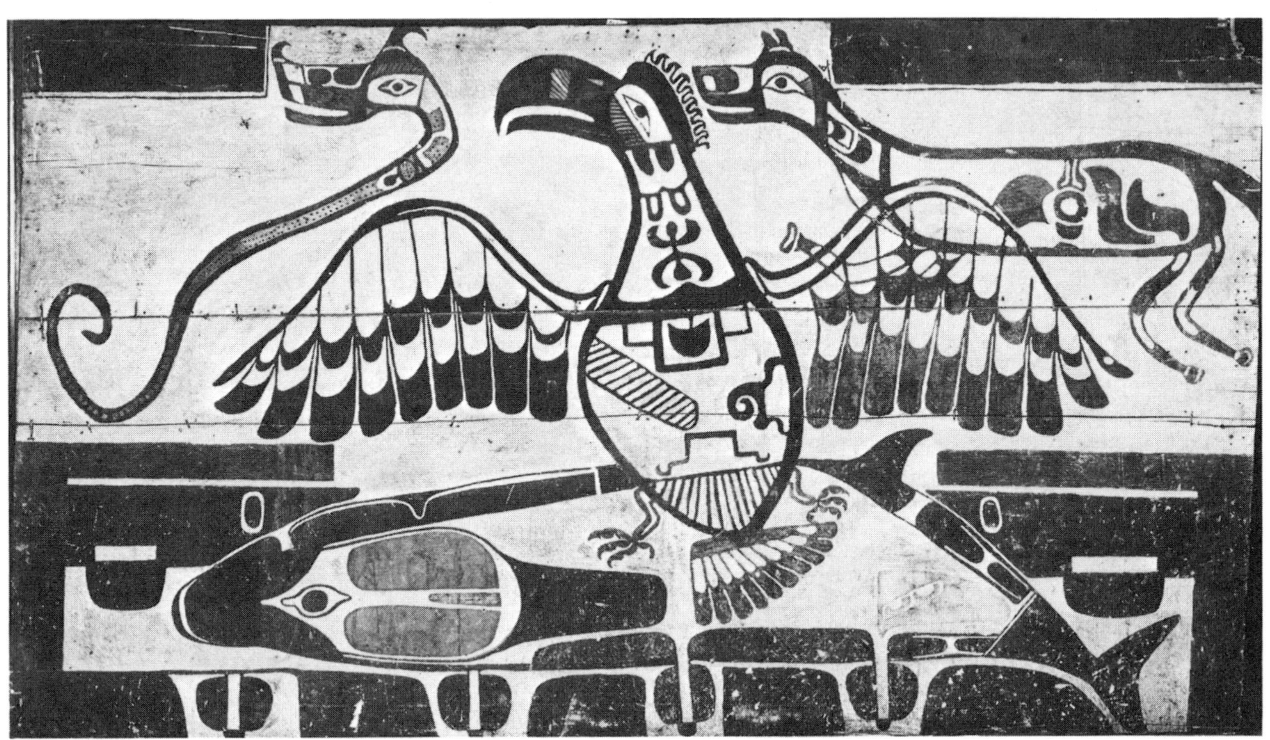

Nootka Indian (no date) Vancouver Island
THUNDERBIRD AND KILLER WHALE
78″ x 114½″; painting on wood
Courtesy of the American Museum of
Natural History, New York, N. Y.

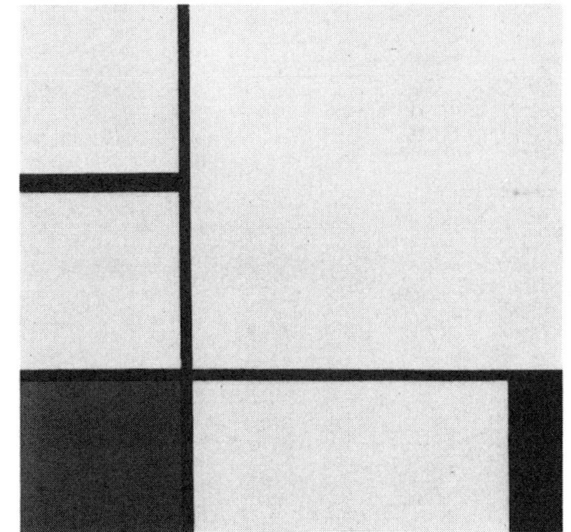

Piet Mondrian (Dutch, 1872-1944)
COMPOSITION, 1929; 19⅞″ x 19¾″
oil on canvas
Yale University Art Gallery
Gift of the Collection Société Anonyme

Although there are various types of patterns suited to differing problems, the type chosen must always be conditioned by the use to be made of the picture. Is it to be seen on a printed page? A huge wall? In a gallery or in a home? Is it to be projected upon a motion picture screen?

These conditions under which we see the picture in turn introduce another factor, the reading time of the picture. If the picture is projected upon a motion picture screen at the constant rate of twenty-four exposures a second, reading time may be as short as one-twelfth of a second. On the other hand, a huge mural may take hours to examine. The pattern of a picture is always modified by this reading time.

Like so many terms used by the artist, this word "pattern" has several meanings:

It may refer to a formal arrangement of elements, polka-dots or stripes, for instance (*116-2*).

It may refer to units of several figurative or geometric arrangements repeated in various ways to create in their entirety a picture constructed of one or more repeated shapes, as in this Northwest Indian design.

It may refer to geometric shapes which often are varied as to size, shape, or color and so organized as to create not repetition but great graphic variety in the order of their structure, as in Mondrian's *Composition*.

Instead of repetitious or varied use of the same or similar elements, a common use of the term "pattern" implies the ordered arrangement of completely different elements which constitute the whole picture surface. Such an order often is referred to as a "free pattern."

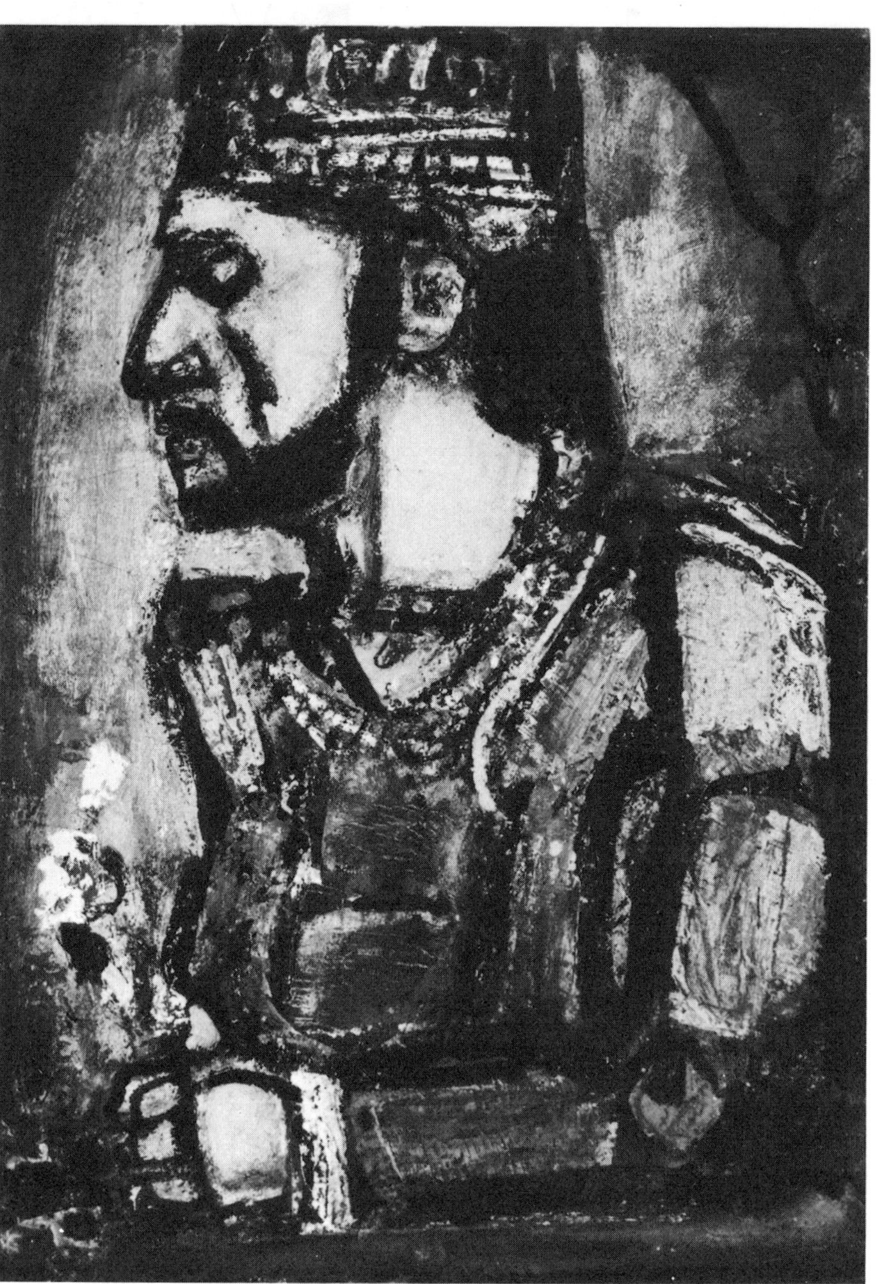

Georges Rouault (French, 1871-1958)
THE OLD KING, 1916-1938
30¼″ x 21¼″; oil on canvas
Museum of Art, Carnegie Institute
Pittsburgh, Pennsylvania
Patrons Art Fund

An overwhelming number of pictures throughout art history fall into the category of free pattern, like *The Old King,* by Rouault. Obviously no two free patterns are alike.

## The Sparse Surface Pattern

Common sense should guide us in determining the complexity of a pattern. If it is too complex, it may create confusion instead of interest. If the pattern is too simple, it may be easily read but very dull.

We may find that a picture becomes dreary because of an overwhelming dominance of large areas. As long as a large area is truly spacious, there may be justification for its existence. A feeling of vastness or true emptiness may depend upon the use of large areas which have been activated in some way to feel spacious. Many fine Oriental paintings are premised on the use of such large areas.

But too often a large area merely looks flat, spaceless. Instead of contributing to a volume or a shape in space, or to true space, the area appears simply as the flat paper, an unfinished portion of the picture surface. The area becomes insistent, pushing us away from the picture. The picture seems remote, and we experience a thinness or sparseness in the surface pattern.

At times an area may be partly spacious and partly flat. In *119-1A*, we feel that the large area around and above the head is spacious only in part. As the area around the head is made larger it becomes flatter (*119-1B*), as it is reduced it becomes more spacious (*119-1C*). The first two patterns seem sparse; the third, more involved.

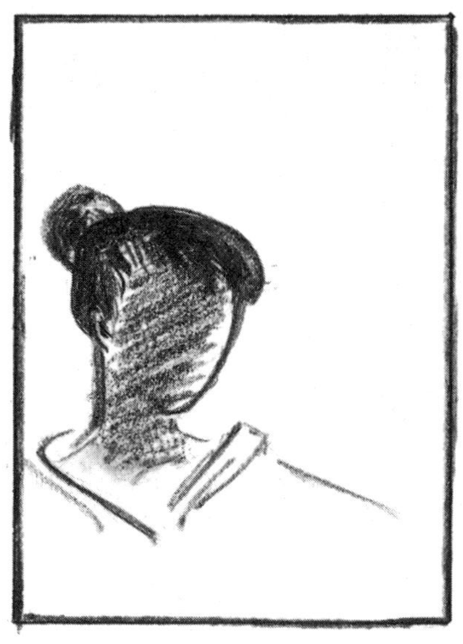

119-1A

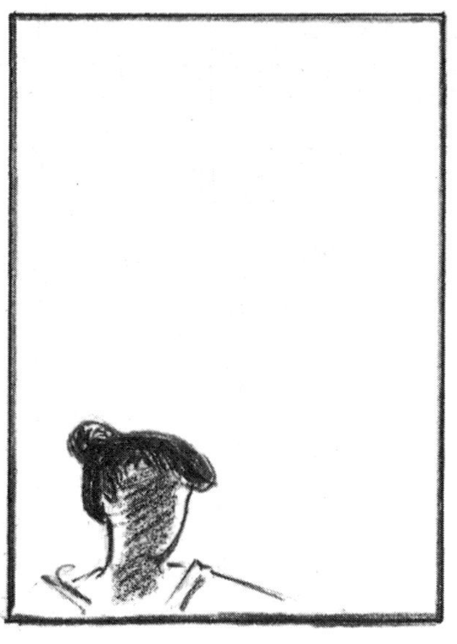

119-1B

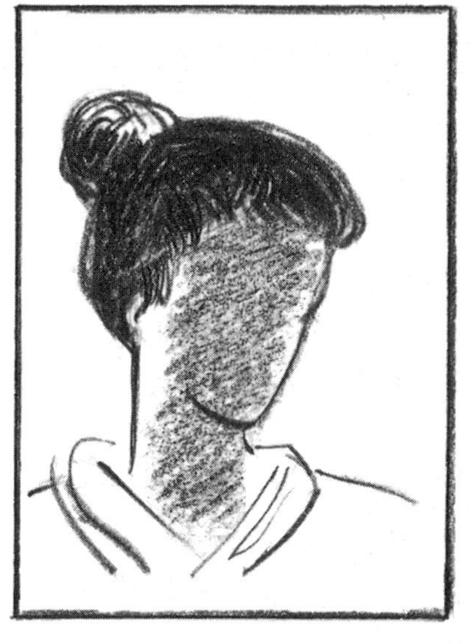

119-1C

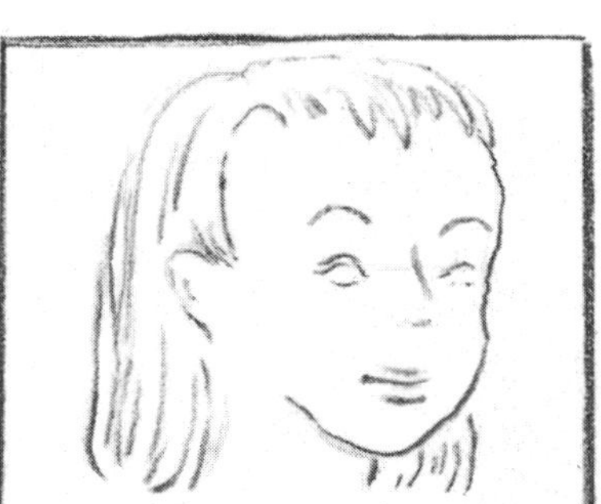

119-2A

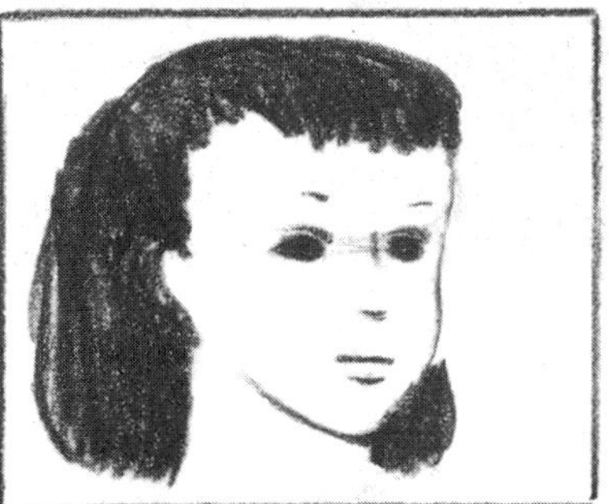

119-2B

## The Confusing Surface Pattern

If we employ an indiscriminate distribution of whites, grays, and darks, the pattern may become spotty and confused. The resulting picture will be uninteresting, dull, or monotonous. In particular we may lose strong impact by focusing the viewer's attention on scattered points of interest. Such random distribution of elements often forces the viewer to concentrate on individual parts, and usually creates an overemphasis on subject matter in relation to picture structure.

In any drawing there is a mysterious relationship between the activity of the lines used to delineate a form and the areas generated by these lines, which become volumes or shapes. Too much line activity gives us an overly busy and noticeable linear pattern (*119-2A*). Too much emphasis upon the enclosed areas usually results in a loss of space and an ensuing loss of scale (*119-2B*), which we will discuss in Chapter 29.

Strangely enough, a factor which is often experienced but seldom is consciously seen can determine the type of pattern to be used. This factor is the accent which contributes so greatly to the luminosity of the picture, as we noted in Chapter 10. The type of accent we stress has a great bearing upon the pattern of the whole picture.

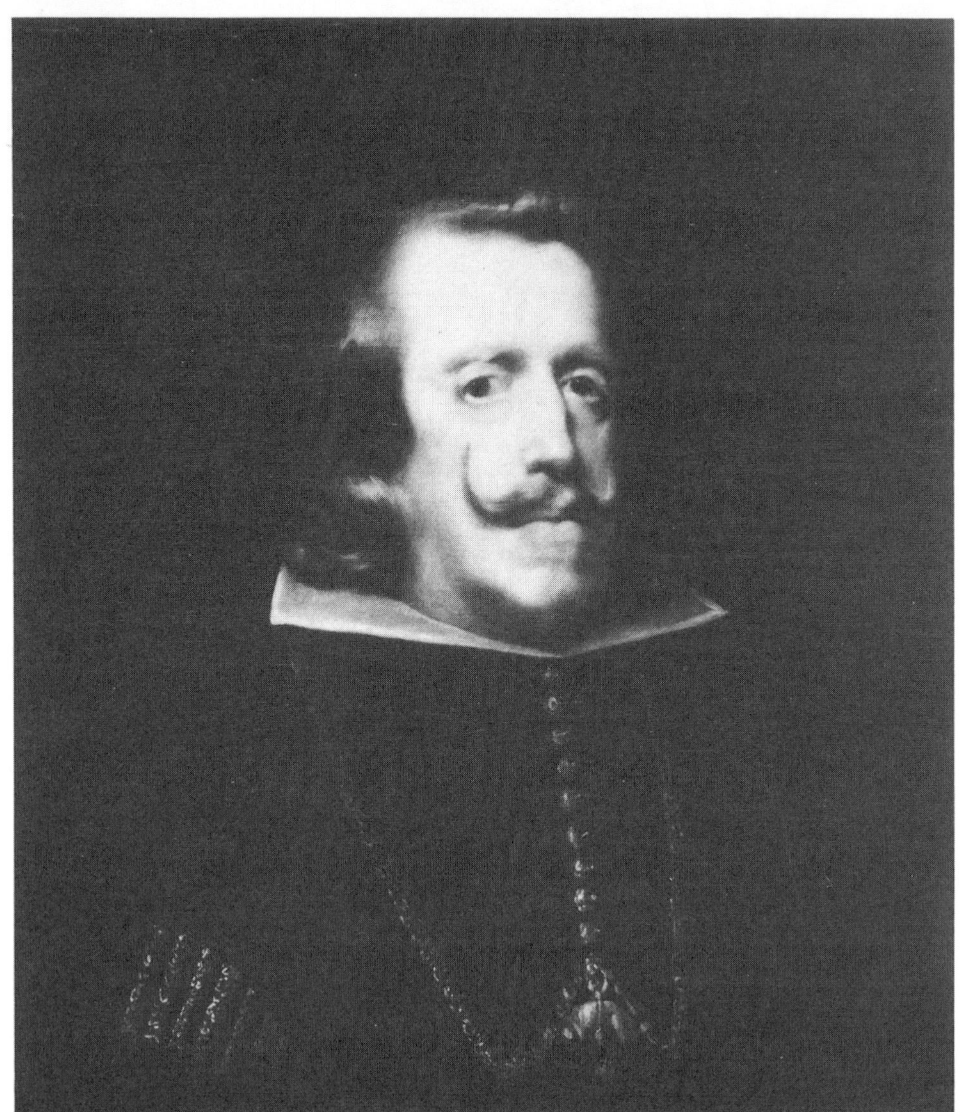

Velázquez (Spanish, 1599-1660)
PHILIP IV, KING OF SPAIN, ca. 1656
23⅞" x 20"; oil on canvas
Cincinnati Art Museum
Bequest of Mary M. Emery



## The Matrix

The matrix is one factor in a pattern that holds the picture together. We may compare the graphic matrix to a stone holding a fossil or to a conglomerate structure of rock which holds together pebbles or gravel. The darks or the lights of a picture constitute the graphic conglomerate which cements the picture surface into an integrated whole. The matrix may be either predominantly dark or predominantly light. If dark, the matrix might be compared to a dark sea surrounding a cluster of bright islands; if light, to a bowl of rice pudding in which raisins are suspended.

The matrix usually is a foil to the encompassed significant elements. As a foil its presence is experienced rather than consciously seen. Though unseen, its structure is of vital importance in most pictures.

## The Dark Matrix Picture

The dark matrix picture is constructed as a dark graphic conglomerate holding together areas of light. There is a preponderance of dark in the picture structure, and light areas are limited in number. Since the lights are like islands surrounded by dark, there is a continuity of dark throughout the picture.

If we place the tip of a pencil anywhere on a large dark area and move the tip, without lifting it, from dark to dark, we often are able to move throughout the entire picture on darks. A few small darks may escape the path of our pencil, those isolated in light areas. Such isolated darks, an eye for instance, can frequently be stabilized by a strong visual relation to other darks in the picture. In his portrait of Philip IV, Velázquez has surrounded the right eye with light but has related it

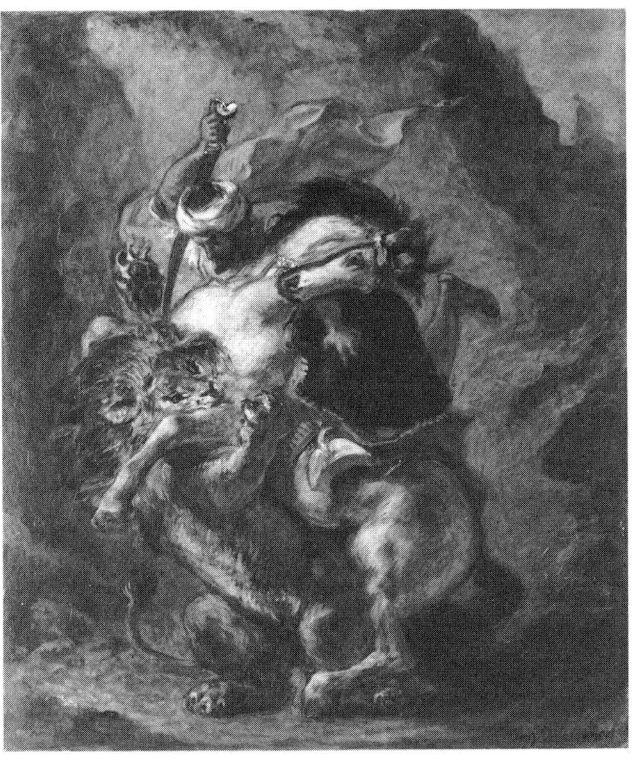

Eugène Delacroix (French, 1798-1863)
ARAB RIDER ATTACKED BY LION, 1849
18″ x 14¾″; oil on canvas
Courtesy of The Art Institute of Chicago
Potter Palmer Collection

Hanabusa Itcho (Japanese, 1652-1724)
BULL AND RIDER; Edo period
36⅝″ x 11⅛″; ink on paper
mounted as a kakemono (hanging scroll)
Seattle Art Museum
Eugene Fuller Memorial Collection

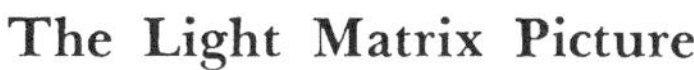

closely to the other eye, which is locked into
the general dark pattern of the picture.

The dark matrix, or binding factor, may be
not only black, but may incorporate dark
grays. This preponderance of dark makes the
lights in the picture seem lighter, and also
makes the use of light accents more effective, as
in Delacroix's picture.

Conversely, the large amount of dark makes
the use of a dark accent less effective. Dark
accents can be used, but they are used
sparingly. Dark shape accents, although sometimes used in a dark matrix picture, usually
are not as dramatic as when they are surrounded
by large light areas, as we noted in Chapter 10.

## The Light Matrix Picture

The light matrix picture is a graphic conglomerate made up of white or light colors
which hold together isolated areas of dark. It
is characterized by being predominantly white,
relieved by a relatively few areas of dark,
as we see in the Japanese painting above.
Just as we are able to move from dark to dark
in a dark matrix picture, so we may move
from white to white, or light colors, in a light
matrix picture. In such a structure we find
that the location of the darks becomes a
critical factor in relation to the whole picture
pattern. The slightest misplacement or overstatement of a dark immediately becomes
apparent.

The large amount of white in the light matrix
picture makes dark accents extremely effective.

122 On the other hand, the use of the white accent becomes limited both as to number and importance.

Possibly one of the greatest hazards inherent in creating the light matrix picture is that of over-delineation. As we add more and more lines in such a structure, we actually add more and more contrasting pigment, or dark. So we inadvertently gray our picture.

This is especially true if we resort to the use of closed shapes. Such a shape, surrounded by line, visually separates from adjacent whites preventing an easy flow from one white area to another. By breaking through the line with white, so that overlapping areas or shapes are brought back into the picture surface, we can assure a continuous pattern of white throughout the picture.

With certain media such as chalks or crayons, it is much easier to lower the values in a dark matrix picture than to lighten a light matrix picture. A gray which seems too light may easily be darkened, but to lighten it may be almost impossible because of the medium.

Naturally, as the darks generated by either line or area are increased in number in a light matrix picture, the effectiveness of the dark accent is reduced.

The use of white or light colors in an abstract way calls for great reductions in the representation of most forms. Since forms in nature are predominantly dark, such reductions are also abstract and thus more difficult to achieve. Generally speaking, the light matrix picture is truly inventive and usually is more difficult to control than the dark matrix picture.

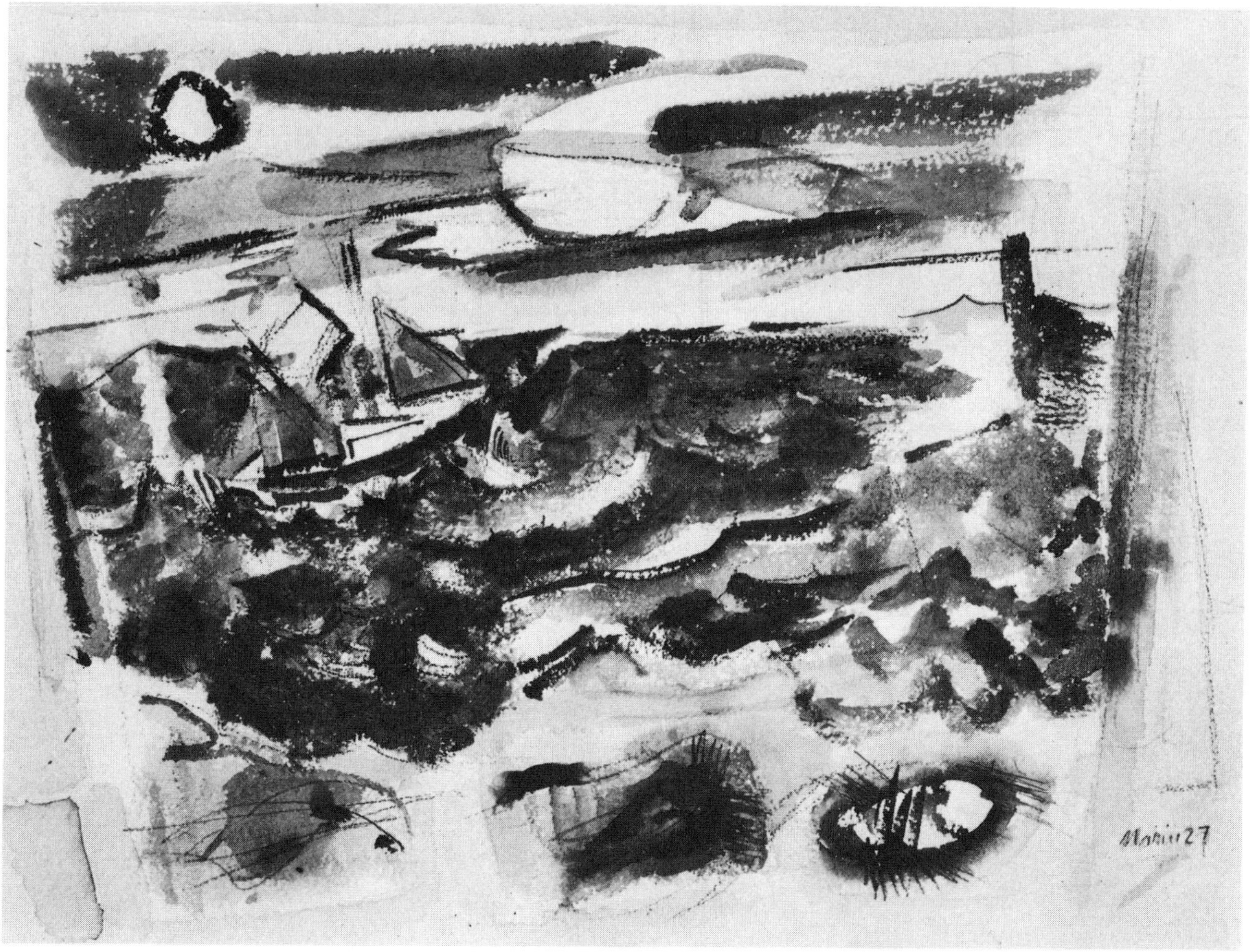

John Marin (American, 1870-1953)
BOATS AND SEA, DEER ISLE, MAINE, 1927
13″ x 17″; watercolor, pencil, on paper
Philadelphia Museum of Art
The S. S. White, 3rd, and Vera White Coll.
(Photograph: A. J. Wyatt)

## The Indeterminate Matrix

Of course, innumerable pictures have neither a strong dark nor a strong light matrix. Successful pictures constructed upon an indeterminate matrix have resulted from an understanding of the matrix and the ways in which the usual matrix structures may be varied, as in the Marin above. Ignorance of such structures usually results in dull, chaotic patterns and an ensuing weak picture.

The knowing designer realizes that white can be made to seem only so white, and dark only so dark. At times he is willing to sacrifice maximum brightness for other attributes inherent in a picture. For instance, given the choice of creating a strong dramatic statement with great impact or one less dramatic but brighter, he probably will choose the former. Or for the sake of a low-toned muted statement, he may well sacrifice brilliance for subdued mood. At times sheer violence of movement may be preferable to brilliance. Such choices made by the artist are many and varied. How bright or how subdued his picture is his option, but his choice is always tempered by the limits of his media and the matrix chosen.

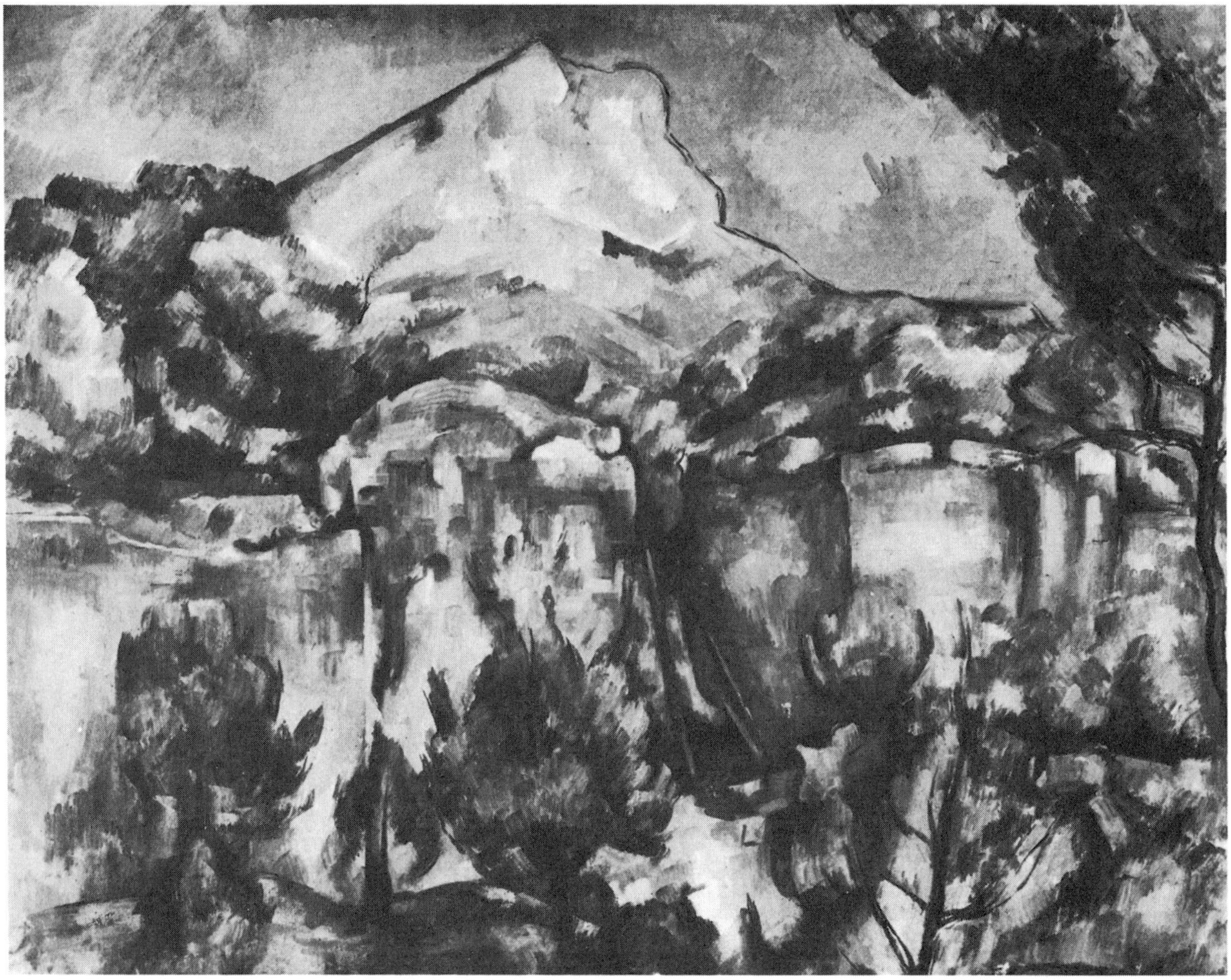

Paul Cézanne (French, 1839-1906)
MONT STE. VICTOIRE SEEN FROM BIBEMUS QUARRY
ca. 1898-1900; 25½″ x 32″; oil on canvas
The Baltimore Museum of Art
The Cone Collection

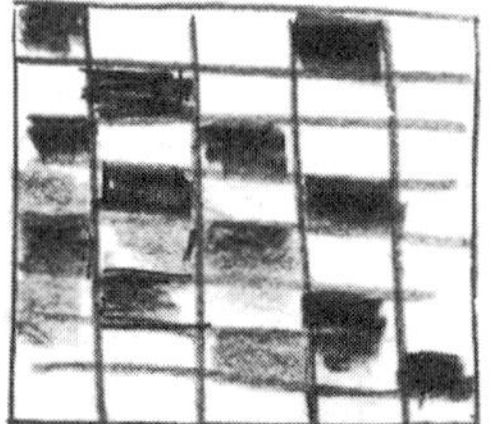
124-1

124    A *checkerboard* pattern, whether geometric or free, is characteristic of many indeterminate matrix pictures. It may be well constructed, but always runs the risk of being not particularly brilliant. A checkerboard itself is a familiar example of such a pattern. It is easy to read, but not particularly exciting or bright. By transposing to a free pattern, we find that variety of shape, color, size, etc., greatly enhances the picture's interest (*124-1*).

Such a structure does assure an alternation of dark and light both from vertical to vertical border, and from horizontal to horizontal border. This creates a unity in the all-over pattern which has great merit. In Cézanne's painting above we see how skillfully he has transposed a checkerboard structure into a fine painting. The organization can be built upon either a dark or light matrix in order to preserve brightness. This picture is another fine example of the principle of the web discussed in Chapter 3.

The *divided* pattern is used over and over again and often causes great difficulty for the inexperienced designer. We may describe this pattern as one which roughly divides the picture into half light and half dark, as in this Goya.

This type of structure, for instance one constructed upon the diagonal of the whole field, introduces so much light in one segment that light accents in the dark area are minimized in intensity. In the same way, dark accents in the light area are reduced in intensity. This is equally true in pictures divided vertically or horizontally.

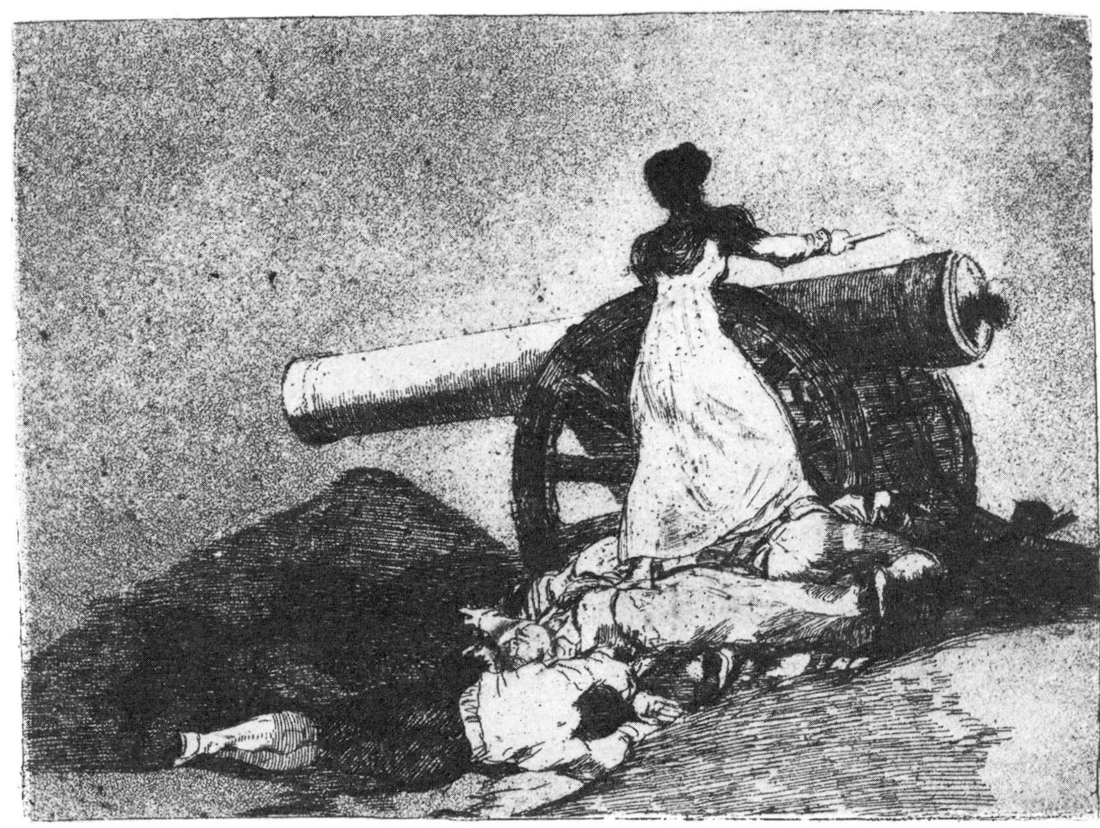



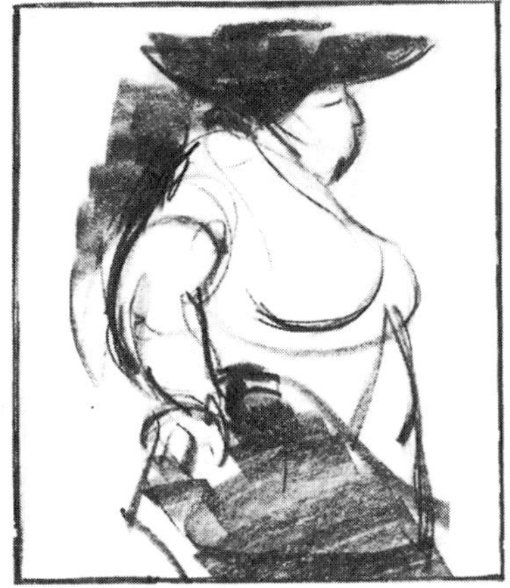

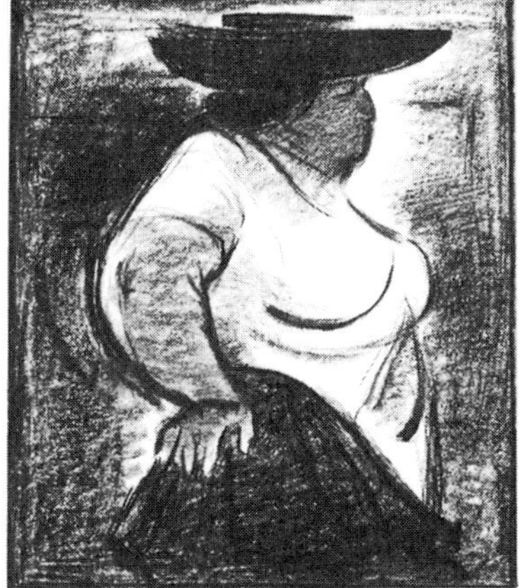



Francisco de Goya (Spanish, 1746-1828)
WHAT VALOR! Plate 7
*The Disasters of War Series*; 1st ed. 1816
13¾" x 9⅞" approx.; etching & aquatint
Achenbach Foundation for Graphic Arts
San Francisco
(Photograph: Schopplein Studio)

The *vignette*, or spot, especially on a white ground, may be completely surrounded by light. In such instances the preponderance of dark in the drawing may call for white accents. Again the divided matrix makes the use of white accents difficult and often ineffective.

In many instances a divided pattern may be transposed into a dark matrix structure (*125-2A*) simply by making the light half of the picture darker (*125-2B*). Of course, this type of correction will not help all pictures and, in certain dramatic statements, may actually weaken picture impact.

So we see that the matrix is mysterious, for it is constructed of both space and volume, or space and shape. It is one of the abstract factors in picture making. Its structure determines the impact of the whole picture. It is intimately related to the pattern of the entire picture and at the same time to the individual shapes employed in the picture. It is an important factor in the control of the accent.

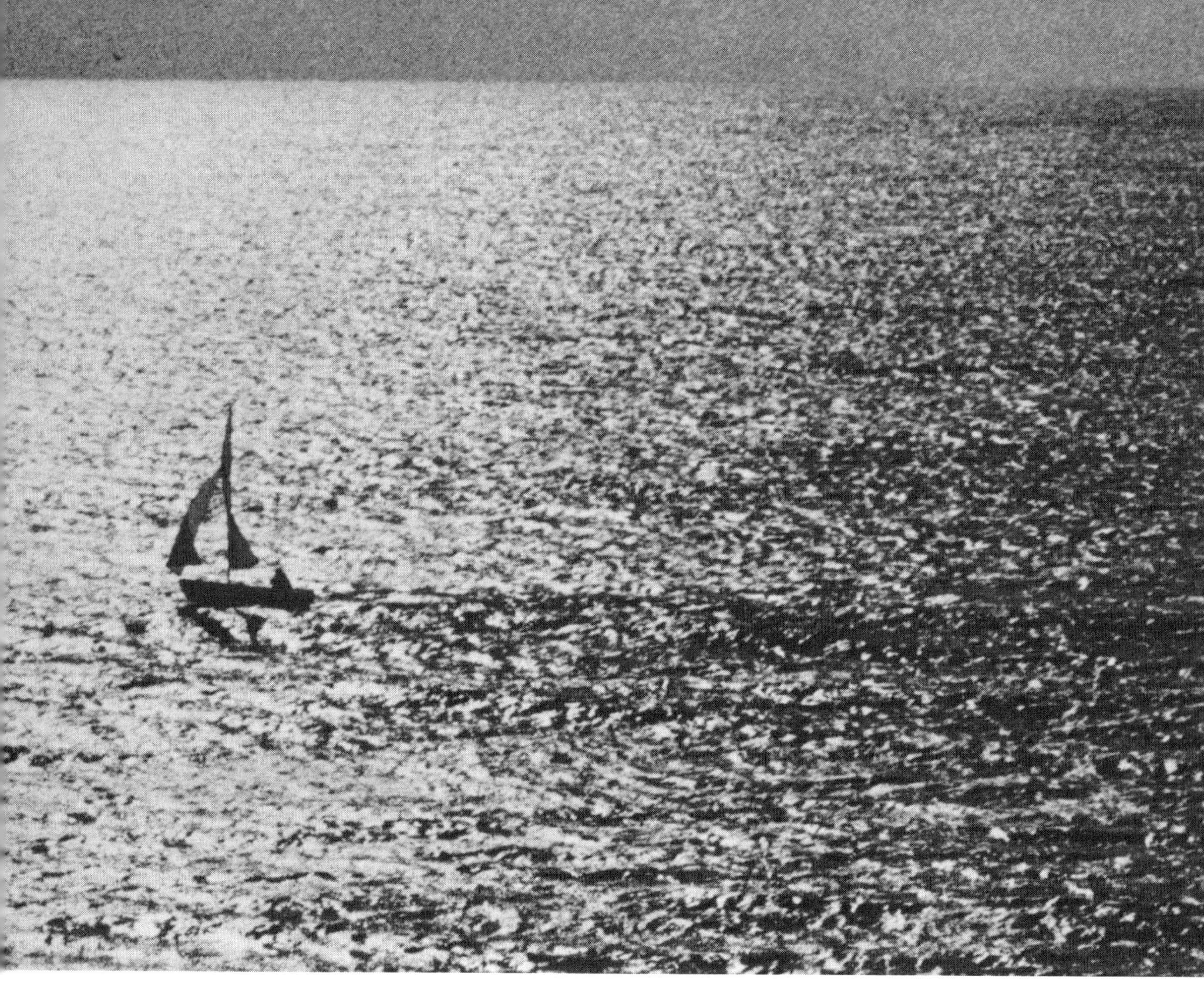

PASSAGE, 1968
(Photograph: Richard Barlow)



# 12 The Passage

### The Passage in Nature

Another picture element besides the matrix plays a dual role—the passage. As we walk along a beach we frequently notice that on the horizon the sky is lighter than the water at one place, yet darker a little farther on. Between these places of contrast the sky and and water are exactly the same value, as we note in the photograph. This transition zone may vary in size from a rather large area to a small point.

We see that this transition zone is a curious combination of distance and direction. It represents the water which appears closer to us than the sky. It also represents the horizontal surface of the water and the apparently vertical sky. How can this zone, which may be a mere point, represent simultaneously such contradictory occurrences in nature? Does it occur elsewhere?

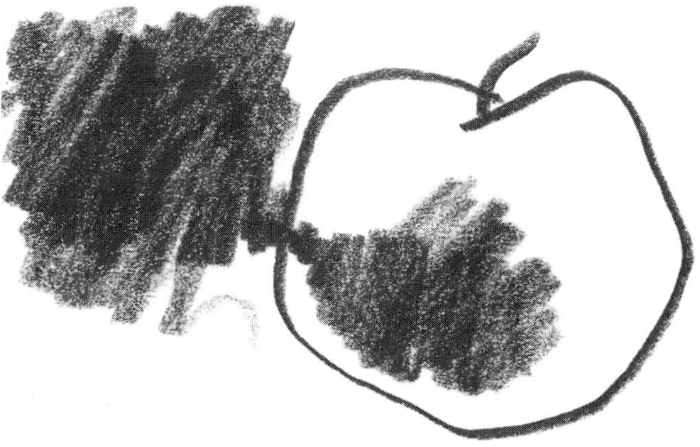

127

We see in an arrangement of familiar forms, such as an apple on a table, the table against a chair, the chair against a wall, that almost every form is both lighter and darker than the adjacent object against which it is silhouetted. Upon close examination, we usually find a transition value common to both the object in front and whatever is behind it. We may have difficulty finding this transition for it is seldom as obvious as in the example of sky and water. In fact, in extreme cases, a piece of black felt on a white surface for instance, we see no transition at all.

## The Passage in Pictures

Once we are aware of this transition, we find that this atmospheric effect in nature is a clue to marvelous graphic controls of the picture surface. Yet in picture terms it is in no way limited to representing merely atmospheric effects. We have discovered what many artists before us have found and utilized, the *passage*.

To illustrate, let us indicate a simple symbol of a form. Now let us make part of the background darker than part of the volume and an adjacent part of the volume the same value (*127*). We see that there is a point on the silhouette of the volume common to both the background and the volume and of the same value as both. This point represents a unique position in the picture, for it is both on the volume and in the background simultaneously.

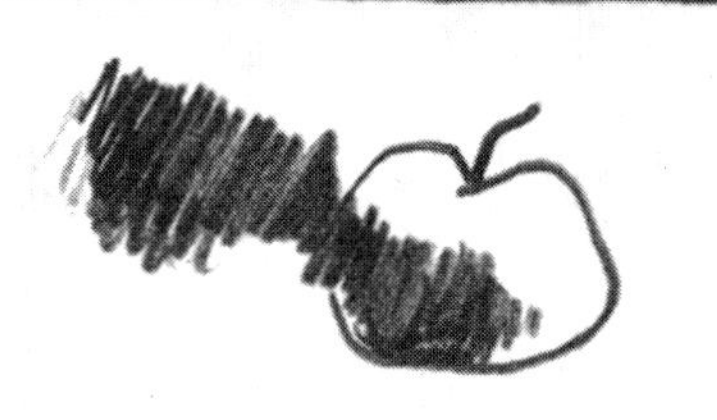

128-1

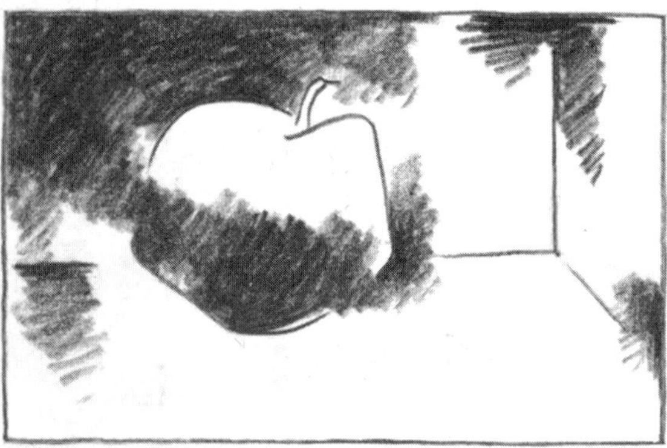

128-2

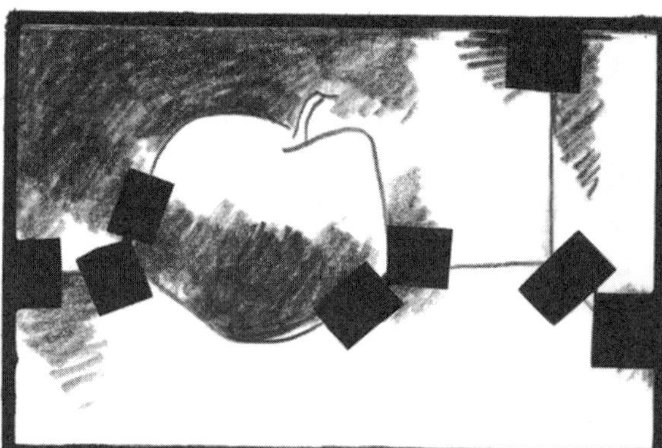

128-3



**The Areal Passage**

As we found while studying the nature of a point in Chapter 5, a point may generate an area (*128-1*).

Here, now, we take a seemingly static point, which represents a position in space, and change it into a graphic area. By doing so we open up whole new lines of investigation in our search for surface control of the picture. We find that this area takes on a special and magic property—it becomes an *areal passage*. This special area lies partly in the background and partly on the volume. It also lies on the picture surface, since it is a flat area. How astonishing that this area can be on the surface, back of the surface, in the background, yet on the volume, all at the same time! This is one of the true enigmas of picture structure.

Here we indicate a volume enclosed by two vertical planes, a horizontal plane and the actual picture surface which is represented by the borders (*128-2*). Between the various planes are introduced a number of areal passages, some white, some gray, some almost black.

If now we stick pieces of masking tape to the surface of the drawing, just covering the passages, we experience vividly the true flatness of the passage. To demonstrate this effect we have utilized a diagram which locates the passages.

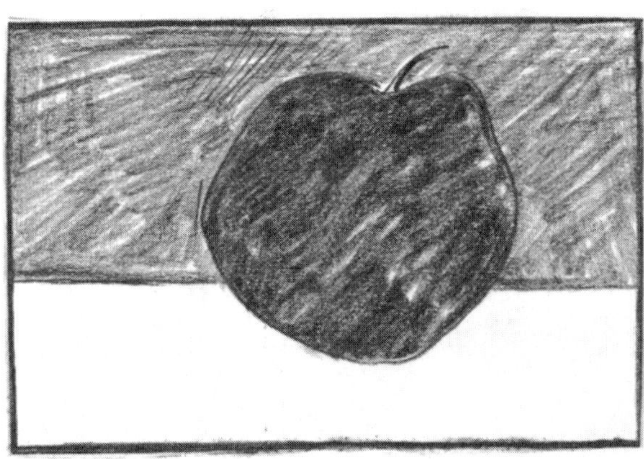

129-2A

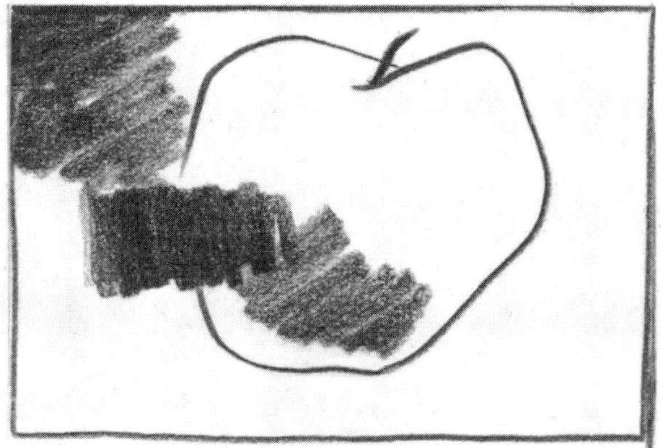

129-1

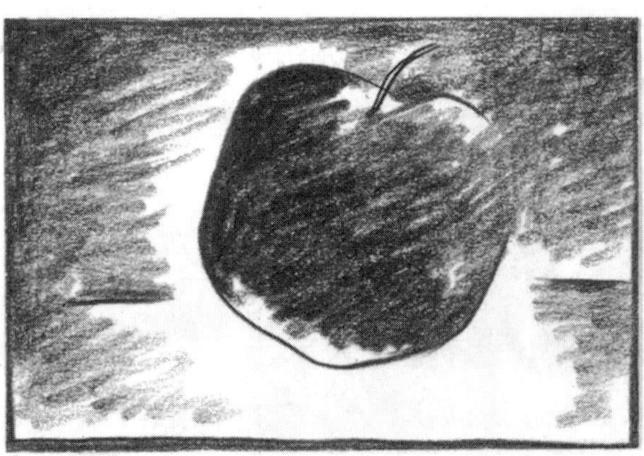

129-2B

If the patch is the same value as its corresponding passage, it will seem to disappear; if excessively large, although of the same value as the passage, it will become a shape unrelated to the volumes involved. If we remove this oversized patch and make the underlying passage the same size as the patch, it, too, becomes an unrelated shape. Actually, a well-executed passage does not really disappear for we are conscious of its presence but not of its shape, and we are reminded constantly of the physical flatness of the picture surface.

The areal passage is an area, not a shape. If it becomes obvious as a shape in itself, we find it separates from the volume and the background and becomes an independent element floating on the picture surface (*129-1*).



As we investigate the passage further, we find that whenever two areas of the same value lying in different planes come together, there is always the opportunity to generate an areal passage (*129-2A*). Usually we must make minor adjustments in the local values of adjacent volumes to create needed contrast between the volumes (*129-2B*). For instance, where the background is adjacent to the volume, it may be made lighter to emphasize the volume. Where the foreground is adjacent to the volume, it may be made to seem lighter by darkening parts of the foreground.

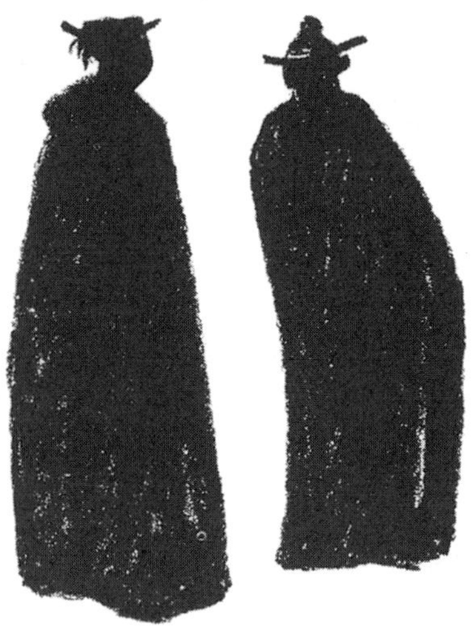

130-1A

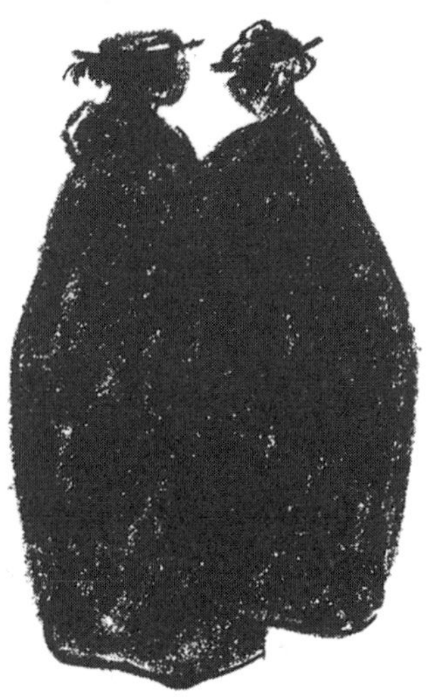

130-1B

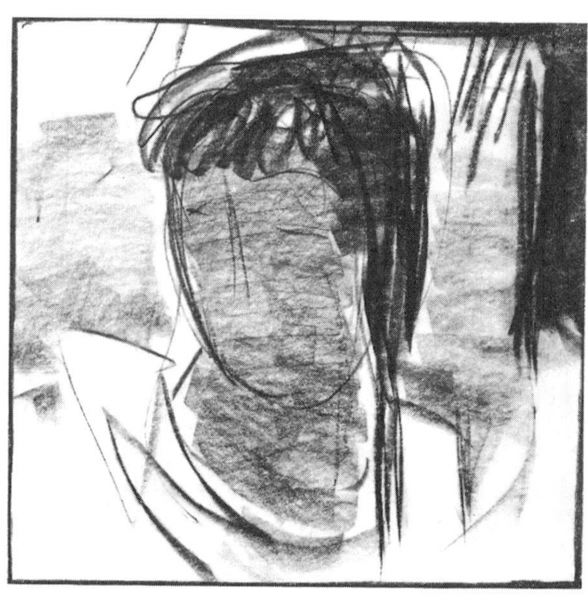

130-2



**The New Shape**

At times we may employ an areal passage to generate a new shape, and then the passage assumes a new function. For instance, let us draw two women in black coats facing each other but not overlapping. Now two distinct shapes are involved (*130-1A*).

Suppose we lap the front figure over the second figure (*130-1B*). The two black shapes now become one black shape. We have generated out of two shapes, a new shape, a third shape. In this case, the areal passage, although not visible to the spectator, is quite large in extent. It contributes to surface control, as any areal passage, should but also creates the third shape, thus vitally affecting the structure of the surface pattern. Such a passage may be of any value, white to black, or corresponding values of color.

Often areal passages are used between internal shape structures almost subconsciously. The value of a top plane of a cheek may be identical with the side plane of a cheek, or of the nose. Or the neck and face may be exactly the same value yet lie in different planes. Usually such passages give us an opportunity to develop new shapes which have a direct bearing on the surface pattern of the whole picture (*130-2*).

**The Linear Passage**

Just as a point may generate an area, so a point also may generate a line (*131-1*).

Just as an areal passage evolves from a point on the silhouette, a position in space where volume and background are the same value, so a line may be generated from the same point. Now we experience a new graphic

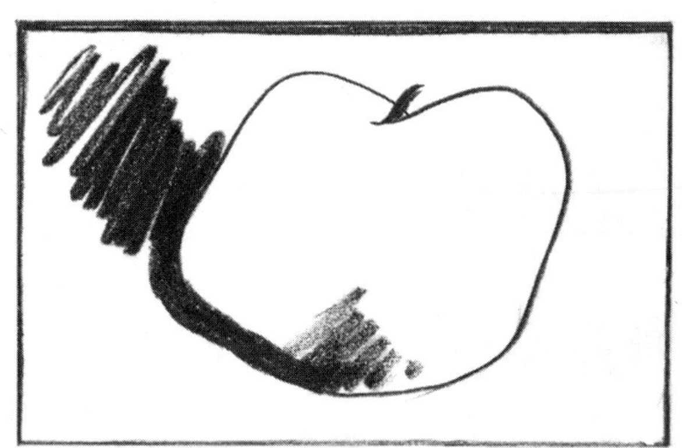

131-2B

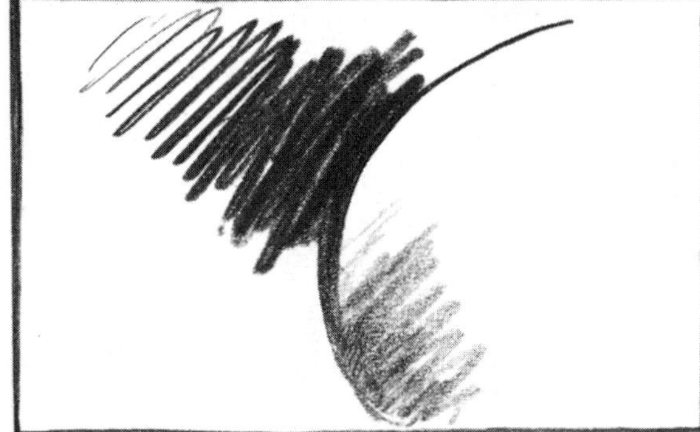

131-2C

131-1

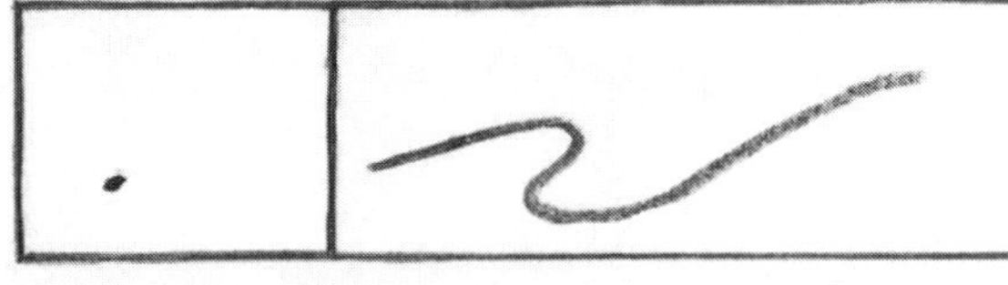

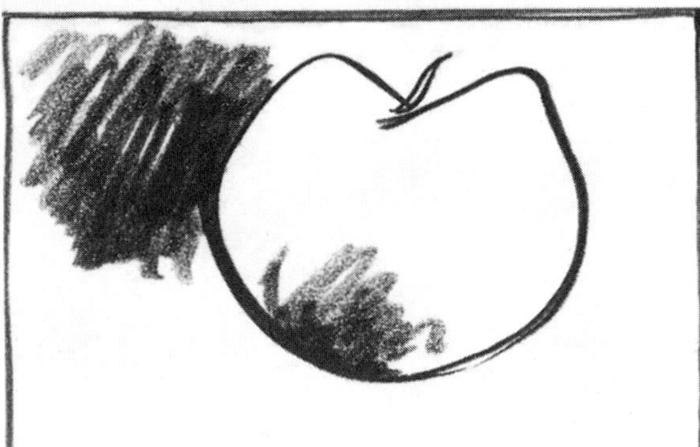

131-2A

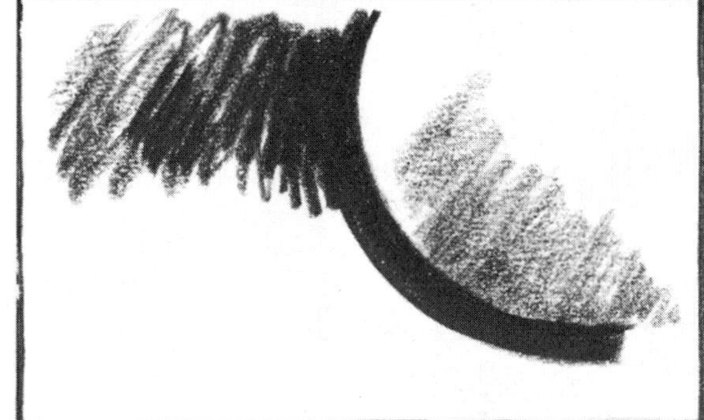

131-2D

event: the *linear passage.* We see that the line connects an area of dark in the background to an area of dark on the volume (*131-2A*).

We see that this connecting line has taken on the function of a passage. The line is in the background, on the volume, on the surface. By exaggerating the thickness of the line these seemingly contradictory occurrences are strikingly demonstrated (*131-2B*). As long as the connection is of a progressive nature, a linear passage is assured; if the connection is dispersive, the linear passage changes character and becomes an areal passage. This should be kept in mind if a strong linear pattern is desired. Since it is a line or an area actually lying on the surface, the passage gives us an opportunity to create dramatic patterns.

The value of the line used as a passage must be identical with that of the area from which it originates and terminates. If both background and volume areas are black, the line must be black.

If the background value is black and the volume value is halftone, for instance, a line must change value as it moves from one area to another (*131-2C*).

Unless the line is the same value as each of the areas which it connects, it becomes not a passage but a line separating two adjacent areas of different values, a line on a value or color separation (*131-2D*). Such a line usually creates a tight, "dry" picture, as we noted in Chapter 7.

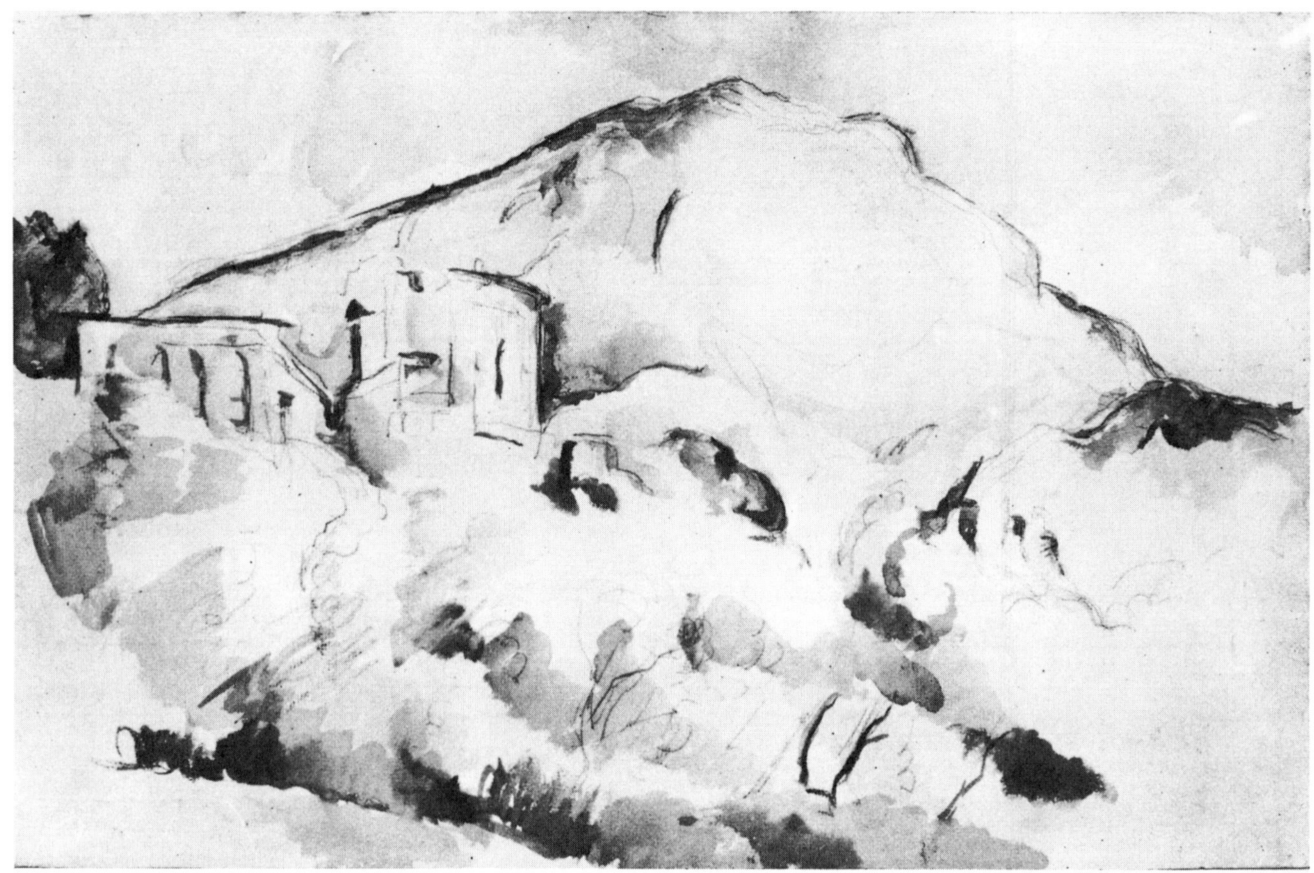

Paul Cézanne (French, 1839-1906)
MT. SAINTE-VICTOIRE
1895-1900; 12⅜″ x 19⅛″; watercolor
Albertina, Vienna



Although a passage may be of any value, a picture often is constructed in such a way that one value dominates the whole passage structure. We may construct a light matrix picture, as we noted in Chapter 11, by utilizing white almost exclusively. And in such a case the passage will be white, or just off white, as Cézanne demonstrates in this landscape.

Or we may build a dark matrix picture almost entirely upon darks or blacks, with corresponding dark passages, as Rouault has done consistently in his picture *The Judges*.

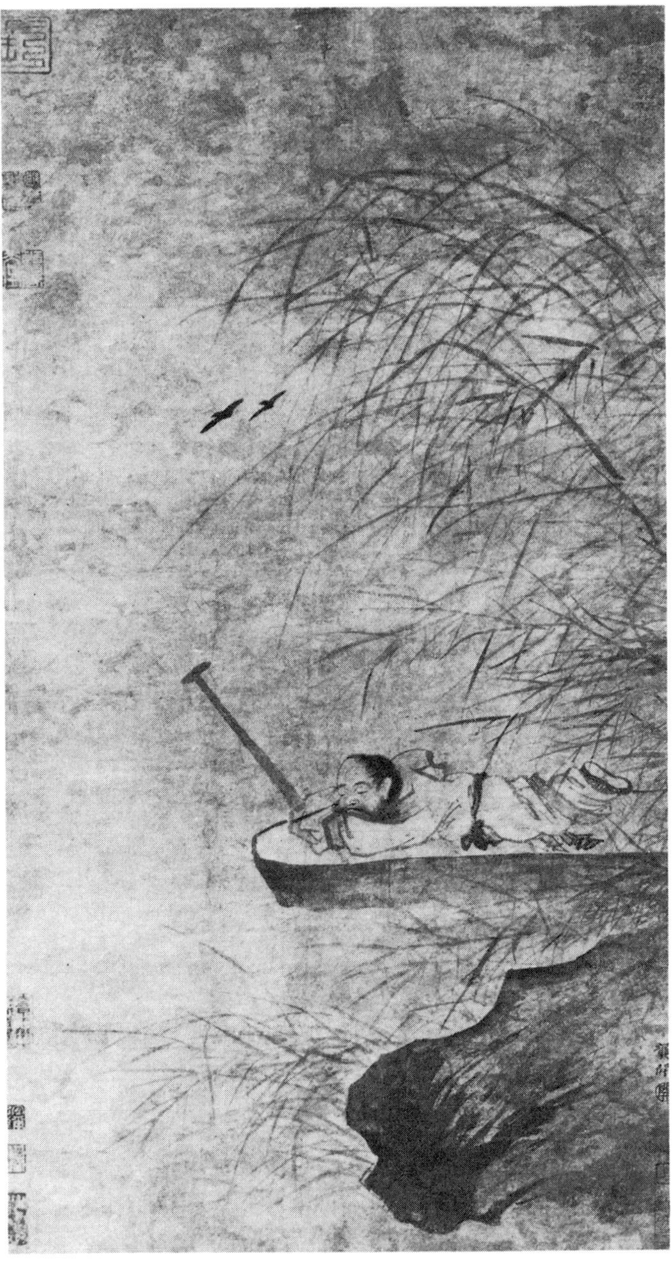

Artist unknown (Chinese, 15th century?)
A MAN ASLEEP IN A BOAT NEAR THE SHORE
Ming Dynasty; 40¹⁵⁄₁₆″ x 21¹¹⁄₁₆″
ink on paper panel
Courtesy of the Smithsonian Institution
Freer Gallery of Art, Washington, D.C.

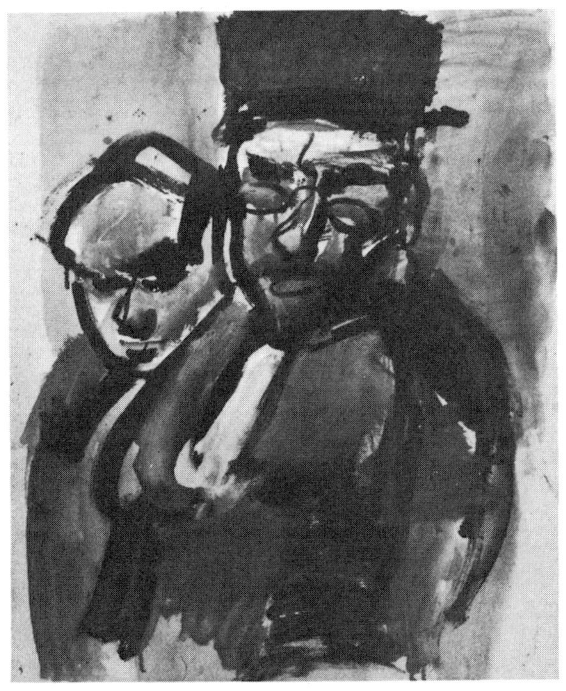

Georges Rouault (French, 1871-1958)
THE JUDGES, ca. 1907; 25⅛″ x 18¾″
gouache on paper
From the collection of the Portland Art Museum
Portland, Oregon (Photographer: Bissell)

We may construct a picture entirely on areal passages, entirely on linear passages, or on both. When we construct a picture entirely upon areal passages, there is a tendency for the picture to be rather soft. To overcome this inherent weakness, we can always employ rather larger contrasting areas with resulting hard edges, which enhance the impact of the shapes.

If we build a picture upon a strong use of linear passages, with a minimal use of areal passages, the results are more dramatic than when areal passages alone are used. The Rouault demonstrates this clearly. Striking pictures have been made in which linear and areal passages have been deliberately separated on the picture surface, but such construction represents great sophistication on the part of the artist, as in the Chinese painting above.

## Passage and Pattern

Strong as the passage is in developing surface patterns, it must not be allowed to create patterns that are spotty. As we move from a dark to a dark on a linear passage, the two dark areas may easily become the same size and result in a chaotic pattern. We may make passages which are successful locally in the picture yet so strong that they destroy the legibility of the picture as a whole.

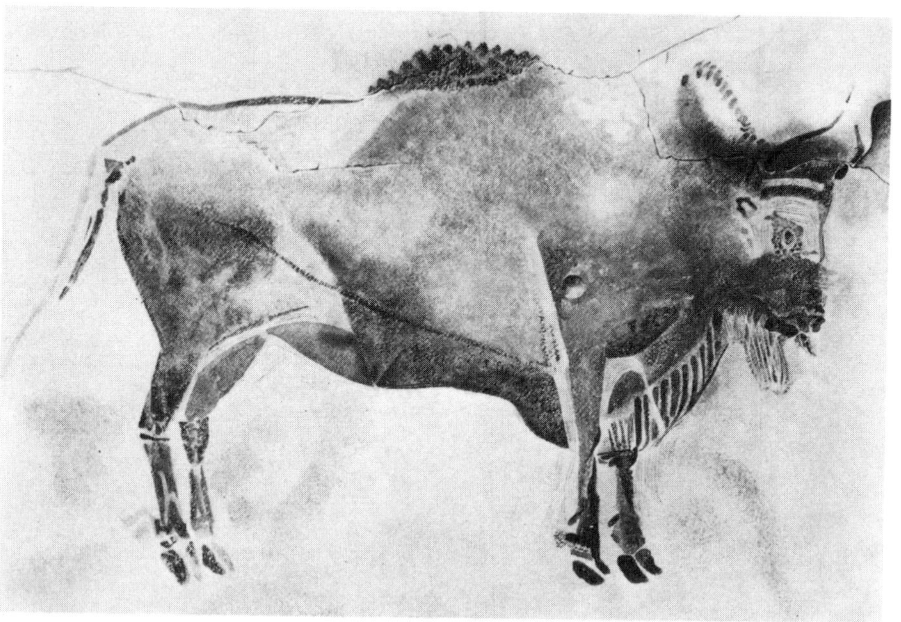



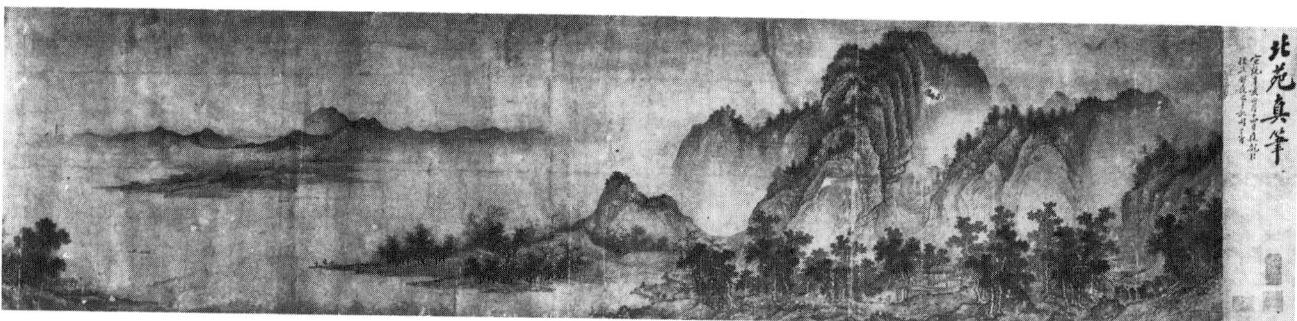

Artist unknown (Chinese, 12-13th cent.)
CLEAR WEATHER IN THE VALLEY; Sung Dynasty
15″ x 52″; ink, traces of color

paper makimono, landscape scroll
Courtesy, Museum of Fine Arts, Boston
Chinese and Japanese Special Fund

134     If we develop passages too locally, for instance, all on one side of the picture and none on the other, or all in relation to the principal volumes and none between background and borders, we are in danger of producing an unbalanced picture. But if we distribute passages in an orderly way through the whole picture, surface control is more easily maintained.

It is generally true that as the picture becomes more and more realistic, or atmospheric, the passage as a surface control becomes less and less noticeable. It does, however, help to bind overlayed volumes and shapes and keep the picture from becoming dry or tight. Natural passage effects, such as the sky and water phenomenon we have noted, do occur, but when expressed graphically they in no way assure structural control.

## Historical Uses of the Passage

The passage is as old as picture making. As early as the Altamira rock paintings and those in Africa, we find skillful use of the passage, especially involving individual symbols. In this bison, from the walls of the Altamira caves, the use of the same value defining adjacent forms which lie in different planes is evident throughout the whole drawing.

Chinese artists employed the passage in the construction of entire pictures. We see in this landscape the common value tying sky, mountains, and foreground into a strong surface pattern.

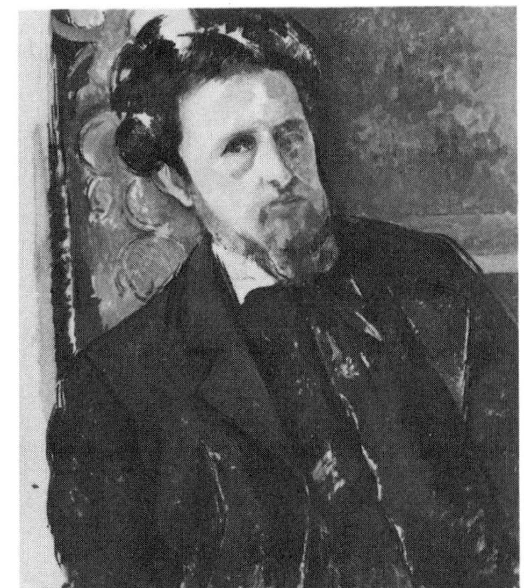



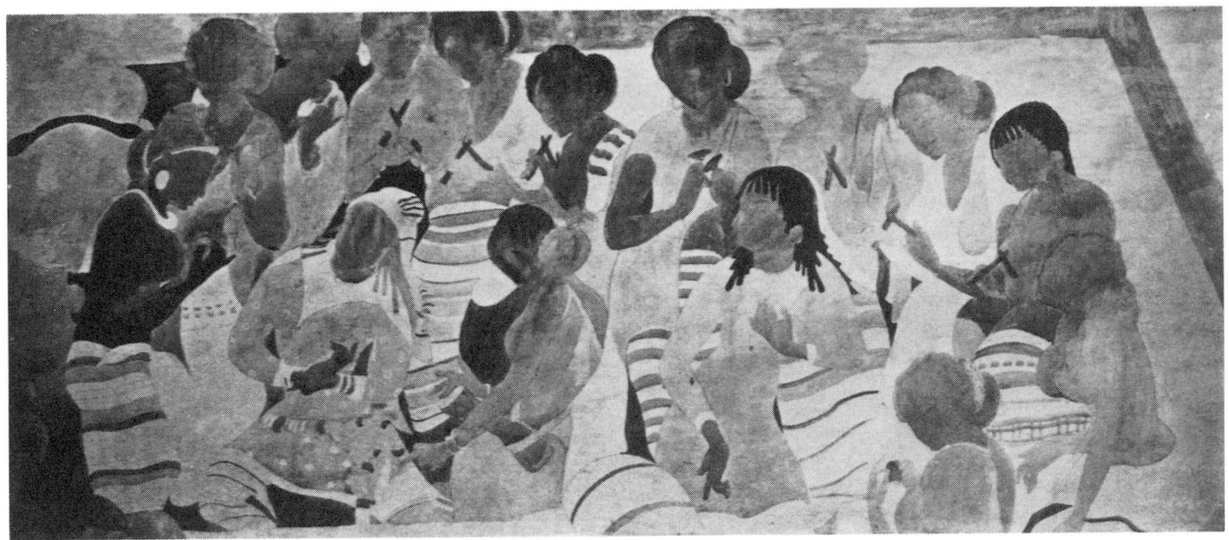

The East Indian painters of the Ajanta caves, and those at Bagh, carried the use of the passage to a high degree of sophistication. In the painting from Bagh above, we see the way the passage has been used to create an involved surface pattern built upon the interweaving of two large circles of figures. The changing value of the figures and the way they are related to each other and to the background is only possible by means of the passage.

Cézanne, searching for strong surface controls, developed pictures which are like texts on the passage. In this portrait we see that the transitions on dark between hair and background, background and left arm, coat and vest, are purposefully designed to make a dramatic shape impact.

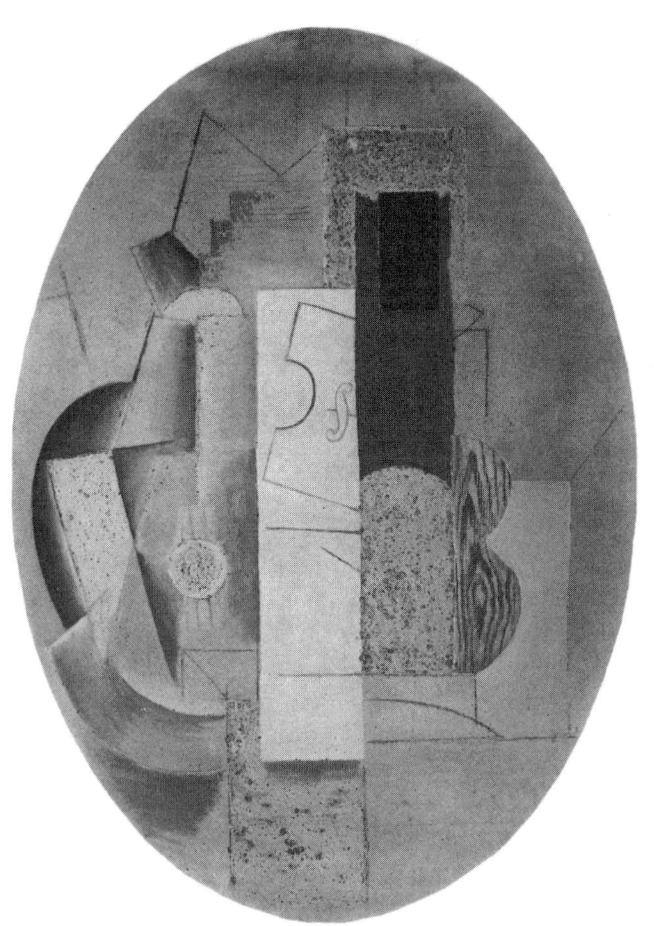

Pablo Picasso (Spanish, 1881-    )
VIOLIN AND GUITAR; 1913; 35¼″ x 25¼″
oil, pencil, cloth, and plaster on canvas
Philadelphia Museum of Art
The Louise and Walter Arensberg Collection
(Photograph: A. J. Wyatt)

Mark Rothko (American, b. Russia, 1903-1970)
BLACK OVER REDS, 1957; 95″ x 81½″
oil on canvas
Mr. and Mrs. Edgar F. Berman, Maryland

136     In the early Cubist period, Picasso and Braque synthesized the passage by reducing it to its essentials. If we study this period carefully we shall find a great variety of solutions to the problem of surface control. Picasso's still life *Violin and Guitar*, involving collage, clearly demonstrates the ingenious use of the passage.

Most twentieth century painters have employed the passage to one degree or another. But, in *Black Over Reds*, the painter Rothko has limited its use. Only at the bottom of the picture is the passage apparent. If the horizontal shape had been continued to impact against the borders the whole meaning of the picture would have changed.

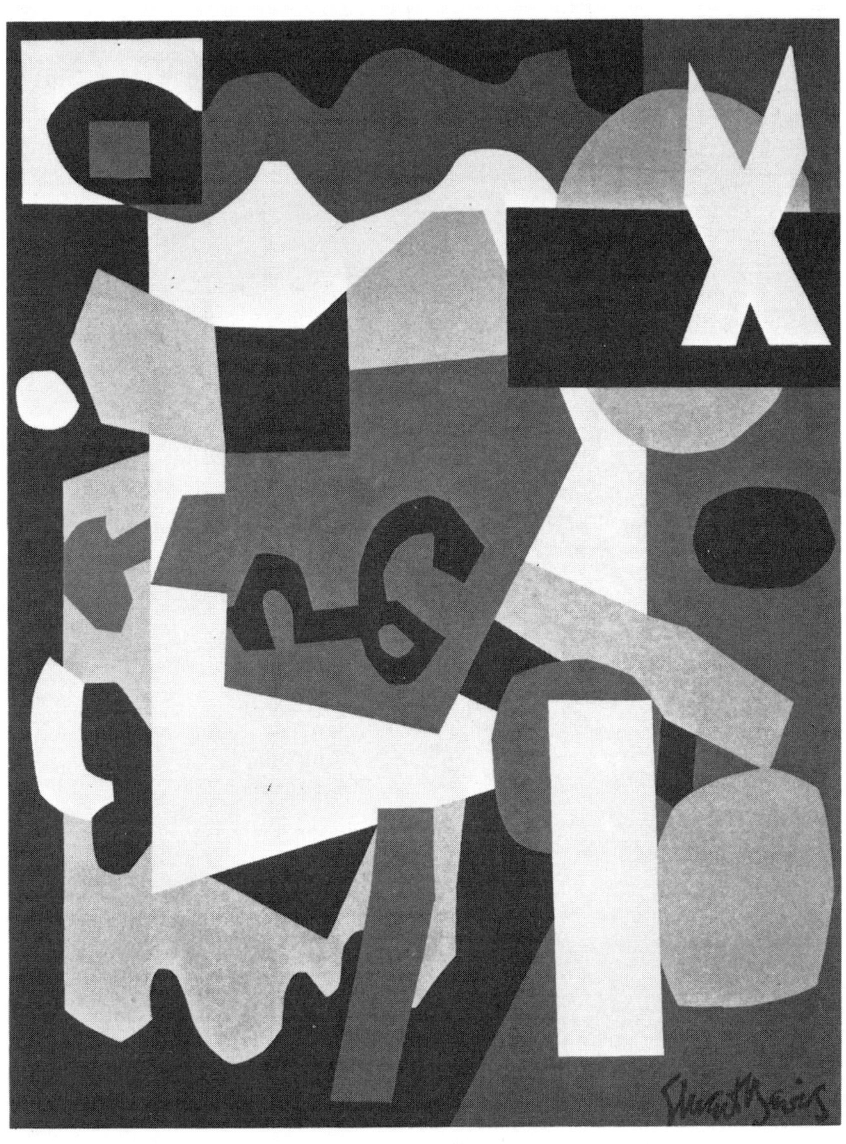

Stuart Davis (American, 1894-1964)
READY-TO-WEAR, 1955; 56¼" x 42"; oil on canvas
Courtesy of The Art Institute of Chicago
Gift of Mr. and Mrs. Sigmund W. Kunstadter
and Goodman Fund

Some painters purposely avoid using the passage and depend upon strong contrasts of line and shapes with hard edges. Surface control in such pictures is based on an exact control of space and volume or shape, with emphasis upon the graphic activity of the elements. We see in this Stuart Davis that almost all the elements have been resolved as separate units, which in their entirety constitute a strong pattern on the surface and in space. Tonal passages are minimized for the sake of strong shape impact.

The passage is only one of many controls which we may employ to stress the surface factor or to bind the picture into a whole. Certainly it is one of the most important. Our mastery of the passage can only result in a better understanding of picture structure and, for us, more exciting picture statements.

# 13 Measuring Depth in Nature

# IV MEASURING DEPTH

**Depth Perception**

In Chapter 1 we noted that as artists we live in a three-dimensional world but work in a two-dimensional world. If our picture is motivated by some occurrence in nature, we must become aware of the depths or distances we perceive in order to simulate such depths in our picture. If our picture is purely imaginative, as the Hogarth shown here, or even non-representational, our graphic symbols always occur in an environment suggesting some degree of space which we also must first experience.

How we interpret depth in picture terms is usually referred to as our space sense. Whether space is considered a visually measurable depth between symbols or an abstract graphic environment, it is one of the most important factors in picture making.

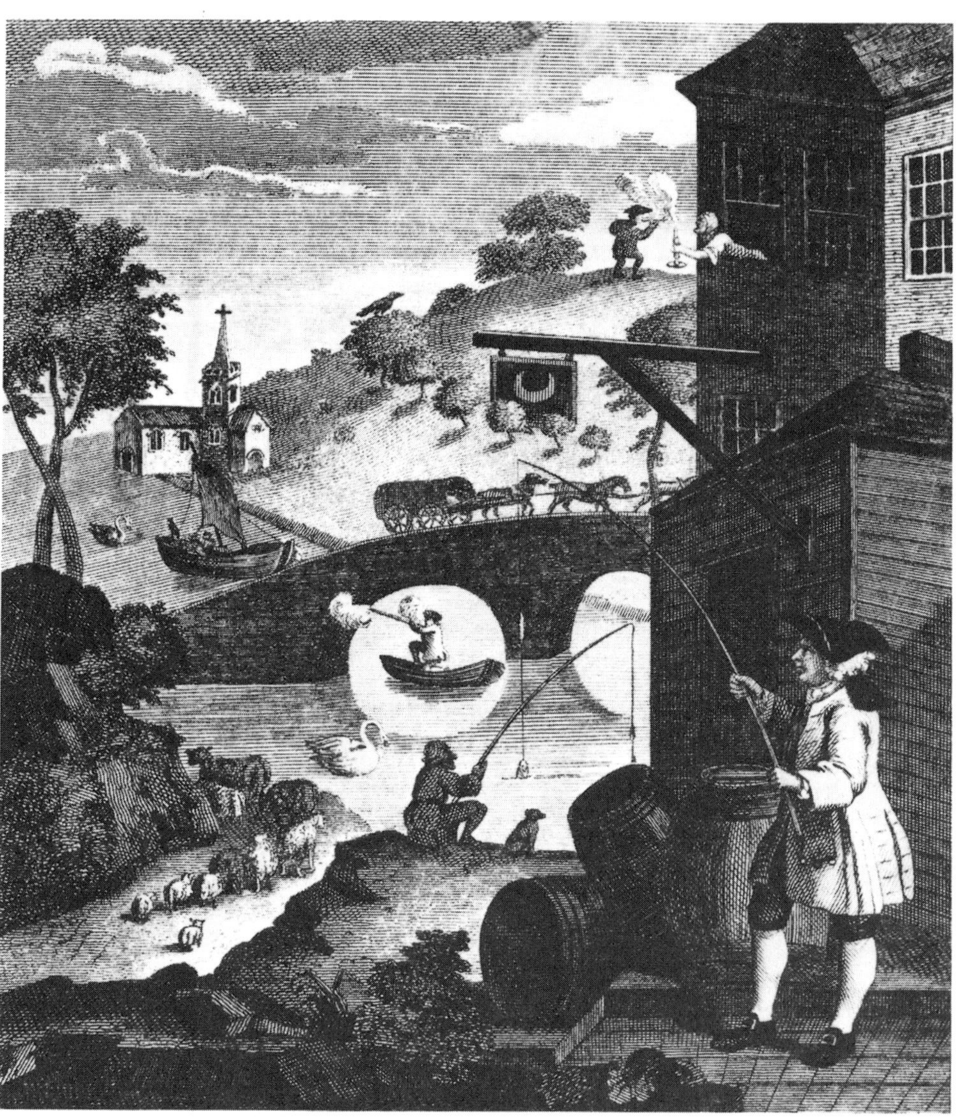

William Hogarth (English, 1697-1764)
FRONTISPIECE TO KERBY (FALSE PERSPECTIVE)
1754; 7¼″ x 6¼″; engraving
The Bettmann Archive

In this space we should be able to suggest the dimensional characteristics of three-dimensional forms. We must be able to measure exact distances, reasonably acceptable distances, even imaginary distances. In addition, we must be able to simulate the distances between shapes that may not be related to volumes. This is especially true in the construction of non-representational pictures. We must be able to create a graphic space in which points, lines, and areas may exist independently of any reference to nature. Yet a sense of graphic space is impossible without some understanding of depth perception in nature.

Many factors affect our ability to perceive depth, especially the effect of action. Action in the things around us, or in the actual change of position of the eye itself in relation to its environment, constitutes one factor of great importance to the artist, especially in the preparation or construction of motion pictures, animation in particular (we explore this in Chapter 31). At this time, however, we shall concentrate on the problem of simulating actual depths in a still picture, showing how we measure in graphic space.

## Range of Vision



In addition to action there are other phenomena of depth perception. Suppose that we stand on a seashore looking out to an unbroken horizon. At first we may feel that the horizon is infinitely far away. But let us see. The horizon is the last bit of the surface of the water that we can see from a fixed observation point. Our view of the sea is limited by the curvature of the earth and by the height of our eyes above the water. The ratio of the elevation of our eyes above the surface to the distance separating us from the horizon can be computed exactly. We find that the horizon is not infinitely far away but is at a finite distance from us.

We also realize that the horizon, although the last part of the ocean that we can see, is by no means the limit of our vision. Quite often certain elements are visible beyond the horizon—a range of mountains may tower above the horizon; the moon may rise above the mountains.

Our range of vision also may be reduced by the introduction of elements that mask out the distant horizon. We may be confined to the interior of a room, or be face to face with a person and experience just a close-up of his features. Our range of vision then may be a matter of only a few inches.

With unaided eyes we may examine something very close or something at an incredible distance in the sky, but our range of close and distant vision may also be enlarged, for the microscope or telescope extend our range many times.

Now let us see how to estimate distances in nature.

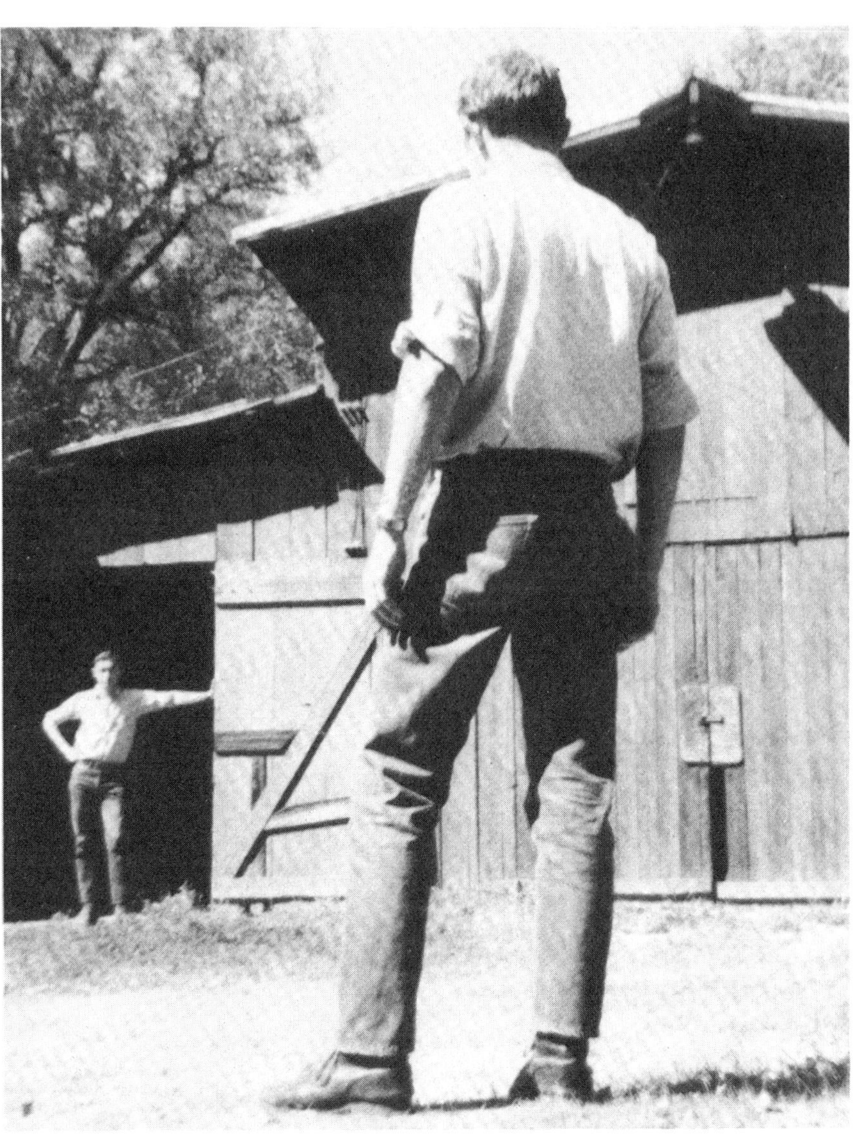

TWO FIGURES AND BARN
(Photograph: Kenneth Graham)

## Measuring Depth by Comparison

When we are children we learn to compare intimate forms as to size and distance. Our own body serves as a yardstick. We compare one finger to another, a foot to a hand. One is larger than the other; one is farther from our eyes than the other.

We later discover more accurate units of measure, some involving incredibly large or incredibly small units of comparison such as the light year or the angstrom unit.

In learning to measure we soon find that to compare one thing to another each must be of the same order and must be compared using an appropriate unit of measure. We compare an inch to a yard, not an inch to a quart, a quart to a gallon, not a quart to red. In like manner, red can be compared to another color but not to fat or thin.

When visually measuring depth in nature, we often compare two or more similar forms which we know are alike but which appear to be different because of the distance between them. Through the logic of overlapping forms we judge the relative sizes of dissimilar forms. For instance, the man in the foreground of the accompanying photograph seems larger than the barn he overlaps. The man leaning against the barn seems smaller than the barn. But we assume that the men are approximately the same size; that the man in the foreground is not a giant; that the barn must be much larger than the man in the foreground, although visually it seems smaller; and that considerable distance must separate the men.

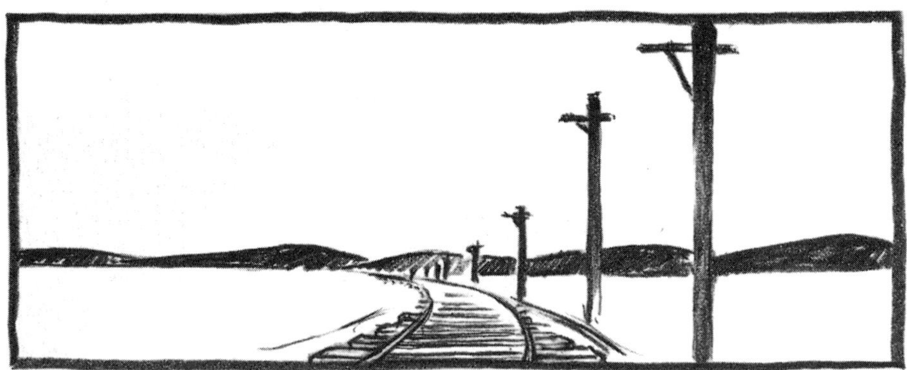

142-A

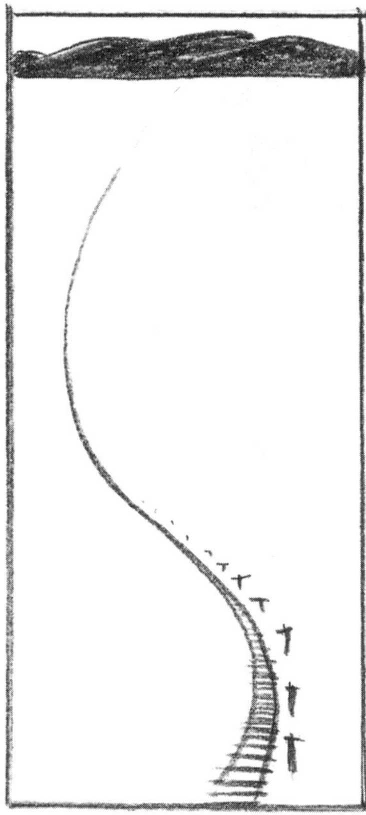

142-B



However, our judgment of depth in nature is not always infallible. An intriguing popular game demonstrates how easily we can be deceived. It is the old size-guessing game. How high is the table? How thick is the beam? How wide is the room? We try to determine the exact dimensions of things close to us, then try to guess the distance of more distantly related forms: How far to the house next door? To the house at the end of the street? We soon realize how easily eyes can be fooled.

We, also, soon discover that it is relatively easy to estimate shallow depths, or short distances separating forms close to us. But as the interval increases between ourselves and the form, determining this exact distance becomes more difficult. For instance, standing on a railroad track, we notice that the short intervals between the ties become almost impossible to distinguish only a few feet away (*142-A*).

By using the distance between poles paralleling the track, instead of the distance between ties, as a unit of measure we are able to estimate depth into the middle distance with fair accuracy. The far distance, however, still can be estimated only roughly. As our point of observation rises higher above the tracks, we are able to distinguish the intervals between the ties for a much longer distance as we can also with the interval between the poles (*142-B*). Yet far distance remains indeterminate.

So we see that no matter how we try to estimate depths in nature, distances between things far from us are much harder to measure than distances between things close to us.

**Binocular Vision**
We rarely stop to think how important two eyes can be in helping us determine depth

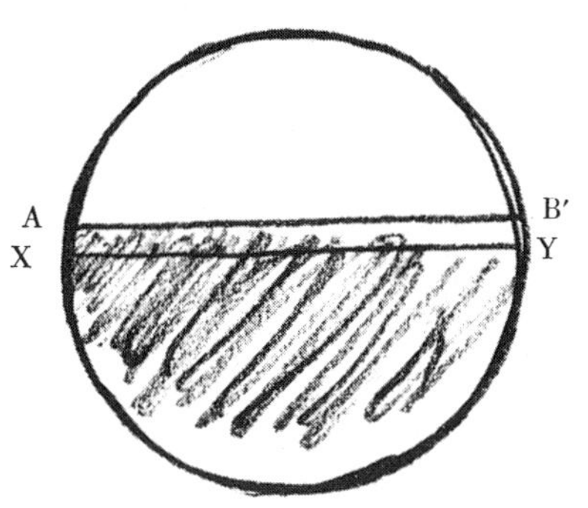

143-D

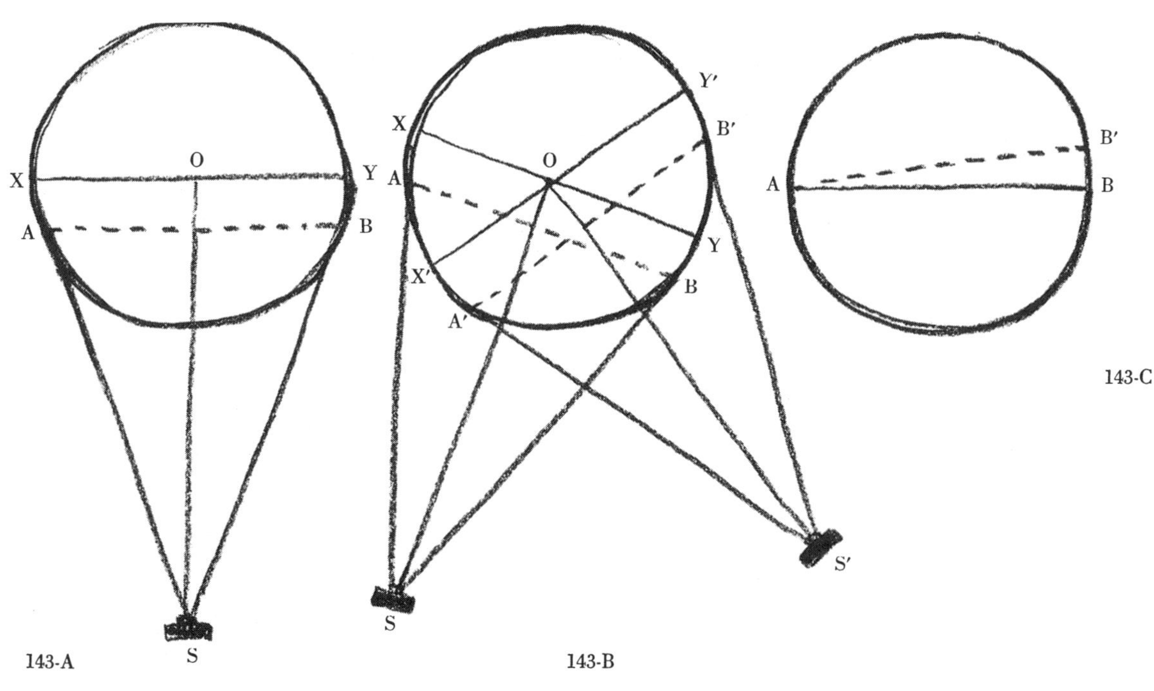

143-A    143-B    143-C

in nature. To recall just how binocular vision works, let us hold an index finger vertically about a foot from our nose. Now close the left eye and view the finger with the right eye. With the right eye we see a little bit of the right side of the finger. Now close the right eye and view the finger with the left eye. Now we see a little bit of the left side of the finger. When we look at the finger with both eyes, we really are looking around it to a certain extent.

To further clarify, let us indicate a cylinder in plan. Diagrammatically it will appear as a circle (*143-A*). At a point not too remote, let us indicate a camera (*S*). A picture taken of the cylinder from this position shows two points *A* and *B* which lie on the silhouette of the cylinder and represent its apparent maximum width. Note, however, that the distance *AB* is slightly less than the true diameter *XY* of the cylinder.

Now let us introduce, at the same distance from the cylinder, a second camera (*S'*). A photo taken from this position would place *A'* and *B'* on the silhouette of the cylinder. *A'B'* will, in turn, be slightly less than the true diameter *X'Y'* of the cylinder (*143-B*).

If these two photos are traced and superimposed, we see that *A* represents the extreme position on the cylinder recorded by the camera at *S*; and *B'* the extreme position recorded from *S'* (*143-C*).

Although each camera respectively records less than half the surface of the cylinder, taken together the two cameras record all the surface from *A* to *B'* which is greater than the surface from *X* to *Y*, which is exactly half the surface (*143-D*).

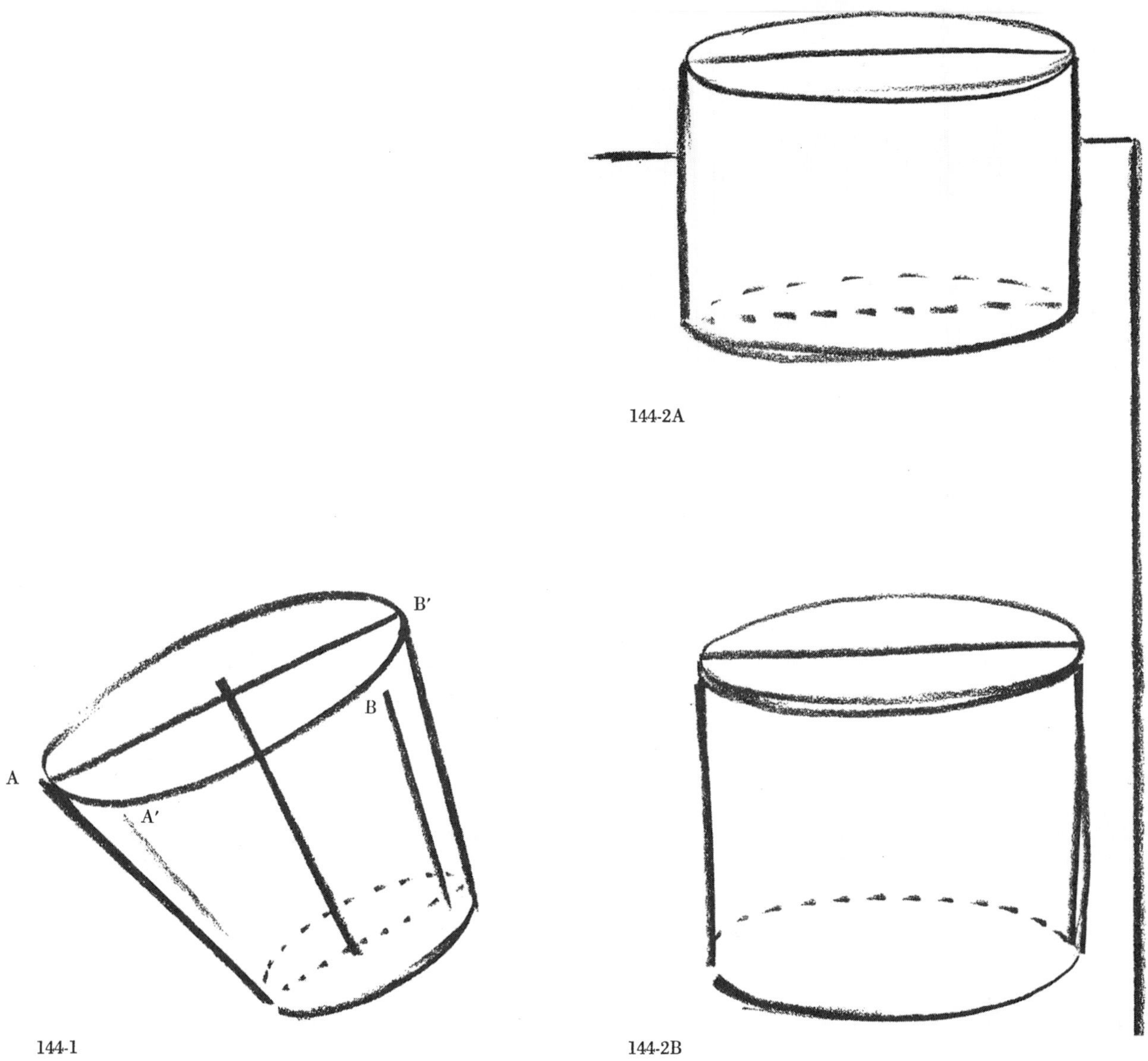




We see now, in effect, that our eyes are like two cameras. They are separated by quite an interval and they usually record simultaneously. When a small vertical object is viewed from close range, we actually do see around corners. With two eyes we see *more of its surface* than with one eye. This surface factor has great significance for us when it comes to picture making (*144-1*).

How this surface factor may be exploited in a perspective drawing may be illustrated with a simple cylinder. Using only one eye we record the cylinder much as would one camera. The top and bottom of the cylinder will appear as true ellipses (*144-2A*). Using normal binocular vision we will actually see more of the surface of the cylinder. To account for this added surface, we can distort the top and bottom ellipses by increasing their curvature on the close side (*144-2B*). This increases our sense of solidity of the volume and gives an added sense of space to our drawing.

As we view things farther and farther away, the effectiveness of binocular vision lessens. Viewing a tree trunk from six feet, we will probably experience a strong sense of dimension and added surface, but from sixteen feet not nearly as much. A tree on a ridge several miles away will look flat. Binocular vision is not a factor at this distance.

## Actual Depth versus Visual Depth

Because we become so accustomed to seeing the
world in terms of perspective we usually
accept a perspective view as the way things
actually are. Yet we know that the edges of a
cube do not actually converge, even though
in many views they seem to do so. Our
perspective world is in most cases a visually
distorted world.

Possibly nothing emphasizes the limitations
of our perspective viewpoint as much as when
we try to build a simple three-dimensional
structure. In order to build even a small box
we must be able to measure, to find true
dimensions which, as we have noted, usually
are determined by means of a ruler or
yardstick of some kind. However, neither a
foot-rule nor a yardstick can be seen all at once
and at the same time be held close enough
for us to make accurate measurements. To
measure a board six feet, one-sixteenth inches,
we must *ignore perspective,* for it is impossible
for us to focus our eyes to encompass a
one-sixteenth inch unit and at the same time be
far enough away to observe the six foot unit.

Large dimensions may be measured with
fair accuracy but such dimensions must be
computed, and again the perspective view
discounted. We can measure a large floor or a
wall in a room, yet we are not able at any
time to see it in its true shape. We can look
at a large rectangular building yet see its
corner as less than, or greater than, ninety
degrees. From the ground a square forty-acre
plot will not appear square, yet we know it has
been determined square by survey.

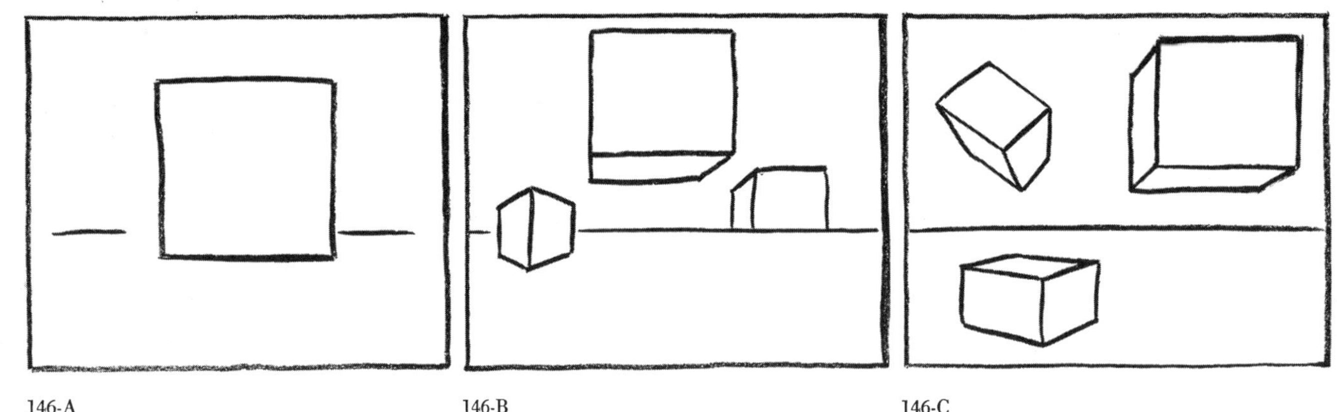

146-A    146-B    146-C

## 146  Aspects of a Cube

Sometimes by carefully examining something very simple we learn to see more complex organizations in a new light. So let us observe a simple form, a cube.

However made, of whatever material, it is possible to weigh, measure, paint, touch, and even taste such a small three-dimensional structure. Although we know it is a cube, it is impossible for us to see each side simultaneously as a square. We can only compare various aspects of the cube which we can see and thus estimate its true form.

We have noted that action, distance, and binocular vision are some factors that determine how we see the simplest form. Other factors are the physical construction of the form, its opaqueness or transparency.

Our position in relation to a structure also has profound effect upon our visual reception of its characteristics. Thus we gather different information depending upon whether we see it from outside, inside, or both. To return to our cube, we may see:

*One side.* By looking directly at one facet of a small cube with one eye or directly at one facet of a large cube with both eyes, only one side will be revealed, and the cube will look square (*146-A*).

*Two sides.* By moving up or down, or side to side, a second side of our cube is revealed. If viewed from almost directly in front, one side will still seem square (*146-B*).

*Three sides.* By moving up or down, or side to side, a cube revealing two sides will reveal a third side. This is the view of objects in nature with which we are most familiar. Such a view gives us the most information concerning a solid volume that we can experience visually at any one time (*146-C*).

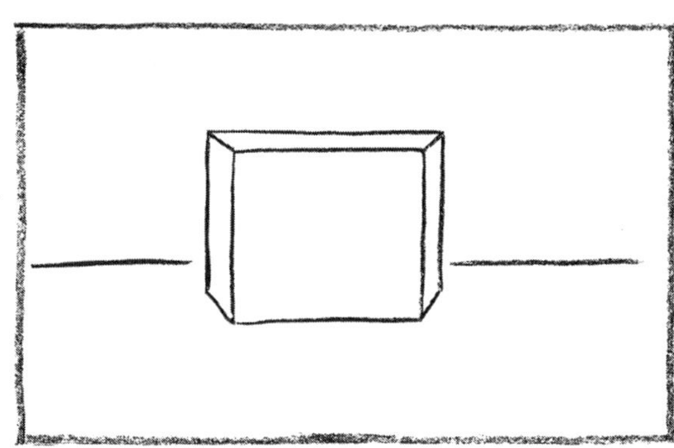

147-A

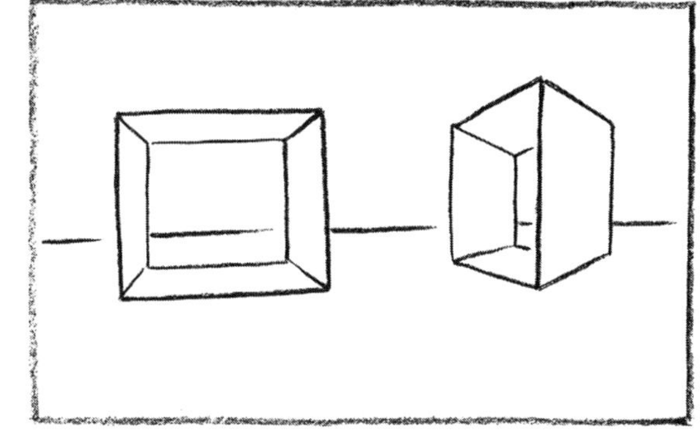

147-B

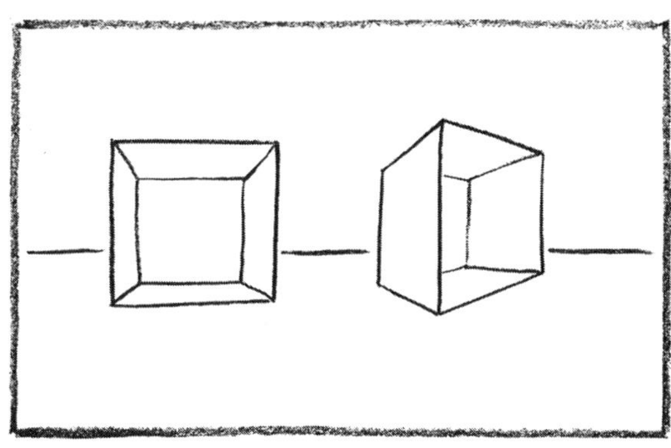

147-C

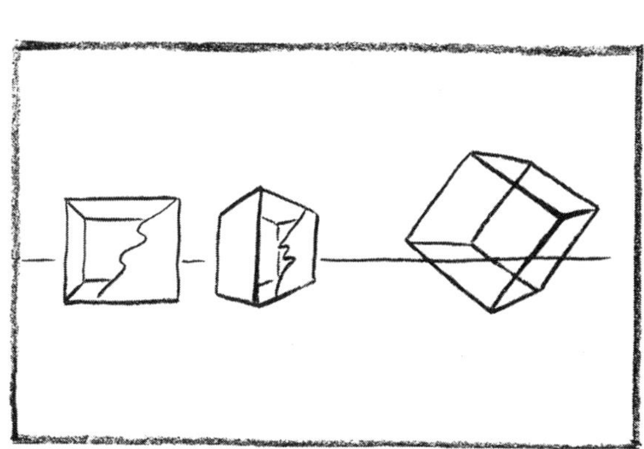

147-D

*Four sides.* Under special conditions, a solid cube seen with both eyes may reveal four sides simultaneously. It must be small enough and be seen close enough to allow binocular vision to function. It also must be seen from a little above or a little below the top or bottom (*147-A*).

If the cube is hollow and the front and back surfaces have been removed, we also may see four sides (*147-B*).

*Five sides.* If our hollow cube has only its front surface removed we have a familiar five-sided structure (*147-C*).

*Six sides.* If the front plane of our hollow cube is semi-transparent, the other five sides will be visible, and we will be able to see all six sides simultaneously. In like manner, if all surfaces are constructed of glass, plastic, or the surface area suggested by wire or dowels, we also see six sides, though not in their true shapes (*147-D*).

All of us have held a small box in our hands, a ring box or a cigarette package. Yet few of us have observed that we are able to see four of its sides at the same time. Even fewer of us have tried to draw this aspect of such a form. Yet out of this observation comes one of the most important graphic controls the artist uses. By discovering and exploiting the potential of binocular vision, a concept known as multiple station points becomes a reality, as we shall see in Chapter 19. But first we need to examine aspects of a graphic box-like structure which is known as the picture box.

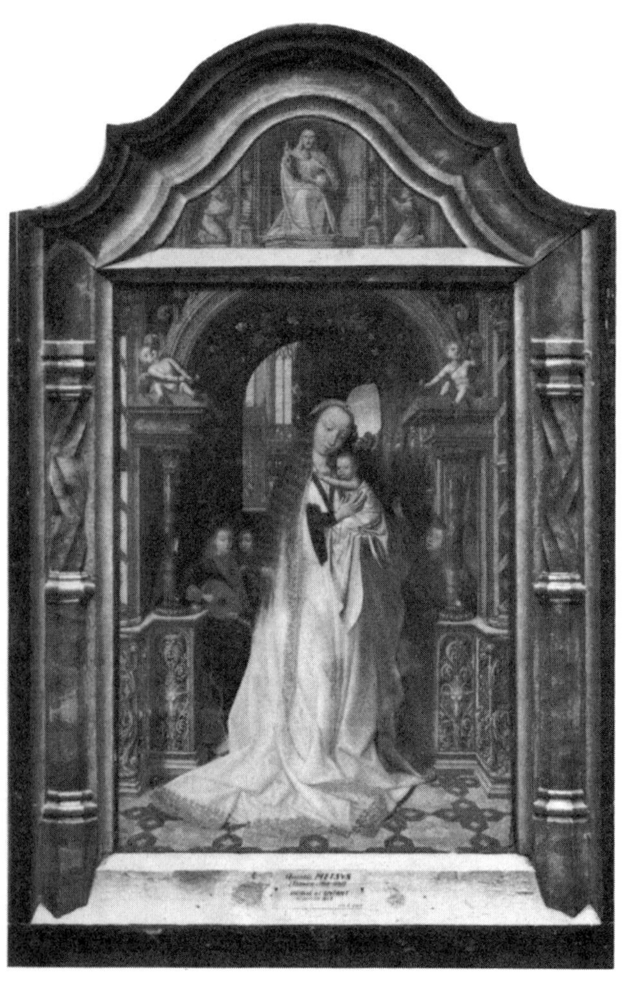

Quentin Metsys (Flemish, 1466?-1530)
MADONNA AND CHILD SURROUNDED BY ANGELS
1491-1515; oil on wood; 21⁷⁄₁₆″ x 14¾″
Musée des Beaux Arts de Lyon
(Photograph: J. Camponogara)

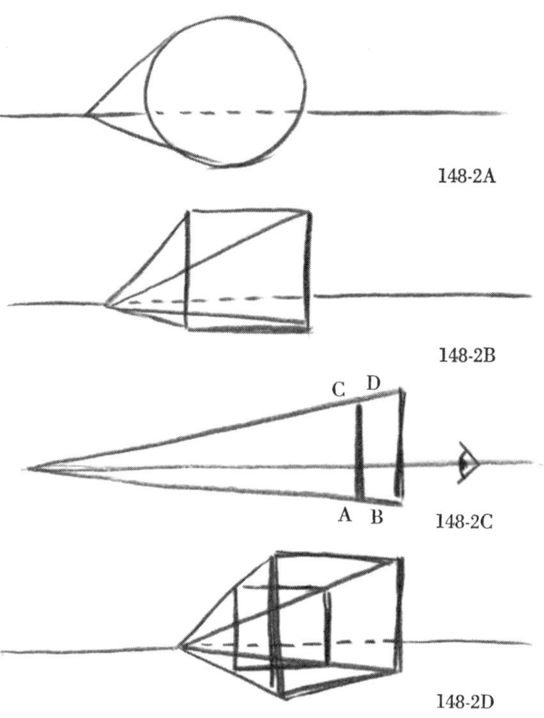




# 14  The Picture Box

## Limiting Picture Depth

Around this Metsys Madonna is a real box-like
frame enclosing and dramatizing the picture.
Within the picture is a painted box-like
structure enclosing and dramatizing the figure.
Let us see how this painted box helps picture
construction.

If we focus our eyes upon one point on the
horizon in nature we create, in effect, a visual
cone. Within this cone things seem in focus.
Things outside of the cone tend to blur. Great
distances will still be indeterminate, but
elements nearby in this cone of vision are
subject to measure (*148-2A*).

If we visualize this cone as a box-like
prism in perspective we relate it more closely
to our accustomed picture shape (*148-2B*).

Suppose now that at an estimated distance of
twenty-five to thirty feet we imagine our
prism interrupted by a backdrop (*148-2C*).

149-A

149-B

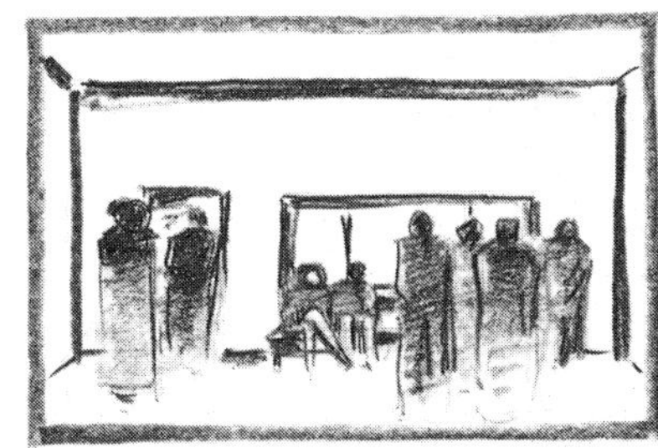

149-C

Everything in back will be cut off. In front of *A-B-C-D* is a shallow box (*148-2D*). Within this imaginary box true measurements can be suggested convincingly.

## The Nature of the Picture Box

The graphic box generated by the backdrop *A-B-C-D* is like a little stage, which is referred to as the *picture box*. As we shall see the picture box takes many forms and its use is constantly changing. But in its classic form it represents a small stage usually viewed from normal standing eye level and easily encompassed by the eye. The distance separating objects on this stage can easily be suggested graphically *(149-A)*.

Into a drawing of this little stage, the picture box, we may introduce any number of appropriate props or objects. A drawn chair or table will take up so much room in this stage, leaving a certain amount of clear floor space. These areas can be estimated visually and expressed graphically with great accuracy *(149-B)*.

Into this graphic stage dressed with graphic props we now can introduce as many symbols of living forms as we desire. Human figures, animals, growth forms of every description, real or imaginary, may be shown occupying the environment we have created in our picture box. The only limit we must impose is that the little stage be confined to shallow depth and a reasonable dimension from side to side or top to bottom *(149-C)*.

 **The Evolution of the Picture Box**
The picture box developed as a solution to
the problem of measuring shallow depth
both in nature and in pictures, a preoccupation
of the artist for thousands of years. Not until
the development of architecture, however, did
the creation of limited depth become a definite
picture problem. Unlimited depth was
suggested in the prehistoric rock paintings
of Europe and Africa long before the advent of
architecture. These pictures were actually
"free drawings" or vignettes. They were not
limited as to overall shape (rectangle, square,
oval), for the surfaces upon which they were
made were indeterminate as to shape and
widely varied in size.

Although tools, utensils, and weapons did
provide the prehistoric artist with some surfaces
of limited shape and size upon which he
could paint or draw, it was not until there were
real walls on which to work that the problem
of measuring depth became significant.

The wall has always been a key to an
understanding of pictures. How the artist
accepts or rejects the wall as a limitation of
graphic depth always affects his attitudes
toward, and his concepts of, picture structure.
Conversely, the construction of the wall
itself affects everything the artist paints upon it.

It is likely that much drawing started as
idle scratching on the ground with a sharp
stick or tool. Scratching the wall may have
been a natural and easy next step. In neither
case was pigment needed. As light falls on the
surface of a wall parts of the scratched or
incised lines catch more light than others. By
increasing the depth and width of a line this

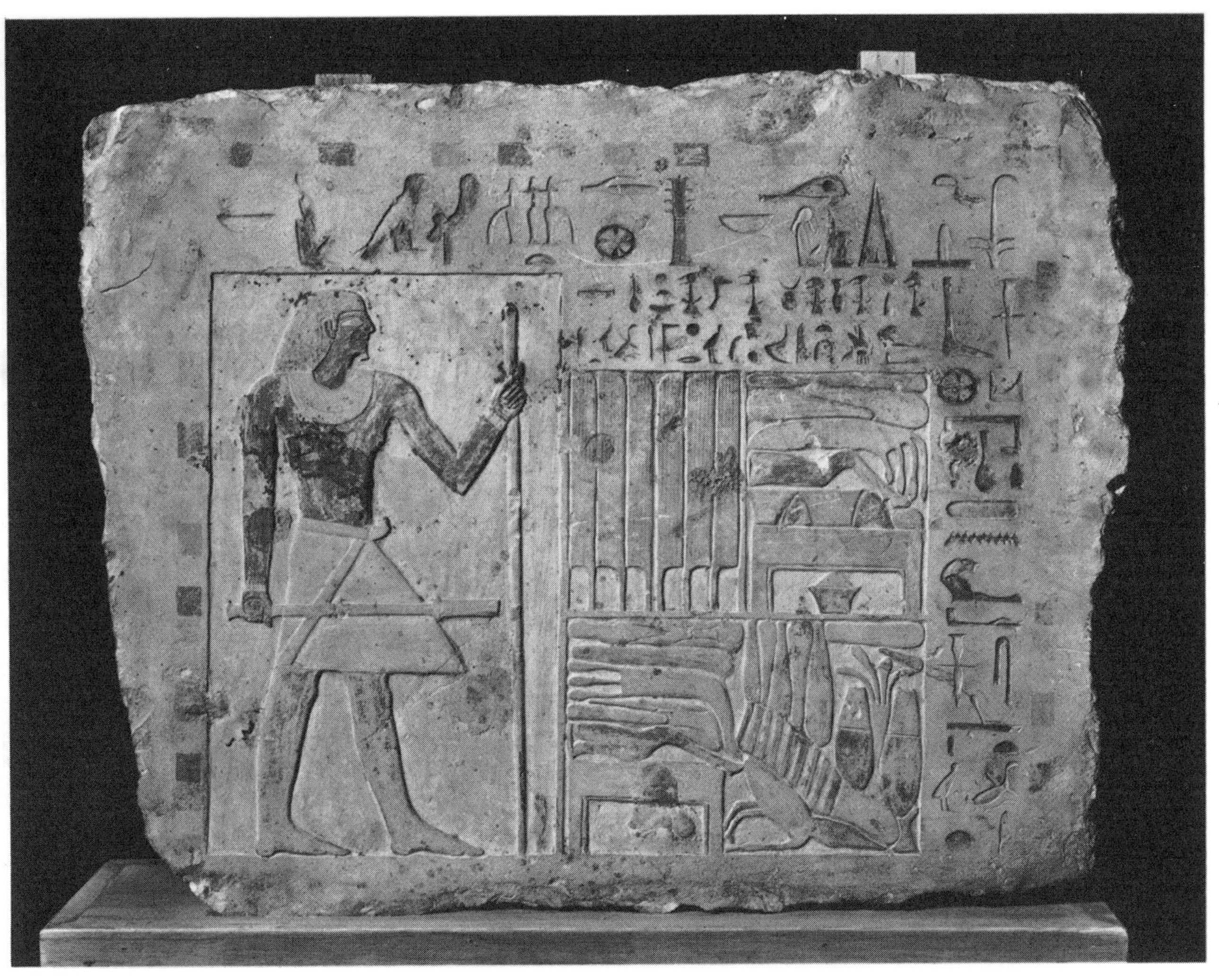

Artist unknown (Egyptian)
TJAWYET, SOLE COMPANION OF THE KING
ca. 2280 B.C.
Egyptian, first intermediate period; 18″ x 22″
limestone stele in intaglio carving with polychrome
Seattle Art Museum; Thomas D. Stimson Memorial Collection
Gift of Mrs. Thomas D. Stimson and Hagop Kevorkian

varying pattern can be changed at will. Of course such a drawing will change as the light source changes, both as to position and intensity.

It is a short step from incised drawing to shallow modeling of sculptural forms, to bas-relief. Such sculpture is a strange and wonderful bridge between drawing and true sculpture in the round.

For example, the image of the head on a coin really is not a drawing in two dimensions, nor is it truly three-dimensional, for much of its depth is merely implied. Behind the head is a flat surface slightly deeper than the rim or the highest projection of the head. This neutral plane acts as a backdrop which shuts out any visual penetration past it.

The ancient Egyptians explored the technique of bas-relief which they developed to a high degree of excellence, discovering both its merits and weaknesses. They soon discovered that incising with line does not perceptibly weaken the strength of the wall, nor does shallow carving. If, however, they attempted to indicate effects of deep space as observed in nature in the carving, the physical and visual strength of the wall was weakened. Possibly another factor dictating the depth of the carving was the amount of labor involved; obviously, the deeper the carving, the harder the work.

The Egyptians rigorously maintained the backdrop or shut-off plane in their bas-reliefs and achieved a limited amount of actual depth in their carvings. At the same time they preserved both actual and visual strength in the walls.

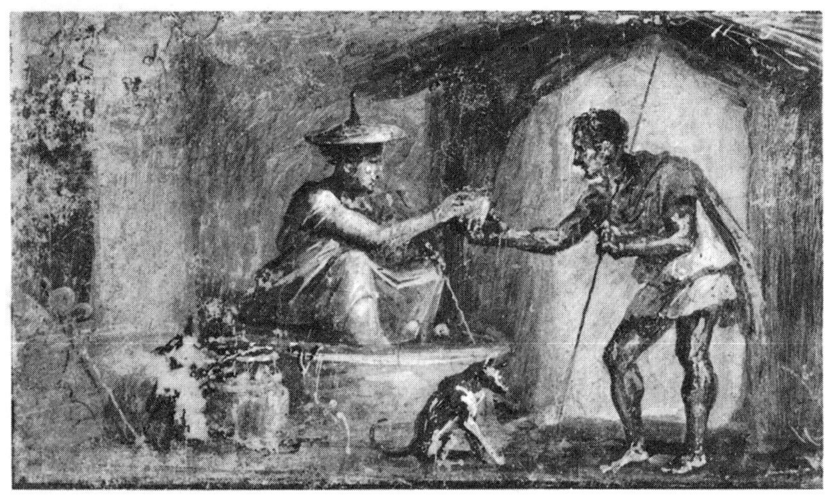

Artist unknown (Roman)
EPISODE IN THE TRAVELS OF ULYSSES
Mural in House of the Dioscuri, Pompeii
1st cent. B.C.; wall painting
Museo Nazionale, Naples
(Photograph: Alinari—Art Reference
Bureau, Inc., N. Y., and
Fototeca Unione, Rome)

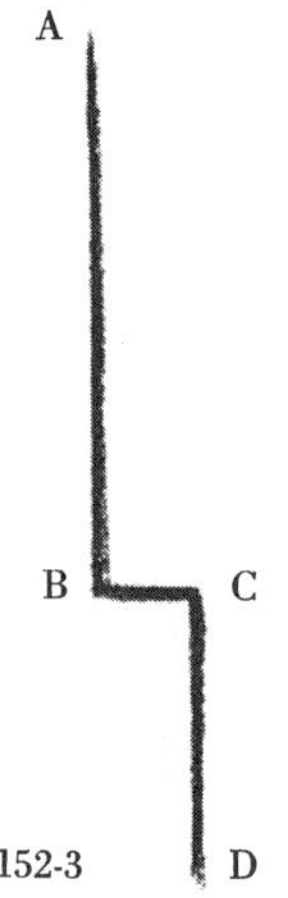

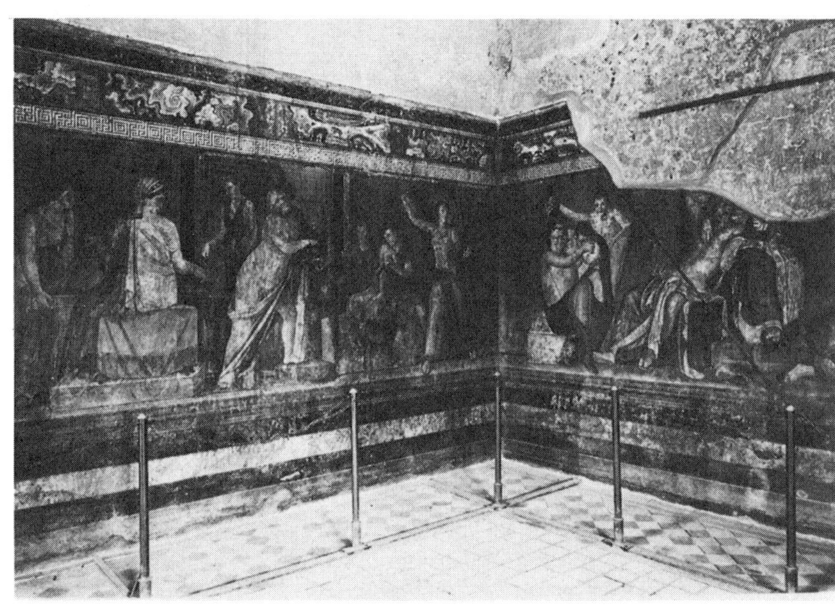

Artist unknown (Roman)
WALL PAINTINGS from the Villa of Mysteries
Pompeii, ca. 50 B.C. Museo Nazionale, Naples
(Photograph: German Archaeological Inst.
Rome, and Fototeca Unione, Rome)

152 From this awareness of the wall's integrity, of its strength and usefulness, came a feeling of respect for the wall, whether decorated or not, which has been handed down by the artist through centuries. He may respect or deliberately violate the integrity of the wall, but he can never ignore the wall itself.

Turning from carving to painting, we observe that the Egyptian painter, who was so intimately related to the tradition of bas-relief, also devised a shut-off plane to limit the depth of his painted picture. In many instances this plane is made to appear as a wall against which figures, animals, plant forms are represented in very shallow depth. In many instances the paintings approach the limited depth of a bas-relief. On the painted or simulated shut-off wall, hieroglyphics often are introduced which, in turn, remind us of the shut-off wall.

In a sense this shut-off plane can be compared to the rear wall of the picture box, for their function is the same. Both limit the picture to shallow depth. But the idea of a picture box as a little stage, a room giving an actual feeling of walls and ceilings enclosing a given space, was not fully realized as a structural factor in picture making by the Egyptians.

In the House of the Dioscuri in Pompeii we find a wall painting, *Episode in the Travels of Ulysses,* which seems to be a bridge between the Egyptian structure involving the shut-off wall and the true realization of the picture box which we find in the early Renaissance. Here we see figures occupying deep space on a stage which implies a ceiling. The characters may well be in a cave which opens into passageways, in turn suggesting added depth.

In the murals of this room in Pompeii we again find a strong bridge from the flat

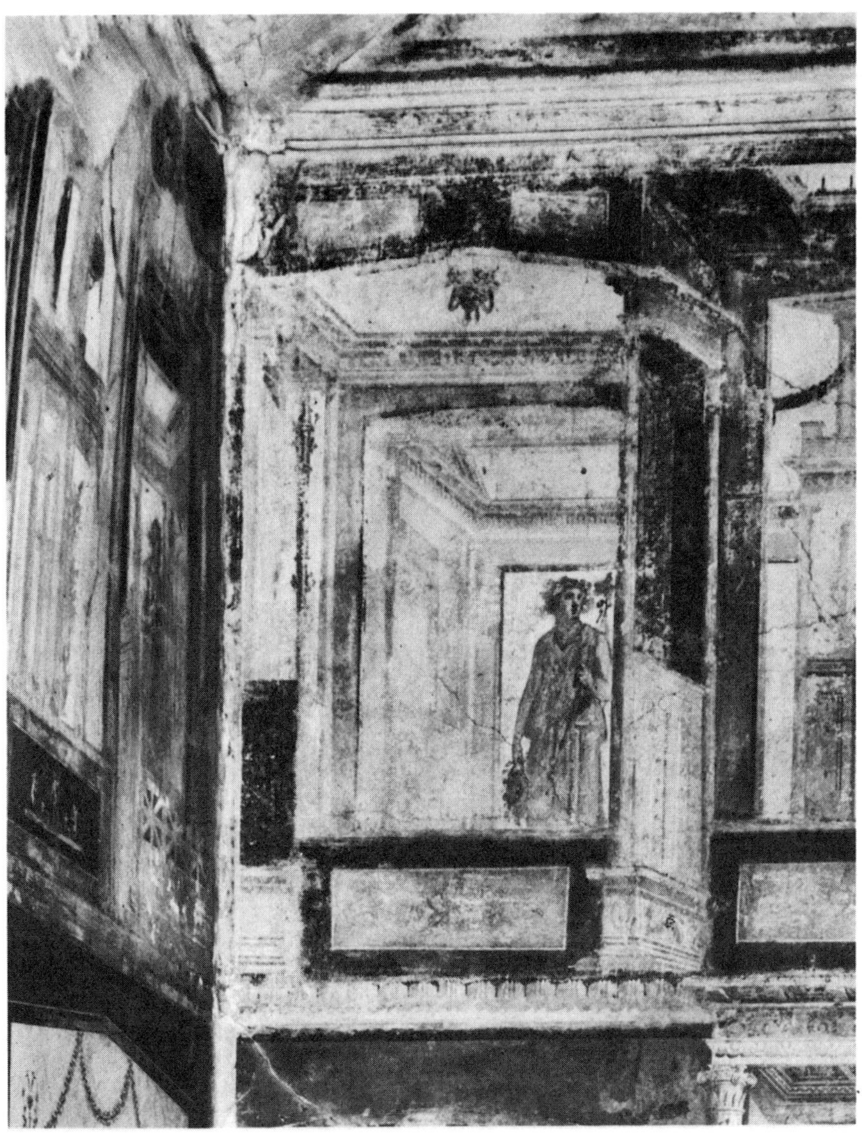

Artist unknown (Roman)
DETAIL OF WALL PAINTING, Ixion Room
House of the Vetti, Pompeii, 63-79 A.D.
Museo Nazionale, Naples

(Photograph: Anderson, Alinari, Rome
Art Reference Bureau, Inc., N. Y. and
Fototeca Unione, Rome)

decorated surface into deep space. We might say that here is half a picture box. On the painted surface *BC* the characters stand as if on a shallow stage (*152-3*). Their heads, however, are silhouetted against surfaces which are defined by rigid panels in the true surface of the wall. *A-D* defines the location of the panels, and also the true surface of the wall. *C-D* defines the front surface of the little stage which visually seems to be some distance in front of the panels. *A-B* and *C-D,* however, are actually in the plane of the wall. By covering the upper parts of the figures, the reality of the space generated on the little stage is apparent. When the lower parts of the figures are covered the shallowness of the space generated by the heads is noticeable.

In the Ixion room in the House of the Vetti, Pompeii, appears a small panel in which a true stage is represented by posts and beams defining a limited space, a true picture box. In it is indicated a single figure, an actor on the stage.

153

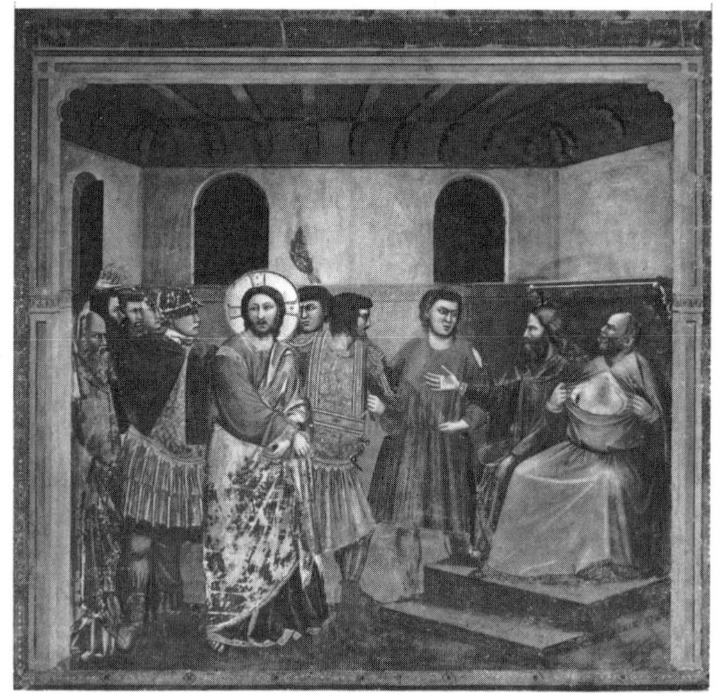

Giotto (Florentine—1266?-1337)
CHRIST BEFORE CAIPHAS, 1305-1306
fresco, Scrovegni Chapel, Padua
(Photograph: Alinari—Art Reference
Bureau Inc., N. Y.)

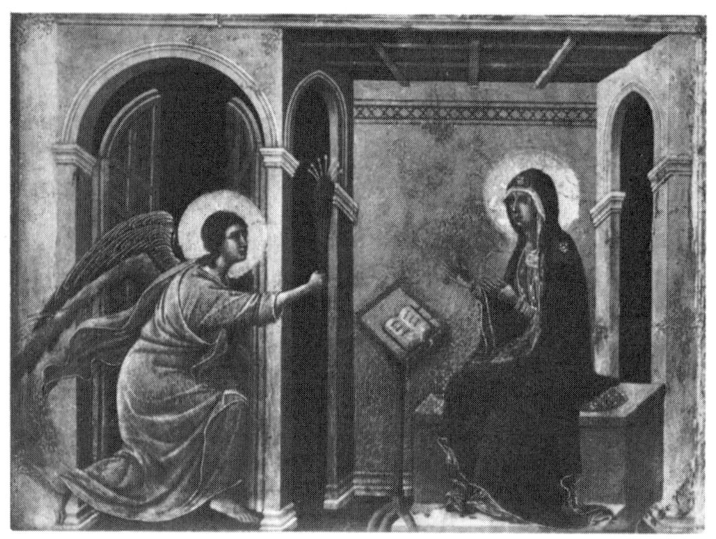

Duccio (Italian, ca. 1255-1319)
ANNUNCIATION OF THE DEATH OF MARY
from Maesta Altar; Siena, 1308-1311
Opera della Metropolitan di Siena, Italy
(Photograph: Alinari—Art Reference
Bureau Inc., N. Y., and Fototeca Unione, Rome)

154     About 1300 A.D. in Italy, we find the beginning of the classic picture box in Western painting. Between 1305 and 1306, Giotto painted the great frescoes in the Arena Chapel in Padua. Here we find examples of the picture box as a true stage enclosed by three walls, a floor, and a ceiling. In *Christ Before Caiphas* we have a stage on which all the action is taking place.

Duccio, between 1308 and 1311, developed the picture box idea with an ingenious variation, introducing a double stage in his *Annunciation of the Death of Mary*. In effect we look into space on the right and through a volume on the left.

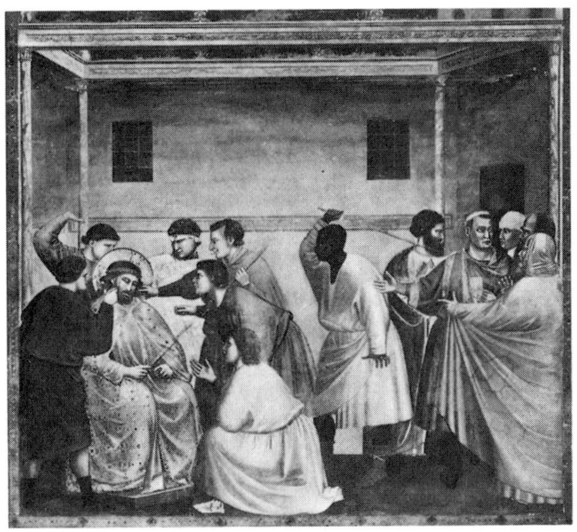

Giotto (Florentine, 1266-1337)
CHRIST DERIDED (THE FLAGELLATION),
1305-1306; fresco; Scrovegni Chapel, Padua
(Photograph: Anderson, Alinari—Art
Reference Bureau, Inc., N. Y.)

Giotto
THE MERCHANTS DRIVEN FROM THE TEMPLE
(Photograph: Anderson, Alinari—Art
Reference Bureau, Inc., N. Y.)

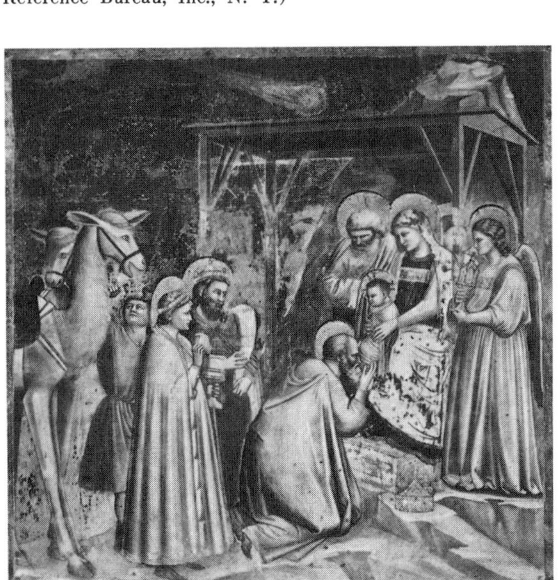

Giotto
ADORATION OF THE MAGI
(Photograph: Anderson, Alinari—Art
Reference Bureau, Inc., N. Y.)

In *Christ Derided,* by Giotto, the actors are partially inside and partially outside an inner box which redefines in skeletal form the true picture box.

In *The Merchants Driven from the Temple,* the picture box has been opened to become a scene out of doors, but opened to only a certain degree. In place of the backdrop of our little stage, Giotto has substituted an architectural structure reminiscent of a second stage. All the action takes place before this empty stage. By association, we sense that the actors are in a confined space much like that of the empty architectural stage. The empty cages also play a part in echoing this sense of measurable depth.

And in Giotto's *Adoration of the Magi,* we find a shelter, again reminiscent of the picture box, shown more closely related to a true landscape. Rocks, sky, and the star are introduced, yet they are still held in seemingly shallow depth. Here again part of the action is restricted to the little stage formed by the shelter, part to the shallow depth in front of it. In this case the shelter as a space box contains and emphasizes the Holy Family, yet restricts the amount of depth we experience.

A thorough study of Giotto's frescoes will reveal an astounding number of variations on the classic picture box. The picture box idea has been used by a great number of artists ever since Giotto's time.

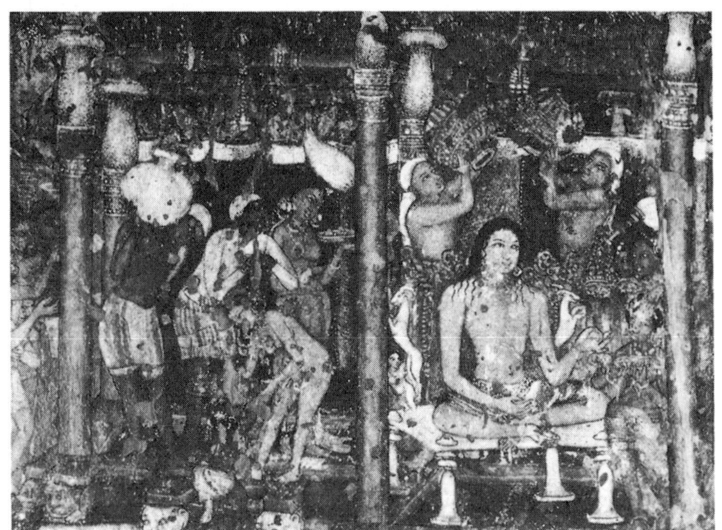

Artist unknown (Indian)
BUDDHA'S BATH, mural from Cave 1
Ajanta, India
Courtesy Archaeological Survey of India
and the Minister of Education
Government of India, New Delhi

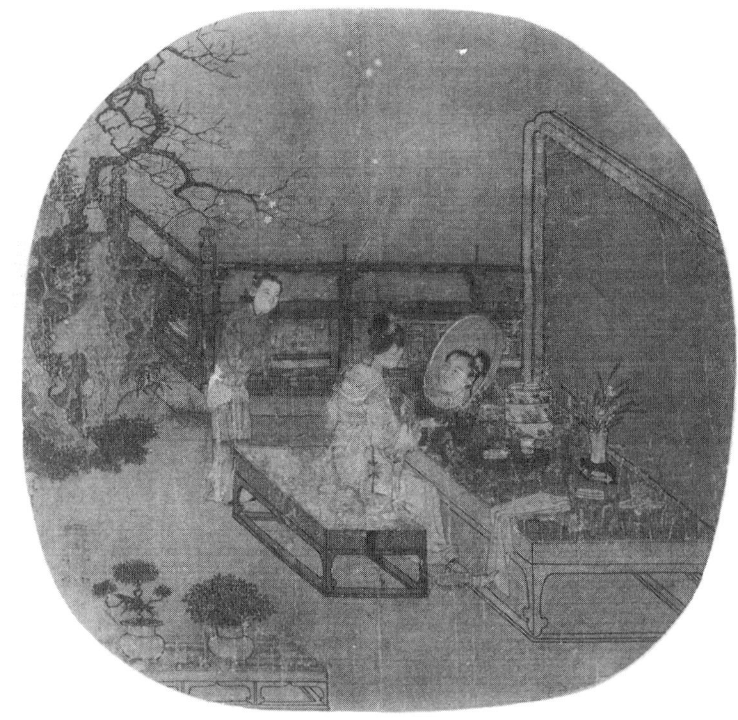

Su Han-Ch'en (Chinese, ca. 1115-1170)
LADY BEFORE A MIRROR IN A GARDEN; Sung Dynasty
early 12th cent.; 7″ x 10″
fan-shaped album leaf; color on silk
Courtesy Museum of Fine Arts, Boston
Ross Collection

156 Western painters were not alone in utilizing the picture box. In the Ajanta caves of India are many examples. These caves, excavated and decorated some time between 272 to 231 B.C., and 700 A.D., represent a startling bridge between the deep space structures of the Renaissance and the stylization of the true Oriental paintings. Interestingly enough, the caves are geographically almost halfway between Tokyo and Rome as the crow flies. A close study of these paintings will reveal the ingenious use of architecture in the control of picture depth.

In Chinese art vast spaces are often depicted, yet we also find the picture box concept. In *Lady Before a Mirror*, we find the background and foreground abstracted into one plane. Part of the scene suggests the confinement of an interior; part, however, leads us into a garden, an extension into deep space. Only through the picture box concept could such a picture be possible.

In this Hokusai we see another extension of the picture box. In this case the conventional stage contains the actors and props. The back of the stage, however, has been removed, and a scene of Fuji substituted. Although the mountain is shown at a great distance from the room, in effect, the scene might be a painted backdrop on a stage. There is little suggestion of space beyond the room.

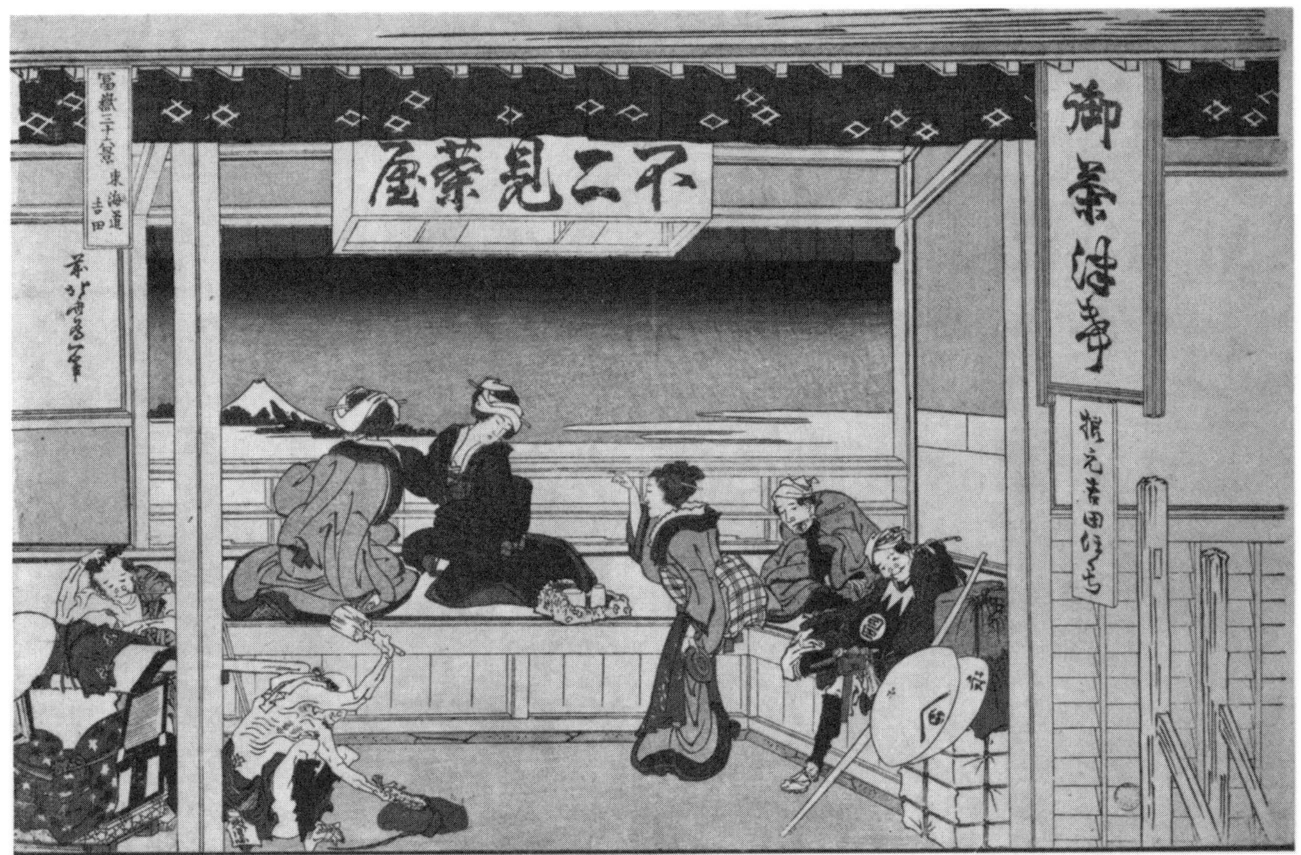

Katsushika Hokusai (Japanese, 1760-1849)
YOSHIDA ON THE TOKAIDO, from
"The Thirty-Six Views of Fuji"
1823-1829; woodblock
The Metropolitan Museum of Art
Rogers Fund

## Limited Use of the Picture Box

The picture box is but one of the methods that we employ to control depth in a picture. For certain kinds of space problems it is the easiest and most useful. However, there are times when its use is not only questionable but inadequate.

An artist involved in depicting great depths will find the picture box concept of little value. We also must remember that not all artists are concerned with limiting depth in a picture. To many artists a sense of unlimited space, a lifelike "window" effect, not strictly controlled depth, is the aim. Yet the picture box is a classic structure which should be part of the practicing artist's vocabulary of skills, for it introduces disciplines of thinking indispensable in the solution of other types of picture structure problems.

The picture box symbolizes our concern for a measurable depth in a picture, which in turn can be coordinated directly to the surface pattern of the picture. Disregard of these factors may lead to undesirable realism, or uncontrolled space, and usually weakens the surface pattern.

As we shall see, a true understanding of the picture box necessitates a special concept of space, a special way of looking at a picture, and certain procedural steps in the actual making of a picture. In our next chapter we shall show how the first step in the control of the picture box, as well as of more complex picture structure, concerns plan and elevation.

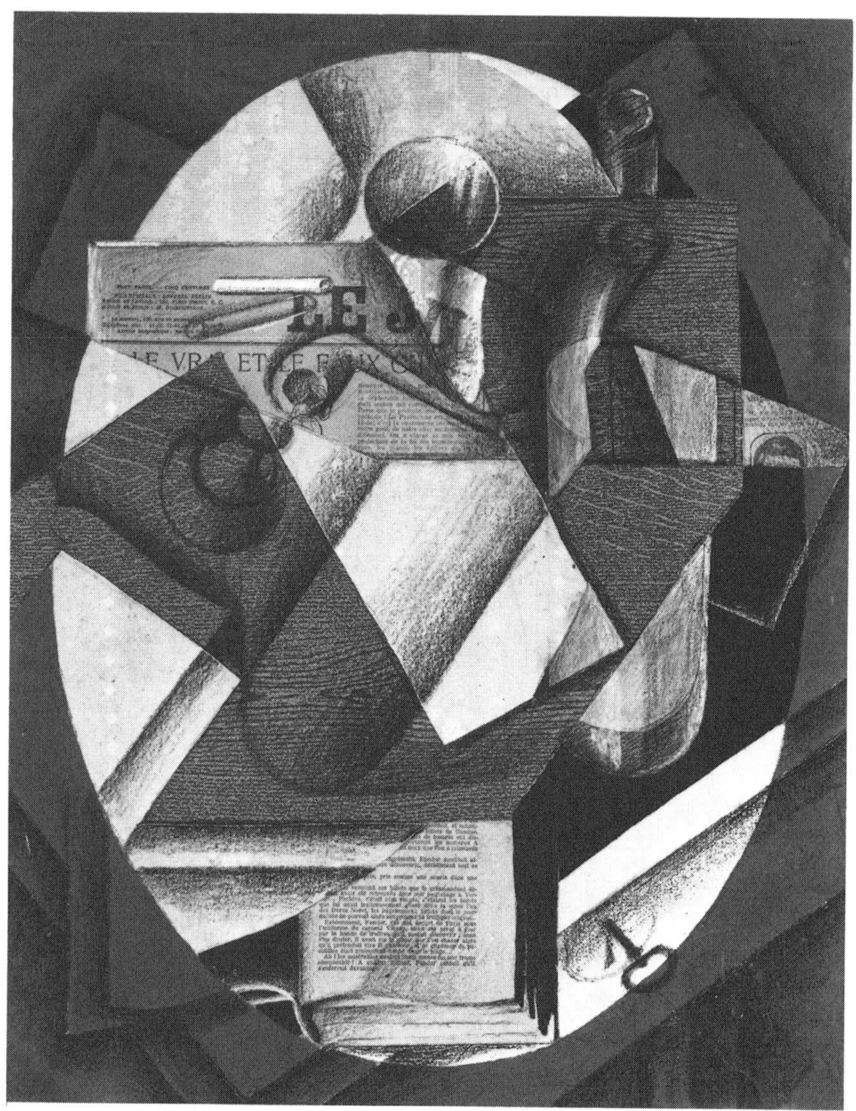

Juan Gris (Spanish, 1887-1927)
STILL LIFE, 1914; 23½″ x 17½″
charcoal, colored papers, printed matter
Philadelphia Museum of Art
A. E. Gallatin Collection
(Photograph: A. J. Wyatt)



# 15 Plan and Elevation

**The Effect of Plan on Our Lives**

Plan is the relation of objects to the intervening space between them, as Juan Gris emphasizes in this still life. Although most of us are not consciously concerned about plan as we lead our daily lives, all of us are in a strange way controlled by plan. When we walk across a room, whether we are aware of it or not, the placement of the furniture affects the direction of our action. The relation of hills to valleys has much to do with our choice of a home-site. The relation of the number of floors to the height of an office building may determine whether we take the elevator or climb the stairs.

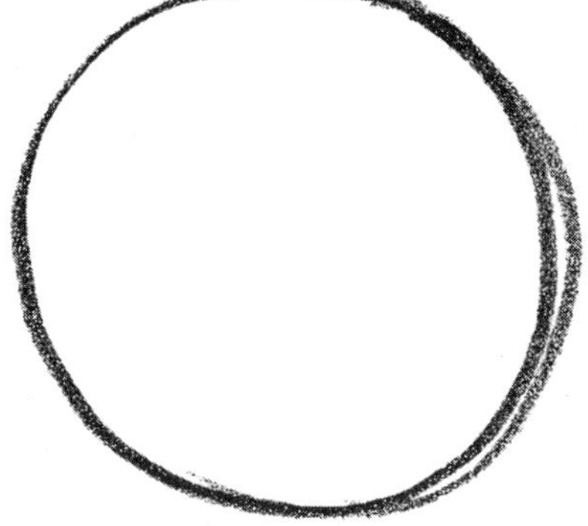

159-A

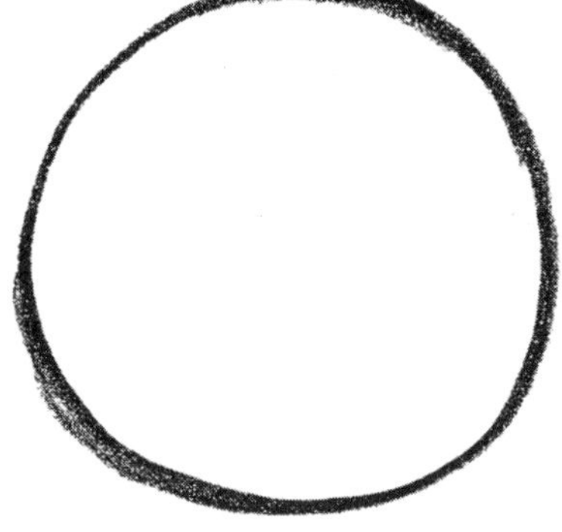

159-B

Not only does the space between forms suggest possible action, but at times it may dictate what we may actually do. To get through a mountain we must go through the tunnel. If we are playing baseball and make a a two-base hit, we must touch first base before going to second. If we are playing chess, we know that the moves of the pieces are limited by the squares of the board. Not only does plan affect action in our everyday environment, but our concept and application of plan profoundly affects our picture structure.

## Observed Plan versus Conceptual Plan

To vary the old saying "a penny for your thoughts," let us give a few thoughts to your penny. For how we look at a penny has special significance in relation to our understanding of plan.

Let us place a penny on a horizontal drawing surface, then look directly down upon it from a foot or so above. If we use only one eye, the penny will look perfectly round. Now let us trace the penny with our pencil. When we remove the penny the tracing will be almost a true circle, the same size as the penny (*159-A*).

Some distance away from the penny on our drawing surface, let us place a marble the same diameter as the penny. When we look directly down upon it, the marble will appear sculptural, three-dimensional. Now if we trace its silhouette upon the surface, the tracing will be another circle, the same size as the diameter of the marble and the penny (*159-B*).

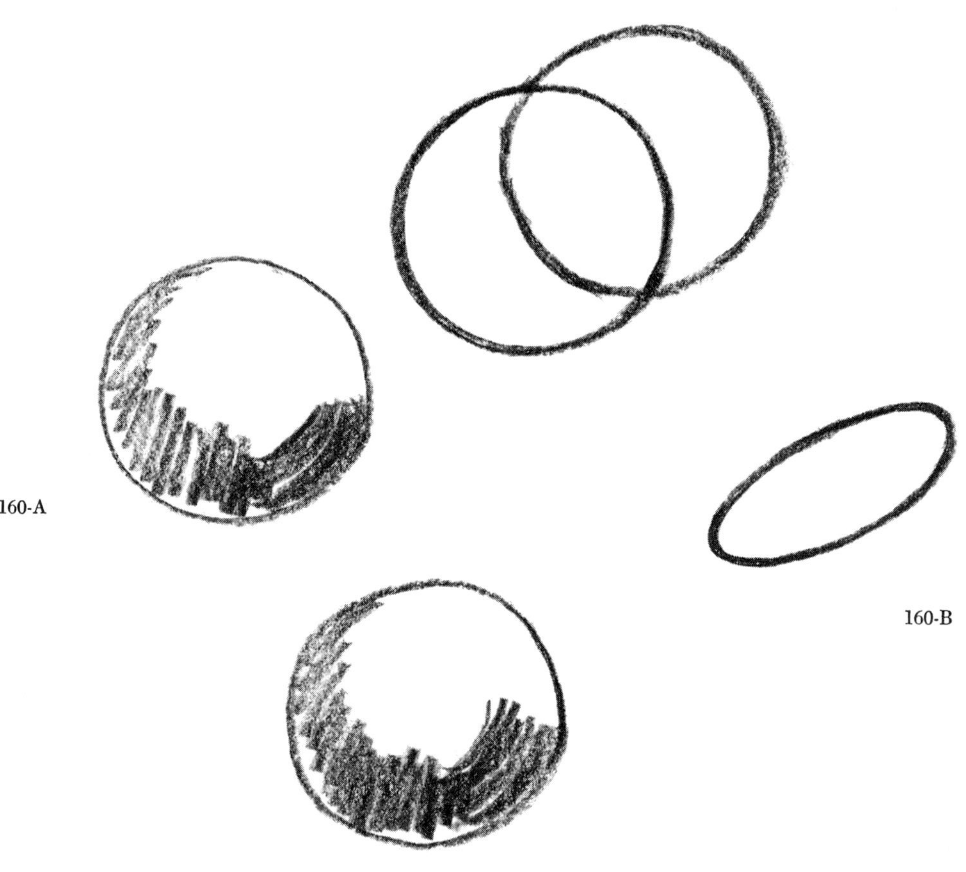




Now let us place the penny about a diameter away from the marble. When we look directly down on the marble, it will be in focus (*160-A*). The penny will be very slightly out of focus, slightly blurred. At first glance both penny and marble appear round. Now let us move the penny farther and farther away from the marble. As we continue to view the marble from our original viewpoint directly above it, a strange effect occurs. As long as we stare at the marble, we cannot see the penny clearly. As the penny is moved farther and farther away, it continues to become more blurred. If, however, without changing the position of our head, we glance over at the penny, we find that it is now in focus and seems to have changed shape. It now appears elliptical (*160-B*).

What actually has happened is that we have changed our plan view of the marble to a perspective view of the penny. For theoretically there may be only one observed plan view, or true view, at any given instant. Everything else we see is in perspective.

Let us again assume a true view of our marble which we have represented as a circle. To actually see the penny in its true shape we would have to move our eye to a position directly above its circle drawn on the surface. The distance between the centers of the circles represents the physical shift the eye would have to make to see each as a true shape involving no perspective.

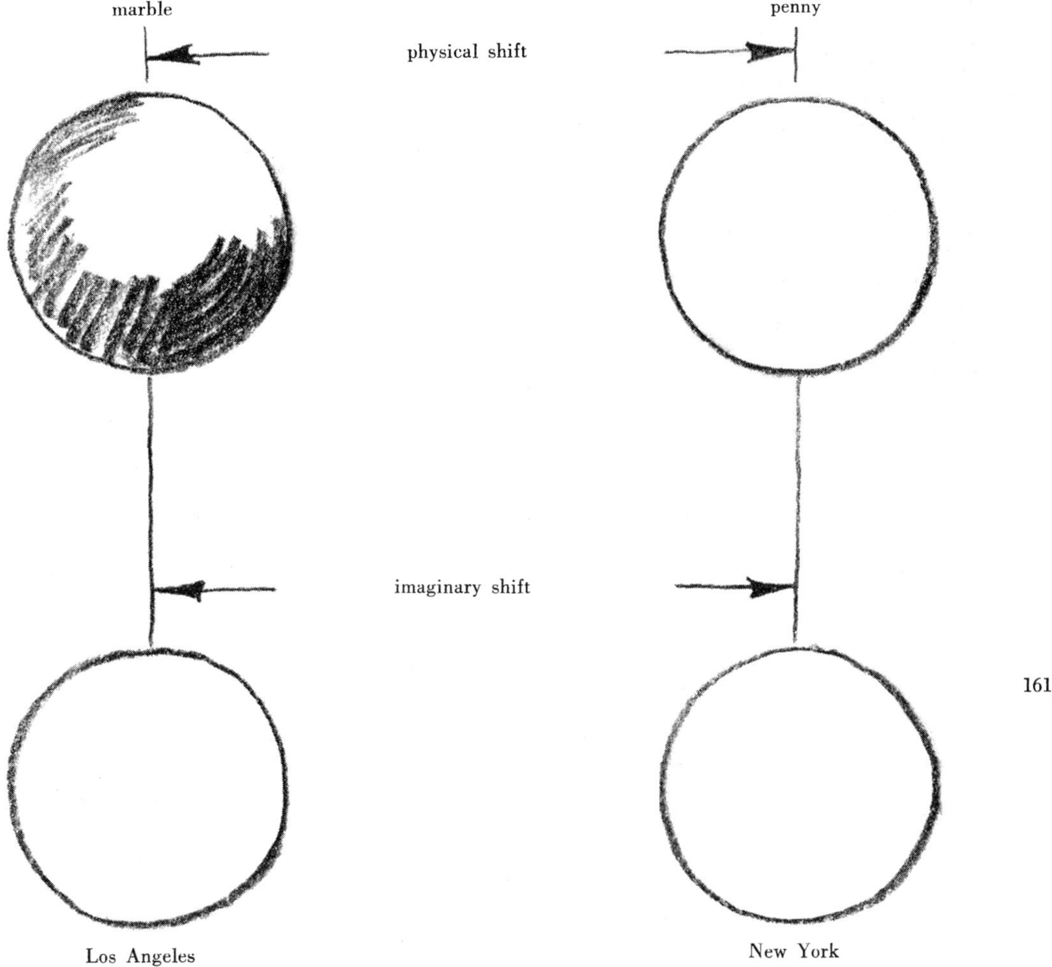



The interval between the circles represents the distance between two true views, whether these views are actually experienced by an observer or not. By accepting the possibility that two independent true views may be represented in one drawing involving no perspective, we introduce a new concept of drawing.

In such a drawing, the position of the observer is abandoned. In fact, the very presence of an observer is no longer necessary, for the dimensions of the true views may be arrived at conceptually. The distance between true views now becomes a part of the composite drawing and ceases to represent an actual shift of an observer. It becomes a finite distance, unaffected by perspective.

The interval between the centers of our two circles represents the distance between two points in space. It might as easily represent the distance between two towns (*161*) or the distance between the earth and a star. Both the interval and the true views have changed function from something observed to something imagined.

As we pursue the development of the true view drawing, which is called an *orthographic projection*, we find that various aspects of this subject have developed into different systems of drawing: isometric projection, descriptive geometry, and the measured Italian perspective. Although all systems of drawing should be of interest to the artist, it is not possible or desirable to explore these at this time. Specific information pertaining to any of these drawing systems may be obtained in any library.

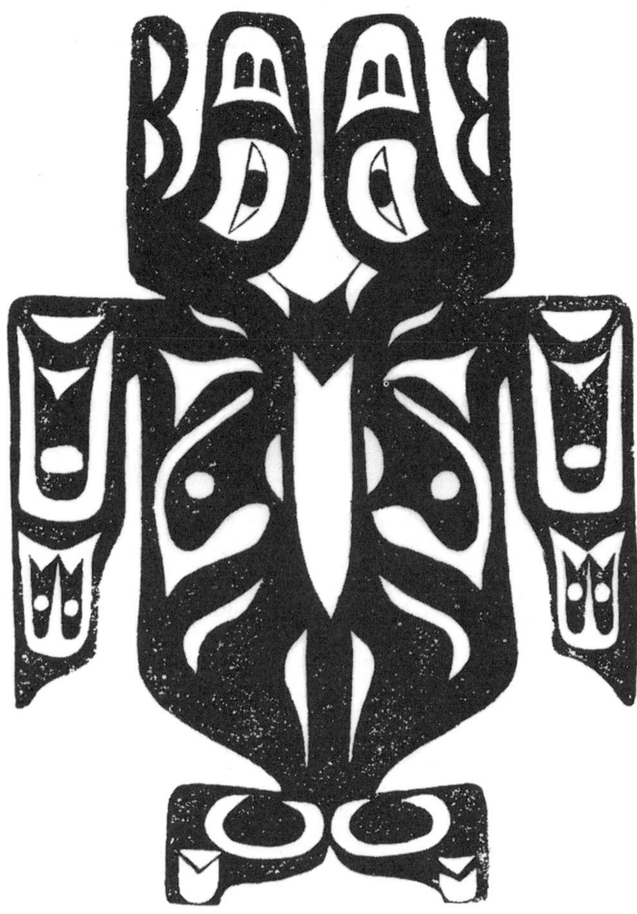

Copy of Haida Indian design of KILLER WHALE from *Indian Art of the United States*; copyright 1941, The Museum of Modern Art, New York

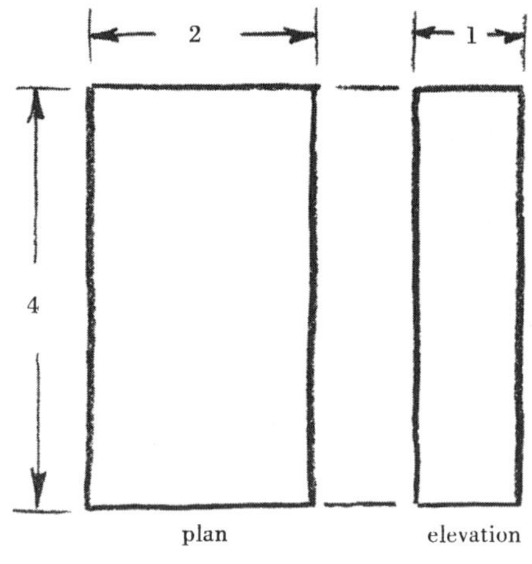



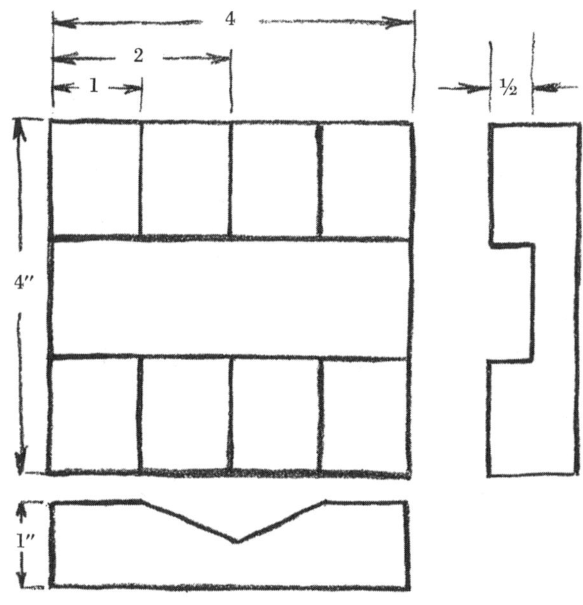



162  We should note, however, that by means of orthographic projection the dimensions of a structure, whether built or not yet built, may be represented. The construction or manufacture of all man-made structures is contingent upon some use of this system, which implies ordered methods of recording true measurements.

In making such a drawing, the size of the combination of true views and their indicated dimensions often are rather small. If the extreme dimensions employed are less than the size of the drawing surface upon which they are made, they may be indicated true size. If larger, they may be indicated by means of scaling. In such a drawing, an inch may represent a mile, or a fraction of an inch, or any imaginable distance.

Primitive artists, children, and the Cubists show an understanding of the logic of a plan view in their pictures. Often no other view explains a form so convincingly, as we see in this Haida design representing a killer whale.

## Plan and the Perspective Elevation

A plan view may or may not be a true view of a structure. For instance, a plan view of a pitched roof in no way gives us a true view of any of its pitching planes. A drawing showing a plan view can never truly describe a three-dimensional structure; other views are necessary.

At times one extra view will give us adequate information, as we see in this drawing, termed "a two-view," of a simple box (*162-2*).

Usually a three-view is necessary to show various aspects of even a simple structure. An architect may use a great number of drawings to explain the structure of a small house, not to mention a skyscraper (*162-3*).

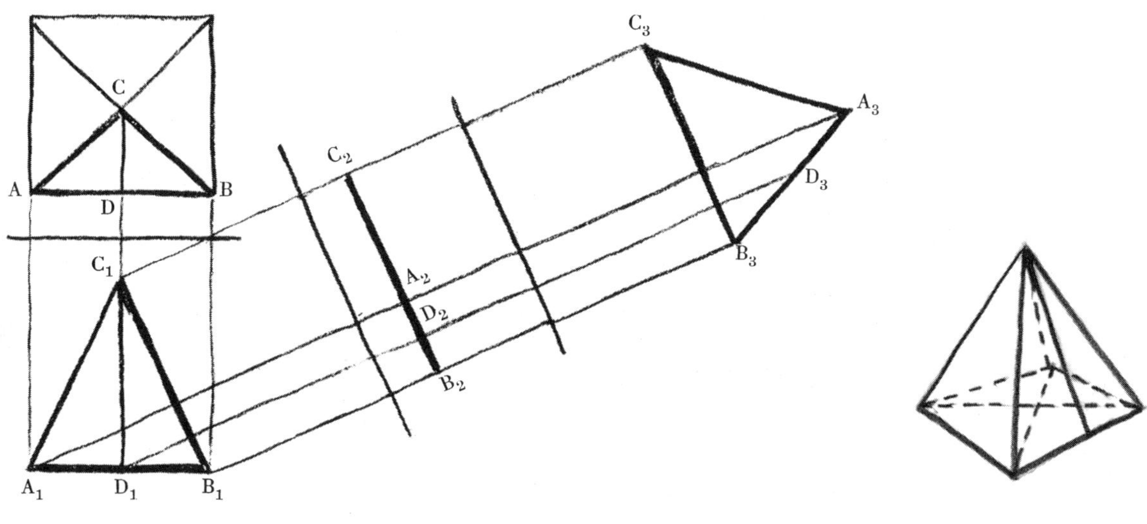


Truly complex structures usually cannot be described with only three views. Information about the construction of even seemingly simple structures, a pyramid for instance, can only be described with auxiliary views. Such drawings fall into the category of descriptive geometry. In this case neither the plan view *ABCD,* nor the elevation $A_1B_1C_1D_1$, describes the true shape of the side of the pyramid. A view $A_2B_2C_2D_2$ gives an edge view, and $A_3B_3C_3D_3$ gives a true view which, like all true views, can be dimensioned (*163*).

To read such drawings takes a special way of thinking. We must learn to build up a mental image of the form being described. This can be done by comparing several views of the form: top view, end view, side view, etc. From the information thus gathered, a concept of the appearance of the complete form emerges. The composite is imaginary.

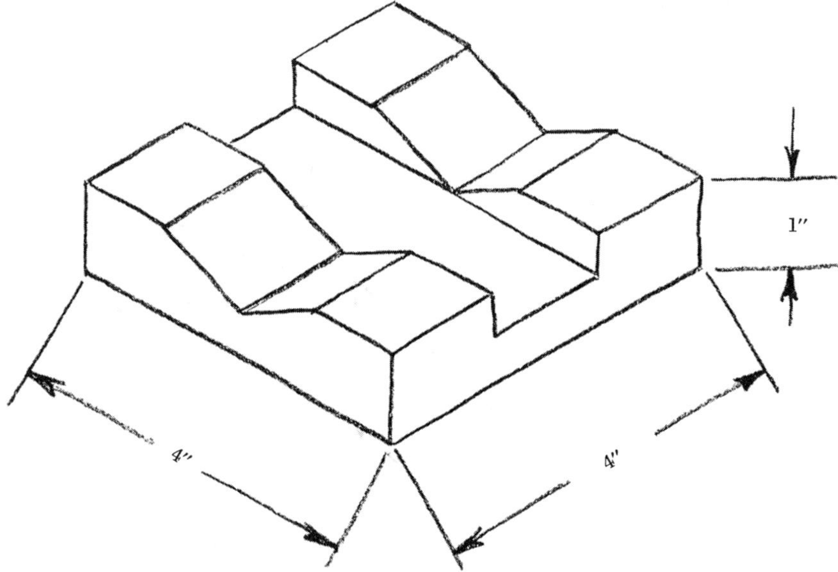



To describe this form to someone not able to read an orthographic projection, other devices must be employed. Either the finished structure must be at hand for demonstration purposes, or perhaps a scale model. Or the true dimensions shown in the three-view may be transposed into an isometric drawing. Here, as shown in our slotted block, the use of true dimensions are incorporated in one drawing (*164*). An isometric, however, always results in a drawing which appears distorted. It is strange that a perspective drawing developed from plans and elevations must be constructed with false views in order to simulate what we might expect to see as "true" in nature.

A perspective drawing implies the presence of a spectator and at least one observation point, or station point. The drawing represents a view of anything, from a single form to a crowd scene, seen from this station point. Theoretically only one element in a perspective drawing is in its true shape. But by the adaptation of certain conventions more than one true view may be introduced. For instance, all shapes parallel to the picture surface, if near the center of the picture, are drawn in true shape.

As we have noted, a perspective drawing is constructed upon lines that seem to converge in the distance. Such a drawing, in this case pulled apart, or "exploded," shows us that it is made up of separate false or distorted views (*165*). When these parts are assembled and seen simultaneously in one drawing, an image is created in some respects corresponding to what we see in nature.

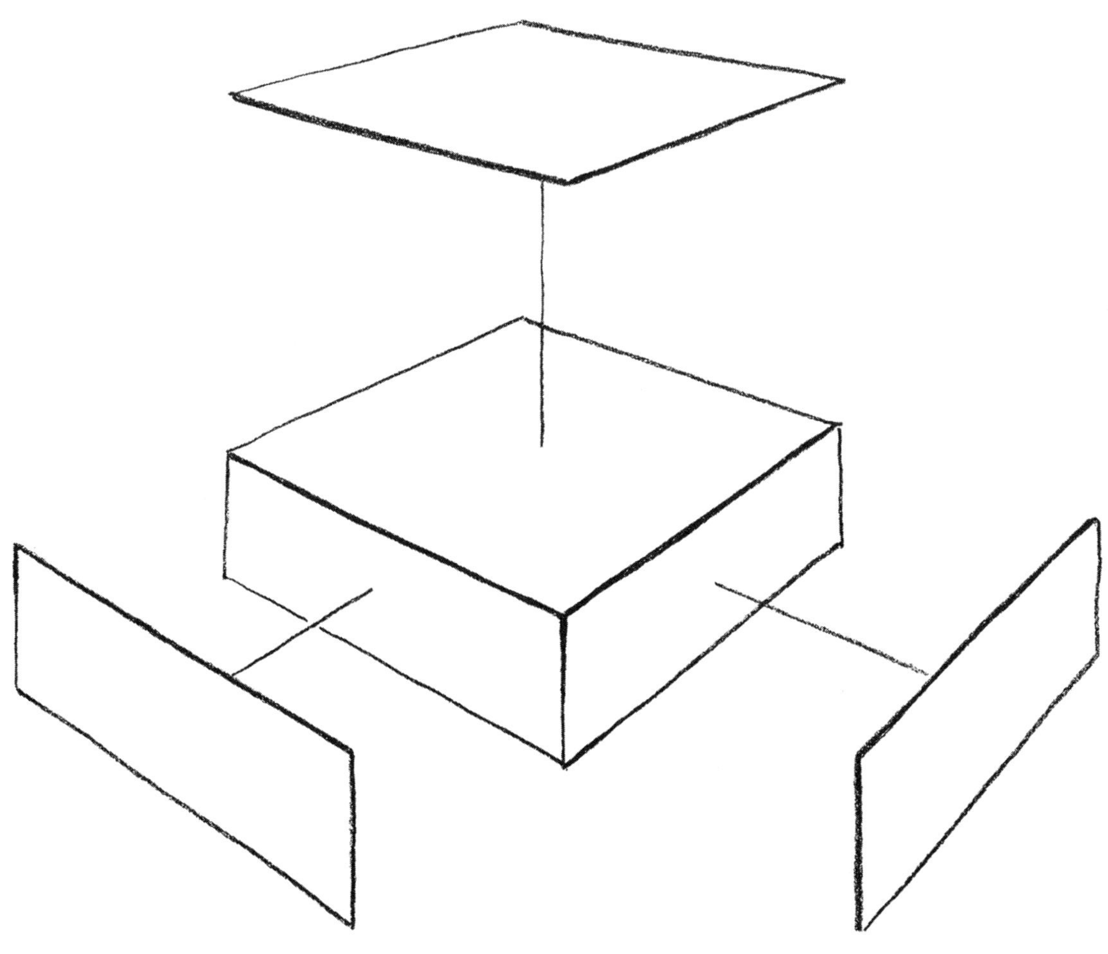



Developing Italian perspectives from plan is necessary in the construction of some pictures. For instance, such perspective views are used extensively in making informative drawings of all kinds. In planning motion pictures, the set designer plots the exact placement of the cameras in relation to the finished set, using carefully made perspective drawings generated from architectural plans. By plotting the position of the cameras in plan and the type of lens to be used, he can then show quite accurately, in perspective drawings, the anticipated appearance of the finished scene.

In all applications of perspective projection rigid limits must be observed. Much of the drawing is mechanical in nature and usually requires drafting instruments. To attain good results, the artist must be highly skilled not only in projection but also in the general skills: color, design, and draftsmanship.

To a tremendous number of artists who make freehand illustrative pictures, perspective projection is objectionable. The whole idea of anything so mechanical is distasteful. This attitude may be based to a great degree upon a lack of understanding of the mechanics of Italian perspective, or upon a lack of realization of the advantages inherent in the use of plan in relation to many perspective drawings.

To overcome some of the objections to the use of conventional plan in picture making, let us first try to discover simple freehand procedures in a field which is so obviously mechanical and complex. Then let us examine a few advantages of using plan in a free way to help make the composing of certain types of pictures more interesting and exciting.

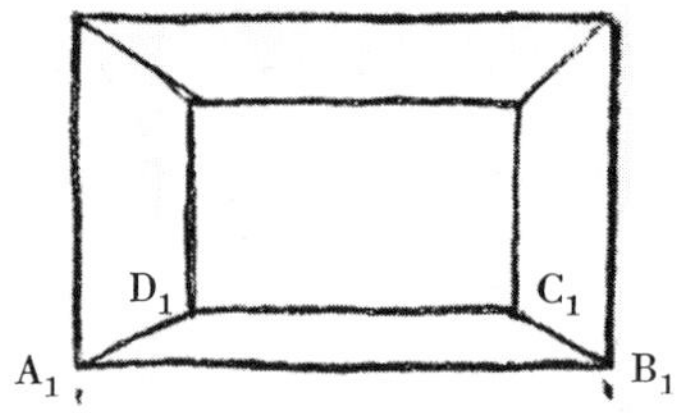


166-B

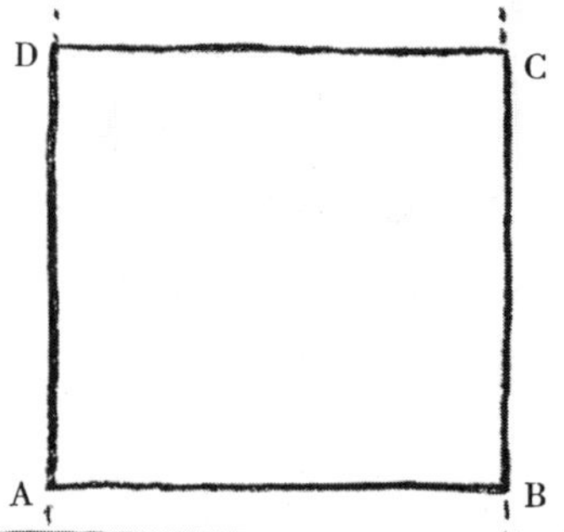


166-A

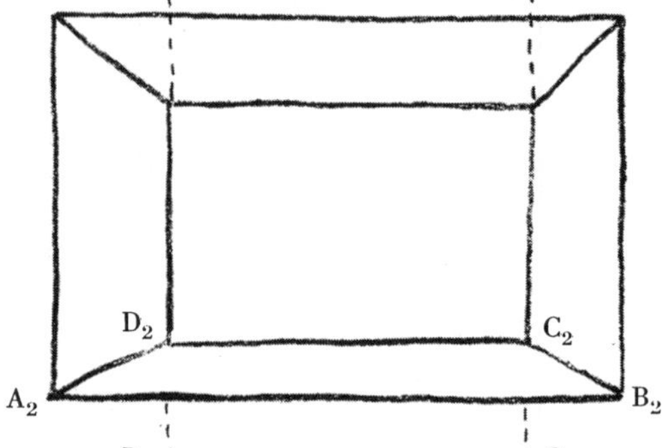


166-C

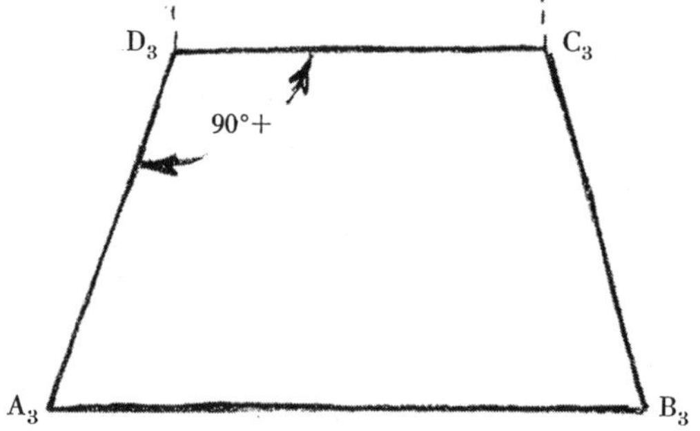


166-D



## Conventional and Non-Conventional Projection

Let us discuss for a moment the conventional approach to making a perspective elevation from a given plan. We will assume that we must draw a box, which could be the interior of our picture box. In plan view, the picture box is a true rectangle *ABCD* made up of ninety-degree corners *(166-A)*. In such a plan the front plane, *AB*, can be established in a perspective drawing, a second drawing, as a vertical plane, $A_1B_1$, which in this case is the frame of the picture (*166-B*). Care must be taken that the two drawings are vertically aligned. $A_1$ must be above or below $A$; $B_1$ above, or below $B$, respectively. The back wall in the perspective $C_1D_1$ is drawn smaller than the frame $A_1B_1$.

In a non-conventional projection, the back wall, *CD* in plan, is established in a perspective as the vertical plane $C_2D_2$. Now the perspective is developed *toward us*, resulting in the frame of the picture $A_2B_2$ being drawn larger than the back wall (*166-C*).

This procedure also results in an unusual exploitation of the plan view. When the front plane $A_2B_2$ in the perspective is projected into a new plan view, it determines a distorted view of the floor $A_3B_3C_3D_3$ (*166-D*). Although this odd shape in a way is reminiscent of a perspective shape, it involves no perspective. It is a true plan view, but no longer rectangular. By adding simple symbols of human figures either little stage can be activated. In plan, the figures may be indicated roughly as circles; in the elevation, as simple chalk indications or silhouettes (*167-A*).

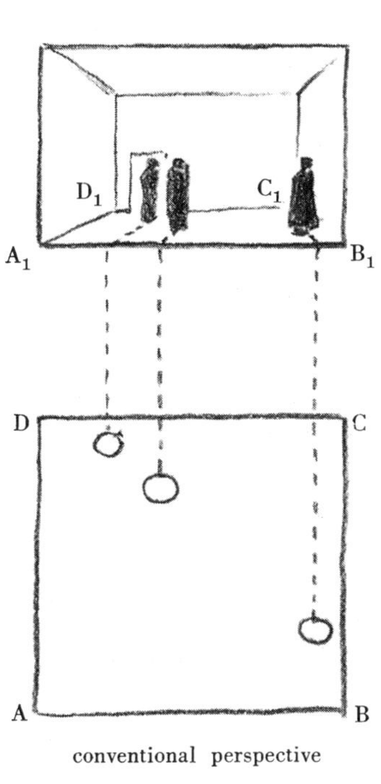

conventional perspective

167-A

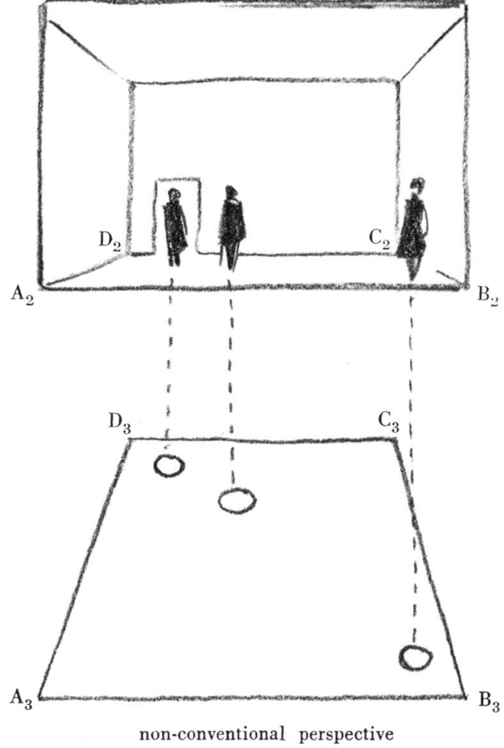

non-conventional perspective

167-B

In both plan and elevation attention should be paid to relative sizes. For instance, the size of a circle should conform to the width of a silhouette in elevation, and the height of a silhouette to its perspective environment.

In conventional projection, *ABCD (167-A)*, a figure close to the center of the picture can be placed directly above or below its corresponding position in the plan. But as its position shifts to either side of center there is no longer a direct up-down relation between the figure and its location in plan.

The difficulty of projecting the conventional way, converging to a vanishing point to locate the figures, is apparent if we try to relate the side wall $B_1C_1$ visually to its plan view *BC*. For $B_1C_1$ is a visible perspective plane, while *BC* is a line having no direct visual relation to $B_1C_1$.



In non-conventional projection no attempt is made to conform to an exact convergence of perspective lines to distant vanishing points in order to determine the location of various figures. Instead, a direct up-down projection is maintained between all of the figures and their corresponding positions in plan *(167-B)*.

The greatest deviation from conventional projection is found when it becomes necessary to draw the side planes of the box. But by distorting the plan into $A_3B_3C_3D_3$ *(167-B)* the error becomes visually negligible. There is a direct visual and graphic alignment between the figures in the perspective and the distorted plan $A_3B_3C_3D_3$. A figure standing in front of the side wall $B_2C_2$ projects as a circle located visually between $B_3C_3$ in the plan view.

It should be observed that in conventional projection, figures indicated in perspective elevation become smaller as they approach the back wall of the picture box. In non-conventional projection, they become larger as they leave the back wall and move toward us. Although the distinction between moving from front to back or back to front may seem pointless at this time, it has great bearing upon the ease with which we build a picture. As we shall see in Chapter 30, it also has a profound effect upon scale. Developing a picture from back to front is a work habit which, once acquired, becomes one of the artist's most valuable tools.

Although this method of projection is in many ways arbitrary, in many ways faulty, it does have one outstanding advantage over conventional projection. It is completely simple. Once the two drawings are aligned, straight up-down projection becomes possible, and necessary adjustments can be made between the two quite effortlessly. It is this very flexibility and simplicity that justifies the use of plan in relation to an illustrative picture. Indeed, the labor entailed in making an Italian perspective projection, except for special uses such as a set design, or an architectural rendering, is seldom justified.

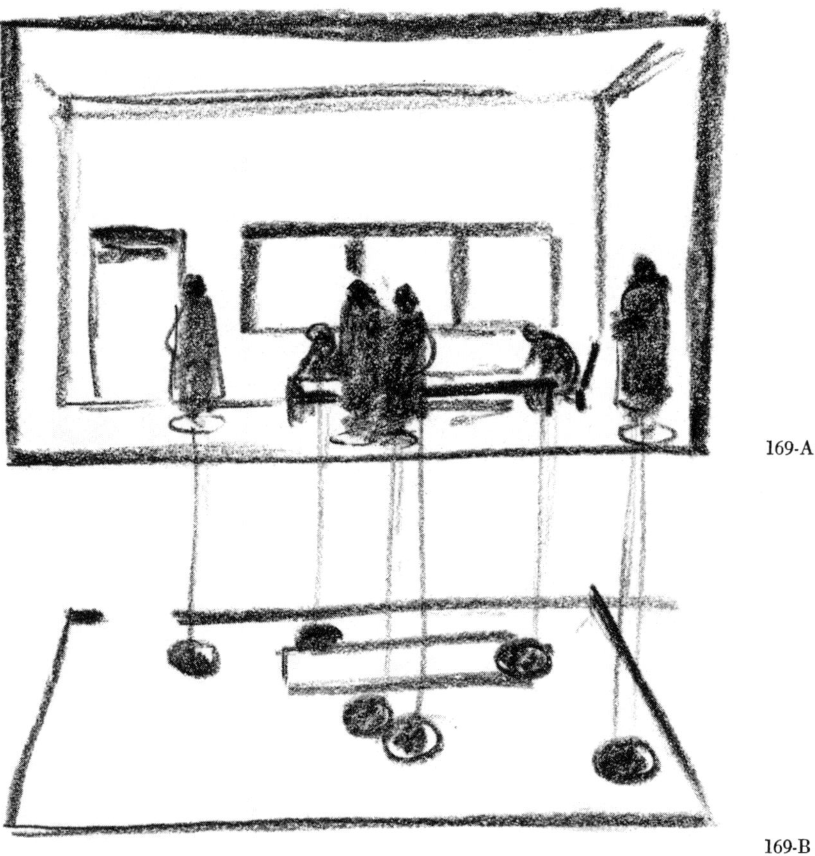

169-A

169-B

## Using Non-Conventional Projection

Our first picture idea often is expressed as
a freehand perspective usually called a
"rough," which is subject to many changes.
As long as the rough suggests a depth of no
more than thirty feet, there is every reason for
us to use a picture box and a simple plan.
When the distance suggested is greater than
thirty feet, the plan will be of little use and
other approaches to picture structure become
necessary, as we will see in the next chapter.

Once we have made our rough we may proceed with the plan. It can be drawn upon the
same paper as the rough, or it can be drawn on
a separate sheet. In either case, as we have
seen, the two drawings must be aligned with
the plan exactly above or below the perspective
rough. It is also suggested that at this time
the back wall of the picture box be drawn
parallel to the picture surface. The reason will
become apparent when we investigate the
rotation of the plan in Chapter 18.

In the plan, the back wall of the picture
box should conform in width to the back wall
in the perspective. And in the plan the side
walls will be diverging diagonals (*169-A*).

We can now project our figures directly up
and down from the rough to the plan and
from plan back into the rough (*169-B*). With
practice we soon learn to work from plan to
elevation and from elevation to plan with equal
ease. In fact, the procedure should be automatic, not involving too much time.

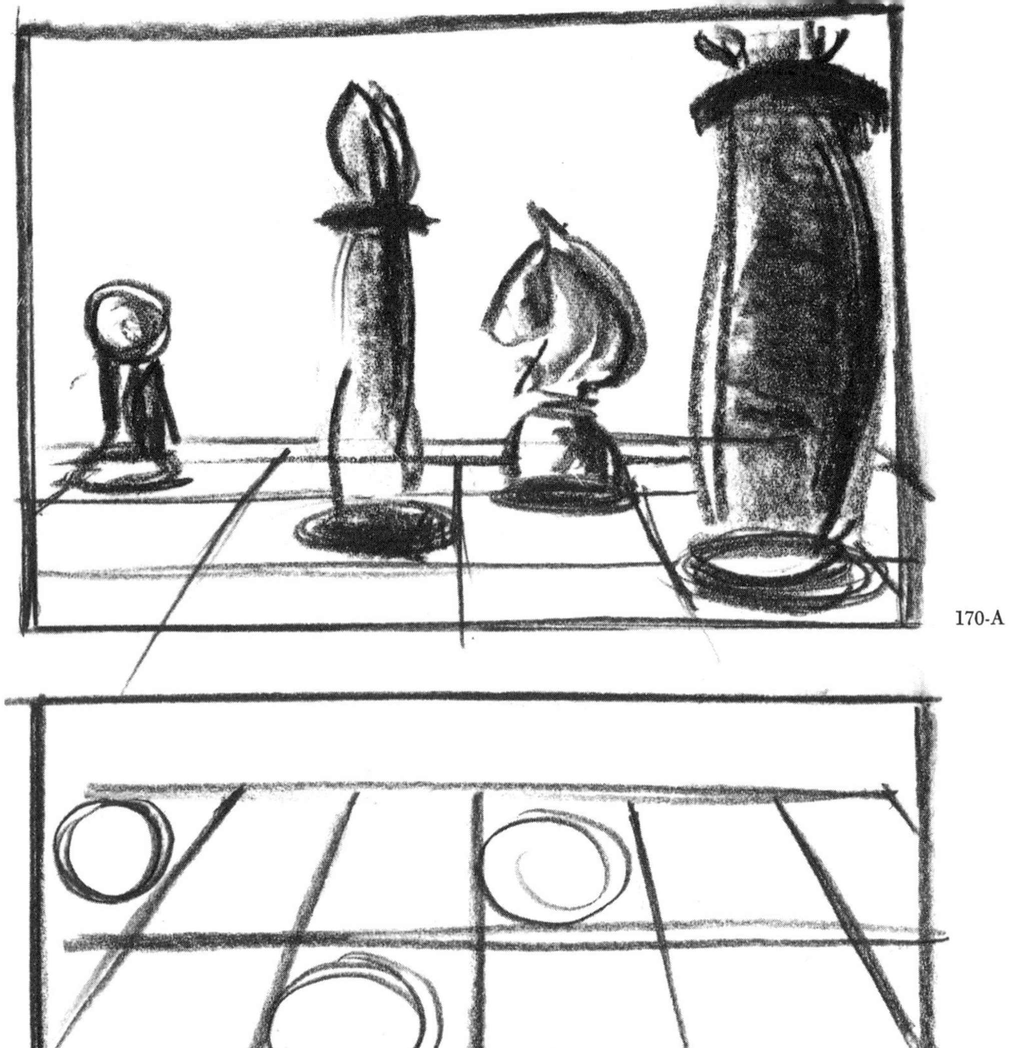

170-A

170-B



In nature we have developed the habit of seeing things in front overlapping things in back. As we adjust our perspective elevation in relation to our plan it is inevitable that one figure somewhere will overlay another. But instead of trying to jam the figure in the rear into the space left over by the front figure, let us reverse the process; let us put the front figure *over* the back figure. In many ways designing a group may be compared to stacking pancakes. We start at the bottom and work up. In the same way we start at the rear wall of the picture box and pile up the figures as a series of overlays coming forward one on top of the other. To use a familiar admonition, "there is plenty of room in the front." It literally never runs out.

At times it is helpful to visualize the picture as a chessboard. First let us indicate the board in both plan and elevation (*170-A, -B*). Note that the rectangular shapes in plan are distorted squares, not squares in perspective (*170-B*).

In the plan view we can locate our chess men as circles. Now, projecting into our elevation, let us indicate on the floor in their corresponding squares a series of rough ellipses. These elements may be adjusted freely both in plan and elevation until a logical order seems to have been attained. Now individual chessmen may be drawn upon the ellipses in perspective.

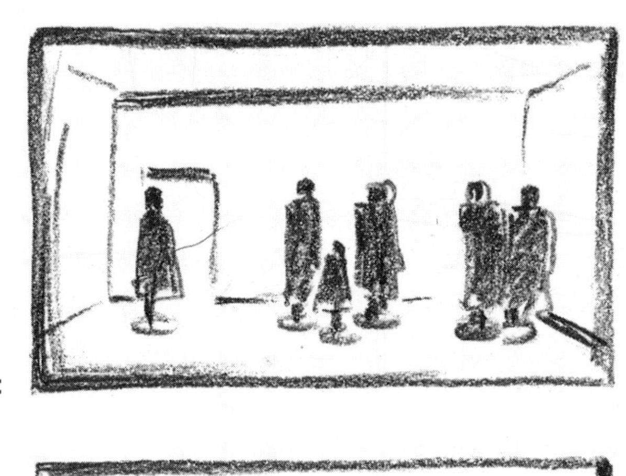

171-C

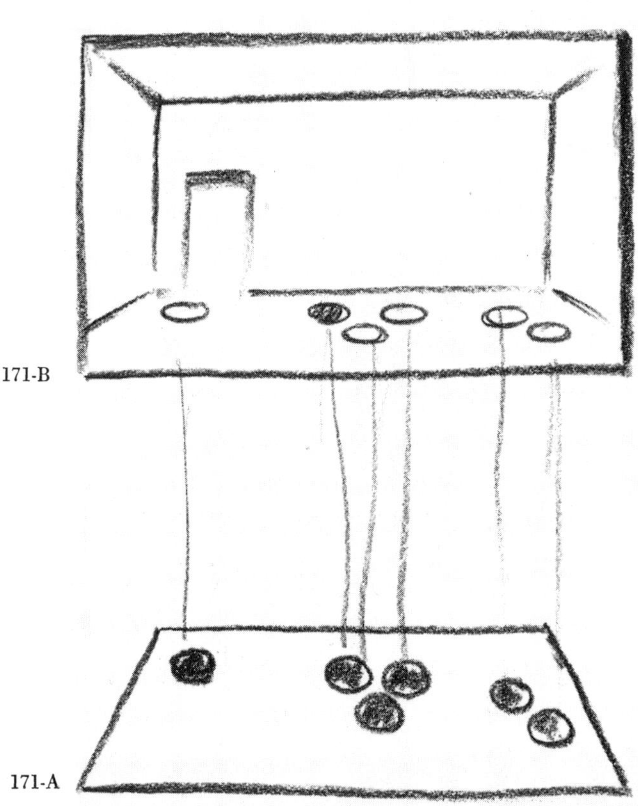

171-B

171-A

In exactly the same way a picture box may be first laid out in plan and elevation (*171-A,-B*). Furniture and props may be indicated in plan and studied to determine their best arrangement, both as to the logic of their location and their effect upon the placement of the figures. When a satisfactory order has been achieved this plan view may be raised into a perspective, not of the figures in elevation, but as a series of shapes on the floor (*171-B*). Upon these shapes the perspective elevations can be built later. These shapes are like shadows cast by imaginary figures or props with a light directly overhead. Or they can be visualized as puddles of water. It is amazing how much bad staging can be avoided by transposing a true plan into a perspective plan.

Once the elevations are developed upon this perspective plan the effect of these on the pattern of our picture can be studied (*171-C*). Now the figures can be adjusted to the original plan and vice versa until we arrive at an exciting pattern on our picture surface.

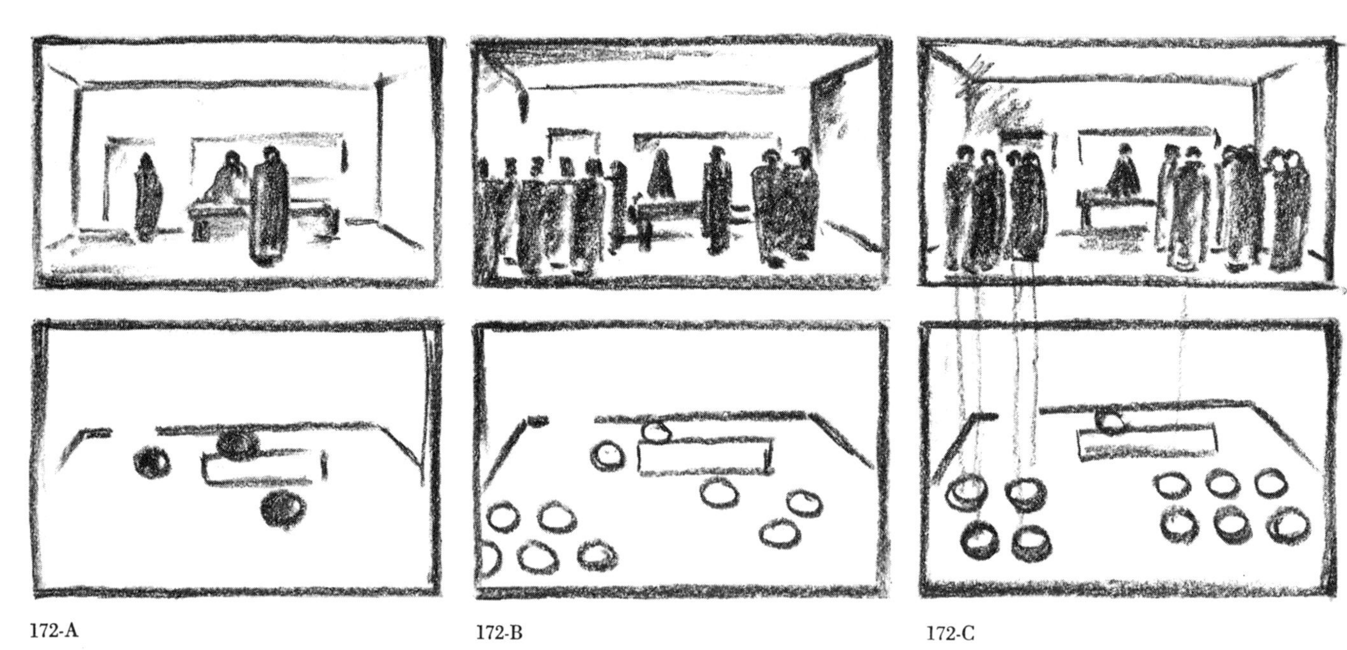

172-A      172-B      172-C

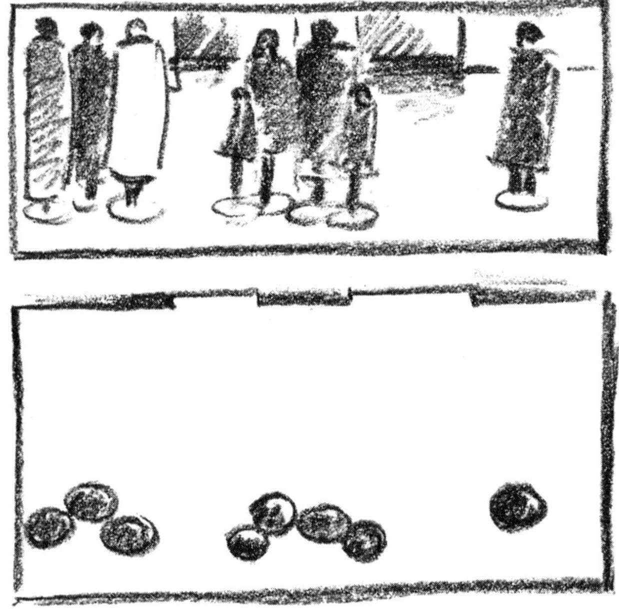

172-D



# 16 Echoing Plan in Elevation

**Plan and Surface Pattern**

When we make a preliminary rough we first establish our thoughts about the general nature of our picture. In contemporary painting this may entail placing a few lines or color areas on the picture surface. No prior plan is involved, and quite possibly no representational subject is involved. If, however, we are called upon to employ a picture box, which justifies the use of plan, the rough also is a preliminary statement of a surface pattern in many ways evolving from plan.

Let us assume that we are to draw a room in which a number of figures are to be placed. In this instance the number of characters is less important than the variety of patterns these shapes may generate.

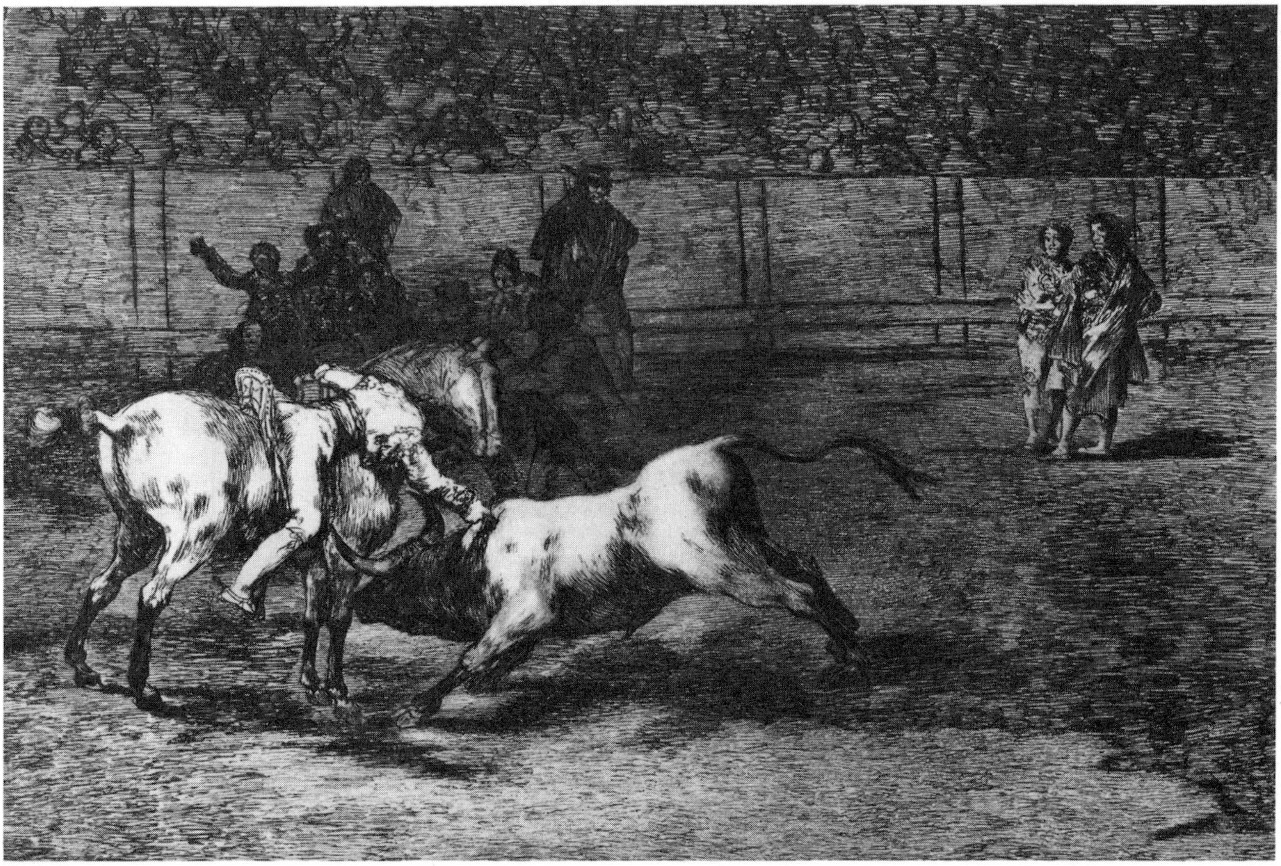

Francisco de Goya (Spanish, 1746-1828)
MARION CEBALLOS, KNOWN AS "THE INDIAN,"
KILLS THE BULL FROM HIS HORSE'S BACK
Plate 23, *Tauromaquia*; 1st ed. 1816
7⅞" x 11⅞"; etching and aquatint
Achenbach Foundation for Graphic Arts
San Francisco
(Photograph: Schopplein Studios)

The accompanying roughs demonstrate the ease with which an elevation may be changed to accommodate a change of position of any figure indicated in the plan. The resulting pattern is a variable, reflecting the order of occurrences in the plan. The number of figures, the number and complexity of the props, and the distribution of these elements profoundly affect the nature of the surface pattern of our picture (*172-A, -B, -C*).

The first requirement, of course, is that the picture be easy to read. Unless the viewer is able to understand what we say, we run the risk of creating confusion and losing him completely. However, if the pattern is too simple, the picture will seem dull and empty. Our viewer will become bored.

Quite often our first rough will seem sparse. In this plan of a street scene, for instance, we find great empty areas (*172-D*). At first the pattern of the plan projected in elevation may seem adequate. Soon, however, we become aware of great emptiness behind the figures. There is a large space in the center of the picture which does not seem to serve any purpose. It is a *graphic hole*. This empty space is especially noticeable when large areas are implied by a strong horizontal, a floor line, for instance.

Now we should not jump to the conclusion that in every picture all floor space should be occupied. At times a large empty area in plan is necessary to tell our story. In this Goya we see that the bull ring is not only a large empty area when seen in plan, but that it is essential to the story. In elevation, the arena is a dramatic shape as well as a space.

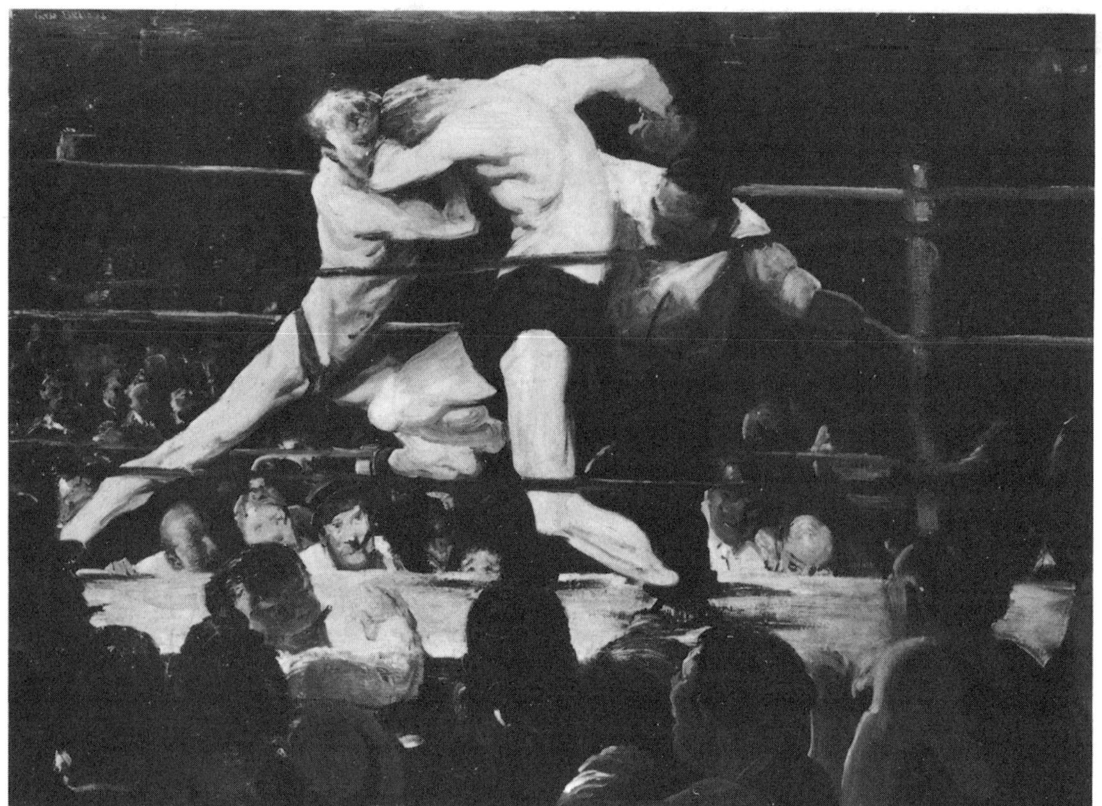

George Wesley Bellows (American, 1882-1925)
STAG AT SHARKEY'S, 1907; 36¼" x 48¼"
oil on canvas
The Cleveland Museum of Art
Hinman B. Hurlbut Collection

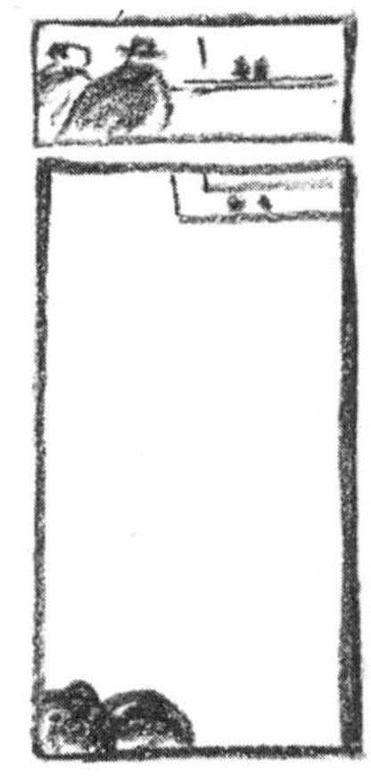

174-2



Similarly, in George Bellows' *Stag At Sharkey's* the fight ring is an essential space necessary to the action. Although the shape of the ring in elevation is interrupted by overlays, we are still aware of the importance of the ring space.

The presence of an undesirable graphic hole in an elevation emphasizes the importance of the work procedure mentioned in Chapter 15: by placing overlays from back to front, stacking them like pancakes, we always know exactly where each is in relation to our plan. Reversing this procedure, working from front to back with overlays, may fill up large areas of the picture surface. But these close overlays usually mask out what is really occurring in plan. For example, this street scene, although too deep for a satisfactory plan-elevation projection, does demonstrate how an overlay in the foreground may hide, or partially hide, a huge hole in the center of the picture. Nothing in the elevation suggests what is happening between the foreground figures and those in the background (*174-2*).

To correct this feeling of emptiness, we may be tempted to locate other characters *between* the front overlay figures (*175-1A*). In other words, when we find an open space between overlays we simply plug a character into the opening much as we would plug a cork into the mouth of a bottle (*175-1B*). Such a procedure usually results in a questionable solution to the space problem suggested in plan. Equally serious, we intuitively see the crowd as comprising many people standing or sitting in such a way that their heads never overlap. Each is in the clear. Each is in a separate little hole.

Now it is true that people tend to live and move in separate space worlds of their own,

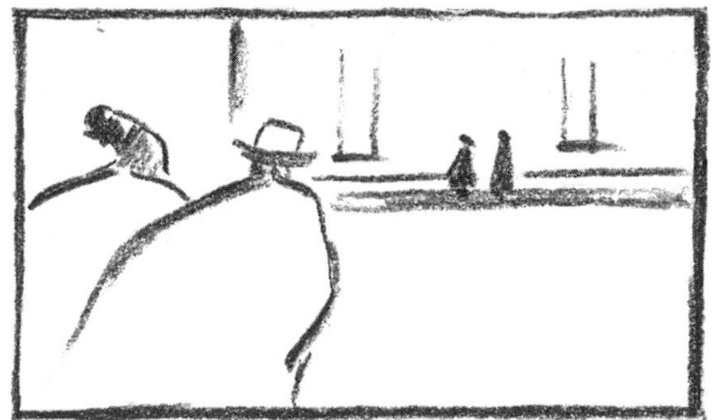

175-1A

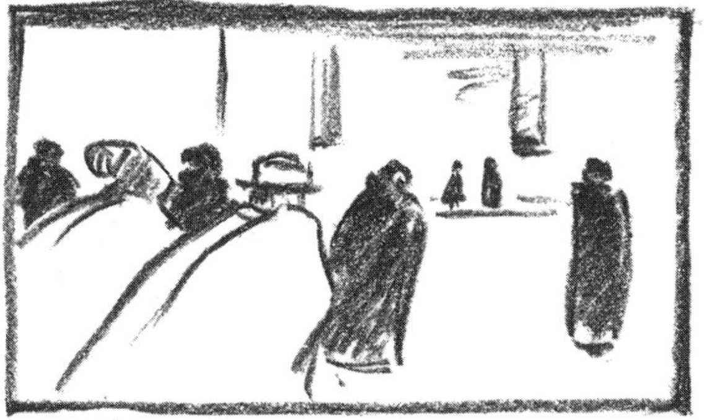

175-1B

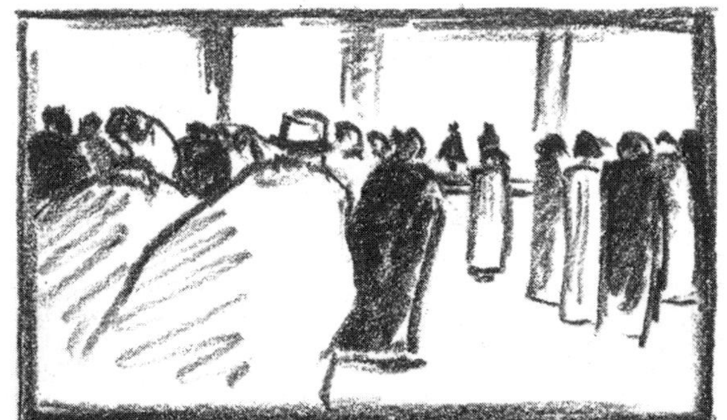

175-1C

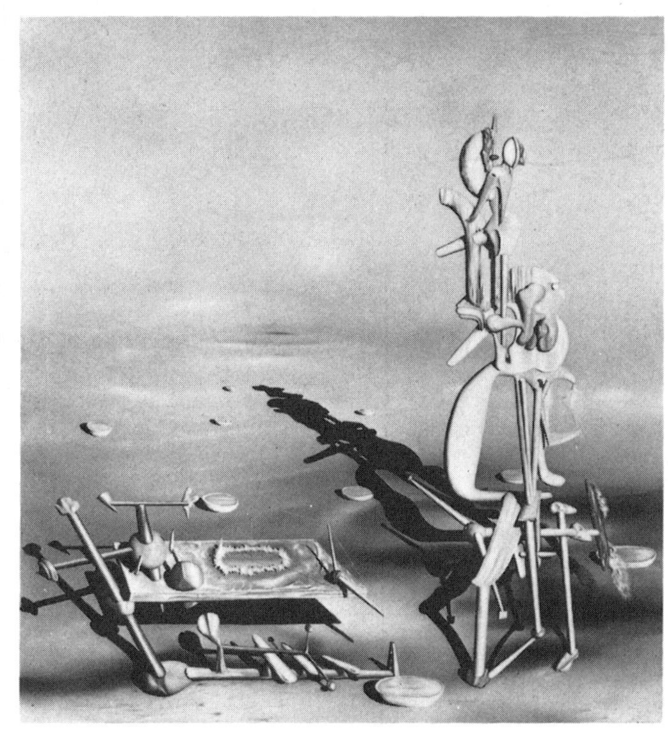

Yves Tanguy (French, 1900-1955)
INDEFINITE DIVISIBILITY, 1942; 40″ x 35″
oil on canvas
Albright-Knox Art Gallery
Buffalo, New York

although at times they may become involved, as when dancing or wrestling. But usually they are entities, each living in an imaginary bubble of space. When, however, we observe people from a fixed point we see them as a series of overlapping forms. As a matter of fact, seeing a crowd of people with each individual standing clear of his neighbor is a rather noticeable and startling occurrence. We might say that the world seems to be made of a never-ending series of overlapping forms. There always seems to be something in back of something else (*175-1C*).

Therefore indicating groups of figures as a series of isolated units often results in a weak relation of plan to elevation and, as we shall see shortly, to questionable surface pattern. Sometimes, however, such an effect of separateness has been purposely exploited to create a great sense of loneliness, as we see in the work of the Surrealists like Tanguy. But most pictures involve many overlaying symbols, and their very complexity creates a sense of completion in the spectator.

The fallacy of plugging holes or filling in the areas between overlays stems directly from failure to consider the effect of plan in constructing the elevation. As long as we continue to search for a space in our surface pattern sufficiently large to allow for the introduction of a new symbol, we are in effect merely constructing our picture as we would a jigsaw puzzle.

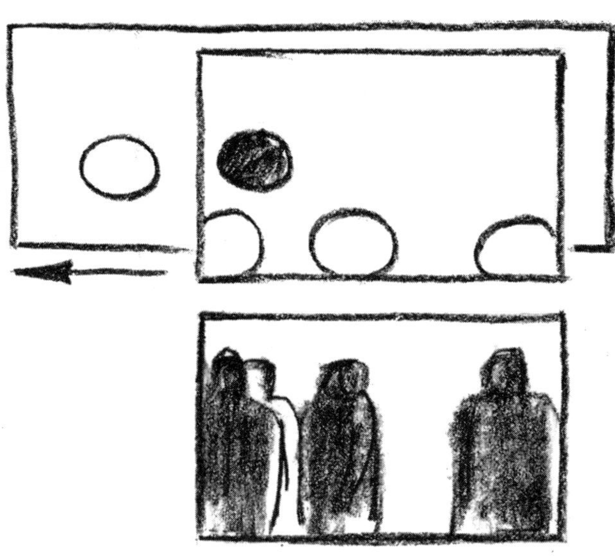

176-A

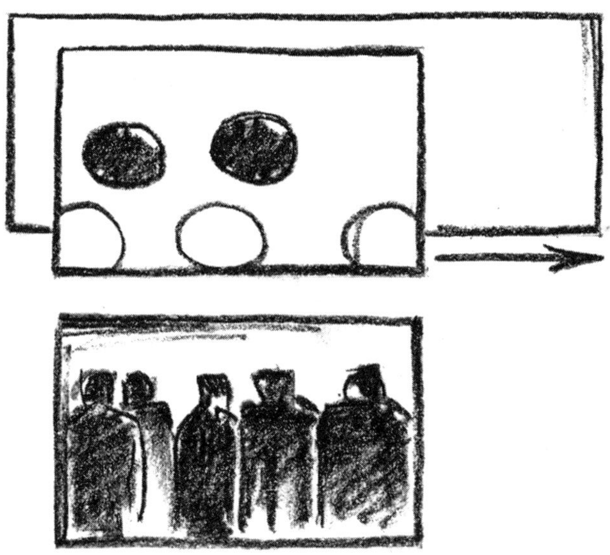

176-B



If we persist in simply plugging holes in the elevation, we find it increasingly difficult to find room in our pattern for partially revealed elements almost covered by the foreground overlays. In addition to this crowded feeling, we also find it difficult to place convincingly a fragment of a head, a nose, or an ear, for instance, in any small free area which may be somewhere in the middle distance of the picture.

Fortunately there is a truly simple procedure which circumvents all this trouble. We again work from back to front. By first drawing the symbol to be overlayed, then placing the close symbol over the more distant one, we never are confronted with the problem of plugging holes between overlays or of drawing small details which have no origin.

In working with the picture box, our first rough may reveal areas of congestion in the elevation when studied in relation to the plan. To clarify important hidden parts, the overlayed symbol in the rear may be shifted from side to side, or the overlay may be similarly moved. In either case, the move should be justified in the plan (*176-A*). This usually means a simple adjustment of the position of one or two of our basic circles. Often such a simple shift from side to side will reveal details of head or hands, or important parts of significant props inadvertently hidden by the front overlays (*176-B*).

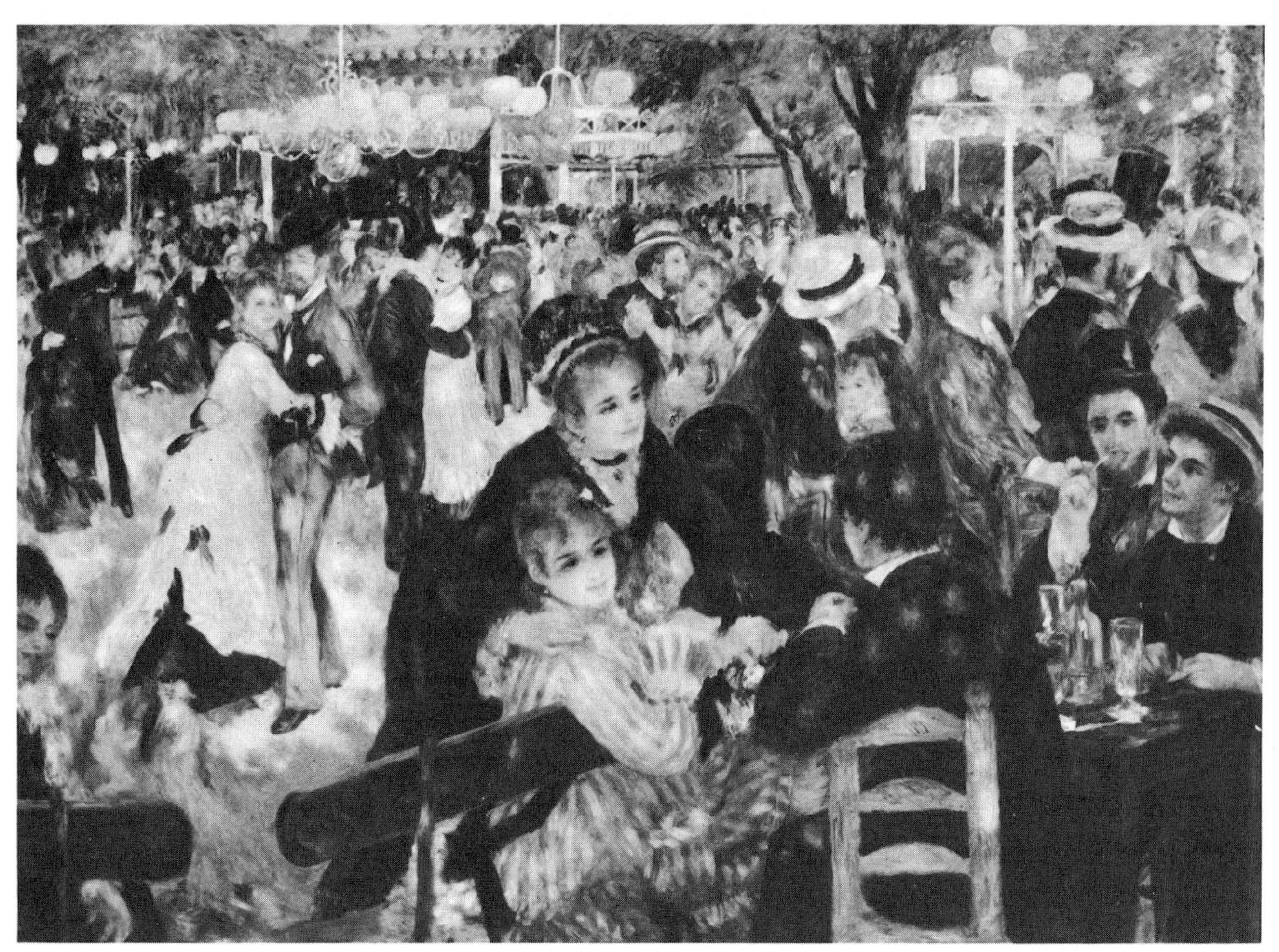

Pierre Auguste Renoir (French, 1841-1919)
LE MOULIN DE LA GALETTE, 1876; 51½″ x 69″
oil on canvas
The Louvre, Paris



At times a complex picture structure will
involve many overlaying groups of figures or
props, as in the Renoir above. In such cases
it is not unusual for the picture to suggest a
depth of more than thirty-odd feet. The
greater the distance involved in our scene,
the longer the plan becomes physically. It is
apparent that if our plan is extended indefinitely it becomes so physically long as to be
unmanageable. Our direct up-down plan-elevation projection is no longer possible. Size
differences due to perspective become increasingly noticeable.

Now instead of trying to force a procedure
which is effective only for short distances,
let us simply abandon it and find easier ways.
However, it is still important to have a concept
of a plan in all elevations, whether or not we
actually draw the plan.

When a picture involves depths greater than
thirty feet but does not pass a range in which
we can still comfortably establish depths
with our eyes, we sometimes call it a "medium
shot," or "medium long shot." Such terminol-
ogy, adapted from motion picture photography,
is descriptive and is accepted by many
artists. The terms "close-up" and "long shot"
also are becoming part of an international
language.

To construct a medium long shot picture,
let us follow another simple procedure: first,
work from back to front; second, control the
location of the overlays by working from a
perspective plan.

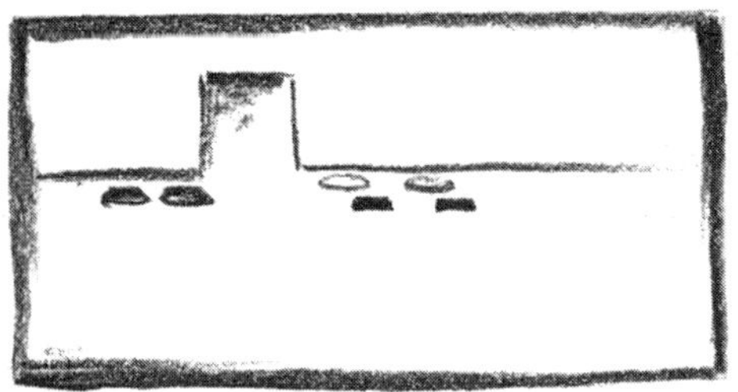

178-A

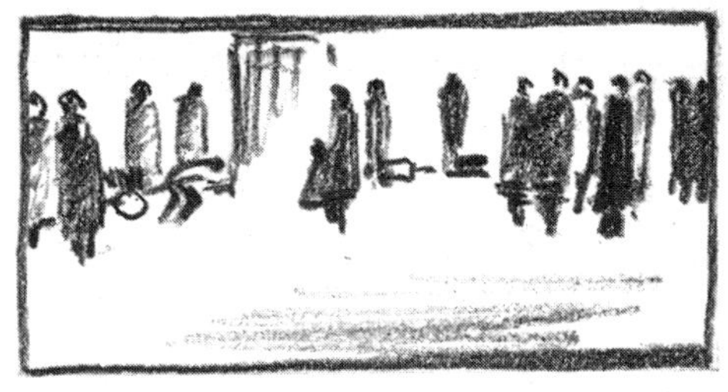

178-E

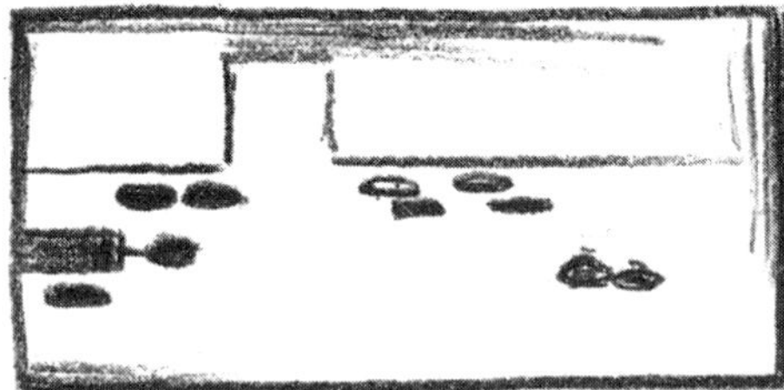

178-B

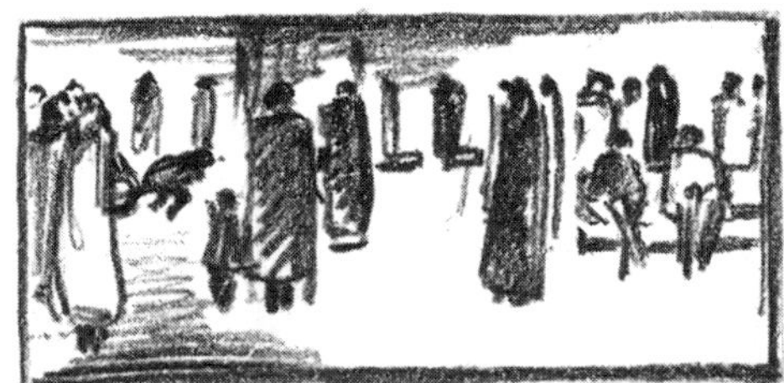

178-F

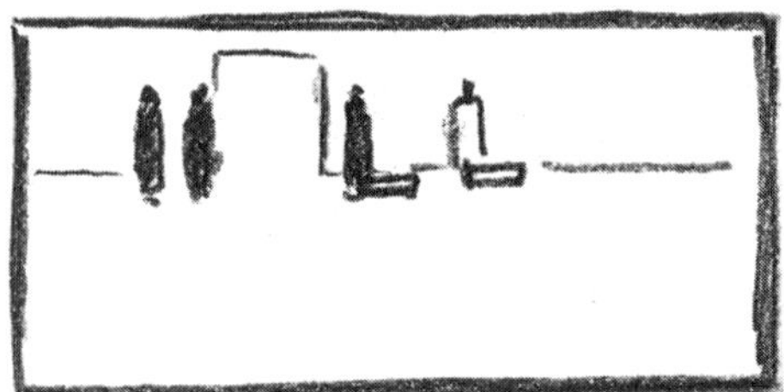

178-C

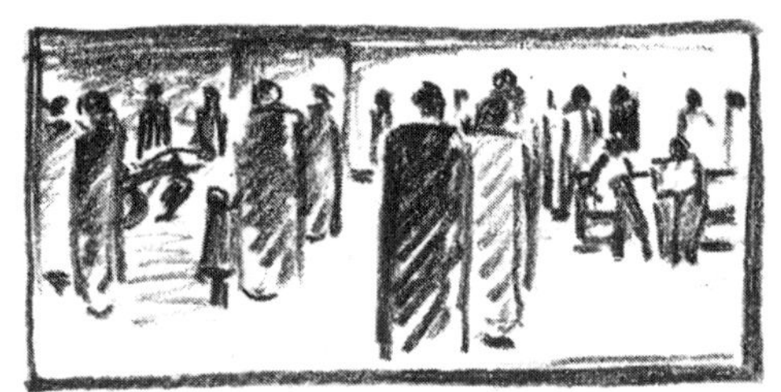

178-G

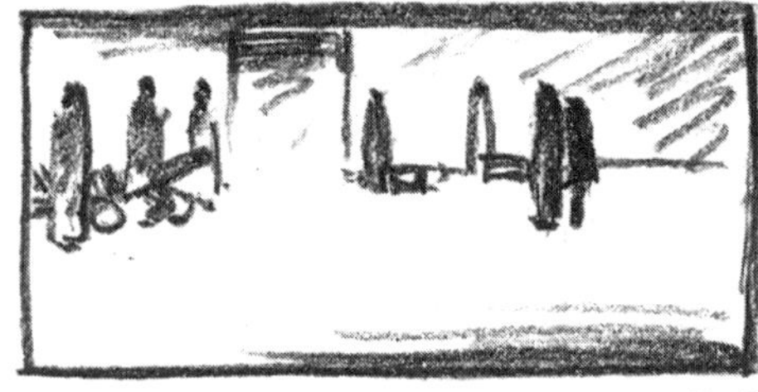

178-D

El Greco (Spanish, b. Crete, 1541–1614)
THE BURIAL OF COUNT ORGAZ, 1586
15′ 8½″ x 11′ 10″; canvas
San Martín y Santo Tomás Apóstol
Toledo, Spain

## The Crowd Scene



To draw a crowd scene such as we might find
in a large waiting room at a railroad station
or airport, first let us indicate a simple
perspective of the room, with a doorway to
give a sense of the size of the structure.

On the floor plane of our rough let us
place the figures first as simple ellipses, which
can later be developed into standing figures.
Similarly, props—baggage wagons, suitcases—
can first be indicated simply as rectangles
(*178-A*). By distribution of these shapes on
the floor, we can determine very quickly the
presence of unwanted empty areas, or, conversely, rearrange the ellipses and rectangles
to emphasize desired empty areas (*178-B*).
Since we are working in deep space, size
adjustments must be made in our indications
to suggest the estimated distance from back to
front. By starting at the *back* wall and gradually
increasing the sizes of the ellipses or rectangles,
this is easily accomplished. In actual practice
the whole procedure takes only a short time.

In a large waiting room our viewpoint may
well be from a standing eye level, the crowd's
eye level. Although other eye levels can just
as easily be used, let us accept the standing
eye level for this picture.

Now let us locate our horizon in relation to
the doorway. Most adult male heads in the
picture will conform closely to this eye level.
Most women and children standing, or seated,
will be drawn with their heads proportionately
related to the accompanying male.

Starting at the back wall, all groups
indicated on the floor plane which are closely
related to the wall may now be indicated as
perspective elevations (*178-C*). These groups
represent a zone roughly ten feet in front
of the wall. Now a similar zone including

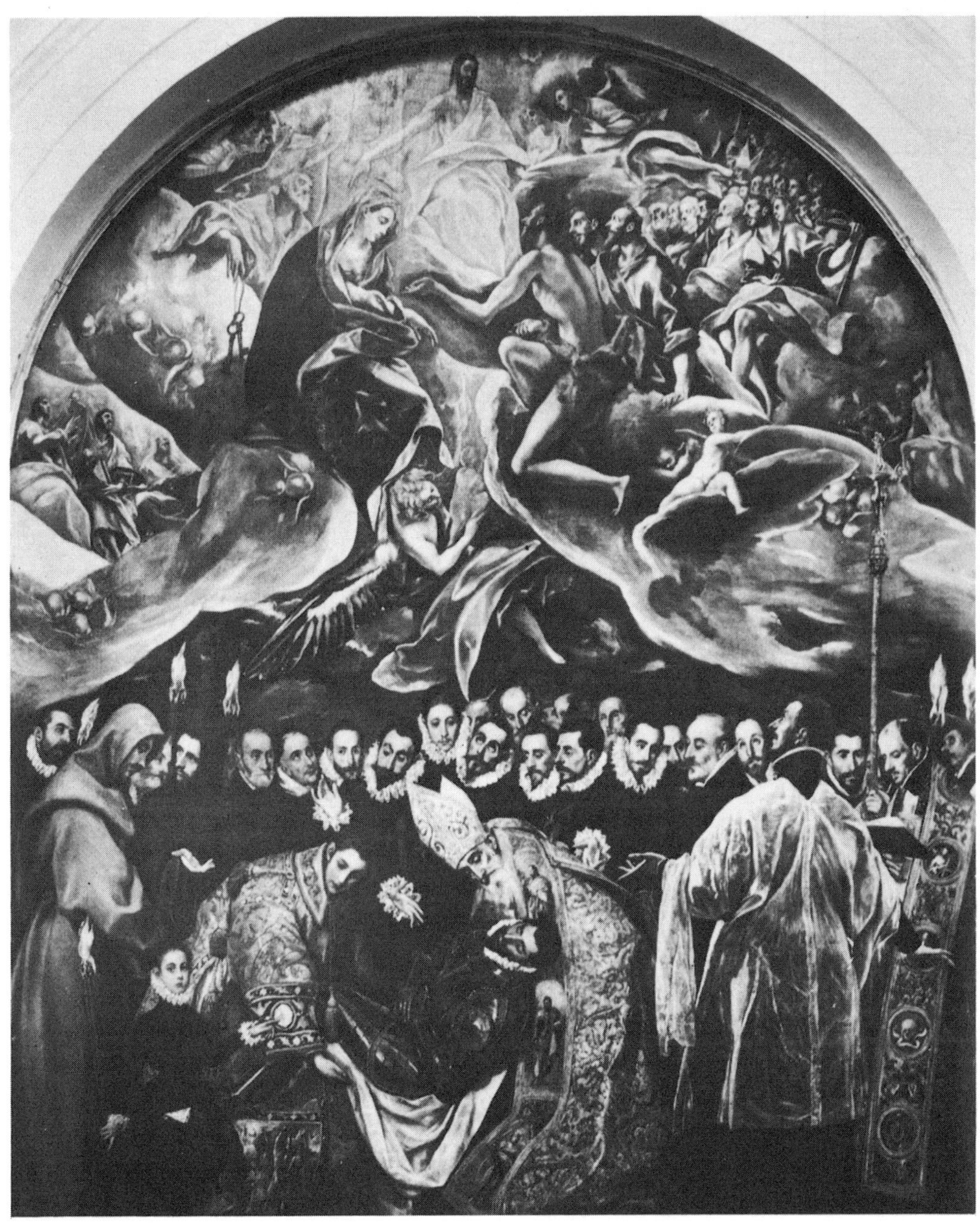

other groups can be raised in elevation (*178-D*). This procedure can be continued until the closest overlays have been accounted for (*178-E, -F, -G*). Naturally, as overlays continue to pile up many figures and props in the background may be partially or completely hidden, as in this El Greco. Strangely enough, by working from back to front such interferences appear normal and valid.

If important information becomes lost by the addition of overlays, a new control of overlays may be employed. If we raise the elevations in our first zone on a piece of tracing paper pinned over the perspective plan, we now may simply pin another tissue over it. On this second tissue, the groups in zone two appear. By moving either tissue number one or tissue number two from side to side, minor interruptions may easily be cleared.

The perspective plan can be divided into any convenient number of zones which, in turn, can be translated into the same number of tissue overlays. Any or all of these overlays may be moved back and forth laterally in order to clarify the surface pattern. At any time a master tracing may be made to bring all of the overlays into one drawing. This procedure may sound formidable but it is performed simply. It can be executed in a few minutes and may save the artist hours correcting a faulty plan later on.

Working from back to front at times presents some technical difficulty. If the picture is laid out in chalks, or a type of paint easily changed, adjustments can be made with minimum effort. But if the drawing is in pen and ink, wash, or fresco, changes may be almost impossible.

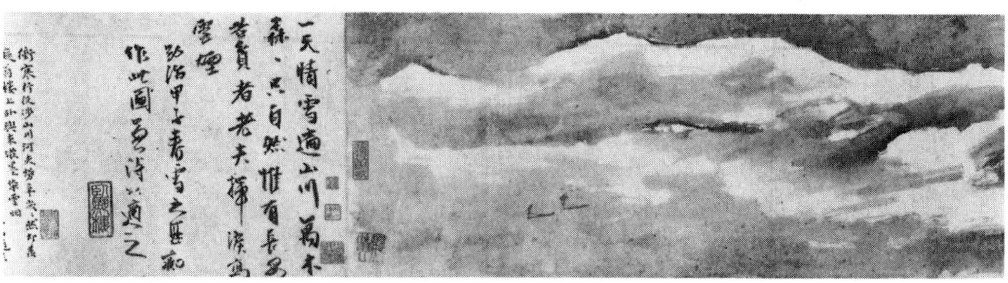
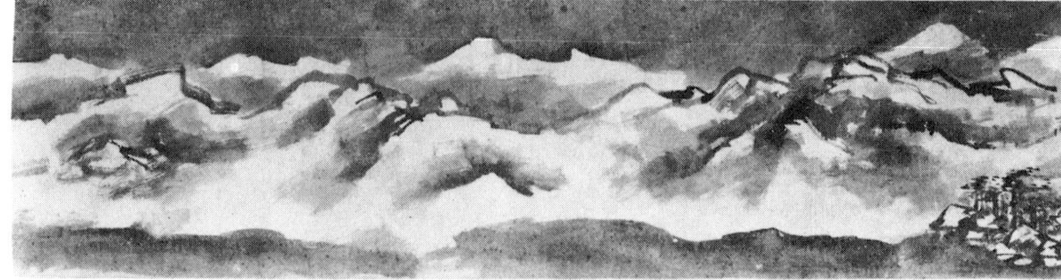
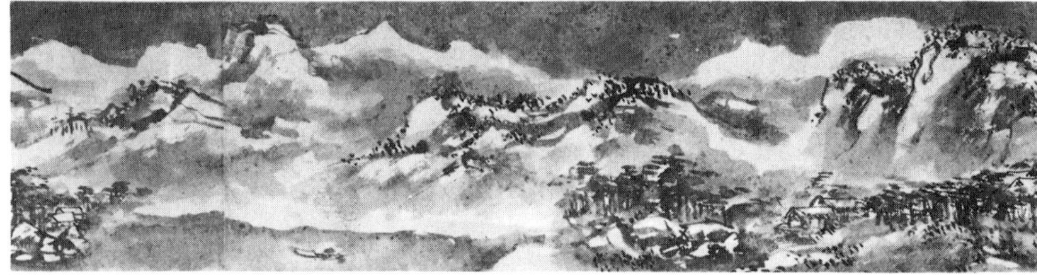
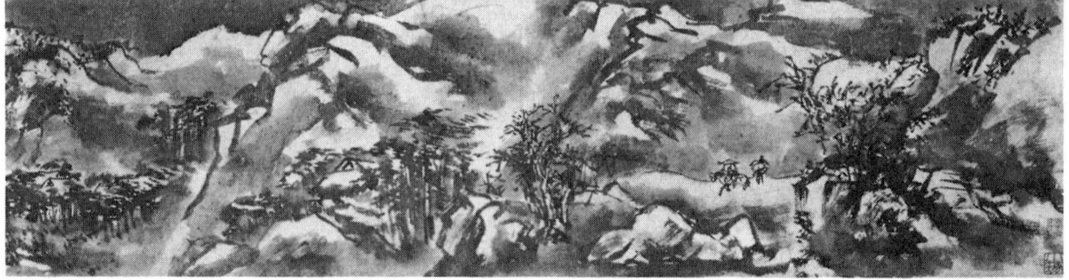

Shih Chung (Chinese, 1437-1517)
SNOW LANDSCAPE, Ming Dynasty; 9⅞" x 125⅝"
paper makimono
Courtesy, Museum of Fine Arts, Boston

Maria Antoinette Evans Fund
Purchase Fund, Ellen Francis Mason Fund
Ellen Page Hall Fund, George Nixon Black Fund

## Controlling Great Depths

180

As we have observed, the dimension of things, or the space between them in the far distance in nature, are almost impossible to estimate visually with any degree of accuracy. Yet the artist from earliest times has never hesitated to construct pictures reminiscent of distant landscapes which simulate great depth.

An artist soon discovers that not only he but others find difficulty in measuring sizes accurately in the distance. To most people a mountain range appears as a large shape or cluster of closely related shapes. In a picture this same illusion may be preserved. By establishing a series of overlays of such clusters, and by working from back to front, the distance factor is implied, though never exactly determined.

A device exploited by the Chinese, who have always excelled in the art of landscape painting, is to build not only from back to front, but also from large to small. In normal perspective, things close to us seem larger than things the same size in the distance. Through habit we believe that all things become smaller as they recede.

By reversing this order, as Wang Shih-ch'ang has in this landscape, two picture controls are achieved. The first, and most important, is one of surface control. In introducing great activity at the top of the picture he assures vertical stability. The second control is based upon the reversal of an expected perspective diminution. With the human figures shown as tiny forms in the foreground and everything else progressively larger as it recedes, a sense of vastness is achieved, and this is the very quality desired in most landscapes.

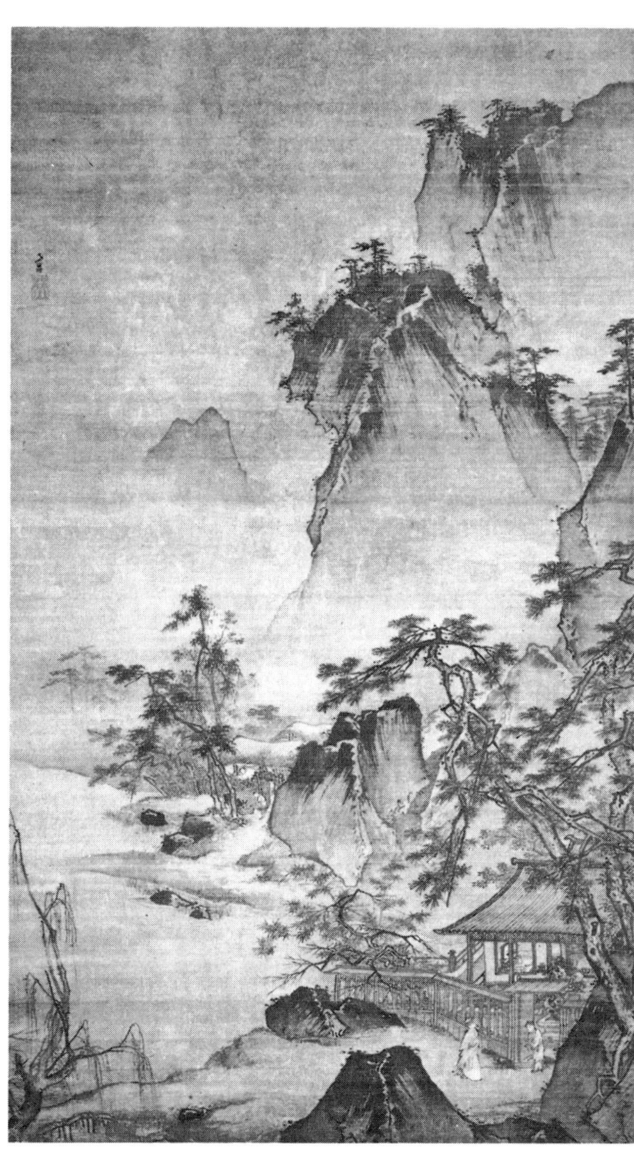

Wang Shih-ch'ang (15-16th century?)
MOUNTAIN LANDSCAPE: Cliffs and a Stream, a Scholar's Abode
Ming Dynasty; 72½″ x 40¹⁄₁₆″; ink and traces of color on silk
Courtesy of the Smithsonian Institution
Freer Gallery of Art, Washington, D.C.

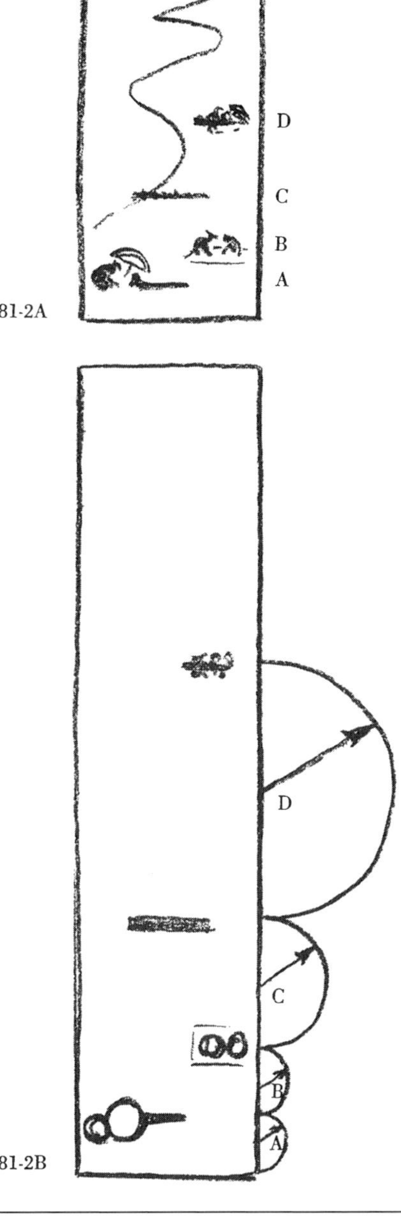



In a landscape showing far distance as well as close foreground, difficulty may arise in correlating measurable depth with the implied indeterminate depth of distant general shapes. The problem is similar to that facing the old-time stage designer when he used a realistic backdrop depicting a street scene diminishing in the distance until it became lost in the foothills. How can real action involving real chairs, stairs, etc., seem convincing against such a false backdrop?

To solve this problem in pictures a special device may be used: zones of activity in deep space are treated as separate little stages. For instance, a group of figures in the foreground of this beach scene (*181-2A*) is represented by zone *A*. Stepping back, in plan a distance equal to zone *A*, we arrive at zone *B*. Here another scene of activity is indicated.

In the same way, in plan, zone *C* is as far back as *A* plus *B*. *A* plus *B* plus *C* equals *D*, etc. In each case we double the distance (*181-2B*).

By estimating these progressively enlarging intervals in our perspective view, a strange effect occurs. The progressively increasing intervals in plan, when estimated in our perspective, are counteracted by the rapidly decreasing effect of perspective in these intervals. The result of this conflict is remarkable. As the distance increases, as we move into the picture, the perspective foreshortening overcomes the doubling, and the intervals slowly decrease.

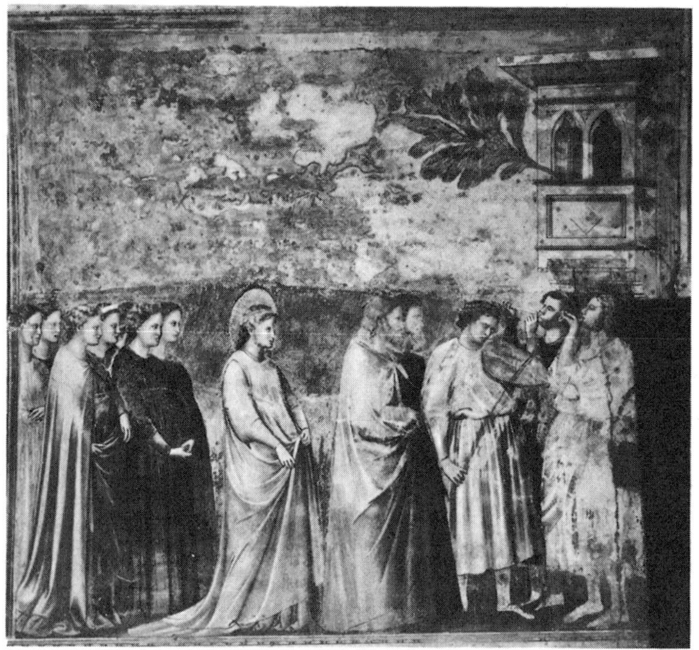

Giotto (Florentine, 1266?-1337)
SAINT JOSEPH CONDUCTS MARY TO HER HOUSE
1305-1306; fresco from the
Scrovegni Chapel, Padua, Italy
(Photograph: Anderson, Alinari,
Art Reference Bureau, Inc., N. Y.)

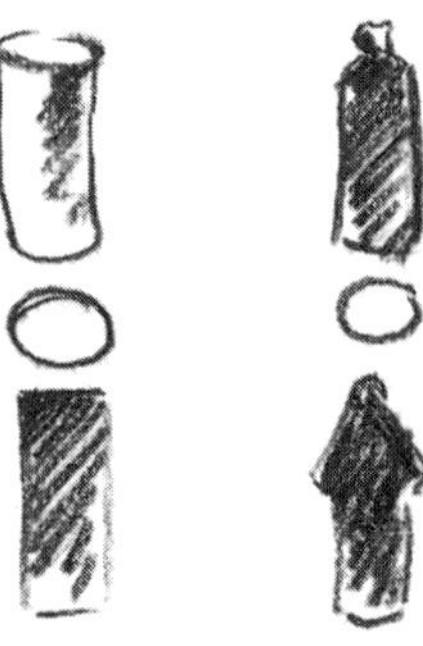

182-1

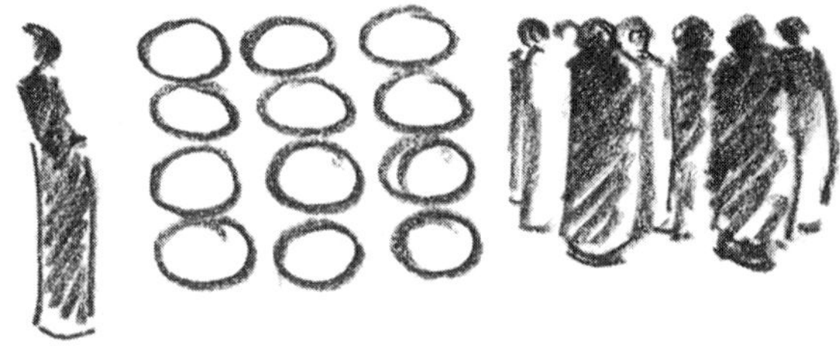

182-2

182 Although this procedure is based completely on guesswork, completely freehand, the effect is one of convincing graphic space because the depth of the distant volumes and the space between them is retained, in contrast to nature in which distant forms and the space between them seem to flatten.

Of course the ultimate challenge to the artist is the control of abstract space. Often such space involves imaginary depths, not depths derived from nature. In such pictures the problem of plan may not arise. We shall investigate the control of such depth in Part VIII.

## Echoing Shapes from Plan in Elevation

As we work from plan to elevation, especially if most of the figures are standing, we notice that we project from a circle to a cylinder, which may be compared to a standing figure (*182-1*). Both standing figure and cylinder are long, slender, three-dimensional forms in relation to their relatively small circular bases. When simplified, these cylinders become thin rectangular shapes. As we see, there is little similarity between a circle and a thin rectangle.

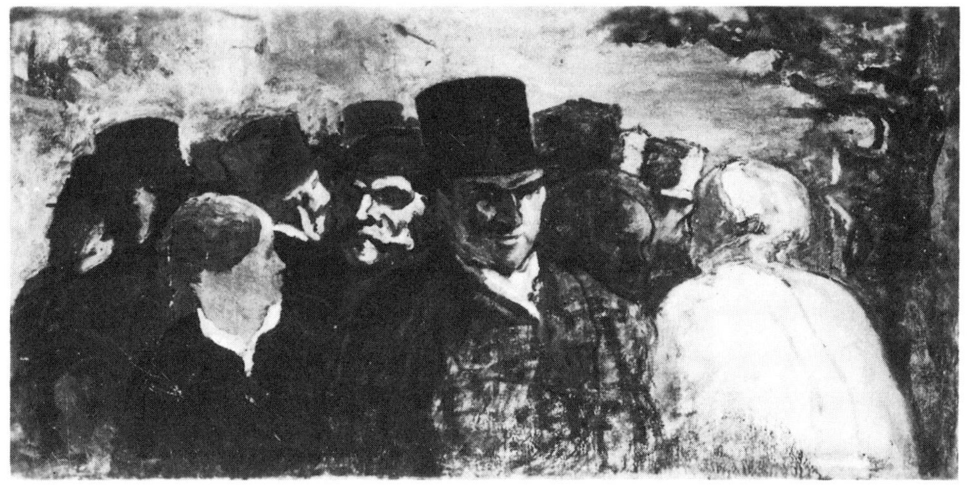

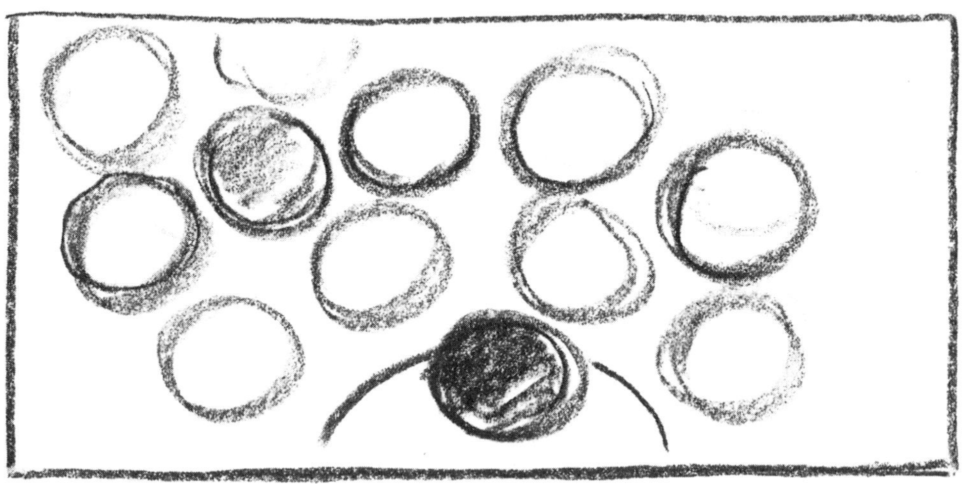

183-2



Suppose, however, that a series of circles, each representing a plan view of a standing figure, are grouped into a square, whose side is equal to the height of our figure (*182-2*). When projected into the perspective elevation at a standing eye level the same as our own, we arrive at a shape which is remarkably similar to our square in plan, as we see in the Giotto above. Moreover, as we look at the square in elevation, we see that visually it becomes a cube. The existence of this cube, through association, helps identify the area above the cube as a space. In the same way the area in front of the cube, or between us and the cube, becomes spacious.

We should remember that the viewer is seldom conscious of the plan of the picture or that the artist even uses a plan in constructing a picture. The viewer does respond to simple large shapes if they are dramatically presented. In Daumier's *The Waiting Room at the Station*, we, as viewers, may not be aware of the semi-circular arrangement of the figures around a core, as indicated in the plan view (*183-2*). But when we discover it, the picture takes on a new meaning.

As we become aware of the incredible variety of shapes which can be generated in elevation from simple changes made in arrangements in plan, we sense the potential for unending change. Picture making becomes an increasingly exciting experience.

# 17  The Horizon

## The Common Horizon

So engrossed have we become in plan and elevation that we may take for granted a picture factor so important that it determines the view of everything we see, both in nature and in pictures. It is our eye level.

Our eye level is like a persistent ghost. Wherever we go, it goes. We know where it is, for it is always directly before our eyes no matter in what direction we look. Sometimes it lies down quietly before us, and we see it as a distant separation of sea and sky. If we look up into the sky or down a well, there it is still in front of us. As we climb a mountain it keeps pace with us. But most of the time it is invisible. Seldom are we conscious of our eye level. Only when it is emphasized in some way, as in the Whistler above, are we aware of its presence.

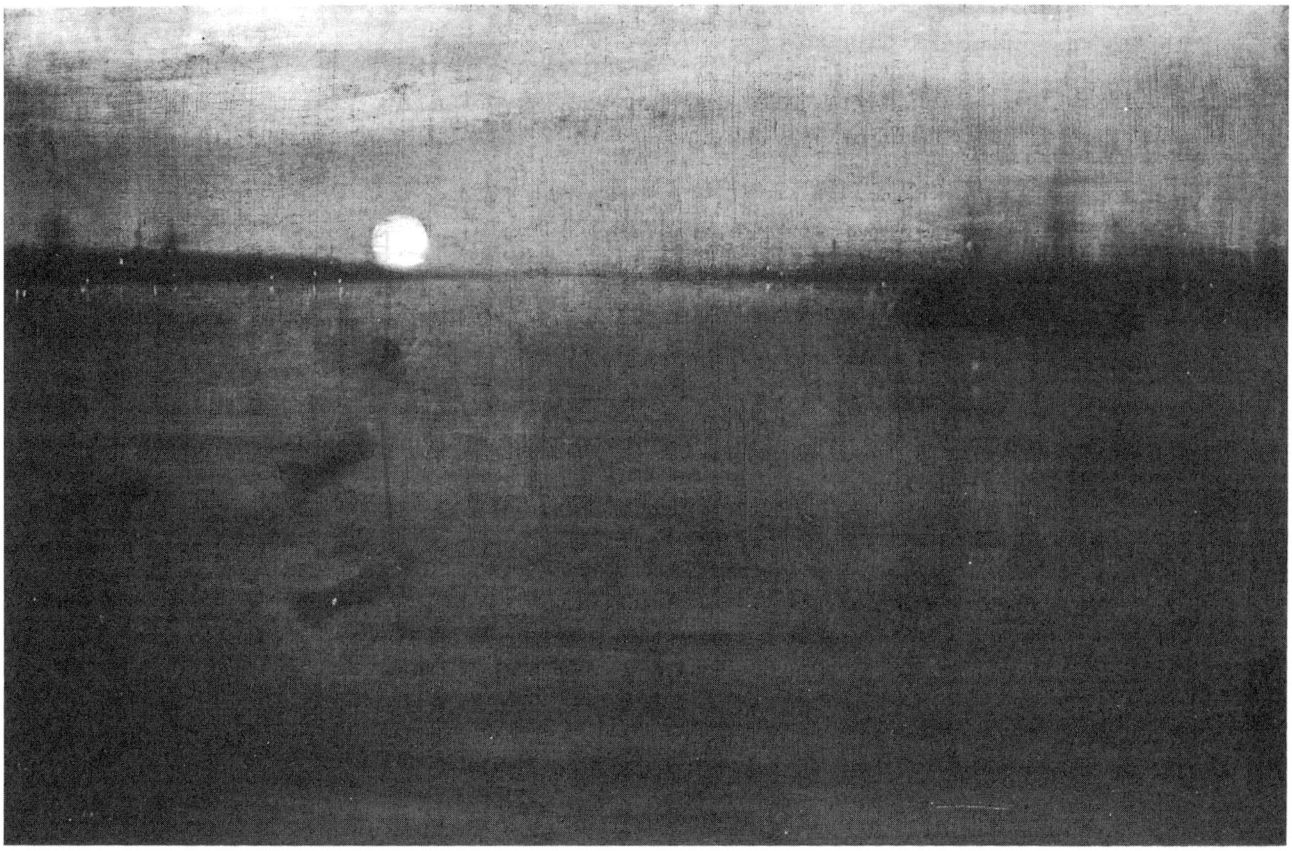

James Abbott McNeill Whistler
(American, 1834-1903)
NOCTURNE, SOUTHAMPTON WATERS
1872 or 1874; 20″ x 30″; oil on canvas
Courtesy of The Art Institute of Chicago
The Stickney Fund

We even have different names for our elusive friend the eye level. If we hold a playing card on edge before our eyes parallel to any plane receding from us in nature, the card will appear as a line. When transposed into drawing terms, this plane on edge becomes a graphic line termed a vanishing line, as we noted in Chapter 3. When the vanishing line is horizontal it is called *the horizon*.

### The Spectator and the Picture Horizon

When we look at a picture we seldom, if ever, are able to project ourselves completely into this imaginary world. Usually some barrier of size, or picture flatness, or color keeps us back. Yet there are times when we do feel that we are almost in the picture, especially if human figures are depicted. Because of our great familiarity with human forms, it is easy to associate ourselves with symbols of people, especially when they are shown in certain settings.

Of all the bridges between spectator and picture none is quite as powerful as the horizon. If the horizon is the same for both spectator and the graphic characters there is a common bond. As spectators we intuitively feel that we are one with the characters. This should not imply that surface control is to be ignored. Although we establish a close relation to the horizon suggested in the picture, a strong surface pattern may still be achieved. In fact, the horizon often is incorporated in the linear structure of the picture surface (Chapter 25).

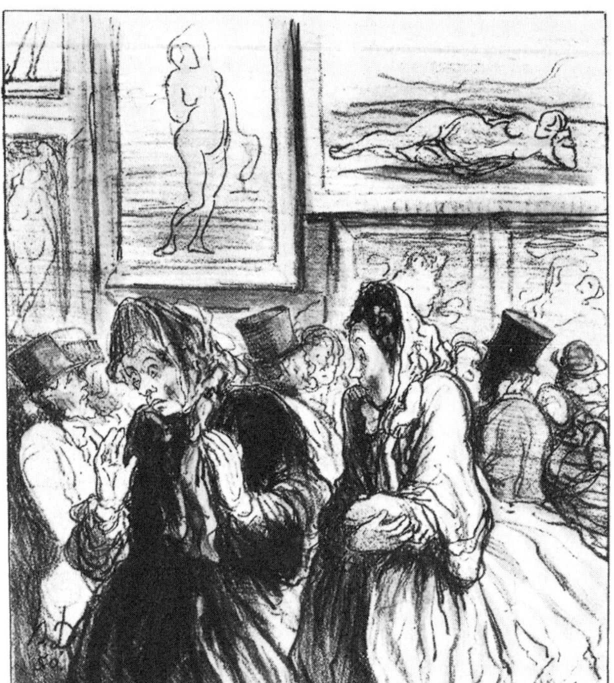

Honoré Daumier (French, 1808-1879)
AGAIN THIS YEAR THE VENUS, ALWAYS THE
VENUS! . . . AS IF THERE WERE ANY WOMEN LIKE
THAT!, 1864
9⅞″ x 8½″ lithograph published
in *Charivari*
Prints Division, The New York Public Library
Astor, Lenox, and Tilden Foundations

Honoré Daumier
ABUSING THE PERMISSION THAT ARTISTS MAY
SHOW MORE THAN THREE PICTURES THIS YEAR
8¹/₁₆″ x 9¹⁵/₁₆″; lithograph published
in *Charivari*, May 13, 1857
Courtesy of The Art Institute of Chicago

Honoré Daumier
THE SAD ASPECT OF THE SCULPTURE PLACED
AMONG THE PAINTINGS; lithograph
published in *Charivari*, July 22, 1857
The Metropolitan Museum of Art
Rogers Fund, 1922

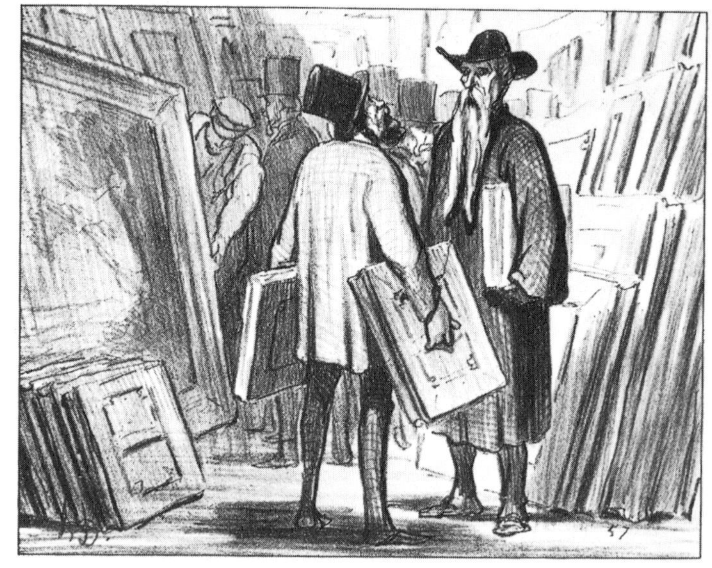

186  In a picture the horizon often is indicated as a drawn line and becomes a means of helping us identify with the drawn characters. Generally speaking, the stronger the indication of the horizon in a picture, the more we feel that it is our own horizon. Suppose, for instance, that we look at a picture of a crowd in which all the people are walking or standing on a level floor, as in the first Daumier. Through association we assume that we, too, are standing, that our eye level is also the eye level of the crowd. In effect, we project ourselves into the picture even to the extent of actually taking the place of a drawn symbol.

If a group is shown in an "up" view from a low eye level, we may feel that we are looking up from a position just above sidewalk level, as in this second Daumier.

If the picture has a high horizon, we may feel that we are above the crowd looking down upon it, as in this third Daumier.

At times we may feel that we are not an intimate part of the scene, yet we still feel that we are interested observers. This is particularly true if we assume a remote station point or remote point of observation, such as we found in the Whistler. We feel ourselves looking across a great expanse to objects in the distance. We are interested in the objects, but do not associate ourselves intimately with them.

There are times when our imaginary location in a picture is not exact. We witness an occurrence in a rather remote way, yet at the same time we are fully aware of the most minute

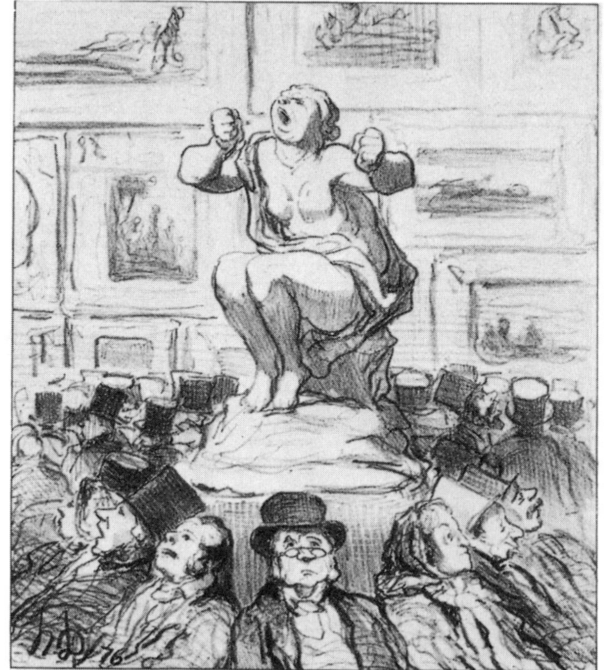

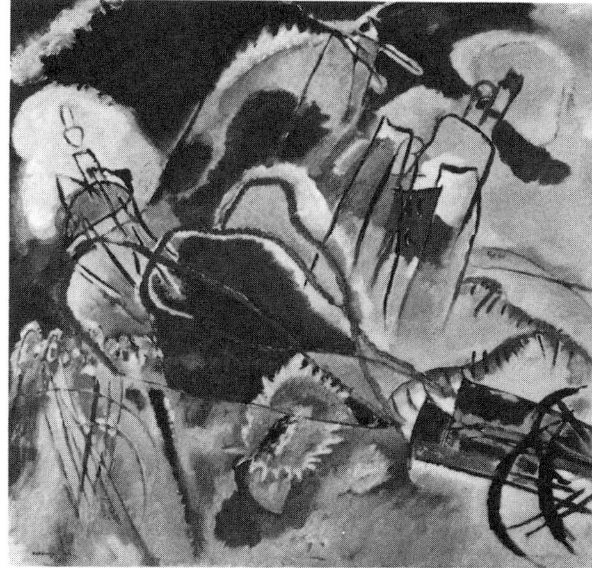

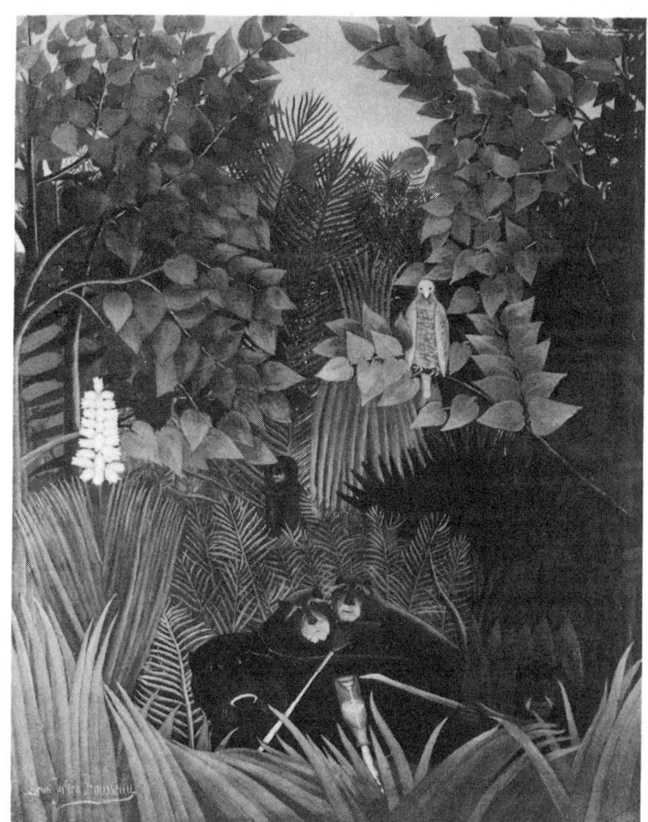

Henri Rousseau (French, 1844-1910)
THE MERRY JESTERS, 1906; 57⅜" x 44⅝"
oil on canvas
The Philadelphia Museum of Art
The Louise and Walter Arensberg Collection

Wassily Kandinsky (Russian, 1866-1944)
IMPROVISATION No. 30, 1913; 43⅝" x 43⅝"
oil on canvas
Courtesy of The Art Institute of Chicago
Arthur Jerome Eddy Memorial Collection



detail, such as we find in the painting of Rousseau. We may well call this our omnipresent station point.

In many abstract paintings, like Kandinsky's *Improvisation No. 30*, the spectator does not assume a given station point. The picture seems to exist by itself in space.

## Perspective Linear Patterns

As we noted in Chapter 5, a line—in this case the horizon—need not be actually delineated. A series of graphic elements so arranged as to create a progressive movement also generates a line. If, now, we organize a series of related symbols: heads, hands, and feet, a linear structure is achieved which may give strong rhythmic linear patterns.

In order to explore a few possibilities of linear patterns let us use only two symbols, heads and feet.

Variations in height of human beings fall into rather broad, simple categories. The adult male, ranging from less than five feet in height to well over six feet, is generally taller than the adult female. Children range from babes in arms to medium tall adolescents. If in our picture we assume a height of about six feet for the male, and five feet, five inches, for the female, the difference is great enough to be noticeable. Naturally, a short fat man can be paired with a tall thin woman, and other such unexpected variations may be used.

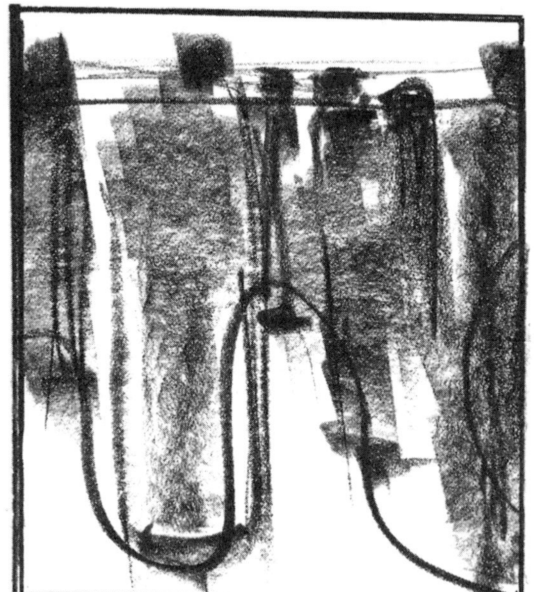

188-1A

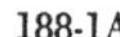

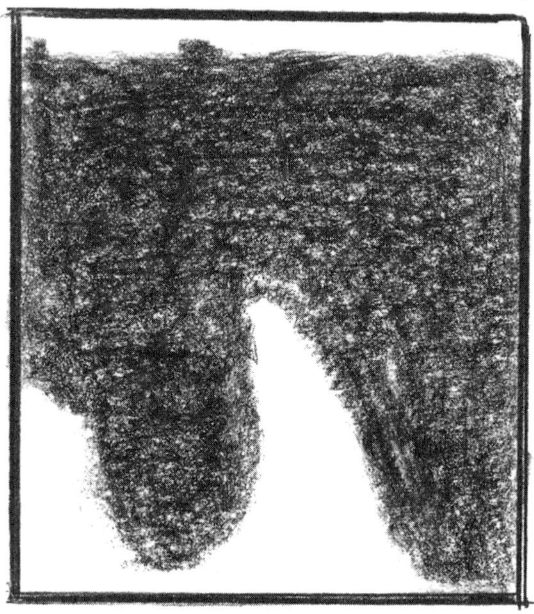

188-1B

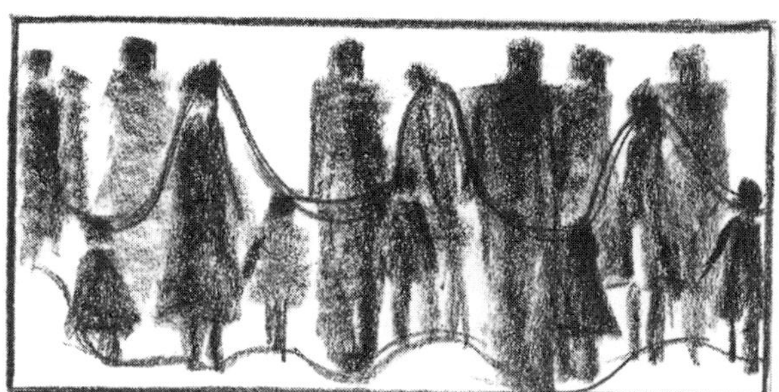

188-2A

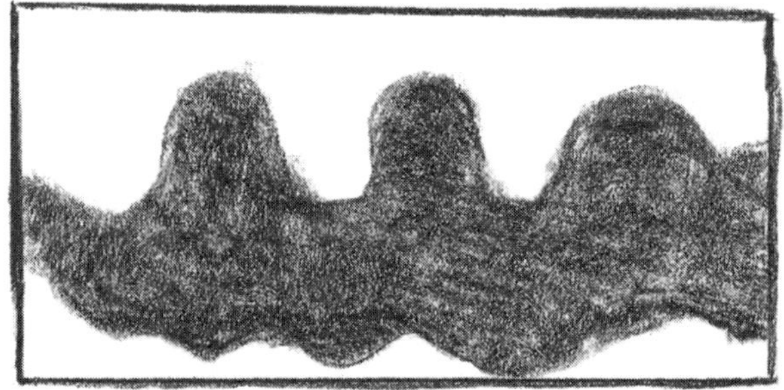

188-2B



Suppose now a group of men are depicted standing, conversing with each other. Their heads may be carried approximately as a straight horizontal line. Their composite eye levels will be very close to our eye level, our horizon (*188-1A*). Their feet, however, will constitute an undulating linear pattern, varying from elements far from us (which will be closer to the horizon) to elements close to us (which will be lower on our picture surface). By careful planning this wave-like curve may be manipulated, varied, made rhythmic or eccentric (*188-1B*).

By adding a number of women, the linear pattern can be made more varied and complex. We may also add children who, because of the great difference in heights, give even more variety to the surface pattern (*188-2A*). We should note that such linear patterns can give great richness to what might be a dull picture structure (*188-2B*). However, they are seldom emphasized to the extent of dominating the picture. The accompanying diagrams show a few possible variations (*189-1A,-1B, -1C*).

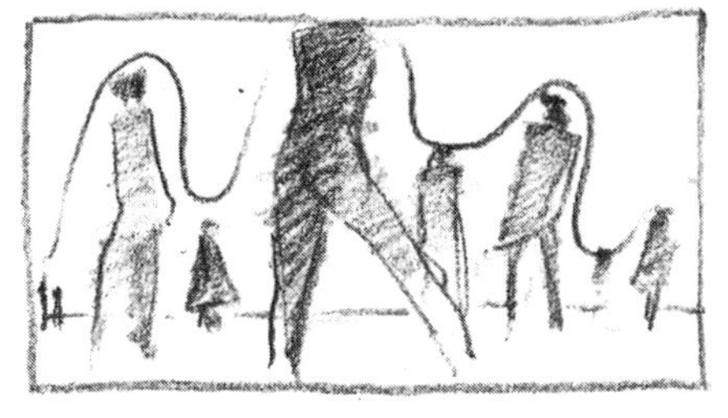

189-1A

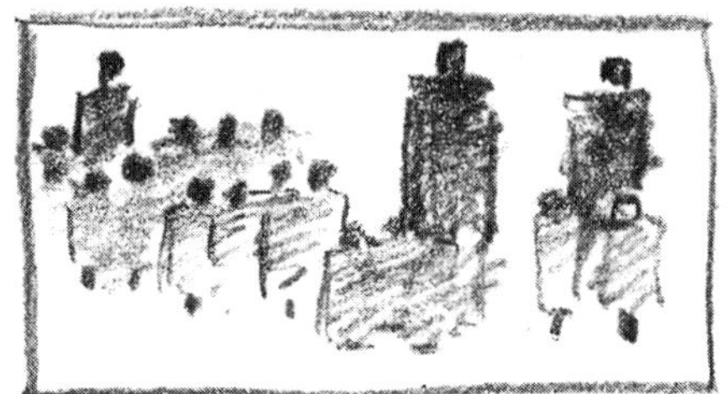

189-1B

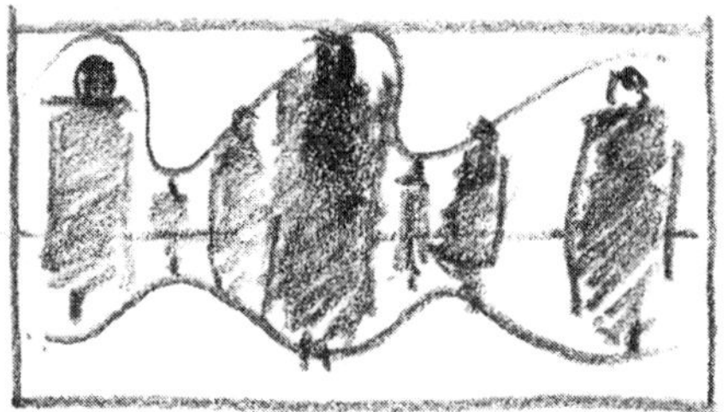

189-1C

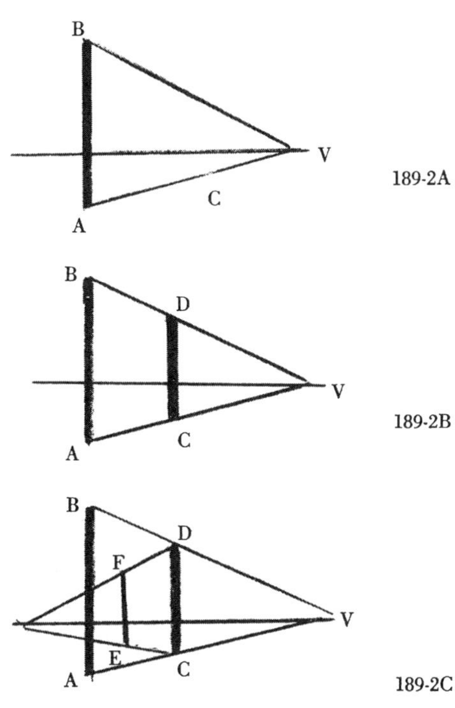

189-2A

189-2B

189-2C

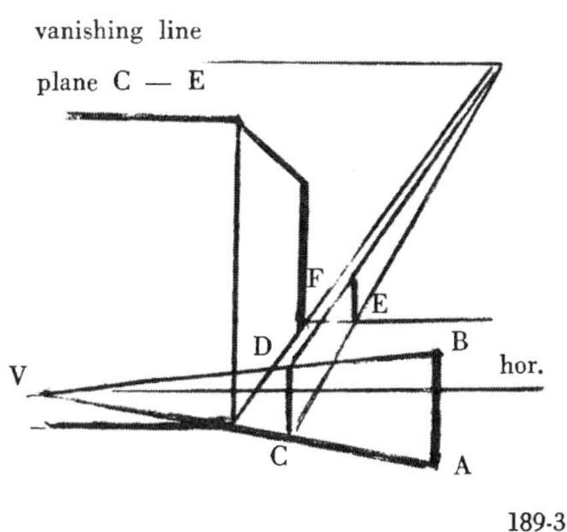


189-3

## Location of Characters in Perspective Depth

Although Italian perspective is a method of drawing which rarely satisfies involved picture problems, its simple system of triangulation often is helpful in placing figures in a picture. A vertical element $AB$ occurs in a plane $ABV$ (*189-2A*). Any element lying in $ABV$ and parallel to $AB$ will be directly related to $AB$. Hence, if we wish to draw at point $C$ a figure in perspective of the same size as $AB$, we simply raise a vertical at $C$ until it meets $BV$ at $D$. $CD$ is now equal in height to $AB$, in perspective (*189-2B*). In the same way the same height may be found at any point $E$ by direct triangulation from either $A$ or $C$ (*189-2C*).

If more than one level is involved, heights may be triangulated from a known vertical at $AB$ to a vertical rising from $C$, a point common to the horizontal plane and the sloping plane (*189-3*). The vanishing line of this sloping plane is found by holding our hand parallel to the plane and through the eyes. When the hand is seen on-edge while still parallel to the sloping plane, we have established the vanishing line. If the drawing is not derived directly from nature, the graphic vanishing line is arbitrarily established in the drawing.

Once the vanishing line is determined, the height $CD$ may be transferred to $EF$ by direct triangulation to the vanishing line $P$ (*189-3*).

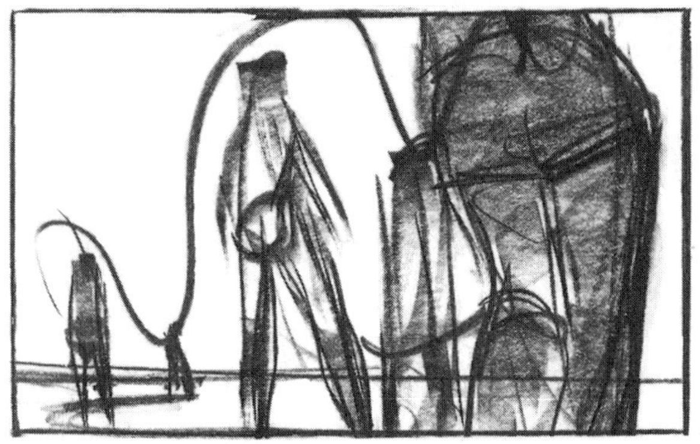

190-1

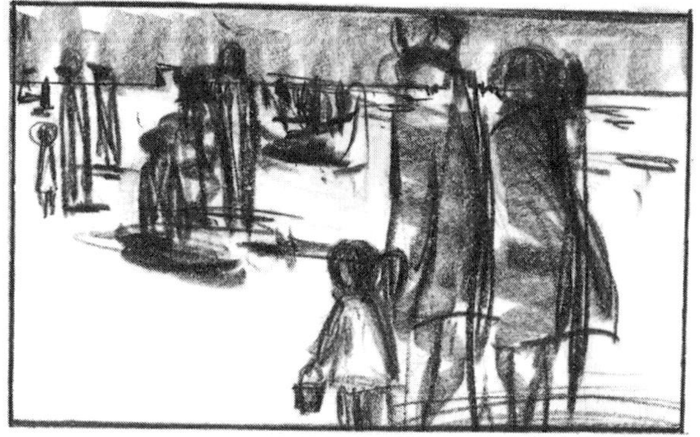

190-2

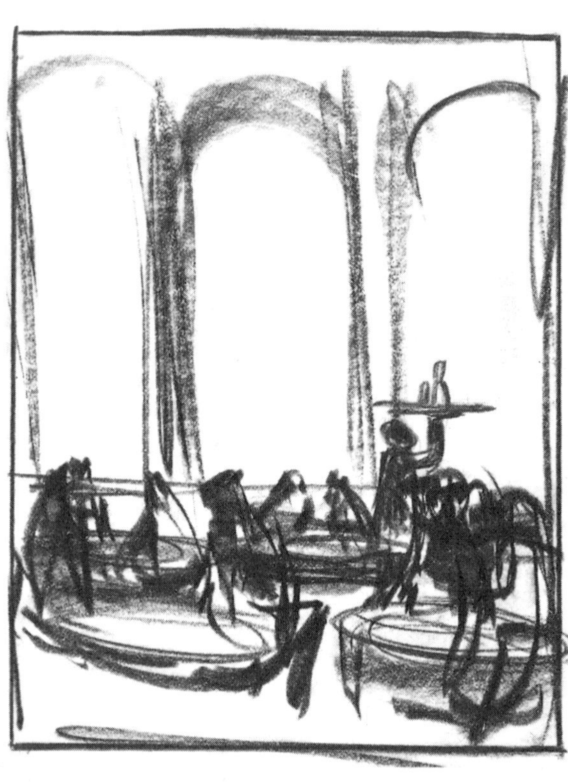

190-3



190     Probably one of the easiest methods of establishing heights in perspective depth is to utilize proportional divisions. Let us assume that we are lying on the beach, which gives us a logical reason to use a low horizon. This horizon may cut below the knee of a person standing in the middle distance. It will also cut all other standing adults at approximately the same place. To establish a figure in the distance, or in a close-up in our picture, we need merely to locate the knees or calves at the horizon and divide the figure in proportion to this division. This method is fast and accurate (*190-1*).

Once a figure is located in relation to a horizon in the picture, other figures can be directly related to the first figure, especially if they are near each other. A man may be established in the middle distance. His wife's head comes to his shoulder, his child's head comes to his hip. Moving forward, once a second man's height is determined, the height of the wife and child also are determined automatically (*190-2*).

In any scene involving many people this method is a sound and direct way to control complex structure, as for example this restaurant scene (*190-3*). All seated persons are at approximately the spectator's eye level. Other customers and waiters are walking between the tables. The heads of the seated figures come a little above waist height of any standing figure anywhere in the room. The heads and feet constitute a linear pattern which adds great interest to the picture.

figure standing	figure seated	figure reclining

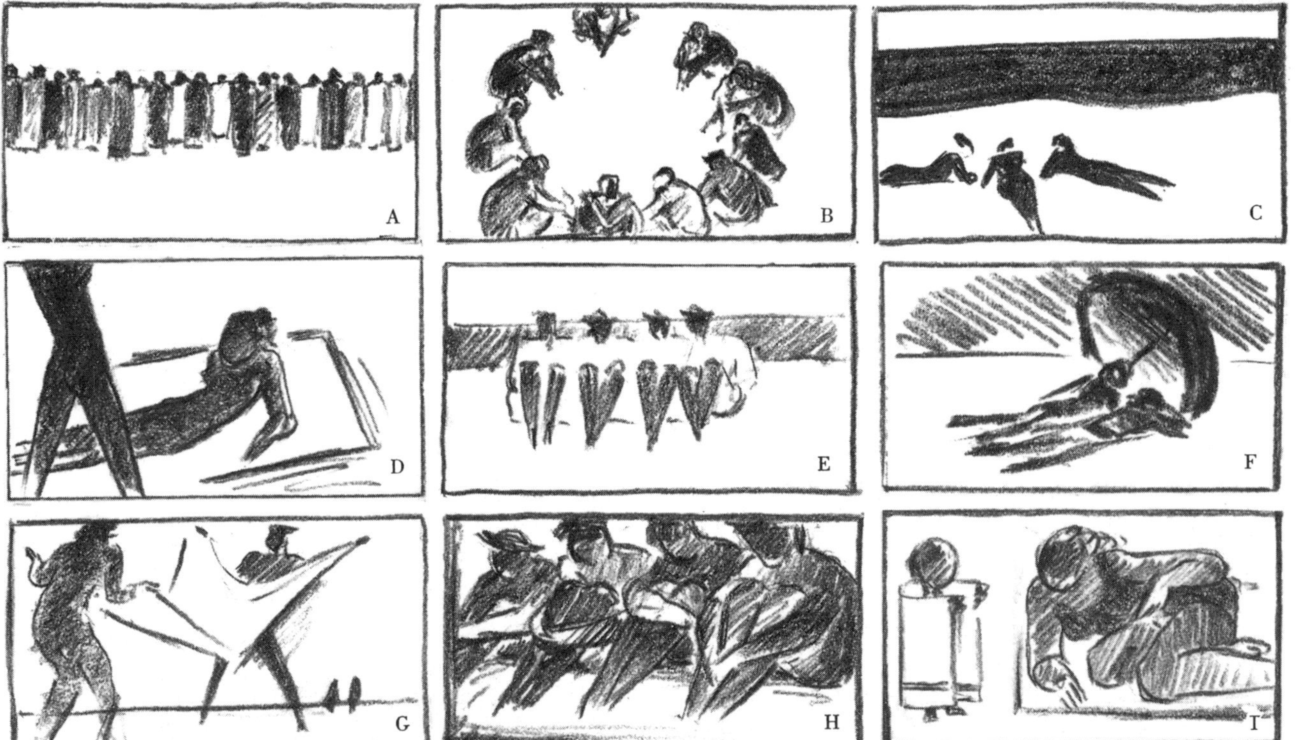

The variety possible in relating the spectator to picture horizon is provocative. These arrangements depicting beach scenes should suggest many others. In each of the accompanying examples a level or horizontal floor plane is assumed.

The free choice of horizon gives us a direct control of picture pattern. By varying our eye level we may generate a constant change of pattern with an accompanying variety of picture impact.

Reading from left to right, we may generate a strong horizontal strip (*191-A*), a circular pattern (*191-B*), or a star (*191-C*). In the second row, we generate a strong right angular shape rotated (*191-D*), a rectangular shape (*191-E*), a cone (*191-F*). The third row achieves a strong diagonal pattern with horizontal stripes (*191-G*), a pattern based on diagonal stripes (*191-H*), and a vertical rectangle and a square (*191-I*).

Given an assignment to develop a number of pictures using crowds, the inquisitive artist or film designer is never at a loss for compositional ideas. As we see here, limiting ourselves to only three eye levels, a vast selection is possible. By adding up or down shots, the vocabulary of expression is extended. By introducing angle shots by rotating the camera, or by introducing violent perspectives, the possibilities become endless.

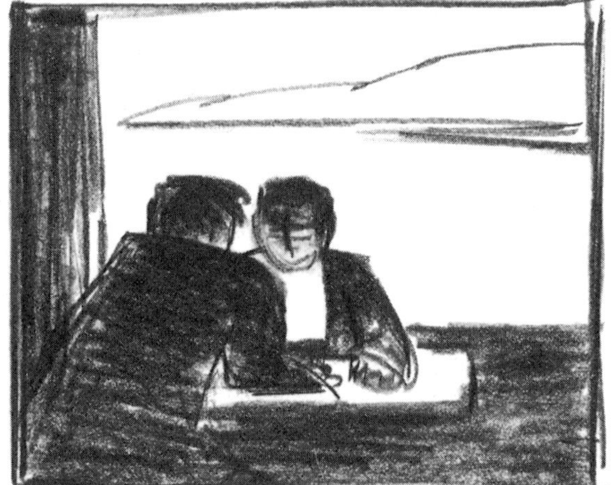

192-A

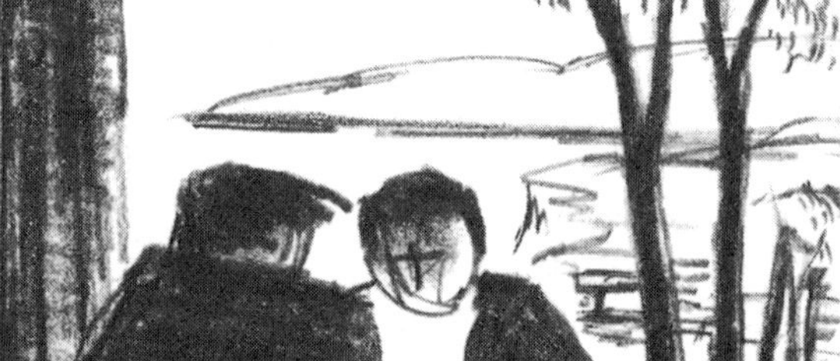

192-B



## The Improbable Station Point

We have noted that the spectator wants to identify with a picture and that he identifies his own horizon with the horizon indicated in the picture. Suppose, now, that we establish a horizon in such a way that when the spectator identifies with it he is made uncomfortable. This can and does happen frequently in pictures. Although the spectator rarely is conscious of what is happening, he may nevertheless become so disturbed that he avoids lingering to look at the picture.

Confusion sometime arises when we make a close-up overlaying a distant background. The spectator feels lost without the expected intervening elements which are so familiar to him in nature (*192-A, -B*).

At times the spectator's views are limited by the architecture suggested in the picture. This is especially true of small interiors. When the choice of horizon violates the logic of the structure, the spectator is disturbed.

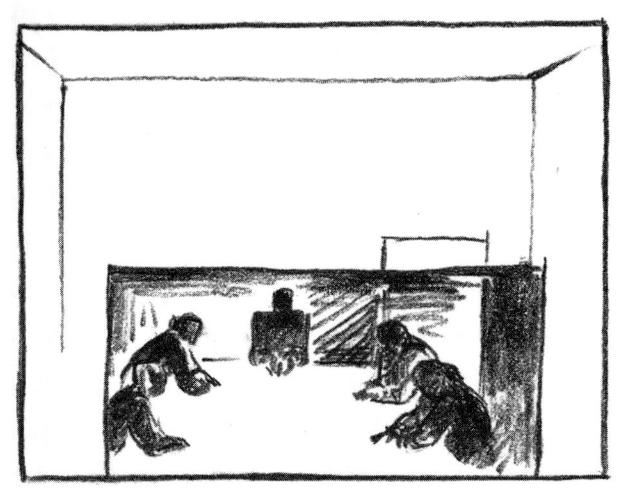

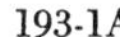

193-1A

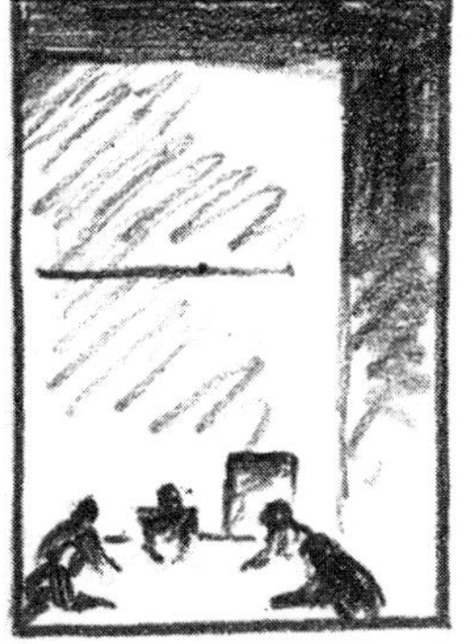

193-1B

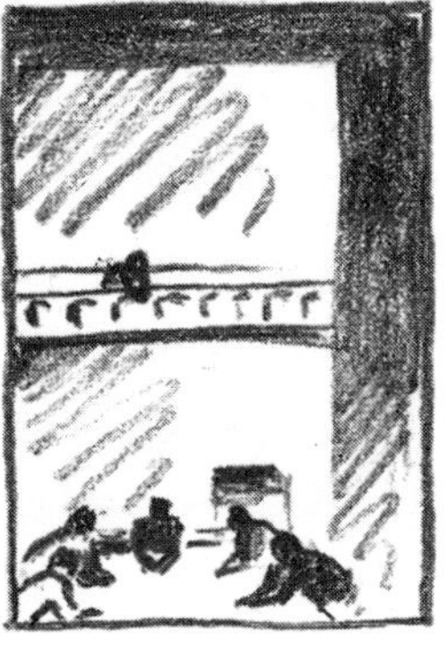

193-1C

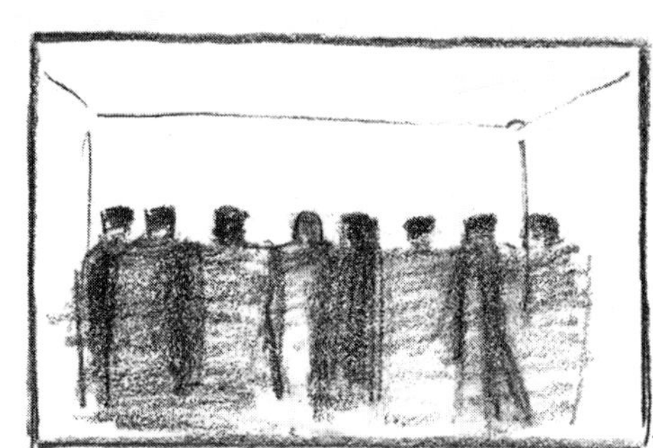

193-2A

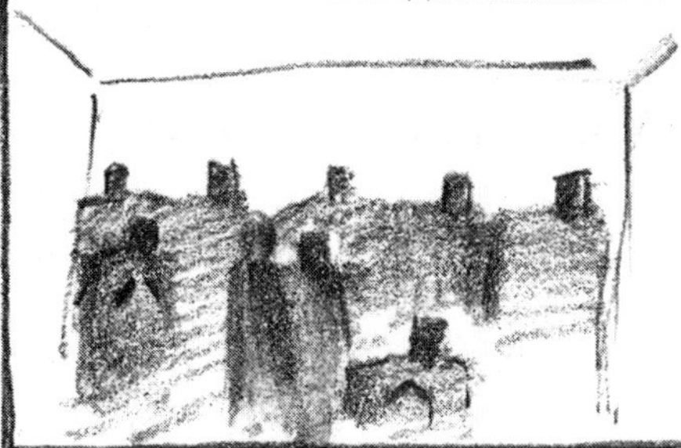

193-2B

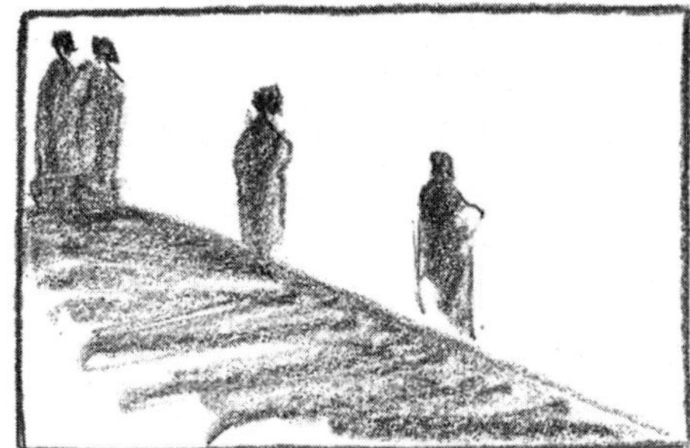

193-2C

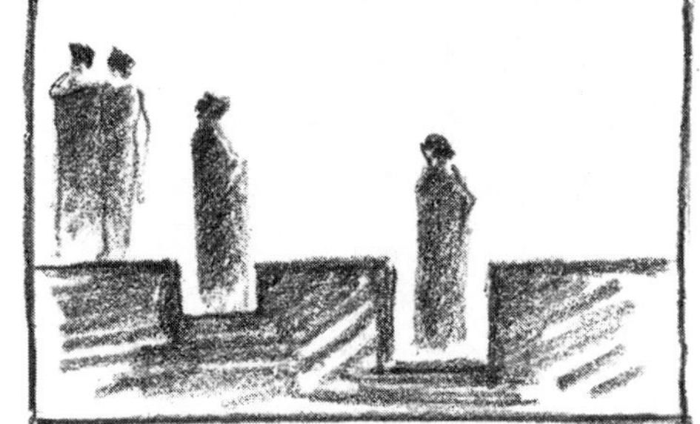

193-2D

For instance, if the picture suggests a ceiling height of eight feet, and we establish the eye level at ceiling height or above, the development of the subject will give a strong down view (*193-1A*). When the spectator tries to justify the horizon in the picture to his own logical location lower in the picture, he finds himself in an improbable position. The same view of the subject related to a high ceilinged room would be less objectionable, although still not entirely satisfactory (*193-1B*). If we place a balcony in the picture, the spectator can identify his position as being at that height, and the horizon becomes logical (*193-1C*).



Of all the disturbing perspectives we create perhaps none is as prevalent as that of the *dropping overlays*. To demonstrate, let us show a simple interior and establish a number of standing figures (*193-2A*). Their eye level will be approximately that of the spectator's eye level. Now, if other figures are introduced as overlays, it may seem logical to lower the level of each overlay to better display each separate head (*193-2B*). This always results in clear staging of all figures, but let us see what happens to the rest of the picture. As we drop the overlays we imply that either the floor slopes down as it comes forward (*193-2C*), or that each overlaying figure, as it approaches, is standing in a progressively deeper hole in the horizontal floor (*193-2D*).

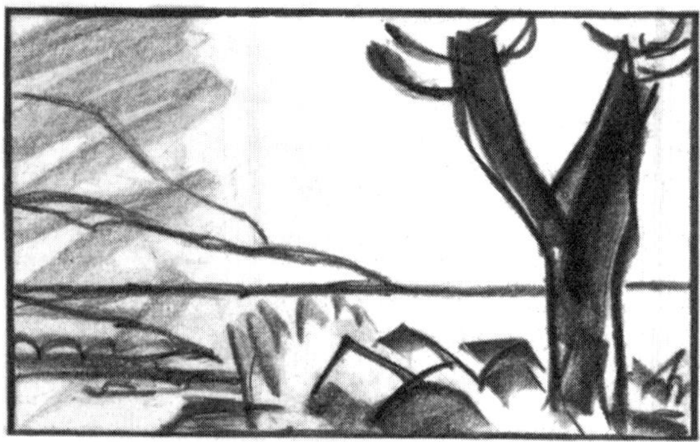

194-1A

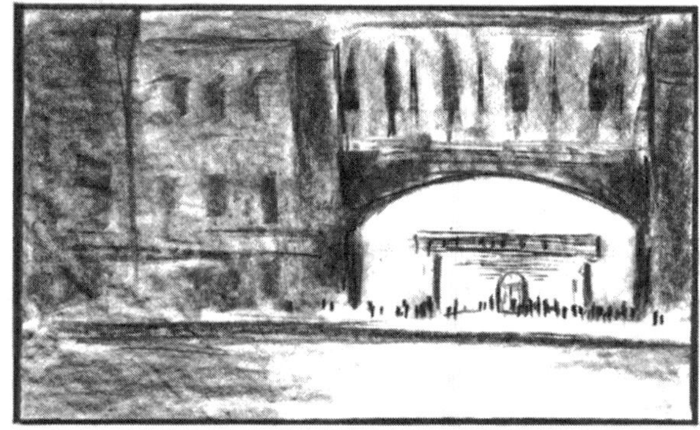

194-2A

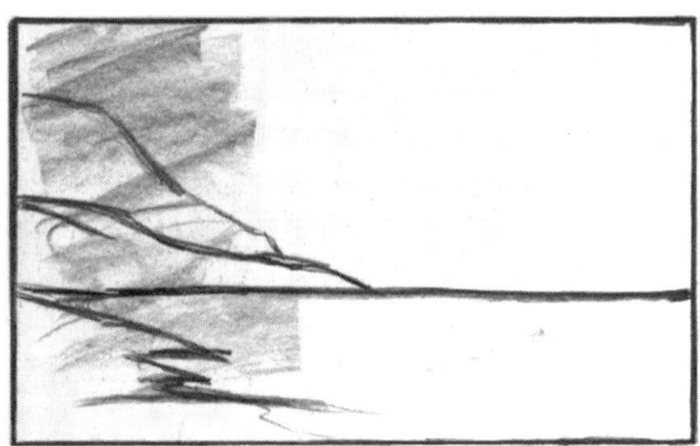

194-1B

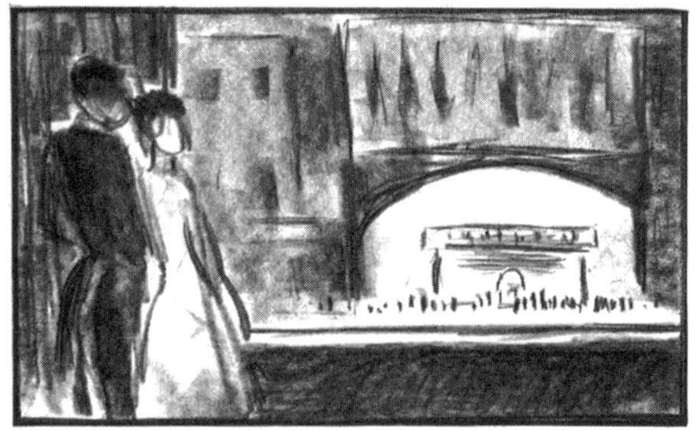

194-2B



On the other hand, the use of overlays can be very effective in giving a sense of security or stability to the spectator. For instance, an overlay of a tree growing on a shelf in the foreground suggests that the spectator too, might be on this ledge *(194-1A)*. Without the overly there is a distant view of a landscape, possibly a bird's-eye view, and the spectator is placed high in the air *(194-1B)*. The overlay gives him a more secure viewpoint.

A street scene shown from a high elevation may be made more intimate, and more plausible, by the introduction of an overlay depicting an interior *(194-2A, -B)*.

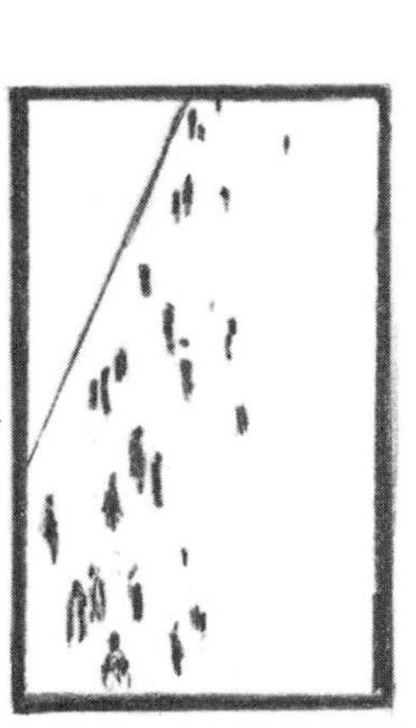

195-1A

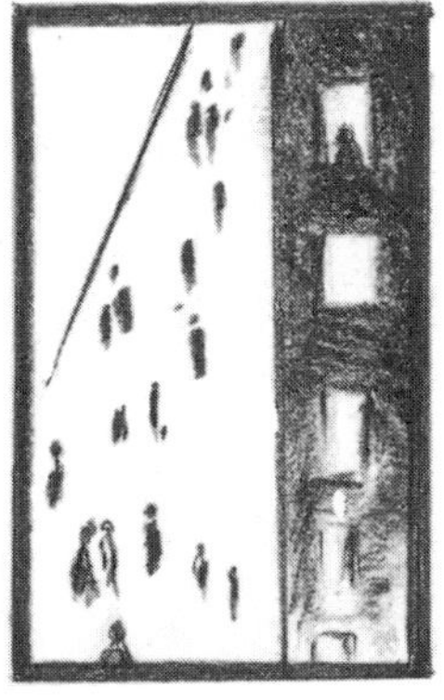

195-1B

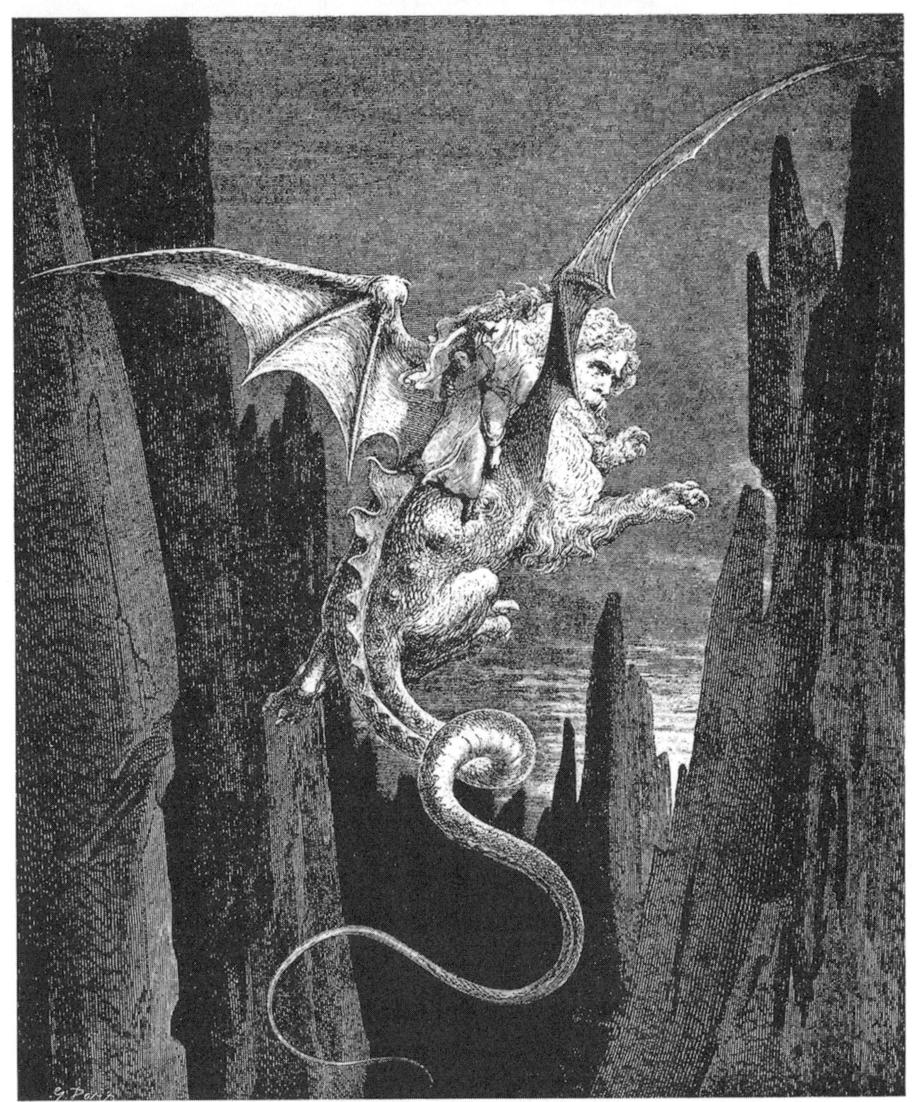

Gustave Doré (French, 1832-1883)
THE DESCENT OF THE ABYSS ON GERYON'S BACK
from Dante's *The Divine Comedy*; 1861
engraving; 8⅝″ x 7″; Courtesy Random House, Inc.
(Photograph: Alexander Hovsepian)

A crowd seen from a high elevation may cause the spectator to feel remote and insecure *(195-1A)*. If we introduce an overlay of a building, the spectator feels through association that he, too, may be in a similar building and again feels reassured *(195-1B)*.

At times an environment is so convincingly established by the story that the station point is seldom questioned. Once Dante establishes the premise of *The Divine Comedy*, Doré's illustrations of angels and devils are accepted in their improbable environments, and the spectator willingly accepts impossible station points, as we see here. Any imaginary space environment once accepted by the spectator permits impossible station points.

We have explored some of the possibilities of plan and elevation, and the relation of the horizon to elevation. Now we return to the plan and investigate the almost infinite number of elevations which may be generated from any given plan.

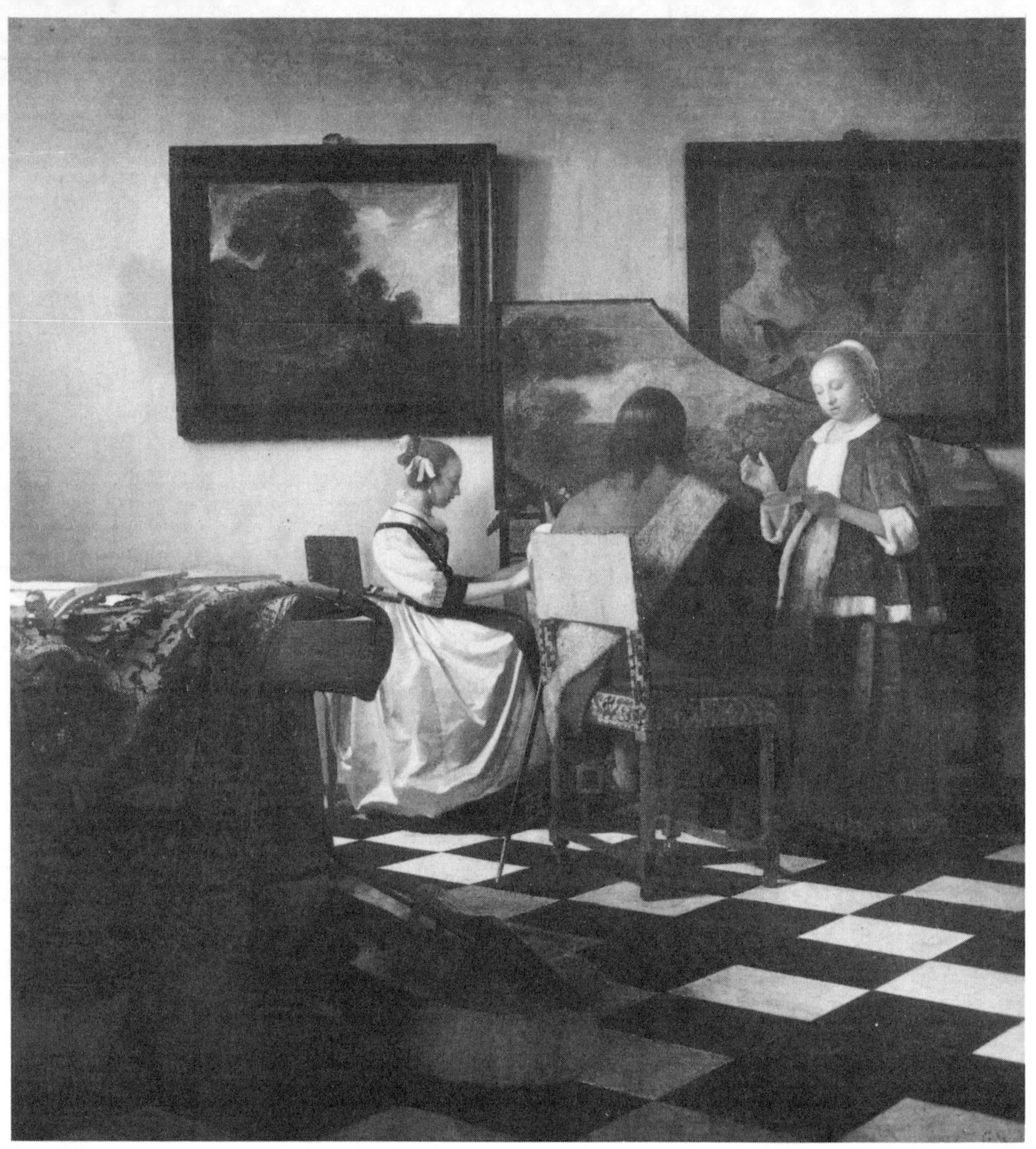



## 18  The Whirling Plan

**A Story Built Around an Object**

To explore the graphic potential in variations of plan and eye level, let us accept a theoretical assignment. Although an artist may be motivated to create a picture by an idea of his own, in many instances the picture problem is assigned by someone else. The person may be a highly qualified art director, or perhaps a client who who knows very little about picture construction. In any case, it is not unusual for the artist to be given only the barest suggestion of an idea. Often an object of some kind dominates the problem suggested: a billiard table, a diving-board by a pool, a telephone. These objects all suggest particular environments which give graphic ideas to the artist as the piano does in Vermeer's *The Concert.*

Suppose that we have been asked to make a representational picture using a grand piano as a theme. What does it suggest? A concert? A

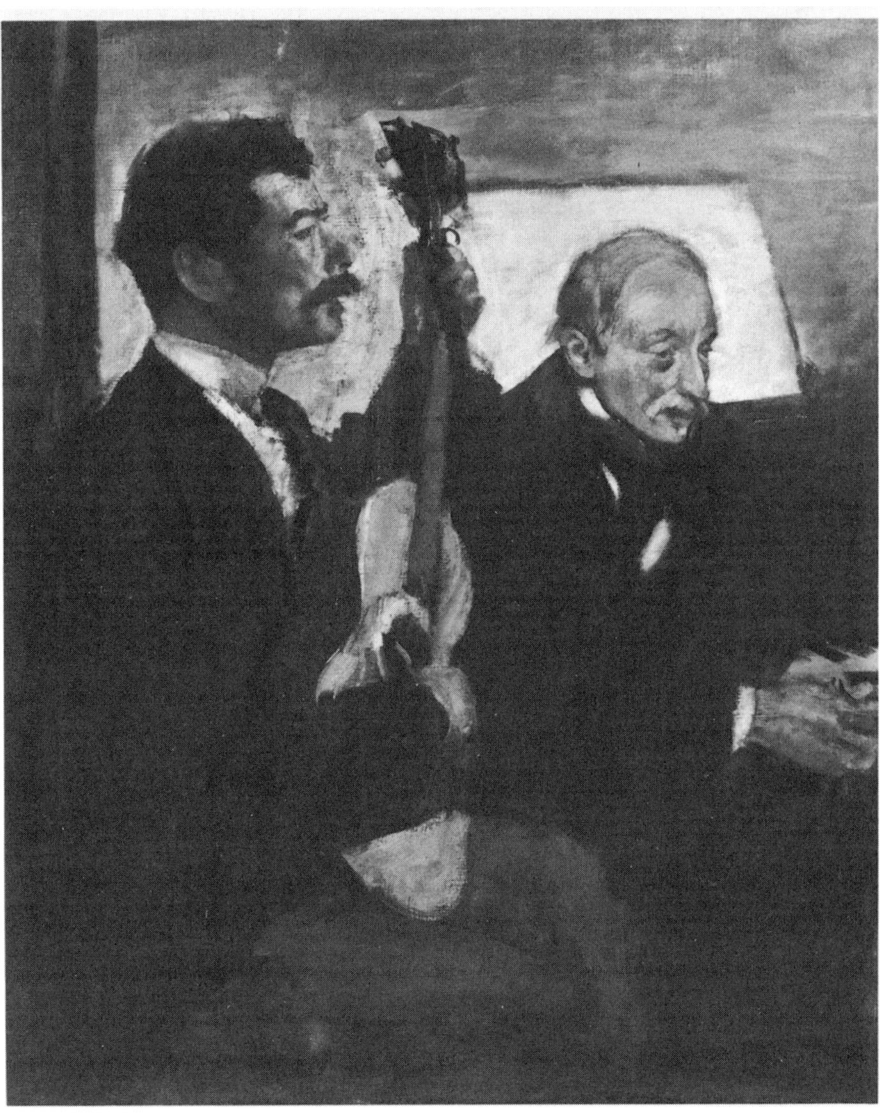

Jan Vermeer (Dutch, 1632-1675)
THE CONCERT, ca. 1662; 27¼″ x 24¾″
oil on canvas
Isabella Stewart Gardner Museum, Boston

Hilaire Germain Edgar Degas (French, 1834–1917)
DEGAS' FATHER LISTENING TO
PAGANS ACCOMPANYING HIMSELF
ON THE GUITAR
1872; 32″ x 25½″; oil on canvas
Courtesy, Museum of Fine Arts, Boston; Bequest of John T. Spaulding

recital? An evening of entertainment at home?
A dance? A party? Why not a party! The more
we consider the idea of depicting a party, the
more intriguing the idea becomes. What kind of
party? A costume party of some kind offers
opportunity to use interesting graphic shapes
and colors. A Halloween party, a birthday
party, a formal party, all suggest great variety,
great visual scope.

The mood of a party often determines its
success. It can be gay, bright, and happy;
spooky, or bizarre. Some parties are fanciful,
imaginative, or romantic. Others, more
reserved, are formal but still pleasant.

In deciding upon the type of party, we are
immediately confronted with the character of
the guests who would participate. A birthday
party usually, although not necessarily, suggests
children, a Halloween party might suggest a
suburban group, a New Year's Eve party may

suggest an adult gathering in formal attire in an
apartment in a large city. Certainly the nature
of the group and the group temperament will
affect what we draw.

Let us decide, for instance, that the party will
be a formal one. Now we have simplified our
choice of costumes. In doing so we also restrict
our choice of shape, especially concerning the
men to be depicted. Instead of the bright,
multi-colored, many-shaped costumes which
might be seen at a costume party, we show the
male characters in conservative dress. This gives
us certain design advantages such as opportunity
to use large dark shapes of the suits, as well as
the piano, to set off areas of intense color or
pastel shades which might be used in the
women's dresses. In this Degas we see how such
dark shapes are used to stage the hands and
guitar.

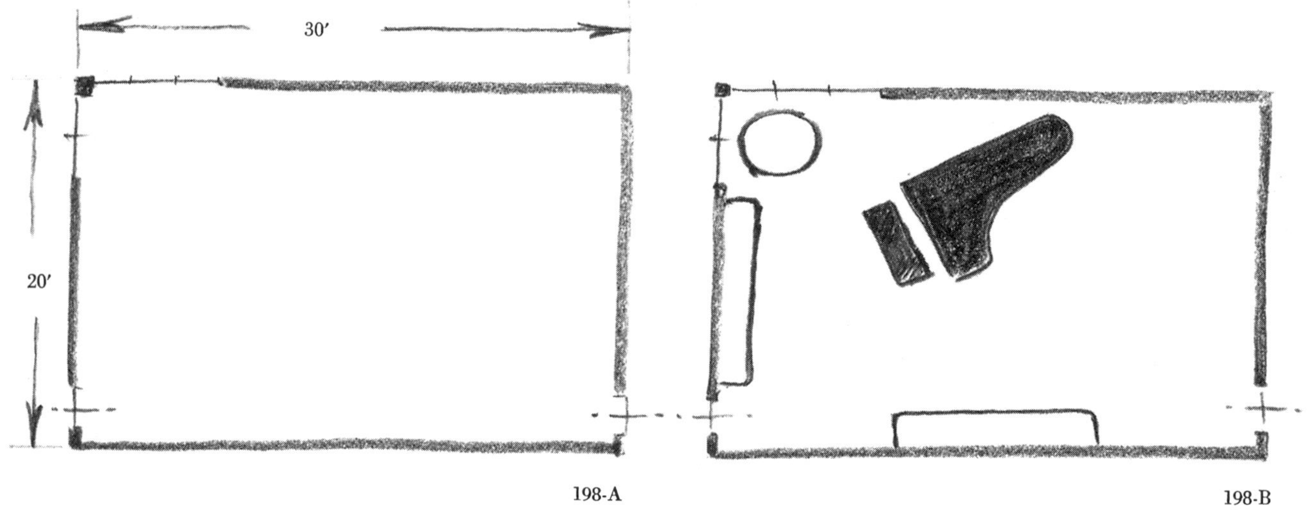



 Now we must set further limits, this time as to the environment. In what sort of room is the party located? To clarify our concept, let us make a plan showing a room thirty feet by twenty feet, by ten feet high. In this plan we might show two doorways and a corner window (*198-A*).

Now let us place the grand piano, the piano bench, and miscellaneous furniture in the room: a few chairs, a table in the corner, a large sofa (*198-B*).

Since our picture must emphasize the piano we might dramatize it by placing a woman singing beside it with a man accompanying her at the keyboard (*199-A*).

These, let us say, are given factors. No matter how we shift them around we must account for all this material.

To these required constant factors we may add as many variables as the subject suggests. In this case by "variables" we especially mean more people. The density of the crowd and the distribution of various groups will depend upon the nature and mood of the party, and also how the groupings work graphically in the picture (*199-B*).

### Rotating the Plan

When deciding upon a picture idea we frequently become so interested in seeing it evolve graphically that we develop our first rough without taking time to explore other possibilities. We may visualize a subject, our party for instance, from the viewpoint most easily conceived, most obvious, most banal. This first rough may block further exploration, for we become so intrigued in perfecting our first idea that we close our minds to other solutions. Then

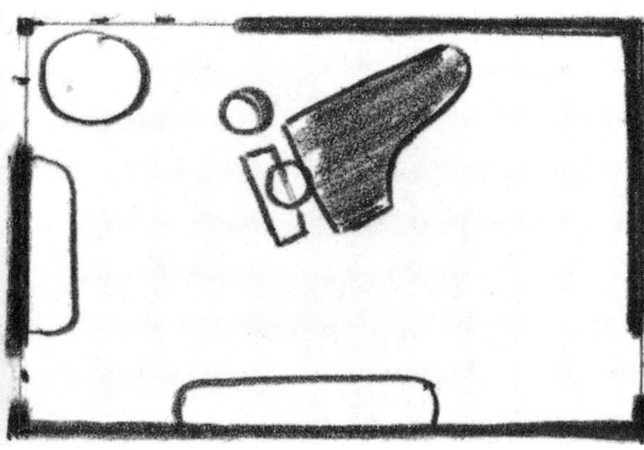

199-A

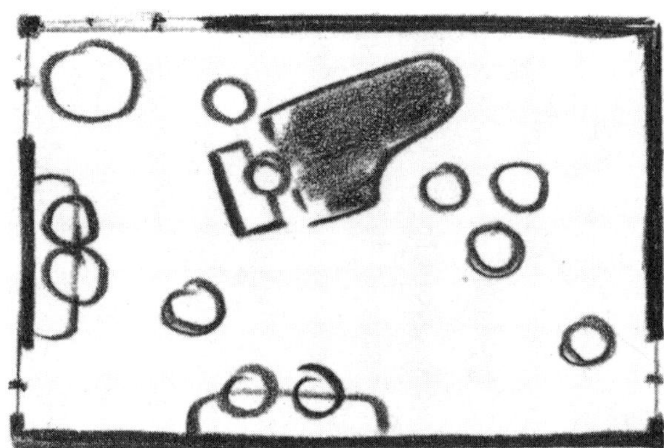

199-B

as work on our first layout progresses we feel little inclined to make major changes, and even less inclined to start entirely new picture structures.

Now there are occasions when deadlines must be met, when the time factor prohibits a full graphic investigation of an idea. Yet in most cases time will be saved by doing so. An error in planning is costly, but not to exploit the graphic possibilities of a picture to the best of our ability is not workmanlike.

To overcome built-in inertia, certain work habits are helpful. First, instead of starting the picture with a single concept, assume that many drawings will be necessary to really exploit the graphic possibilities of the assignment. A series, a great number of drawings should be generated, all pertaining to the basic idea. By making many roughs we arrive at a new way of visualizing a picture and a new way of exploring its graphic potential.

Certain procedures, if followed, will give us a variety of picture ideas all built around the basic problem, the piano. From these we may develop the idea best answering the needs of the assignment. In one sense these procedures are mechanical, but in another they are truly inventive. We do start with a single drawing, a plan, but as we whirl it around we generate a series of perspective elevations, all from one plan but each a new picture idea.

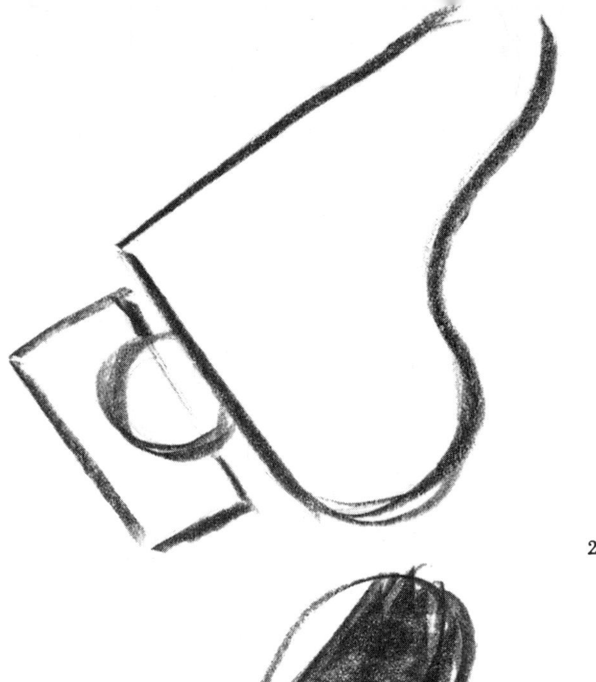



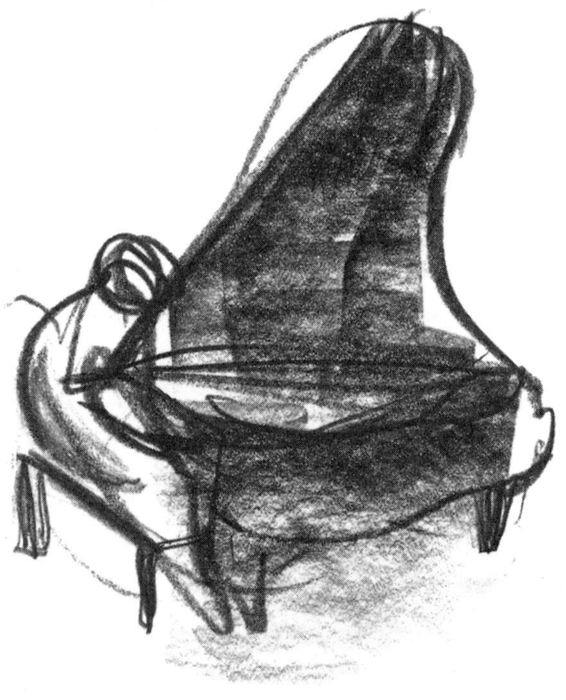



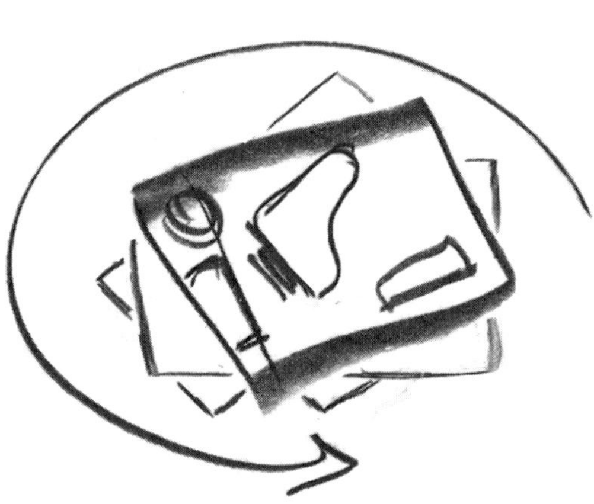



 To perform this miracle we must organize our drawing table in a simple way. It must be large enough, or the drawings small enough, to accommodate two drawings aligned up and down.

One of these drawings will be the plan of our room and the piano (*200-1A*). It is important that the plan drawing be small enough that it may be turned into various positions easily. Placing the plan near the top of the table with the perspective elevation taped directly below and aligned vertically with the plan usually allows a little more freedom to work. (*200-1B*). Occasionally the elevation may be placed above the plan.

Although only a single plan is used in this particular procedure, elements in the plan may be adjusted to provide for necessary changes in the perspective elevation. For instance, a group drawn around the piano may mask out the man at the keyboard. By adjusting the plan arrangement slightly, a corresponding change will occur in the elevation which will help clarify the picture.

If the composition is at all involved, tracing paper laid over the original plan allows for adjustments without redrawing every part of the plan. Several tissues may be superimposed before such adjustments need be transferred to the master plan.

One perspective elevation developed from the plan by a straight up-down projection is only one of many picture possibilities. To develop a a new layout we simply choose another viewpoint. By rotating the plan we are ready to proceed with a new projection. Thus by rotating one plan we generate a great many elevations (*200-2*).

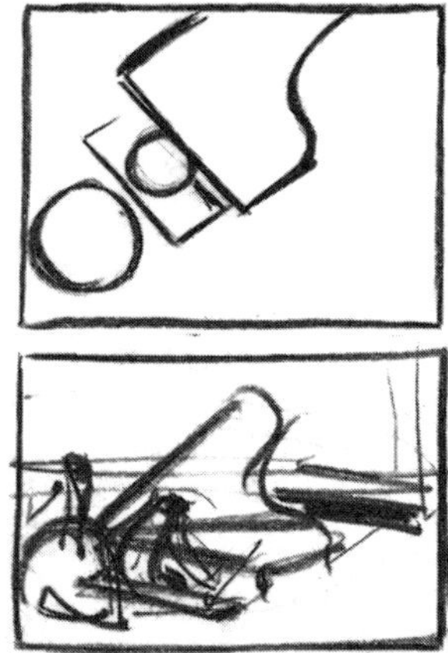

201-1A

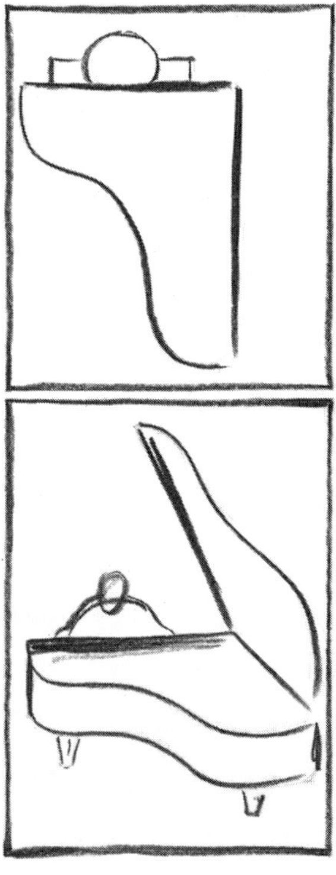

201-1B

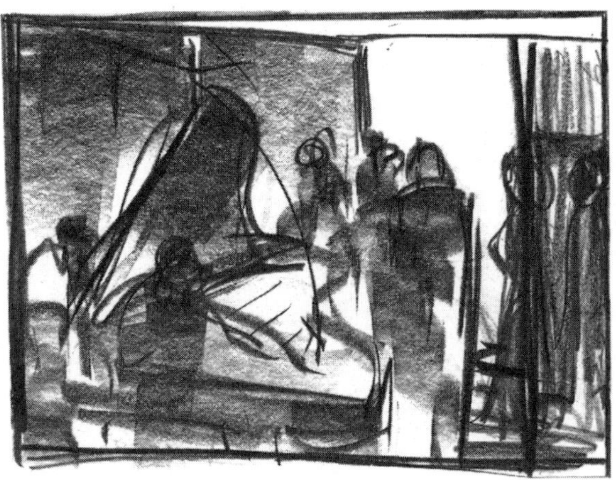

201-2

201-3

As we whirl the plan we soon find that certain views result in more satisfactory elevations than others. We must remember that the problem is to display the pianist and the singer. As we see here, a view over the pianist's back assures us of a clear view of the singer, yet still retains a view of the pianist's actions (*201-1A*).

A view looking down the strings into the face of the pianist, gives us a clear view of the singer only if the top of the piano is closed. If it is open, we may have difficulty staging the singer in the clear (*201-1B*). In such a case a slight change in the plan, possibly moving her to the other side of the pianist, will give a clear view.

A side view of the piano, with its top up, gives a dramatic shape against which other figures may be staged (*201-2*).

At times a view may incorporate important architectural features. For instance, the corner window might be used as a contrasting shape against which the activity of the party can be silhouetted (*201-3*).

Since we may have as many figures in the picture as we wish, the number of picture patterns resulting from different arrangements of characters is almost infinite. Coupling the whirling plan with various crowd arrangements multiplies our choice of layout to an impressive degree.

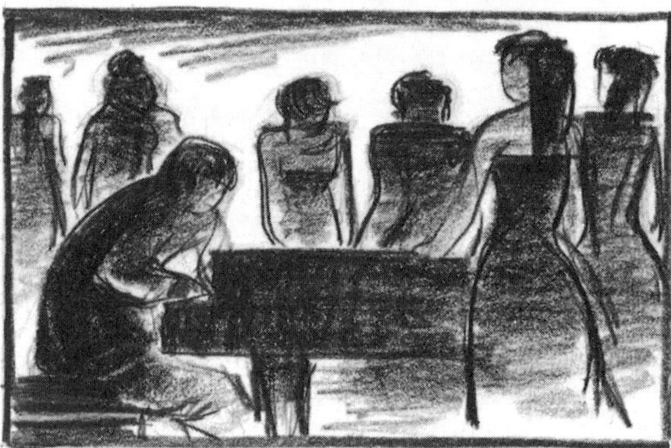

202-1

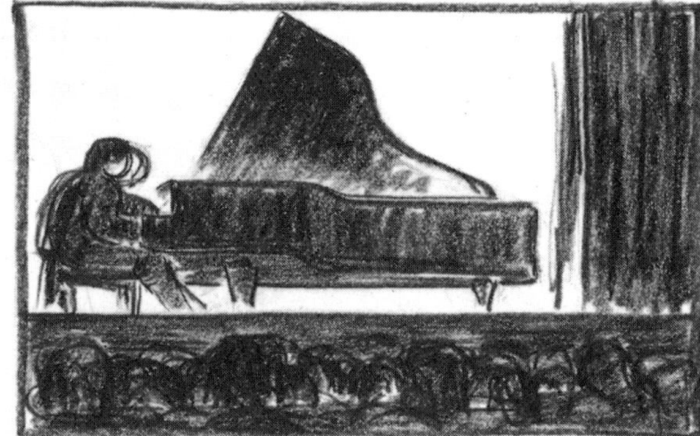

202-3

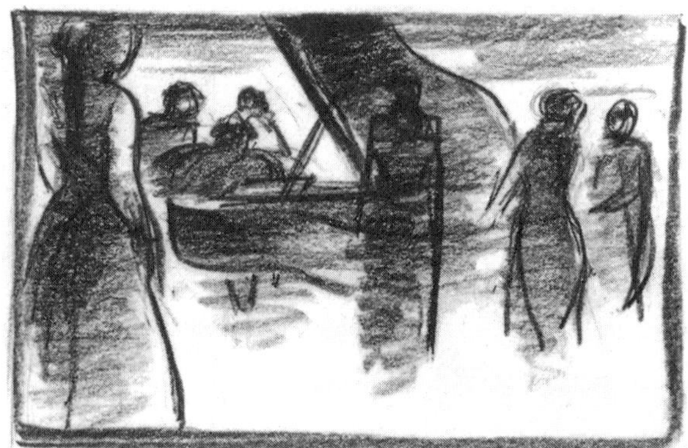

202-2

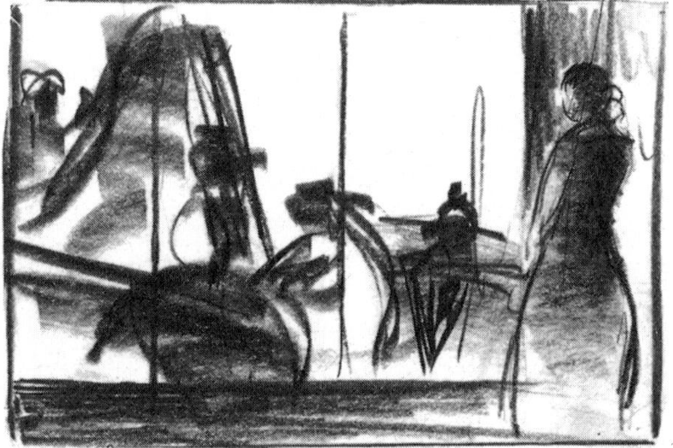

202-4

202 In any picture in which human symbols are involved we must decide the location of the horizon and, as we shall see shortly, whether or not more than one horizon is required. In solving the present problem, variety may be achieved by taking a viewpoint as if seen from a seated position (*202-1*). By recalling that our horizon, if we are seated, divides all standing figures in approximately the same proportional way, we should have little trouble with our layout (*202-2*).

Although not encountered in our present problem, the introduction of staircases, balconies, and other architectural features often suggest possible new eye levels, each suggesting unusual elevations (*202-3*).

Visualizing our plan as a small stage, we note that our viewpoint is limited by the walls, windows and doors, so that we have to imagine ourselves somewhere inside the four walls, except for the possibility that we might look through the window or doors into the room (*202-4*).

Makers of motion pictures also encountered this limitation in the early days. How could they maneuver large cameras in a narrow hall or tiny room. The answer was direct and logical: they removed a wall, as had been practiced on the theater stage for years. In special instances openings were provided in a wall to accommodate the camera.

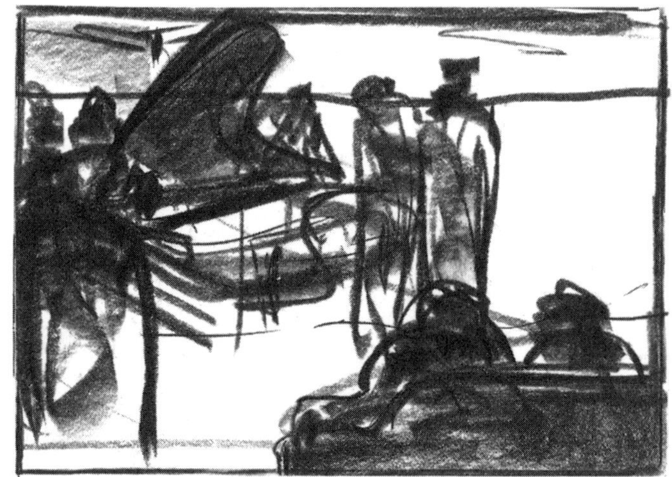

203-A

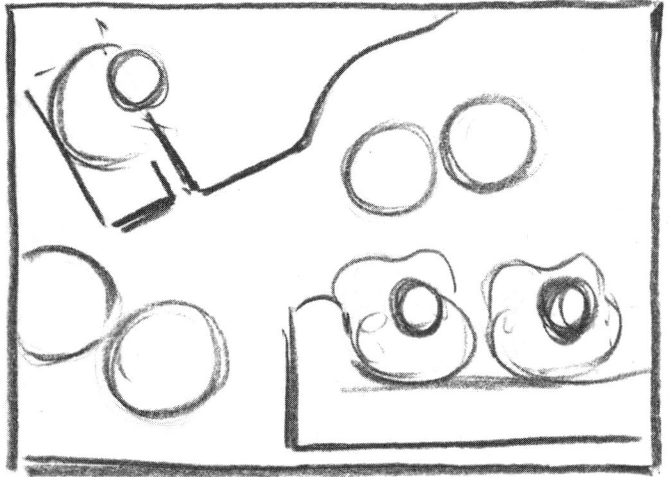

203-B

When we work from plan we too can take such liberties. For instance, if we arrange the picture so that the spectator looks past a group seated on a sofa in the foreground, we are, in effect, removing a wall, for in our plan we see the sofa is close to the near wall (*203-A, -B*).

## Varying the Viewpoint

There are limits to this arbitrary choice of viewpoint, for if it is too extreme the logic of our station point may be questioned. Our viewpoint of the party from a standing, seated, or reclining position has much to do with the mood of the party. But a viewpoint near the floor, as if we were reclining, might be considered inappropriate for a formal party. For certain dramatic reasons, however, it could be successful. A horizon far above the crowd, a bird's-eye view, may not seem logical either, since the room height we set is only ten feet.

It is helpful in determining whether or not an unexpected view is overemphasized to note whether interest is in the picture or in the station point of the spectator. The artist may choose any station point he desires as long as the spectator's interest remains in the picture itself. If, however, the viewpoint dominates the rest of the picture, we feel a disturbing shift of attention similar to that which we feel when a spotlight wanders from a stage singer. We lose interest in the singer and become interested in the operator of the light.

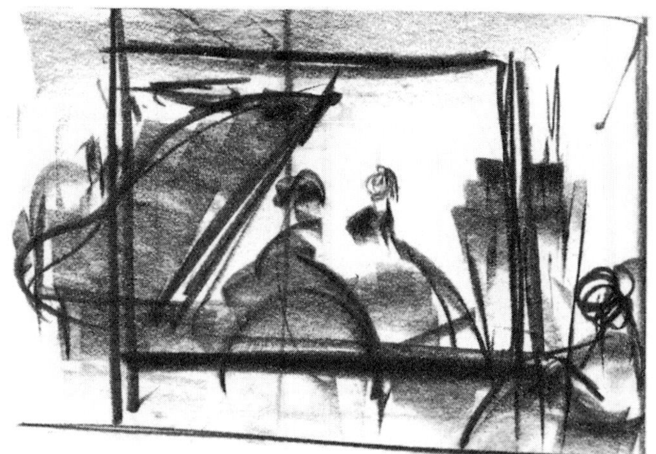

204-A

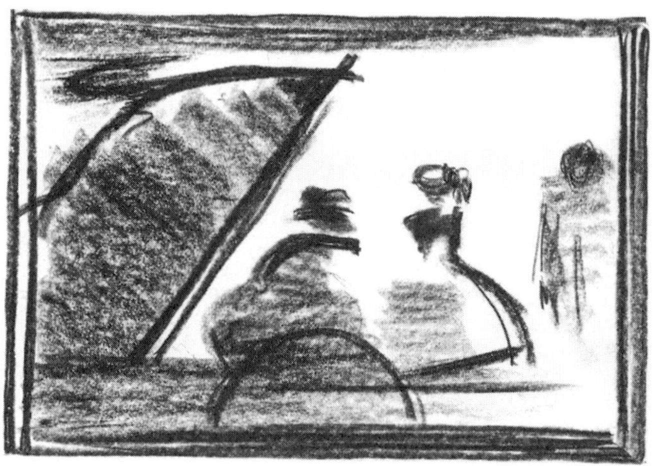

204-B



We also must realize that the reading time of a picture has much to do with our choice of an appropriate station point. An up-shot from the floor into the face of a dying villain may be appropriate for the cover of an adventure magazine or a momentary scene in a motion picture, for in each case the picture will be seen only a short time. But as a station point for a picture to be seen for any length of time, a mural in a hospital waiting room, for instance, where we already are upset, a violently distorted view is hardly appropriate. However, a violent viewpoint in a mural planned to be seen but a short time may be dramatic and effective.

### Moving In and Out

As we explore the potential of the whirling plan we may encounter certain difficulties. We may feel that the perspective projection is remote. The actual size of our drawing may contribute to this feeling, for it must be fairly small in order to be manipulated. In addition, the characters may seem equal in interest, resulting in a dull surface pattern.

To overcome some of the difficulties we can again adapt a technique which has been exploited by the motion picture industry. This device is known as *trucking*. The camera moves in on the actor to create a close-up view, or away from the actor to create a long shot.

A common technique in a motion picture story-board is to indicate a truck by means of a border, often red, within a larger layout (*204-A*). This shape, when enlarged in a second

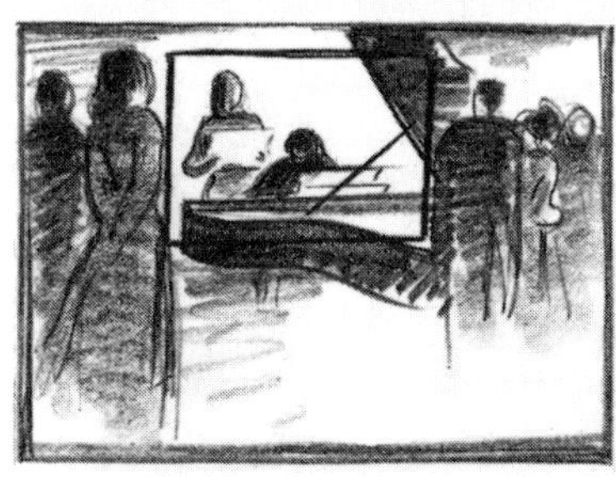

205-A

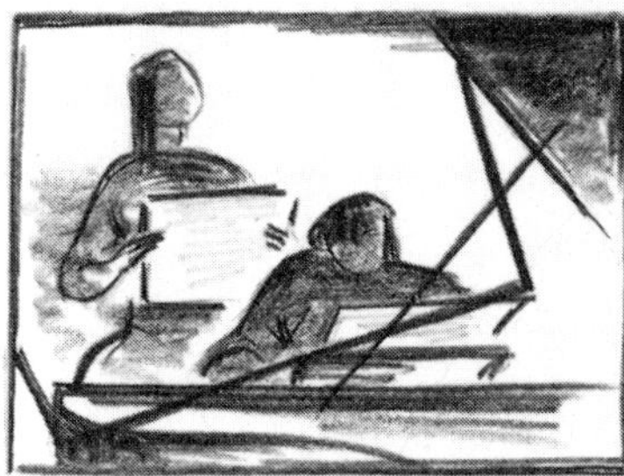

205-B

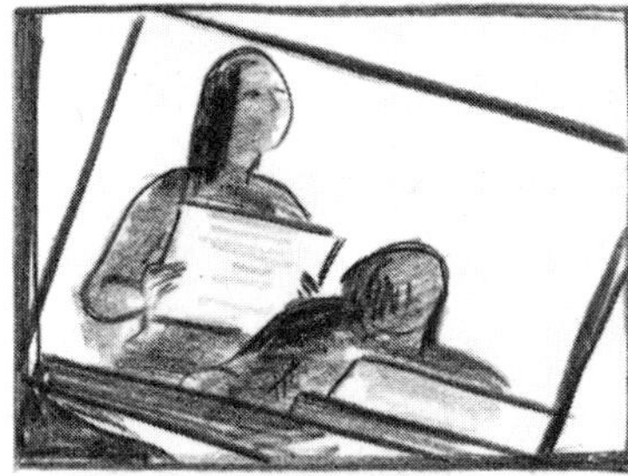

205-C

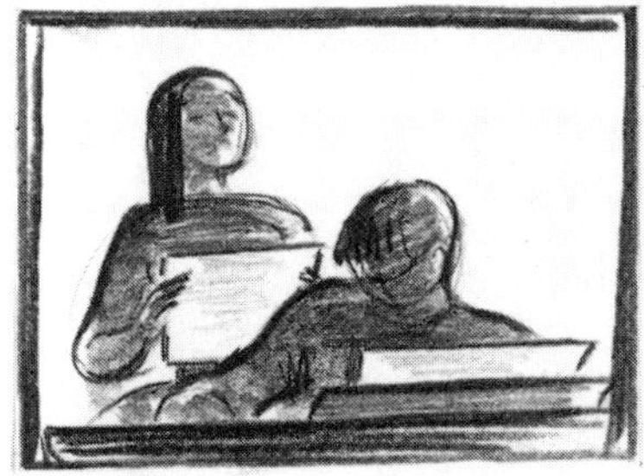

205-D

drawing, usually conforms to the proportion of the screen (*204-B*). Similar procedures may be followed in still picture designing.

To adapt the trucking technique to a still picture a simple procedure may be followed. Using the perspective elevation, for example, we find that the area near the pianist suggests a new layout (*205-A*). By indicating in our rough a border, which may be the same proportion as the original rough, we achieve a closer view, or a close-up (*205-B*). If now we enlarge this detail to the required size of our layout we are, in effect, moving closer to our subject (*205-C, -D*).

As we shall see in Chapter 32, there is often great value in maintaining a series of pictures all the same size and proportion. By preserving a constant size, we achieve a variety of views at different distances from our subject. From these we may choose the best answer to our assignment.

So we find that instead of developing a picture from our first thought, our first rough, we can explore many possibilities by utilizing the whirling plan. With the rotating plan many elevations may be generated. In addition to these new picture ideas, the exploitation of various horizons extends the picture possibilities. Then by moving in and out, other compositional ideas evolve. As we restudy segments of the rough revealed by this moving in and out, we create more exciting, more varied surface patterns. Even though our final picture may be only a single illustration, it will reflect a richness achieved only by such thorough graphic investigation.

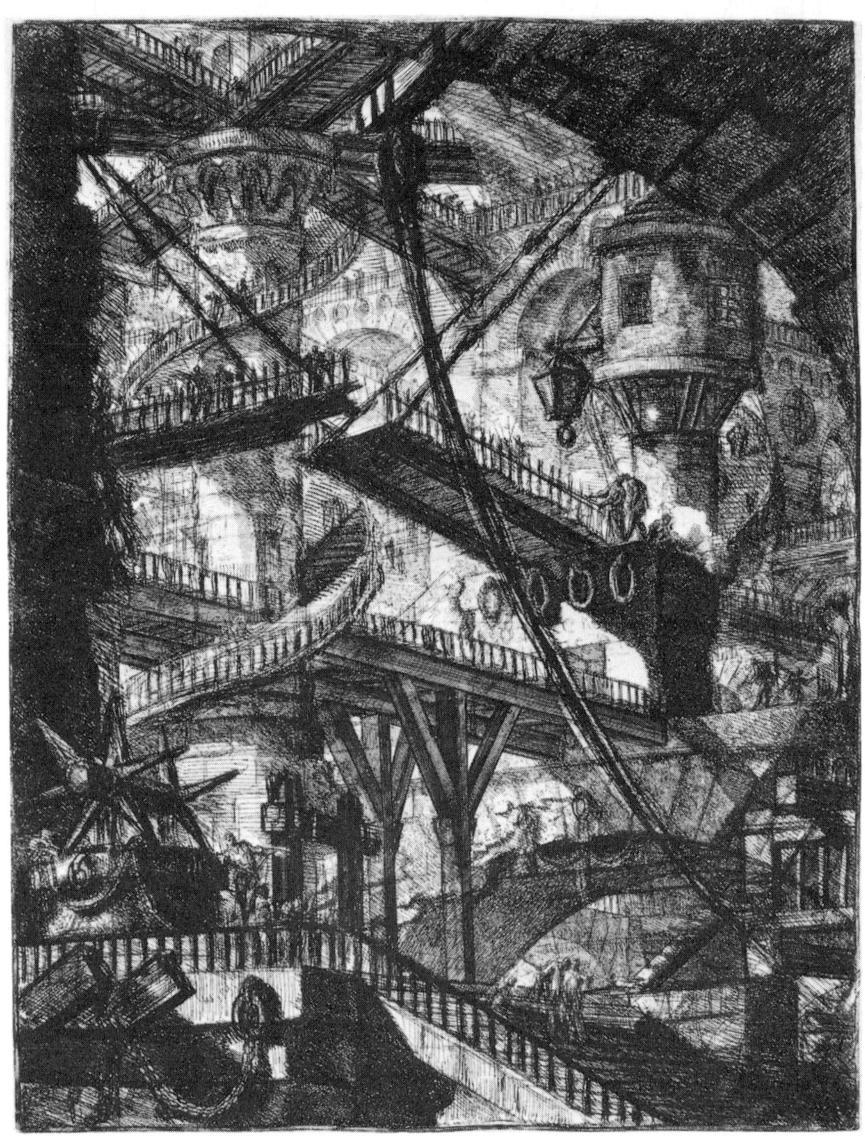

Giovanni Battista Piranesi (Italian, 1720-1778)
THE PRISONS (Pl. VII) Piranesi Edition of 1761
21⅝″ x 16⅛″; etching
National Gallery of Art, Washington, D. C.
Rosenwald Collection



# 19 Multiple Station Points

## The Limitations of the Single Station Point

We have discovered a number of graphic possibilities in varying the plan and elevation and adjusting the horizon. These possibilities are premised upon depicting the subject matter from a single station point, as Piranesi does so well. But there are times when a single station point seems inadequate, especially if used in conjunction with Italian perspective.

Strangely enough, the Italian artist who perfected scientific perspective was one of the first to find it unworkable in many of the great mural problems which were so much part of the Renaissance world. For instance, an Italian perspective picture on a large scale emphasizes the position of the spectator rather than the picture.

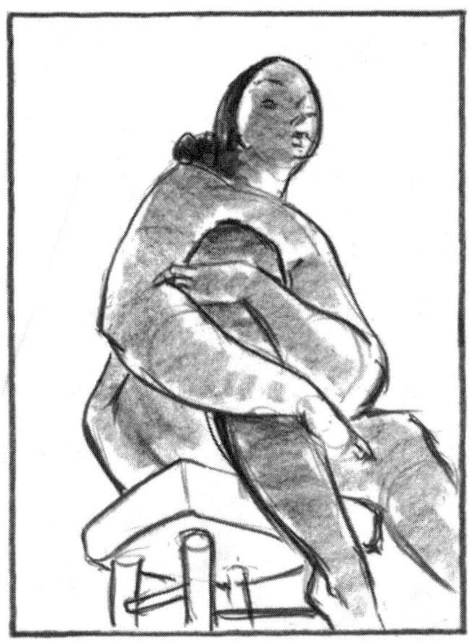

207-1A

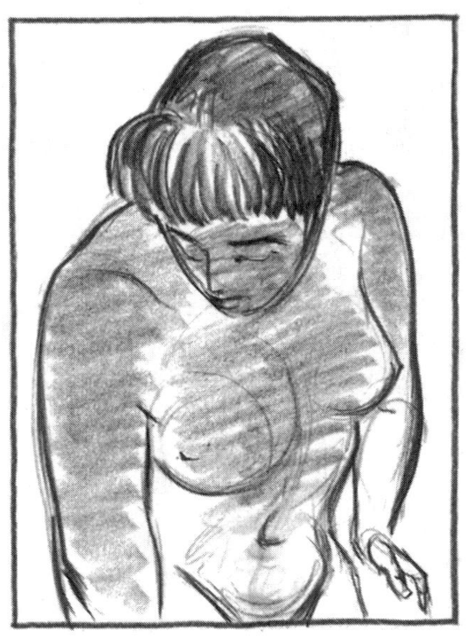

207-1B

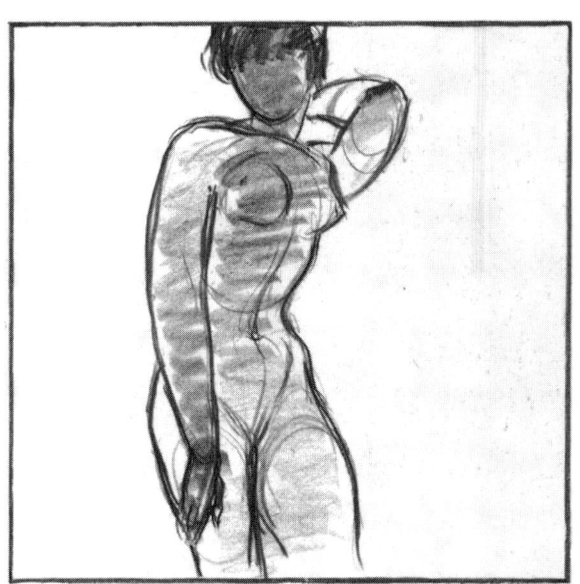

207-2

Possibly the greatest weakness of Italian perspective is revealed when applying it to the drawing of the human symbol. If a low eye level is established in a picture, the figure becomes a series of forced views, all from down-up (*207-1A*). If a high horizon is accepted, everything is seen in an up-down view (*207-1B*). Although at times such perspective may be used, in most instances we are not comfortable with these violent views.

A perspective view may be correct as far as a photographic projection is concerned, yet may create most distressing visual distortion. A violently foreshortened arm, for instance, may be correct in an Italian perspective drawing, yet it may look like a stump in relation to the rest of the picture (*207-2*). More important, discrepancies in size and space-volume relations frequently result in a badly scaled picture.



As we have noted, Italian perspective is based on making a picture as if viewing nature with a single eye. We also have noted how drawings can be modified and adjusted using the effect of two eyes, or binocular vision. Now, expanding the thought, what would happen if we could see with three eyes? Or four? Or an unlimited number of eyes or station points?

The clue to such extension lies in what we have learned about binocular vision. By seeing partly around a small object we bring into play two station points, one for each eye. By extending the interval separating these station points to any desired distance, we can, in effect, extend binocular vision into a new dimension. We can now depict large objects from distant station points and simulate a binocular effect.

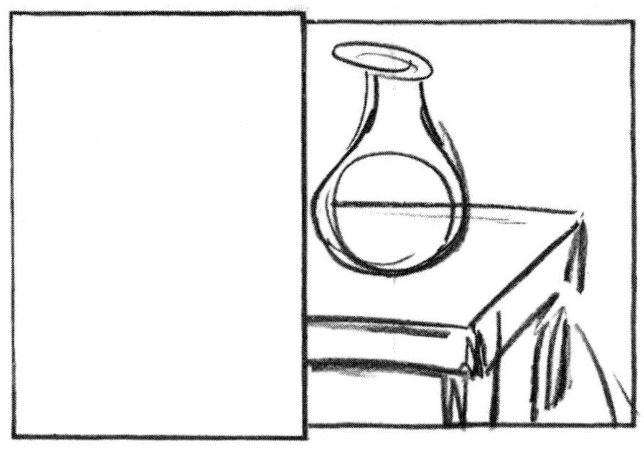

208-A

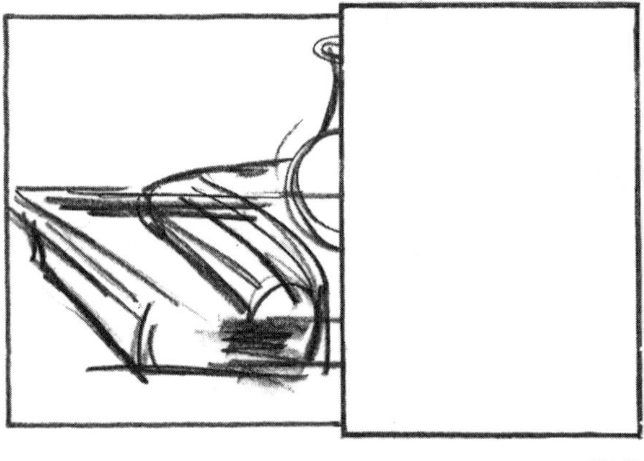

208-B

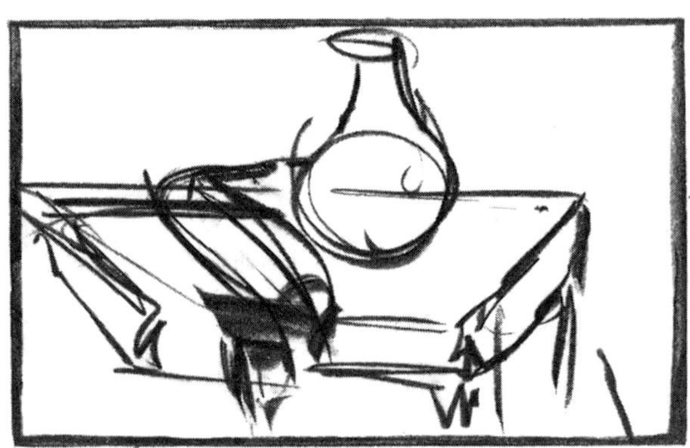

208-C

208 For example, let us draw a table somewhat differently than we would if using Italian perspective. Accepting the fact that we have two distinct principal station points, we might say that first we draw the table from one side (*208-A*), then walk around and draw it from the other side (*208-B*). In the same way we can look down upon the table top. At times it is advantageous to visualize ourselves actually assuming new station points (*208-C*).

For instance, in this drawing (*209-A*) a dozen different station points have been employed. The result is an examination of the figure from different views in an extension of surface as we experience it in normal binocular vision, except that this awareness of surface is multiplied many-fold.

By assuming many views we are also able to exploit various perspective differences which otherwise may be canceled from one station point. In the accompanying drawing (*209-B*) both upper and lower legs appear approximately the same length from one station point taken at knee level. The effect of normal perspective differences due to foreshortening is lost, resulting in a flattening of the drawing.

As we have noted, with one eye fixed in one spot we would record visually as does a still camera: one aspect of the whole object at a time. Actually our two eyes also involve peripheral vision and are really not at rest.

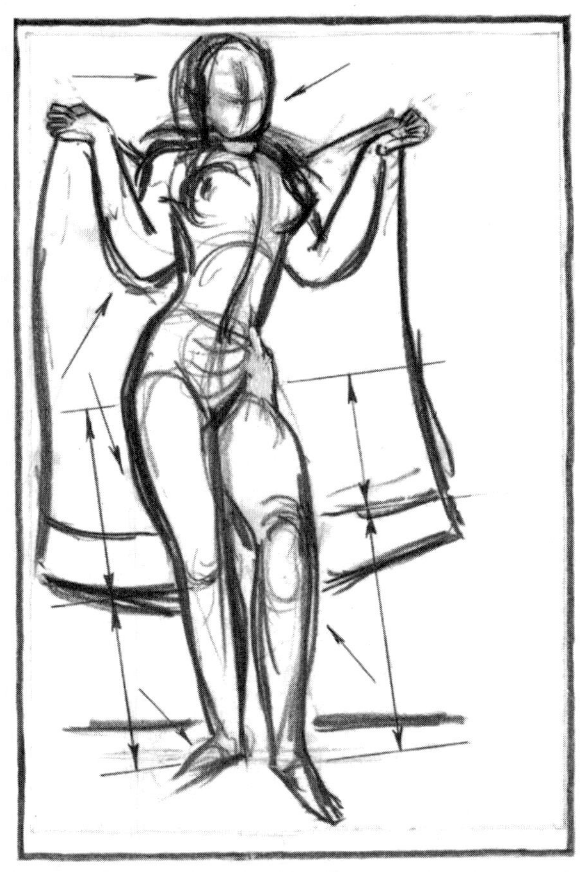

209-A

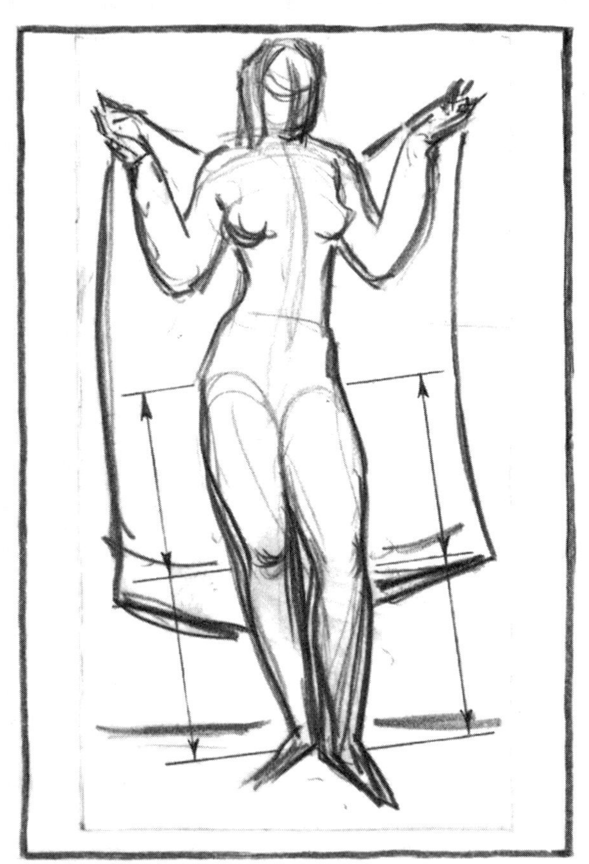

209-B

With many station points, or many eyes, we see an object from many views. But we do not see these views simultaneously. Reading time is involved as we move from viewpoint to viewpoint. We may compare this scanning, this continuing examination, to the same type of scanning possible with a motion picture camera. Both involve an unfolding of views, both involve the factor of reading time.

When we look at a standing figure in nature from a distance of four to six feet, it is impossible to see head and feet simultaneously. An Italian perspective drawing cannot account for this fact. True, both head and feet may be indicated in such a drawing, but in no way does this conform to what we actually see, though that is the prime aim of scientific perspective.

With the introduction of many station points in a picture, a sense of change, a sense of things happening in time, is communicated to us. As we shall see in Chapter 26, this ability of ours to scan a picture can be exploited to give intriguing controls of the picture.

Using multiple station points we are able to explain the physical aspects of a form more thoroughly than with one station point. Much of this is due to our ability to see more of the surface and to indicate it graphically, an extension of binocular vision.

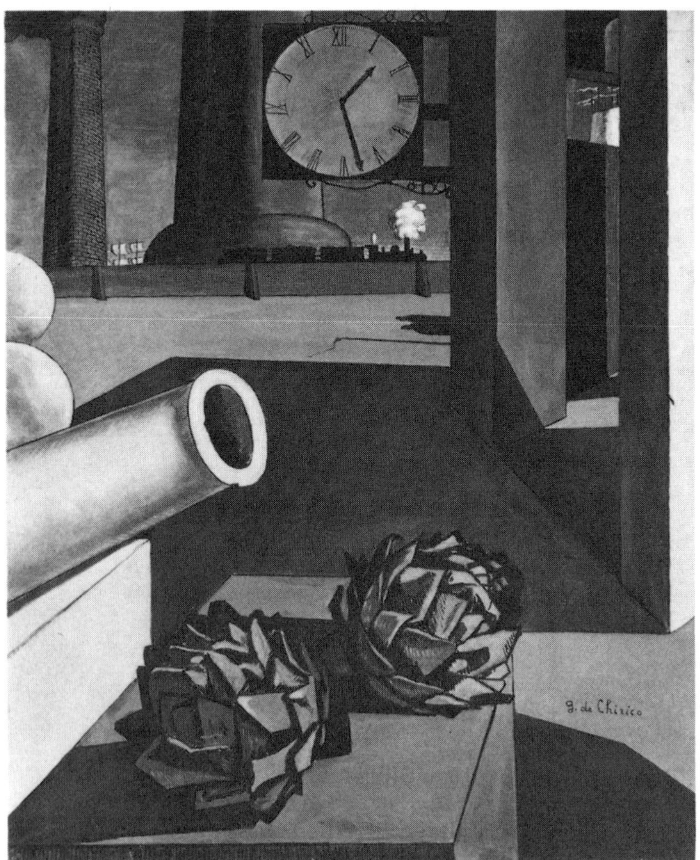

Giorgio de Chirico (Italian, 1888-    )
PHILOSOPHER'S CONQUEST, 1914
49½″ x 39¼″; oil on canvas
Courtesy of The Art Institute of Chicago
The Joseph Winterbotham Collection

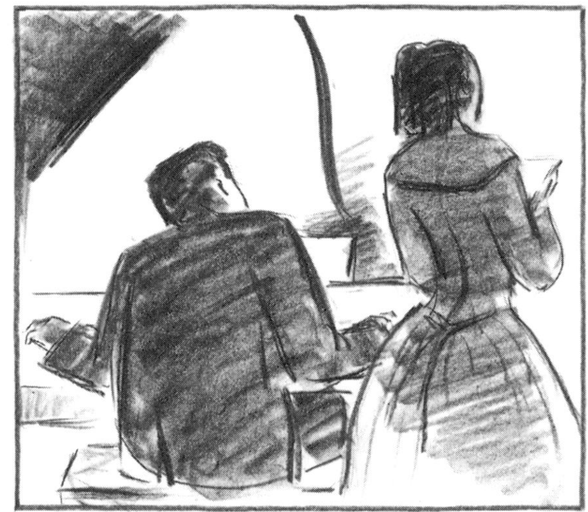

210-2

 **The Extension of Binocular Vision**

In a picture the true limits of binocular vision may be violated purposefully, in effect introducing new station points. With multiple station points figures and objects may be shown in the distance as if seen from close at hand. By so doing, the limits of Italian perspective are violated and a new dimension is introduced. By means of such a device de Chirico gives us a view into the distance never experienced in nature by anyone. The result is super-depth, a depth beyond actual experience. Many artists have explored this mysterious depth, often with startling results. It has a great weakness, however, for it makes control of picture surface difficult.

One use of multiple station points which tends to be overlooked is in delineating crowd scenes. Often the complexity of such a picture problem blinds us to the graphic realization of the individual figures. They tend to seem remote, to flatten. Once the basic relations of figures to architectural structures and props are established, we can correct this flattening effect by exploiting the potential of multiple station points.

As an example, the piano bench in our party problem in Chapter 18 usually must be related in perspective to the floor and piano. But the views we take of the pianist or the singer are subject to great variety (*210-2*). As we scan the figures in a crowd the up-down, side-to-side, down-up views reveal the individual forms with new intimacy resulting in a true sense of scale (Chapter 30).

El Greco (Spanish, born Crete, 1541-1614)
ST. JAMES THE GREAT, ca. 1583
16⅞″ x 14⅝″; oil on canvas(?)
Courtesy The Hispanic Society of America, N. Y.

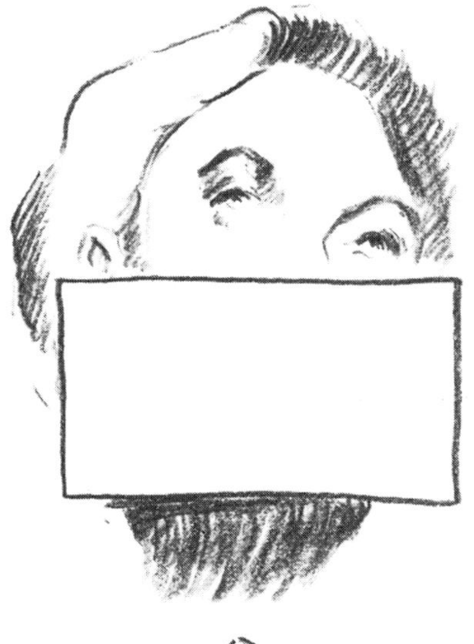

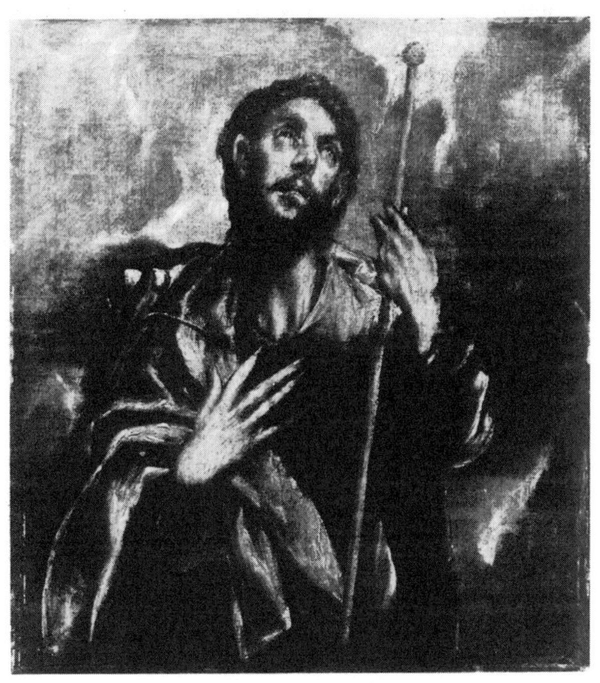

211-2A

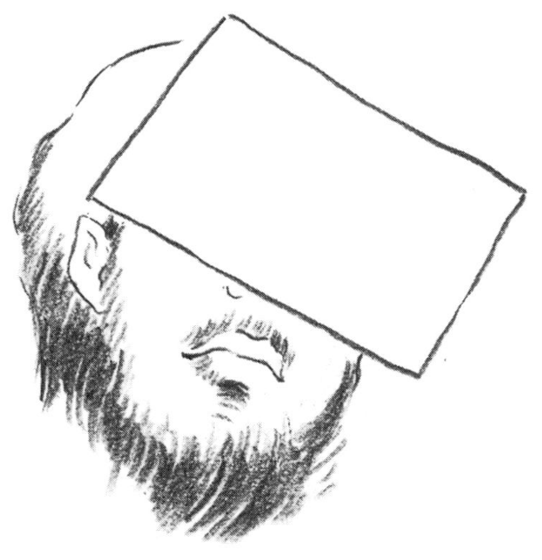

211-2B

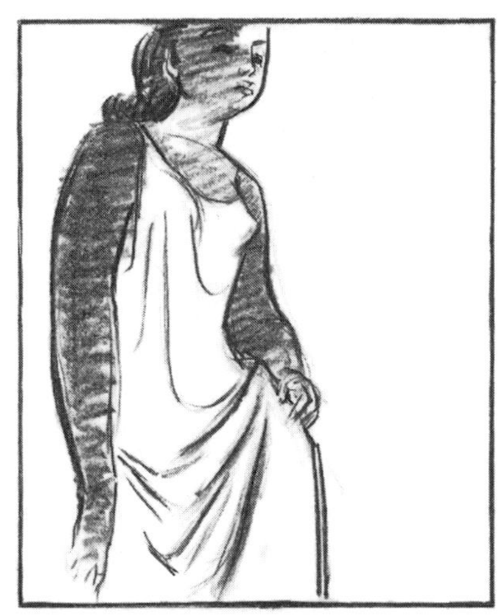

211-3

To demonstrate how successful the use of multiple station points can be, let us examine the accompanying El Greco. If we take a plain white card and progressively cover parts of the painting with it, we emphasize the views from the various station points used. For instance, we look up at the upper part of the head (*211-2A*), but down upon the lower section of the face (*211-2B*). We look into the upper part from the right hand side of the head; but more from the front and left side for the lower part. We look up under the brow, but down on the cheek bones. We look up under the upper lip, down on the lower lip, and so on throughout the picture.

In fact we scan the picture in time. By flipping the card rather rapidly, first covering the upper part, then the lower, the comparison of upper and lower part will give us a sense of true animation.

Multiple station points are easily achieved graphically if the subject in nature is seen at very close range. To view an entire figure in nature we must take a more distant station point. This does not imply that we may no longer employ multiple station points in depicting the figure at this greater distance. But we now find that we must adjust certain parts of the picture arbitrarily in order to give the up-down, side-to-side, or down-up view.

If we utilize only one station point, an up-shot of a standing figure often focuses undue attention on the unimportant area under the chin, detracting from a clear staging of the head to the detriment of the whole picture (*211-3*). Emphasizing in a middle long shot a cluster of station points around a focal part such as a head permits a remarkably clear display of the whole figure.

211

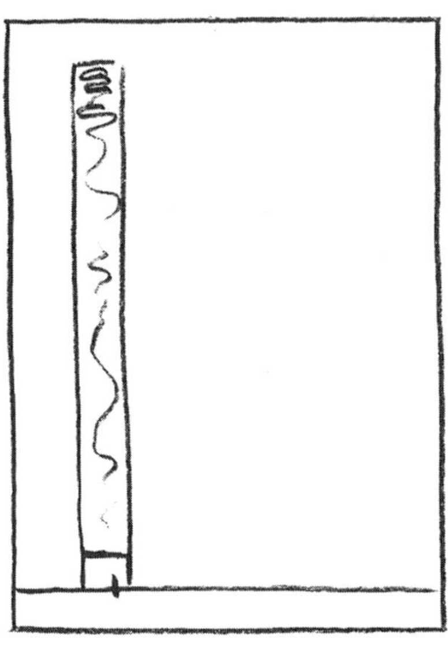

212-1A

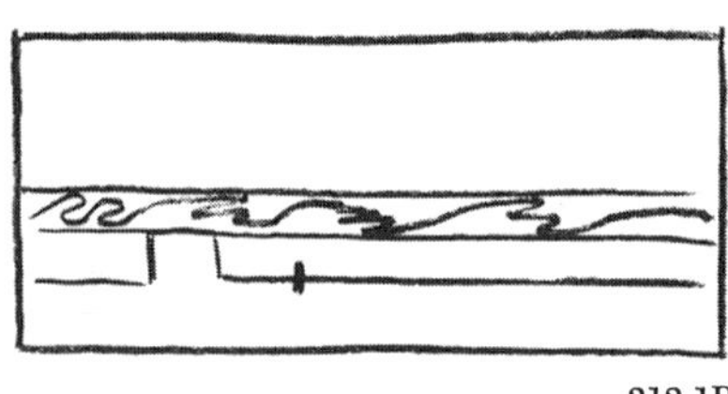

212-1B

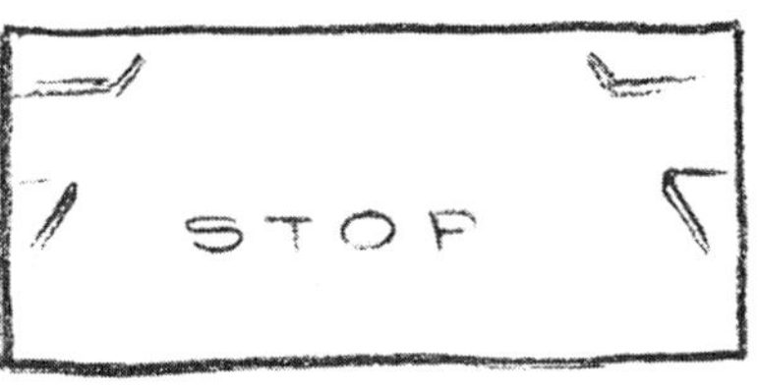

212-2A

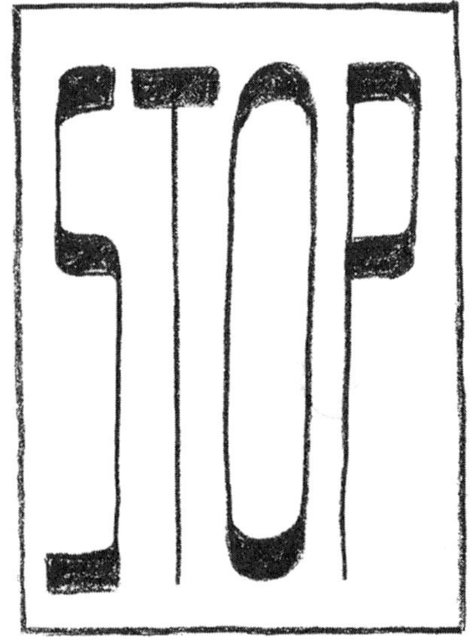

212-2B

## 212   Multiple Horizons

Most pictures, whether originals or reproductions, are relatively small, so we tend to ignore certain problems inherent in making mural structures. The actual size of the picture has profound effect on what the artist may or may not do in his design. The shape of a wall-sized picture is of equal importance.

Suppose in a large waiting room or foyer we see a mural rising high above us. The artist has accepted a horizon ten feet from the ceiling; our true eye level is sixty or seventy feet below. We find ourselves in an uncomfortable physical relation to the picture, for it is impossible for us to actually assume the same viewpoint that the artist did to construct the picture. The same picture reduced in a reproduction may not be quite so objectionable (*212-1A*).

Similarly, in extremely broad mural statements, the farther the elements of the picture are from either side of the spectator, the more the actual perspective distortion he will experience. To correct such real distortion certain graphic distortions must be utilized in the mural. These, in turn, unless skillfully designed, will be disturbing to anyone looking at the mural from any view but the station point determined by the artist (*212-1B*). Most of us have seen this effect demonstrated by a "STOP" sign painted in violent perspective on a pavement. The sign seems to read like normal lettering when seen from an automobile approaching it (*212-2A*). Seen from any other viewpoint the sign is difficult to read, the lettering is distorted (*212-2B*).

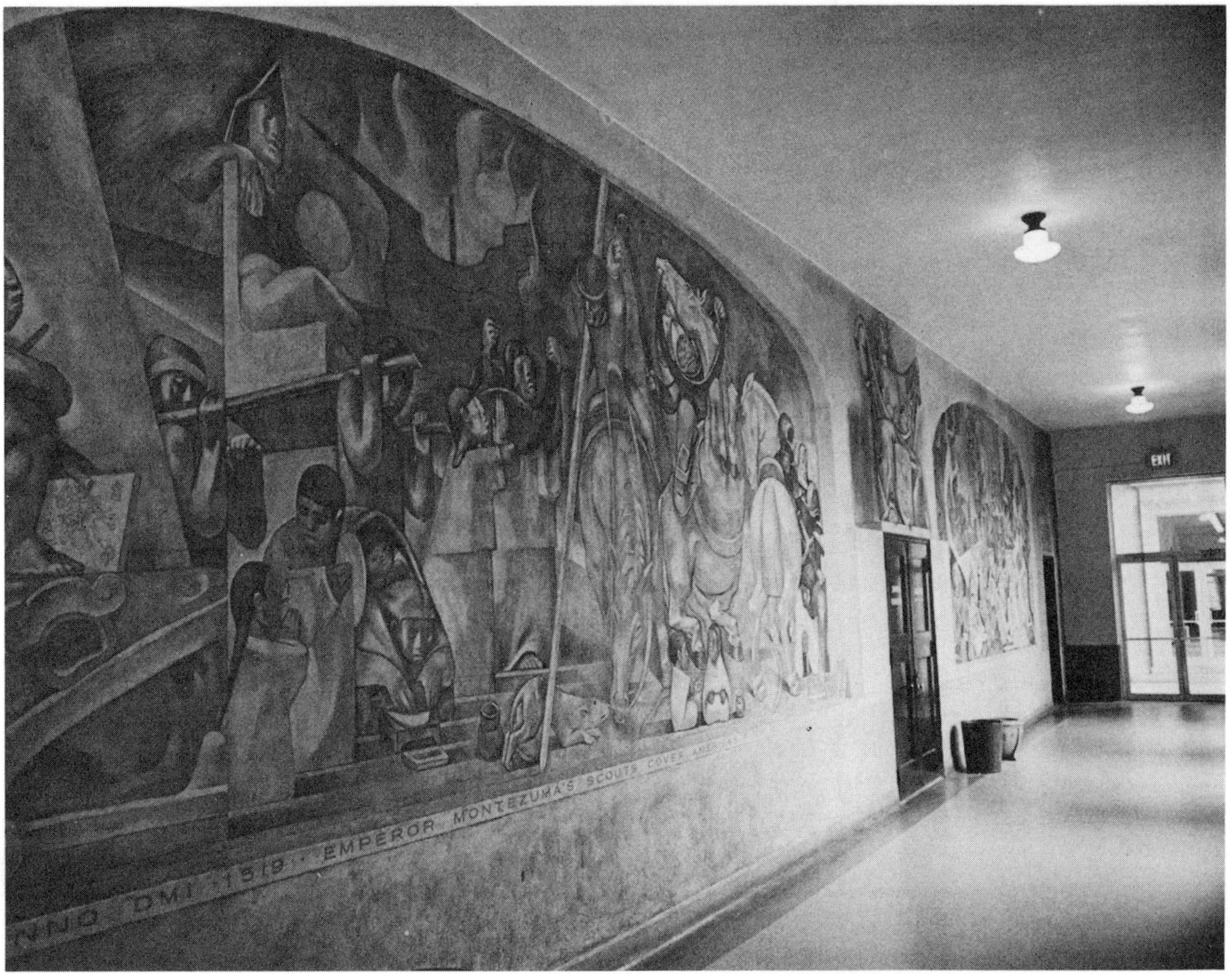

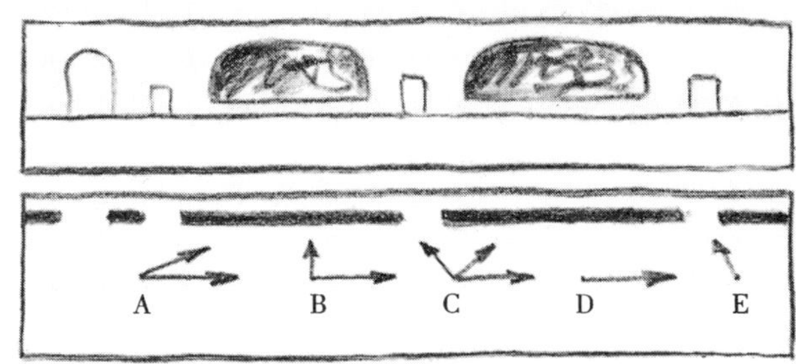

213-2

Frequently a single station point is inadequate for a huge mural. A mural by Jean Charlot in the Journalism Building at the University of Georgia is eleven feet by sixty-six feet divided into two panels located in a corridor only ten feet wide. In order to see the mural a spectator must walk the length of the corridor. In doing so he passes through a constantly changing number of station points. As he walks slowly down the corridor he looks ahead from *A* to the first panel, then directly at the first panel from *B,* then back to it from *C.* As he moves along the corridor he looks ahead to the second panel from *C,* directly at it from *D,* then finally, as he approaches the end of the corridor he looks back at the panel from *E.* Each new station point required a special design solution in the execution of the mural (*213-1B*).

To see any large mural the spectator's eye must wander over its whole surface. In doing so his head must turn, which implies a change of viewpoint. Usually this is not enough: the spectator must actually move his position and view the picture from many station points often separated by a distance of several feet.

If the spectator is far from the wall he will be able to respond to the full graphic impact of the large shapes and pictorial structures of both line and color. But as he walks toward the wall he soon is unable to see the entire picture surface. However, as he walks closer he is able to respond to small detail, intricate patterns, subtle textures indistinguishable from a distance.

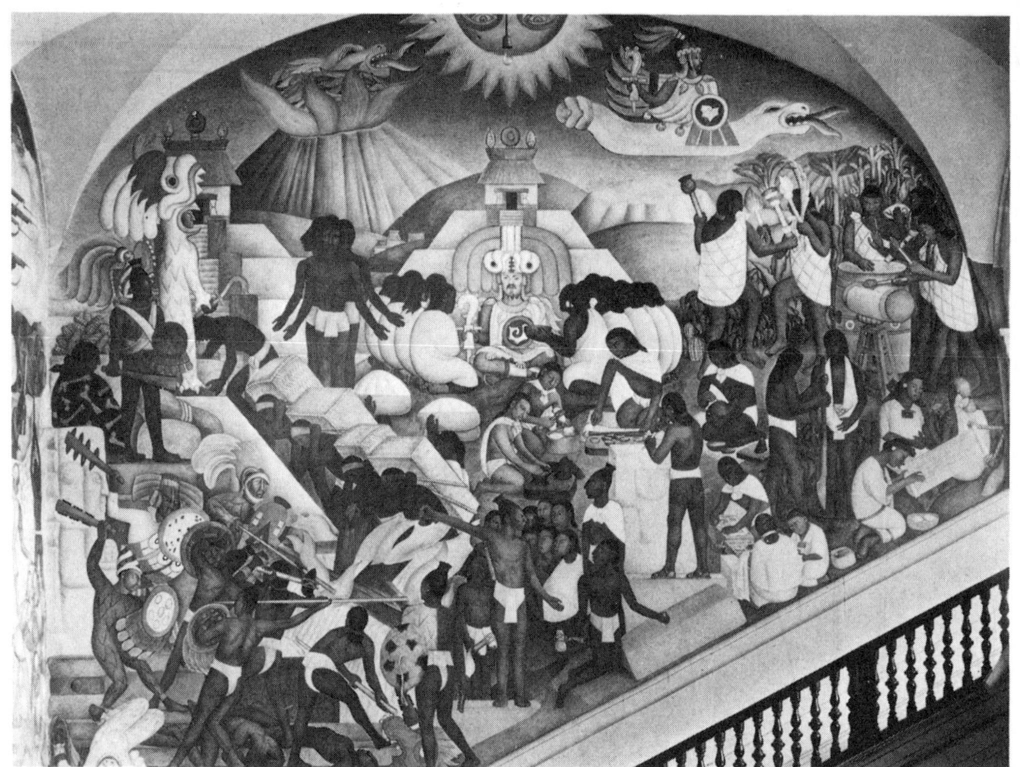

Diego Rivera (Mexican, 1866-1957)
THE MYTH OF QUETZALCOATL, side panel
right, fresco in National Palace
Mexico City, 1932
Courtesy Sr. Jorge Hernandez Campos
Instituto Nacional de Bellas Artes
Mexico, D. F.

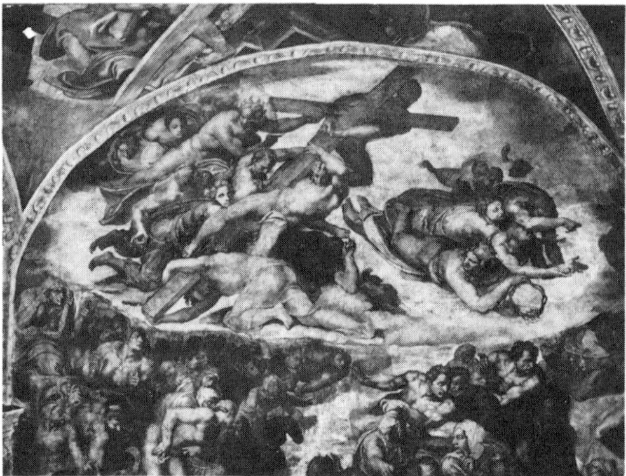

Michelangelo
Detail of THE LAST JUDGMENT

214     Sometimes in order to see a large surface it is necessary to move vertically from one floor level to another. In such cases a view from the ground floor level establishes a normal eye level quite low in the picture, to which the spectator may easily relate. The same wall seen from a higher level puts the spectator in an awkward position in relation to his original horizon which is now far below his eye level. To modify this discrepancy a second horizon, or a horizontal simulating or echoing the first horizon, can be introduced at the higher level, as Rivera does here.

At times a large mural actually may have no single horizon, no one station point. This is possible through the use of multiple station points. An excellent example of such a picture is Michelangelo's *The Last Judgment*.

Should we receive a commission similar to Michelangelo's we would be faced with many major decisions. Since the room is sixty-eight feet high, the height of a good-sized office building, the spectator's single eye level, if drawn near floor level, would throw everything near the ceiling into violent perspective. If, on the other hand, a horizon were introduced high, near the ceiling, everything low in the picture would be thrown into gross distortion and the spectator placed in an imaginary position high above ground. Obviously an Italian perspective solution will not work.

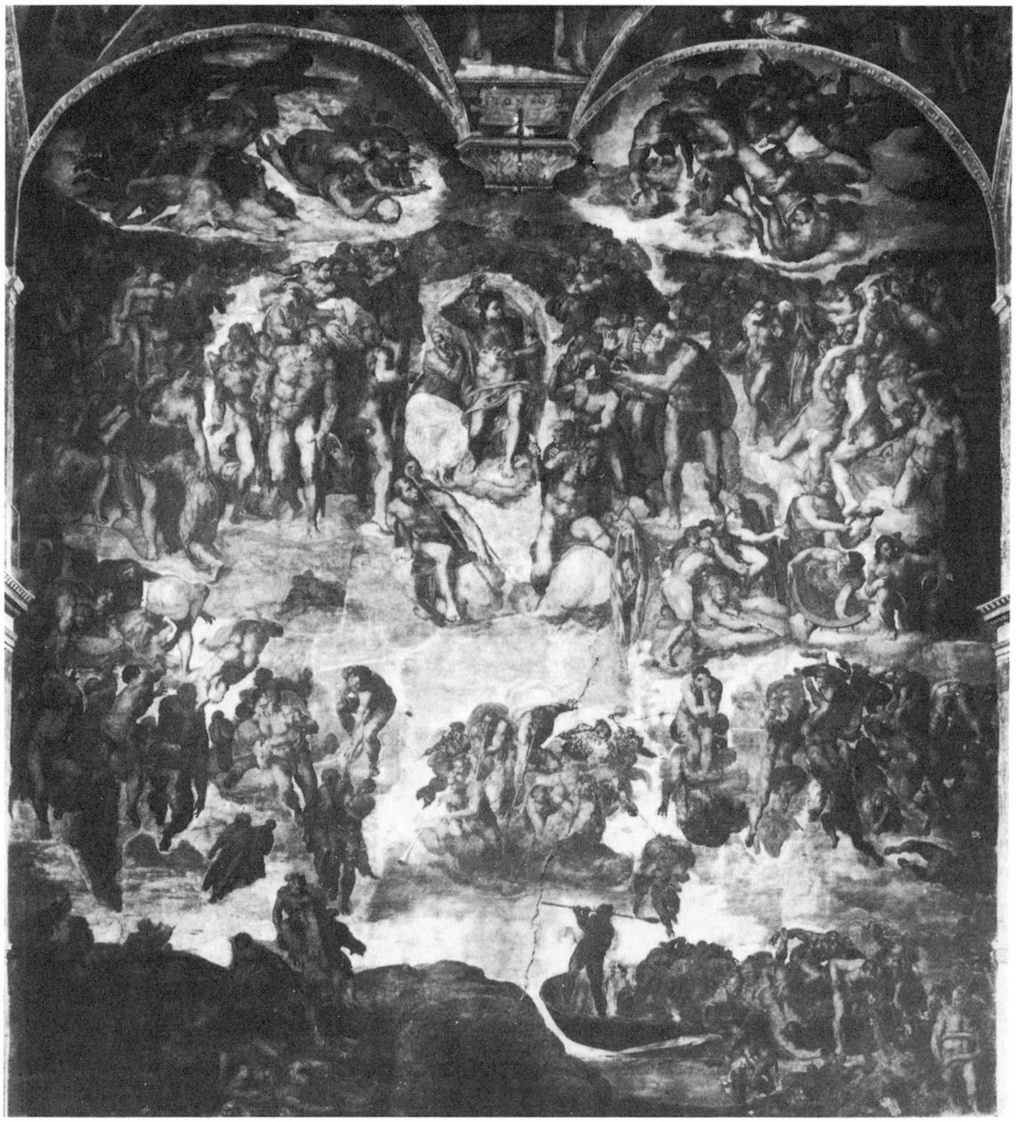

Michelangelo (Italian, 1475-1564)
THE LAST JUDGMENT, 1534-1541
48' x 44'; fresco, Sistine Chapel
The Vatican, Rome

We could circumvent the problem of controlling such a huge wall in a single perspective drawing by partitioning the wall into a number of clusters. In this way each cluster would become a picture viewed separately, yet related closely to the other clusters.

In drawing any single cluster we could also treat it as if viewed from many station points, as Michelangelo does. In each cluster we can look down-up, side-to-side, up-down, and nowhere feel a single true horizon.

In drawing any single figure in any cluster again we may bring into play as many viewpoints as we need to display the important parts. In designing the whole wall we would probably find it necessary to use literally hundreds, possibly thousands of station points, just as Michelangelo does.

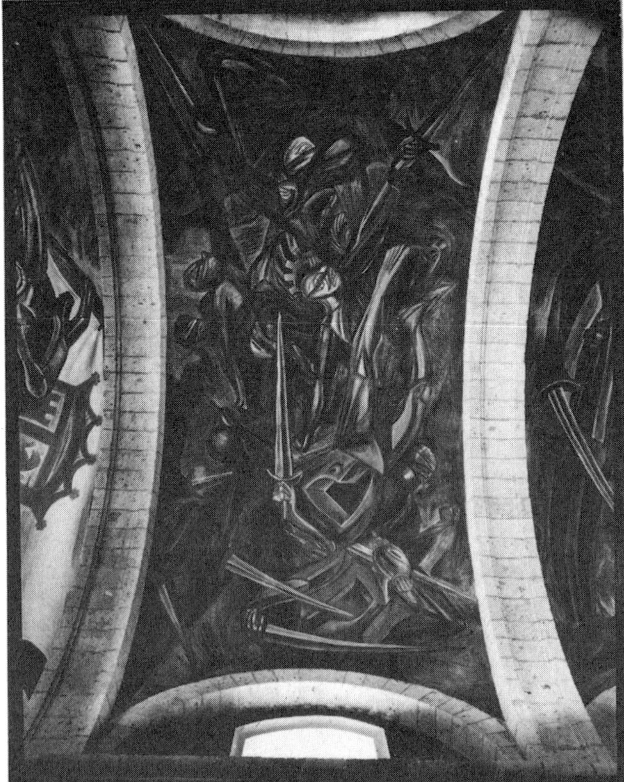

Orozco
Barrel Vault, Orphanage
Guadalajara, Mexico

José Clemente Orozco (Mexican, 1883-1949)
Frescoes on site at the Orphanage
Guadalajara, Mexico
Courtesy Sr. Jorge Hernandez Campos
Instituto Nacional de Bellas Artes
Mexico, D. F.

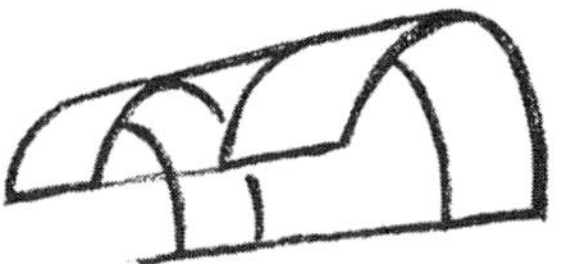

216-2

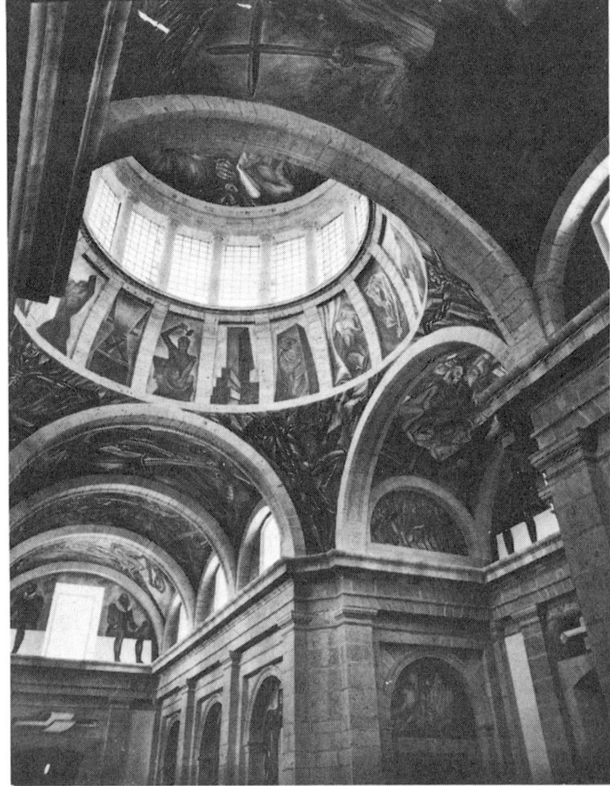

216    In painting ceilings in large architectural structures the painter must so design the murals that they may be read from a series of station points assumed by the spectator as he wanders around on the floor beneath. In the Orphanage in Guadalajara Orozco was faced with the monumental problem of decorating a whole building including barrel vaults and a circular dome.

To look at a section of a barrel vault (*216-2*) the spectator must assume at least one station point at each side of the vault and one at each end of its section and look upward. As he does so the design reverses graphically. This has been accounted for by the artist, as we see here.

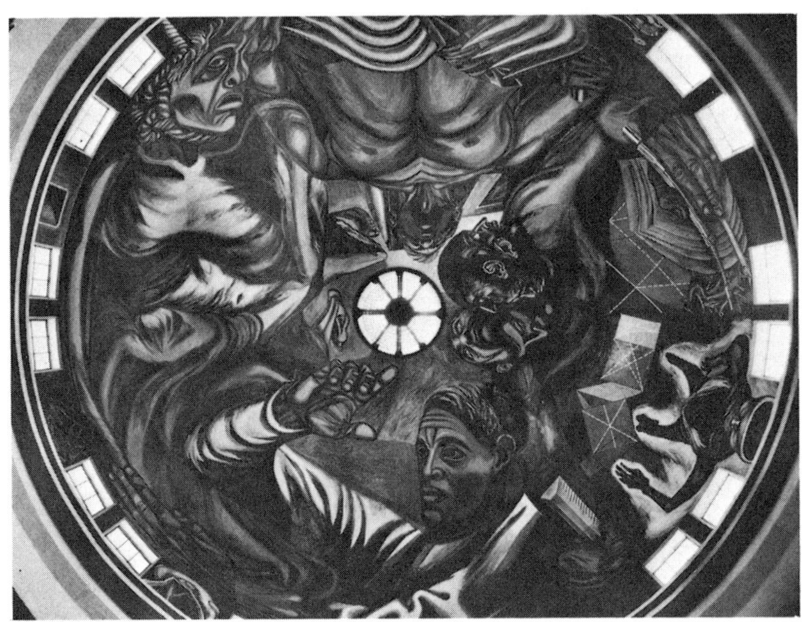

Orozco
Frescoes on Cupola Ceiling
University of Guadalajara

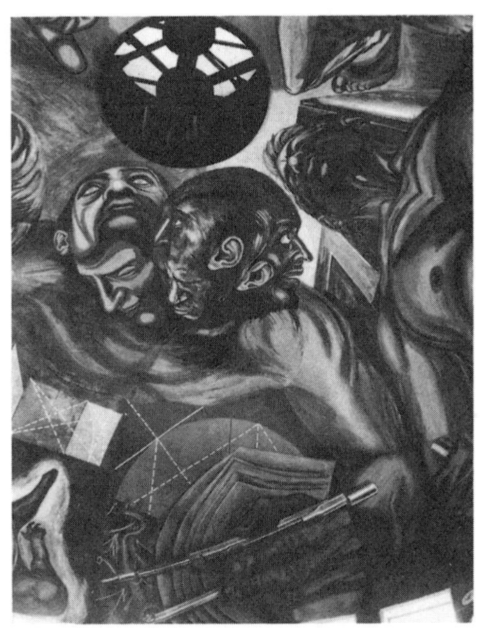

Orozco
Detail of Cupola Ceiling

In studying the cupola of the Auditorium at the University of Guadalajara the spectactor must observe it while making a three hundred-and-sixty-degree turn. Instead of turning ourselves we can hold this reproduction above our heads and slowly turn it in a complete circle; the various heads depicted in the mural will slowly emerge one by one while others drop out of focus.

Another example of Orozco's ingenious use of multiple station points is found in this detail from the same ceiling. In this case the composite of five heads also accommodates the actual turning of the spectator's body.

Our most familiar contemporary "mural" experience is the motion picture. When we sit in a theater watching a live action picture on the screen, we see what the camera has recorded as it constantly scanned things in nature both stationary and moving. Visually we experience a constant change of viewpoints. In large murals which are always stationary the spectator is often in motion. Paradoxically, in viewing motion pictures the spectator is stationary.

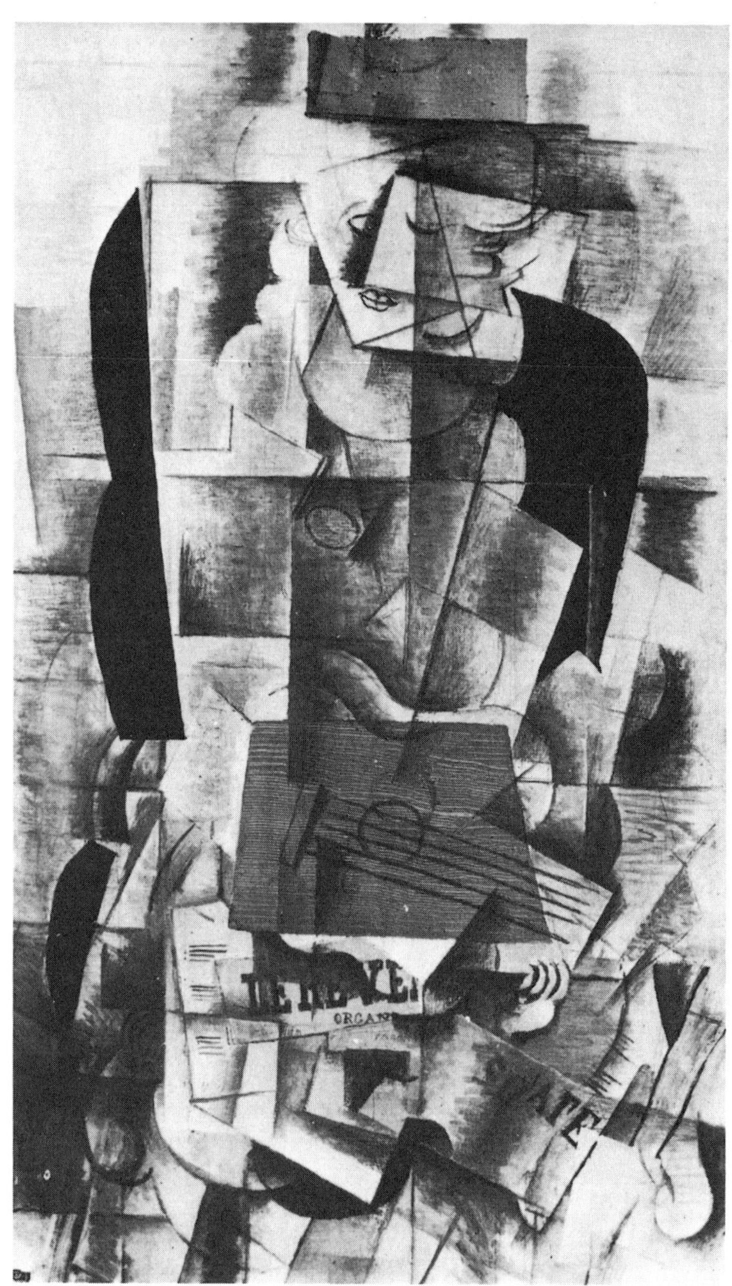

Georges Braque (French, 1882-1963)
YOUNG GIRL WITH A GUITAR, 1913
51½" x 29½"
Musée National National d'Art Moderne, Paris

## The Copernican Viewpoint

Once the artist is liberated from a single fixed station point, his whole concept of picture making changes. No longer is he bound by a Ptolemaic point of view as reflected in a fixed viewpoint with the world revolving around it. Now the artist is free to choose as many station points as he feels necessary. He sees his subject from a Copernican point of view: he can show aspects of form not visible from any one station point.

These aspects of a structure are truly conceptual rather than visual. The surface of a three-dimensional form can be shown as a flat shape, a development, like the label of a tin can unrolled on a flat surface. Section views can be combined with perspective views. In fact, any observation pertaining to a subject, whether actually to be seen or not, can be incorporated in a picture structure, as demonstrated so well by Braque and other Cubists in still pictures. Contemporary film and future technological developments in film offer even greater challenge and opportunity for the artist in the exploitation of multiple station points.

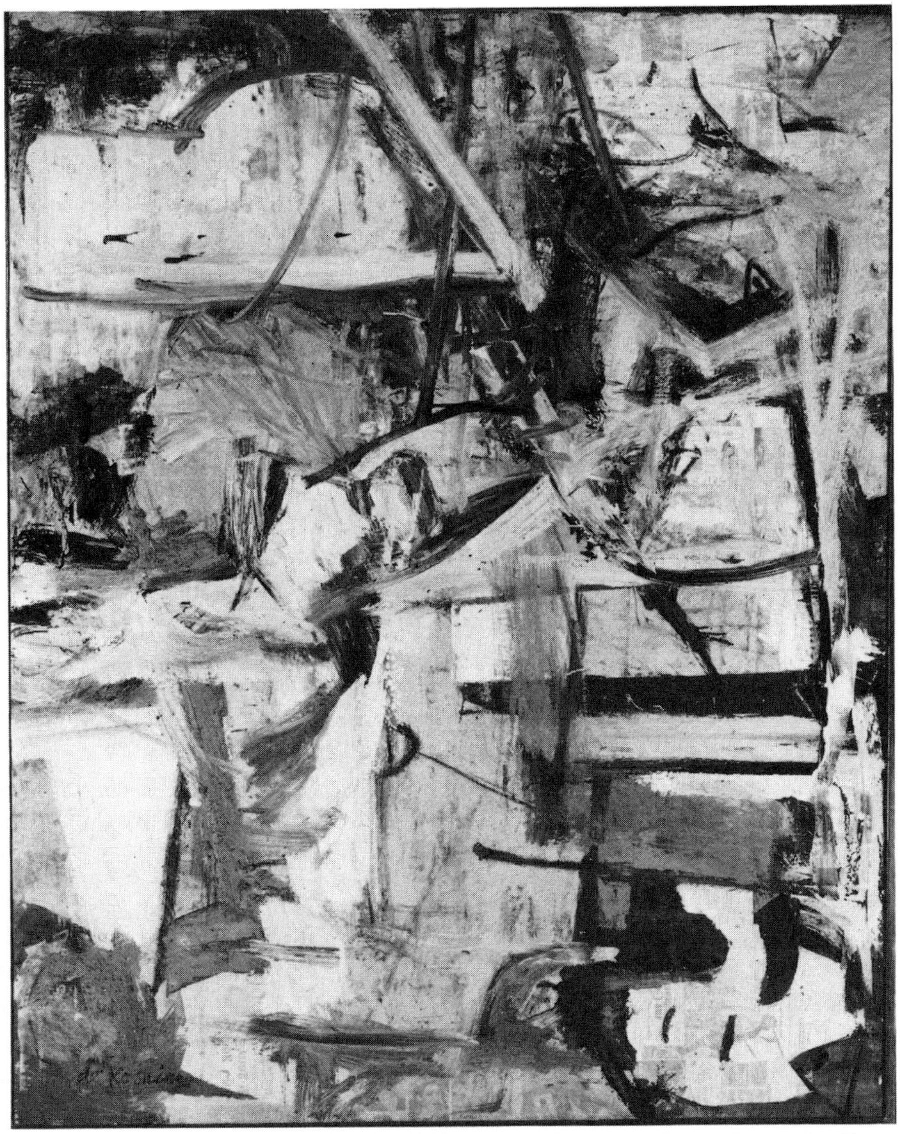

Willem de Kooning (American, b. Rotterdam, 1904–   )
EASTER MONDAY, 1956; 96¼″ x 73⅞″
oil on canvas
The Metropolitan Museum of Art, N.Y.
Rogers Fund, 1956

In other words it is possible to accept an omnipresent view of things around us as well as of our own actions. We may learn to see ourselves at the dinner table as remotely as we view the motion picture of the same scene. By so doing we begin to see the dining table in plan as a core around which we and our family are seated. Once we have liberated ourselves from the confines of perspective views we may recognize innumerable internal structures invisible to the human eye. We may visualize ourselves inside the human body or climbing up inside the stem of a plant.

Once liberated from a fixed station point the artist is free to dispense with realistic subject matter. Now he can turn to an exploitation of purely graphic elements. With these he can find new ways of arousing the emotions of the spectator. This leads naturally to the evolution of personal or semipersonal symbols which again opens up new worlds of expression to the artist, as de Kooning demonstrates in his *Easter Monday*.

## 20 Action and Movement

## V GRAPHIC MOVEMENT

**A Confusion of Terms**

In discussing any subject, especially one as complex as picture making, we need a vocabulary which is simple yet capable of explaining special and complex ideas. Usually, familiar words are chosen and then given emphasis or specific meaning in relation to the subject under investigation. And herein lies the danger. Too much special meaning given an old accepted term may render it incomprehensible; yet to invent a new word means developing a jargon perhaps even more confusing. And so we find a semantic problem in using the words "action" and "movement" in discussing pictures.

The words "movement" and "action" seem synonymous and are used by most people almost interchangeably to indicate any alteration of position. The artist, however, faces an involved problem. He must be able not only to distinguish

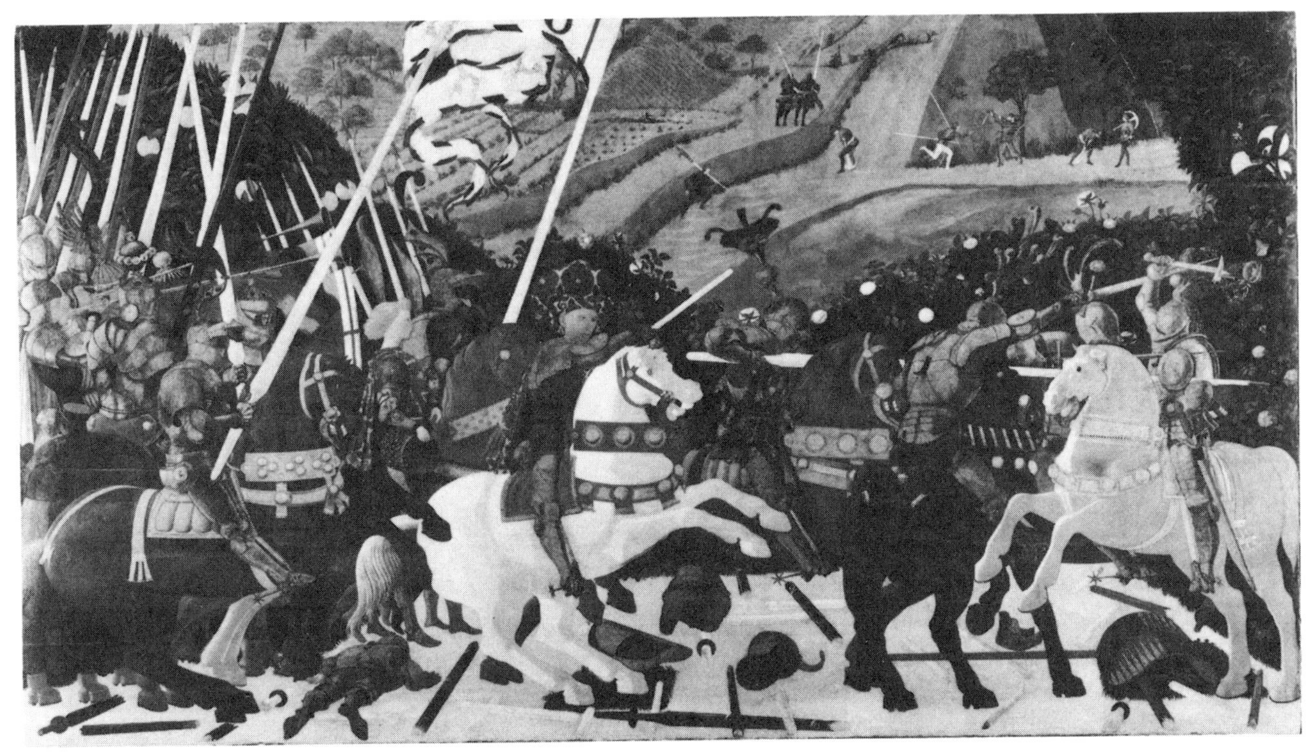

Paolo Uccello (Italian, 1397-1475)
THE BATTLE OF SAN ROMANO, ca. 1455
72″ x 125¾″; oil
Reproduced by courtesy of the Trustees
The National Gallery, London

between an action and a picture of an action, but also he may wish to generate in us special subjective responses to his picture which he calls "movement."

For instance, if we see a man riding a horse we say he is performing an action. Now let us look at a painting of a man on horseback, as in the Uccello above. We no longer are looking at an action but merely at a picture of an action. The still picture reminds us of action, but there is no real action for there is no actual change of position.

## Types of Action

*Physical action* implies a change of position of an object in nature. Today we also experience action through motion pictures or television.

*Cinematic action,* as we shall call this phenomenon, occurs when we are aware of a change of position of one or more still images when seen in special sequences at controlled time intervals on a screen. Our response to motion pictures, whether generated by live action, stop-motion photography, or animation, is nearly as genuine as if we witnessed true action in nature.

At times we experience the effect of action in our surroundings when the position of our eyes changes in relation to stationary objects in space. Such effects we call *apparent actions.* Most of us have experienced the sensation of watching an adjacent bus or train slowly begin to move, only to realize shortly that it is our own vehicle which is under way, not the other. Or as we watch from the window of a moving vehicle, rows of trees in an orchard seem to turn like spokes in a slowly spinning wheel.

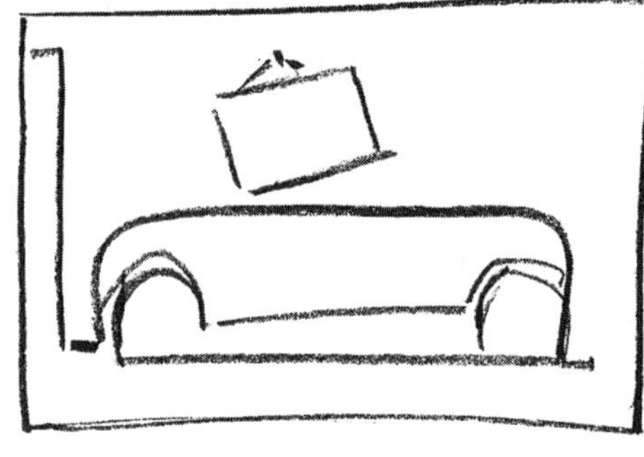

222

Another illusion of action, *optical action* is an animation effect resulting from alternately opening and closing our eyes while focusing upon a stationary object. This action, entirely the result of binocular vision, is easily demonstrated if the object is the end of our nose. It may be made to seem to wiggle, to be truly animated.

### Movement

The term *movement* is used by the artist in a very special way which has nothing to do with action. To use a familiar example, suppose as we sit in a room we notice that the picture on the wall facing us hangs askew. Something about its misplacement bothers us. The more we look at it, the more agitated we become. As a rule we either straighten the picture, take it down, or leave the room. One thing is certain, we cannot comfortably live with the tipped picture (*222*).

In this instance we view an absolutely still arrangement of things in nature, yet we are physically and emotionally distressed. We experience a compelling, emotional reaction to the relative positions of the tilted picture and the floor, wall, or furniture. This emotional reaction, the result of comparing relative positions of one visual stimulus to another, or to accepted visual references, the artist calls "movement."

This effect termed movement may be found in nature, but it is found and used most often in graphics. We see that the tilted picture on the wall and a drawing of the tilted picture both disturb us, although not necessarily to the same degree.

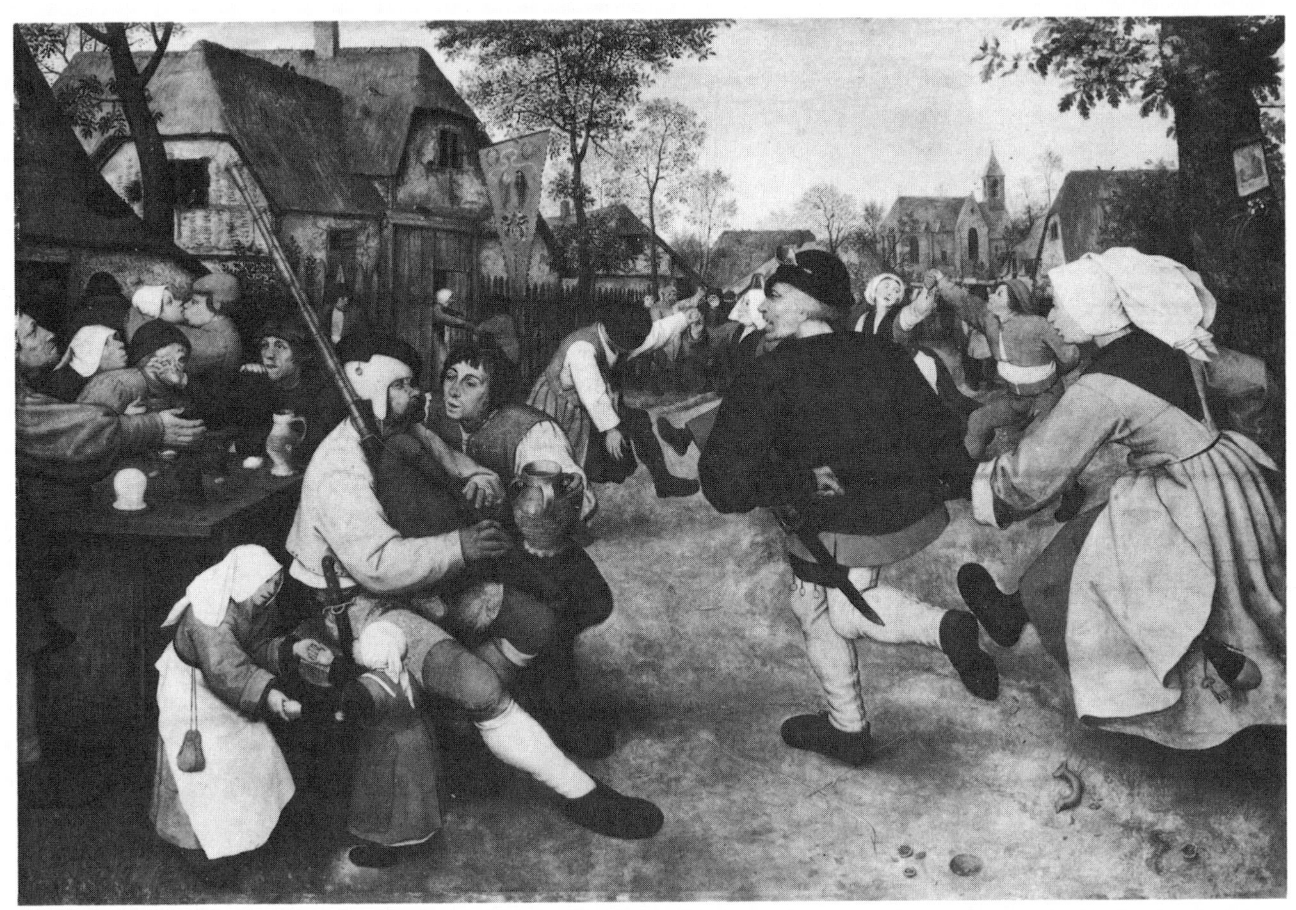

Pieter Bruegel (Flemish, ca. 1525-1569)
THE DANCE OF THE PEASANTS, ca. 1568
44⅞″ x 64⁹⁄₁₆″; oil on wood
Kunsthistoriches Museum, Vienna

## Gravitational References

The experience of movement often is based on
a disturbance of our gravitational sense, our
sense of the vertical and horizontal. Almost
everything we see in nature in some way
relates to these invisible gravitational references. If things seem to be insecure or pre-
carious we become aware of the lack of the
true vertical or true horizontal even more.

When translated into drawing terms, various
graphic stimuli may be utilized as references.
These, in turn, may emphasize the presence
of the vertical and horizontal to reassure us
of our gravitational orientation, as we see in
Pieter Bruegel's *Dance of the Peasants*. A
picture without a suggestion of either the
vertical or horizontal may seem unstable.

It is not imperative that all pictures have
vertical and horizontal graphic references, but
we should be aware of the function of such
elements whether they are used or not. As we
shall see in the following chapters, conscious
violation of vertical and horizontal references
constitutes one of the most powerful tools of
the graphic designer.

## Forces and Shapes

To understand further what the artist means
by movement, we must pursue our investigation
of forces in nature and how they are represented in graphic terms.

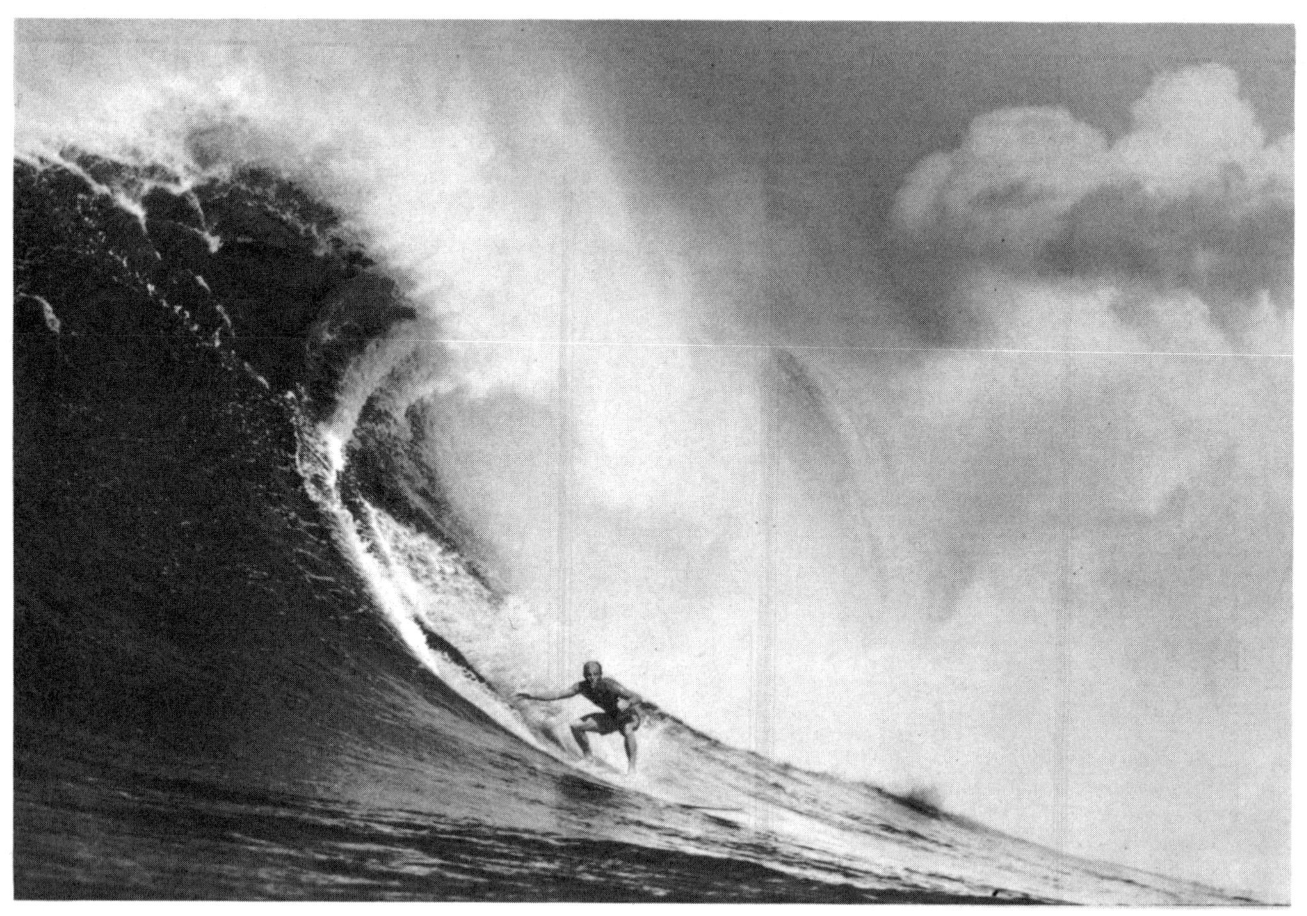

SURFER
(Photograph by Dr. Don James
Culver City, Calif.)

224 Many shapes and forms we see in nature are affected by hidden forces or are manifestations of them. We have noted how gravity affects almost everything we see, yet we cannot see gravity. The wind blows the field of grass, yet we cannot see wind. Our hand blurs as it moves rapidly in front of our eyes, yet we cannot see speed.

A number of other invisible forces in nature also are made evident by the reactions of visible structures. The following list of these other forces should stimulate further investigation: An understanding of muscular forces manifested in the action of animate forms—human, animal, bird, insect—is imperative to the study of drawing of living creatures. Mechanical forces manifested in actions of inanimate forms, a speeding car for instance, or chemical forces, explosions, smoke or fire, challenge the artist to discover graphic solutions. Another

category worth investigating is often called Acts of God. These are forces whose sources are far beyond our control—cloud patterns, lightning, wind, rain, earthquake, and wave action, depicted here by James and Hokusai.

Forces, then, not only affect all action but can generate it. In so doing, forces drastically act on many shapes we see. A soaring kite is not just a familiar shape, it is a shape which is a manifestation of forces being exerted.

Now when transposing into picture terms we frequently must represent as a still shape on our picture surface a vibrant, energy-charged form which is in action in nature. But often our close association of visible form to invisible force is so taken for granted that we thoughtlessly draw a static or projected shape, neglecting to suggest how the shape is generated.

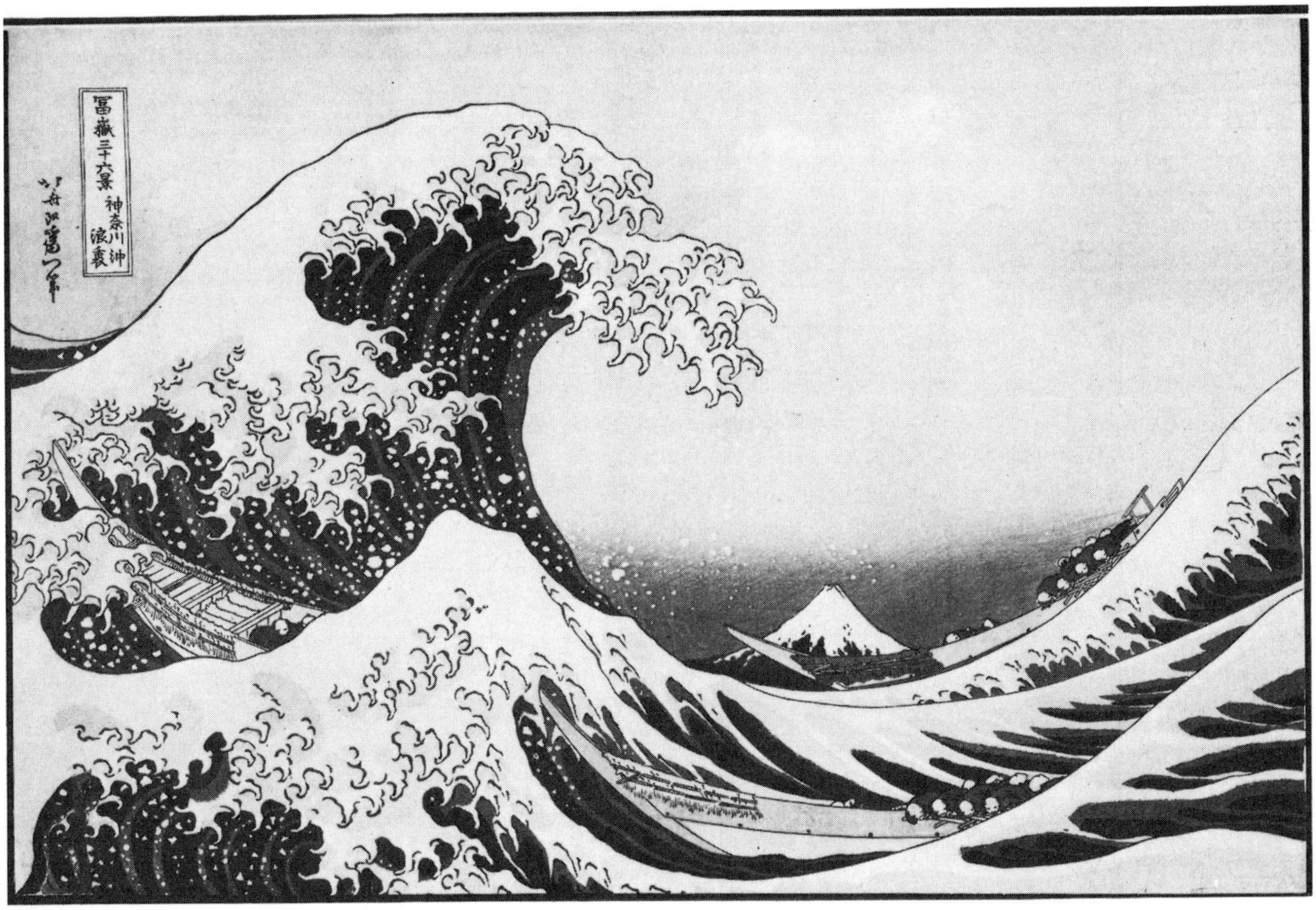

Katsushika Hokusai (Japanese, 1760-1849)
THE GREAT WAVE OFF KANAGAWA, from
"The Thirty-Six Views of Fuji"
1823-1829; woodblock print
The Metropolitan Museum of Art, N. Y.
Bequest of Mrs. H. O. Havemeyer, 1929.
The H. O. Havemeyer Collection

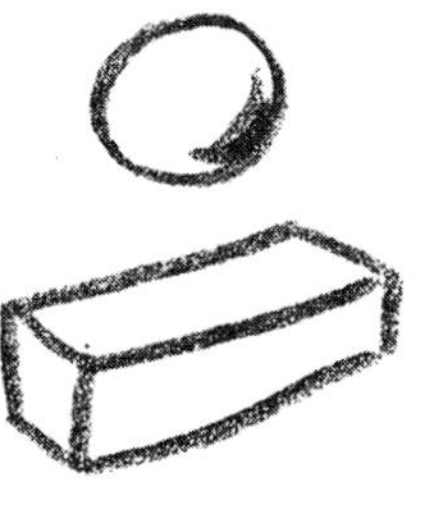

225-2A

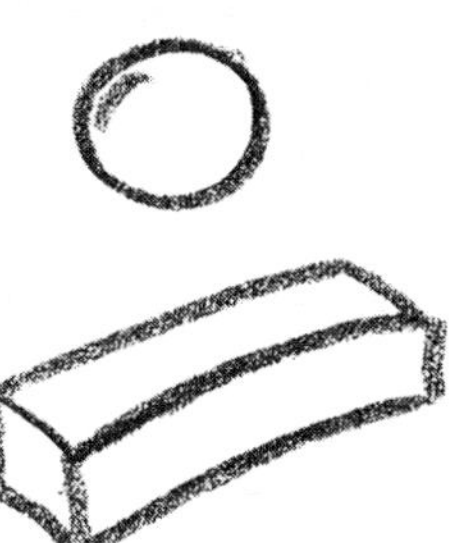

225-2B

Such an interpretation, when drawing drapery for example, frequently results in a wooden arrangement of lifeless folds.

Here, then, is another clue to picture structure: the way a force is interpreted in relation to shape affects the structure of the whole picture. For instance, in making a drawing of a figure in action, a system of shapes must be organized which reflects or suggests the forces which make such an action in nature possible. Yet this is not enough, for the organization of shapes may be unpleasant, dull, too factual, or too active to create a successful picture structure.

Let us again consider gravity as a force having profound significance in picture making. If we wish to make a symbol seem particularly heavy we encounter special drawing problems, for a picture of something heavy in no way assures us that the spectator will respond to the image as being heavy. To realize a sense of weight as an attribute of the subject, we must employ certain devices which dramatize graphically the illusion of gravity acting upon the symbol.

For example, let us draw a ball bouncing on a surface or platform of some kind. By bowing the graphic structure of the surface the ball will seem to be attracted to the surface. The attraction between the two is dramatized. The space generated contributes to both the movement and the sense of weight in the sphere (*225-A*). However, by reversing the direction of the surface, the same sphere may be made to float in the air (*225-B*).

225

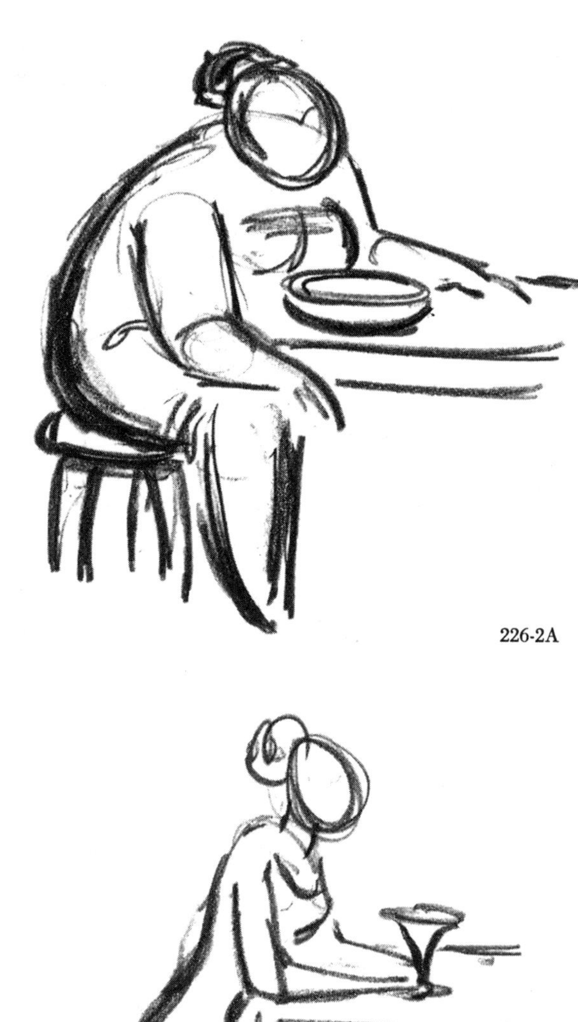

226-2A

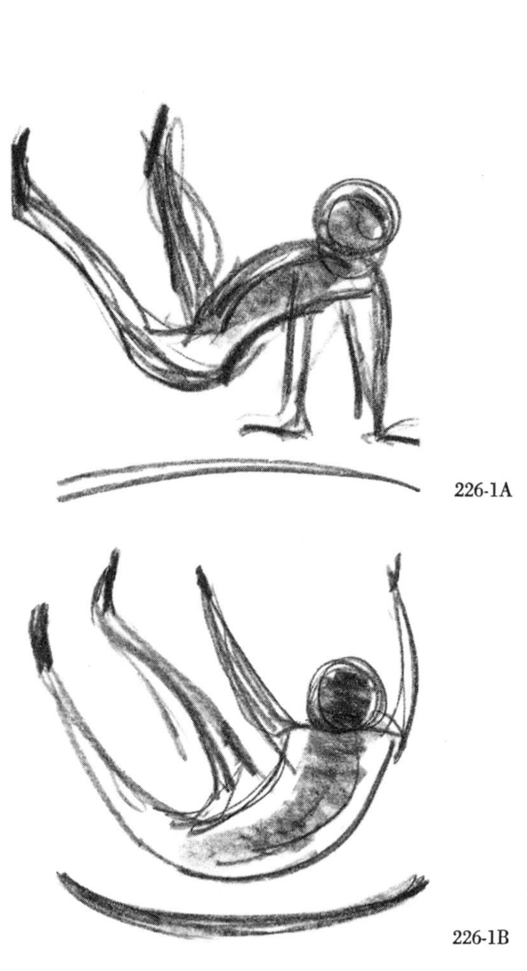

226-1A

226-1B

226-2B



Similarly, a figure may be shown slipping, his feet in the air. By manipulating the drawing of the sidewalk, he may seem to be propelled into the air (*226-1A*). Or the direction of his fall may be reversed by generating a strong directional movement emphasized by cupping of the sidewalk (*226-1B*).

By an association of forces we can make a heavy object seem heavier by finding elements which accommodate or respond to the downward thrust of the image. For instance, we might compare a heavy figure to a squat bowl on a table top. The dominant direction is down. The reaction in the stool opposes this downward thrust by bowing slightly (*226-2A*).

A slender figure shown perched on a stool may be compared to a wine glass whose dominant thrust is upward. By a manipulation of forces, in this case accomplished by "squeezing," both wine glass and figure are given a quality of buoyancy (*226-2B*).

In certain pictures a quality of weightlessness may be desirable, especially in non-representational pictures. This can be achieved by minimizing gravitational references. Graphic elements may be so accented that tensions between them generate an upward movement. In highly illustrative pictures using figures such as angels, the natural muscular tensions which result from contact with resisting surfaces may also be minimized as may the effect of gravity on garments and drapery.

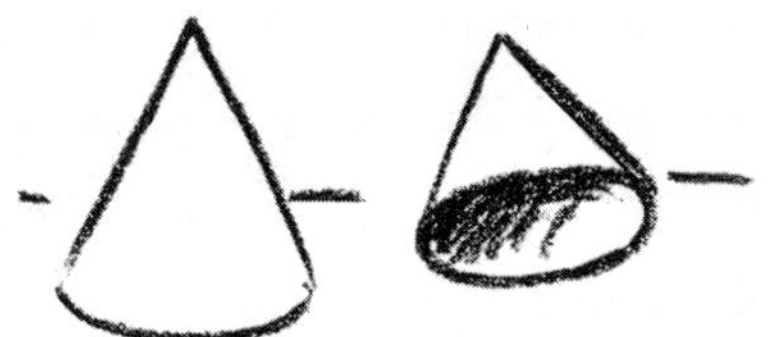

227-1A

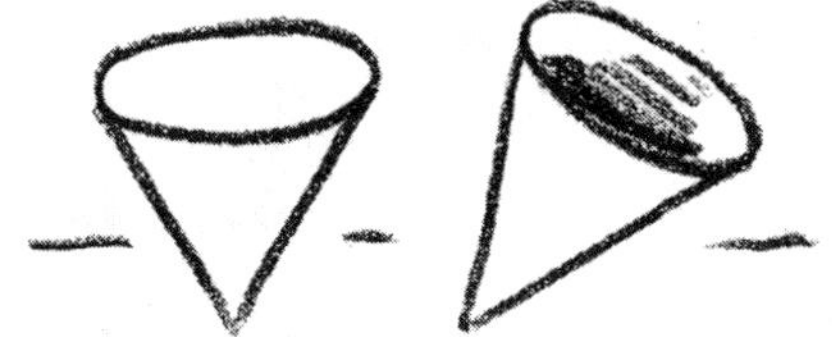

227-1B

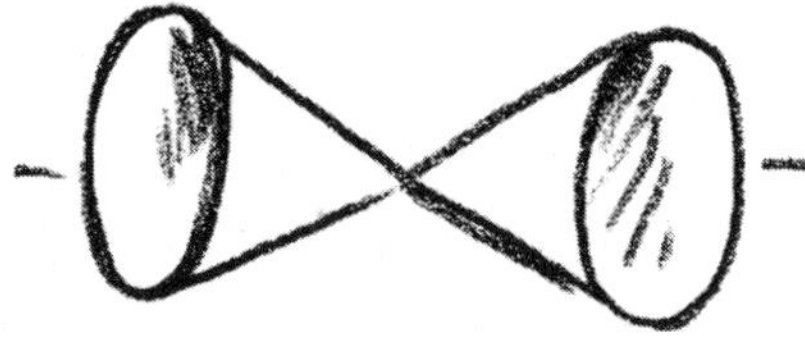

227-1C

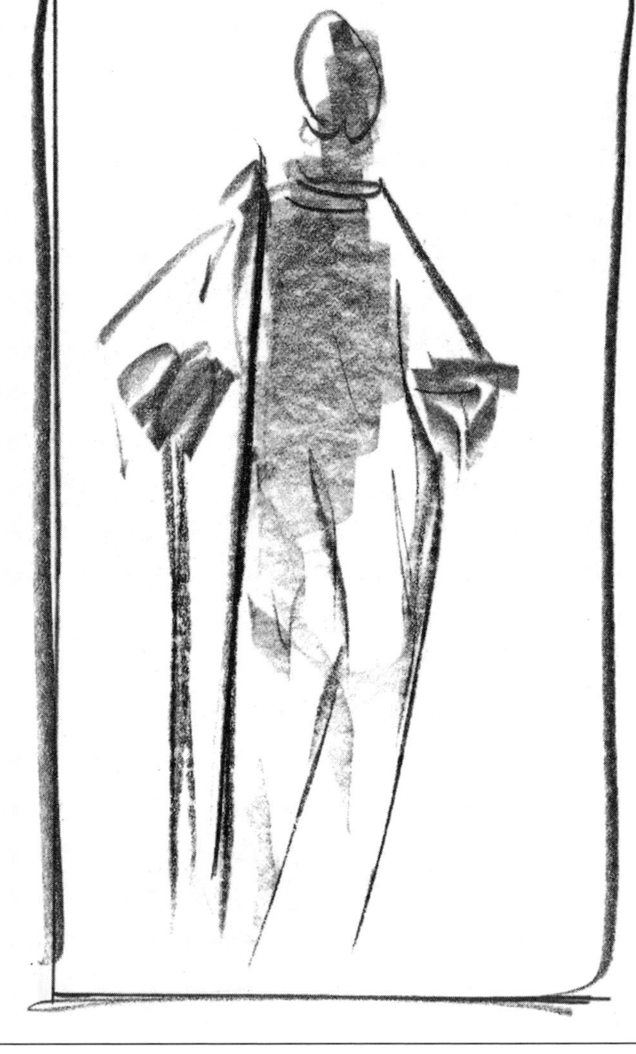

227-2

## Equilibrium and Balance in Nature

Sometimes forces are exerted yet no action results. Then we witness the phenomenon of equal forces negating each other. In nature, if one of these equal forces is increased slightly and momentarily over the other force, action then results. For instance, when a cone is lifted slightly from the surface and then released, it returns to its original stable position (*227-1A*). It is in a state of *balance*. If poised upon its tip and then displaced by a slight application of force, it falls into a new position. When on its tip, it is in an unstable position. It is in a state of *equilibrium* (*227-1B*). A third condition exists when a cone is on its side. A slight push, and it changes its position in relation to us, but not in its basic relation to the surface upon which it rests. It is in a neutral position (*227-1C*).

Before we can delineate a form our first problem is to determine whether the form in nature is in a state of equilibrium or in a state of balance. A standing figure in nature can be at rest, for it is not in action, yet it is in an unstable condition. It is in a state of equilibrium. The muscular forces of the body are counteracting the pull of gravity (*227-2*). When the forces being exerted change, the state of equilibrium is destroyed, and the figure goes into action.

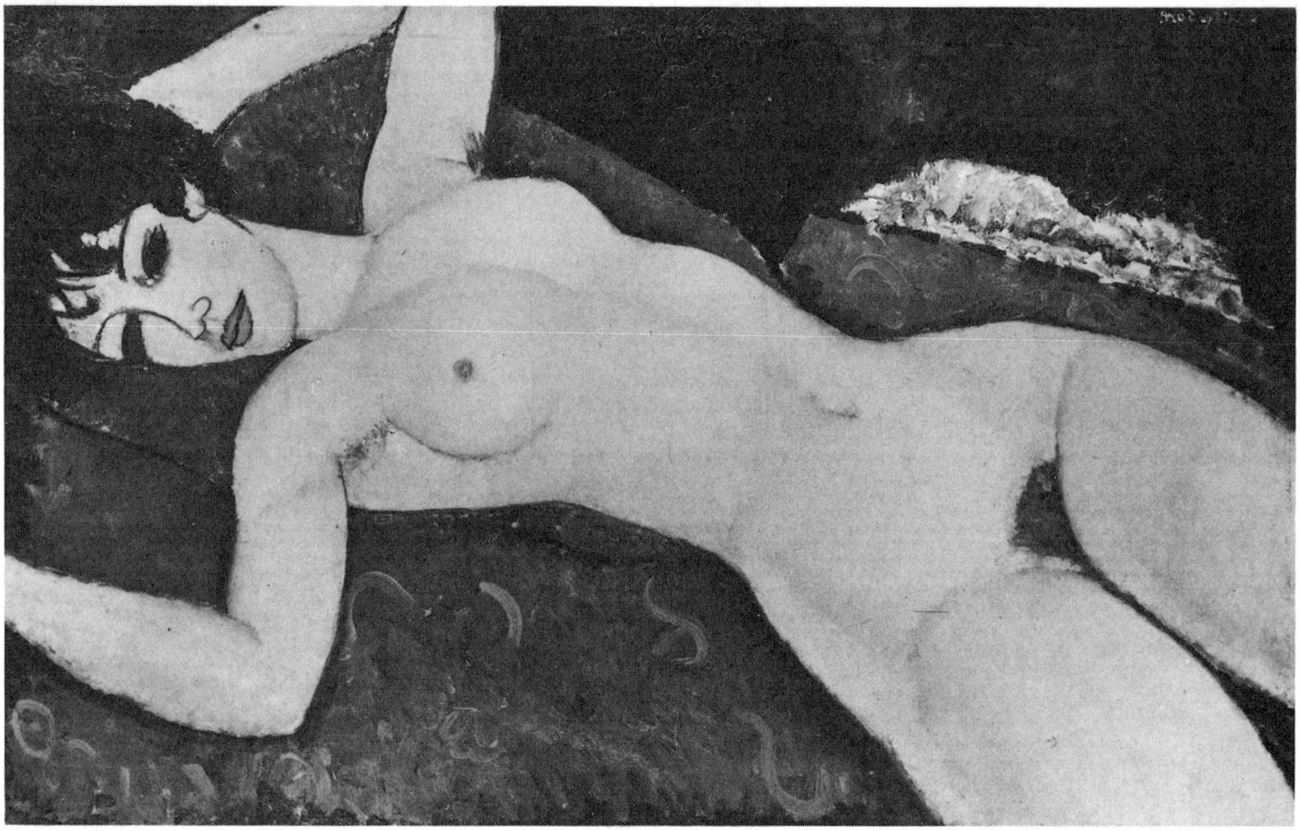

Amedeo Modigliani (Italian, 1884-1920)
NUDE ON A CUSHION, 1917
23½" x 36¼"; oil on canvas
Collection Gianni Mattioli, Milan
(Photograph: Bacci Attilio)

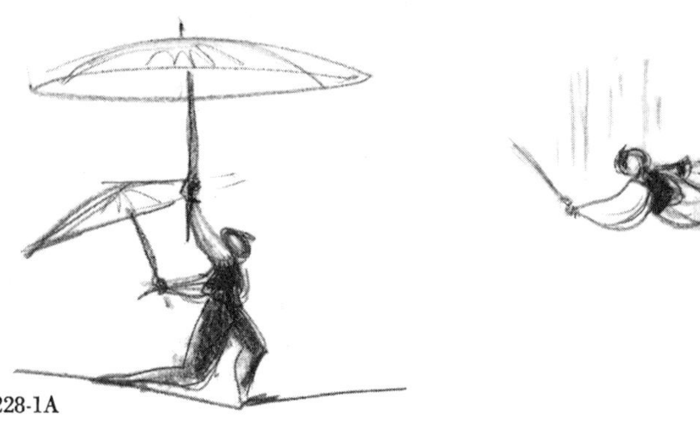




A reclining figure in nature, on the other hand, is in a stable condition. The force of gravity overwhelms any resisting muscular force. Any slight change due to the exertion of a muscle does not generate a whole new set of actions. The figure is like the cone in a stable position. It is inert, like a sack of potatoes. It is in balance.

A figure in action, for instance a tight-rope performer, demonstrates how a state of equilibrium is sustained from position to position. The unstable condition is constantly changed, but not overwhelmed, by gravity (*228-1A*).

If, however, the performer should fall, the force of gravity becomes an important factor in the story. In this case the action, the fall, and gravity are complementary (*228-1B*).

## Graphic Equilibrium and Graphic Balance

A picture may represent a form in either a state of equilibrium or balance, like this reclining nude by Modigliani. However, this does not assure that our picture, as an entity, is in either a state of equilibrium or in a state of balance. In fact it may well violate both conditions and be in a state of graphic imbalance. That Modigliani has achieved a picture in a state of equilibrium has nothing to do with the fact that the nude is reclining.

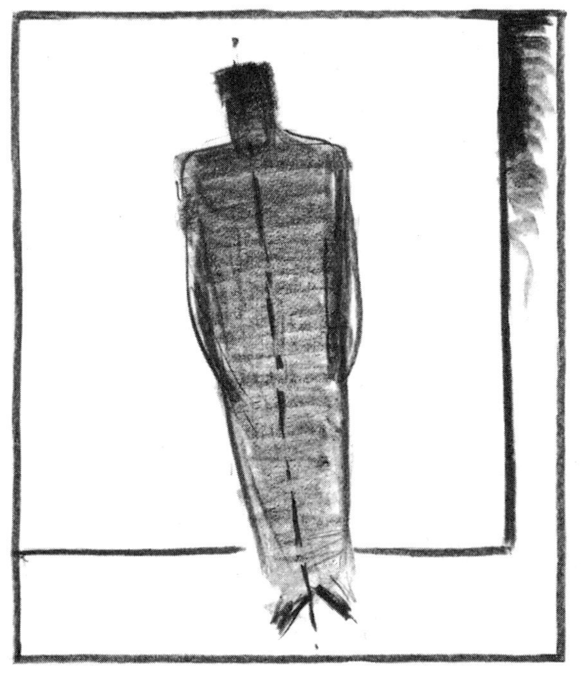

229-A

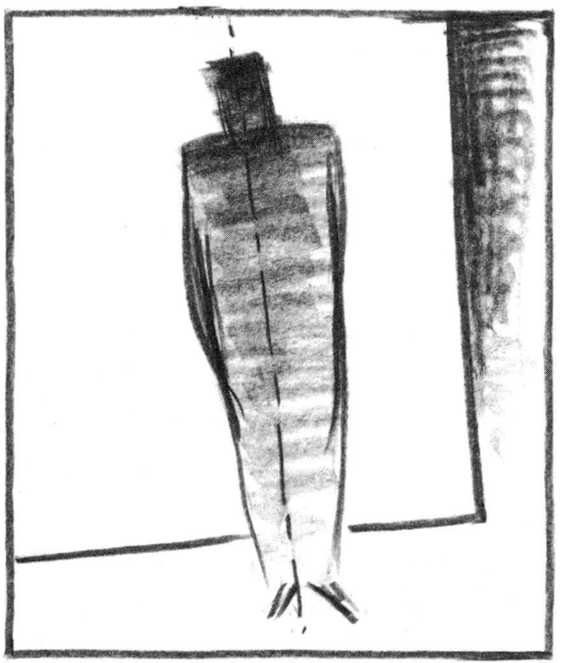

229-B

To clarify, a person seated comfortably in an easy chair is in a state of balance. The same person running down the street, the weight of his body distributed so that it is compensated by his forward action, is in a state of equilibrium. But in a drawing of either condition, new factors are involved. As we have observed, picture elements are but symbols of forces. A picture as a whole is a manifestation of an organization of forces expressed graphically. How these forces interact in the whole picture determines whether a picture itself is in a state of equilibrium, in a state of balance or imbalance.

The actual lines of a picture, the direction of a progressive shape, the relation of the symbol to the borders, and so on, may all contribute to either graphic equilibrium, graphic balance, or graphic imbalance. In *229-A* the figure seems to be falling, to be off-balance. The same figure, *229-B*, in relation to a rotated background is in a state of equilibrium, as is the picture as a whole. We should note that an organization of volumes or shapes may be neither vertical nor horizontal yet may imply a condition of equilibrium.

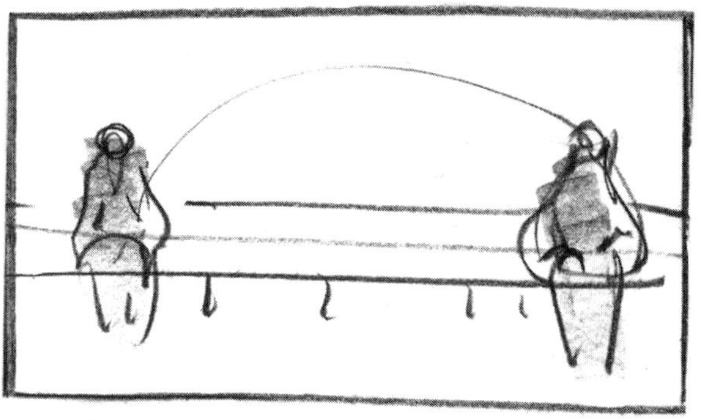

230-1A

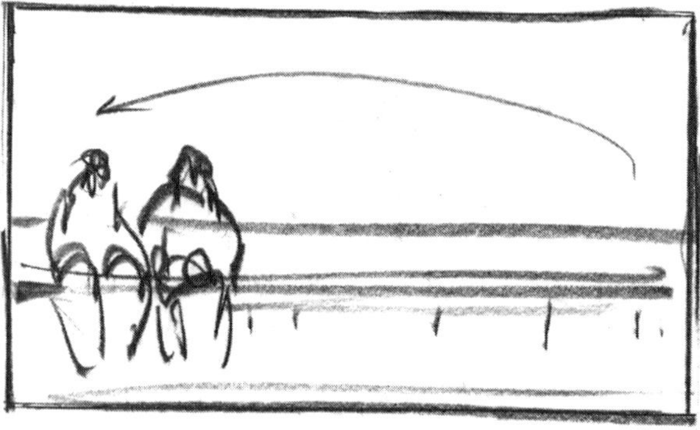

230-1B

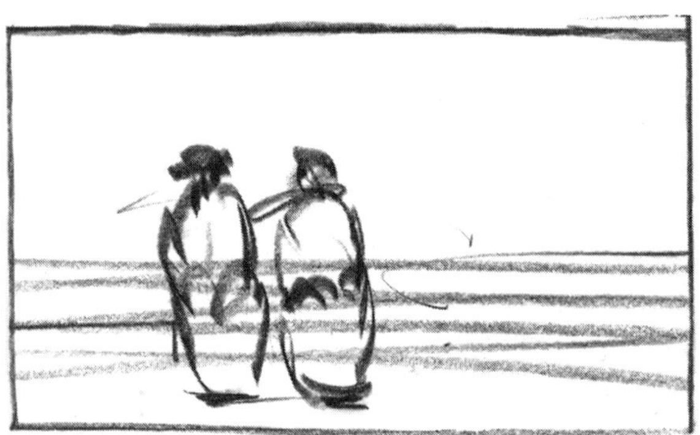

230-1C

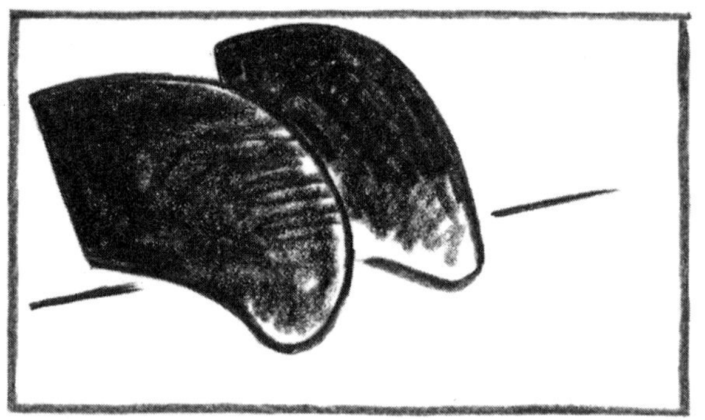

230-2


Two figures, each in repose, may be shown seated on a bench (*230-1A*). Each figure is in a state of balance. The picture itself is in a state of balance. Graphically it is dull, uninteresting. Most of the forces of the picture cancel each other. The quality of energy, so important in a picture, is slight.

Yet it is impossible not to generate some tension between various elements of the picture, as well as between them and the borders. Some energy is developed even in a balanced picture. However it has little intensity.

If now the two figures are jammed against a border, we create undue tension between border and symbols. We sense a congestion. The picture is now in a state of imbalance (*230-1B*).

By restaging the images, by placing them in a position of suspension in relation to the whole picture, we begin to feel the full effect of the borders, the bench, the enveloping space. Although the images, singly, are in balance, the picture in its entirety is now in a state of equilibrium (*230-1C*).

Graphic equilibrium need not be contingent upon the representation of action, or even upon things in nature. A graphic force, a strong concentration of interest in one area of the picture surface, may be so overwhelming that the whole picture may seem to tip, to wheel. By overstating a movement of the symbols in relation to the borders, the artist forces our eyes to return constantly to one overpowering area of the picture. A state of imbalance again exists (*230-2*).

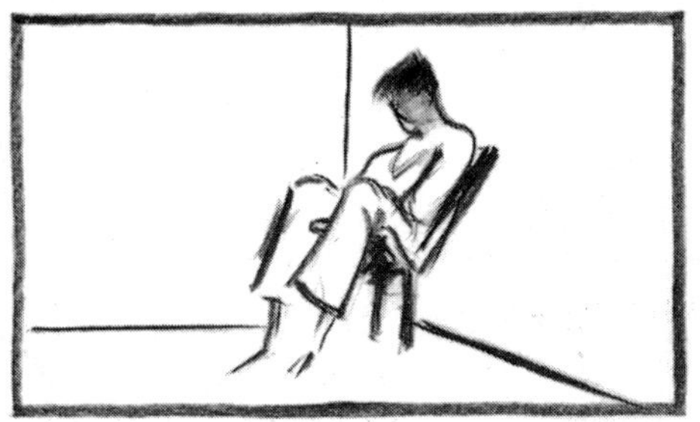

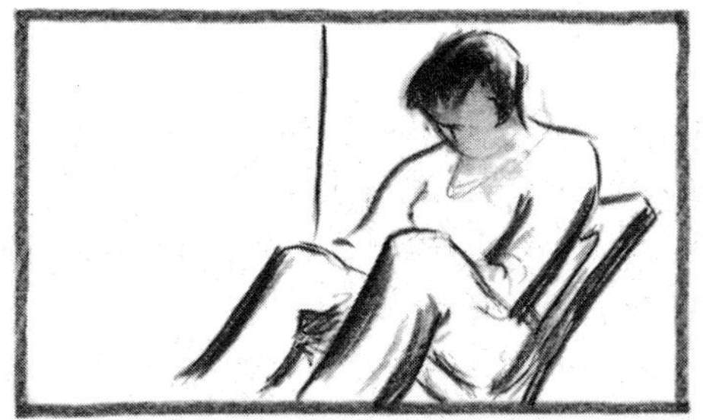

231-A                                          231-B

We find at times that a drawing of a stable condition of a symbol, a figure tipped back in a chair against a wall for instance, is convincing, is in balance because the opposing diagonal of the floor maintains the picture in a state of equilibrium (*231-A*). But if we assume a closer view of the same organization, the diagonal is lost and the picture is now imbalanced. The figure now seems to be falling (*231-B*).

## Rhythmic Actions in Nature

Another response generated in us by effects both in nature and in pictures is termed *rhythm*. Rhythm is the recurrence of elements in alternation with opposite or differing elements. Strangely, although we are surrounded by things constantly in action, or apparently in action, we become aware of rhythmic patterns of action only occasionally. A man rowing a boat, hammering, marching is involved in actions repeated within a limited time span. This is also true of actions repeated with variations, a dance, exercises, work routines such as hauling, pushing, etc. When we become aware of such underlying patterns of action, we also are aware of patterns of change. These patterns generate what we know as rhythm, which is an emotional response.

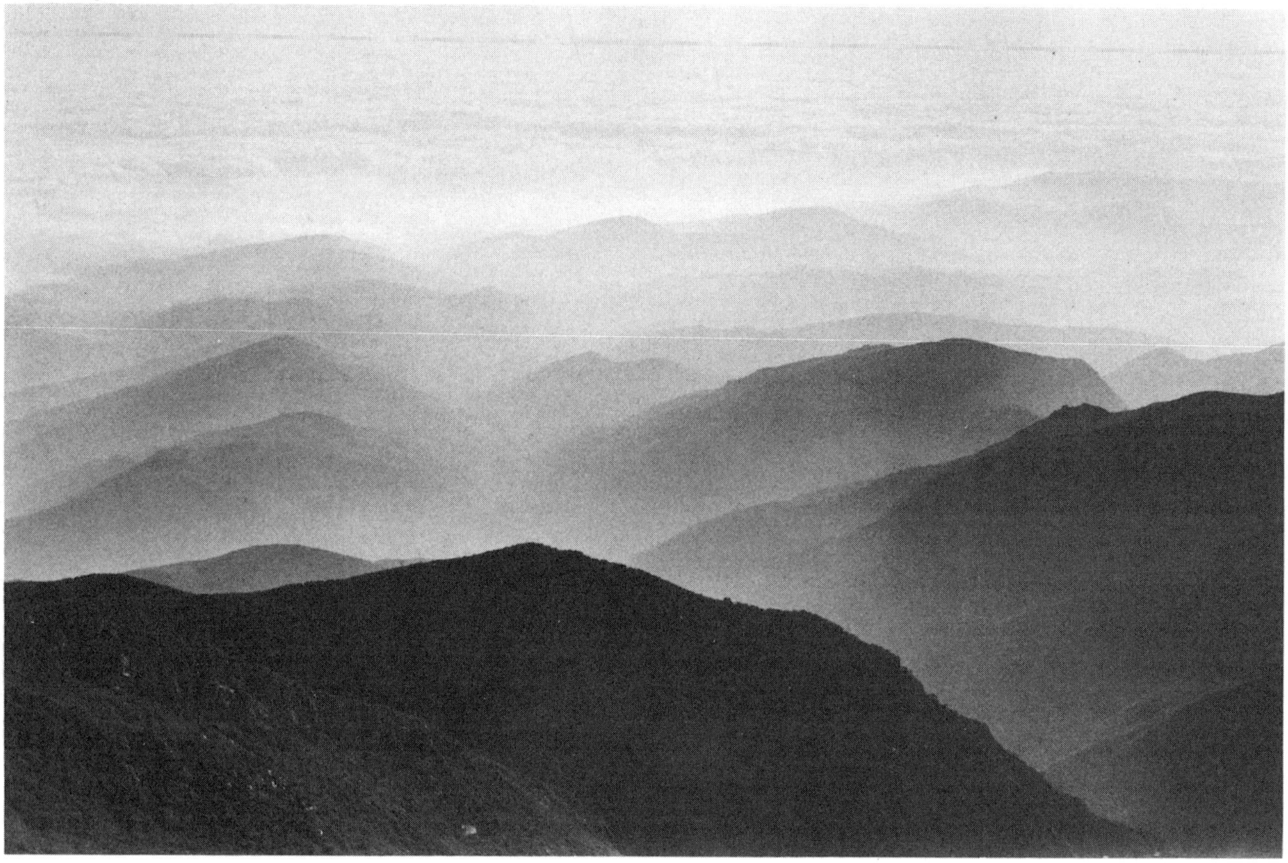

SAN MARCOS PASS, 1967
(Photograph: Richard Barlow, Hollywood)

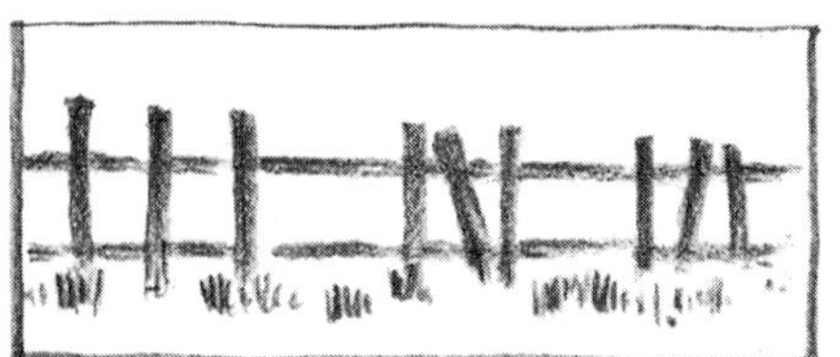

232-2A

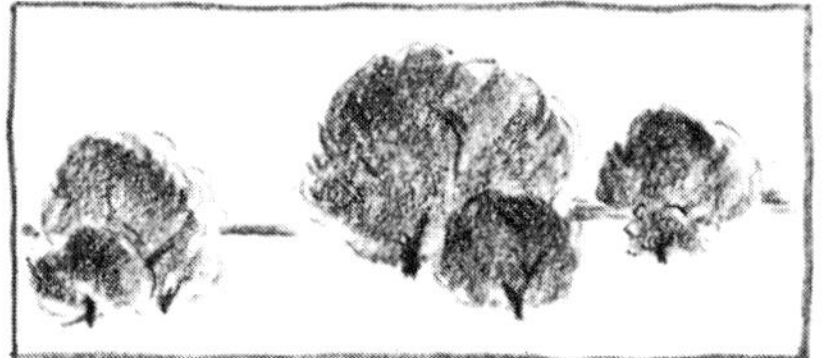

232-2B

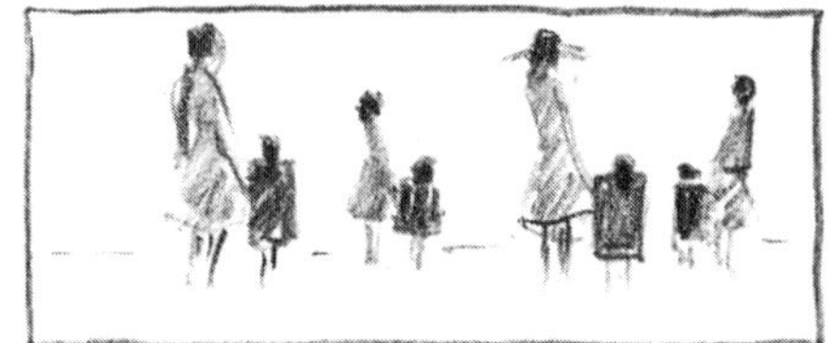

232-2C

## Rhythmic Movements

A similar response may also be generated in us by special organizations of inanimate forms in nature. Such disturbances in us are subjective and are called *rhythmic movements.*

The contour of a mountain range may induce in us a sense of undulation as our eyes drop from a peak to a valley, only to rise again to another peak. Repetitions with variations in the arrangement of pickets in a fence or telephone poles in a line may likewise induce a comparison of related positions, and thus generate rhythmic movement (*232-2A*). Large and small forms in nature may be so arranged that we become aware of rhythmic repetition with size variations (*232-2B*). A pattern of tall and short, high and low, forces our eye to compare relative positions. Color, texture, and pattern all play a part in creating rhythmic movement (*232-2C*).

As in nature, a picture may indicate the relative positions of graphic symbols in such a way as to generate rhythmic patterns such as tall and short, large and small, etc. Often these symbols represent inanimate objects or may be non-representational shapes. A picture in which rhythms are a dominant feature is often referred to as a rhythmic picture, as for example this painting by Edward Hopper.

### Movement and Picture Control

We now see that movement is a subjective emotional reaction. It is something in us, not in things around us. Action implies a real or apparent change of position. Movement is generated not by a change of position, but by the way we compare the relative position of things which usually are stationary in nature and are always so in a still picture.

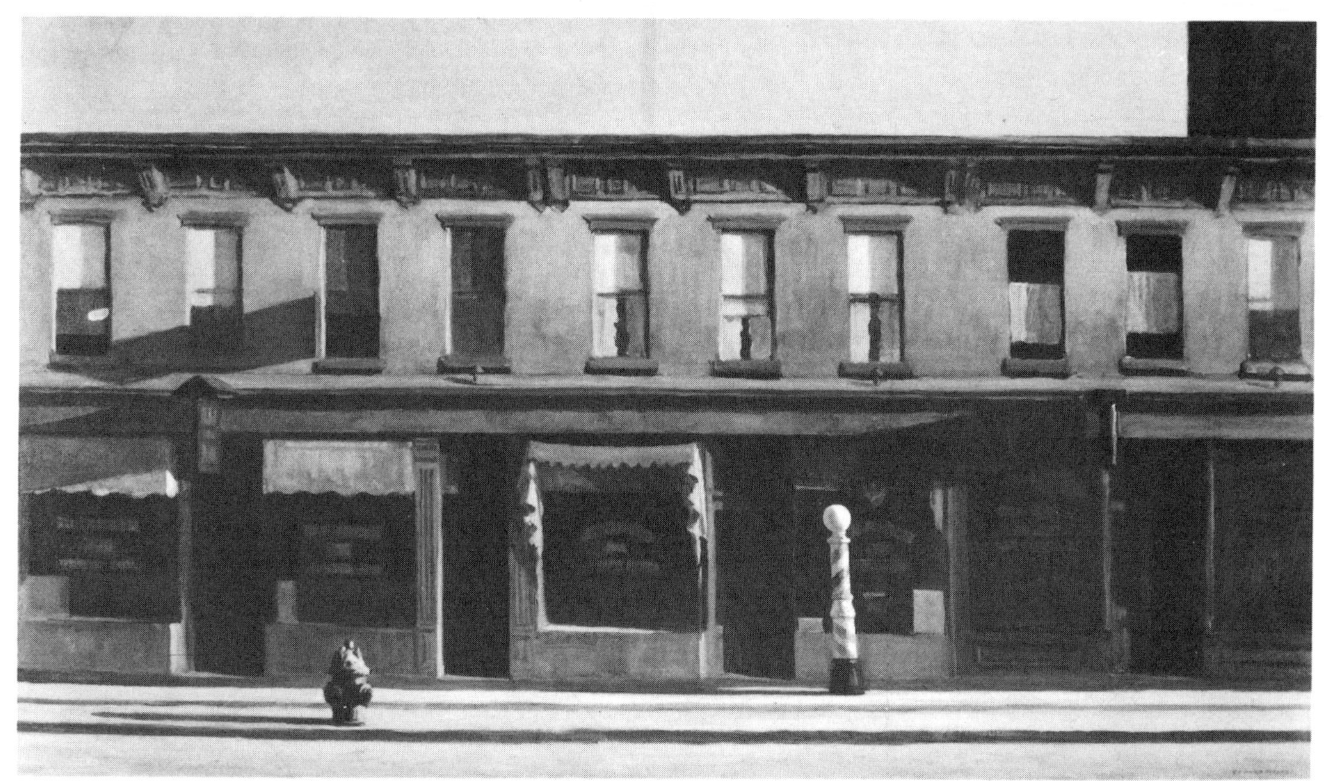

Edward Hopper (American, 1882-  )
EARLY SUNDAY MORNING, 1930; 35″ x 60″
oil on canvas
Collection of The Whitney Museum
of American Art, N. Y.
(Photograph: Soichi Sunami)

In actual practice we often refer to the order of an arrangement that generates movement in us as "having movement." Or we may say that a certain arrangement of forms in nature or symbols in our picture "has movement." This common use of terms in an objective sense is permissible as long as it is understood that in graphics the arrangement itself never moves, it merely arouses in us an emotional response which constitutes true movement, subjective movement.

To some degree all pictures involve movement, for comparing the positions of any two symbols generates some movement. But when movement is not understood and controlled, or when it is generated accidentally, results are usually chaotic, lacking vitality, energy.

The ordered control of movement makes possible the ultimate control of the whole picture. Usually this is conscious control by the artist, but at times the use of movement may be intuitive. When such intuitively generated movement is successful, as we find in much primitive art, it is truly exciting; when unsuccessful, it results in confusion.

So we see that although action is a major factor in most people's lives and often is a contributing factor in the imagery of a picture, it is only one of the factors of interest to the artist. He may dramatize action graphically or ignore it completely. Movement, on the other hand, cannot be ignored either by artist or spectator, for it is the force which holds any picture together. As we shall see, movement is essential to all pictures.

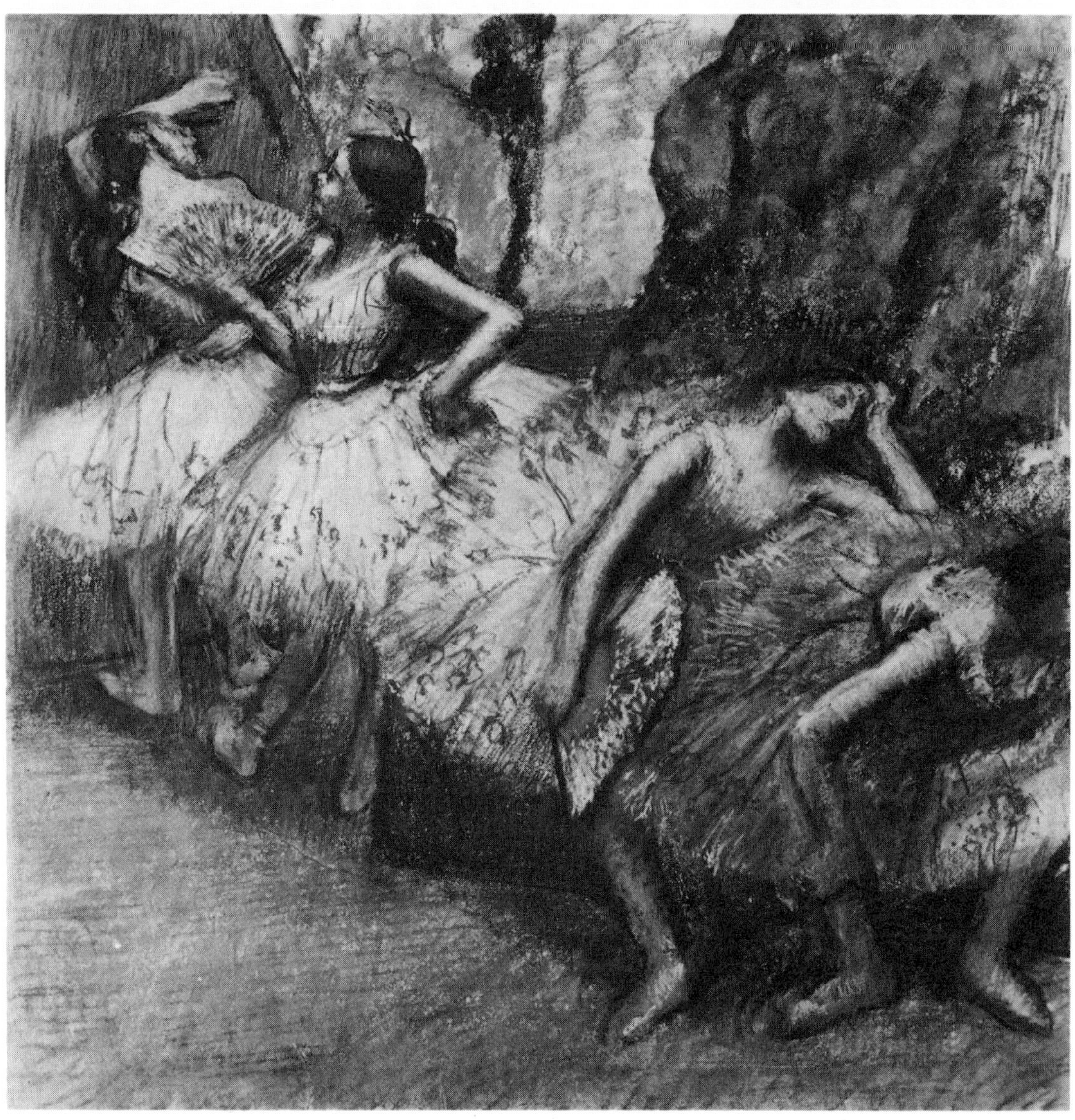

Hilaire Germain Edgar Degas (French, 1834-1917)
BALLET DANCERS IN THE WINGS, 1900; 28″ x 26″
pastel on paper; mounted
City Art Museum of Saint Louis, Mo.



# 21 Perspective Movement and Picture Movement

### The Positional Relation of Forms

As we have noted, movement is generated when we compare the position of one thing to another. The things we compare may be forms in nature, volumes in a drawing, or shapes, lines, or colors which may represent things in nature, or may be abstract. Strangely enough, in daily life we seldom are especially concerned with the relative position of things around us. We recognize the fact that two feet stand on a surface. We rarely are aware of the angle at which they are placed. When we really compare their positions, then we experience movement. For example, we feel a strong graphic movement as we compare the positions of the feet of Degas' ballet dancers.

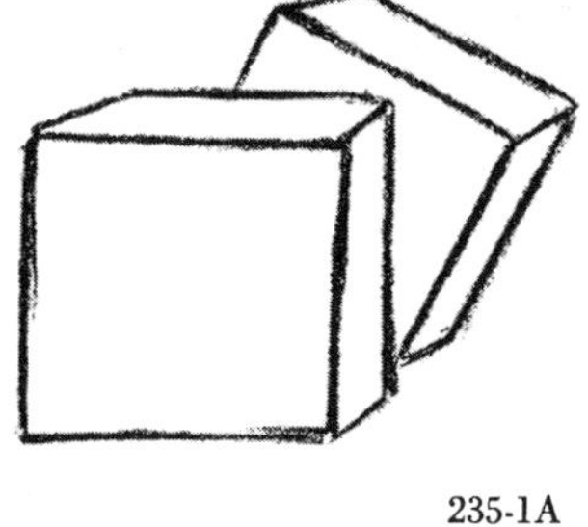

235-1A

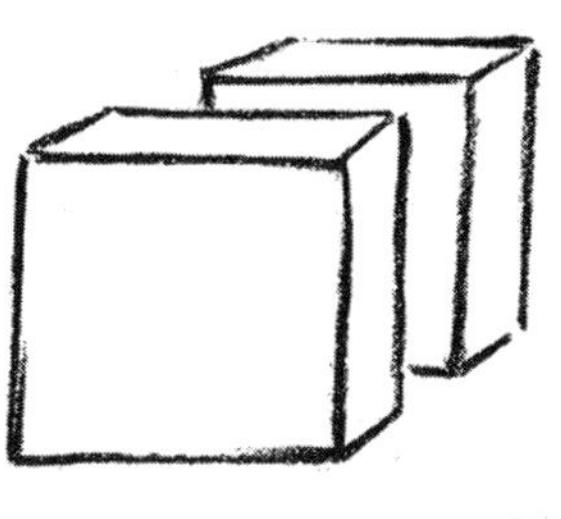

235-1B

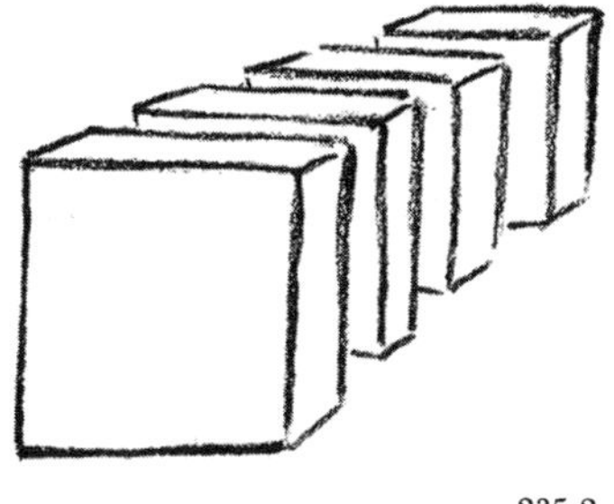

235-2

In most cases in comparing positions, we establish one dominant element as a reference against which we judge or measure. This may be a strong vertical, a strong horizontal, or some other strong element in the picture. For example, if the rows of trees in an orchard in a picture converge to a distant point, this point may overpower our awareness of either the vertical or horizontal, and it becomes the dominant reference of the picture.

As we justify the position of an element in relation to that of a strong reference we try subconsciously to align them in some stable way. In doing so we experience movement. Here we see the tipped box (*235-1A*) as a disturbance; a violation of the order achieved in the second drawing (*235-1B*) which is more easily comprehended, more stable.

## Three Types of Movement Patterns



As we try to form simple movement patterns from the haphazard arrangements we find in nature we discover that such patterns have certain characteristics.

The *straight line* movement pattern results from an organization of elements arranged so that we experience their straight alignment as a simple progressive movement. When we compare their relative positions we feel this progressive movement as a straight line (*235-2*).

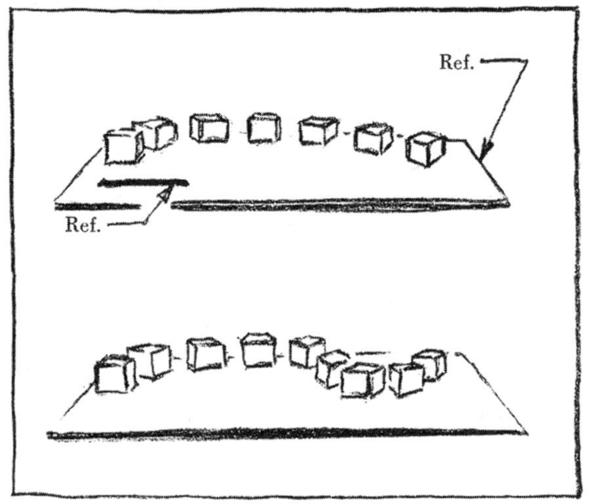

236-1

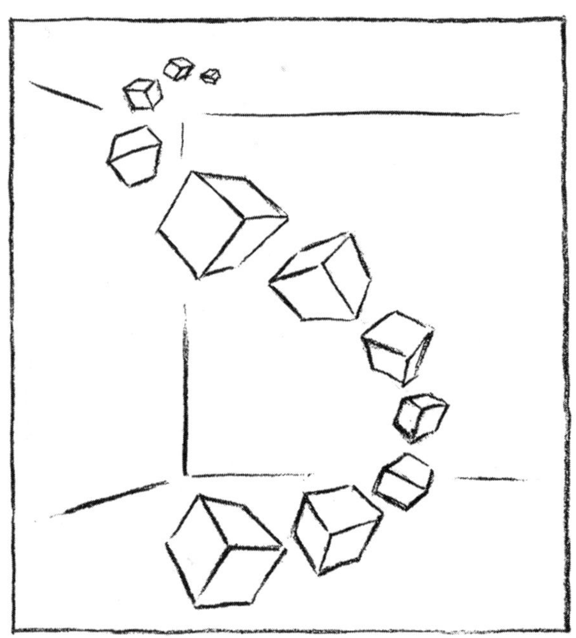

236-2

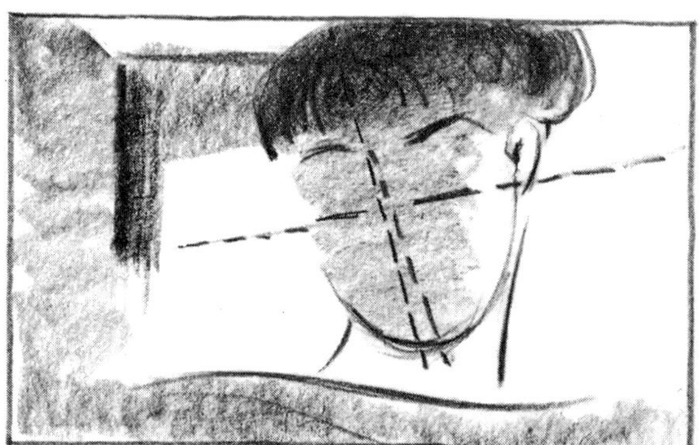

236-3



236     The *curve* movement pattern is an organization of elements so arranged in relation to one reference plane that we are conscious of a progression of elements that continue to change their angular position in relation to a straight line reference in this plane. This pattern results from a continuing opening or closing of the elements to each other. Quite often the pattern reverses direction. In either case a curve movement pattern results (*236-1*).

The *spiral* movement pattern is an organization of elements so arranged in relation to three reference planes, all at ninety degrees to each other, that the position of each element successively changes direction in relation to each of the three reference planes. In so doing they generate a spiral movement pattern (*236-2*).

This movement, which is rather difficult to visualize, is by far one of the most commonly experienced movements in nature. For instance, the action of a form in nature occurs in a three-dimensional environment which usually implies a change of position in relation to three fixed references normal to each other. To explain such action graphically we must draw the various important parts of the body not in relation to one reference plane, but to all three. A head usually tips and turns in relation to two vertical walls and a horizontal floor, or their equivalents. In a drawing, the symbol of the head must explain this tipping and turning toward or away from our three fixed references, either drawn or implied (*236-3*). Of course a form or volume may be intentionally made parallel to one of the references.

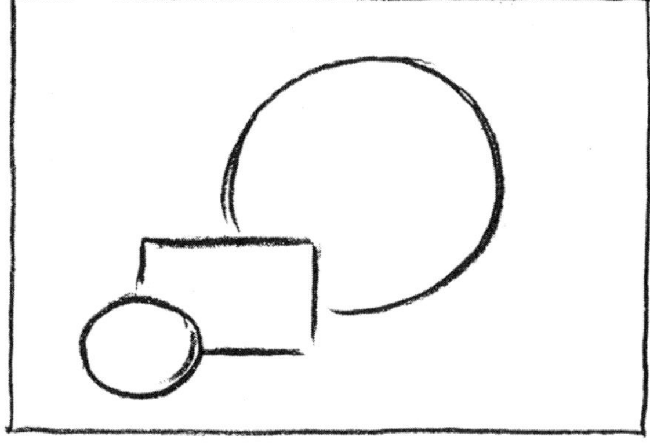

237-1

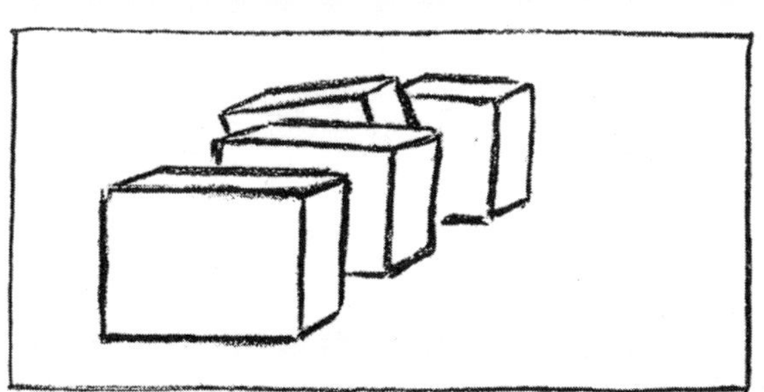

237-3

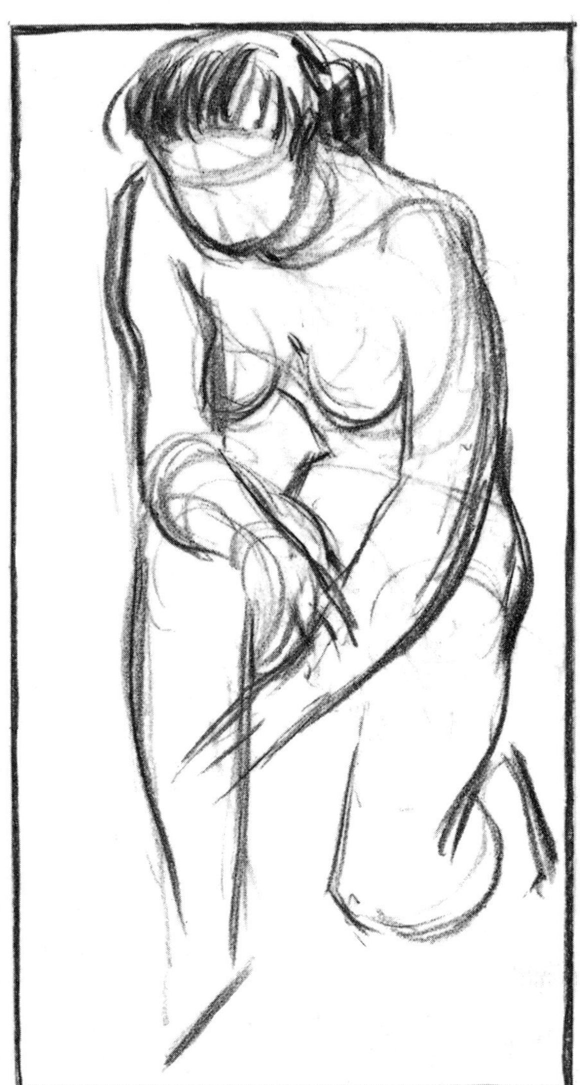

237-2

## Countermovements

The relative positions of elements, whether in
nature or pictures, are seldom mechanically
aligned. An element may contribute to a straight
line, curve, or spiral movement yet in itself be
counter to this movement (*237-1*). At times such
counters may be of great value in emphasizing
a dominant movement. We might compare
such a countermovement to a passing car which
approaches our own at great speed. Our own
speed is seemingly enhanced by the speed of the
oncoming car.



In the same way, one movement pattern may
act as a counter to an entirely separate movement pattern. In the accompanying drawing
(*237-2*) the dominant movement pattern generated by the related positions of head, torso,
and left leg is often called the "line of action,"
a misnomer. It should be called a "line of
movement." The movement generated by the
right leg is a countermovement, as is that
generated by the arms. Both enhance the
principal movement.

We should note, also, that the size, shape,
or color of the elements generating a movement pattern may vary, for whatever their
size, shape, or color it is our response to the
relative positions of elements one to another
which constitutes a movement pattern (*237-3*).

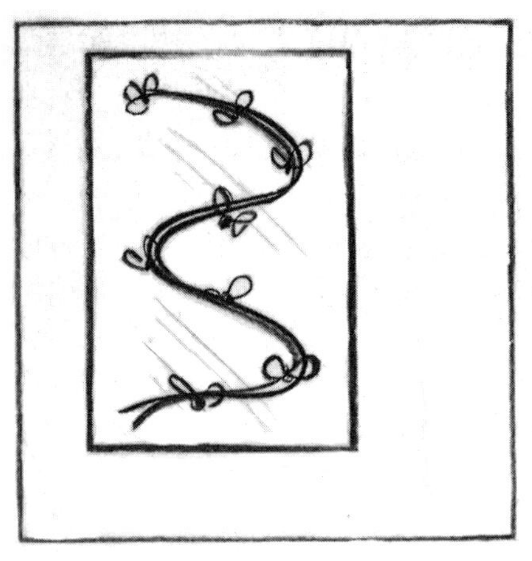

238-1A

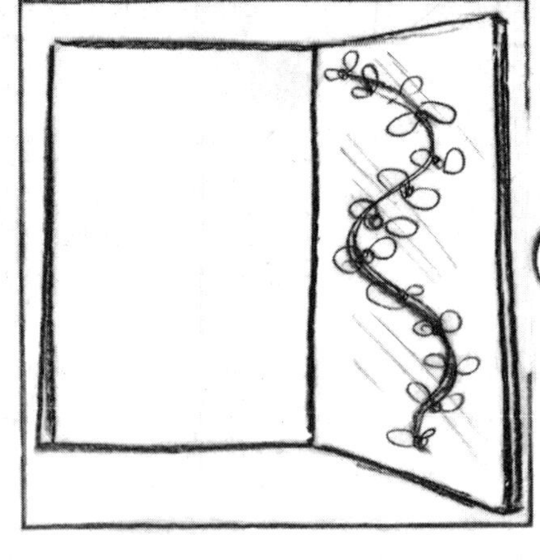

238-1B

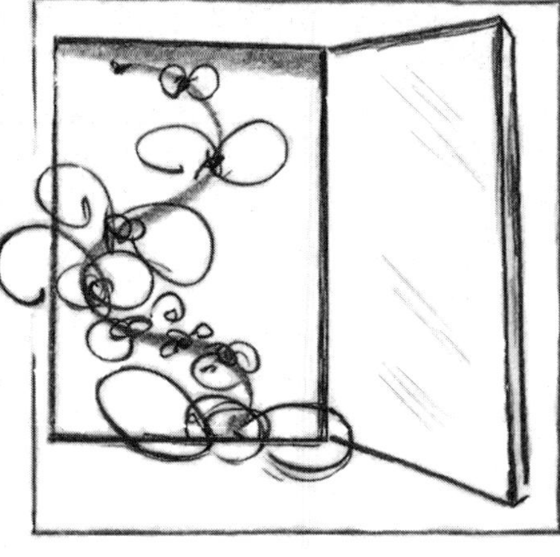

238-1C

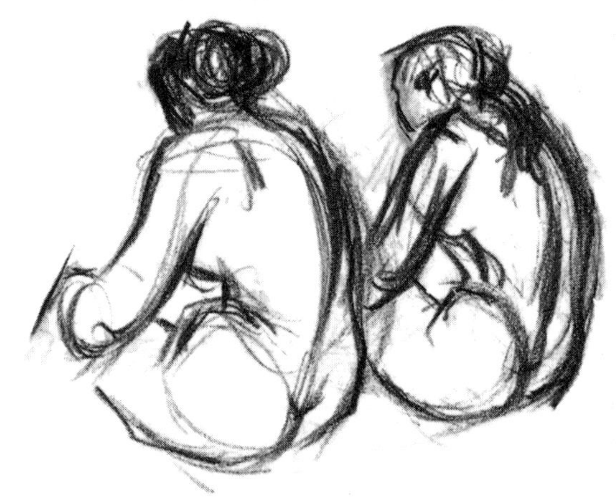

238-2

238-3A          238-3B

 **The Curve versus The Spiral**

Because the curve and spiral movement patterns are sometimes difficult to distinguish from one another, great care must be observed to avoid confusing the two in one drawing because there is a different amount of space generated by each. If a spiral pattern is desired we may apply a simple work rule: never align any two adjacent volumes in such a way that a straight or curve movement pattern results. Of course there are certain cases in which a spiral movement should not be used. The hinged units of the middle finger, for example, almost always generate a straight or curve movement pattern, not a spiral.

To illustrate the difference between a curve and spiral movement pattern let us imagine that we look directly out a window at a fly crawling on the window pane (*238-1A*). The fly moves erratically from side to side and up and down. Its size appears the same no matter how it moves in its relation to the glass or to us. Its path is a simple curve pattern.

Now suppose we open the window at an angle to us. (*238-1B*). As the fly crawls on the glass its size does not change in relation to the pane, but as it moves in and out from us its size does seem to change; it seems to become larger, then smaller. The fly still generates simple curves which may look like spirals to us.

Now imagine that the fly flies off the window pane following not a straight path but a constantly changing flight pattern (*238-1C*). As it approaches us it seems to get bigger; as it recedes from us it seems to get smaller. Its size constantly changes both in relation to the window, the pane, and to us. Its flight path is a spiral.

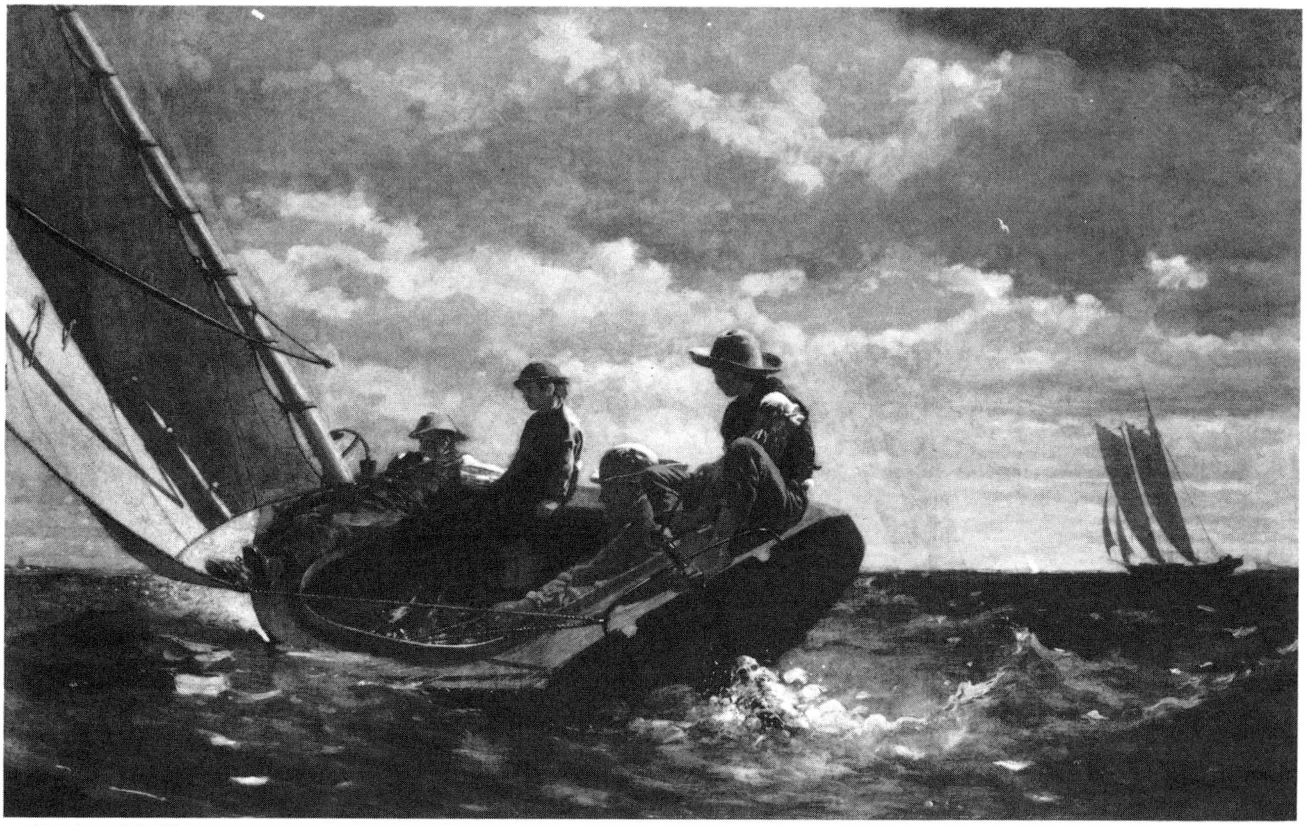

Winslow Homer (American, 1836-1910)
BREEZING UP, 1876; 24⅛″ x 38⅛″
oil on canvas
National Gallery of Art, Washington, D. C.
Gift of the W. L. and May T. Mellon Foundation

The actual projection of the movement patterns, the curve representing the fly's progress while walking on the closed window, may be the same as when it crawls on the open pane or when it flies through the open window. Yet each is different from the point of view of the fixed references or of the spectator (*238-2*).

So we see that two human figures, each drawn performing basically the same action, may differ profoundly as to movement patterns. One, by means of slight disturbances between adjacent parts, generates a spiral (*238-3A*); the other, by the alignment of adjacent parts, generates a series of reverse curves (*238-3B*).

## Movement Through Perspective Organizations



A picture often is based on some occurrence in nature, but we should be aware that most arrangements of forms in nature tend to be disorganized in a movement sense. To create orderly movement patterns from such disorderly arrangements is one of the primary concerns of an artist like Winslow Homer. To the visually chaotic world he must learn to bring visual order, to transpose his observations into graphic terms. Usually he must organize his symbols into some type of movement pattern. This may be a strong spiral, straight line, or curve movement pattern, or other type of movement control which we will investigate shortly.

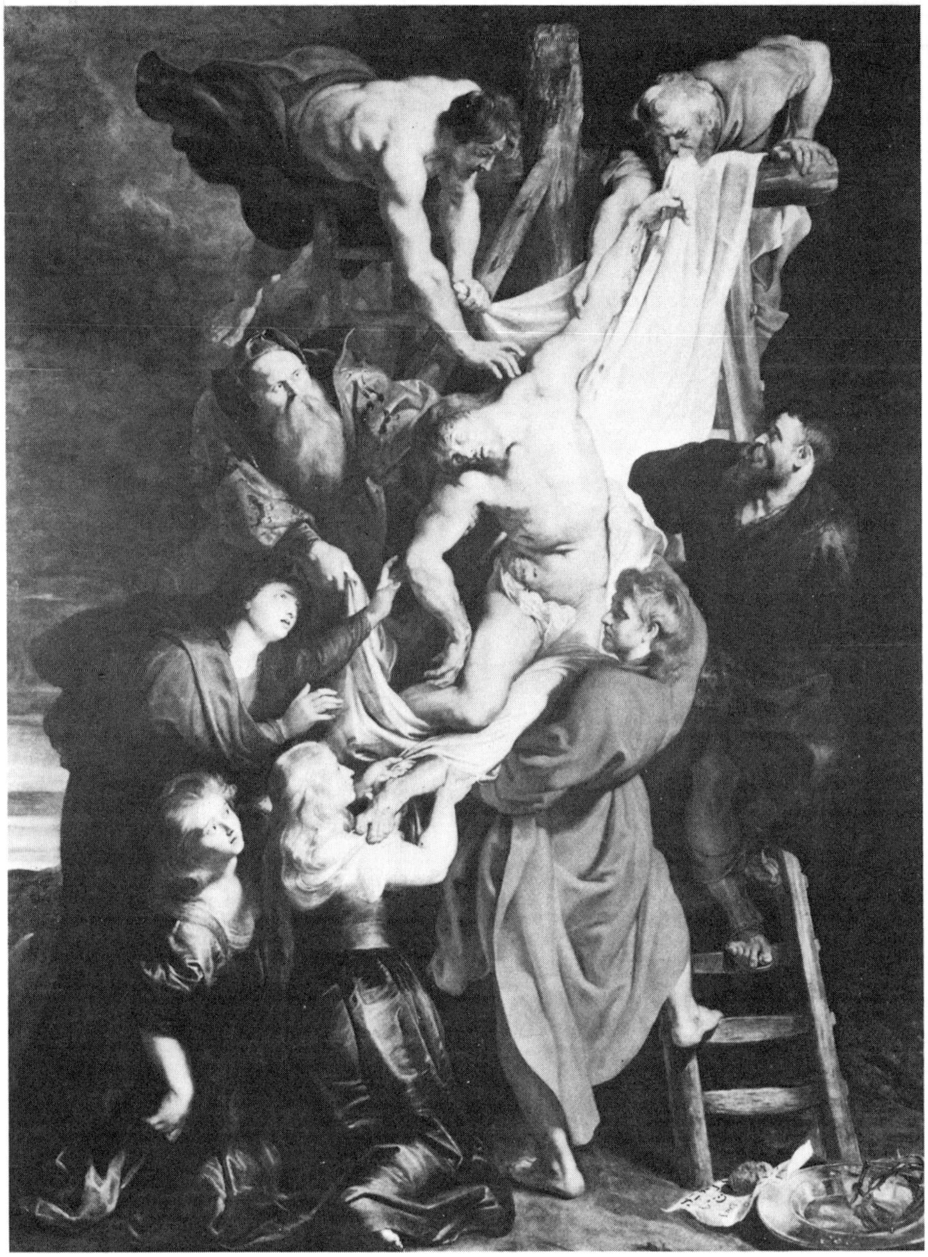

Especially by exploitation of spiral movement do graphic symbols representing three-dimensional realities in deep space become possible. Most Renaissance pictures are built on strong spiral movement patterns. In such pictures three-dimensional sculptural symbols combined with deep three-dimensional space lend themselves easily to the creation of realistic atmospheric effects, sunlight, shadow, etc. Such pictures, like the Rubens above, usually represent a perspective world. For this reason movements generated by comparing relative positions of symbols of three-dimensional forms are referred to as perspective movements in order to distinguish them from other types of graphic movements.

**Picture Movements**

Perspective movements are generated in us when we compare the relative positions of two or more forms or volumes. But we also experience movement by comparing the relative positions of two or more two-dimensional elements in or parallel to the picture surface. Such comparisons of positions, or the arrangements which make such comparisons possible are called *picture movements*.

Learning to experience movement is similar to learning other skills. We learn not through our minds alone, but also through our bodies. We cannot learn to ride a bicycle merely by thinking. We cannot merely *think* playing a violin. In the same way much that we learn of drawing and painting we must learn with our hands and eyes, not only with our brain. In fact it is often the case that a person who is too analytical has difficulty

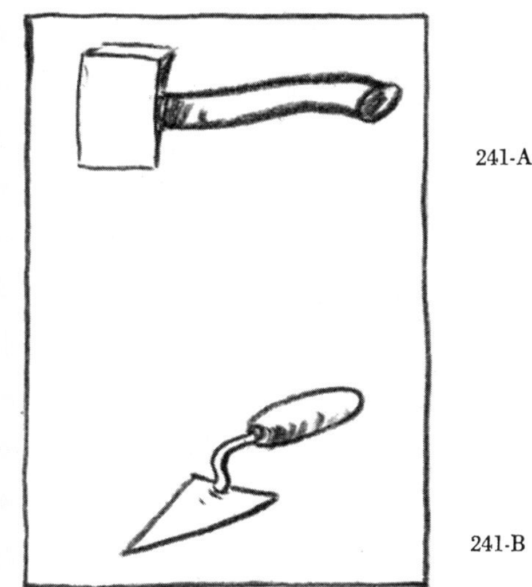



Peter Paul Rubens (Flemish, 1577-1640)
DESCENT FROM THE CROSS, 1611-1614
165½″ x 126″; oil on wood
Antwerp Cathedral

adjusting to the attitude of the artist. In addition to thinking with his brain an artist positively must learn through his eyes, ears, body, and especially his hands.

To learn to distinguish between perspective movements and picture movements let us strike our picture surface, our drawing board, with the edge of our extended hand. The hand is now like a hatchet. It chops (*241-A*). It represents a perspective plane making an angle to the picture surface. Any such chopping action suggests perspective movements in deep graphic space.

As we strike the surface we experience a definite type of physical reaction in our hand. If we strike hard enough we experience real pain. Always we feel that we are cutting the surface.

Now let us place our hand palm down, flat on our picture surface. The hand is now like a trowel. It spreads (*241-B*). No matter in what direction we stroke the surface, our hand never leaves it. As the gliding hand assumes new positions it is reminiscent of a graphic shape generating picture movements.

As our hand glides over the surface we experience an entirely different type of physical reaction than the brutal chopping. Now we feel a smooth action, sensuous, pleasing. The hand gliding on the surface symbolizes a picture movement, in contrast to the hand chopping which symbolizes a perspective movement.

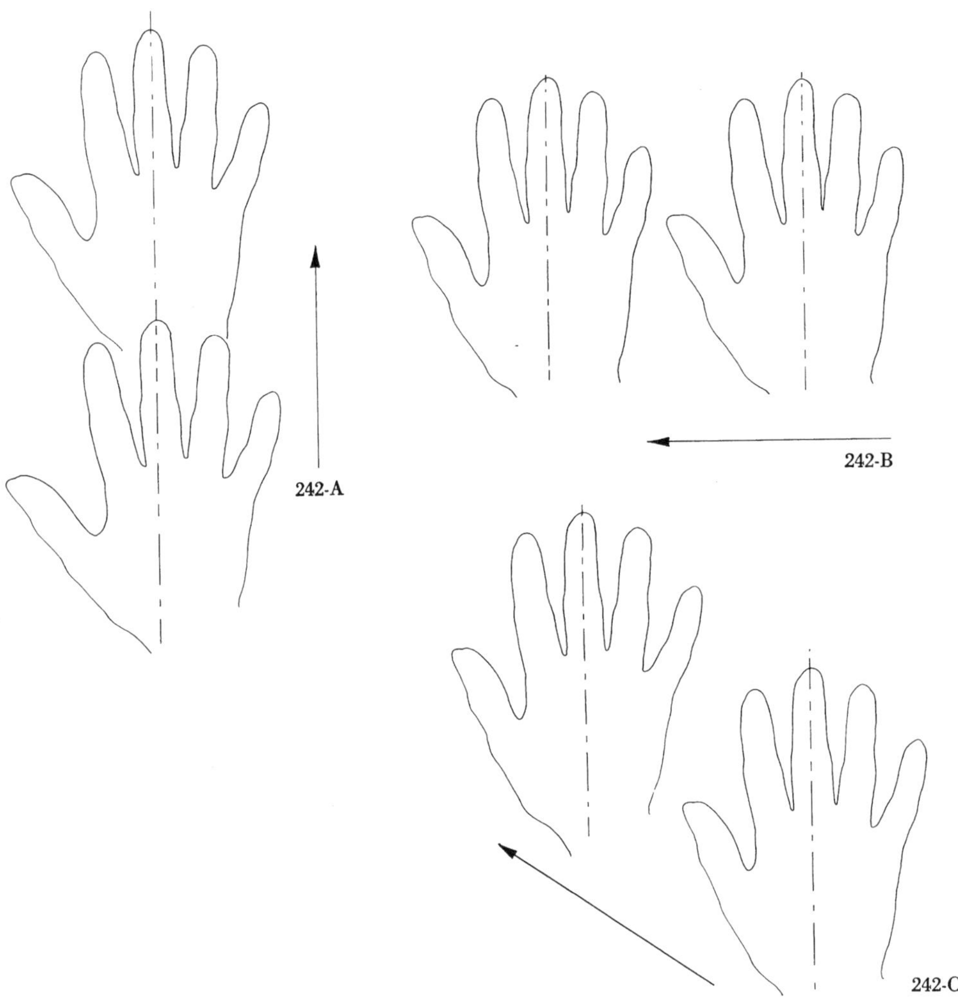




The hand may chop in an almost infinite number of directions, for it is moving in deep three-dimensional space. But when moving in two dimensions on the picture surface, the hand is confined to two characteristic actions, the slide and the rotation. How we move the hand determines which type of movement we generate. The direction of the action of the hand is determined by the position of its axis, the middle finger.

**The Slide**

In generating a *slide* the hand moves only in relation to a strong directional reference. This usually is a vertical or horizontal but may be a powerful diagonal lying in or parallel to the picture surface. As the hand moves, the middle finger is always kept parallel to the reference. As the hand moves it should preserve a constant pressure on the surface.

If we respect these restrictions we find that we may move the hand up and down to give a

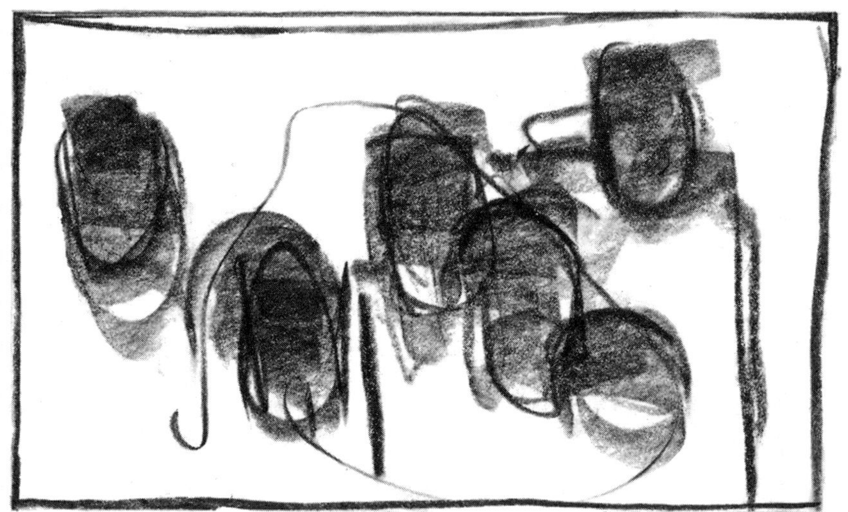

243-A

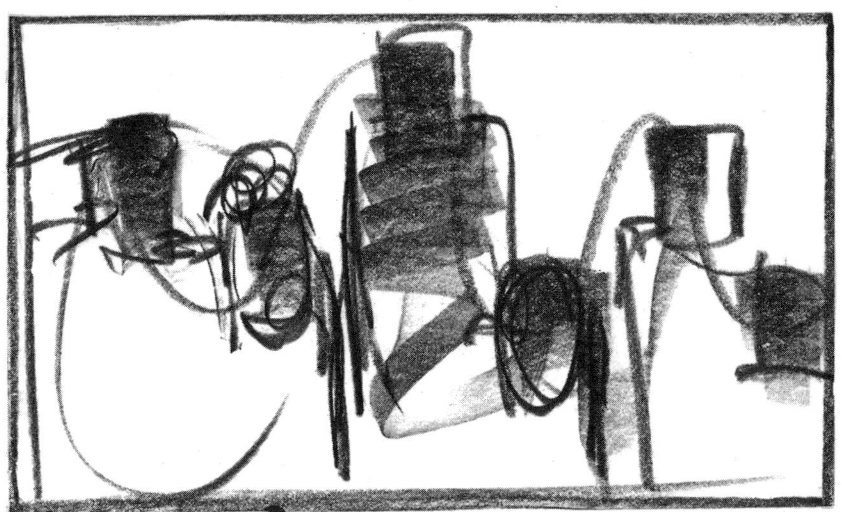

243-B

true vertical action of the middle or axis finger
(*242-A*). Or we may move the whole hand
from side to side with the middle finger always
parallel to the vertical reference (*242-B*). We
also may move the hand in a diagonal direction
provided that the middle finger is constantly
kept vertical (*242-C*). Of course the direction
of the reference determines the ultimate action
of the hand. If the reference is horizontal then
all of the actions outlined will conform to this
new reference. As we shall see this is equally
true when a diagonal reference is employed.

To transpose the slide into picture terms, in
*243-A* we are conscious of one head being
related by slide to another. In *243-B* we may be
more aware of the linear pattern generated by
the positions of the heads than by the slide
relations which make this pattern possible.

243

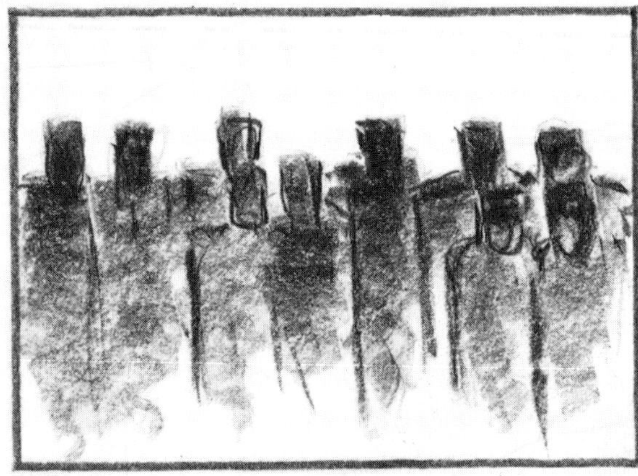

244-A

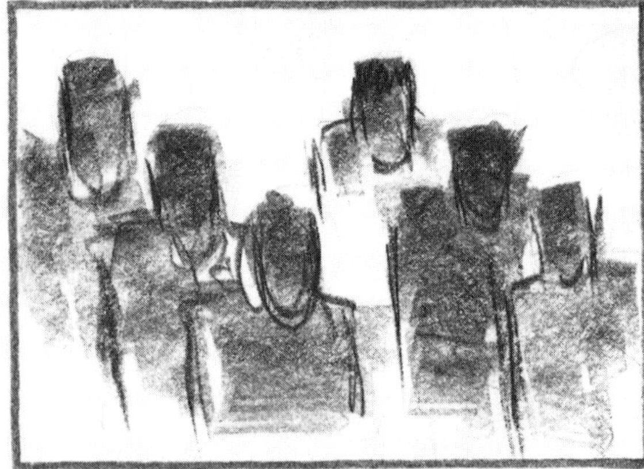

244-B

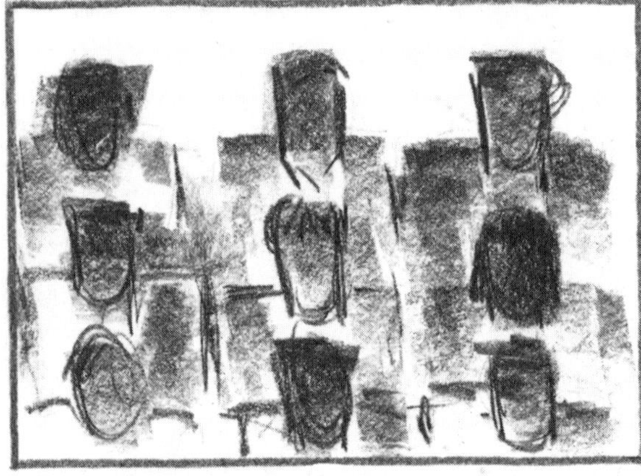

244-C

244 There are many such patterns which grow out of picture movements. And many, although detrimental to a pure slide, make exciting patterns. An example might be an ordered arrangement of standing figure symbols (*244-A*). Each cluster may be visualized as generated by slide and each cluster in turn related to the next cluster by slide. In looking at the picture we notice that with the heads we have generated a strong straight line which divides the entire picture surface off-center proportionally. But of even more interest is the rhythmic count of the heads, 1-2, 1-2-2, 1, 1-2-3-4. Such a count constitutes an order different from picture movement but possibly equally exciting.

In the same way, by means of slide, a strong diagonal pattern may evolve which will dominate the picture (*244-B*). Diagonal, vertical, or horizontal patterns are quite common. Through variations such pictures create great interest which may be generated by picture movement yet not entirely satisfy the requirements of a true slide (*244-C*).

As a rule the greatest difficulty in realizing a successful slide is overcoming the expectedness of a vertical or horizontal arrangement. First, such arrangements are so prevalent in nature that we accept them without thought or reaction. Second, the vertical and horizontal arrangements are used so frequently in most pictures that to make a vertical or horizontal relation a graphic event calls for expert judgment and skill. To be effective, a slide, and a rotation as well, must dominate the whole picture construction. To contribute energy to the picture they must become events.

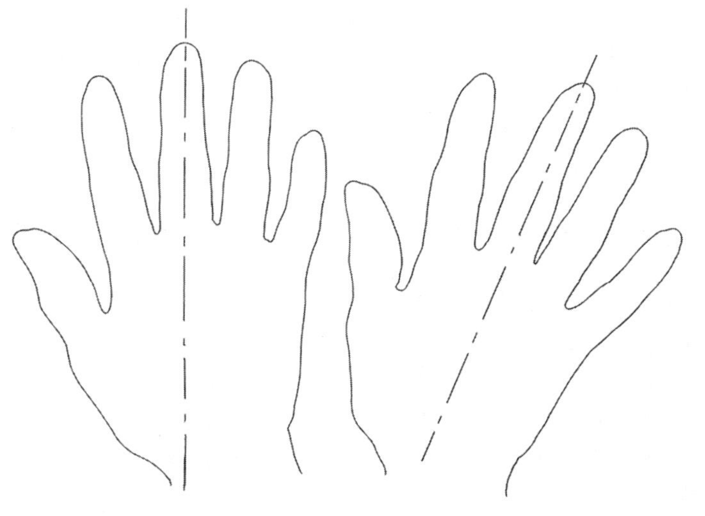

245-A

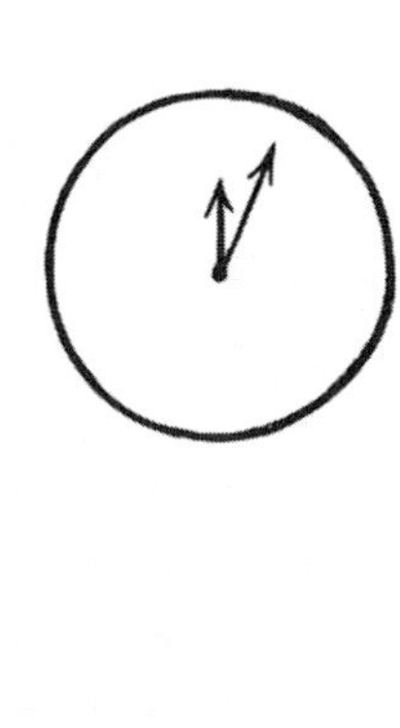

245-B

## Rotation

We have illustrated and explained a slide; now let us demonstrate the rotation in a similar manner. To generate a rotation the middle finger is moved in a slight arc from the reference (*245-A*). Its action is much like the minute-hand of a clock moving away from the hour-hand, but of course our hand may move in either direction (*245-B*). As in the exercise demonstrating the slide, as the hand moves it should preserve a constant pressure on the picture surface.

When the axis, the middle finger for instance, is in a slight diagonal relation to the reference and a strong affinity or tension of one to another is preserved, the resulting movement is called a *rotation*.



When there is weak affinity of the axis of a shape or volume to a reference, the axis no longer wants to align itself to the reference. The resulting movement may be angular, linear, etc., but not a rotation.

## Limits of Rotation

Once more we are aware of the mysterious factor of energy manifested in a picture. What is it? We cannot see it, but when it is present we feel and respond to it. Tension, our awareness of a relation of positions of two or more elements, is a factor essential to picture making. Without it rotation or slide is impossible. The tension between the axis of a shape or volume and reference should be an event.

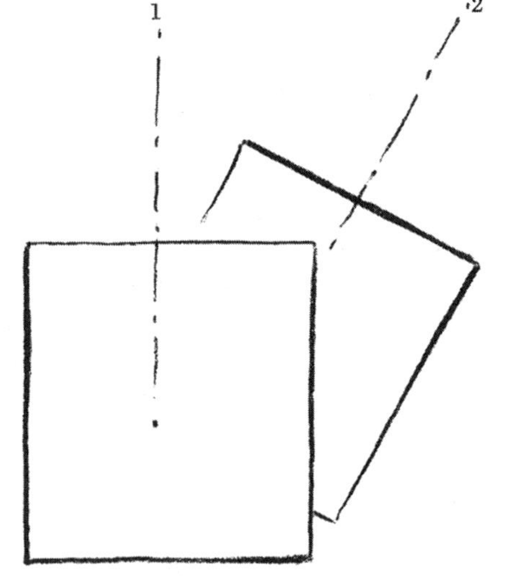
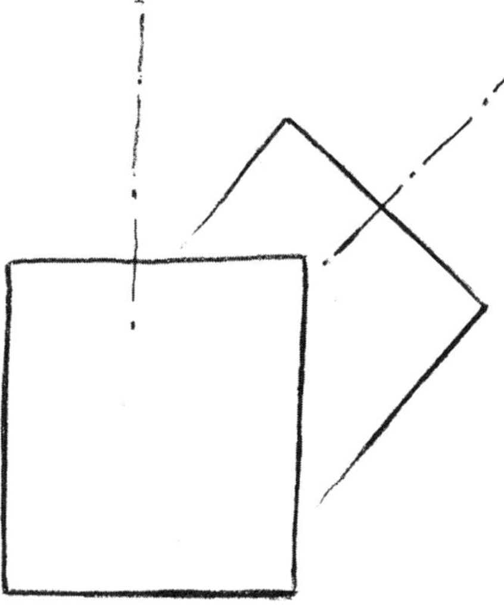
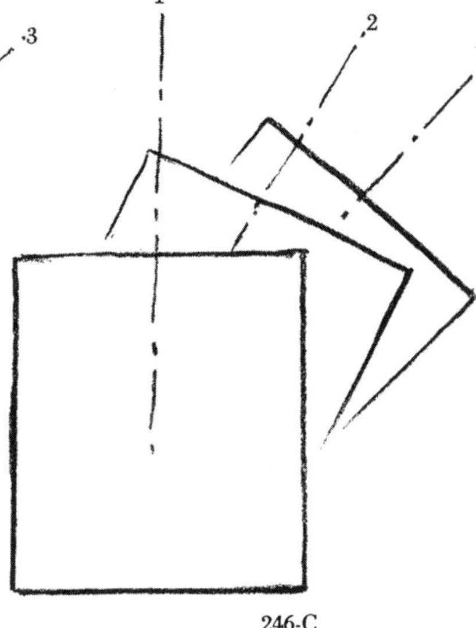







246    A shape or volume displaced in relation to its reference is either in a state of equilibrium or in a stable condition. When in the first state, the shape or volume is much like that of a small iron bar attracted by a magnet. But if the iron bar is moved in an arc so that its axis ceases to be in tension with its reference, rotation no longer exists. The shape or volume has now assumed a new stable position. It is no longer in a state of equilibrium in relation to the reference.

**Bridging Through Series**

At times when we go past a rotation into a new stable position we can still recapture the lost tension by making a new drawing. For instance, card 2 is related to card 1 as a rotation (*246-A*). Card 3 is in a new position and does not constitute a rotation (*246-B*). Card 2 placed between card 3 and card 1 generates a series and a condition of rotation in the order 1, 2, 3. Such a relation is often called a rotation series (*246-C*).

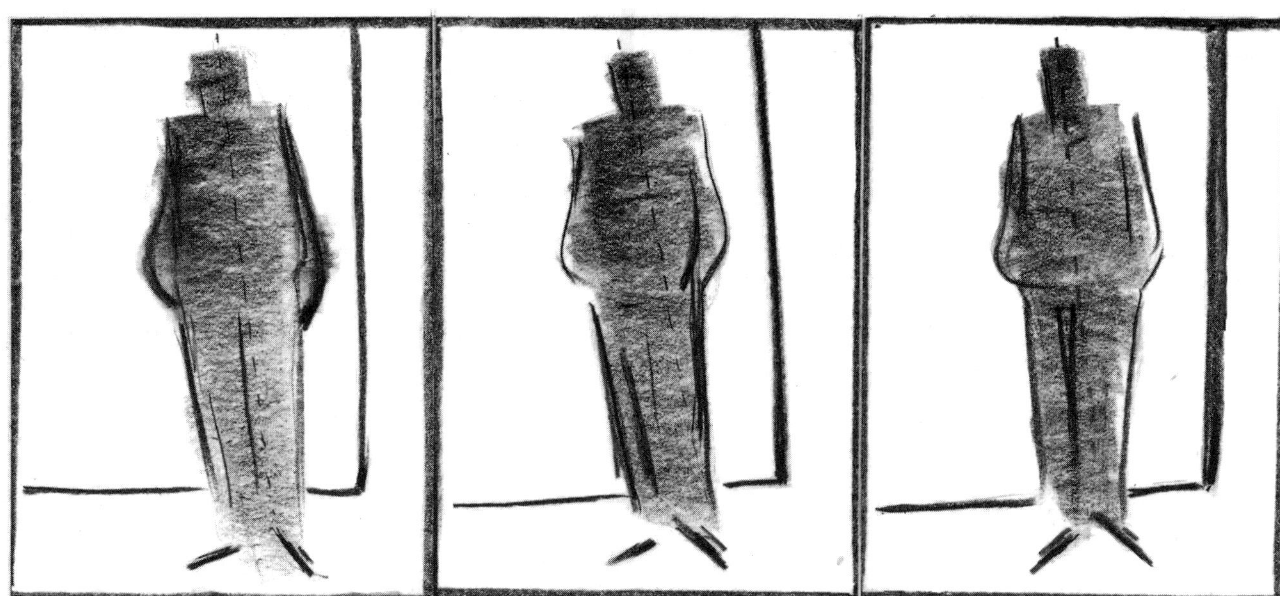

247-1

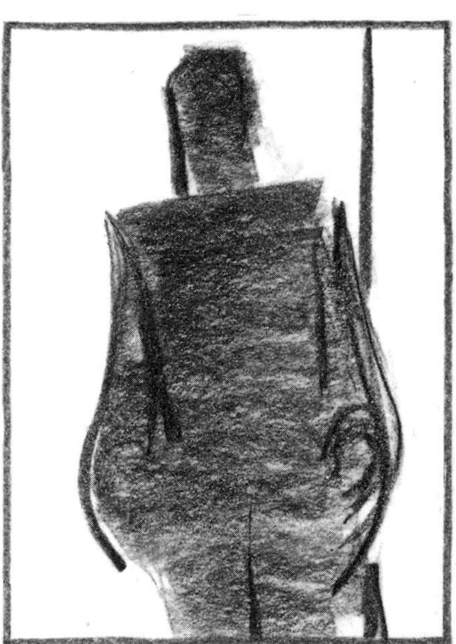

247-2

A rotation series may be used to unify the whole picture. The axis of various shapes in overlays, subject, and background may be tied together by means of such a series. A border of a rectangular picture often serves as one element of a series and most often as a reference. As we shall see in Chapter 24 the edges of some shapes constitute picture lines which may be used in the generation of rotations much as axes are used.

When we rotate a standing figure in a picture, especially if we show the feet in relation to a strong horizontal, we may throw it off balance. To correct this disturbing condition we can introduce a simple bridge between figure and background. By rotating the background we put figure and background into a strong right-angle relation. There is a significant difference between rotating the background and throwing it into perspective (*247-1*). In the rotation the

ninety-degree angular relation of wall to sidewalk is preserved, giving a strong angular and shape relation to the corners of the picture. The perspective, while correcting the off-balance condition, does not relate so strongly to the whole picture.

A device which proves most helpful in also correcting such an off-balance condition consists of cutting in closer to weaken the relation of the figure to a horizontal reference (*247-2*).

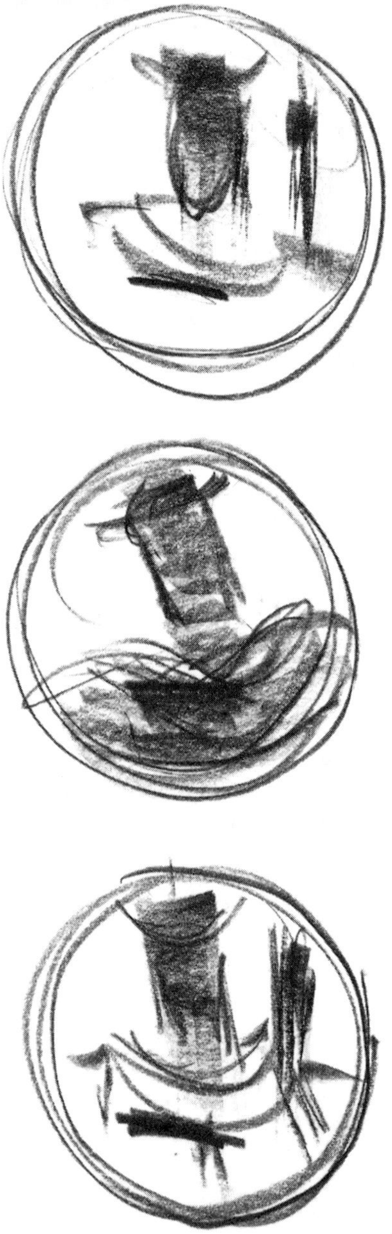

The captions for the images:

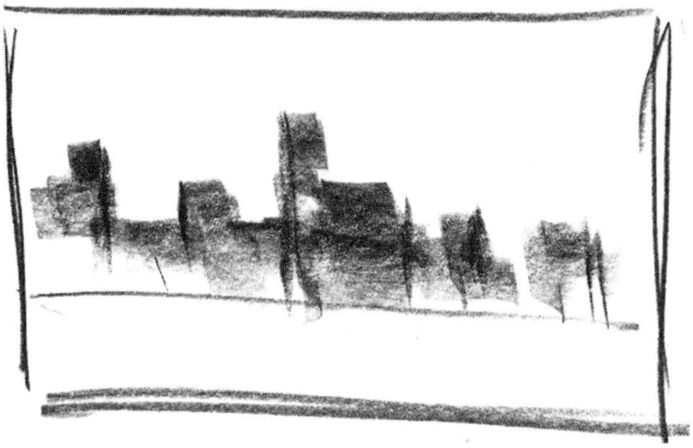

248-2A

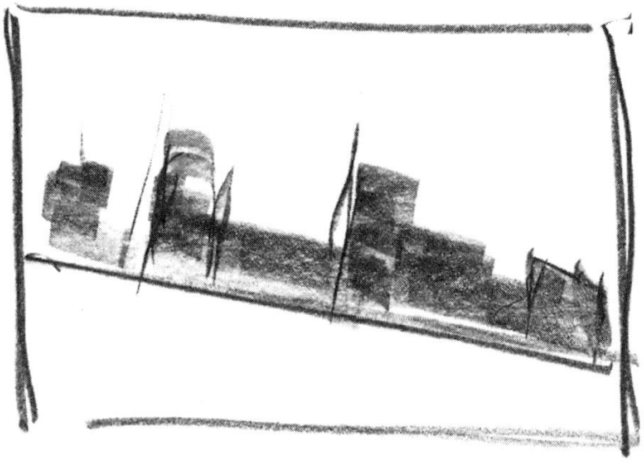

248-2B

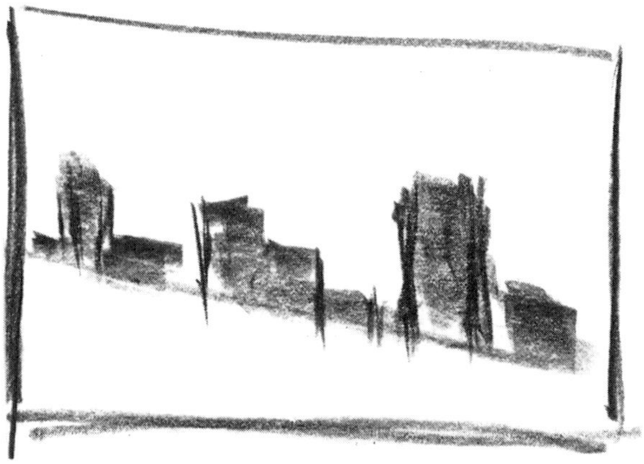

248-1      248-2C



## The Circular Picture

When we design a circular picture we find that the vertical and horizontal borders we usually use as convenient references are sorely missed. To overcome this graphic lack we must relate the positions of our symbols to imaginary gravitational references which we frequently can reinforce with supplementary verticals and horizontals.

The importance of these references is immediately apparent when we attempt to rotate a figure in a circular picture. Instead of the figure rotating, the whole picture begins to wheel, to revolve (*248-1*). To rectify this false movement and to restore the true rotation of the figure, we have but to introduce a strong vertical or horizontal, or both, into the picture. Immediately the whole picture is stabilized, yet the agitation of the rotation is preserved.

## Rotation of the Whole Picture

Rotation becomes a device through which we can add interest to pictures which tend to be graphically dull. For instance, if we paint a landscape showing a flat meadow with a city silhouetted on the skyline, the buildings are in a vertical-horizontal relation to the flat ground and to the horizon (*248-2A*). The projection of this arrangement seems ordinary, dull. Now using the same material, let us simply rotate the whole picture in relation to its borders. Nothing has changed. The buildings are still at right angles to the meadow. Yet the picture is different. It is more disturbing, thus more interesting (*248-2B*).

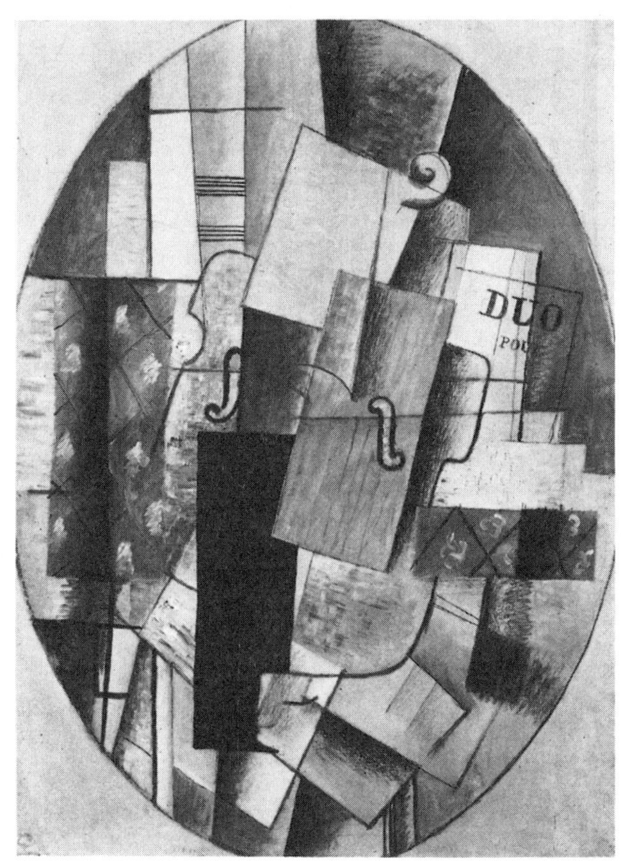

Georges Braque (French, 1882-1963)
OVAL STILL LIFE (Le violon), 1914
36⅜″ x 25¾″
Collection The Museum of Modern Art, New York
Gift of the Advisory Committee
(Photograph: Soichi Sunami)

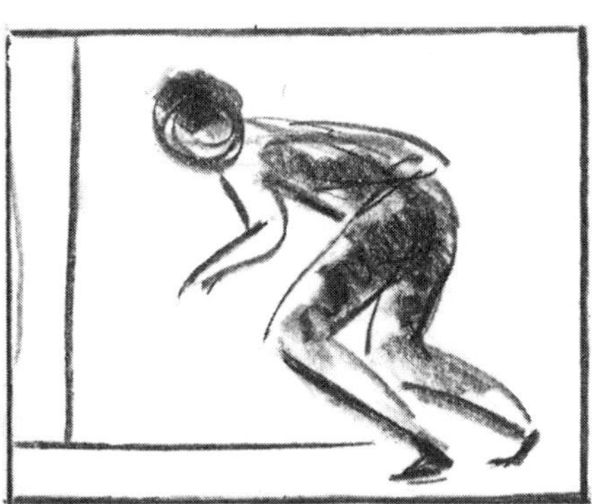



249-2A

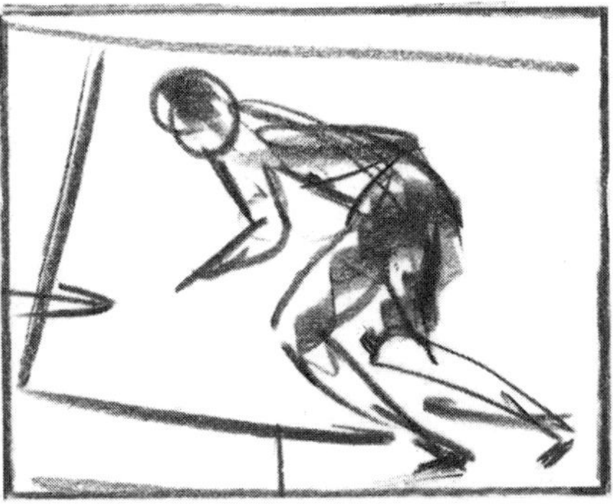

249-2B

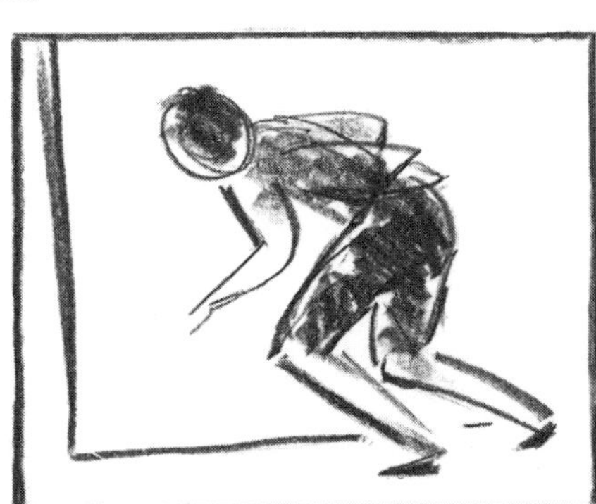

249-2C

We must be careful to distinguish such a rotation of the whole picture from a normal view of the same city built on a hillside. In the latter condition the vertical and stable buildings are no longer normal to the hillside *(248-2C)*.

At times artists have felt the need not only to create added agitation through a rotation of the whole picture but also the need to remind the spectator of the physical reality of the picture surface. By rotating the picture out of itself part of the surface is exposed, or at least seems of a different nature than the portion rotated. This device was frequently used by Cubists such as Braque.

## Rotation and Diagonals



When we draw a figure in action, a man running for example, we show a symbol already in a state of equilibrium. We equate his off-balance position against his implied speed *(249-2A)*. For this reason the drawing is graphically disturbing even without rotation. But at times an action picture may be intensified by the use of a rotation. The background or overlays may be rotated as a device to support the action *(249-2B)*, or as a counter to intensify the implied action *(249-2C)*.

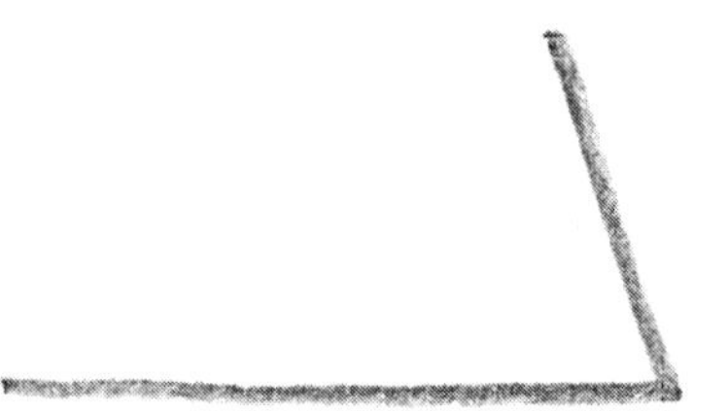

250-1A

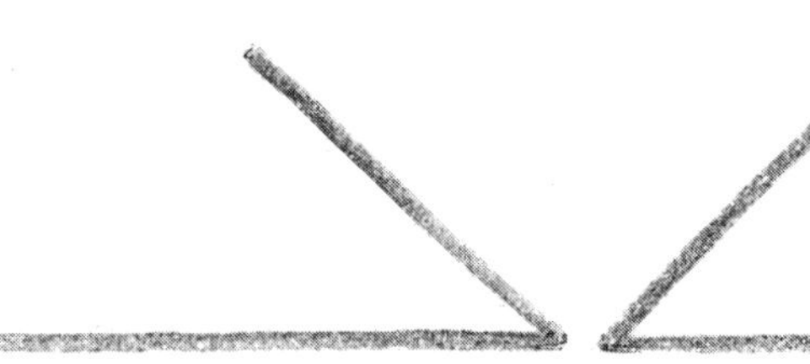

250-1B

250-1C

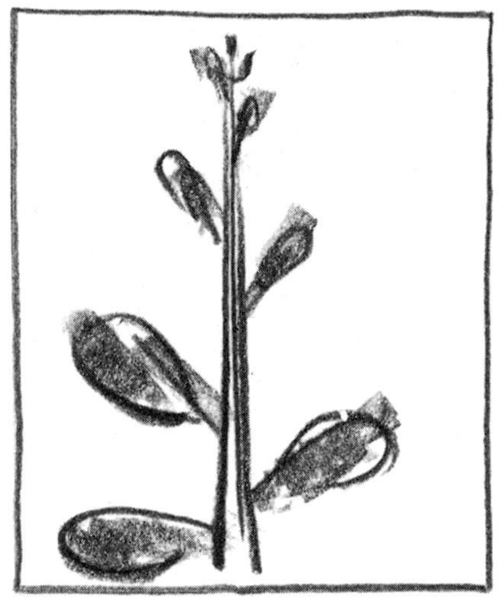

250-2A

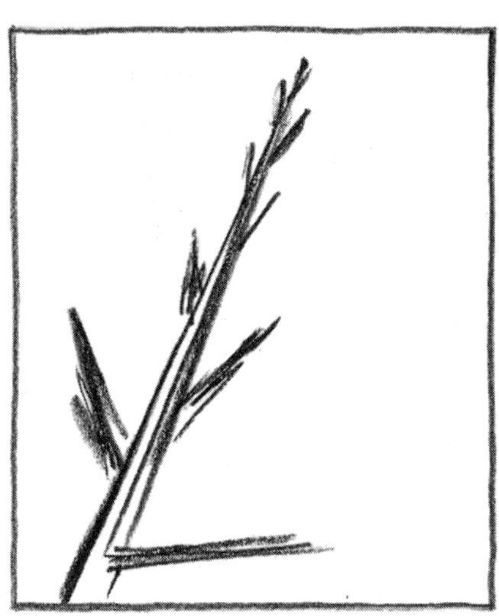

250-2B

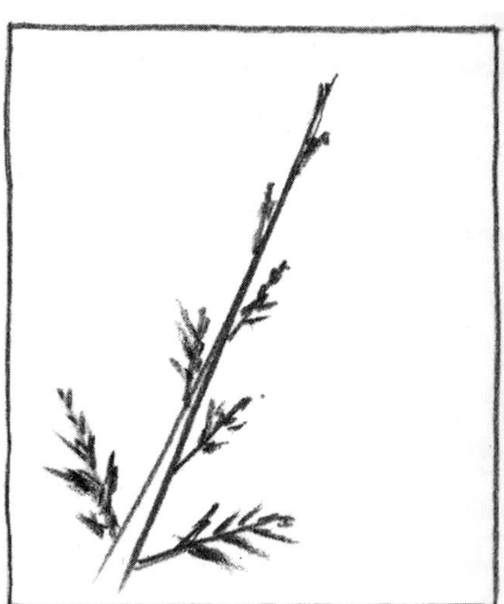

250-2C

250    In graphic motion picture work, because individual views are seldom held on the screen for long, great liberty is often taken by using violent action drawings. This is also the case in certain types of illustration where reading time of the picture may be very short. In such cases violent diagonal structures are used in addition to rotation.

We have seen that as long as a diagonal has a strong affinity for an established reference, whether vertical, horizontal, or diagonal, it generates a rotation. It is dynamic; in a state of equilibrium (*250-1A*).

Suppose now that the diagonal frees itself from the tension of the vertical and assumes a new position somewhere between the vertical and horizontal. If it approaches the horizontal too closely it may well become locked into a horizontal rotation. In this intermediate new position it is more disturbing than the vertical. Not only is it unique in the order of verticals and horizontals and as such is an accent, but also it may arouse in us the idea that the line is falling (*250-1B*).

The addition of an opposing diagonal at the same but reversed angle stabilizes the arrangement. The diagonals are now balanced. Our original diagonal has lost all, or nearly all, its energy (*250-1C*).

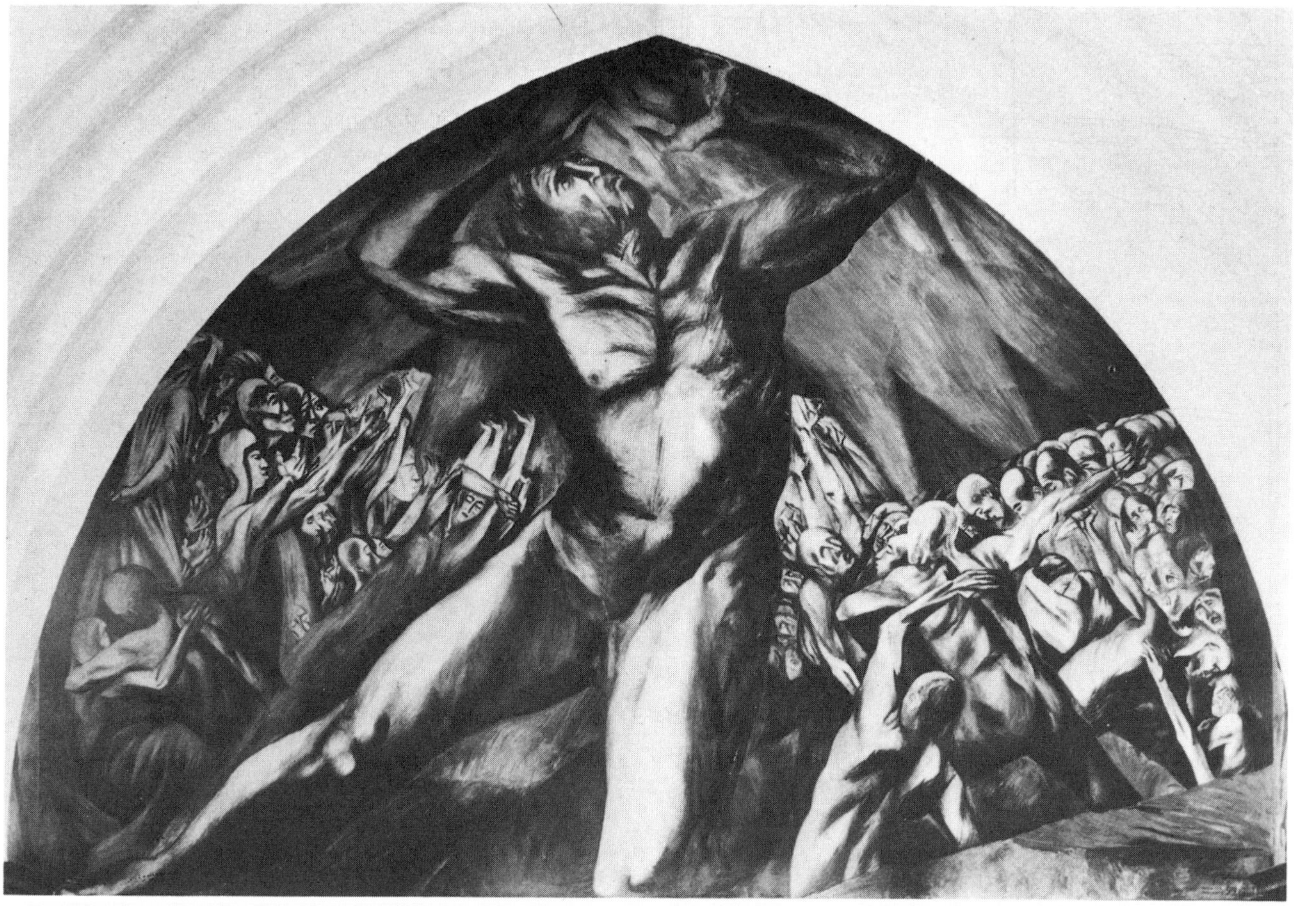

José Clemente Orozco (Mexican, 1883-1949)
PROMETHEUS, 1930; 20′ x 26′; fresco
Pomona College, Claremont, Calif.
(Photograph: Robert C. Frampton)

Ordinarily a picture constructed upon diagonals is more disturbing than one constructed upon verticals and horizontals, as Orozco demonstrates in his *Prometheus*. Yet the use of diagonals may also result in a stable, static arrangement (*250-2A*). The direction of a number of diagonals which counteract each other results in a balance. The same arrangement rotated results in a more dynamic use of the diagonal structure, making a more disturbing, more interesting picture (*250-2B*).

As we add detail one factor becomes more apparent. The activity of the rotations and diagonals is only partly responsible for the added interest. Excitement is also added by increased shape activity (*250-2C*). Both shape and color can be used to achieve movement in pictures.

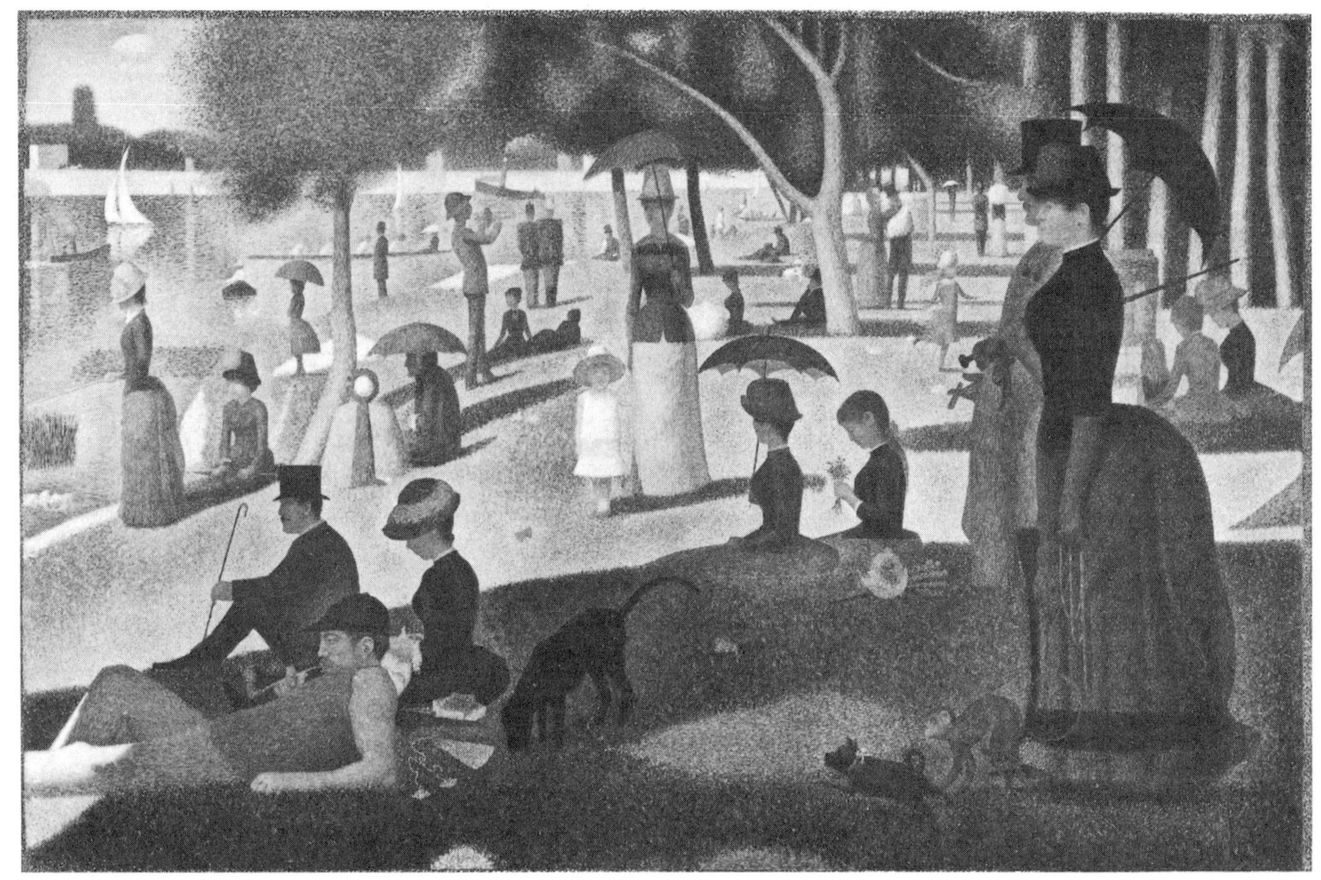

Georges Seurat (French, 1859-1891)
SUNDAY AFTERNOON ON THE ISLAND OF
LA GRANDE JATTE
1884-1886; 81″ x 120⅜″; oil on canvas
Courtesy of The Art Institute of Chicago
Helen Birch Bartlett Memorial Collection



## 22 Movement of Shape and Color

**Shape Movement**

Elements which generate picture movements
may be areas of flat shapes, or points, or lines.
Such elements may or may not be symbols of
three-dimensional forms. As we find in much
non-representational work, a colored shape may
in no way represent anything three-dimensional.
But various combinations of two-dimensional
elements may suggest volumes and believable
space. For instance, a flat silhouette may read as
a convincing volume (*253-1*). In the same way
simple volumes such as Seurat uses may be
predominantly two-dimensional in impact.

253-1

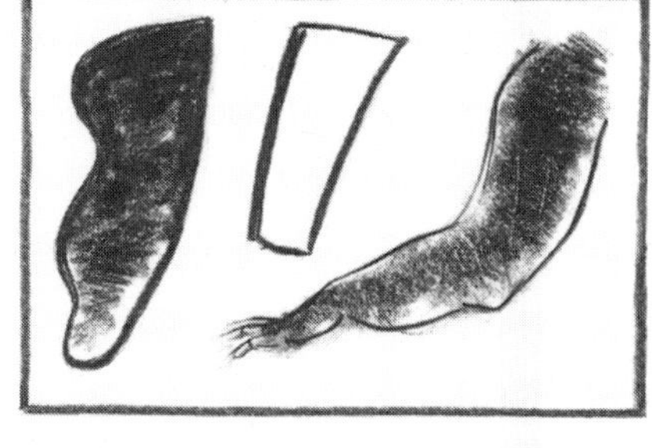

253-3

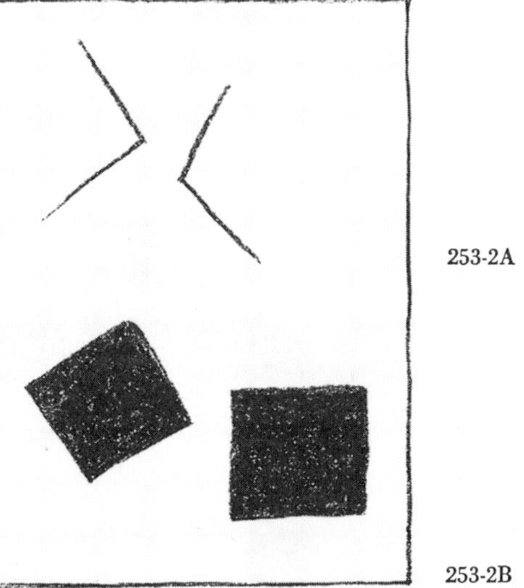

253-2A

253-2B

253-4

We have noted that the positional relation of one shape to another constitutes movement. The relation of two shapes or two lines or the tension between them depends on our awareness of the affinity of one for the other (*253-2A*). Without this tension, this affinity, such comparison cannot come about. Without tension there can be no movement (*253-2B*).

As we proceed we should be aware of the force of the tensions exerted, for as we saw in Chapter 21, the dominant movement of a graphic organization may suddenly be changed by a slight overaccenting of a part, resulting in an entirely new order of movements.

When we look at a rectangular shape we are aware of the elongated proportional relation of length to width. The shape need not be a geometric construction; it may be irregular, such as the silhouette of an arm. We may often clarify the direction of such a progressive shape by drawing or implying its center line or axis, even though in most growth structures it is almost impossible to determine such a line with exactness (*253-3*).

At times a shape may be characterized not by progression but by its tendency to spread or disperse from a center. It may have no dominant axis. A circle, a star, a square are directionless in themselves but by their relation to another shape, or to a fixed reference, they may generate direction (*253-4*).

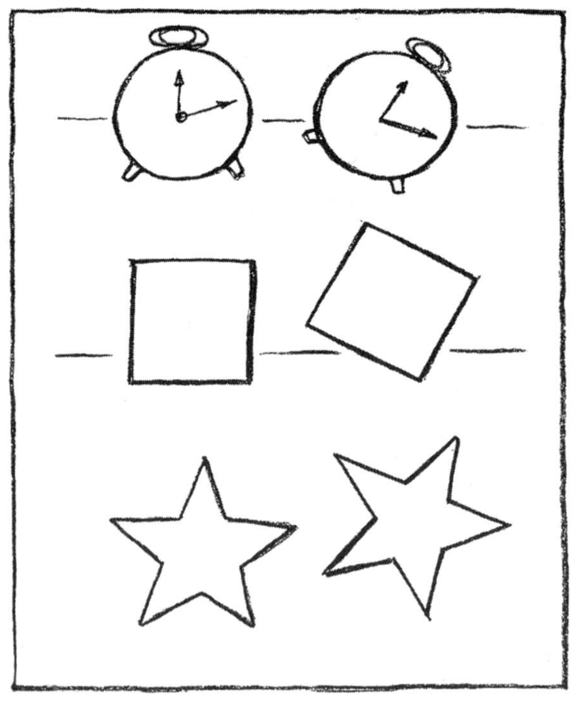

254-1

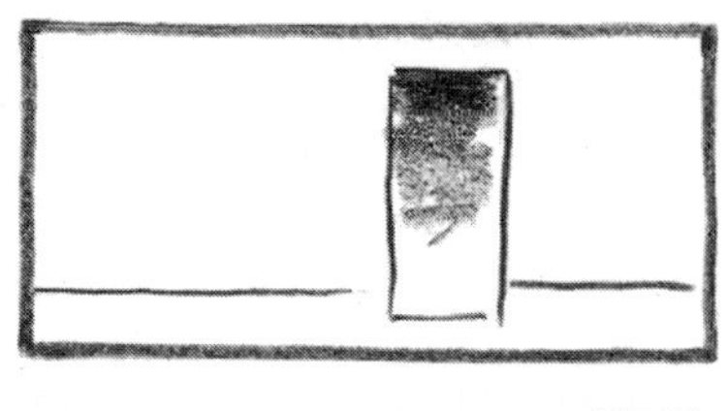

254-2A

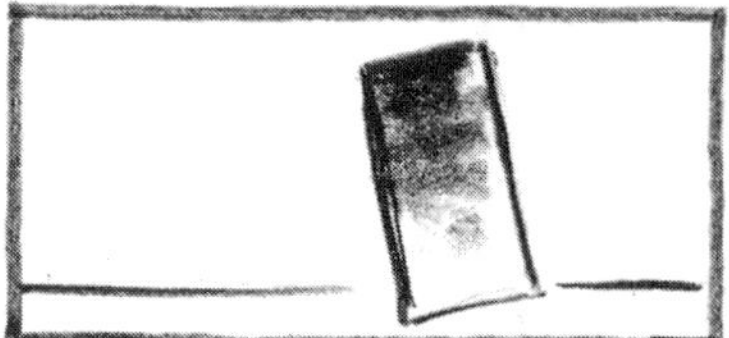

254-2B

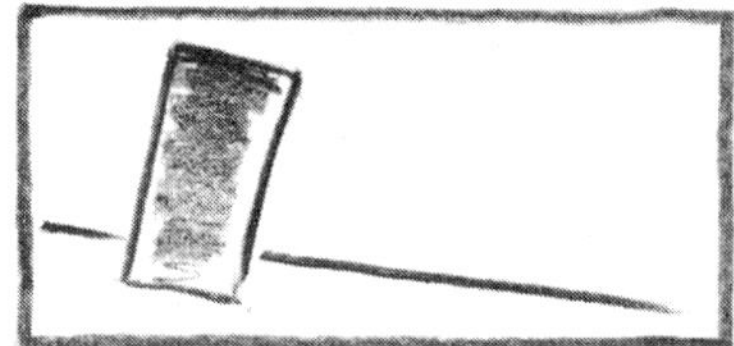

254-2C

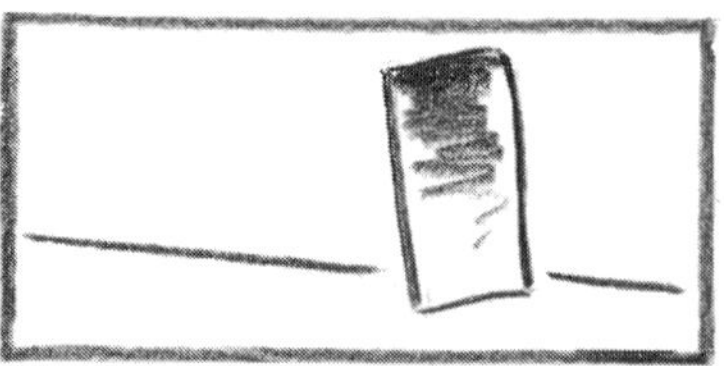

254-2D

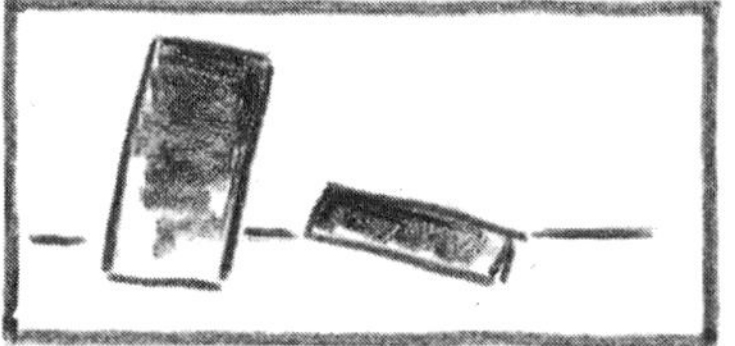

254-2E



We identify the direction of an axis with our gravitational references. Thus an elongated structure is referred to as having a vertical axis when in or near a vertical position; a diagonal axis in a diagonal position, and a horizontal axis in a horizontal position.

At times a spreading shape may be given direction by relating its internal structures to established references. Thus the clock can be tipped, as can the star and square which are built around invisible gravitational axes. A strong reference line makes such differences in direction more apparent. The star, for instance, when balanced on one point, by association to a strong reference, seems to topple. The same effect may be achieved with the square. When such a shape is given direction it is always in conjunction with an established reference either graphic or imaginary (*254-1*).

## A Vocabulary of Expression

In making or studying pictures the question often arises concerning the degree of excitation generated by the various graphic factors.

We have seen how perspective movements may be exploited to heighten emotional reactions. For instance, Peter Paul Rubens evolved a system of painting built upon a spiral movement, a spiral carried not only in the large volume relations but also in the smallest detail. Every brush stroke, even in his huge murals, was related to the spiral. Such swirling, dramatic pictures owe much to his exploitation of perspective movements.

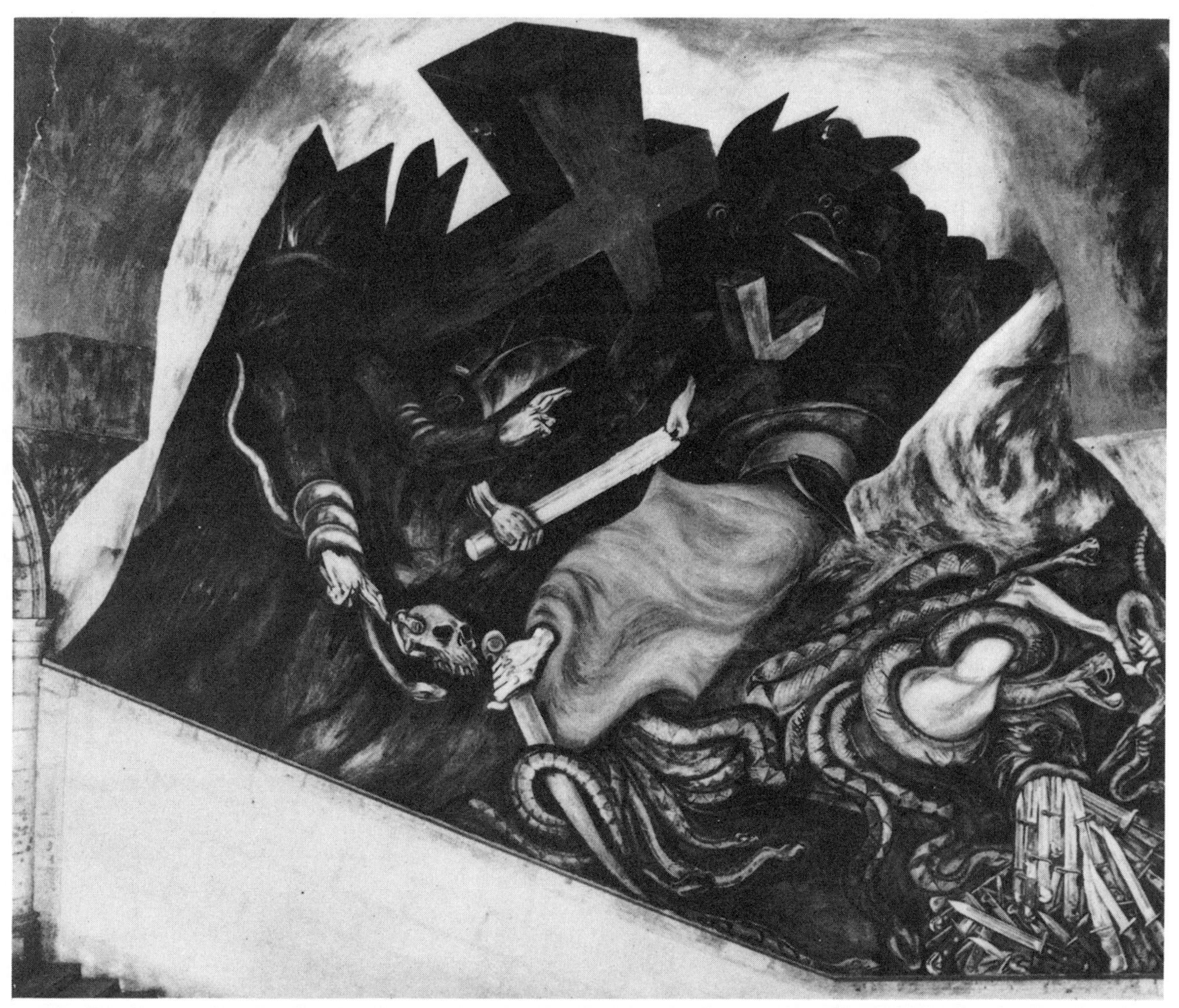

José Clemente Orozco (Mexican, 1883-1949)
THE OBSCURE FORCES, 1936-1939, fresco in
the Governor's Palace, Guadalajara
Courtesy Sr. Jorge Hernandez Campos
Instituto Nacional de Bellas Artes, Mexico, D. F.

(Photograph: Courtesy Manuel Alvarez Bravo
the Editorial Fund for Mexican Plastic Arts
from the book *Mural Painting of the Mexican
Revolution, 1921-1960*)

We have also seen how picture movements, rotation or slide, have profound effect upon the degree to which we respond emotionally. Orozco's huge mural tumbling down the wall of the stairwell is one of the truly great examples of the dramatic use of shapes moving in the surface of the picture.

But movement is not enough. For, as we see in the Orozco, the shape impact of the darks silhouetted against the light sky, the ponderous blacks throughout, the bright, elongated details of candle and blades all contribute to the brutality and power emanating from the picture. It is an example of shape, perspective movements, and picture movements all functioning at the same time. But, as we see, the various activities are not stressed to the same degree. Here the perspective movements have been subordinated to the shape impact and picture movements. In all successful pictures we find this variety in the intensity of different types of movement.

As artists we must be able to compare the intensity of a movement or of a shape. We must be able to play such activities against each other and know their relative strengths.

In condensed form let us review: the stable position (*254-2A*), the rotation (*254-2B*), the rotation of the whole picture (*254-2C*), and one of the infinite variations created by the addition of new elements, the double rotation (*254-2D*). In conjunction with these conditions we often use the diagonal as a vital part of many picture constructions (*254-2E*).

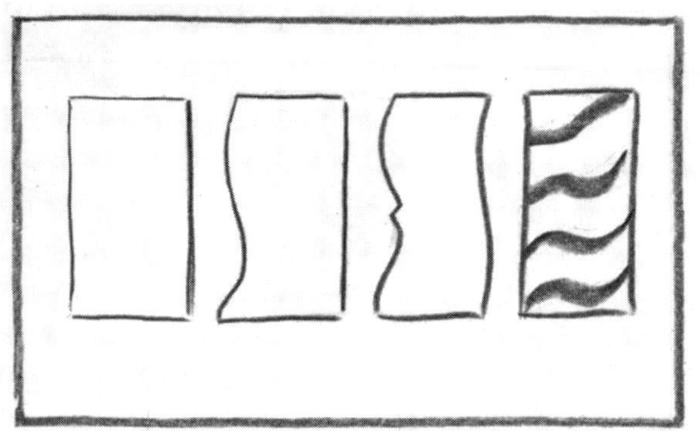

256-1

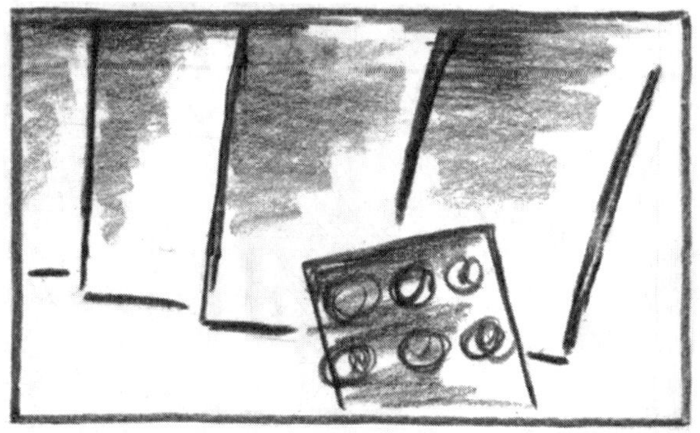

256-2C

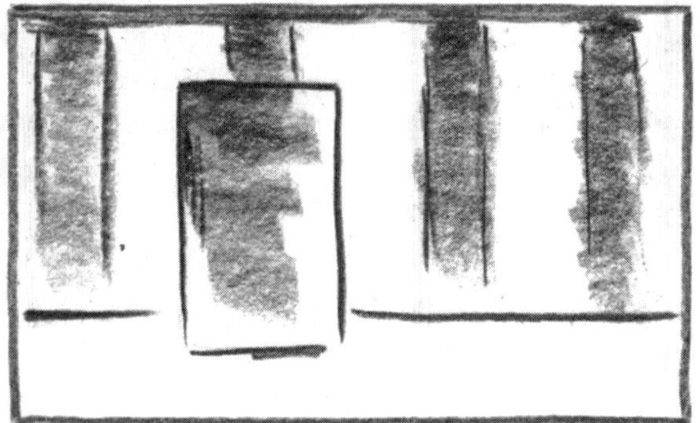

256-2A

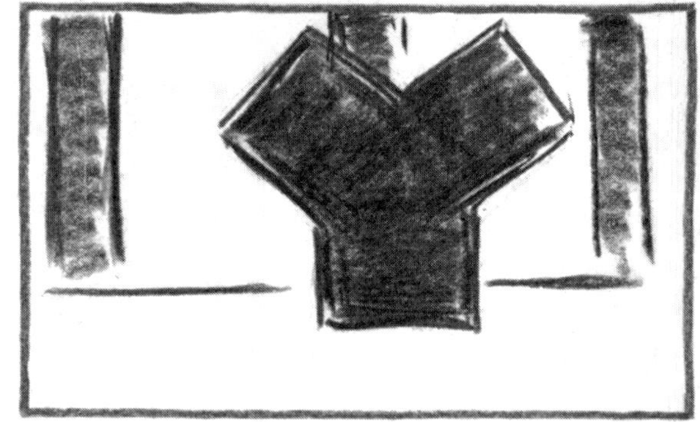

256-3A

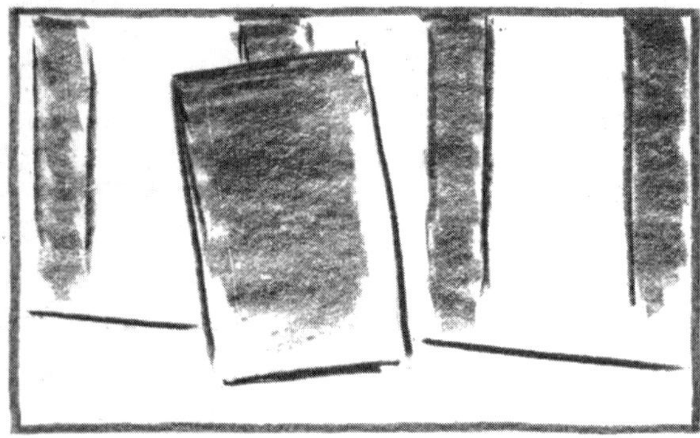

256-2B

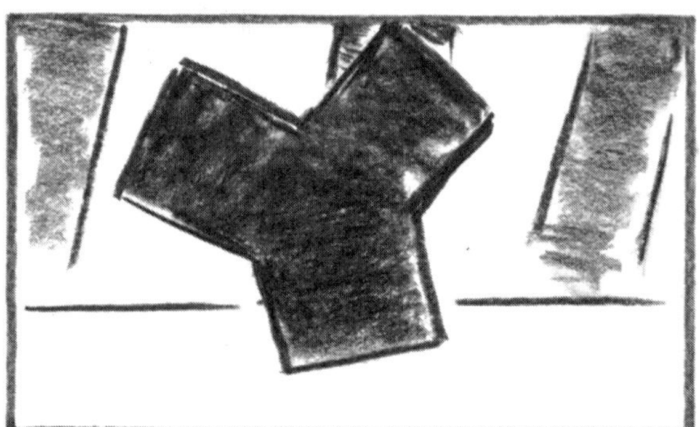

256-3B

256     To control movement we may adjust the activity of a simple rectangular shape. By breaking its rigid contour, by letting it evolve into a new shape, or even by application of surface pattern, stripes, spots, etc., more or less visual activity can be attained. In the same way background and overlays may be varied from extremely simple to elaborate, thus permitting control of their movement in the picture (*256-1*).

We now find a new type of comparison. Now we can estimate the relative importance of an element in the foreground or the background not by shape activity or visual activity alone, but by its shape activity modified by movement. In the accompanying diagrams the background activity of each arrangement is considered in relation to the activity of the subject, both as to shape and movement. In each picture these relative activities are estimated in terms of the surface patterns. In *256-2A* a simple disturbance in the background brings it forward to compete with the simple rectangular subject. In *256-2B* the background can be more violent because of the rotation of the subject. In *256-2C*, the rotated, ornamented subject necessitates great disturbance in the background in order to bring it up into the picture surface. If a more active shape is introduced as subject (*256-3A*), the background in turn can be more active as to both movement and pattern (*256-3B*).

However, graphic activity added in the background to overcome needed detail or interest in the subject may become distracting (*257-A*). One method of accomplishing the same goal is to bring the background forward by means of picture movements such as a rotation, while keeping it simple as to shape activity (*257-B*).

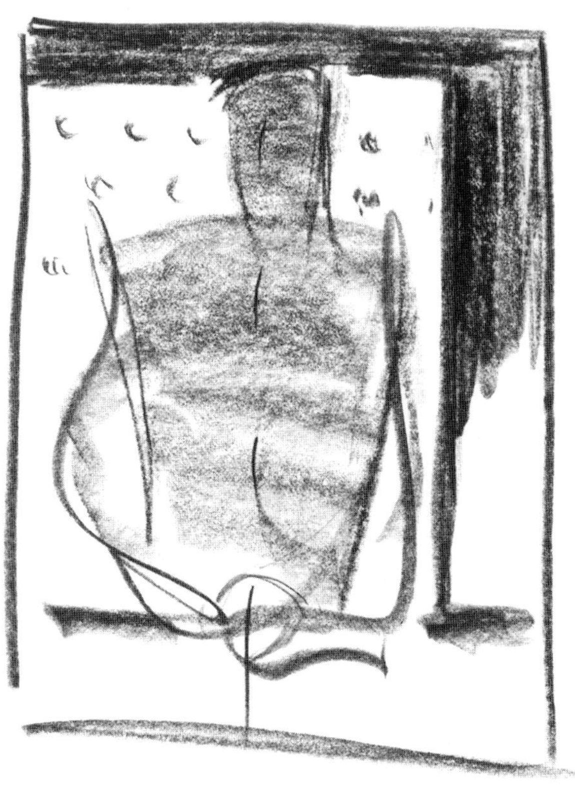

257-A

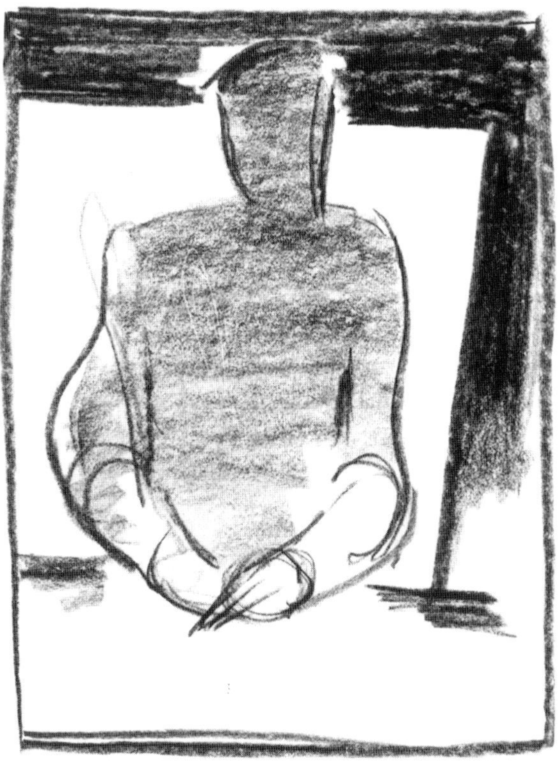

257-B

We discover that the number of combinations of activities of shape and movement is countless. We have considered only a few in relation to one simple element as subject. As elements are increased, as multiple backgrounds occur in section, or as overlay is placed over overlay, the complexity increases proportionately.

In examining this aspect of picture structure we must have clear understanding of our goals: control of movement gives us a way to arouse specific emotions by varying the intensity of a picture at will. Our picture may be quiet, explosive, bright, gay, somber, or dramatic. This pertains not simply to expressions on a face, but to the whole picture. With control of movement we develop a new vocabulary of expression.

## Color Movement



Of particular concern to the artist is the relation of color to the position of a shape in deep space. We have often noticed that at times there seems to be a harmonious relation between the color of a form in nature and its position in depth. A distant hill seems muted in color, a flower in the foreground astonishingly bright.

However, we also have noticed how bright lights in the distance, shiny surfaces gleaming miles away, violently colored sunsets seem contradictory to the usual positions in nature. We rationalize such disturbing effects for we realize that the bright light is not at the end of our nose, it is far away in the hills.

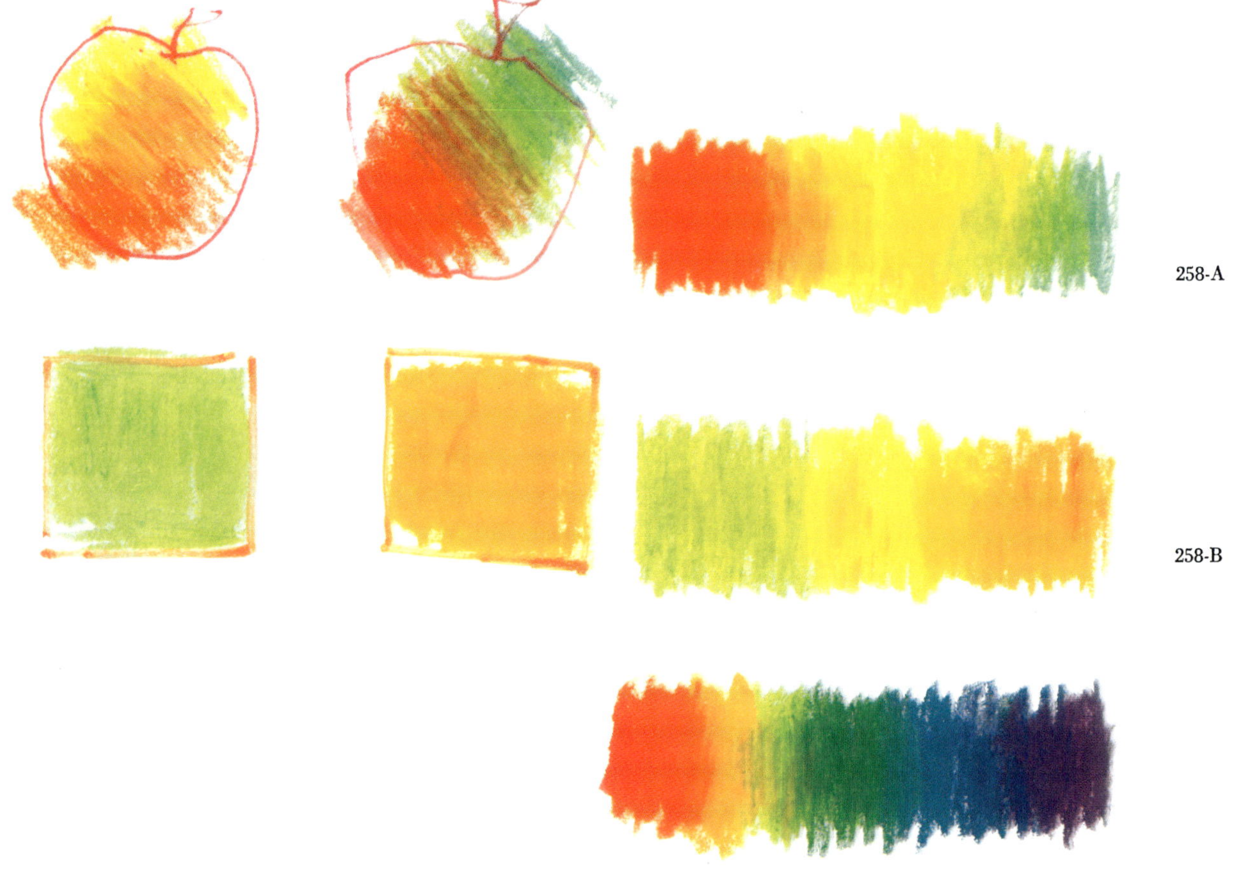

258-A

258-B



Regardless of effects seen in nature, the locating of a color in deep graphic space must also be tempered by consideration of the picture surface. Instead of blending an image of a mountain into the distance, thus possibly negating surface control, the artist might paint the mountain a bright color or emphasize its dramatic shape in order to bring it back to the picture surface. In other words, color bears a different relation to the shape to which it is associated in picture depth than it does to a similar form in nature.

All color areas, as we have seen, have the property of approaching or receding in relation to the picture surface. All color areas also are subject to visual expansion or contraction in relation to other color areas. It is because of this flux, this evasive quality of color, that the artist must temper or adjust color, not merely to locate a shape in picture space but to control its occurrence in the surface pattern. This simultaneous occurrence of a color both in picture depth and on the picture surface is another graphic paradox which must be mastered.

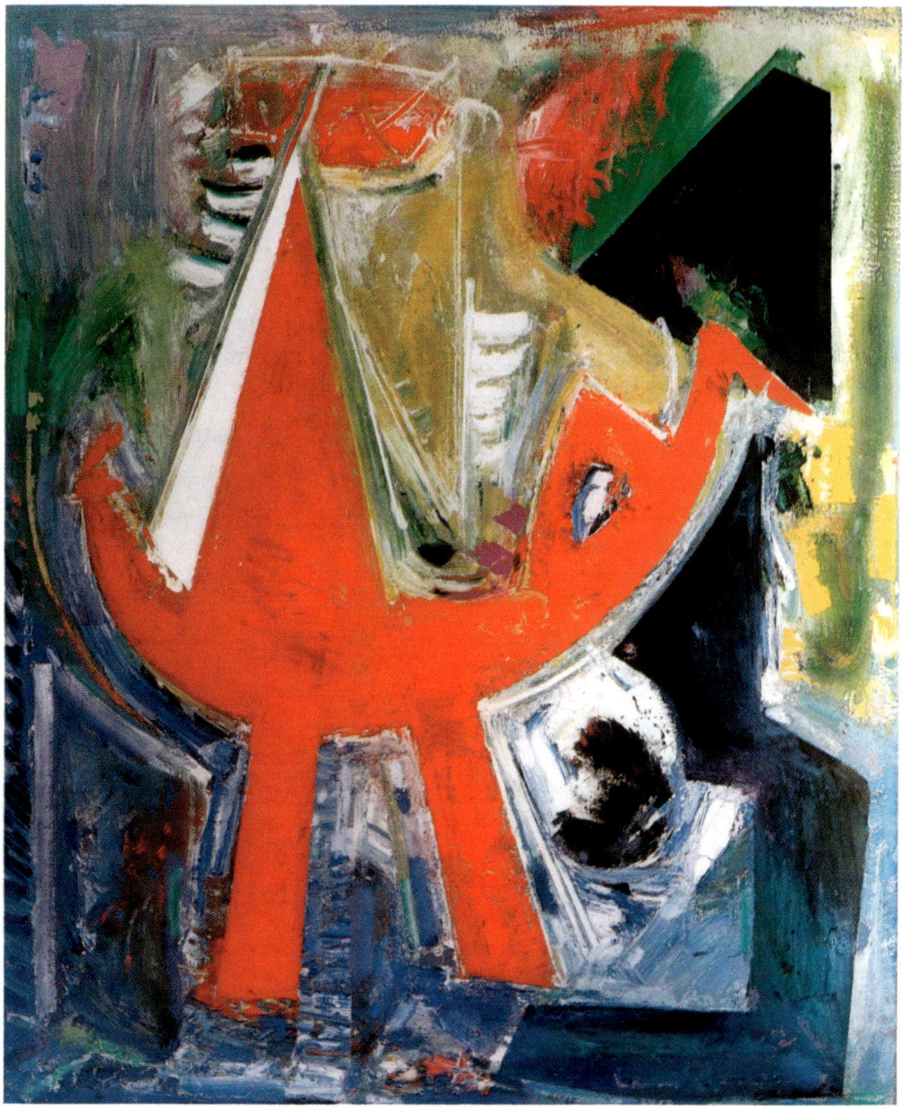

Hans Hofmann (American, b. Germany, 1880-1966)
FLIGHT, 1952; 60″ x 48″; oil on canvas
Los Angeles County Museum of Art
Gift of Mrs. Vicci Sperry through the
Contemporary Art Council

Color as an attribute of a graphic symbol, whether point, area, or line, affects the degree to which we respond to it as a graphic stimulus and as a result affects our awareness of its location in the picture. When we compare relative positions of two or more such colored symbols we experience color movement.

Color movement, as in the generation of any movement, is contingent upon comparison of the position of two or more related elements, in this case colors. Thus, if we are aware of the occurrence of a yellow in the foreground of a picture, for instance, and then of other yellows dispersed throughout the picture in an ordered way, the act of identifying and locating these related yellows may generate in us a sense of movement. Such a device, however, may soon become obvious.

To overcome such monotony the artist often resorts to the method of incorporating two or more related and *separate* colors in any given shape. He may involve both a yellow and an orange in one shape. Then in an adjacent shape, a green and a red. The yellow in the orange acts as a bridge to the yellow in the green, and so a color movement may result. In the same way the red also may act as a bridge (*258-A*).

At times movement may be achieved by the association of two color areas involving a common color. Thus a yellow green and a yellow orange use yellow as a bridge (*258-B*). By establishing a series of such bridges the eye is encouraged to compare their relative positions and so movement is generated. In Hofmann's *Flight* we see how green is used as a bridge between orange-red and purple-blue.

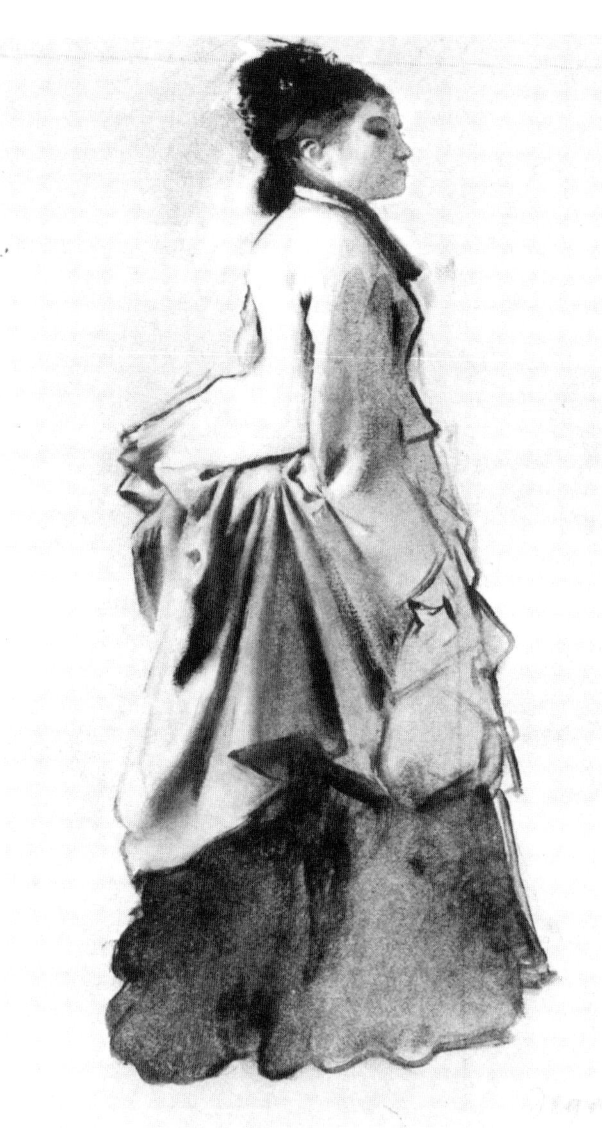

Hilaire Germain Edgar Degas (French, 1834-1917)
YOUNG WOMAN IN STREET COSTUME, ca. 1872
12¾″ x 9⅞″; brush drawing in oil
Courtesy of the Fogg Art Museum, Harvard University
Bequest of Meta and Paul J. Sachs



# 23 The Straight Line in Drapery and Growth Forms

# VI THE STRAIGHT LINE

**A Vocabulary of Line**

When we make a drawing of a three-dimensional form, as Degas' *Young Woman in Street Costume*, we seldom duplicate lines in or on this form for there are few, if any, such lines present. Certain stains or patterns at times may be seen on the surface of a form, but they rarely occur as structural elements. Occasionally a form of linear nature such as a clothesline or a telephone wire may be expressed as a line. These forms, however, are seldom encountered as picture subjects.

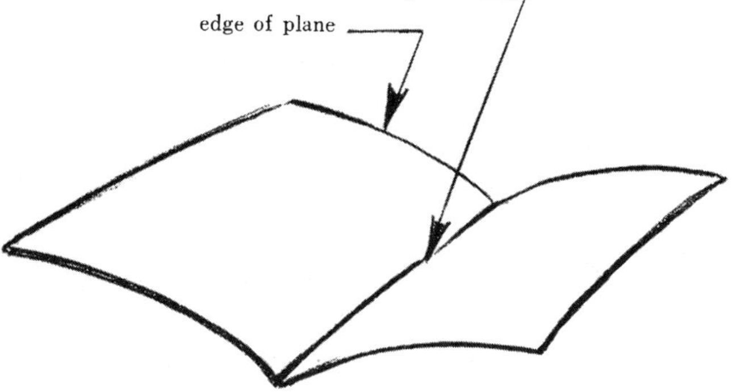


261

The lines we use in drawing fall into several categories: first, lines intimately related to the sculptural or three-dimensional visual aspect of the form, its edges and creases; second, arbitrary lines such as cross-sections of various kinds which further explore the form; third, gesture lines which in no way directly suggest the actual form, but do express the movement, action, mood of the form; fourth, skeletal lines which may act as gesture lines; fifth, design organizations not derived directly from the form but which arouse associations related to the form. For now let us look chiefly at those lines most closely related to the form.

Although few true lines exist in nature, we usually refer to an order in nature which can be expressed linearly as being actually linear. Thus an edge of a surface, or a crease resulting from folding a piece of paper are referred to as being lines, yet both are products of areal relations (*261*).

Such lines fall into categories of occurrences which we experience when looking at a form in nature. It often comes as a surprise to many to discover that a cube, a form with which we are so familiar, is constructed of three types of lines, and only three:

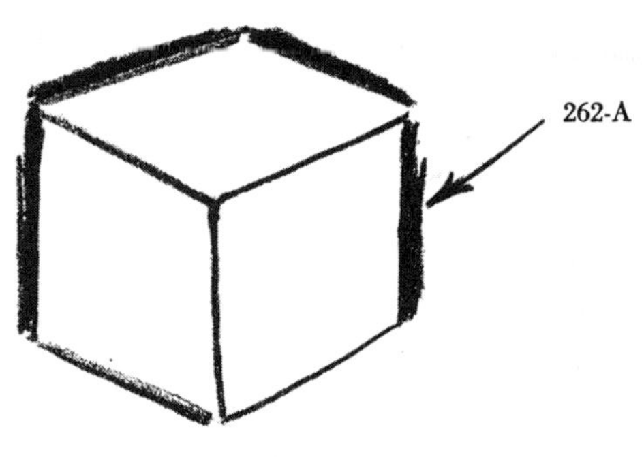

262-A

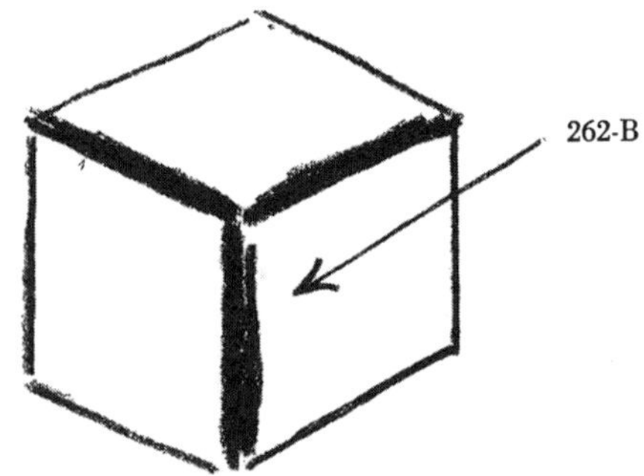

262-B

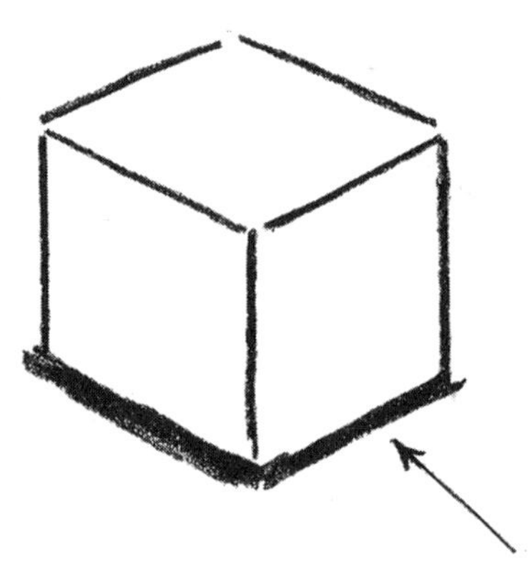

262-C

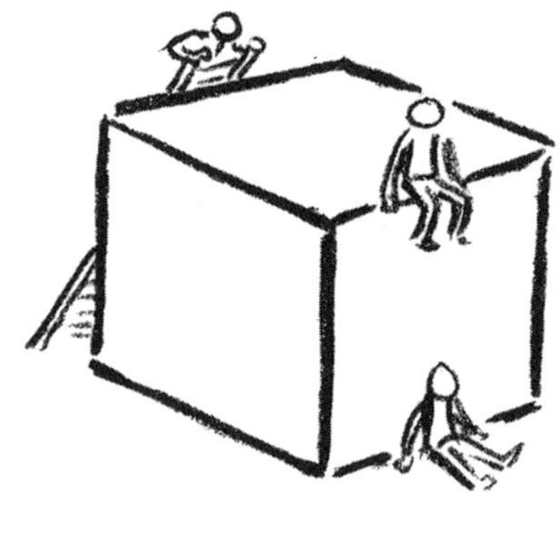

262-D

262    The *outside edge* is a line representing the last portion of a flat surface or plane as we look past it into space (*262-A*). In this view of a cube there are four such lines.

The *inside turning edge*, or *hip*, is the intersection of two planes which move away from this intersection into depth. We always find the intersection closer to us than one of the planes. We look *at* the intersection. In this view there are three such turning edges (*262-B*).

The *inside turning edge*, or *gutter*, is the intersection of two planes which move toward each other (*262-C*). We look into the intersection. In this view of the cube we see two such turning edges, or gutters.

We look *past* the outside edge.

We look *at* the hip.

We look *into* the gutter (*262-D*).

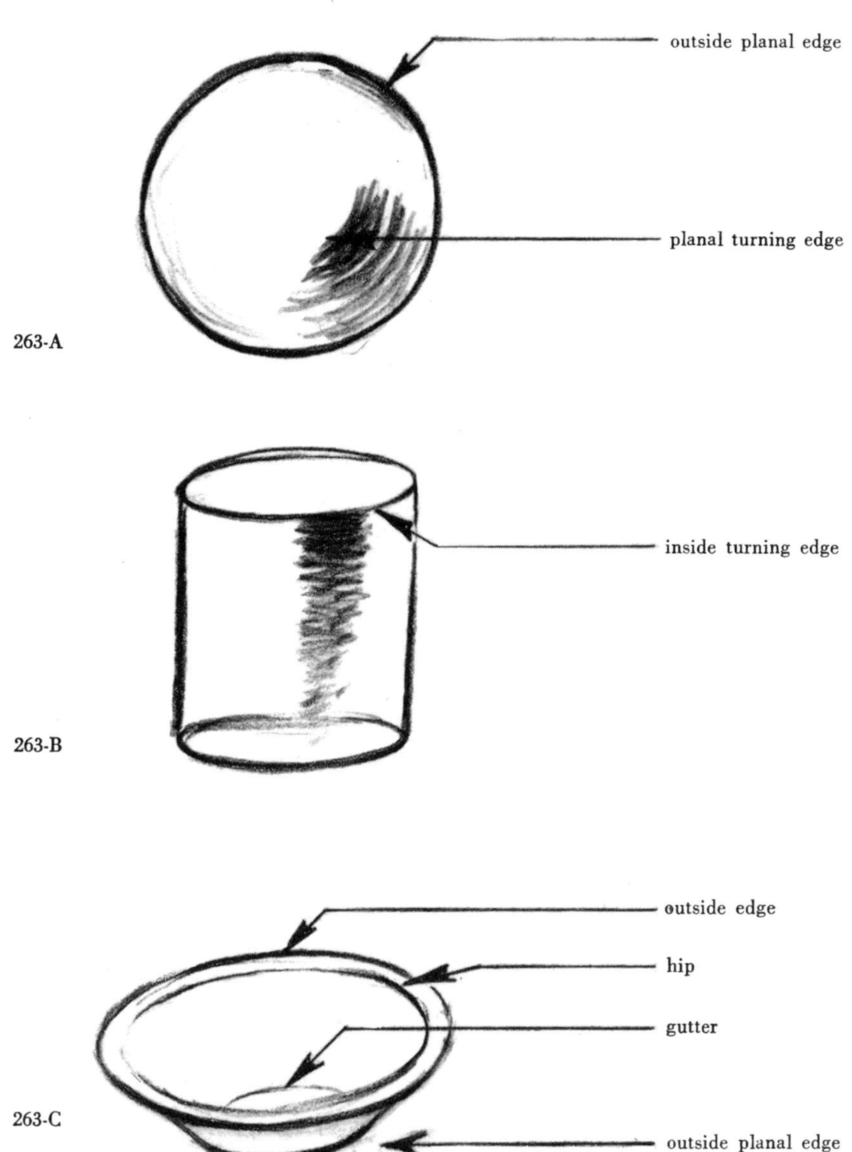


In warped or curved surfaces, such as a sphere, a bowl, a piece of drapery, we find simple modifications of these three characteristic lines. The silhouette of a sphere is the last part of the form visible as the surface turns away from us (*263-A*). It is a line, but of a different order than the outside edge of the cube. It is a planal line. It is an edge view of a theoretically infinitesimally thin plane. It is the *outside planal edge*. This edge usually can be explained with a line (*263-A*).

On the curved surface of a sphere, or other curved surfaces, an inside planal turning edge may be established (*263-B*). In a line drawing this turning edge usually is implied rather than delineated. More often it is expressed tonally.

The planal turning edge may be a hip or gutter (*263-C*).

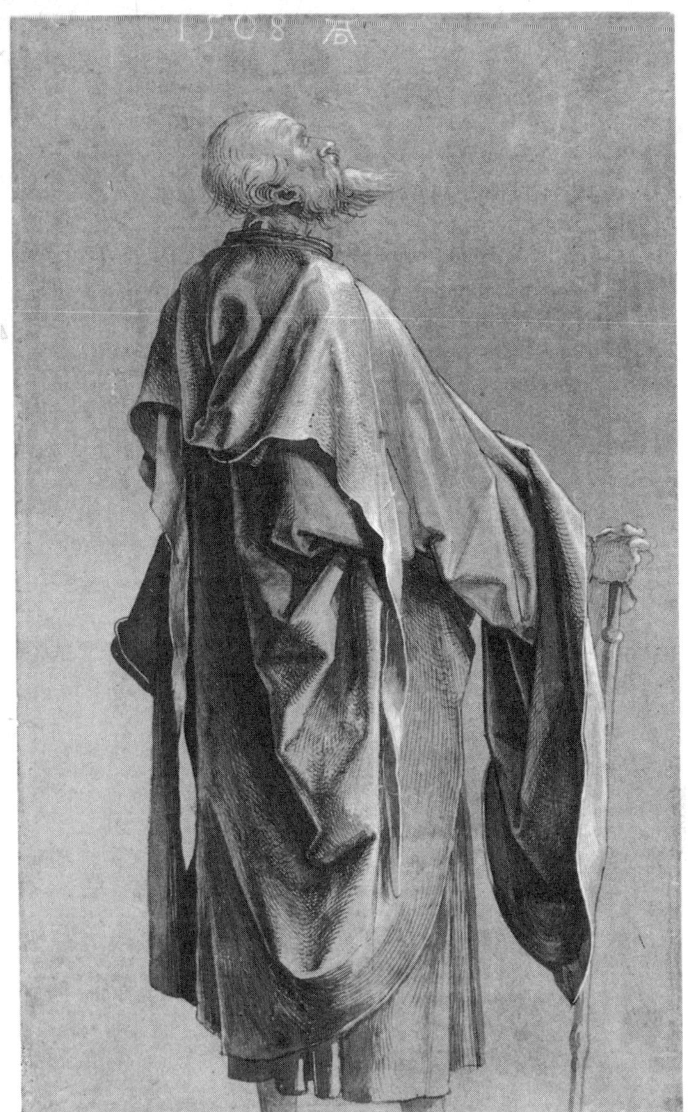

Albrecht Dürer (German, 1471-1528)
STUDY OF DRAPERY FOR AN APOSTLE IN THE
HELLER ALTARPIECE, 1508; India-ink drawing
heightened with white

Print-cabinet, Berlin Museum
Staatliche Museen der Stiftung
Preussischer Kulturbesitz
(Photograph: Walter Steinkopf)

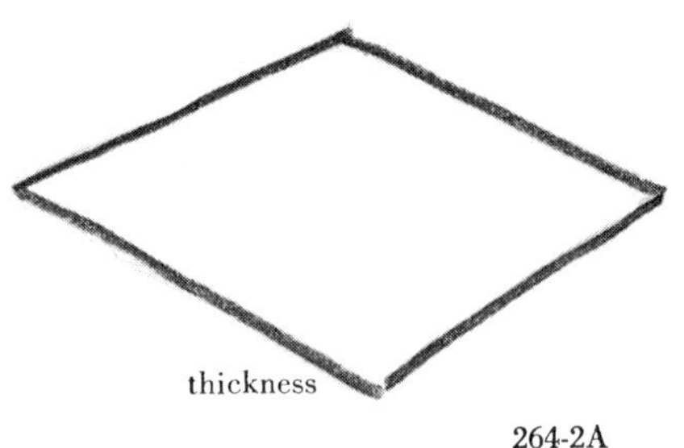

264-2A

264-2B

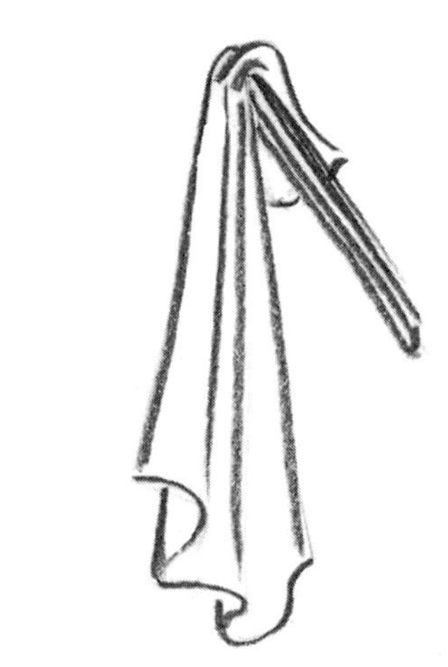
264-2C

## 264 Drapery

In drapery we see the fusion of straight and curved lines; flat and warped surfaces. Since drapery is a three-dimensional structure, its linear identifications are the same as any solid structure. How these systems of line interrelate in the delineation of drapery is one of the truly intriguing drawing problems, as Dürer's study demonstrates.

When we look critically at most drapery in nature we are overwhelmed by the almost infinite variety of forms it assumes. A shirt being worn, or the same shirt thrown on the floor, a sheet hanging from a clothesline, or draped around a figure, are familiar examples. Now there are millions of variously proportioned men and women who are capable of wearing an infinite variety of shirts of various sizes, patterns, styles, etc. Somehow we must try to find a control, a way, to bring order out of this seemingly chaotic variety.

No two arrangements of free drapery are likely to be the same. A piece of manufactured clothing, a coat for instance, may be identical to another, yet once worn it assumes an individuality, a personality of its own. The visual shape aspect of this multitudinous array of forms constitutes the variable of our problem.

Fortunately there are constants, factors which always remain the same. Any piece of drapery, no matter what its shape, texture, or pattern, no matter how it is constructed, has two attributes: first, it has three sides, because it is a three-dimensional form or organization of three-dimensional forms; second, it has weight.

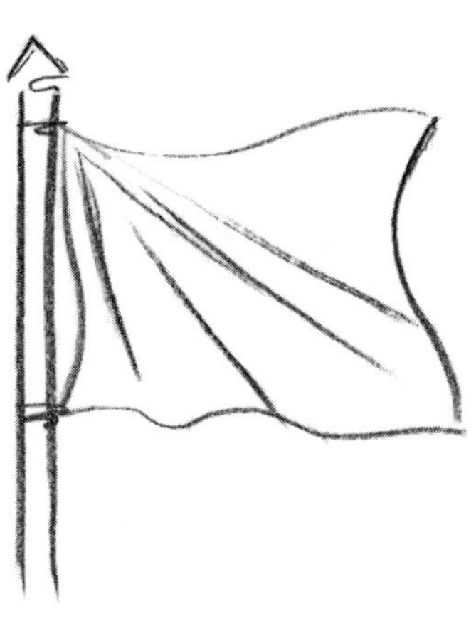

265-1A

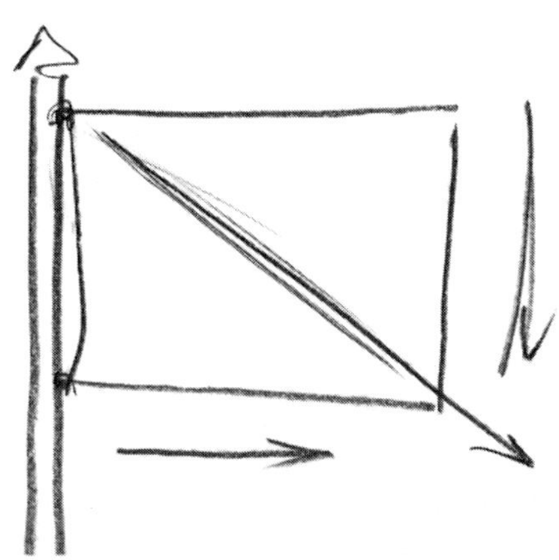

265-1B

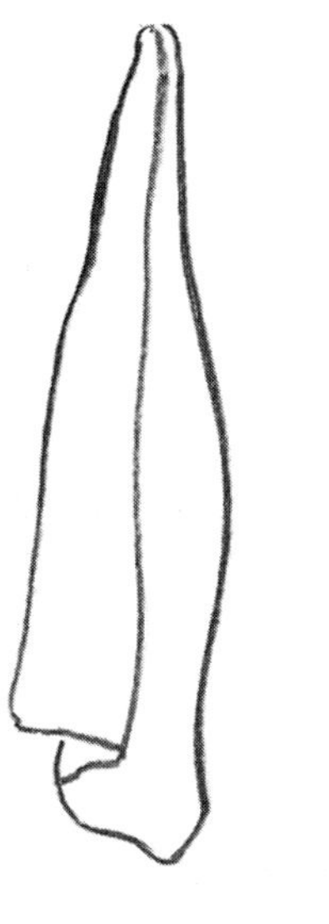

265-2A

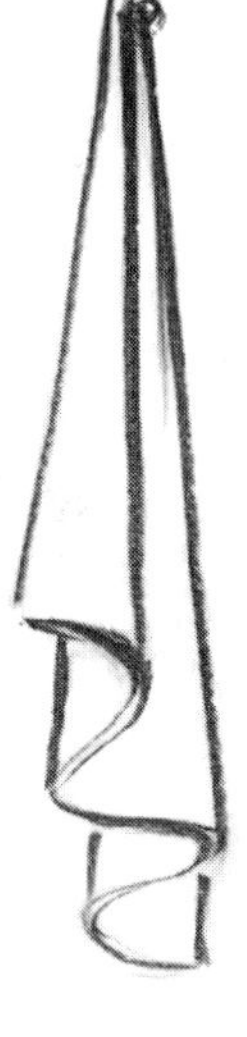

265-2B

For example, suppose we place a piece of heavy toweling on a flat surface. Its width and length are easily observed. Its thickness, however, may escape our attention since the fabric is thin. Yet it is a modified cube, a true three-dimensional form (*264-2A*).

Let us disturb the drapery by pushing it with our hand or a pointer (*264-B*). Now a magical thing takes place. By exerting a force against our three-dimensional form, we generate a whole new series of three-dimensional forms known as folds. If we lift the piece of drapery away from the surface on which it lies with our pointer, the material hangs as a number of new folds (*264-C*).

The movement of the material is reflected in a new and changing order of folds. In other words, a fold is a reflection of, or the manifestation of, a force or forces being exerted against the drapery.

Drapery often changes fold pattern because of the force of gravity acting upon the material, which always has weight. If a flag ripples in the breeze (*265-1A*) its visual form is modified by two forces, gravity and wind (*265-1B*).

When translated into drawing terms, the recording of these invisible forces through the way they are manifested in the folds contributes much to the energy of the whole picture. It is our option whether to draw drapery as we see it as a shape or to draw it as a symbol of forces. The loose edge of a piece of material may be portrayed objectively as a wobbly line (*265-2A*), or as a straight line which suggests the direction, the weight, the idea that the force of gravity is being exerted, and that it is being resisted by the support from which the material hangs (*265-2B*).

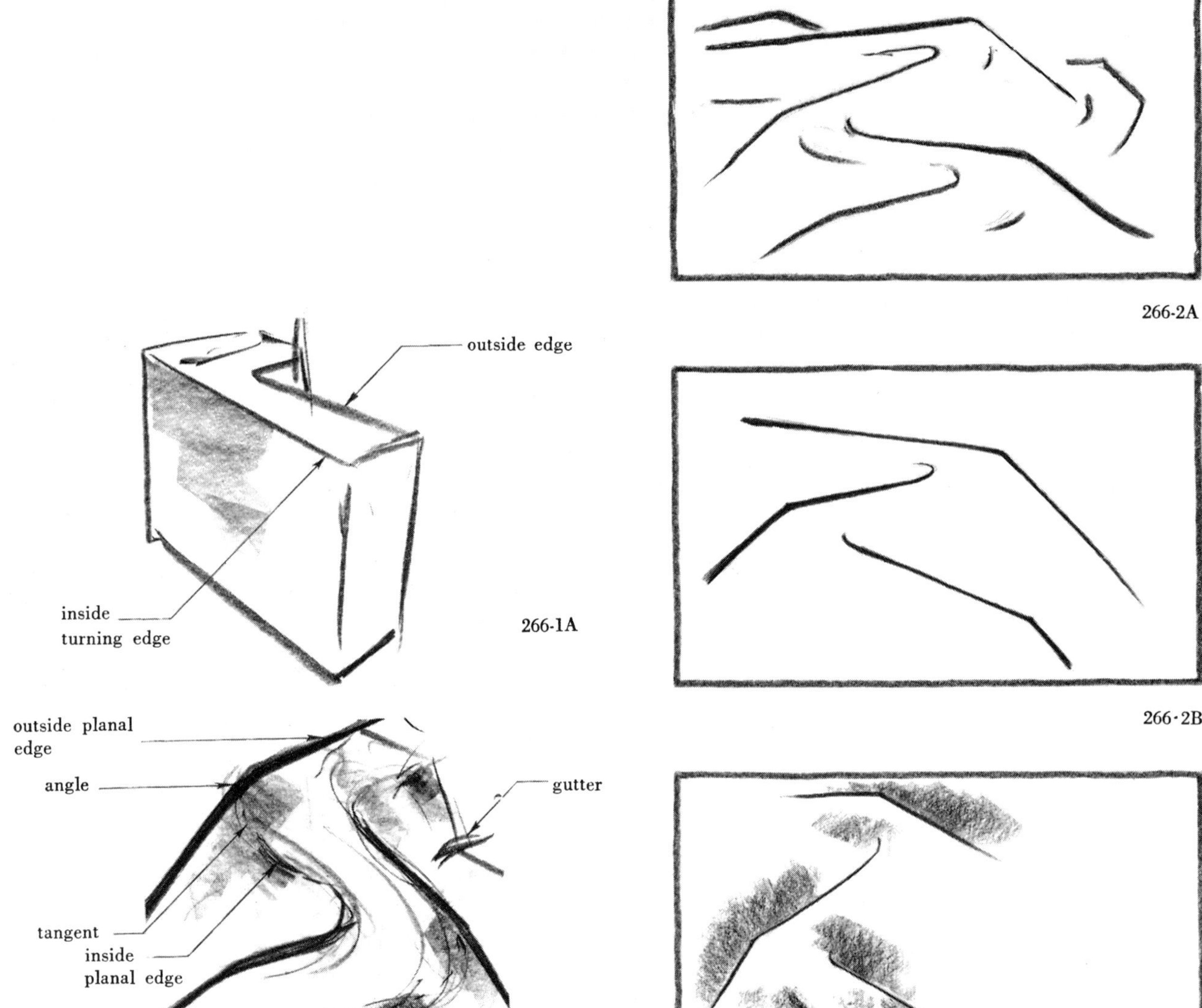




Drapery seldom resolves itself into orderly folds lying principally in one plane. A fold crumples, reverses, and often seems to suggest no force or direction at all. In drawing an inert mass of folds, or a dominant reverse of a fold, we find that if certain relations are respected we can bring order out of seeming disorder.

Unlike a cubic structure which is characterized by the impact of a plane against a plane (*266-1A*), the fold is constructed primarily of warped surfaces. The outside edge of the cube becomes an outside planal edge in the drapery; the inside turning edge of the cube becomes an inside planal edge in the drapery. We should note that rather than a sharp corner which we see in the cube, the corresponding intersection in the drapery is planal, and the inside planal edge is found to lie on the *tangent* leading out of the outside planal edge (*266-1B*).

Usually outside planal edges control the general movements of an arrangement of inert drapery. Plotting these lines first can help determine the basic design in our picture. The hips, or inside planal edges, may next be related to the outside lines to generate volume. The gutters usually are developed last, further revealing the large internal structures of the shapes, the secondary shapes (*266-2A*).

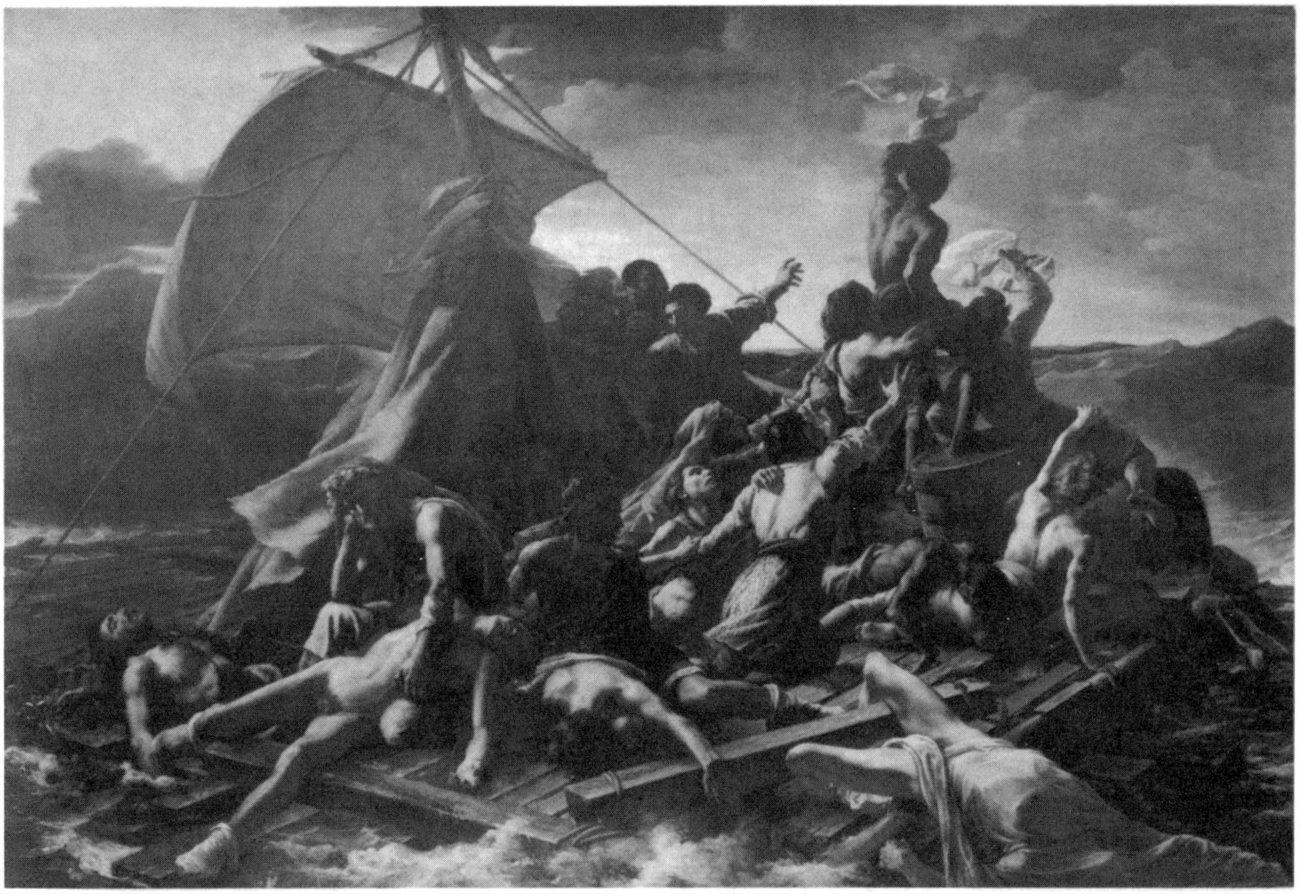

Théodore Géricault (French, 1791-1824)
THE RAFT OF THE MEDUSA, 1818-1819
16'1" x 23' 5⅞"; oil on canvas
The Louvre, Paris

We should note, also, that as a fold changes direction, its outside planal edge can be expressed as an angular change (*266-2B*). The legs of this angle can be expressed as straight lines. Further, the angle generated by the outside planal edge implies the presence of a new, or third, fold.

If the drape is to be indicated tonally, a flat passage inside or outside the angle will make the use of modeling or rendering unnecessary. An accent on the inside turning edge, used for contrast, not shade or shadow, may prove helpful at times (*266-2C*).

## Drapery as a Transition

It is surprising how frequently we find pictures combining symbols suggesting the figure, architectural or manufactured forms, and drapery. The reason becomes apparent when we consider the picture in design terms. Architecture is hard, non-growth, man-made. It usually involves flat surfaces and straight lines. The figure is a growth structure involving numerous curved surfaces and curved lines. Drapery has both straight and curved lines, flat and curved surfaces.

In both nature and drawing, drapery is the transition between architecture and the figure. It displays the same linear and areal structures found in both and may help reveal such structures by binding them. Consider clinging robes, a wet dress, draped forms, as Géricault uses drapery here.

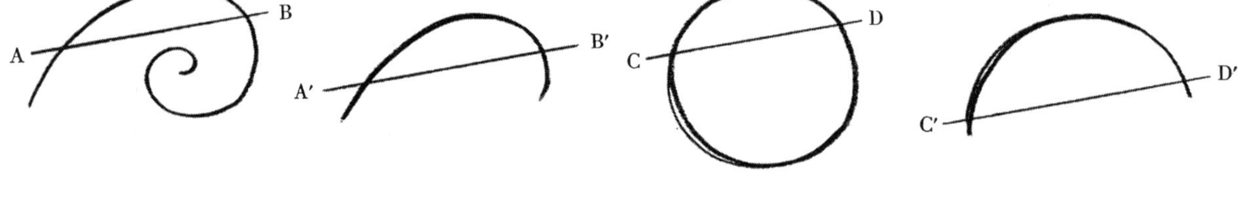



268-A        268-B        268-C        268-D

268     When we transpose the visual shape of a piece of drapery into a graphic shape manifesting forces at work on the drapery, the use of the straight line becomes mandatory. The straight lines in drapery in conjunction with the straight lines inherent in most symbols of architectural structures, and straight lines discovered in growth symbols, constitute a potential order. By relating each to the other, and to the picture surface itself, we develop a dynamic control of picture design.

### Growth Forms
When we look at the human figure, or an animal, or for that matter almost any growth form, we are struck with the preponderance of curved or warped surfaces over flat surfaces.

As we begin to draw such organizations we tend to be overwhelmed by the number and complexity of these curved surfaces. Instinctively we resort to the use of curved lines. In fact there is a dearth of straight lines, at first, either observed in the growth form or actually used in our drawing of it.

Yet we realize that there are only two kinds of lines—straight and curved. By restricting ourselves to only one, the curve, we narrow the scope of our design, weakening the picture impact tremendously.

We soon discover that a preponderance of curves used to express what is already soft or curved in nature frequently results in a soft or mushy drawing. Such drawings, constructed primarily on curves, tend to look bulbous or pneumatic.

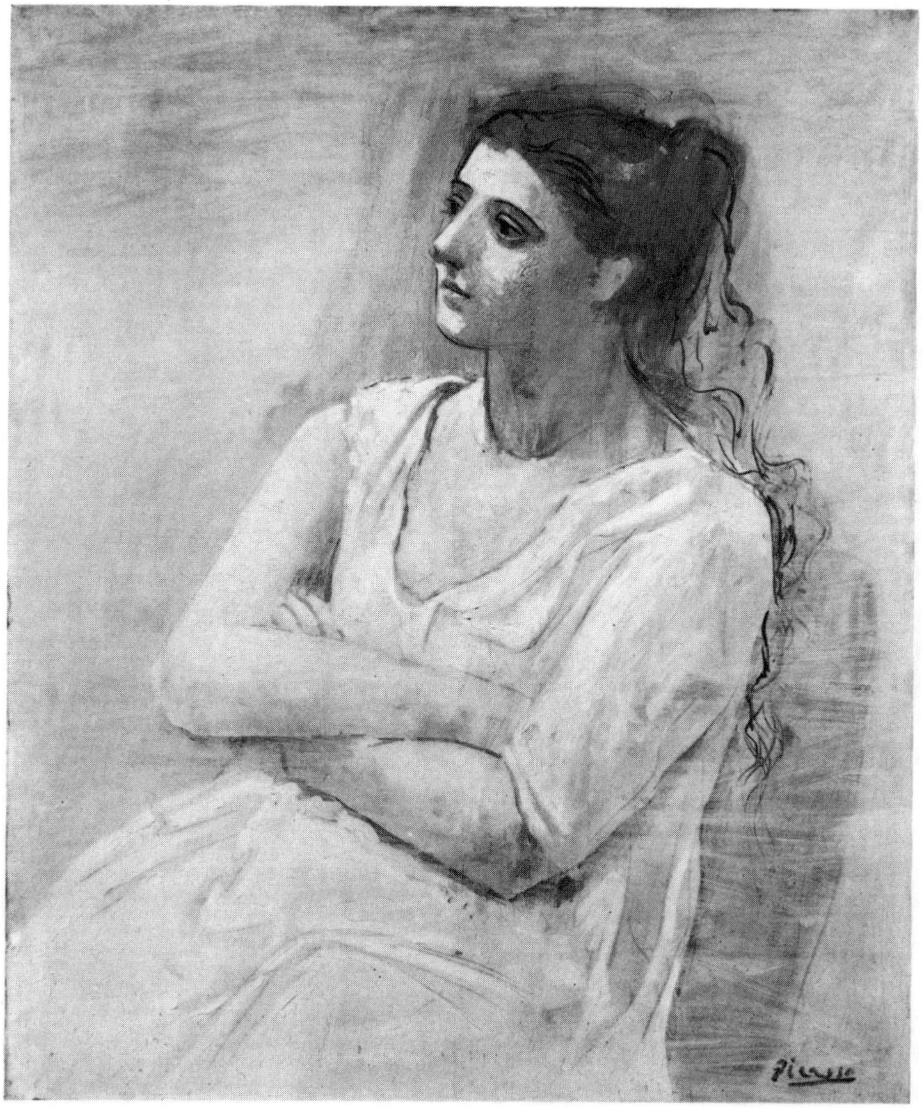

Pablo Picasso (Spanish, 1881-  )
WOMAN IN WHITE, 1923; 39″ x 31½″
oil on canvas
The Metropolitan Museum of Art
The Rogers Fund, 1951; from The Museum
of Modern Art, Lizzie P. Bliss Collection

By introducing straight lines we add a vital structural ingredient to our design. At the same time the straight line implies the presence of flat surfaces or planes which complement the curved surfaces of the growth symbol, as in Picasso's *Woman in White*. Finding and using such lines is one of the first tasks in drawing.

### Finding Straight Lines in Growth Symbols

When we examine a snail's shell, or a fern's frond, we discover a certain type of curve. It is the spiral. It represents a constant ratio of change. In other words, as the curve opens or closes (*268-A*), one segment of the curve is flatter than an adjacent portion nearer the center, or eye (*268-B*). Such a curve, modified in many ways, is characteristic of most lines observed in numerous growth forms, particularly the human figure.

With the exception of the eyeball, and it is not quite spherical, there are no true circular or spherical forms in the human figure. We might say that nature abhors a circle, especially in the growth form. To the designer this has great significance. A circle (*268-C*), or any segment of it (*268-D*), is characterized by a curve which neither opens nor closes as does the curve of a spiral. The circle is a flat, mechanical curve. As such, it lends itself to special types of design, especially those based on space-breaking rather than on any use of the growth symbol. In fact, when a circular segment is used in a growth symbol its presence usually is noticeable and is most often unwelcome.

 270

In delineating a muscle form, a shoulder, for instance, the line expressing it constantly changes. At times it closes, becoming more curved; at other times it opens until it is almost straight. Here, then, is an opportunity to introduce straight lines into our drawing of a form which at first glance seems to be organized only of curves *(270-A)*.

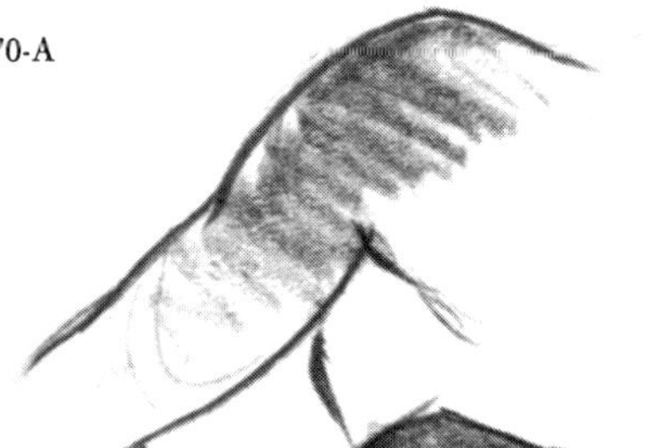

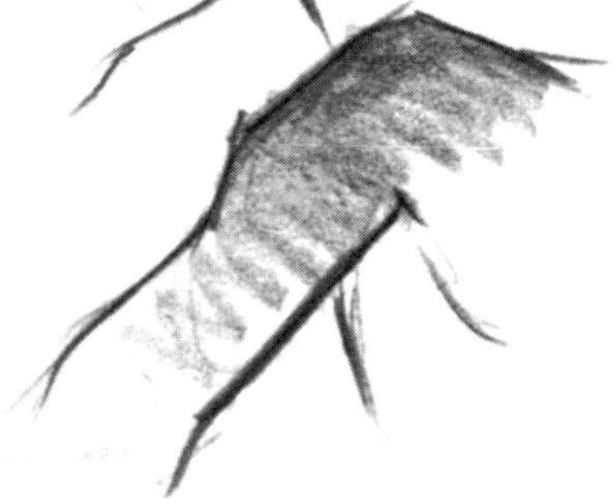

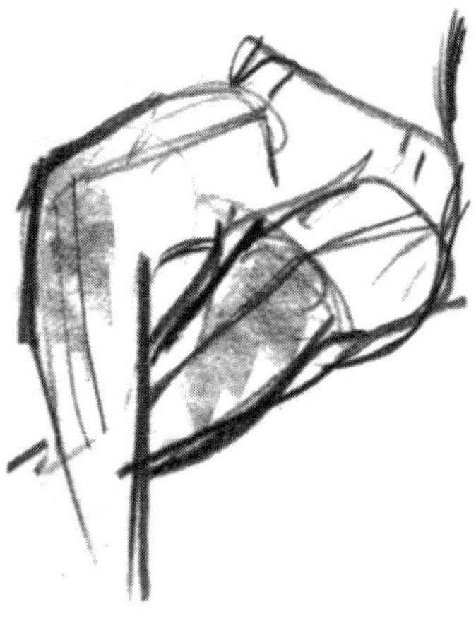

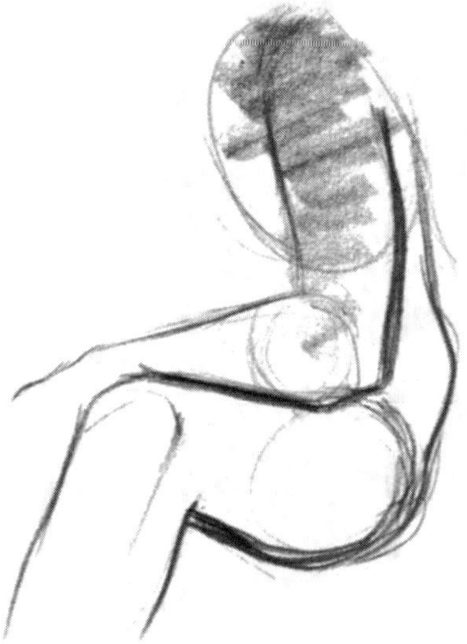

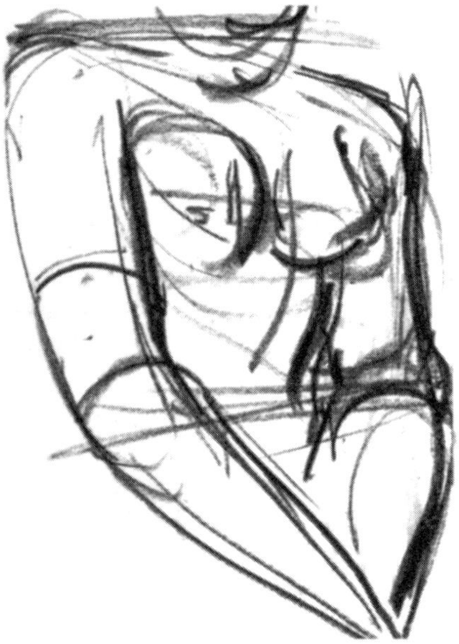

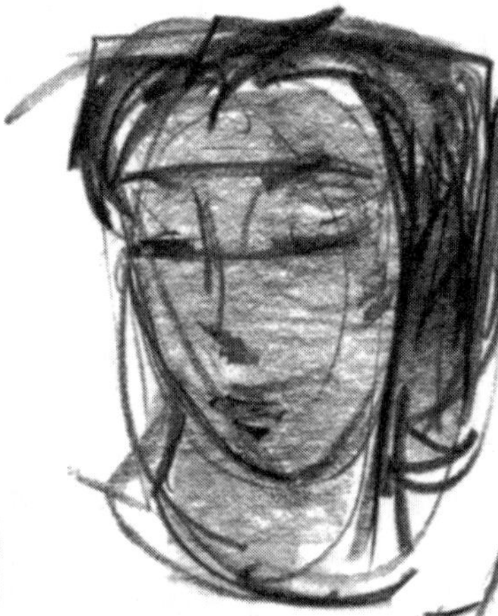

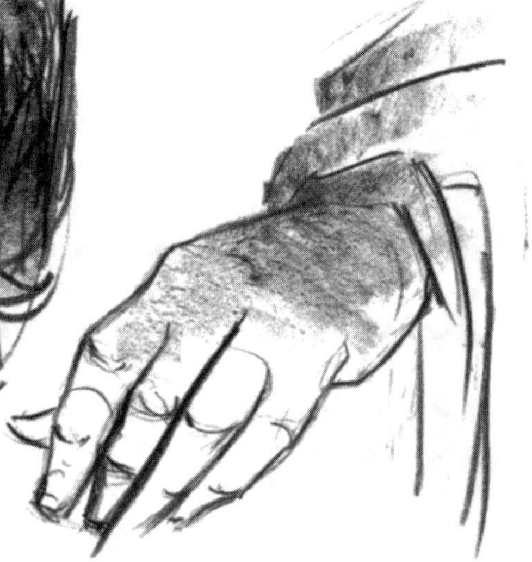

Now if we examine the zone where one muscle overlaps another, we find that the upper form usually takes precedence in interest. Usually the overlapped form can be expressed with a straight line *(270-B)*.

In the same way, when two independent units are overlapped, the closer form may give us more information or attract our interest more strongly. The overlapped form often can be indicated with one or more straight lines *(270-C)*.

The straight line occurs frequently where one form crosses another, resulting in physical contact *(270-D)*. The point of tangency may be generated into a straight line, often of considerable length.

When two touching parallel forms create a gutter, the gutter may be simplified and expressed as a straight line. This is seen, for instance, where an arm, a curved form, presses against a torso, which also is curved *(270-E)*. The straight line used between such volumes emphasizes the true nature of the growth symbol, and also acts as a vigorous design element *(270-F)*. A straight line may be used between any two curved forms pressed together to form a crease and between forms such as fingers, toes, the hair and flesh *(270-G)*.

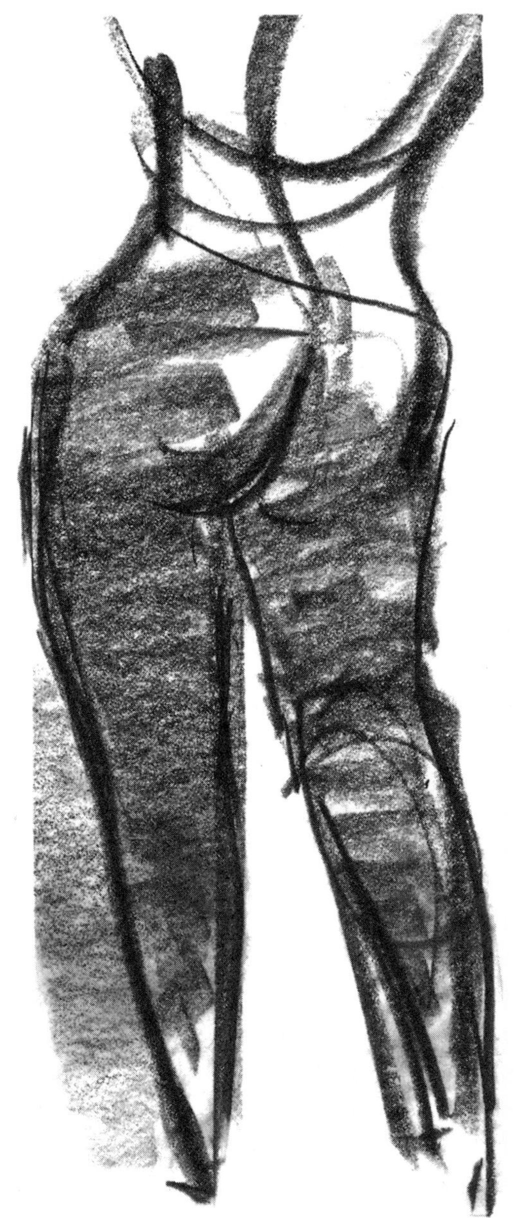

271-1

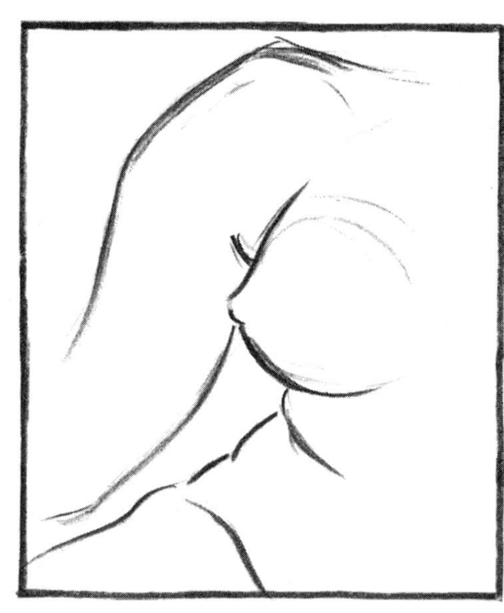

271-2A

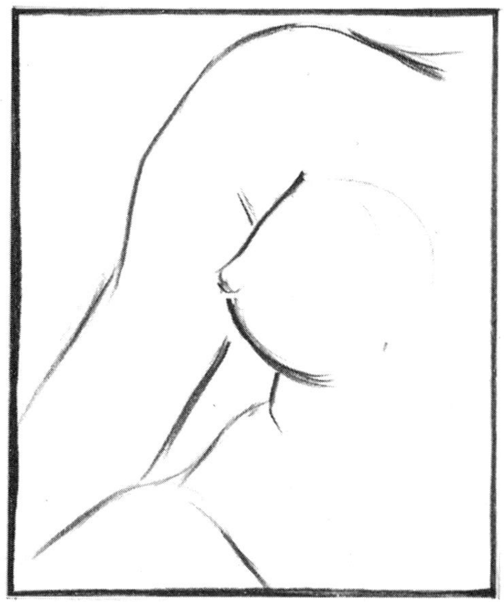

271-2B

At times a straight line may be exploited to intensify a symbol which portrays the exertion of a strong force, a pull, a push. The straight line is especially useful if we wish to contrast a bent member at rest with a straight member that is working, as we find in a simple standing pose (*271-1*).

There is always the opportunity to interject straight lines for design relief. Too often we find in a picture a series of curves on a silhouette, one following another with no straight-line relief (*271-2A*). Much more vigor can be achieved in the picture by simply using straight lines. Similarly, many adjacent curves within a shape may require straight-line reinforcement to avoid a mushy drawing (*271-2B*).

The body is constructed upon a bone skeleton 271 which is hard, covered by soft, muscular flesh. This is a clue to the design of human or animal symbols. The angles, flat planes, straight lines are hard; curved, warped surfaces frequently are soft. This design contrast, hard against soft, allows the exploitation of the straight line in seemingly soft growth forms.

As we explore nature we constantly find more places where a straight line can be visualized. These suggestions can be realized in a generous use of straight lines as we transpose from nature forms into drawing terms. If the design develops beyond a figurative or abstract statement into a non-representational one, the use of straight lines in the picture may be equally desirable.

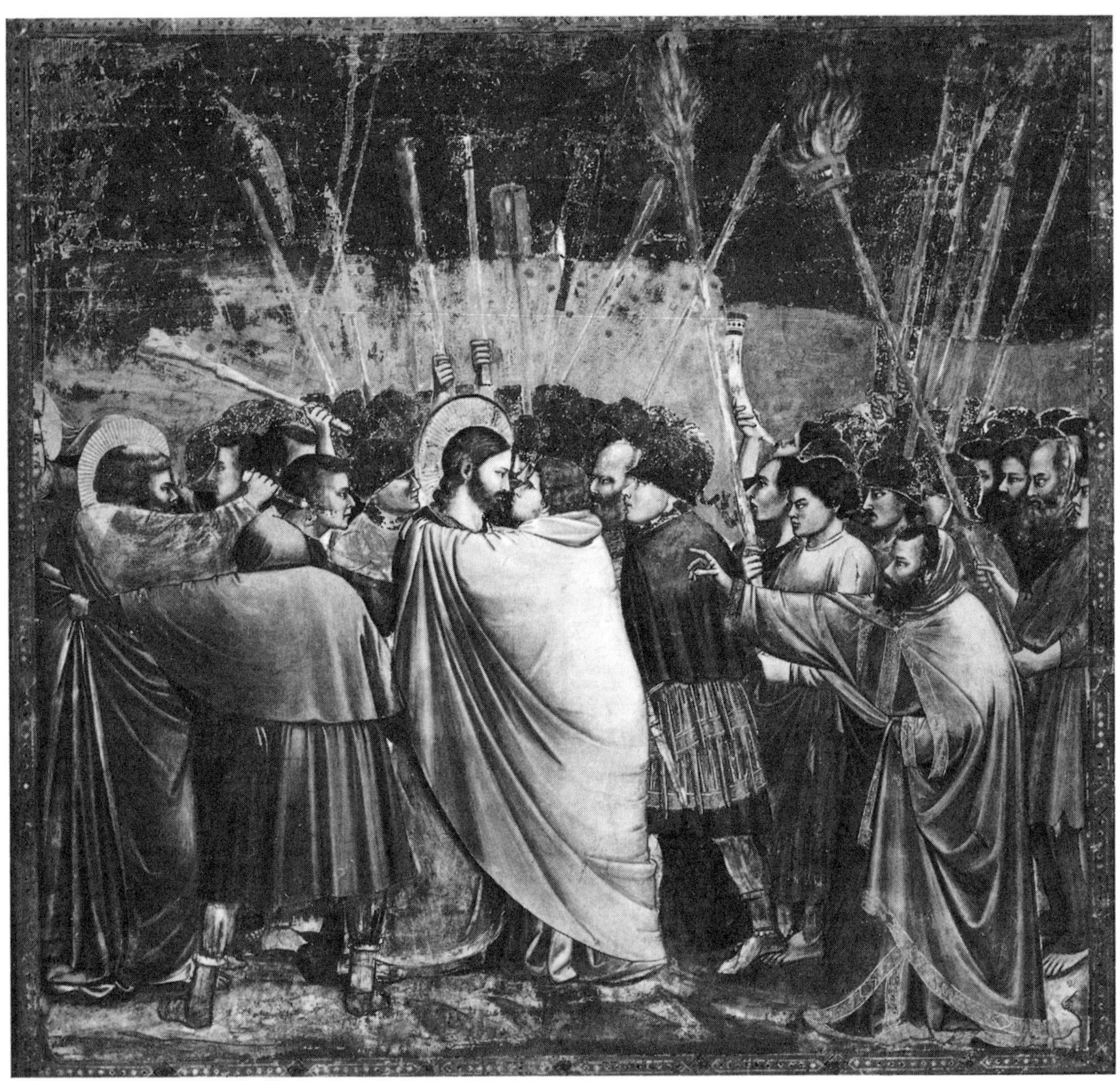

Giotto (Florentine, 1266?-1337)
THE KISS OF JUDAS, 1305-1306
fresco, Scrovegni Chapel, Padua
(Photograph: Anderson, Alinari, Rome
Art Reference Bureau, Inc., N. Y.)



# 24 The Picture Line

### The Unique Line

Although we might say that any line on the picture surface is a picture line, to designate lines which have specific functions we must give special meaning to the term *picture line*.

A picture line is a straight line which always functions in at least two ways, often more, in a picture. The picture line divides the surface, it may help define a volume or shape, but at the same time it will relate in a very special way to other picture lines, to implied references, or to the borders of the picture, as we see in the Giotto above.

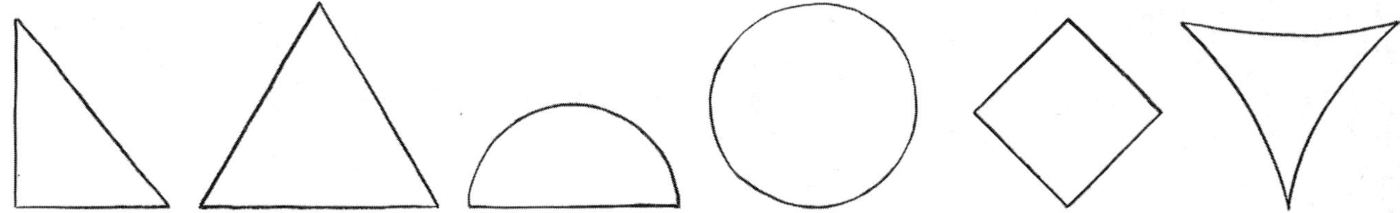



**The Borders as Gravitational References**
Before further investigating picture lines we
should recall what we noted in Chapter 20
about our gravitational senses. We have certain
built-in senses common to all human beings.
Among the strongest of these are our sense of the
vertical and the horizontal. These gravitational
senses are developed to a high degree. We are
irritated by a tipped floor or a door jamb which
is not plumb. We have noted our physical
reaction when we see a tipped picture on a wall.

We find that the vertical and horizontal
borders used in many pictures reinforce our
gravitational senses. In other pictures if only
one border is vertical or horizontal it only
partially reinforces these senses.

Some borders do not contribute directly to
our gravitational senses. Most obvious is the
circular border. The square on corner is also a
rather weak gravitational reference, for it is
prone to tip. Irregular picture shapes, equally
unstable, are often encountered in mural
painting and ceramics (*273*).

So particularly when borders of a picture
are vertical or horizontal do they serve as
powerful references. We relate comfortably to
such borders, we feel secure, at ease. The fact
that a border may be a physical, constructed
boundary, such as a frame or an architectural
structure, is in itself reassuring.

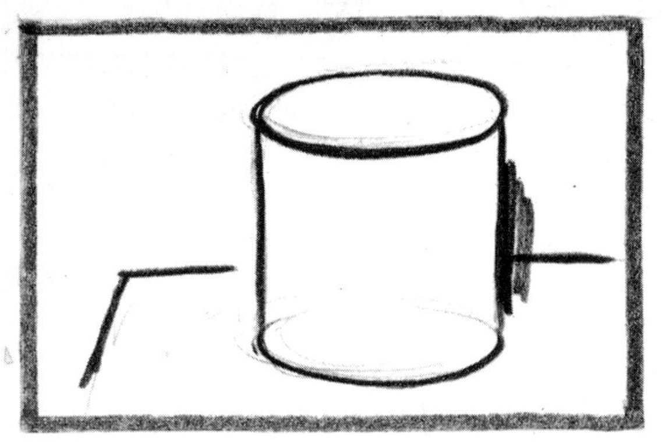

274-A

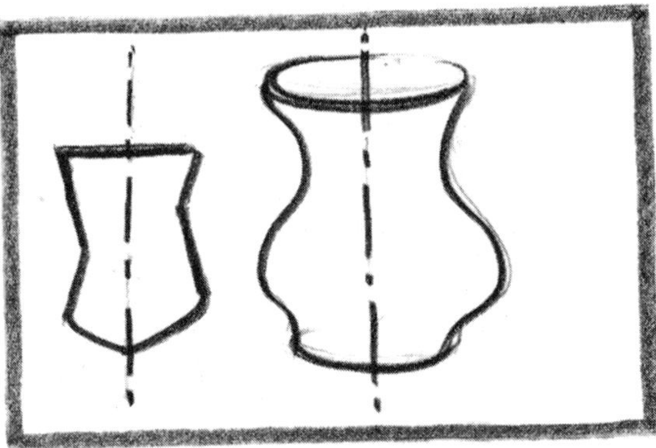

274-B

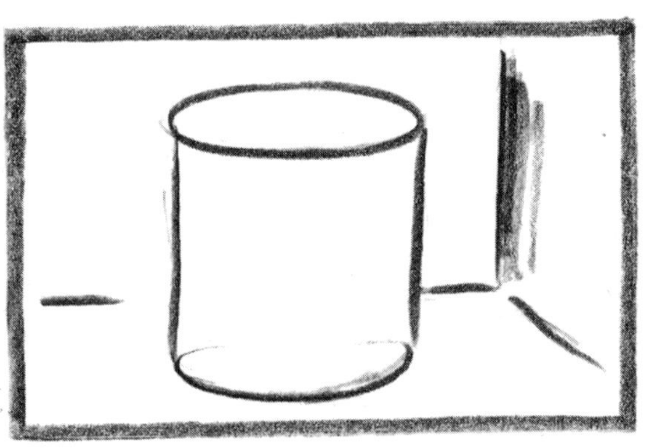

274-C

## The Graphic Echo of the Borders

274

If our picture has strong vertical borders we can introduce a vertical line somewhere between the two vertical borders in order to echo and reinforce our gravitational sense with a true graphic reference actually in the picture.

Such a straight vertical line may be found on the edge of a shape, and it may at the same time determine a volume (*274-A*).

It may be used as a core of a volume or as a center line of a shape (*274-B*).

It may occur as a gutter line between volumes or on the intersection of planes (*274-C*).

In each instance the vertical line introduced parallel to the vertical border, or to an implied vertical when a vertical border is not actually present, serves more than one function: first, it reinforces our gravitational sense; second, it is in some way related to the symbols indicated in in the picture; third, it usually has some relation to the borders. This straight line conforms to our particular definition of a picture line. In a picture with strong horizontal borders, a horizontal line may have similar function.

## Dividing the Whole Picture

To use picture lines in dividing the picture we must have a clear realization of the picture as a whole. We have continually emphasized the importance of the picture surface, to the picture as a thing, to the picture as a whole. We have discussed various ways of maintaining awareness of this picture entity. Although it has been the

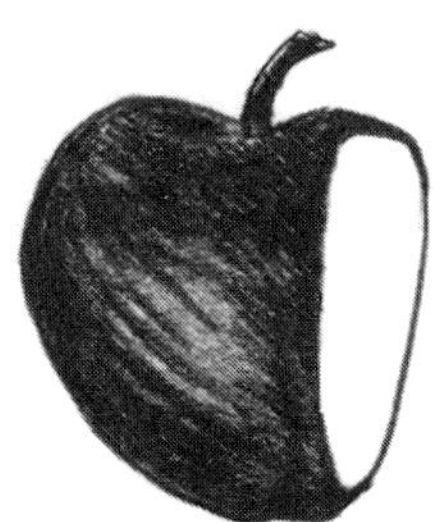

275-1A

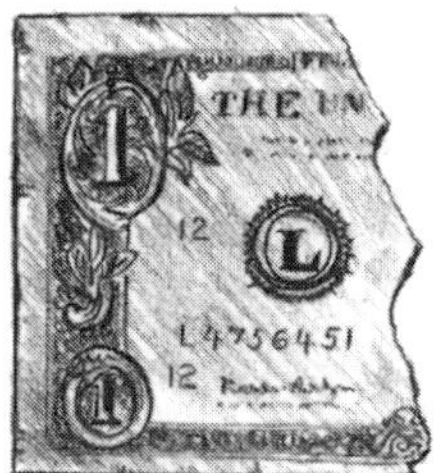

275-1B

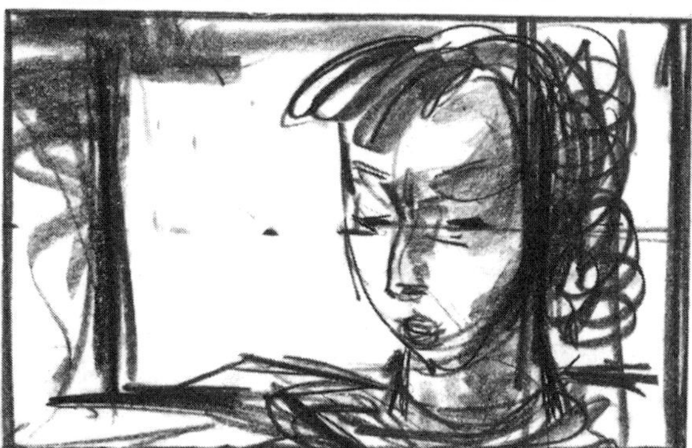

275-2

concern of most artists throughout art history, this factor of picture making, this awareness of the whole, seems most elusive. To illustrate wholeness let us examine an apple.

Now an apple is a thing. It is a whole. We usually accept this quality of wholeness without question. It is a non-event. Suppose, however, that we are handed two-thirds of an apple (*275-1A*). We are immediately intrigued. What happened to the rest of it? We are suddenly aware of the wholeness of the apple by being deprived of some of it.

As another illustration, let us consider a dollar bill. Usually we accept its size, shape, and significance without examining it closely. But we have heard that if more than half of a bill is torn away the remainder can no longer be redeemed as legal tender. So when we are handed only part of a dollar bill it becomes an event, for we must then compare the fragment to a whole bill (*275-1B*). We become acutely aware of the total size and shape of a dollar bill as we visualize the part as a whole.

Now let us look at a picture divided by a vertical or horizontal straight line. Even though the line may not extend from border to border, it affects our eye sufficiently to create a visual division, a division of the total picture shape (*275-2*). Such a division of a picture is like the torn dollar bill. When we see only a part of the picture, we search for the whole. If we are aware of the division, we also become aware of the whole which is divided. Once we have sensed the whole, the picture becomes a physical reality with definite physical properties of size and shape.

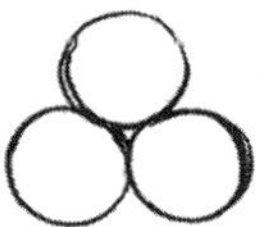

276-1A

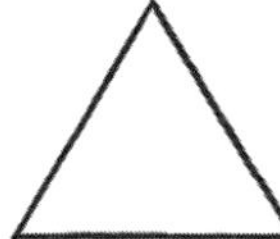

276-1B



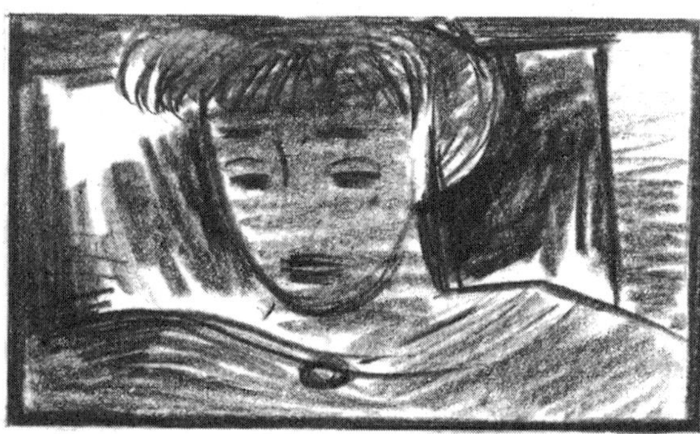

276-2A

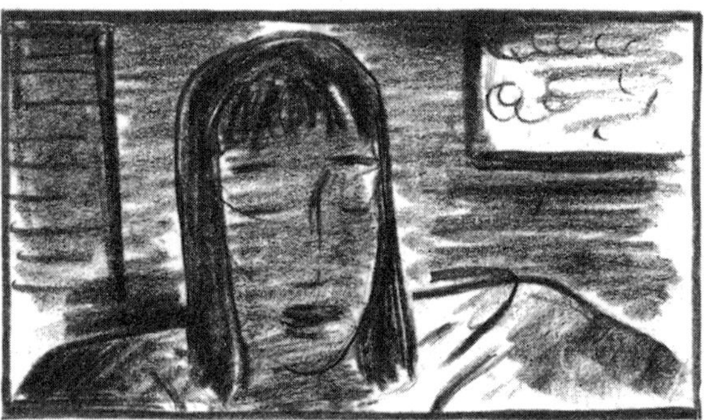

276-2B

276    As we have emphasized, the impact and reality of a graphic image is often stronger than our awareness of the reality of the physical picture. Yet these two realities can be so welded that they become a satisfying whole. The use of the picture line is one device which has helped skillful artists realize this unity.

**Rotating the Picture Line**

Although some device is almost always used in a picture to reassure the viewer that up is up, or down is down, we should not always expect to find actual drawn verticals or horizontals in every picture. Often these gravitational references are imaginary. In the accompanying drawing, the three circles constitute one of the most stable organizations of shapes, yet there are no visible verticals or horizontals, in fact no straight lines anywhere (*276-1A*). Yet they really do exist, even if invisible. They occur between the centers of the circles and constitute a fixed stable triangle which satisfies our gravitational requirements (*276-1B*).

In complex pictures at least one vertical and one horizontal usually is used. In the case of a circular picture such references are even more necessary, especially if there is a rotation within the circle.

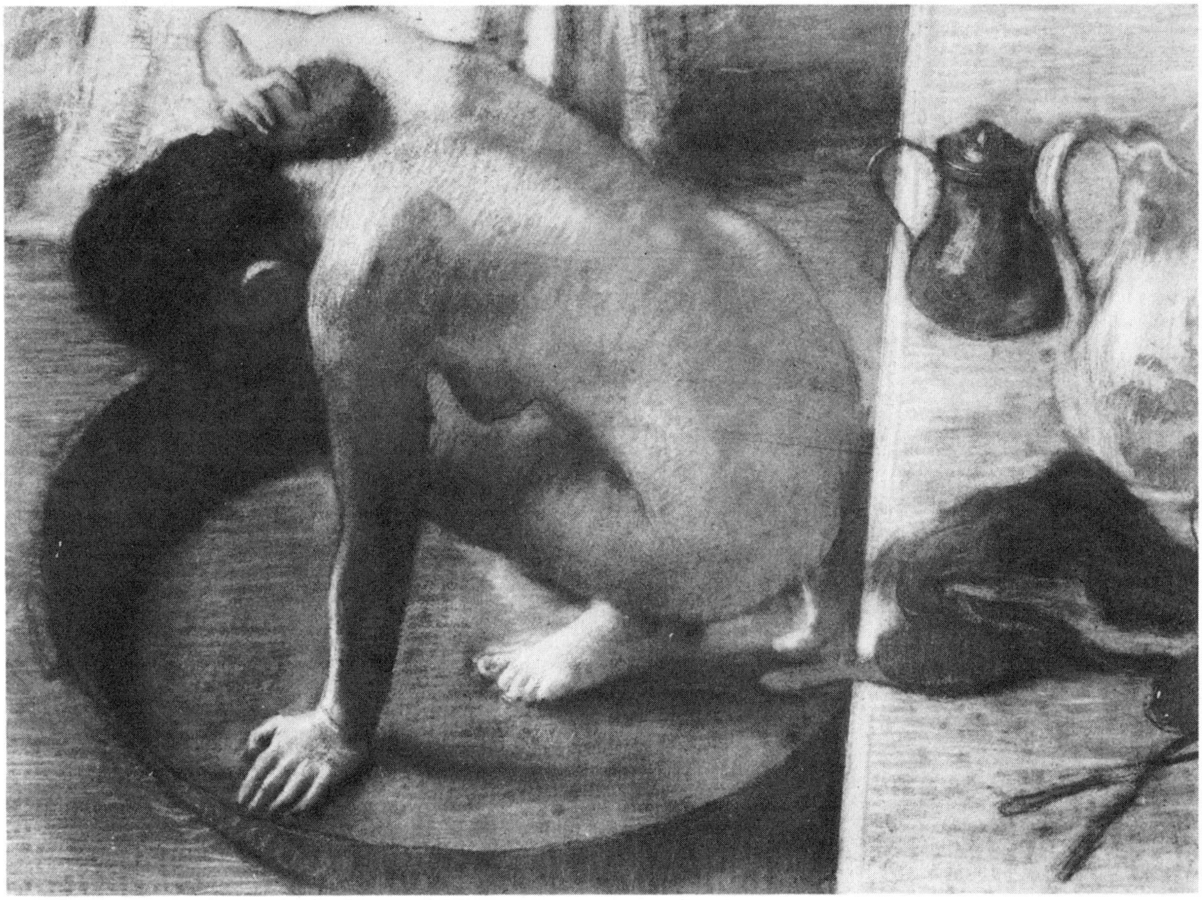

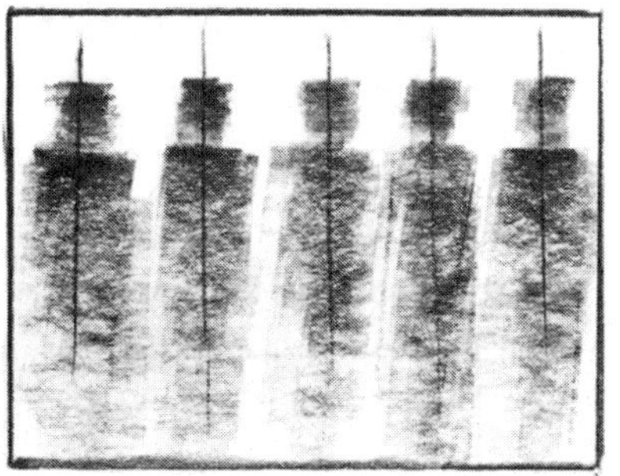 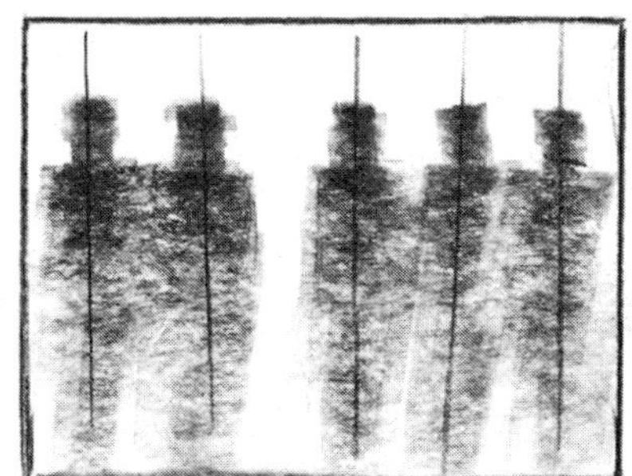 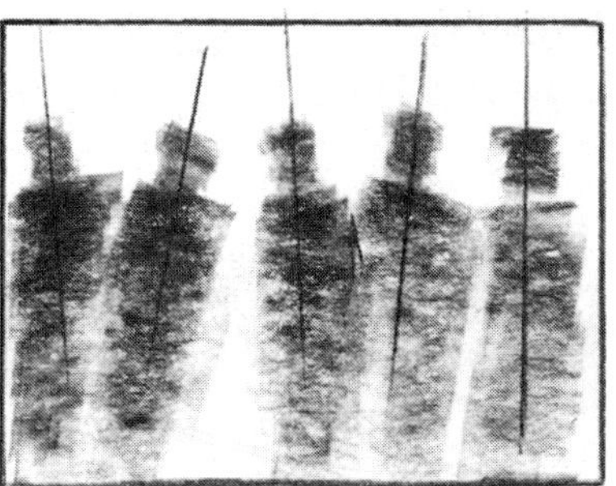

277-2A   277-2B   277-2C

A picture line is often rotated out of a border (*276-2A*). Such a line may effectively divide the whole picture surface since a picture may be divided on a diagonal as well as vertically or horizontally. This rotated picture line can now be used as a reference for other picture lines and other linear organizations related directly to the diagonal picture line, rather than to the vertical or horizontal border.

We often find that the surface of the entire picture may be divided first by a picture line, as in Degas' *The Tub*. Then, within one of the areas generated by this picture line, secondary picture lines are rotated to the picture line (*276-2B*). Since the primary picture line relates to the whole picture, the secondary lines also relate to the whole, but indirectly.

Several picture lines may be used to divide the whole surface. Such divisions may be quite regular (*277-2A*), or grouped in such a way as to divide the surface into easily recognized parts (*277-2B*), or so organized that movements of the total number of picture lines constitute a new unifying order (*277-2C*).

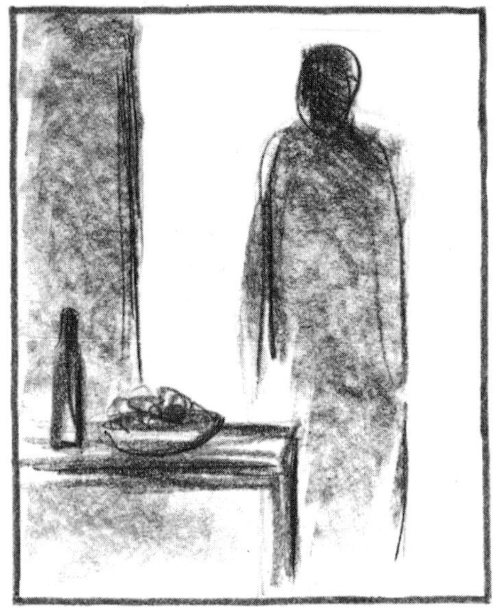

278-1A

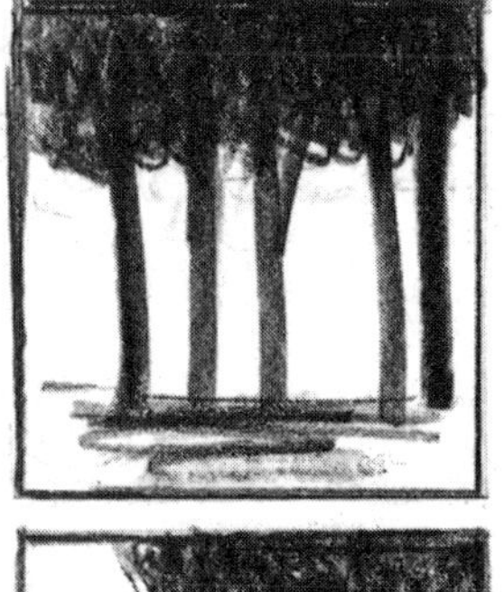

278-2A

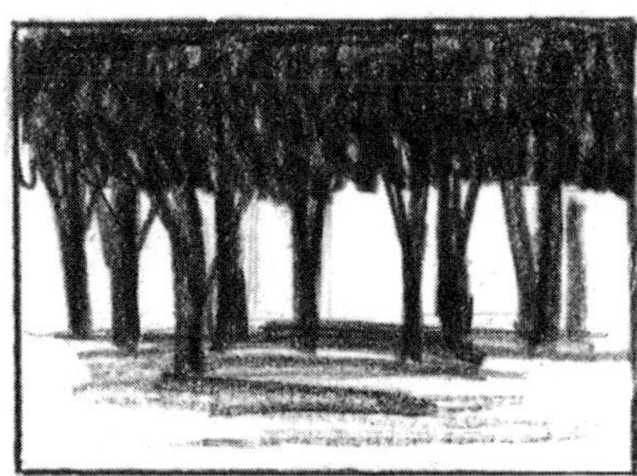

278-2B

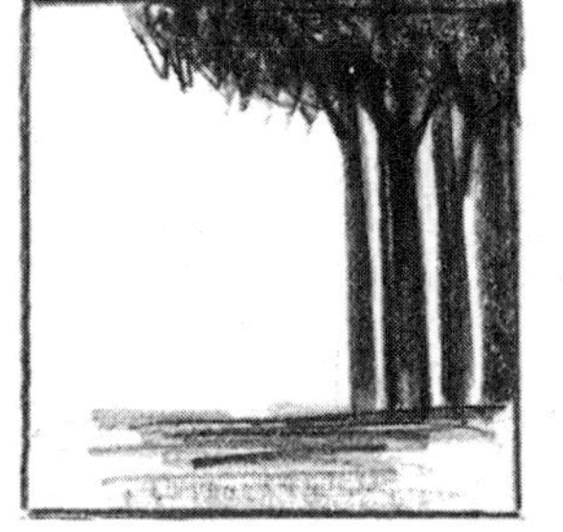

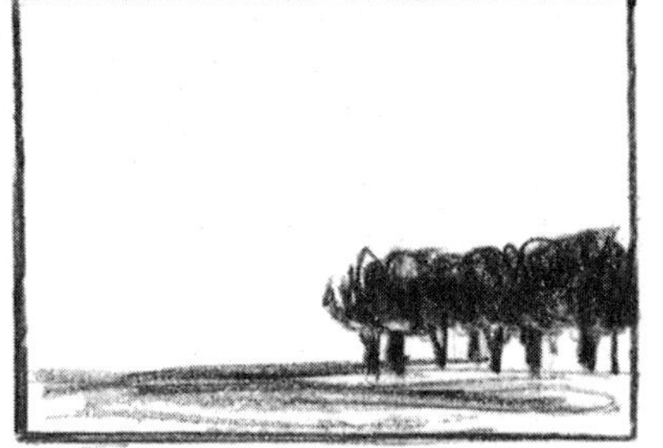

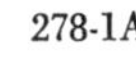

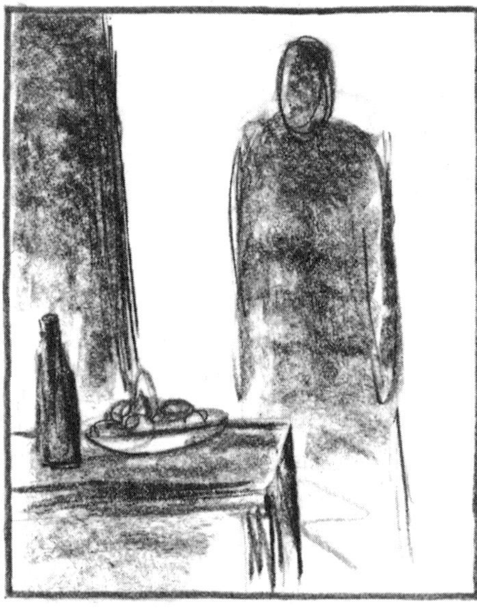

278-1B

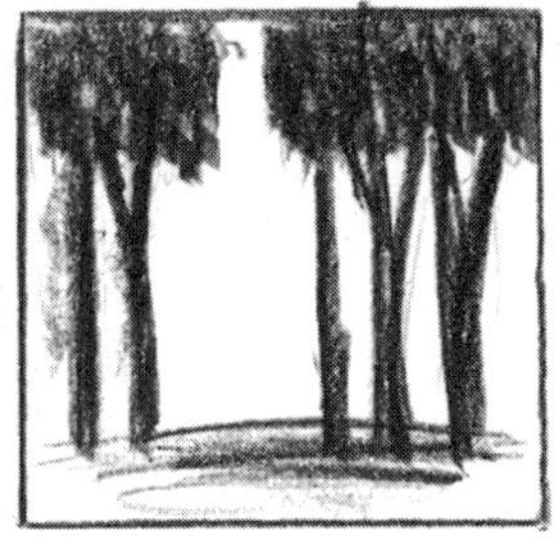

278-2C

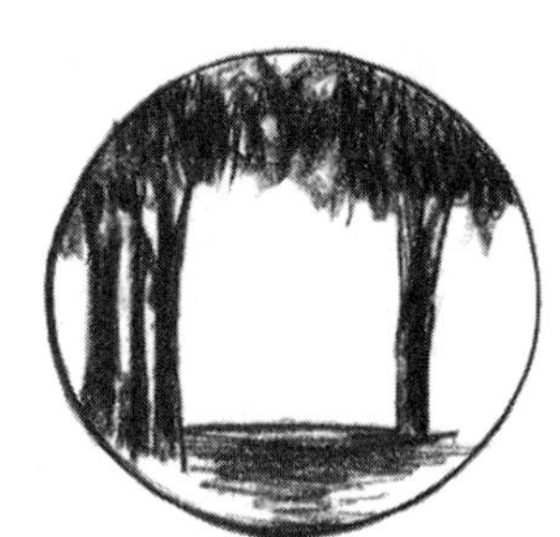

278-2D

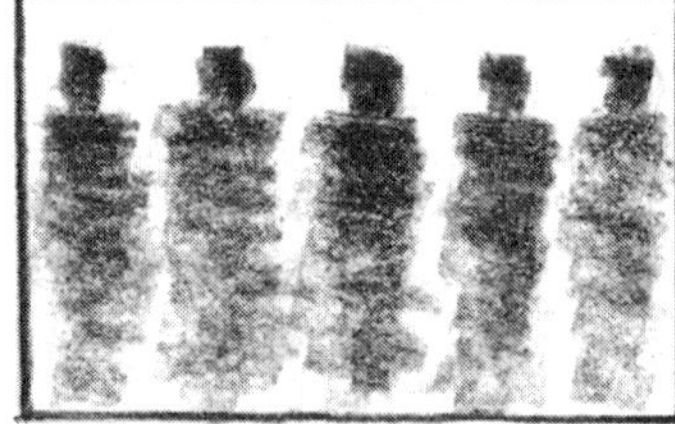

278-3A

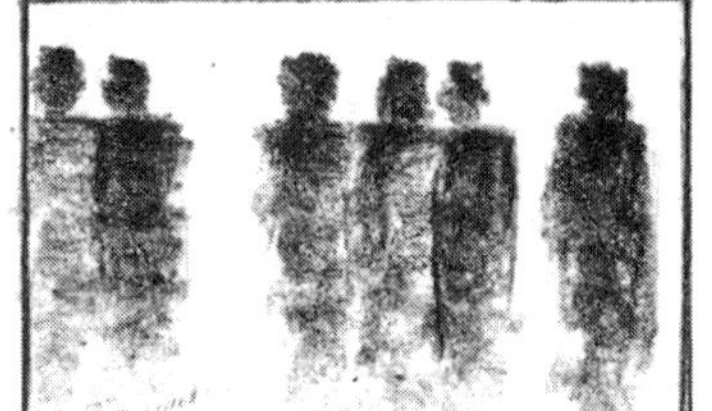

278-3B

## Picture Lines in Depth



We have seen how any vertical or horizontal picture line is directly related to a corresponding border or strong gravitational reference. A picture line may also be related to a shape or volume in the far distance, to the principal subject, or to a shape or volume in an overlay (*278-1A*). Each of these also will relate in some way to the borders, except in the case of vignettes.

A series of picture lines lying in the foreground, subject, or background may be related through slide or rotation to constitute a strong linear order (*278-1B*). These may be oriented to a vertical or horizontal border, or to a dominant picture line.

Thus we find that the picture line is a marvelous and truly graphic control. As we found with the passage, the picture line may be on the surface, and at the same time in deep graphic space. We also found that an active shape may be placed in back of a passive shape, yet both may appear to lie in the picture surface. In the case of picture lines we have a similar paradox. A vertical line in the background can be in the same plane, the picture surface, as a vertical line in the foreground. Such is the magic of graphics. Not only is such a relation possible, it is necessary. By the skillful use of picture lines we are made aware of the picture surface in a truly graphic way.

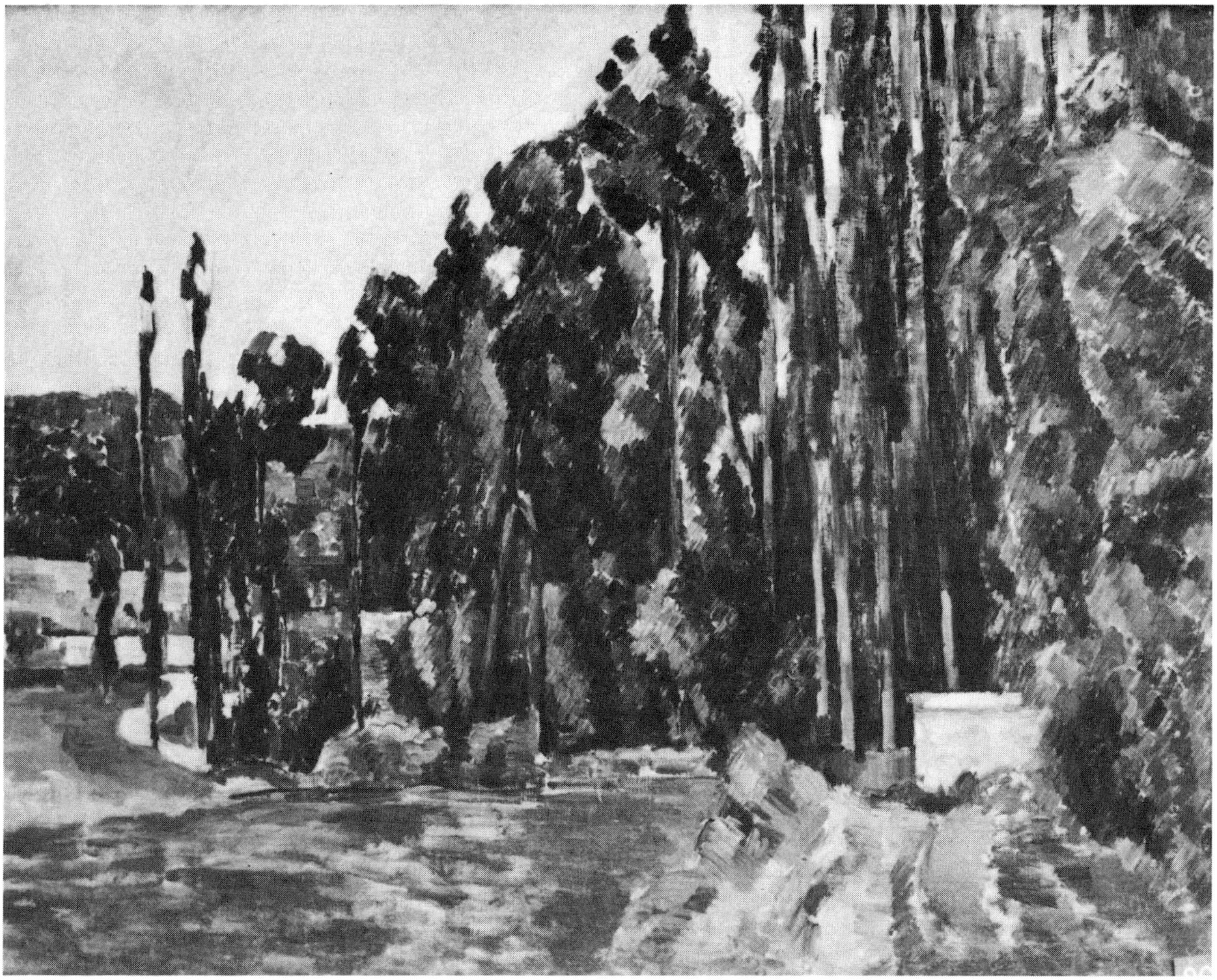

Paul Cézanne (French, 1839-1906)
THE POPLARS, 1879-1882
25½" x 31⅞"
oil on canvas
The Louvre, Paris

## Picture Impact Through Picture Lines

Picture lines help us emphasize or minimize the dominant shape of a picture. We can make a vertical picture look higher (*278-2A*); or a horizontal picture look wider (*278-2B*); a square picture can be made less square (*278-2C*); a round one, less round (*278-2D*).

By using picture lines as dividers we can overcome monotonous organizations (*278-3A*). This, of course, leads directly to the development of rhythmic pattern controlled by picture lines (*278-3B*).

In Cézanne's *Poplars* we find an adaptation of rotated verticals. This device is called the *walking verticals*. Although not always generated only by picture lines, we see how effectively the rocking motion ties the surface together as a whole.

As we saw in Chapter 21, an extraordinary degree of graphic excitement may be generated through rotation and the use of diagonals. Usually rotations of shapes or volumes are intimately related to picture lines. Rotations, slides, diagonal structures are usually enhanced by the use of picture lines.

Since the picture line is an abstract element, it can help us avoid the overly-realistic picture because picture lines do not exist in nature. They are purely the concept of the artist. Thus the use of picture lines can create graphic impact without dependence upon subject matter interest. Yet we must be careful, for picture lines do not automatically guarantee a good picture. In fact, if picture lines are used awkwardly, results may be disastrous.

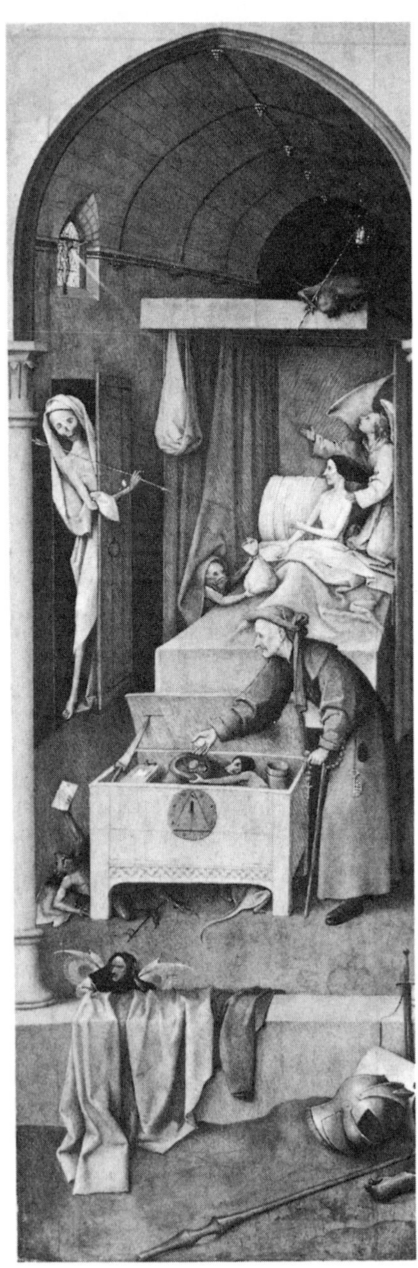

Hieronymus Bosch (Flemish, ca. 1450-1516)
DEATH AND THE MISER, ca. 1483-1484
36⅝″ x 12⅛″; oil on wood
National Gallery of Art
Samuel H. Kress Collection, 1952



# 25 Divisions of the Surface

## Harmonic Divisions of the Picture

As we have seen, the picture line is a way to strengthen our awareness of the picture as an entity. Harmonic divisions of the picture surface make us compare a part to the whole. In so doing the physical characteristics of the picture are emphasized, counteracting the often overwhelming illusion that the picture is a window.

But how can we divide the picture surface to avoid monotony and create harmonic parts? Over the centuries artists have pondered this question and have devised many ingenious solutions, one of which Bosch shows us here. Let us examine some others.

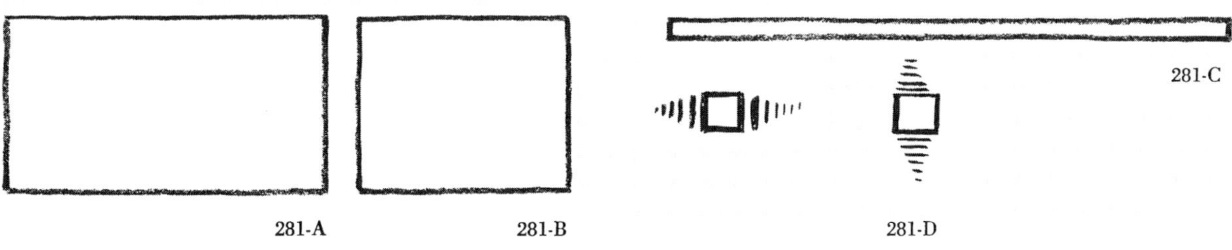

281-A 281-B 281-C

281-D

## The Comparison of Dimensions

As we look about us in nature we constantly are aware of certain rectangular structures, the wall of a building, a table top, a rug. Although we are seldom aware of the exact proportional relations of such rectangles, almost subconsciously we distinguish between long and short sides (*281-A*). When the sides are equal, or nearly so, we sense that the rectangle is square (*281-B*). Also we are aware vaguely that the rectangle and the square are different. In the same way an extremely long rectangle such as a yardstick seems of a different order from either the square or the familiar rectangle (*281-C*).

If we closely observe the size relations which characterize these differing rectangles, we find that our eyes can be rather easily deceived. It is difficult to determine just how much longer one side of a rectangle is than its adjoining base.

Even judging the equality of the sides of a square presents some difficulties. Our success often is influenced by factors affecting the image which originate not in the rectangle, but in its environment (*281-D*).

However, determining the exact ratio which exists between the side and base of a rectangle is of vital importance to the artist. He must paint or draw on canvas of specific size, design for magazine pages of particular shape, or compose for a motion picture screen of certain proportions. He usually must determine the ratio of side to base of such rectangles with exactness. Then, with this ratio in mind, he proceeds with the picture divisions, informing the spectator by graphic devices just what he is doing.

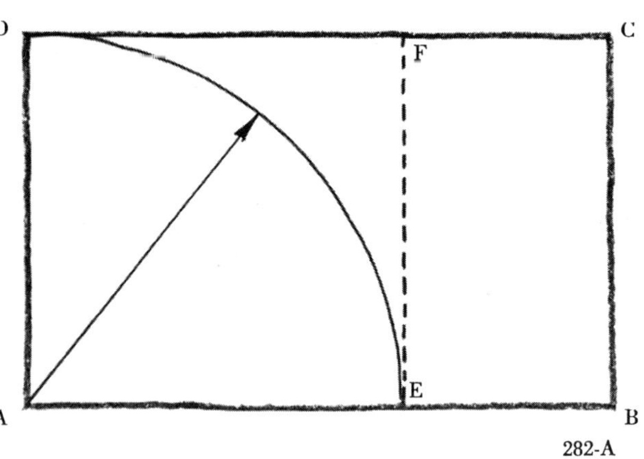




Rembrandt (Dutch, 1606-1669)
THE GOLF PLAYER, 1654; 3¾″ x 5⅝″
etching, second state
Seattle Art Museum
Manson F. Backus Collection


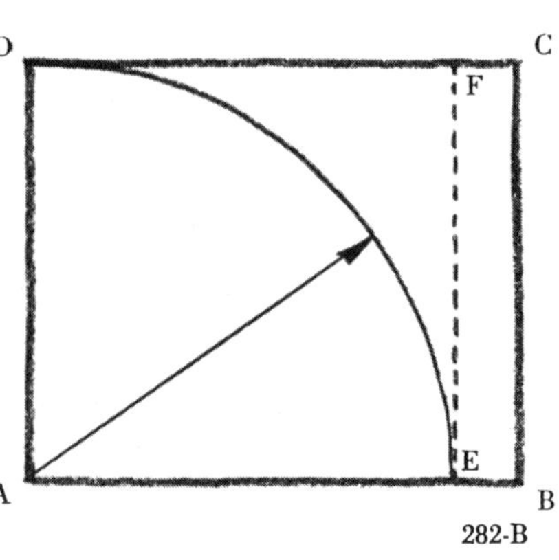



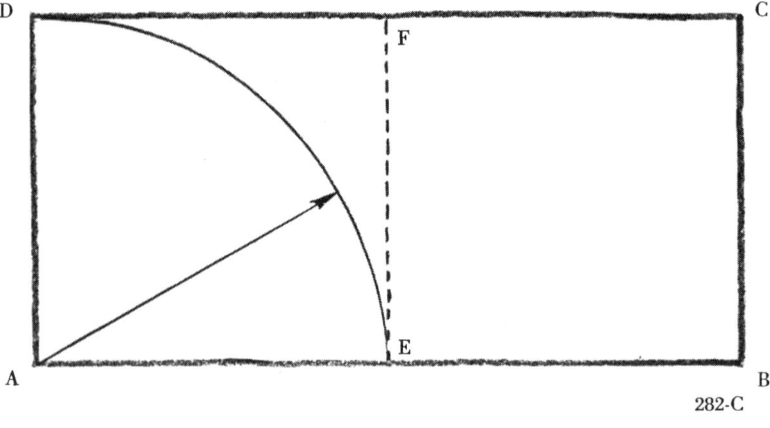



282     An ancient graphic device is to echo the length of a side of a rectangle in its base, or conversely, depending upon which is shorter (*282-A*). In rectangle *ABCD* we find *AD* is shorter than *AB*. Let us lay *AD* upon *AB* by striking an arc from *A* to *E*. *AE* is now equal to *AD*. Now if *EF* is made parallel to *AD* it divides the rectangle into two parts: *AEFD*, a square; *EBCF*, a rectangle.

If now *EB* is made shorter and shorter, *ABCD* approaches a square (*282-B*). In the same way as *EB* becomes longer and longer *ABCD* approaches two squares (*282-C*). As *EBCF* approaches the square, the visual difference between *AEFD* and *EBCF* becomes more difficult to estimate accurately. When we arrive at two squares, *EF* divides *ABCD* into half. As we shall see, dividing a picture in half often results in monotony, yet with special handling such a division may be used.

We see in *282-A* that a division through *EF* generates a simple geometric relation. The resulting rectangles *AEFD* and *EBCF* bear a strong relation to each other, for we are compelled to compare them as related shapes. We also are aware that the two are integral parts of the whole picture shape. And through this division we generate a special new shape, the square.

### The Peripheral Transfer

The device of laying the short side of a rectangle into its long side, thus generating a square, is so commonly employed that it has a name. The French word, *carré*, is used.

This method of arriving at the square, called a *peripheral transfer*, leads naturally into similar transfers generating other squares on

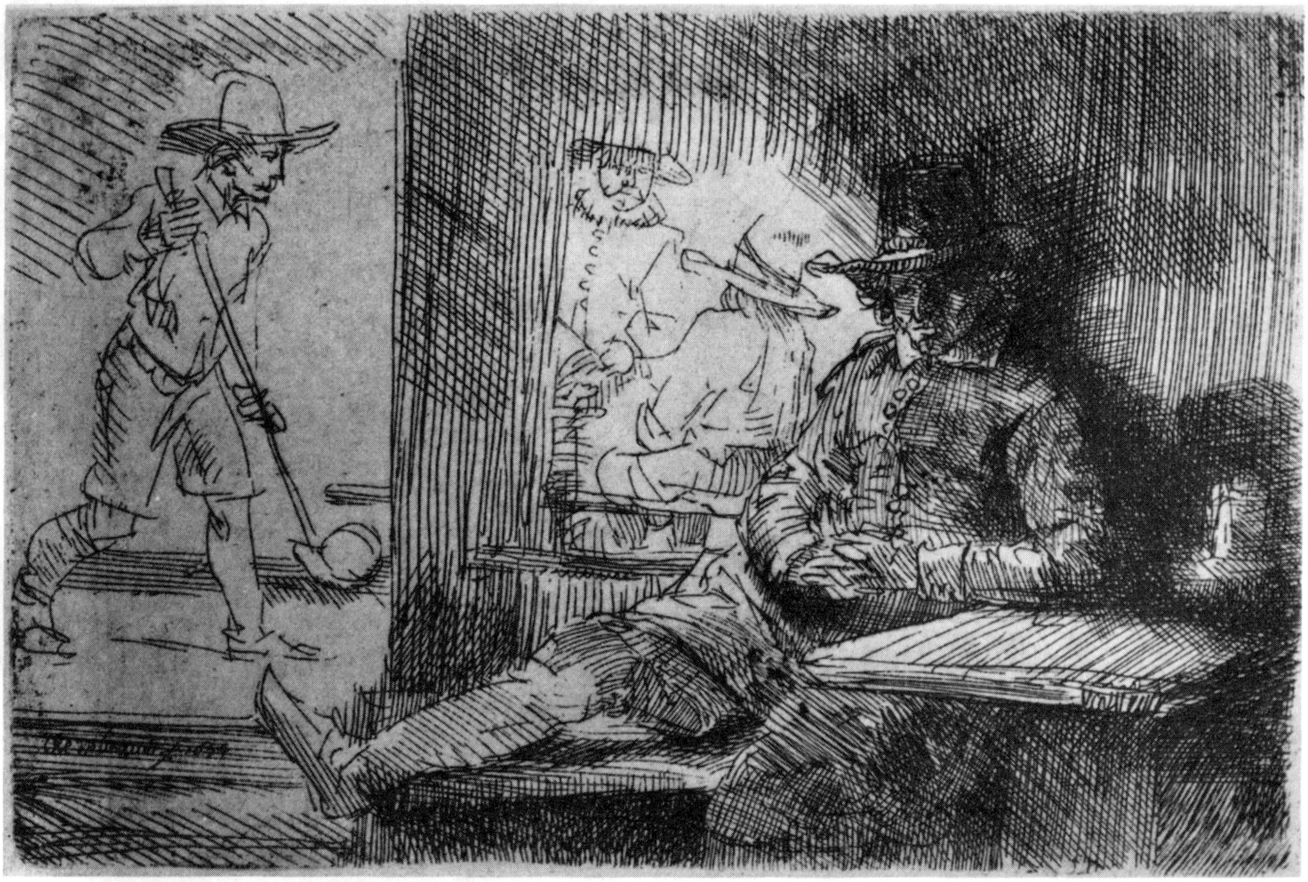

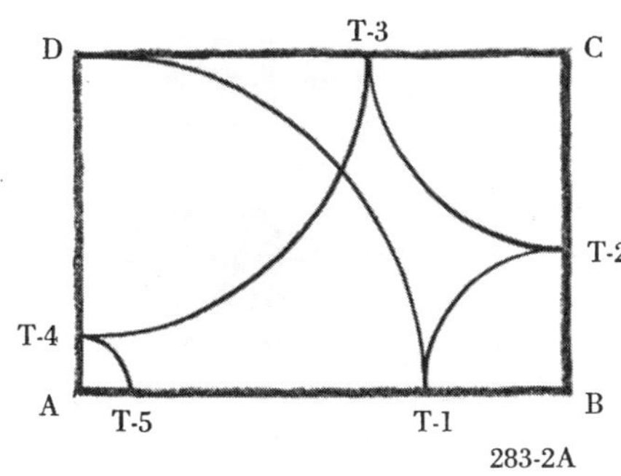
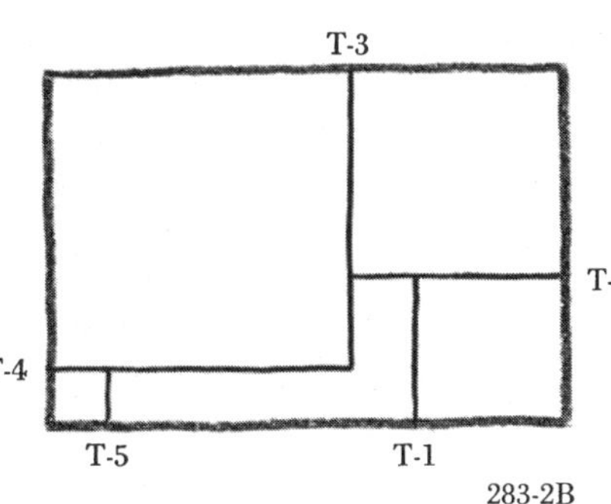
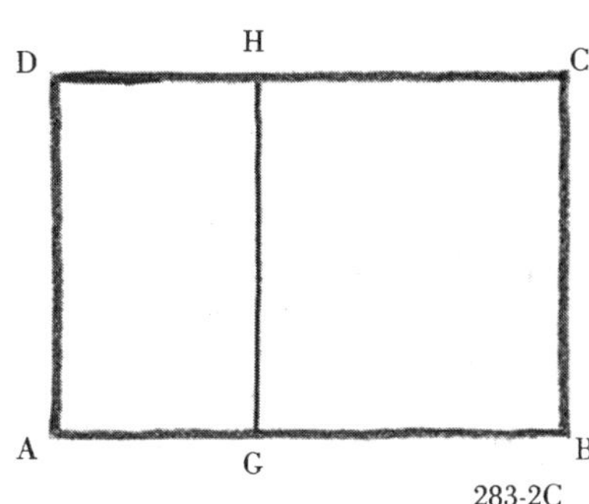

283-2A  283-2B  283-2C



the picture surface. In *283-2A*, *DA* is transferred to *AB*, giving us transfer one, or *T-1*. *T-1* can now be transferred to *T-2*. *T-2* transfers to *T-3*, and so on.

Horizontals and verticals drawn through these transfer points generate a series of squares: *T-1-T-2*, *T-2-T-3*, etc. This method of breaking the picture into a series of squares *(283-2B)* is often called Rembrandt's *whirling square,* for he was partial to its many uses.

## Arbitrary Divisions of the Surface

Returning to our rectangle *ABCD* suppose that we wish to ignore the rotation of *AD* to *AB*, giving us a square, and arbitrarily divide *AB* at *G*, which seems to give a pleasing ratio of *AG* to *GB* *(283-2C)*. Although such a division may result in a satisfactory relation of areas

*AGHD* and *GBCH*, it is not the same as our first division because a square, which is an event, is not generated.

Of course not all pictures lend themselves to the device of the whirling square. Very long rectangular pictures, pictures just off the square, square, round, or irregularly shaped pictures call for other attacks.

For example, if we transfer one side of a square to its base, we reach an impasse. If we desire a vertical division of a square we have several choices: first, we can divide the square into half with the consequent danger of developing a symmetrical picture. Or we can divide the base into thirds, quarters, fifths, etc., and such divisions then can be transferred peripherally.

Velázquez (Spanish, 1599-1660)
THE SURRENDER OF BREDA, ca. 1635
10′ x 12′ approx.; oil
Museo del Prado, Madrid

284   But now a strange thing happens. If we transfer a two-thirds division of the base of the square into its side, and then make a second transfer, we end with a one-third or two-thirds division again (*284-1A*). In the same way a quarter division soon exhausts itself (*284-1B*).

A method practiced by many artists is to arbitrarily divide a side into "what seems right" (*284-1C*). Unfortunately, such divisions although pleasant in themselves, do not transfer well. Often such arbitrary divisions are made throughout the whole picture with little or no attempt to make transfers of any kind. Although occasionally successful, such an attack usually precludes certain harmonic repeats of proportional relations possible with other approaches.

## Cancellations

In any method of dividing the surface, care must be taken to avoid cancellations. Too many transfers almost always result in an equality of divisions which give a static picture. Transferring from left to right, then making similar transfers from right to left is certain to result in such equalities (*284-2A*). A simple rule to follow is to transfer in one direction only, not utilizing too many transfers. Too many proportional relationships often mean no relationships. Structures which tend to nullify each other may be used, however, if one or the other is subordinated (*284-2B*).

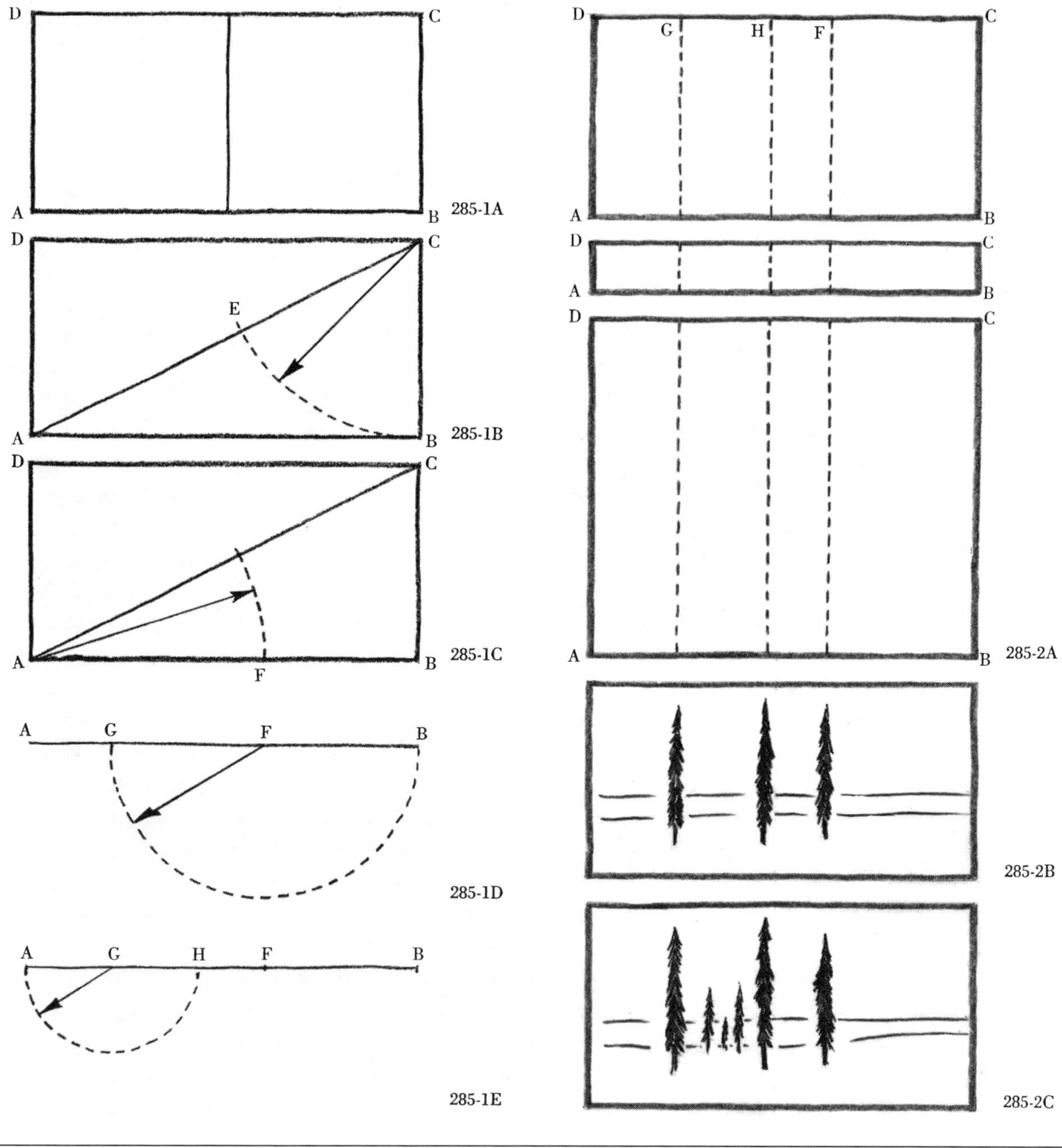


## The Golden Section

The golden section gives us a unique proportional ratio. When the short side of a divided line is transferred into the long side it divides the long side into such a proportional ratio that the remainder, transferred back into the long side again, gives us the same ratio. This transfer may be continued indefinitely within the limits of the drawing tools employed. Such linear divisions usually are translated into areal divisions giving a ratio of shapes, as in Velazquez' painting above.

There are several ways to arrive at this ratio, but one of the simplest is to construct a one-by-two rectangle, or to abut two squares (*285-1A*). Upon the diagonal *AC* transfer *CB*, giving point *E* (*285-1B*). Now from *A* transfer *AE* to the base *AB*, giving *F* (*285-1C*). The proportional relation of *AF* to *FB* is known as the *golden section*.

If now *FB* is transferred into *AF*, giving *G*, *AG* is the same ratio to *AF* as *FB* is to *AF*, or short is to long as short is to long (*285-1D*).

When *AG* is transferred into *GF*, giving *H*, *HF* is the same ratio to *GH* as *AG* is to *GF* (*285-1E*).

The base of a rectangular picture, no matter whether square or very long in relation to its height, may be divided and subdivided in this way, always preserving this constant ratio of short to long or, as this special ratio is called, the *mean* and the *extreme*.

We find that each division is related to the whole, yet no two divisions are alike (*285-2A*). Not only may the whole picture be so divided (*285-2B*), but the divisions in any one area may be continually subdivided (*285-2C*). The golden section is unique, it is the only division of its kind.

Diego Rivera (Mexican, 1886-1957)
TRIUMPH OF THE SOCIAL REVOLUTION
1932; cartoon of mural
National Palace, Mexico, D. F.
Courtesy Sr. Jorge Hernandez Campos
Instituto Nacional de Bellas Artes

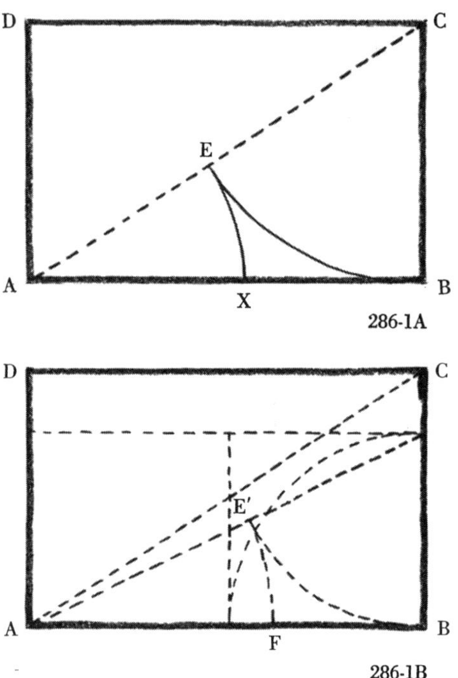

286-1A

286-1B

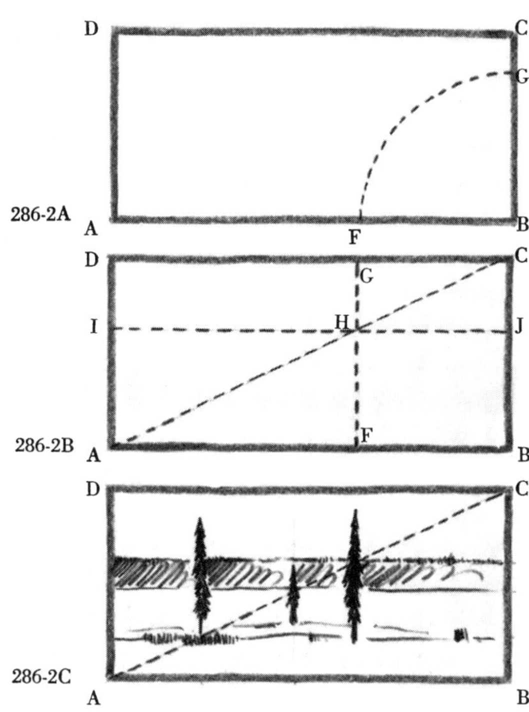

286-2A

286-2B

286-2C

286     It should be noted that the golden section is a special ratio which must be constructed. In *286-1A, BC* is greater than one-half *AB*. By transferring *BC* to the diagonal and then *AE* to the base *AB* we arrive at *X* which is *not* the golden section. To divide *AB* into the mean and extreme ratio, the secondary one-by-two rectangle *ABC'D'* must first be constructed to find *F'*, the true golden section of *AB (286-1B)*.

This procedure at first may seem laborious but after one works with the golden section for a very short time the division can be made visually with as little trouble as dividing a line or area visually in half.

## The Diagonal Transfer

The peripheral transfer is useless when we attempt to transfer the golden section, for if we attempt to transfer the golden section of *AB* to the side *BC*, we get *G*. It is apparent that *G* is not the golden section of *BC* (*286-2A*).

But all is not lost. By first drawing the diagonal *AC* and then raising a vertical through *F* to *G* we intersect *AC* at *H*. A horizontal through *H* gives *IJ*. *J* is now the golden section of *BC* (*286-2B*).

By first transferring any proportional division of *AB*, a half, a quarter, a golden section, to the diagonal by means of a vertical, the proportional division of the base may then be transferred to the side *BC* by using a horizontal. This simple diagonal transfer is used by almost all artists. It, too, soon becomes automatic (*286-2C*).

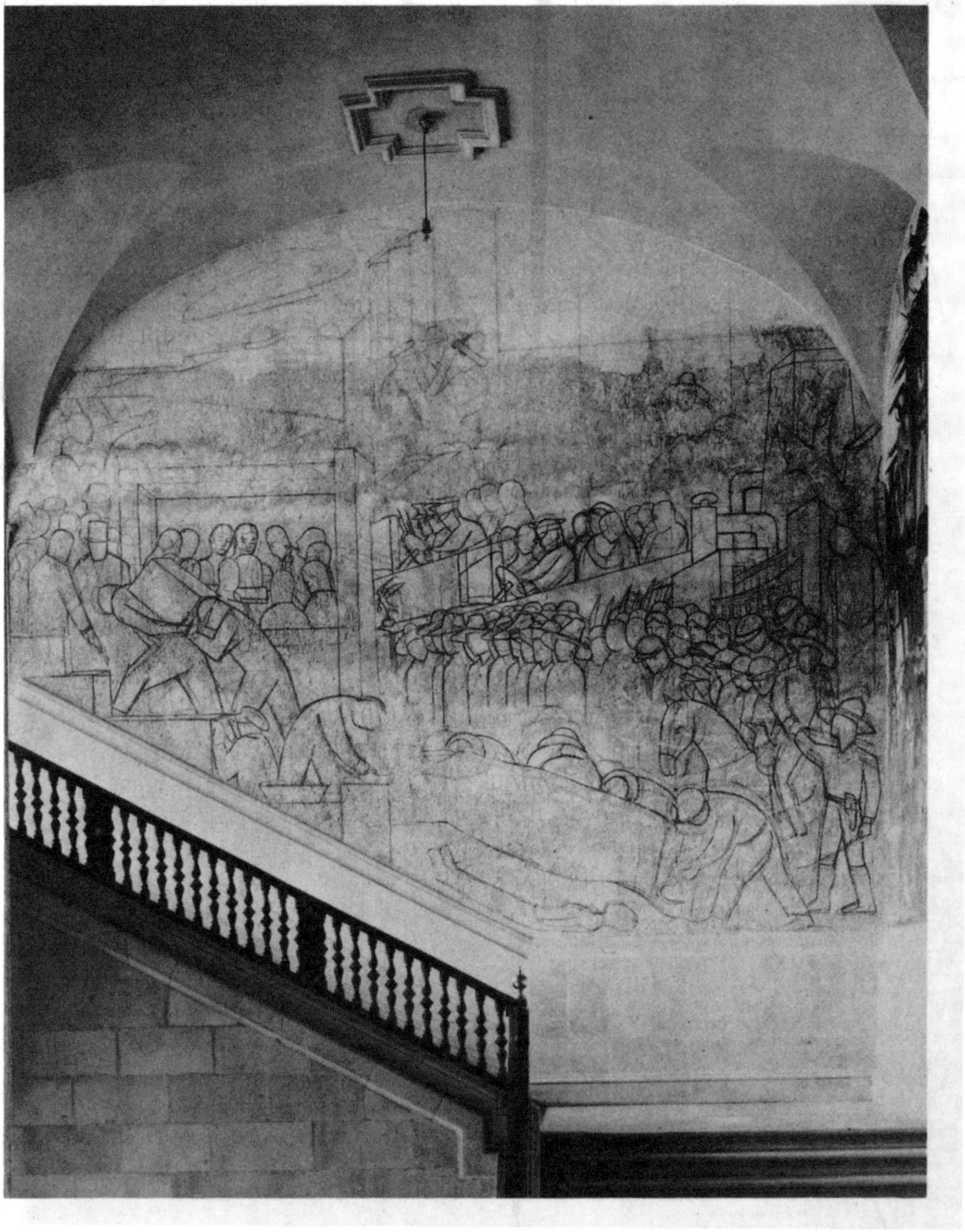

### Linear Ratios

By using either the peripheral or the diagonal
transfer we may continue to divide the whole
picture surface into a series of proportionally
related areas. A method of proportional
divisions based primarily upon the division of
a line was exploited by Diego Rivera.

Like many mural painters he was confronted
with the problem of controlling sizes and
relative positions of picture elements which
often could not be seen simultaneously because
of the huge size or unusual shape of the wall
on which he worked. For instance, in painting
a figure high up in one corner of a wall
perhaps one hundred feet long, it was impossible
for him to compare the figure on which he was
working with a figure low in the opposite corner.
To compound the problem the whole wall
might be so located that at no time could it
be seen in its entirety, as we found in studying
Charlot's mural in Chapter 19.

To help establish a proportional control
Rivera often divided a line on his surface
into what he called "six-ten," or three-fifths,
which is extremely close to the golden section.
Since any length could be so divided, diagonals
as well as verticals and horizontals, a unity of
proportional ratios was thus achieved. Of course
he might have chosen a half division, or a
third division, but the results would have been
too apparent, too obvious. Ratios of height to
width, location of features, proportional break-
up of architectural graphic props all could be
harmoniously related in this way.

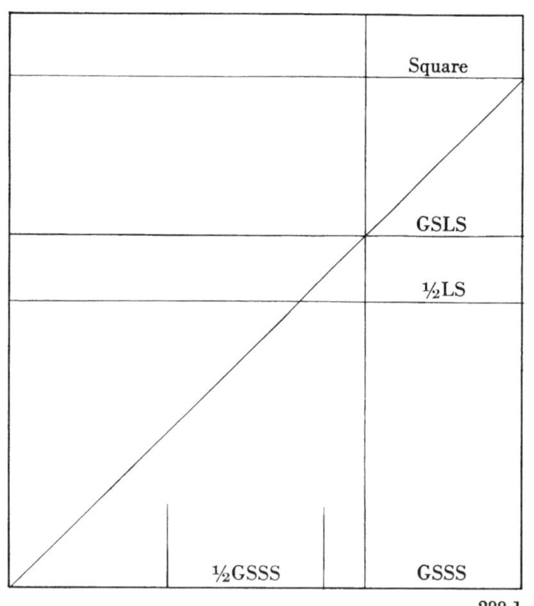


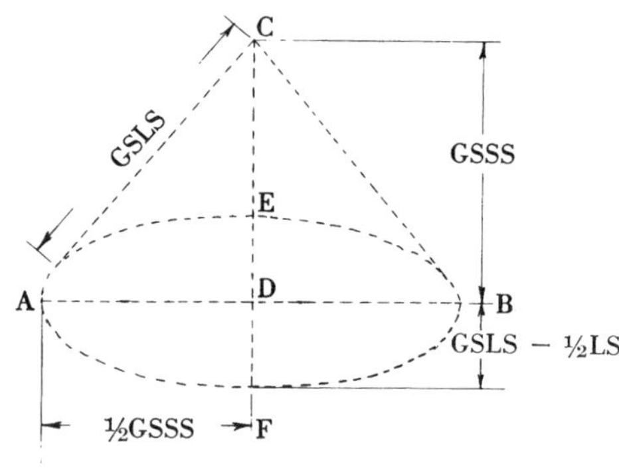


KEY
Square or Carré
Golden Section Long Side—GSLS
Golden Section Short Side—GSSS
½ Golden Section Short Side—½GSSS
½ Long Side                           —½LS
½ Long Side minus
Golden Section Long Side     —½LS − GSLS

288-2

El Greco (Spanish, b. Crete, 1541-1614)
VIEW OF TOLEDO, 1600-1610
47⅝″ x 42¾″; oil on canvas
The Metropolitan Museum of Art
Bequest of Mrs. H. O. Havemeyer, 1929
The H. O. Havemeyer Collection

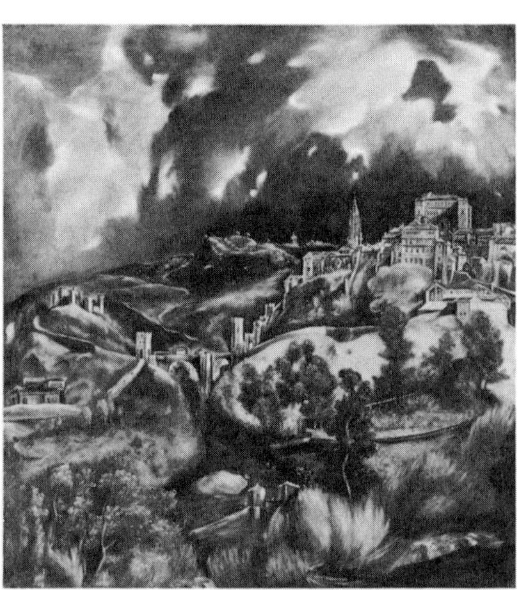

## The Grid

288

The geometric divisions of a picture constitute what is known as a *grid*, a series of lines crisscrossing the picture vertically, horizontally, and often diagonally as well.

When used properly the grid has been of great value to many artists. Much of its success, however, depends on how it is derived and how it is executed in the finished picture. The proportional relations generated in making a grid are intriguing in themselves, yet this is not the problem; the problem is to make an exciting picture. Overconcern with a grid has been a real trap for the young picture maker. Almost always he becomes involved with a grid before he has a clear concept of his picture. Soon he is hopelessly entangled in a maze of mechanical lines and divisions from which a free and rhythmic picture rarely evolves.

Starting a picture by making a grid is like trying to draw or paint in a strait jacket. It is better to have no grid than to start a picture this way. But the grid has intrigued a vast number of great artists, among them El Greco.

## The Moving Format

The moving format offers a dynamic use of a geometric device within a grid. Its intriguing possibilities are demonstrated in El Greco's famous picture, *View of Toledo*. Space does not permit a complete analysis of this picture but the accompanying diagrams should clarify the function of the moving format.

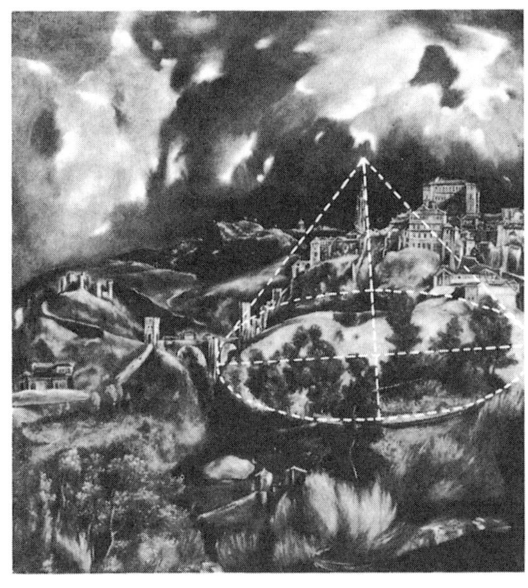

289-A

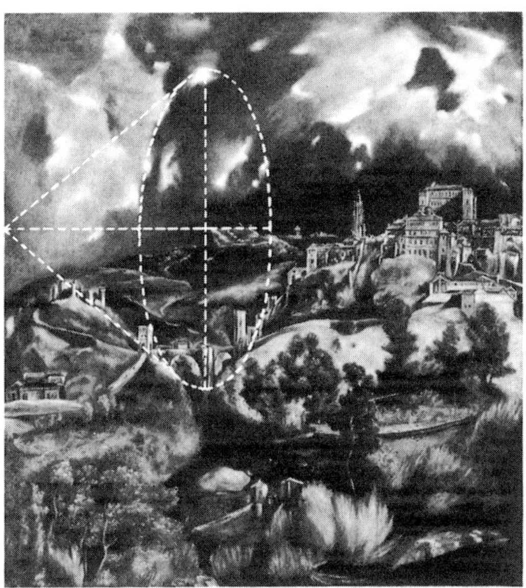

289-B

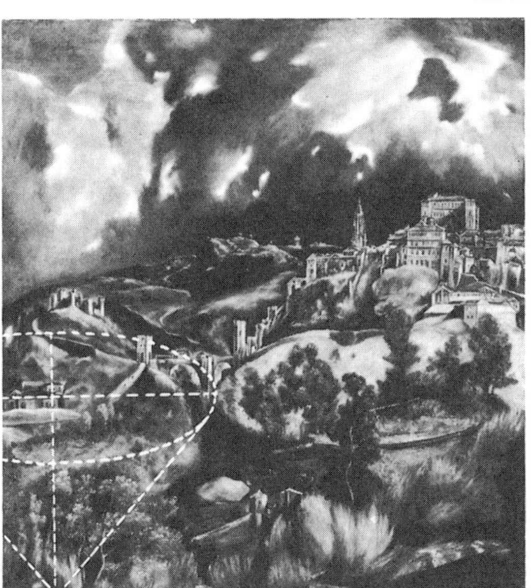

289-C

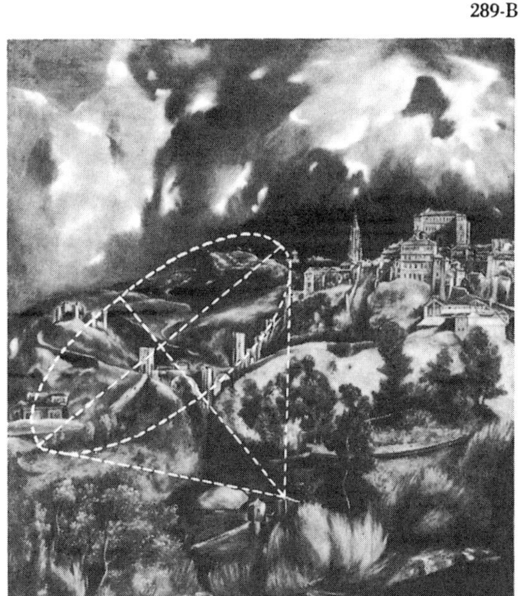

289-D

A grid favoring the carré, the golden section, and half the golden section is the foundation of the geometry *(288-1)*.

A format, or template, cut from cardboard or indicated by the dotted line, is in the form of a geometric cone *(288-2)*. All of its parts are derived from the grid *(288-3)*.

Directly above the cathedral spire in the picture is a bright spot which is the key to the geometry (upper left). By placing *C* of the format on this spot we find that the elipse of the format just matches the elliptical meadow *(289-A)*. Now by rotating our format around *A* (upper right) until in a vertical position, we generate an elliptical picture anchored by the vertical support of the bridge *(289-B)*.

By rotating the format into various positions using *A, B, C,* or *D* as pivot points a constant unfolding of views will expose important features of the picture structure *(289-C, -D )*. A new position of the format that supports a strong picture line or dominant shape will reveal other amazing relations in the picture.

In El Greco's picture structures we find an ingenious melding of the basic shapes of his images with the geometry of his picture. In many of his pictures we are aware of a strange angularity of shape, but angularity of a very special kind. El Greco delighted in the exploitation of the *sheared square*.

El Greco (Spanish, b. Crete, 1541-1614)
THE HOLY FAMILY; ca. 1592-1596
51⅞″ x 39½″; oil on canvas
The Cleveland Museum of Art
Gift of the Friends of The Cleveland Museum of Art
in Memory of J. H. Wade

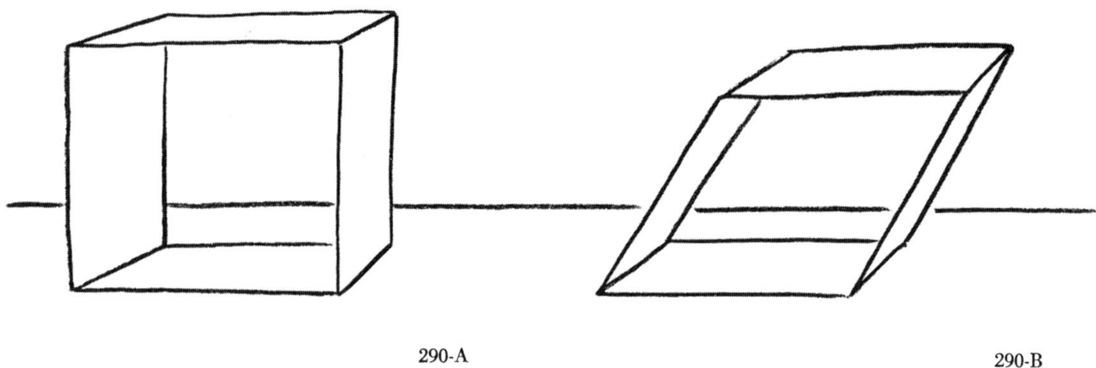

290-A            290-B

290

To visualize this shape, let us imagine a wooden box with both ends removed (*290-A*). If we sit on this box it probably will begin to collapse. Its end, the square, now becomes a parallelogram (*290-B*).

We see that the figure of the Christ Child in El Greco's *Holy Family* roughly defines this shape. In a great number of El Greco's pictures this shape is emphasized not only in the head, body, and hands, but throughout the whole picture.

To achieve unity, many of the principle picture lines are also diagonals, as we see here. By directing a picture line so that it cuts from one border to another, often from a third to a half, a golden section to a quarter, half the golden section to a corner, and so forth, both the sheared square and a strong diagonal pattern are achieved. Were the head shapes predominantly round, this unity would be lost.

**Geometric versus Intuitive Picture Divisions**
The geometry of a picture, whether consciously or subconsciously attained, is always a concern of the artist. No matter how involved his structure may be or how elemental, he works on a surface which must be disturbed. Even if a picture consists of one line or one shape, its placement is always in relation to the whole picture surface and for this reason always involves at least one proportional relationship.

The artist's intuitive sense of rightness may often be as valid as a geometric truth. For this reason picture geometry in its truest sense is a strange mixture of simple mechanical divisions modified by the artist's hunch.

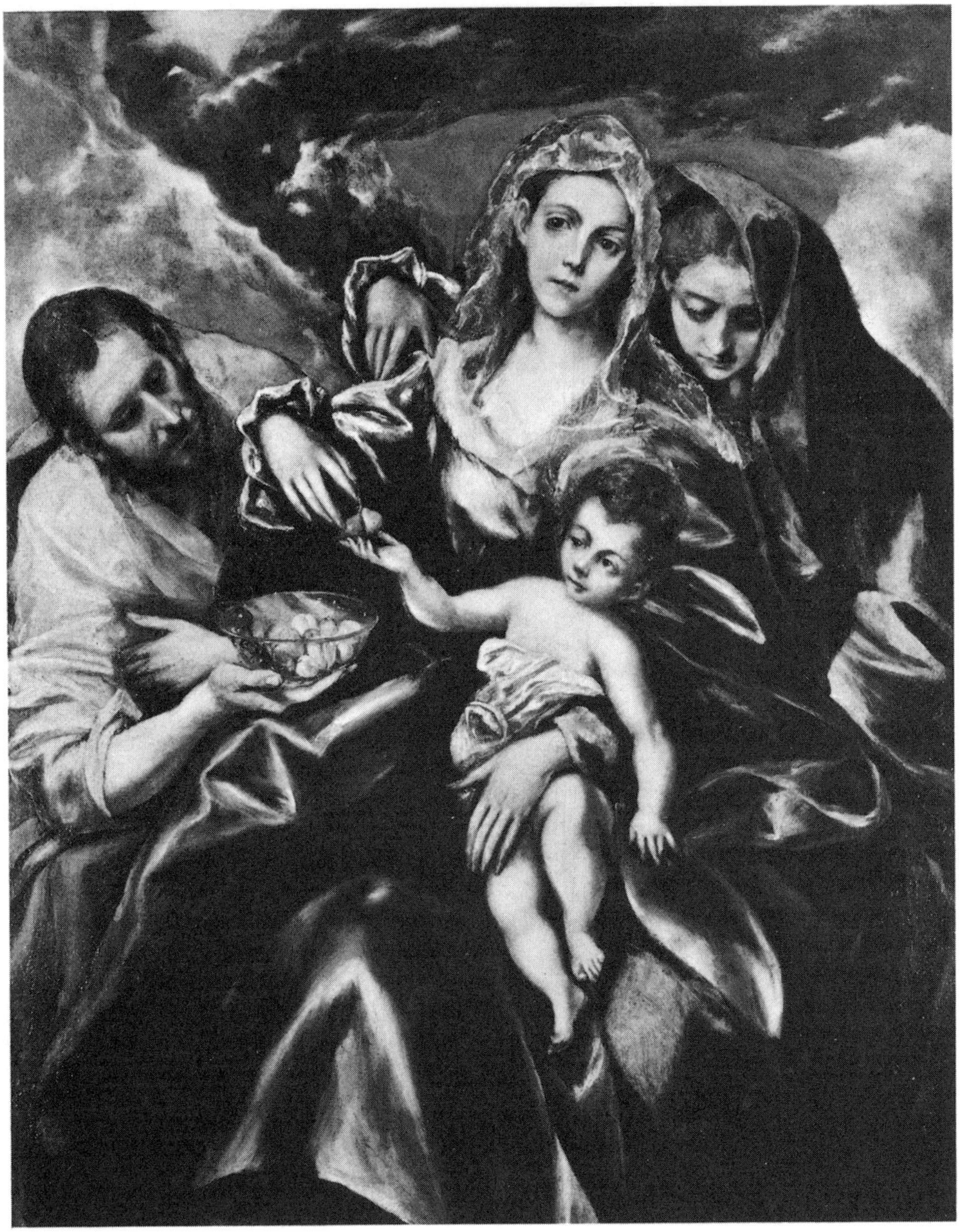

For instance, a rectangle divided vertically exactly in the middle is a mechanical division. But we have noted that the division may not appear equal to the artist, especially if the halves are different colors, so he will shift the true center until the sides appear equal. One center is mechanically correct; the other intuitively or visually correct.

Although the intuitive division may be performed in a non-mechanical way it still is an order, it still is a division, it still results in a simple geometric relation. Picture geometry is the process of measuring and relating lines and angles of surfaces and volumes. Whether this is done mechanically or intuitively makes little difference if an exciting picture is achieved.

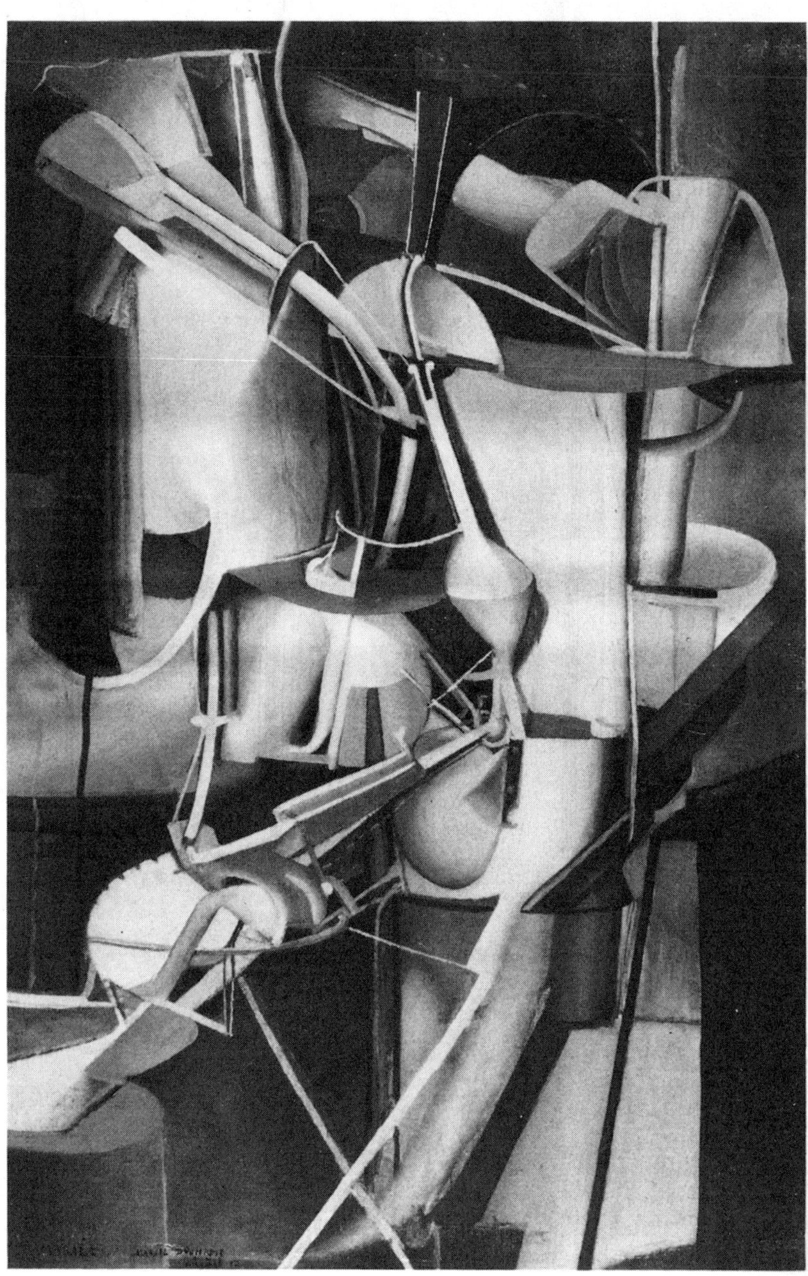

Marcel Duchamp (French, 1887-1968)
THE BRIDE, 1912; 35¼″ x 21¾″
oil on canvas
Philadelphia Museum of Art
The Louise and Walter Arensberg Collection



# 26 Scanning

**Directing the Spectator's Eye**

We use our eyes so often that most of the
time we are unaware of their existence. We
are even less aware of how we see, or how the
eyes may be directed to see in a predetermined
pattern. For instance, in reading these lines
few of us are consciously aware that we are
reading from left to right in horizontal lines,
or that through accepted spacing and punc-
tuation our eyes are forced to follow groups or
clusters of letters. To illustrate: "le tu scha
nget hi so rd er" is somewhat more difficult to
read and understand than "let us change this
order."

# VII DIRECTING
# THE EYE

Now the artist is faced with an even more difficult problem than the writer. The spectator has not been trained to read a picture the way he has been trained to read a book. So the artist must find graphic controls so strong they will force most of his audience to see the elements of his picture in the order he has planned.

The next few chapters are devoted to investigating how the eye sees, how it reads a picture, and how a competent artist, Duchamp, for example, attempts to direct the eye of the spectator by graphic devices.

## Movement of the Eye in Viewing Nature

First let us try to understand a little more about how our eye sees things around us in nature. If we walk down the street and pass a large brick wall, we say to ourselves, "It's a brick wall, I know it is for I have seen it." But have we seen it? Or, more pertinent, how have we seen it? A parallel is often noted between the way the eye and the still camera record. If we take a clear photograph of the wall we have a record, but this may not necessarily be a record of what our eyes have seen of the wall.

The still camera records with equal emphasis every brick, every line of mortar. Yet as we look at the wall we are able to see clearly only a few bricks, only a small portion of the wall at a time.

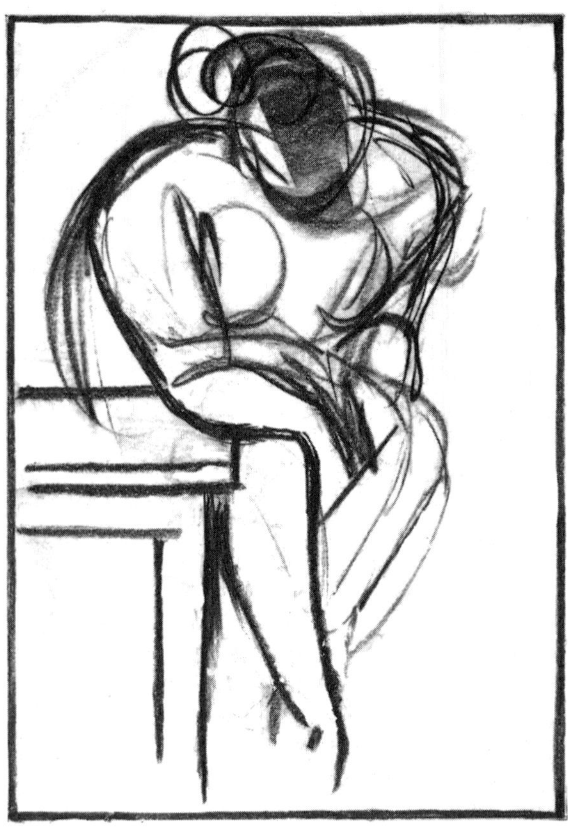

294

294     Suppose, now, we substitute for a still camera, a motion picture camera. As this camera scans the wall, moving up, down, across, it makes an unfolding record of different aspects of the wall. This is more nearly the way our eyes scan the wall. For the eye records not only things it focuses on at any instant in time, but also, like the motion picture camera, it records a constantly evolving continuity of visual events in time.

The eye records a pattern of individual impressions which we are able to remember, thanks to our computer-like brain. It is the memory of these related visual impressions that makes comprehension through vision.

Both the eye and the motion picture camera record things either stationary or in motion. Both are subject to motion themselves. Both record a continuing occurrence in time. This time factor makes it possible for the artist to determine the order in which he desires the spectator to scan the various parts of his still picture.

In one sense the eye has a flexibility of focus even greater than that of the motion picture camera. It can particularize with great ease. When we look at a person partially overlapped by some form, a table for instance, we usually grasp first an overall impression of the whole—the figure seated at the table. Next, we recognize separate forms or parts of forms, a foot, a head, the table, etc. We may also see

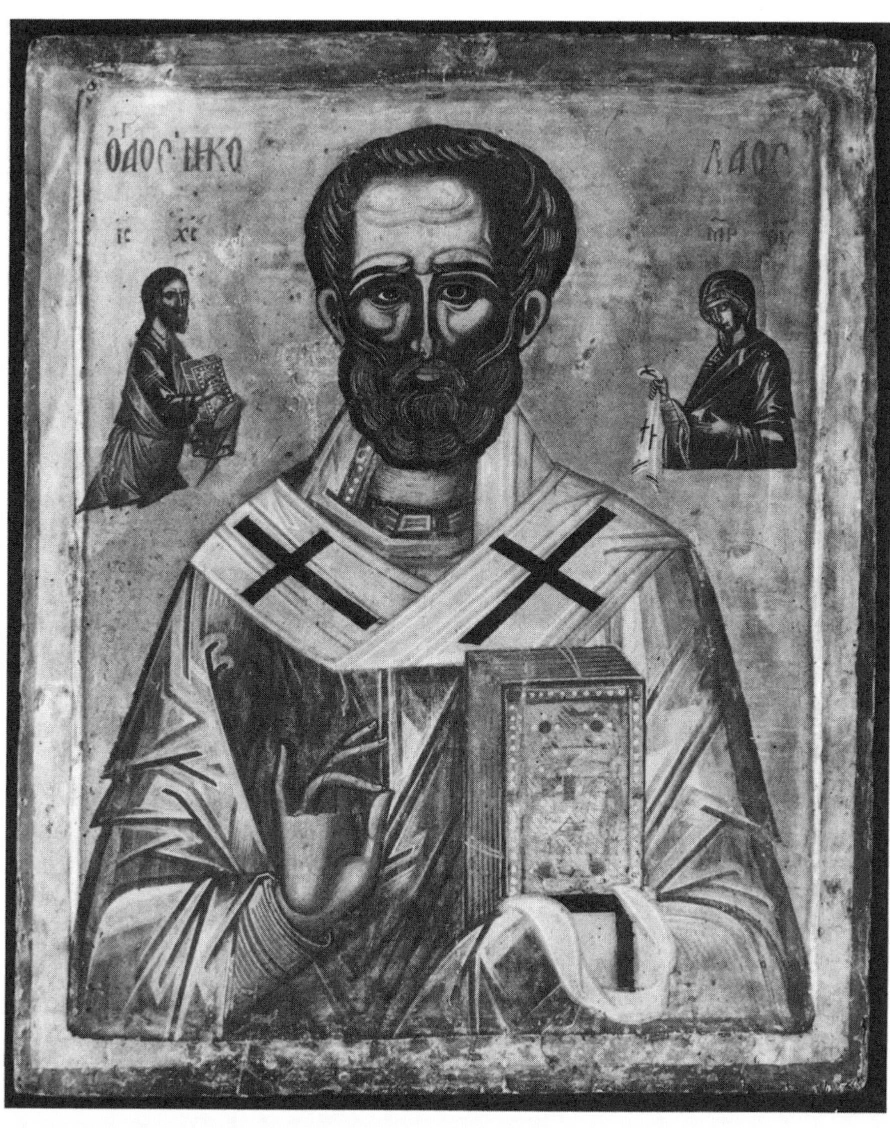

Artist unknown (Greek)
ICON: SAINT NICHOLAS, 17th century; 27½" x 22"
polychrome and gold leaf on gesso panel
Seattle Art Museum; gift of Ernest N. Patty
in memory of his wife, Kathryn Stanton Patty

clusters of forms such as clasped hands or folded arms as large units. Normally we do not scan along the edges of forms in nature. Yet this is possible. We can force our eye to follow an edge from foot to knee, to table, to right arm to head (*294*). But it is indeed a strange and awkward way to view our world.

Of course we may draw a three-dimensional form in nature as a continuous linear silhouette. But the line used is seldom an exact projection of the observed silhouette in nature. Adjustments must be made to diminish an overemphasis on flatness, if a volume is desired.

In like manner, if a shallow space picture is required, similar to this icon or a Japanese print, the continuous silhouette must be carefully designed to accommodate the highly styled shapes which make such pictures successful.

Although our eye usually sees forms in nature as three-dimensional units, it often tends to scan the configurations or edges of a flat shape, either in nature or in a drawing. In fact, our ability to follow the contour of a shape seems part of our ability to recognize its flatness. Our inability to break down the shape into overlapping or protruding parts also makes us sense its flatness. Further, if we are unable to sense indentations or piercings of the shape, we feel its flatness even more strongly.

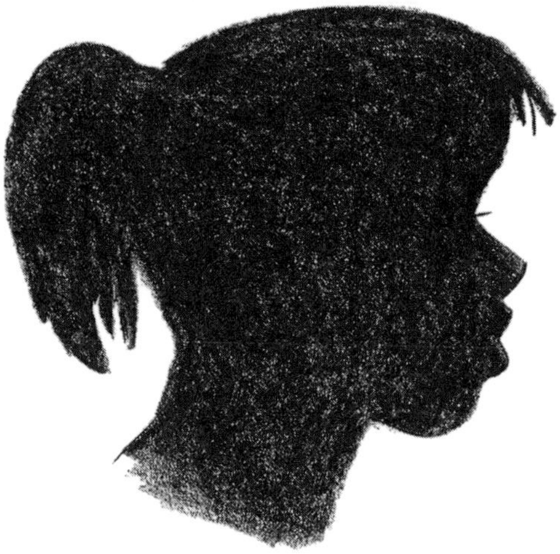

296-1

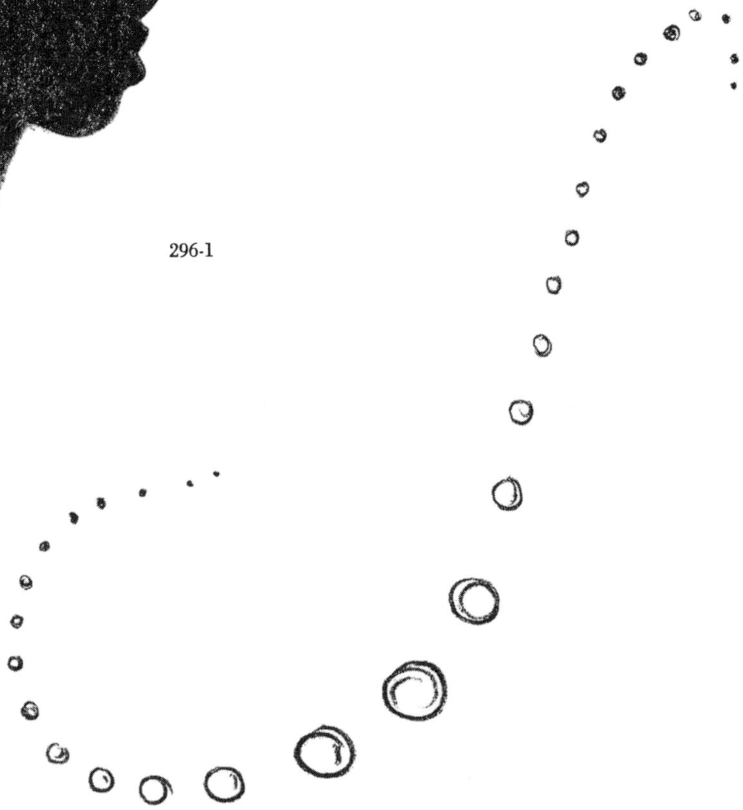

296-2

Of course, there are exceptions. A flat black silhouette may seem three-dimensional through association (*296-1*). Internal structures, however, are still difficult to visualize and parts of the shape usually will remain flat visually.

Now if the eye normally does not scan the edge of a three-dimensional form in nature yet does scan the edge of a flat shape, how does it scan a three-dimensional graphic image on the flat surface of a picture? This question has always puzzled artists. One concept, which may or may not be valid scientifically, has proved of great help to many artists since the inception of drawing. This is the control of the movement of the eye through space patterns generated graphically in the picture.

## Space Patterns in Nature

To explore this concept let us visualize our eye as a house-fly. Of course we all know that our real eyes are firmly encased in our heads. We can follow the flight of a fly in the room, but only from our relatively fixed station point. But by accepting a Copernican attitude we can pretend that we are actually watching our own eye as it flies around in space. Our eye becomes the fly continually moving in space. Now let us pretend that we see what the fly sees as it zooms around real space in nature.

In diagram *296-2* the fly is represented by a small graphic symbol, a dot. Its change of position is shown by the series of such symbols, its nearness or distance from us by change in size, the further away, the smaller the dot.

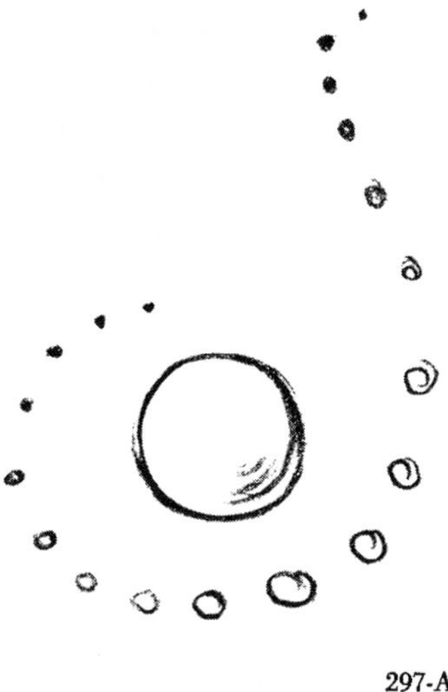

297-A

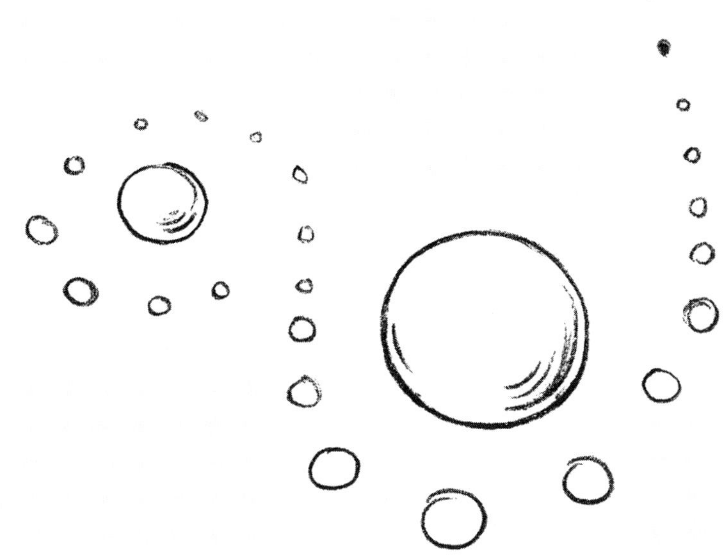

297-B

Suppose, now, that we try to visualize what the fly would see as it scans one or more forms in nature. As it flies toward us it may notice a form in space, a sphere. To get a better view it changes its flight pattern and begins to circle the sphere. Its path describes a circle. Unfortunately, unless it is distracted, it may continue this course indefinitely. Its flight pattern becomes repetitious and dull (*297-A*).

As the fly sweeps around the sphere it may become aware of a second form to its left, another sphere (*297-B*). The fly is undecided now whether to continue around the first sphere or to reverse its flight pattern and swing around the second form to examine it more closely. It decides to look at the second sphere. Then, just as it is becoming satisfied by this second form, its attention is again captured by the first. It reverses once more and flies over to take another look at the first sphere. In so doing, it becomes trapped in a fixed pattern, a reverse loop or a figure-eight. Though not as repetitious or dull as the circular action around one point, the flight pattern still is monotonous.

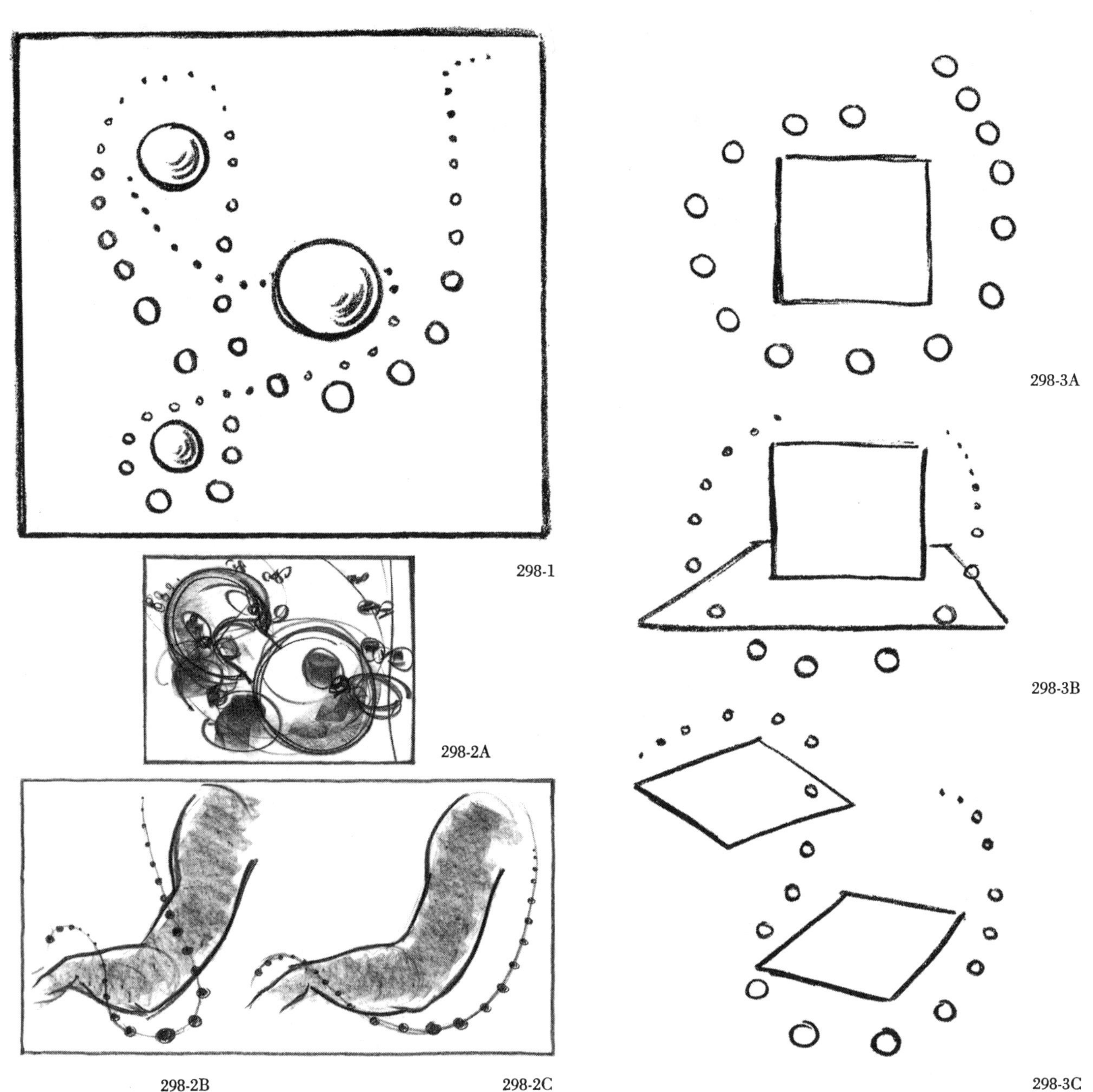

298-1

298-2A

298-2B    298-2C

298-3A

298-3B

298-3C



If a third element is added, a third sphere for instance, the fly's attention is diverted from the second form to this new form (*298-1*). Instead of returning to the first sphere, the fly now begins to examine the new form. Suddenly a magical effect is produced. We now see the fly reversing and changing direction in a series of new and varying loops. Interest is not only captured, but sustained. There is no longer monotony, but variety. If more forms are introduced, this variety is enhanced. This within reason, of course, for introducing too many forms may lead the fly into an erratic instead of an orderly flight pattern.

We notice that if any two forms in nature are connected, like the knobs of a dumbbell, the fly's flight pattern often tends to reverse on this connection (*298-2A*). An arm, for instance, may be seen as a series of forms each serving as individual cores (*298-2B*), but it also may serve as a large unit around which the fly can move (*298-2C*).

We have observed the fly in action around sculptural forms in nature. But sometimes the fly encounters very flat shapes. If its flight is parallel to us, this implies that the shapes, too, must be parallel to us (*298-3A*). But the fly can also describe a spiral path if the flat shape is at an angle to us, or if the flat shape is parallel to us but in deep space (*298-3B*).

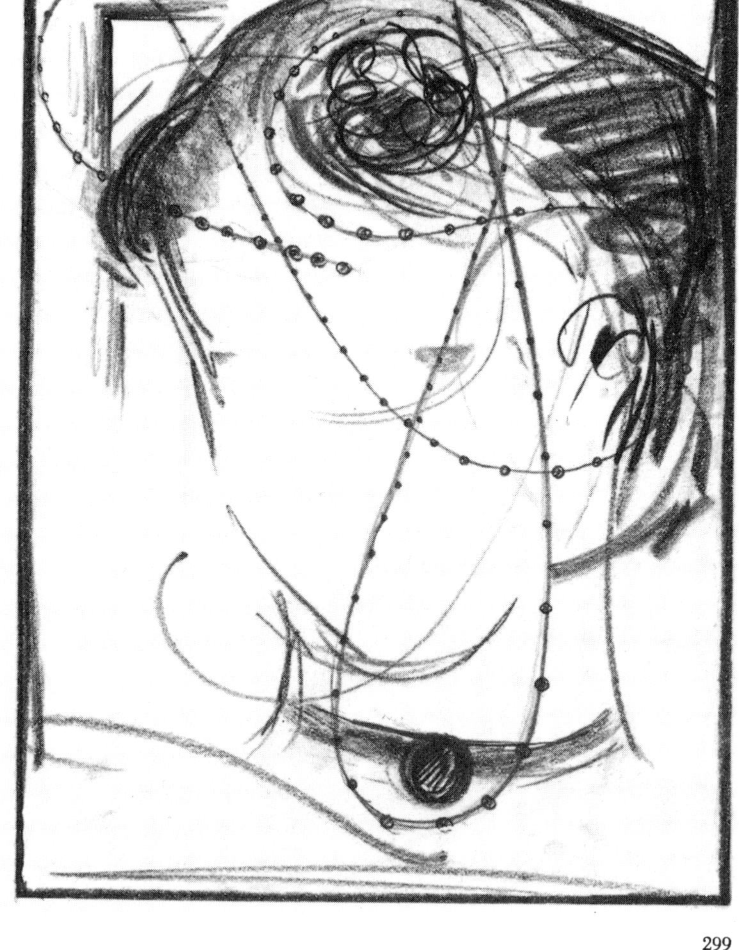



If the fly generates a spiral while scanning two or more flat shapes, it implies that the shapes are in deep space in nature. The fly must reverse its course as it moves between them, and so the flight pattern is similar to that between two forms (*298-3C*).

**Movement of the Eye in a Drawing**
Now for all practical purposes the flight pattern of the fly in nature is characteristic of the movement of our eye in viewing a picture. We need but to substitute graphic space for actual space and the parallel is complete. Of course there are certain limitations since graphic space is a picture of actual or imaginary space.

In a drawing, not only shapes and volumes but any part of a shape or volume usually may act as a pivot around which our graphic eye may move in graphic space. The pivot may be a strong contrast of color, a strong light-dark accent, or a concentration of lines, points, etc. As an accent, the pivot may lose its identity as a volume or shape yet still function as a point of interest which can be scanned, and around which the eye reverses its direction. Such interest points are often referred to as tension points. Thus the whole head, the corner of the rectangular shape, the flower in the hair, the brooch are all tension points (*299*). Such points, when emphasized and exploited, define space through which our eye moves in a picture.

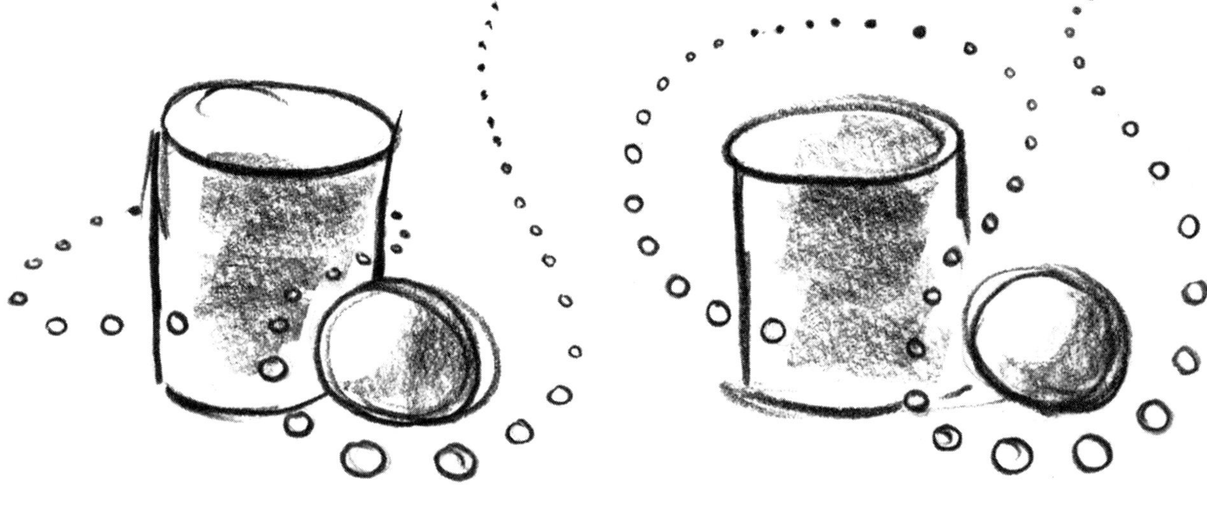

300-A                                                    300-B



300    Now we come to another enigma of drawing. If the eye constantly travels through graphic space, does it or can it actually circle in back of a volume in a picture?

To find an answer, let us once again compare our eye to the house-fly. The real fly has no difficulty in circling back of a real form and emerging on the other side (*300-A*). For an instant it may be lost from view, but it is a real fly, moving in real space. But now the parallel to the fly as our graphic eye in a picture breaks down. When a volume interrupts its flight pattern in a picture, instead of "going behind" the volume our graphic eye flits to some other tension point in the picture. Thus control of its flight pattern is lost. The difference between the flight of the real fly emphasizes the difference between space in nature and the illusion of space in a picture.

Fortunately there is a way to keep the eye circling and looping around in a picture, never becoming lost, always in graphic space, yet never out of control (*300-B*). This introduces a special interpretation of graphic space—the space trough.

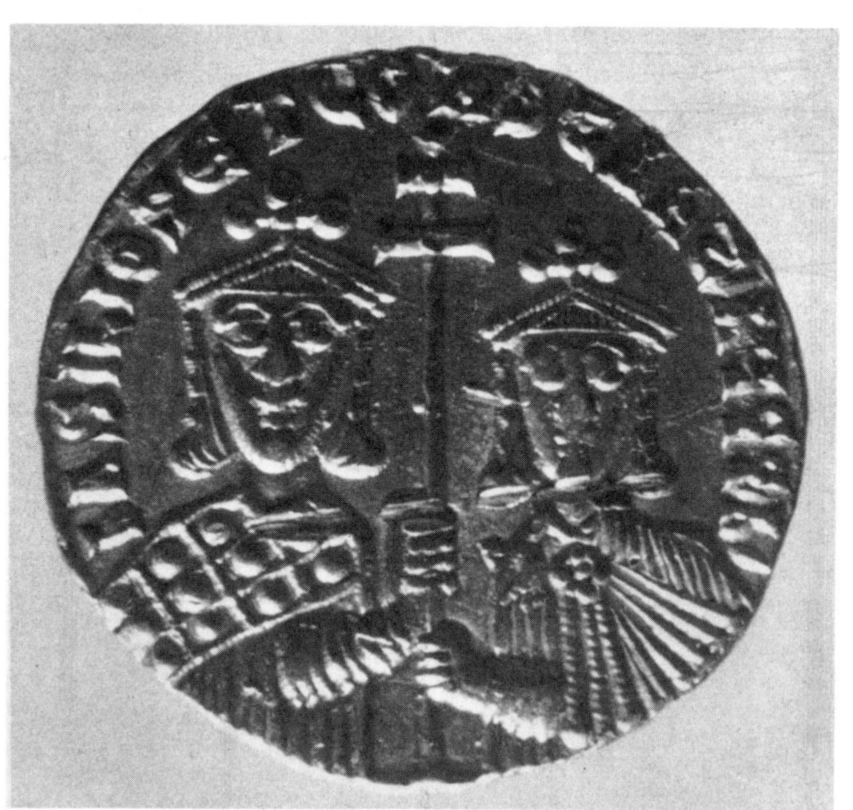

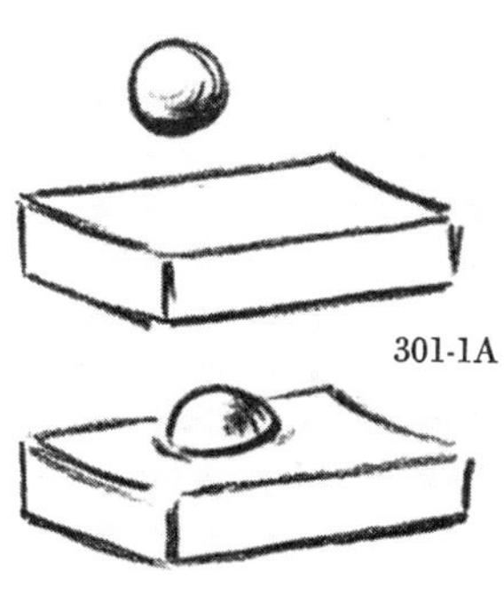

301-1A

301-1B

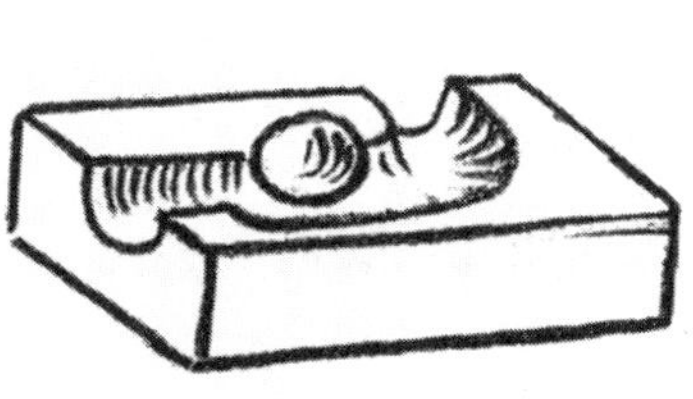

301-1C

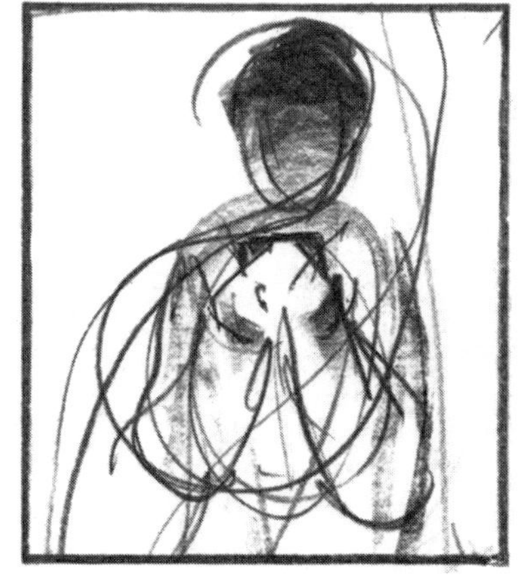

301-3

## The Space Trough

To investigate this interpretation, suppose we visualize the picture not as a fully three-dimensional representation, but as a bas-relief. If we can imagine a sphere and a slab of clay *(301-1A)* with the sphere pushed into the clay *(301-1B)*, and then a trough dug around the sphere *(301-1C)*, we discover a new way of visualizing picture space. Our eye now moves through the space-trough and around or over the sphere, but does not go behind it.

As another illustration, if we place the point of a pencil in the area adjacent to the head on a coin such as we see here, the point of the pencil is in a shallow space-trough. We can move the point all around the head, in front of it, and even through the head in shallow places. The point of the pencil is always in the trough, it never travels *back* of the head, yet the image on the coin still seems spacious.

Each artist must determine for himself the depth of the space-trough he desires in his picture. It is another graphic puzzle. The trough is deep, and yet it isn't. It is in space and yet on the picture surface. We can visualize our eye moving from deep in the picture to a point very close to us, and yet it still is in a trough which encircles, which crisscrosses, which loops around and in front of the volumes *(301-3)*. The space-trough is one of the mysteries of drawing. Though not easily seen, it is easily managed once it is understood, and it becomes a valuable means of controlling the eye.

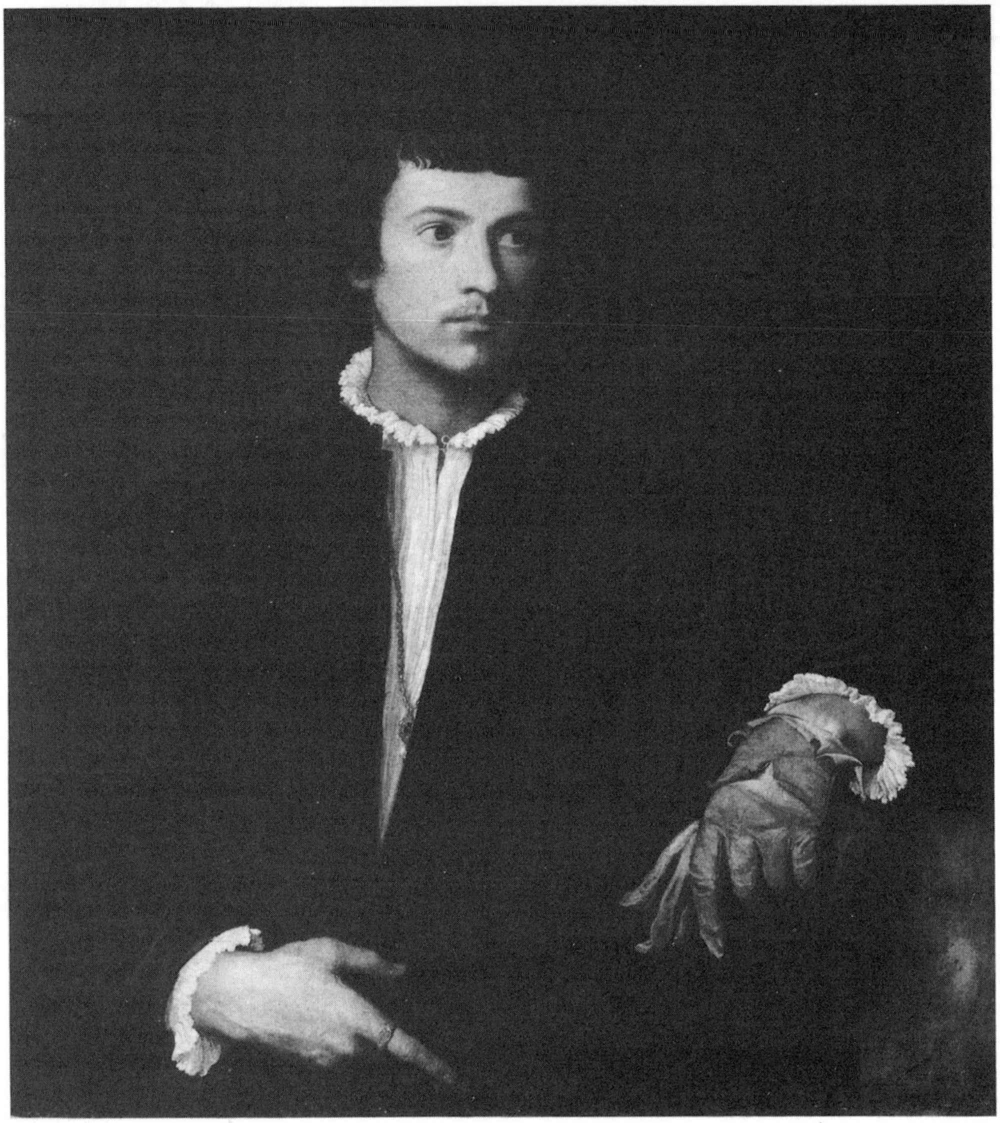

Titian (Italian, ca. 1477-1576)
THE MAN WITH THE GLOVE, 1510-1520
39⅓″ x 35″; oil on canvas
The Louvre, Paris



## The Graphic Environment

As the eye sweeps through the trough between two volumes, its path is affected by the distance separating them. The eye always follows the path of least resistance. If the space-trough is too narrow, or too tortuous, the eye will seek simpler paths through which to glide. If a strong tension exists between two volumes and no congestion exists, the eye will move smoothly through the trough generated. But if we increase the space between volumes, the tension between them decreases and the movement of the eye becomes more difficult to predict. As the tension between volumes continues to decrease, our sense of space becomes less intense until finally it may almost cease to exist.

Theoretically, as the volumes become more and more remote from each other we will be able to concentrate on only one, which we will see as a separate and independent unit. Actually the unit is never alone. It is in an environment, a space; it has a foreground and a background, no matter how vaguely defined. It is this environment, this space which allows our eye to scan a picture.

## The Time Factor in a Still Picture

Now we come to a marvelous factor in picture structure, the introduction of a true time factor in a still picture.

If we study the flight pattern of the fly in nature as it moves in spiral flight, we see that a variable time factor is present. When far away or climbing, the fly seems to move more slowly than when close to us or diving around a form. The actual speed, whether far or near, can be a constant. But in perspective in the

spiral flight of the fly, there will always be an apparent change of speed. In the same way a natural rythmic flow is generated by the movement of the eye through the picture.

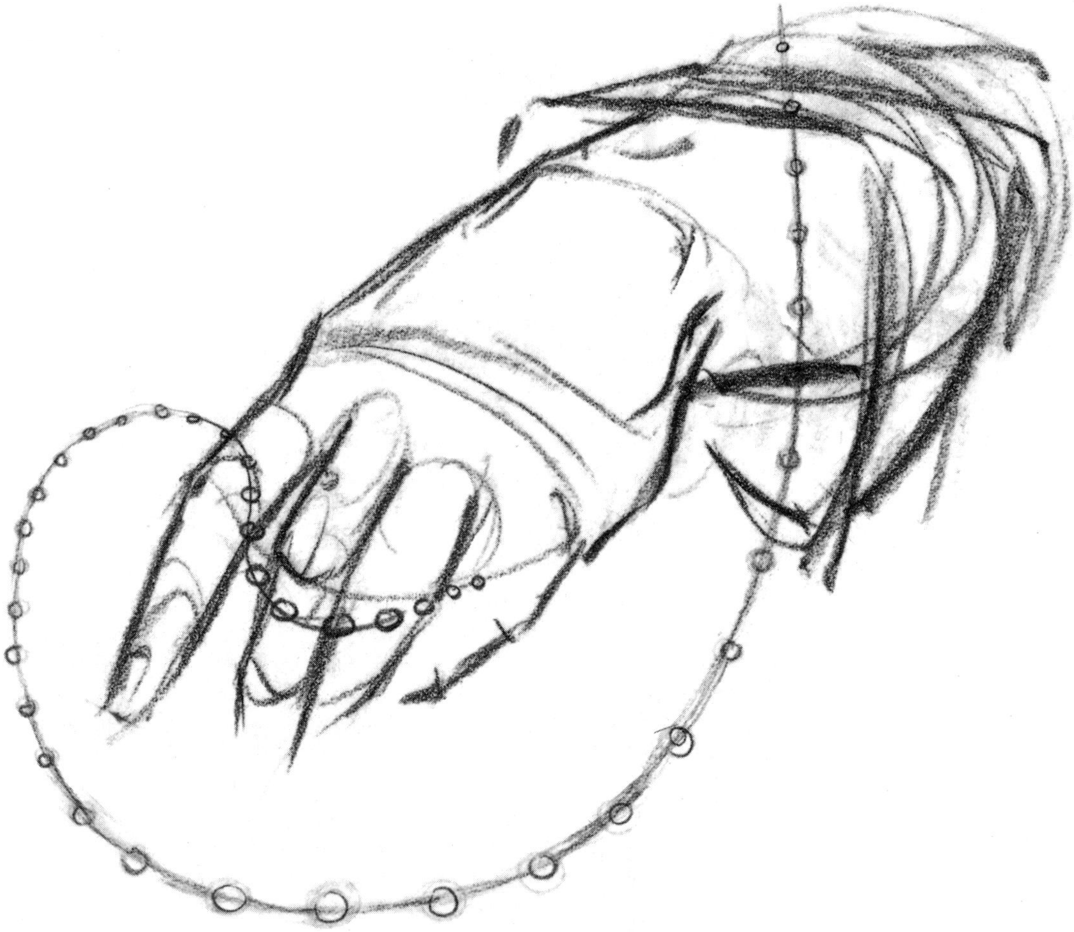

If the eye is moving rapidly downward, it will increase speed as the pulling effect of the bottom border is felt. The mysterious attraction of the borders to the volumes in a picture directly modifies the speed and direction of the eye as it moves through the picture, as we note in Titian's painting above.

In first scanning the large elements in nature or a picture, the eye's movement is usually rather rapid. Later as this scanning slows down, all the elements, even small ones, are eventually examined. Thus the eye first may see the hand as a unit, a cluster of parts; later, in secondary loops, it will glide around each part of the hand to examine it in detail (*303*).

As a rule we find that the eye travels rapidly through large, clear space-troughs. It moves more rapidly downward in a clear trough than upward in a similar trough, as it approaches the top border. In the same way, in order to examine details, the eye must be moving slowly but still in a minor trough. Generally speaking, the eye moves more rapidly around a whole cluster. The more active the cluster, the clearer the trough must be.

When we understand this change of speed in scanning, we begin to see the possibilities of creating rhythmic patterns of eye movement in a picture.

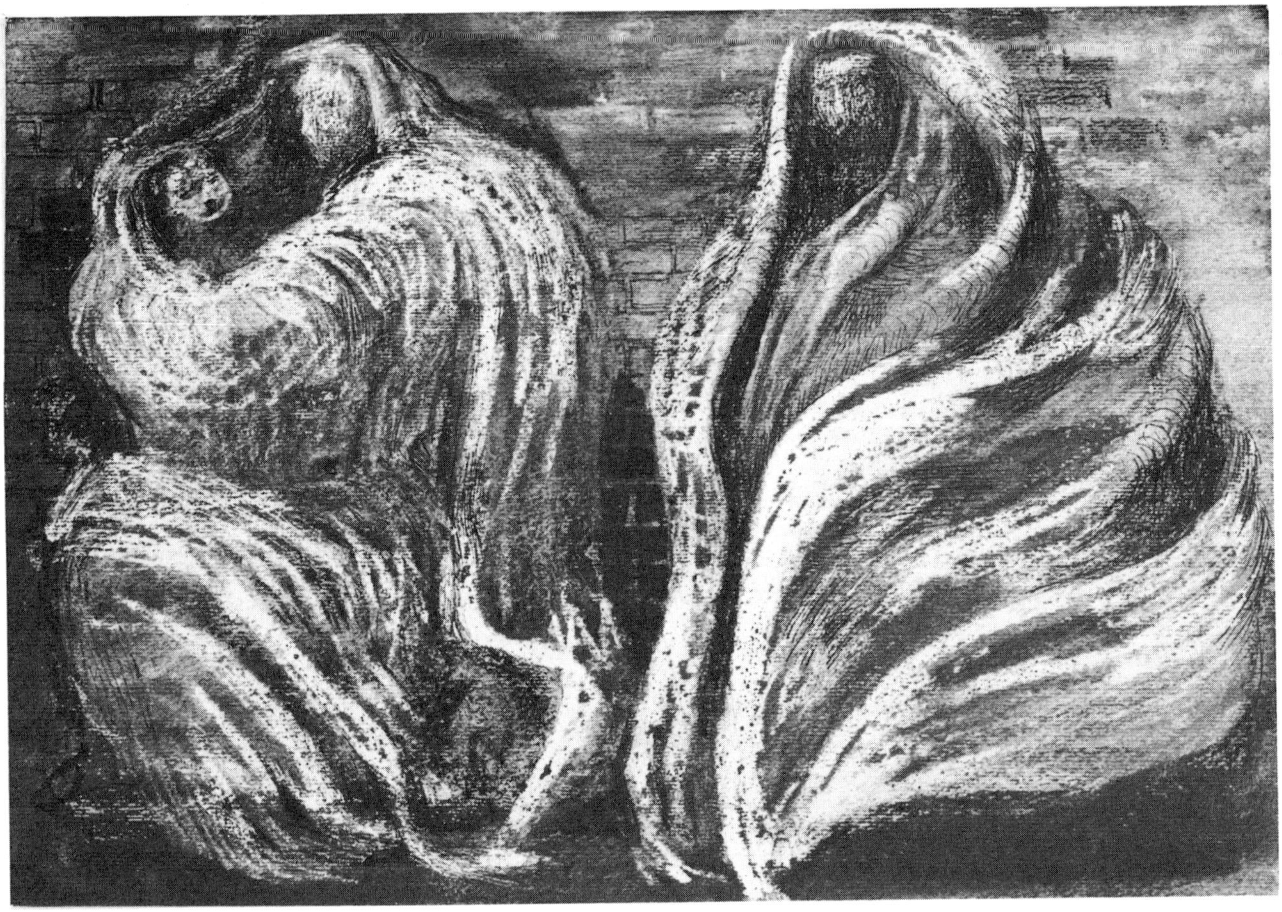

Henry Moore (English, 1898-  )
TWO SWATHED FIGURES, 1941; 15″ x 11′
chalk, pen, and watercolor
Courtesy City of Manchester Art Galleries



## 27 Centers of Interest

**Capturing the Spectator's Eye**

Speaking of flies and eyes, a long time ago
Mary Howitt put it rather well:

> "Will you walk into my parlor?" said
>     the spider to the fly;
> "Tis the prettiest little parlour
>     that ever you did spy."

Here in metaphorical terms is an important
problem confronting the artist. How is he
to lure a passerby, a spectator, often an
antagonistic spectator, into looking at all
the wonders of his picture when he, the artist,
is not there to explain? For it is one thing to
make a picture; it is another to capture the
attention of a spectator and to hold his interest.

### Recognition

As we noted in Chapter 1, if we are able to see the whole picture at a glance, no matter what its shape or size, we first become aware of its general nature. We quickly place the picture image into certain categories or families: a portrait, a landscape, a seascape, a still-life. It may be abstract, like Henry Moore's *Two Swathed Figures,* or non-representational. It may fall into special categories of cartoon or caricature, or a school of contemporary art. In any case, first we become aware of the nature of the picture before we respond to its specific content.

### Examination

Now that we recognize the type of picture, we begin to see it as a graphic organization. We are attracted to certain parts of the picture more strongly than to other parts. Only later do we examine secondary details. Then, if we are sufficiently interested, eventually we will try to comprehend any significant disturbance on the picture surface.

What we see first is determined by the way in which the artist controls our eye. Such an event doesn't just happen; it must be planned. The artist, like the spider, must lure our eye into the picture and then hold it there. This path followed by our eye in first looking into the picture is called the *entry.*

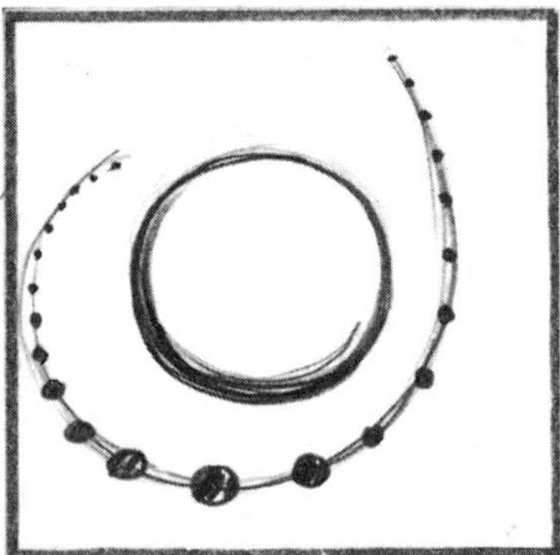

306-A

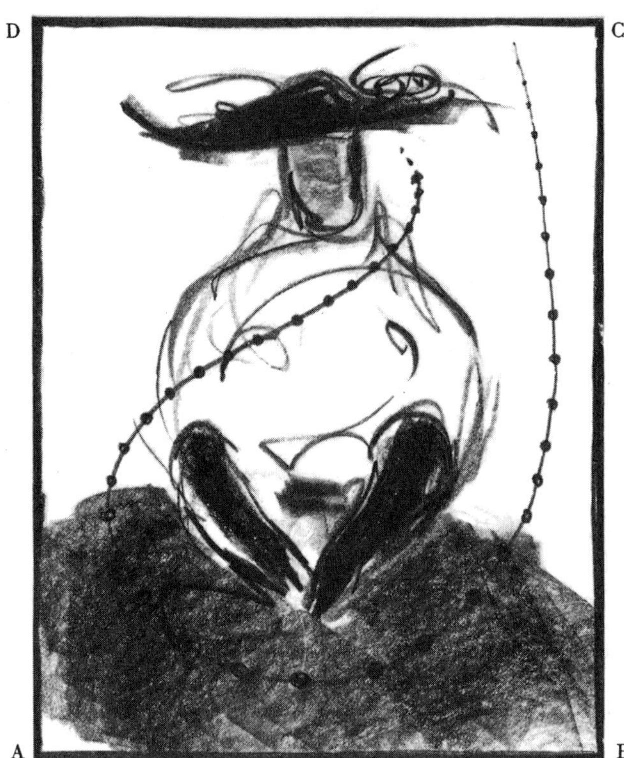


306-B



**The Entry**

The entry is dependent upon the way the artist
locates his centers of interest. The artist realizes
that we soon tire of only one center of interest.
Such a picture may be described as a bull's-
eye, a strong concentration of interest in one
point. If interest is confined to one form, one
shape, a dominant color in one area, the eye
circles around it like the fly circling the single
sphere, as we noted in the previous chapter
(*306-A*).

To overcome this monotony, a second point
of interest, the *foil*, is introduced to distract
the eye. Thus the hands in *306-B* attract the eye
moving through the picture and bring it close
to the bottom border. Just as the eye begins to
scan the hands, the foil, it becomes aware of
the head, and moves up to view it more closely.

Once the eye has entered the picture it flies
through space and around cores just as the fly
did around the dumbbell. But as we have seen,
if the eye continues to loop around two cores
the pattern becomes monotonous, we lose
interest. In the classic entry the same danger
exists. After leaving the foil, the eye usually
returns directly to the center of interest and if
not diverted will return to the foil, creating
a monotonous figure-eight movement.

Now in spite of the danger of creating
monotony, this figure-eight pattern of scanning
has been exploited successfully by many artists
in designing the classic entry. Its success is
due to a careful subordination of one of the
elements of the figure-eight. For instance, the
cluster of hands, the interest point low in the
picture, acts as the foil. The eye is aware of
this foil but not arrested or overwhelmed by it,

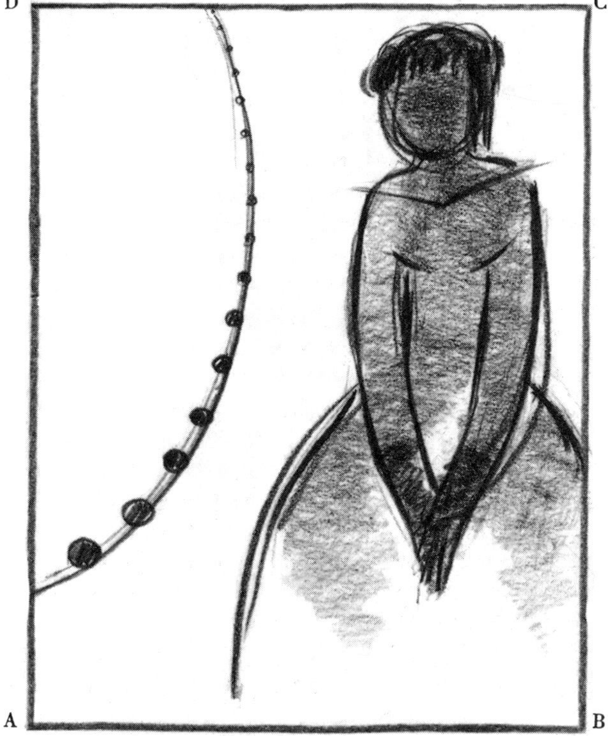

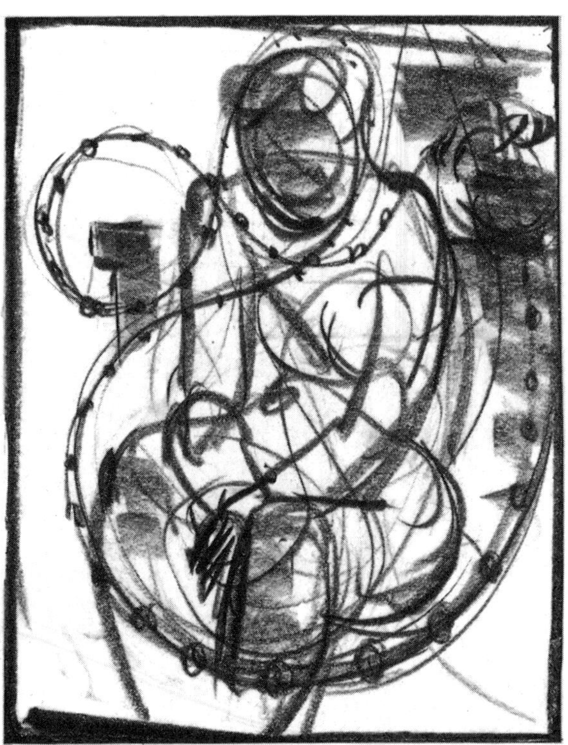

307-1

307-2



and it continues its course through the picture, returning to the head which is the center of interest.

In *306-B* we see a clear space-trough through which the eye moves easily. The eye is attracted downward because of the strong pull of the bottom border, then it is pulled toward *BC* between the figure and border. As it sweeps into the space-trough it moves toward the figure and foil, for the attraction of the figure is greater than the pull of *CD*.

If we place the figure very close to *BC* a large trough opens between the figure and the border *AD* (*307-1*). As the eye sweeps into the picture it is overwhelmed by the extreme pull of *AD* and *AB*. It tends to leave the picture and as a result our interest in the picture as a whole is lessened. The figure seems remote. Any subsequent movement of the eye through the space encompassing the figure will seem congested.

To break the monotony of the figure-eight movement, secondary loops of the eye always may be introduced (*307-2*). Here the eye makes one loop around the foil, the hands; a second loop around the head, the center of interest; a third loop around the knob of the chair; a fourth loop back around the accent in the background; and then a loop back around the head. The movement of the eye through this diagram is an example of the control which can be established.

We should note that each reverse allows the eye to scan an interest point from a new point of view, a new direction. Since the center of interest is dominant, the eye will continually return to it. Eventually every part of the picture will be examined by the moving eye.

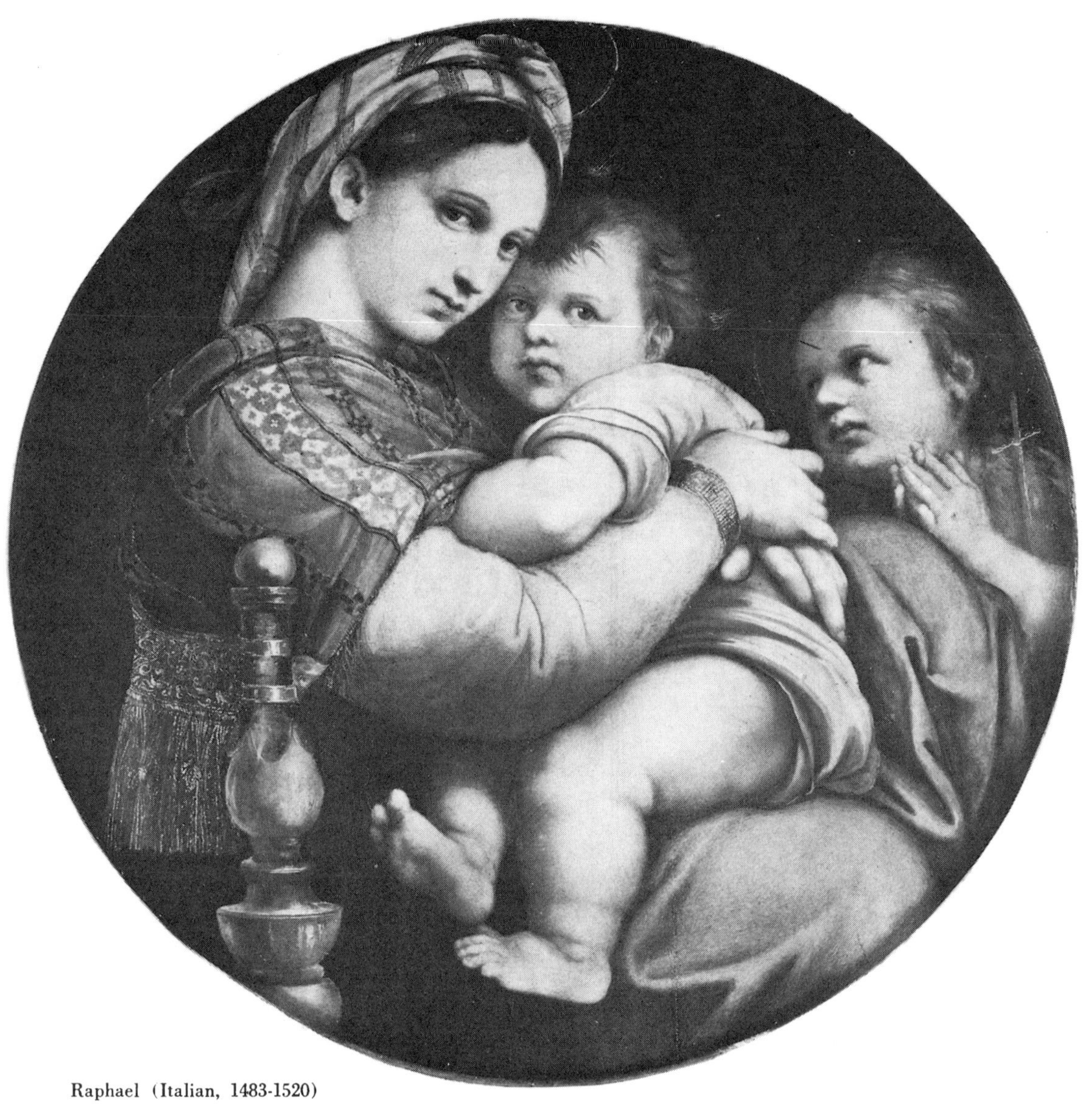

Raphael (Italian, 1483-1520)
MADONNA OF THE CHAIR, 1512-1514
diameter 28″; oil on wood; Pitti Gallery
Courtesy Superintendent of Galleries, Florence
(Photograph: Alinari-Art Reference Bureau, Inc., N. Y.
and Fototeca Unione, Rome)

## The Entry Determined by Field Size and Shape

The classic entry is only applicable if we can
see the whole picture as a unit. Units vary in
size. There are small pictures, miniatures, book
or magazine illustrations made to be seen at
close range. There are easel pictures made to
be seen from short distances, or some may
even reach the size of ten or twelve feet yet
still be easy to read. All such relatively small
pictures can be encompassed by the eye as
single units. However, as we have noted, many
mural paintings are so large that we cannot
see them as units but must see them a part
at a time. Although the eye still scans the
various parts through space-troughs, the entry
of necessity must vary in such large pictures.

The shape of the field also affects the entry,
for not all pictures are rectangular. Because of
the great variety in field shapes, especially in
mural structures, the entry may vary greatly,
the pattern of loops may be drastically affected
by such unusual picture shapes.

The border of a circular picture, for example
Raphael's *Madonna of the Chair*, evidences
the same basic forces that we find in a rectangle.
There is a strong border pull, not just straight
down but to the left and down. If we imagine
the knob of the chair removed, our eye sweeps
around the right foot and returns to the Child.
With the knob intact, our eye pulls around
the foot and knob, then returns to the Madonna's
head, the true center of interest.

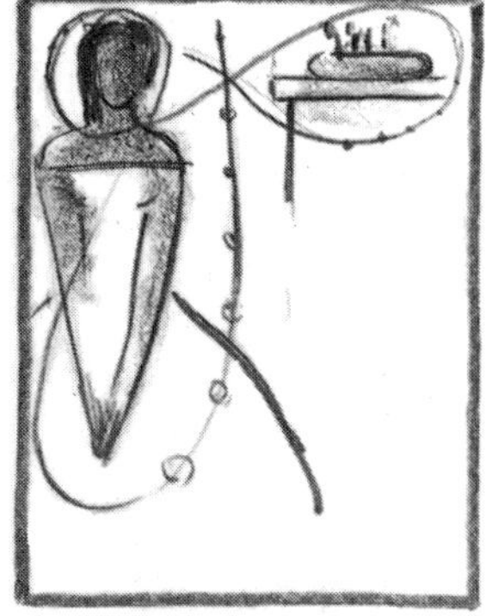

309-1A

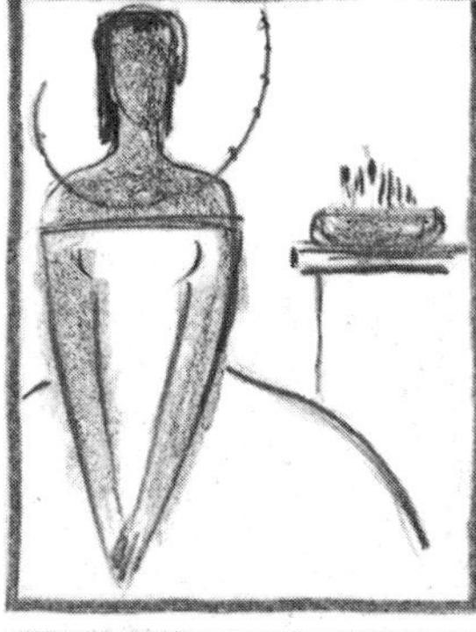

309-1B

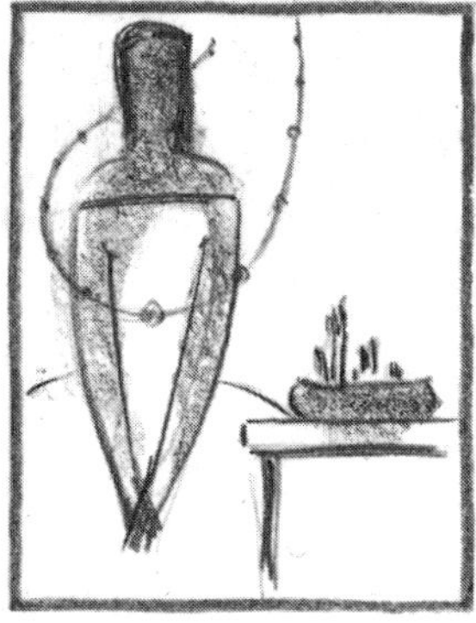

309-1C

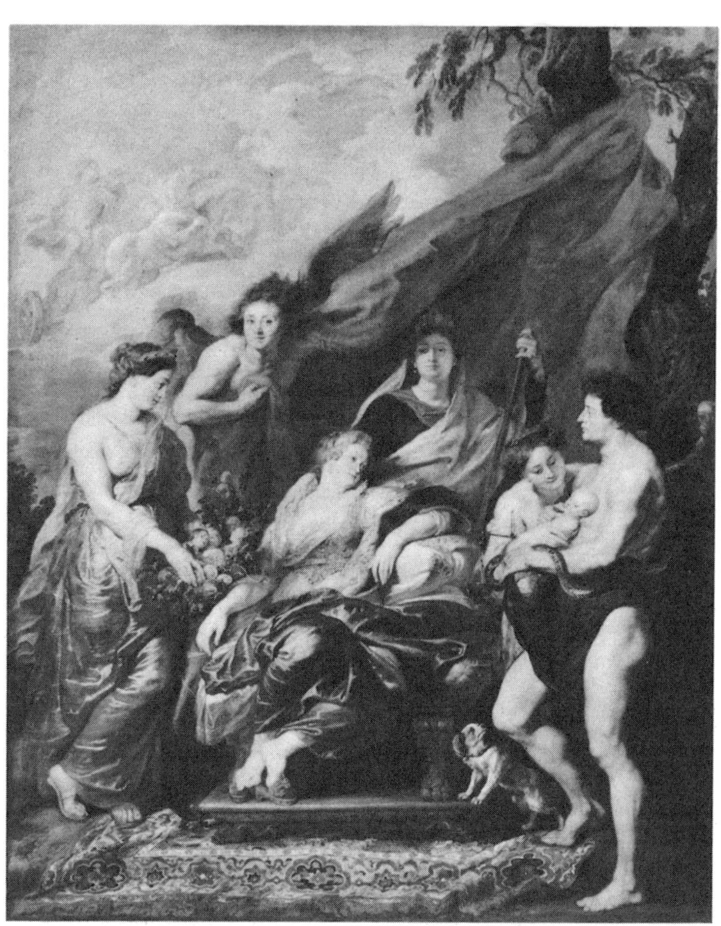

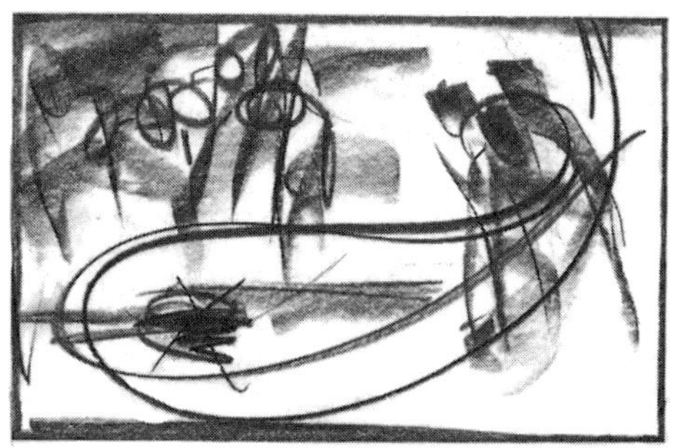

309-2

## Jamming the Entry

Generally speaking, the more open and clear the entry the easier the picture is to read. This is not to say that there can be no graphic elements in the trough, usually there are (*309-1A*). Such elements when in back of the subject may be subordinated easily. However, if an element occurring in the background and also in the trough becomes too insistent, the pattern of the entry will be altered, or destroyed (*309-1B*). If an overlay is placed between the spectator and the trough, the entry may be weakened or completely changed (*309-1C*).

At times the center of interest may lie between the entry and the right border, in which case the foil may be established low and far to the left (*309-2*). Our eye sweeps around the foil and back to the center of interest. In the Rubens above our eye sweeps down through the trough, around the very strong foil, the knee, and back to the true center, the child.

We should note that Rubens' paintings are fine examples of the classic entry, and demonstrate that the center of interest may be located almost anywhere in the picture. A variation of the classic entry is the delayed entry, which we will discuss shortly.

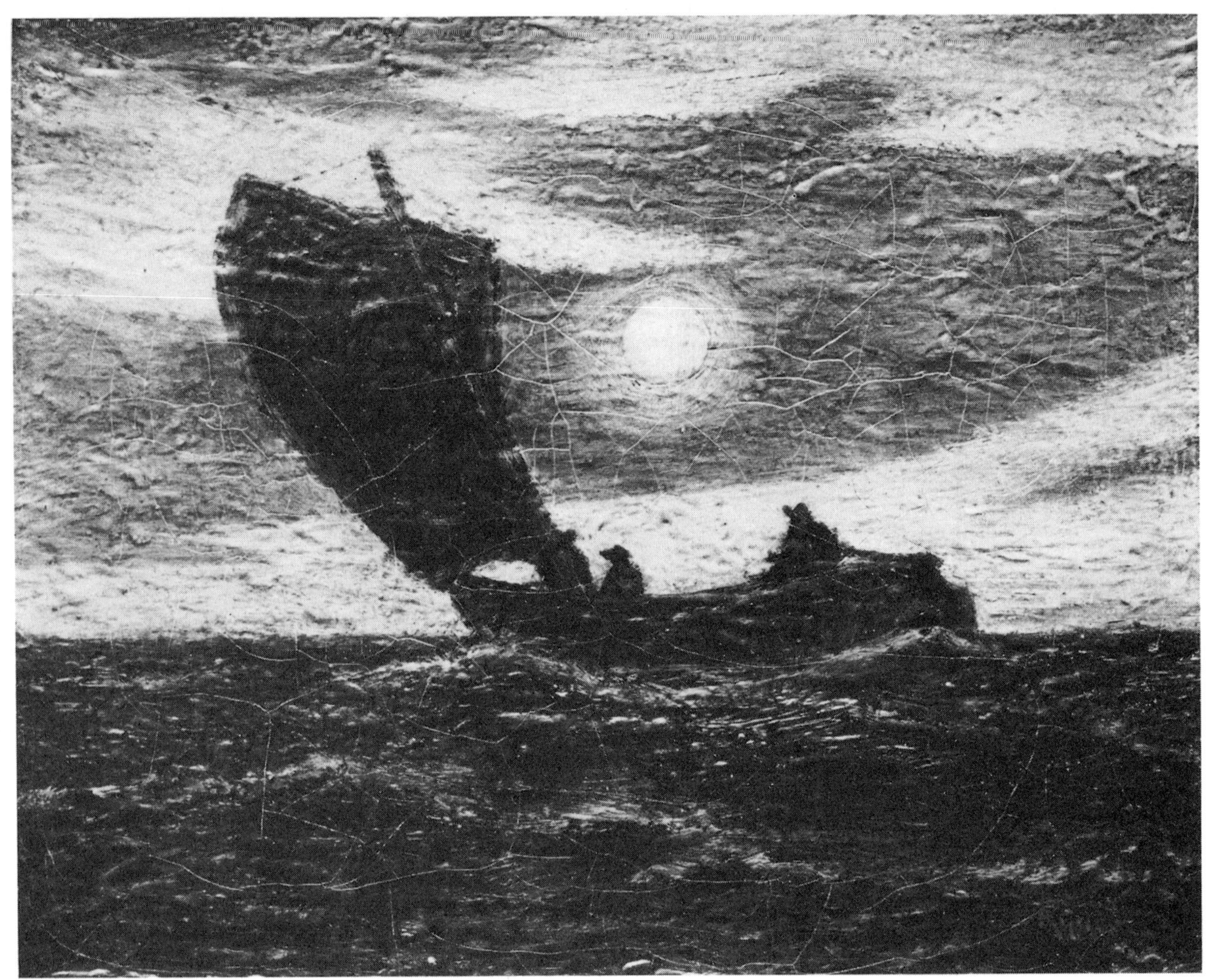

Albert P. Ryder (American, 1847-1917)
TOILERS OF THE SEA, date unknown
10" x 12"  oil on canvas
Addison Gallery of American Art
Phillips Academy, Andover, Massachusetts
(Photograph: Andover Art Studio)

## The Single Unit Structure

310

Although the single unit picture is difficult to make exciting, it does allow us to study the movement of the eye in its simplest terms. And some artists have made highly successful single unit pictures. In Chapter 2 we showed a painting built around a single shape, Malevich's circle. This Albert Ryder, although made up of many large, important shapes, is primarily built around one shape, the boat.

For demonstration purposes the following diagrams suggest elemental ways to plan eye movements in single unit pictures. Such planning in the early stages of picture making can save many hours of work later. One crowded element may perhaps necessitate reworking an almost completed picture. It is better to locate the difficult spot in the early stages than to find it later when change becomes a serious matter. So let us follow the eye movements as indicated in the diagrams.

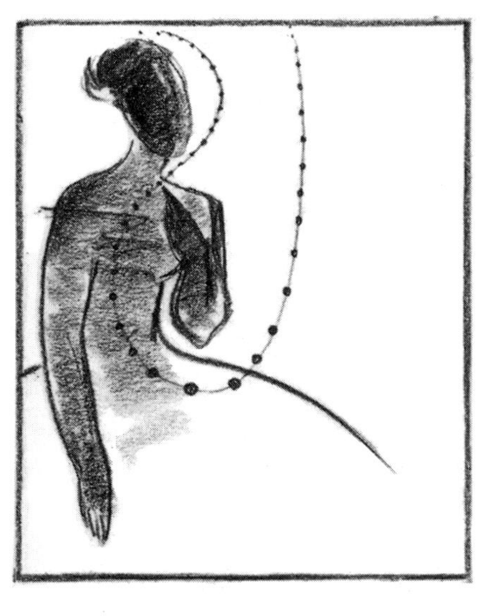 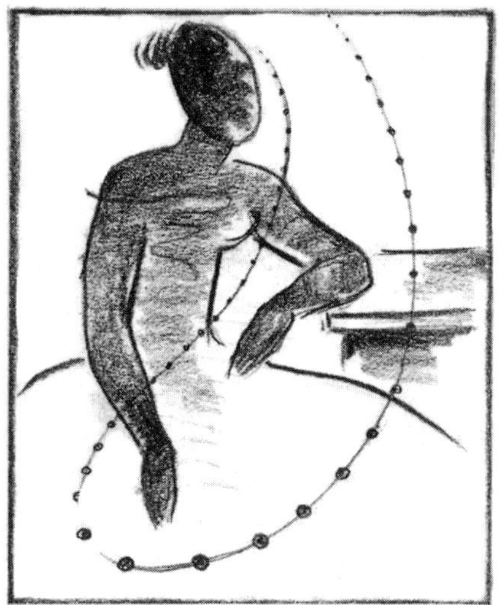 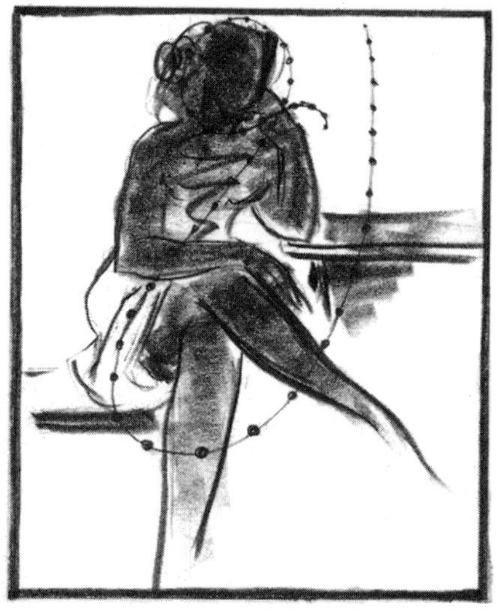

311-A 311-B 311-C

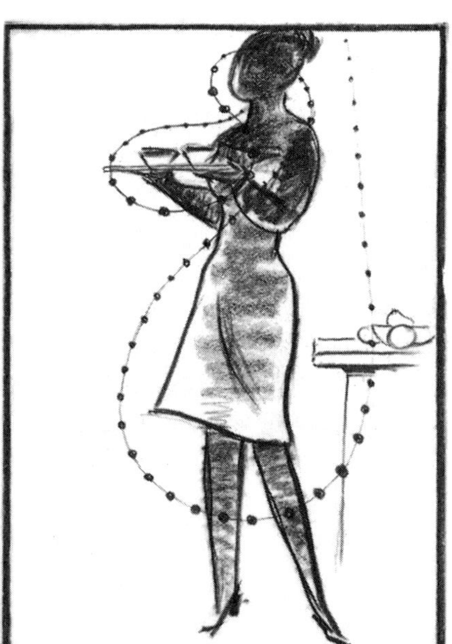 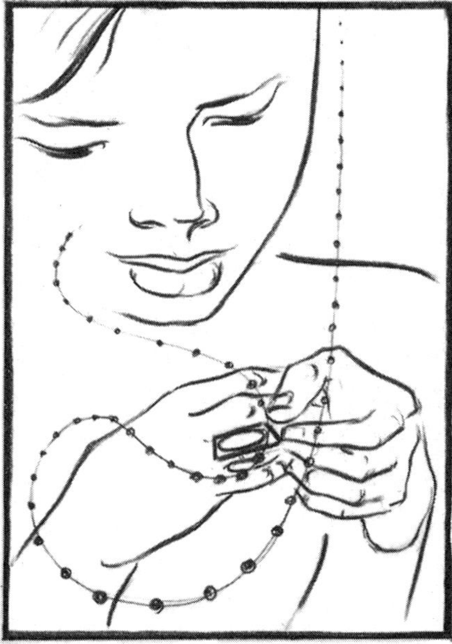 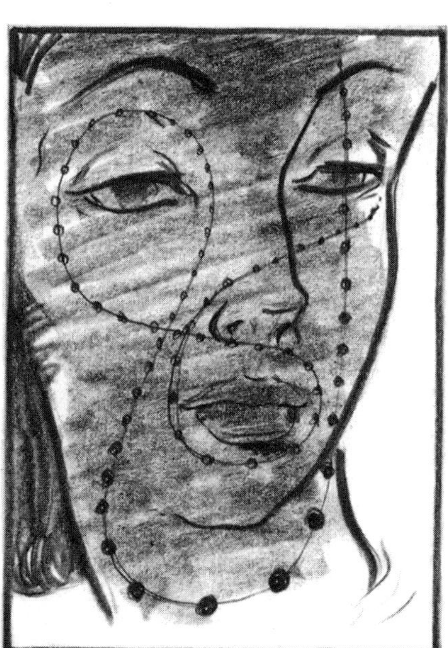

311-D 311-E 311-F

*311-A.* The pattern is clear. The left elbow is the foil, the head is the center of interest, the right hand is seen on the second loop.

*311-B.* The right hand is the foil, the head is the center of interest. The left hand in this case is close to the border, so it will be seen later.

*311-C.* The knee is the foil, the head the center of interest, the left hand the third point of interest. The right foot is seen later.

*311-D.* The corner of the hem of the dress is the foil, the head the center of interest, the hands constitute a cluster which is the third point of interest. The objects in the background are seen later.

*311-E.* At times the center of interest may not be the head. If we desire to make another part of the body, or a specific object, in this case a ring, the most interesting point, we may do so by varying the pattern the eye describes. By cutting through the head we make it more difficult for the eye to encompass it. The eye, sweeping around the cluster of the hands, reverses around the heel of the right hand, the foil, then returns to the ring, the center of interest.

*311-F.* The chin in this close-up becomes the foil; the right eye, the center of interest. The mouth becomes the third point, the left eye is seen next.

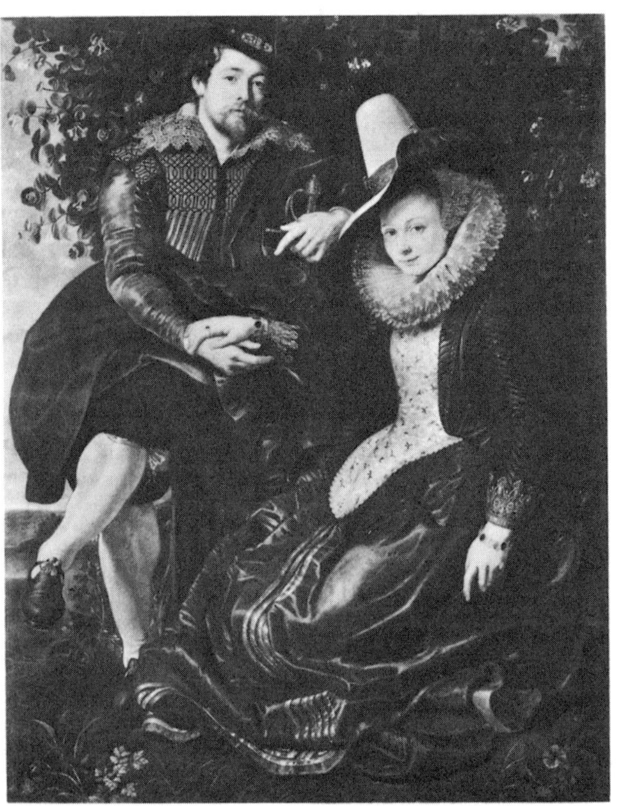

Peter Paul Rubens (Flemish, 1577-1640)
RUBENS AND ISABELLA BRANT IN THE
HONEYSUCKLE
ca. 1609; 70½" x 53½"; oil on canvas mounted on wood
Alte Pinakothek, Munich

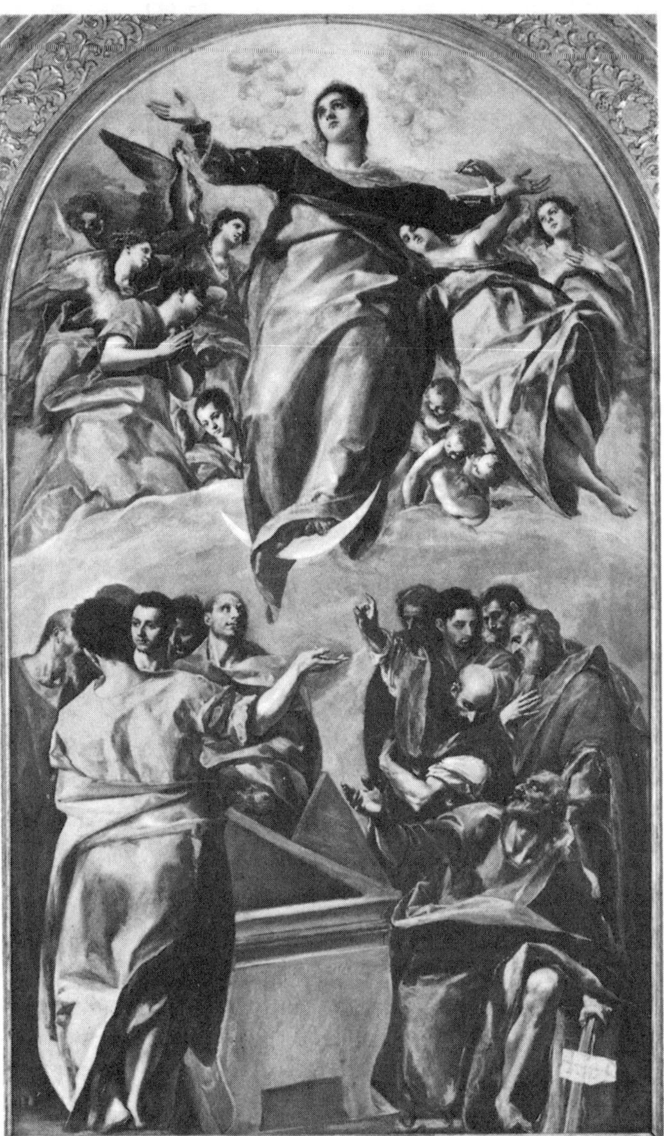

El Greco (Spanish, b. Crete, 1541-1614)
THE ASSUMPTION OF THE VIRGIN, 1577; 158" x 90"
oil on canvas
Courtesy of The Art Institute of Chicago
Gift of Nancy Atwood Sprague

312   **The Multiple Unit Structure**

In a multiple unit structure, of course, the
plan of eye movement is more complex. For
example in a double portrait, as this Rubens,
the problem is to determine which head should
be seen first. Isabella Brant's knee is enveloped in swirling folds low down in the
picture. This becomes the foil. Our eye sweeps
back to her head, the primary center, then
loops around the clasped hands, finally arriving
at Rubens' head high in the picture. This
picture exemplifies how the trough leading
around the foil may be interrupted yet still
permit a clear entry.

El Greco's *Assumption of the Virgin* is a very
large picture, over thirteen feet high. The
problem of organizing upper and lower groups
so that they feel compatible is very difficult.
El Greco solved it by introducing a huge
trough sweeping over the whole group of figures
on the right. Our eye caught in this trough
sweeps down and between the coffin and the
extended arm of the figure on the left. It
swings around the elbow and back up to the
central figure, the Virgin, again following a
trough marked by her knees and the space
between her shoulders.

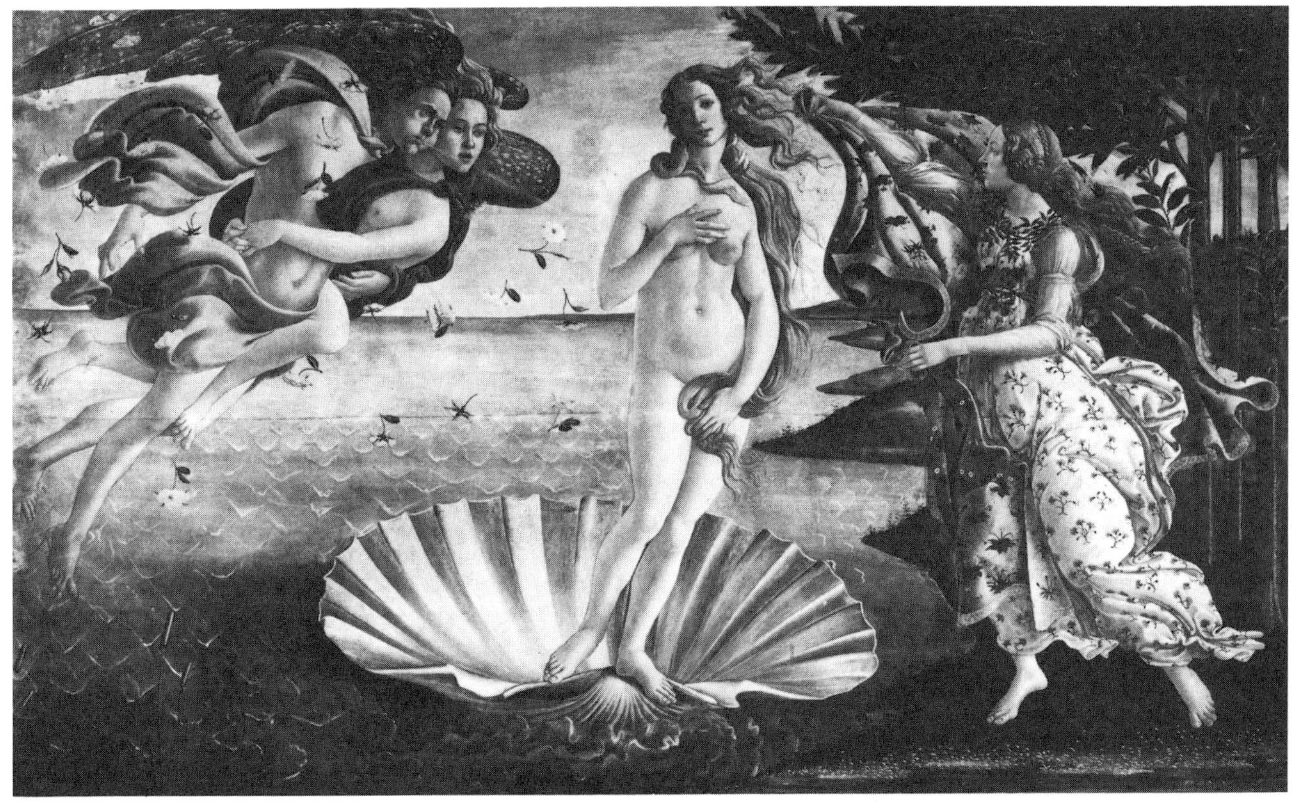

Sandro Botticelli (Italian, 1444?-1510)
THE BIRTH OF VENUS, ca. 1486; 68⅞" x 109½"
oil on canvas; Uffizi Gallery
Soprintendenza alle Gallerie
(Gabinetto Fotografico)

In Botticelli's *The Birth of Venus*, we observe 313
a rather unusual entry. Our eye sweeps down
through the trough next to the right arm of
Venus, reverses on the edge of the shell, then
returns to her head; next, to her left hand,
then seeks out the head of the figure on her left.
But for the dark pointed land masses to the left
of the Venus, the entry would have been to
her left, leading down and around the hinge
of the shell, then returning the whole length
of her body to her head.

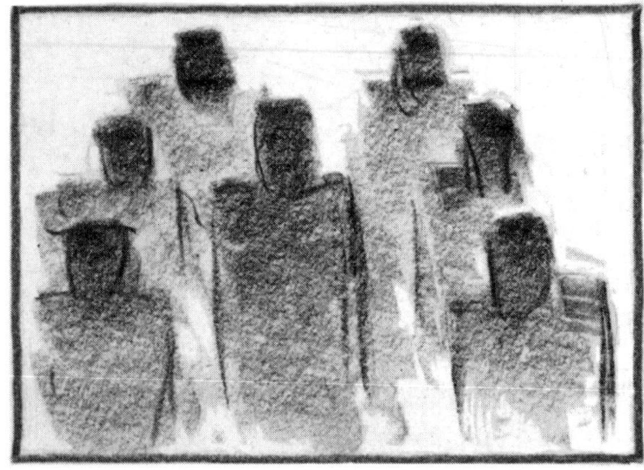

314-A

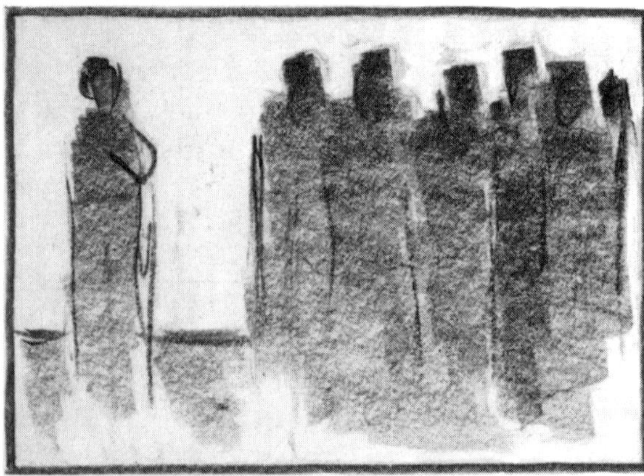

314-B

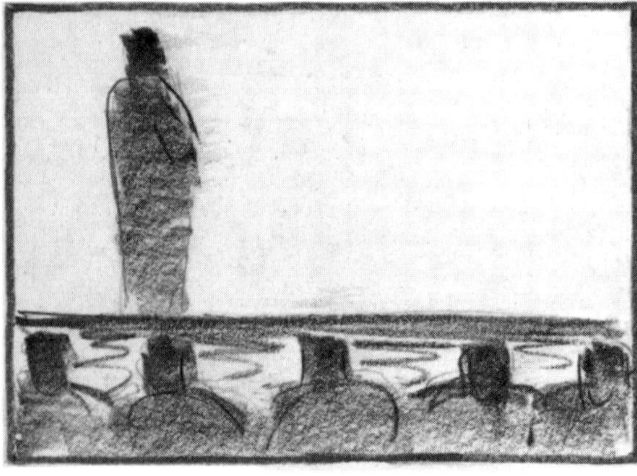

314-C

314 **Varying the Center of Interest**

There are many ways of establishing a center of interest, which may be located almost anywhere in the picture. If the picture contains many figures it is always possible to establish the true center of interest by painting it bright red or green. The same end can be achieved by drawing an arrow pointing to the principal figure. In either case the solution is a bit obvious.

We can also create a doughnut effect by encircling the center of interest with secondary figures (*314-A*). All such solutions derive from the bull's-eye structure. Once we see such a point it becomes difficult to look at anything else in the picture. Unfortunately, if we habitually develop a bull's-eye structure our limitation becomes noticeable especially if we create a series of pictures.

The doughnut structure also depends on interest through isolation (*314-B*). If a symbol, a figure, a head, is isolated in an immediate environment of unimportant volumes, or as a spot in relation to large unimportant areas or shapes, it becomes a visual target (*314-C*). Again we have trouble taking our eye away from such a point. We have a center of interest, true, but this way of achieving it creates great danger of sacrificing the whole picture for one point.

Instead of depending upon the bull's-eye structure, which almost always results in monotony, we can develop great variety by exploiting the movement of the eye as a means of determining the center of interest.

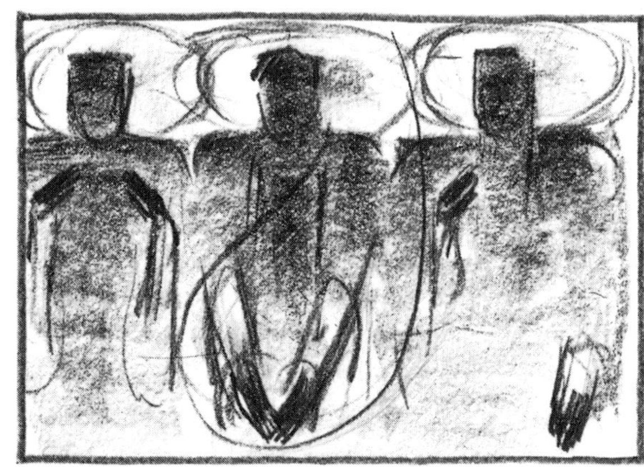

315-A

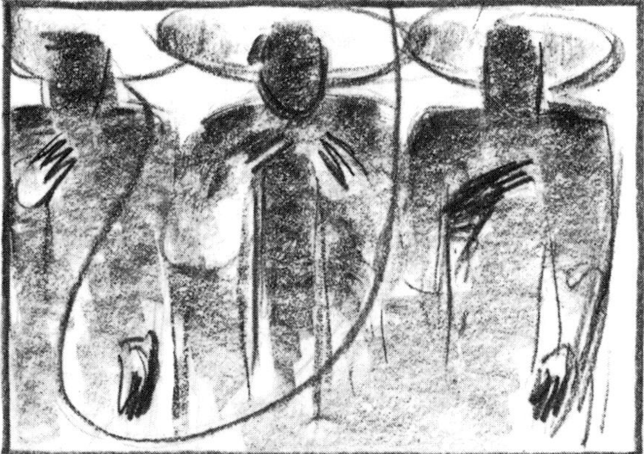

315-B

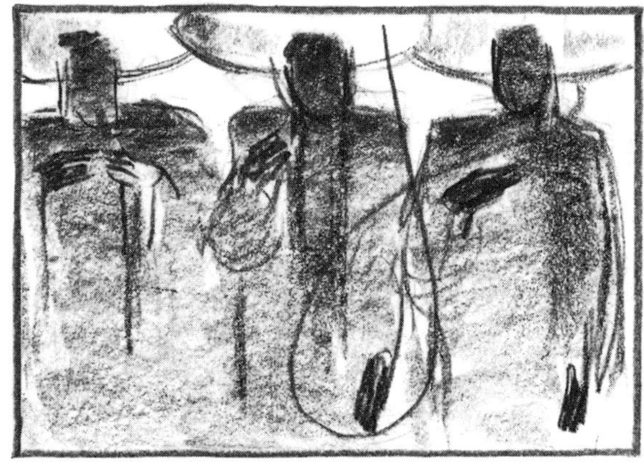

315-C

For instance let us consider the problem of forming a group of three figures into a frieze. By varying the position of the hands the entry may be varied also and interest centered on any particular head desired. Thus in *315-A* by placing the right hand close to the head on the right and jamming the left hand close to the border, a very large trough is opened up. The cluster of hands of the central figure low in the picture is the foil, the eye returns to the central head, the center of interest.

In *315-B,* by moving the right hand a little farther from the head on the right and by lifting the hands of the central figure, the left hand of the figure on the left becomes the foil and the left head becomes the center of interest.

In *315-C,* by dropping the left hand of the central figure, it becomes the natural foil, our eye is next attracted to the right head, the center of interest.

### The Delayed Entry

So far we have demonstrated the classic entry so often employed by artists to draw our attention in a direct way to the center of interest without depending upon the bull's-eye effect, or isolation. But some artists, especially Pieter Bruegel, the Elder, deliberately delay our reading of the center of interest. He achieves this delay by forcing our eye first to move through a series of loops around interesting but secondary points of interest. After two or three loops he leads the eye to the true center of interest.

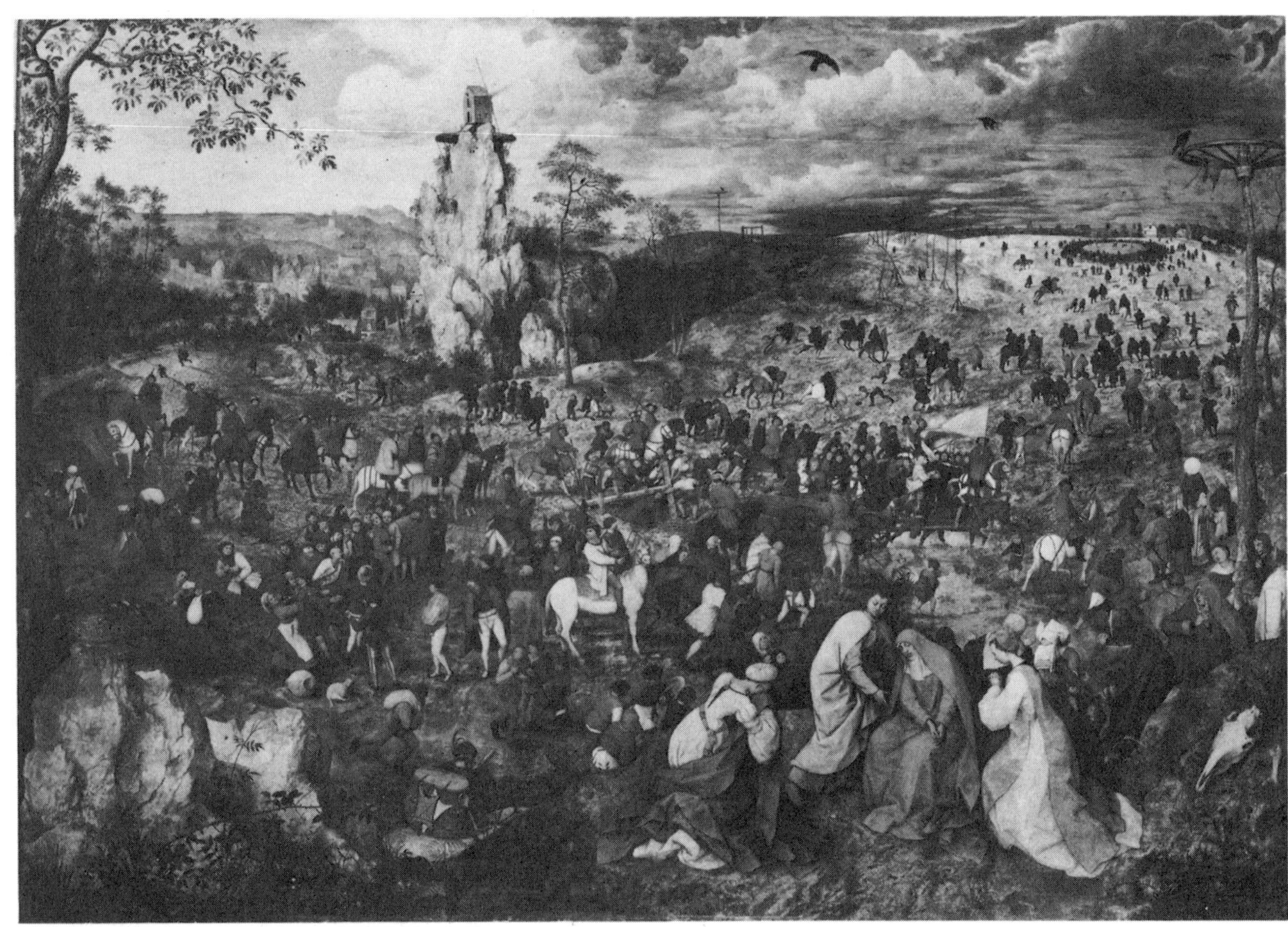

Pieter Bruegel the Elder (Flemish, ca. 1525-1569)
CHRIST CARRYING THE CROSS, 1564
wood; 48¹³⁄₁₆″ x 66¹⁵⁄₁₆″
Kunsthistoriches Museum, Vienna

316    In this Bruegel, *Christ Carrying the Cross,* we find after some time that the picture concerns Christ carrying the cross. The Christ actually is very near the geometric center of the picture, but is a tiny figure surrounded by a great number of figures. The picture is dominated by the large cluster of figures in the foreground, which is comprised of a smaller cluster of three figures, and a single figure. In the background is a dominant volume, a large rock formation. Back of the large cluster, but prominent in the central foreground, is a rider on a white horse. Our eyes encompass all these points of interest before the Christ is disclosed.

The device of the delayed entry is used by few artists, but it is effective because it introduces an element of intrigue; like a puzzle it baffles us, but unlike a puzzle it does not confuse us. Intrigue, no matter how attained, introduces the element of mystery so essential to a picture. In fact we might say that if there is no mystery there is no picture.

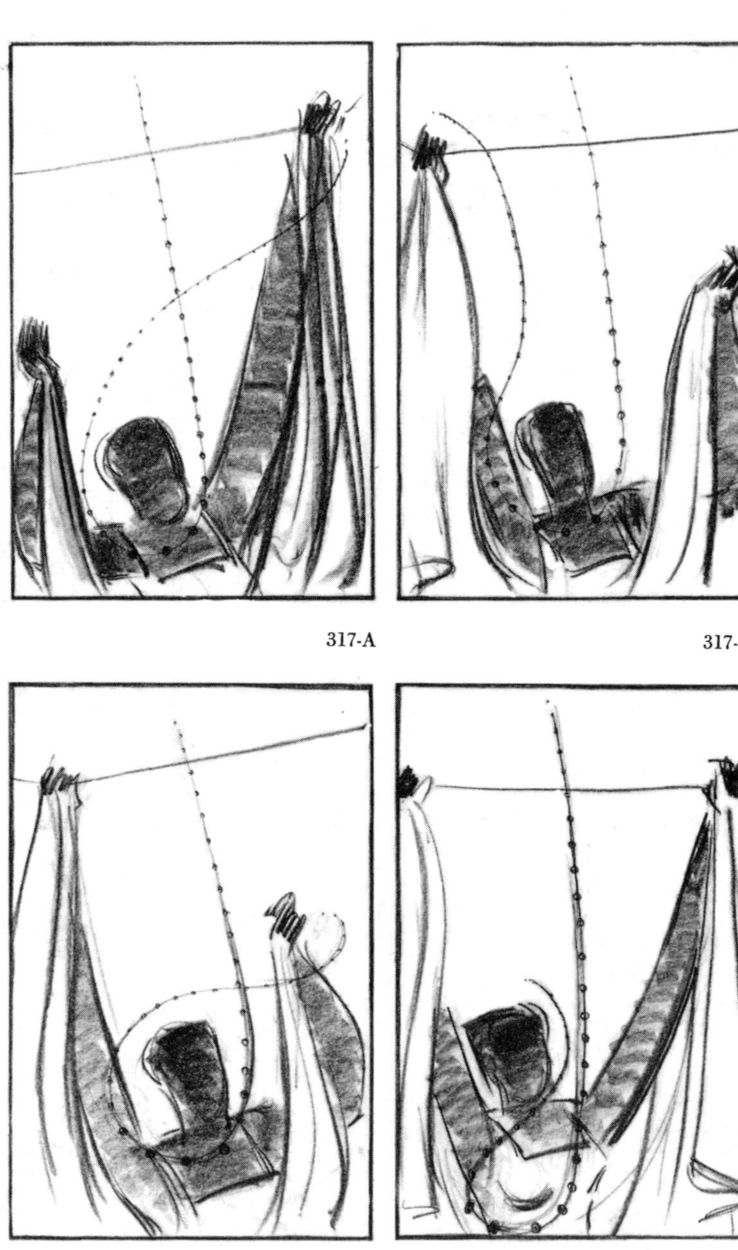

317-A                                                    317-B

317-C                                                    317-D

## The Relation of Cores to Borders

As we have seen, the determining factor in reading any shape or volume is the space around it, the space-trough through which the eye must travel. As a general observation we note that the eye always travels in the easiest way possible, much like the flow of water. If we pour water upon the ground, the water avoids high points, rushing into lower points surrounding them. If a connecting depression is deeper than its adjacent gully the water will rush into this low point or channel.

Just as we can force the eye to move through a clear trough, so we also are able to control the trough through which the eye moves. As we jammed the entry, so we can jam the space-trough. In short, by jamming an important part, placing it in close proximity to a border or another important part, we prevent the eye from  moving easily between the two elements. In the accompanying diagrams the eye is forced to read a special center of interest.

*317-A.* The head is the foil, the right hand is jammed, the left hand is the center of interest.

*317-B.* The head is the foil, the left hand is jammed, the right hand is the center of interest.

*317-C.* The head is the foil, the right hand is jammed, the left hand is the center of interest.

*317-D.* The breast is the foil, both hands are jammed, the head is the center of interest.

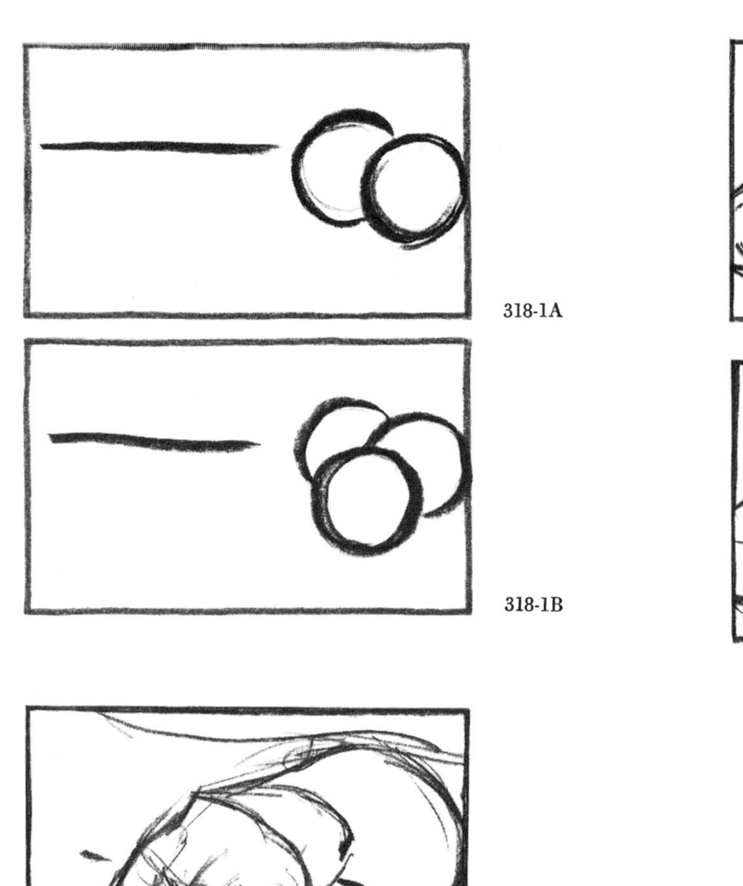

318-1A

318-1B

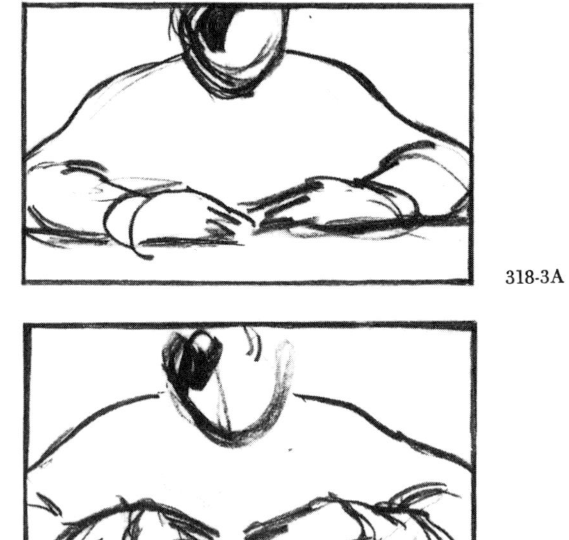

318-3A

318-3B

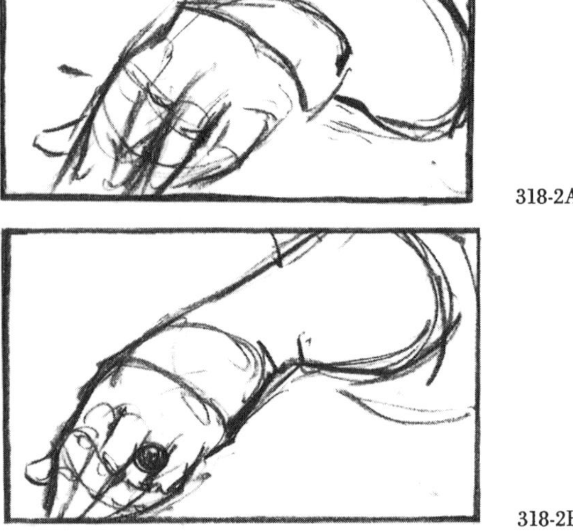

318-2A

318-2B



## Cropping

Eye movement and centers of interest also can be altered by *cropping* the picture, or reducing its size. The term cropping is used for lack of a better one. It is a term used extensively both in still photography and in the commercial design field. It is a poor term because it implies that for some reason or another a completed picture must be altered, either to accommodate some requirement in its use or to improve the composition of the original. In either case some compromise with a prior graphic statement is implied.

In examining the relation of our elements again, we see that the control of space is essential to achieve legibility. Usually when a dominant element is made tangent to a border, usually through faulty cropping, a congestion arises which makes our eye return to it continuously (*318-1A*). As this point is not important to the picture's story, our interest in important parts of the picture is distracted. By introducing a foil in front of such a congestion point, we force the eye through the trough formed by the close volume and the border (*318-1B*). Our eye moves past the objectionable point, thus the whole picture reads more easily.

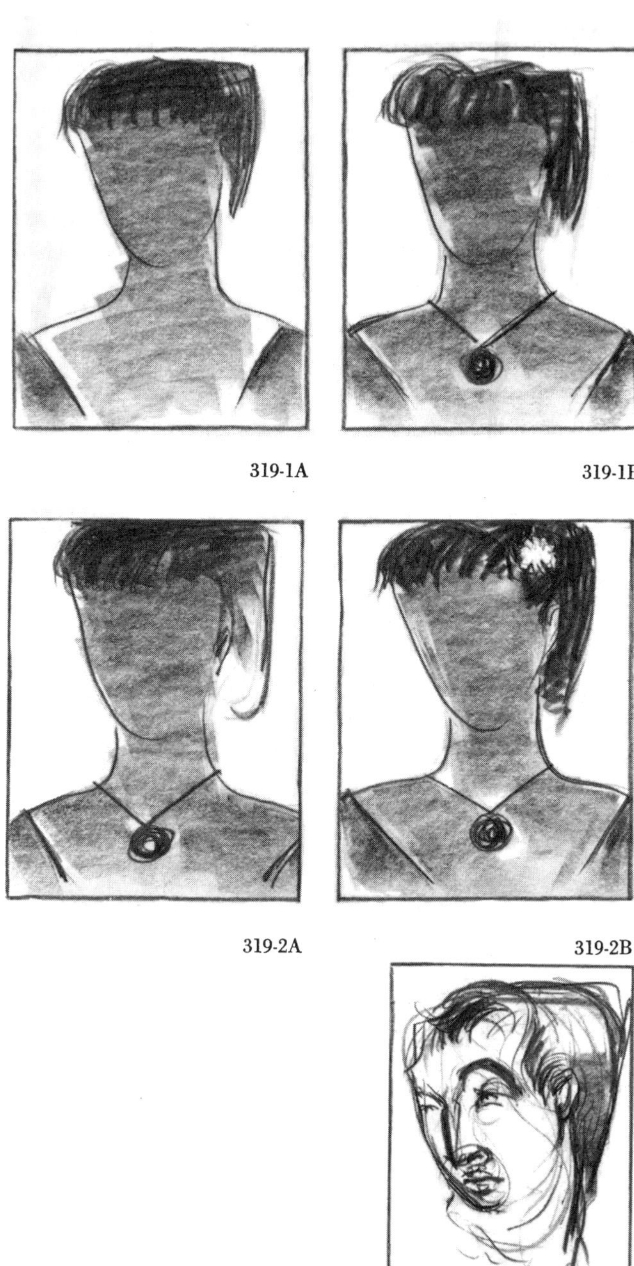

319-1A       319-1B

319-2A       319-2B

319-3

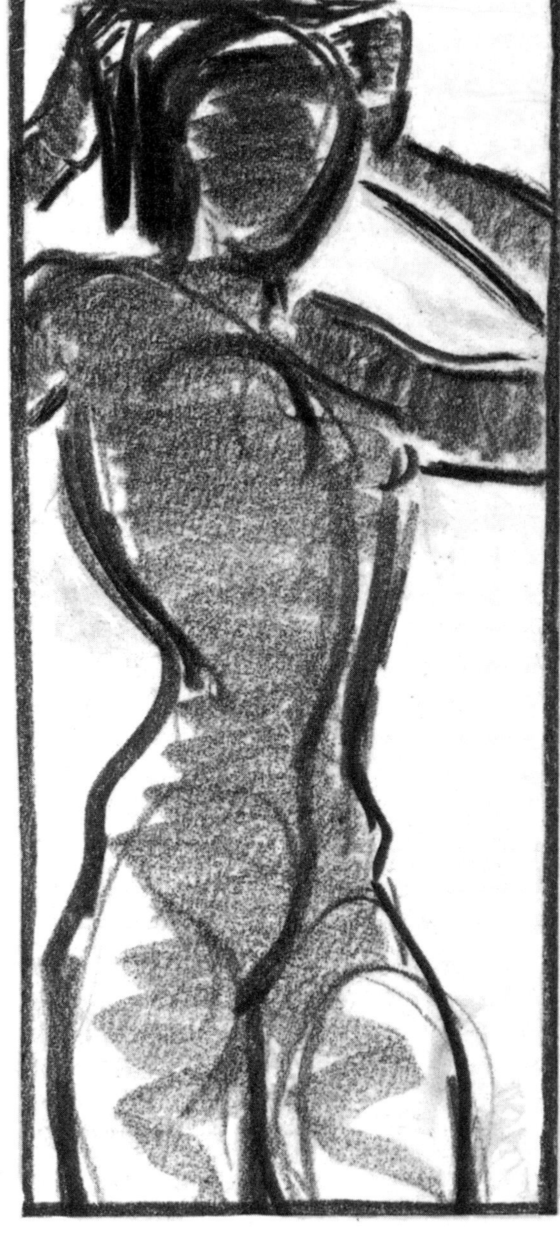

319-4



A hand cropped by the border becomes a powerful point of interest at the point of tangency *(318-2A)*. By introducing a ring as a foil our eye is drawn away from the unfortunate congestion *(318-2B)*. The eye moves through the trough set up by the ring and the border.

In a similar problem, the elbows may be cropped tangent to the border creating little targets *(318-3A)*. By carrying the elbows out of the picture and using the heels of the hands as cores, the eye is redirected from the trouble spots *(318-3B)*.

A picture may inadvertently fall into a single unit arrangement. In a portrait the head may become a target *(319-1A)*. By introducing a brooch, for instance, the eye is led low in the picture, the ornament becomes the foil, and the classic entry is now obvious *(319-1B)*. If, however, the ornament is cropped too close to the border, congestion immediately results.

At times it is desirable to crop an important part, the head for instance *(319-2A)*. By introducing a core, a flower, an ornament, or a concentration of hair forms, the eye is led away from the intersections of the parts of the head and border, and great space is achieved *(319-2B)*.

An eyebrow, an ear, or any part of the body which serves as a core can be used in a similar way to direct the eye through a trough determined by the core's relation to a border *(319-3)*.

A figure cropped at all four borders may be made spacious by careful planning of the tension points or cores suggested within the structure of the figure *(319-4)*.

**The Controversy Over the Entry**

The subject of the classic entry is controversial. Some artists pooh-pooh the idea of an entry of any kind. They suggest that we look immediately at the center of interest as we would at a target, at a bull's-eye. The serious weakness of this concept is that it refutes the premise that the borders of a picture are really symbols of forces, which was demonstrated so dramatically by the Malevich in Chapter 2.

Another school of thought suggests that we enter a picture from the bottom, that our eye moves up through the picture to the center of interest. Certainly there is some truth in this observation in relation to very high murals. But this entry is premised upon the fact that the foreground is closer to us than the horizon in nature; therefore the assumption follows that we begin at the base of the picture if we wish to see something in the middle or far distance of the picture.

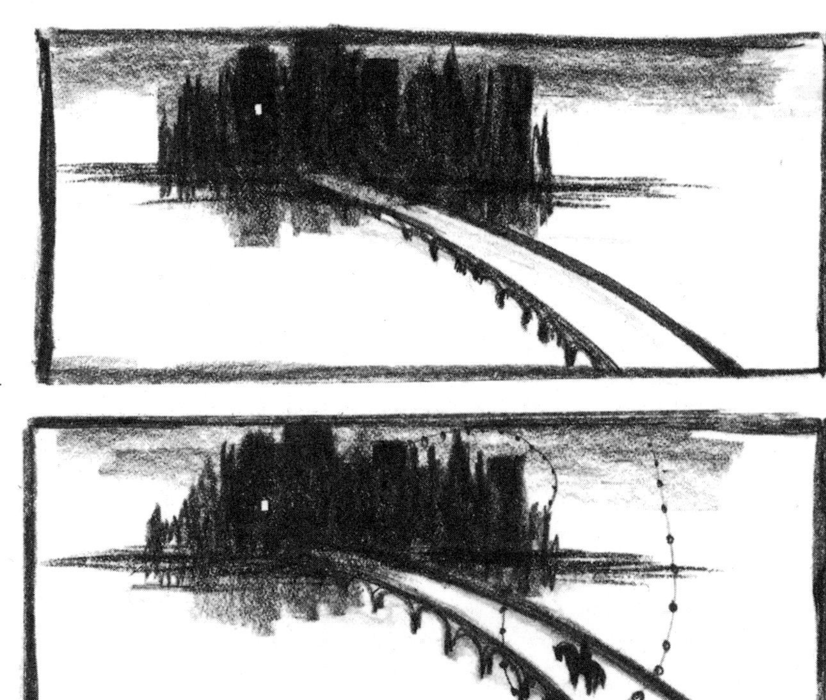

321-A

321-B

In applying this concept, strong diagonals driving from foreground into the distance are commonly used *(321-A)*. Unfortunately such use of diagonals is based upon a perspective concept of picture structure which makes control of the picture surface extremely difficult. In order to retain surface control it may help to introduce a foil near the base to interrupt the diagonal. The eye is forced back into the upper part of the picture not on the diagonal, but by means of a loop *(321-B)*.

There is yet another school of thought which suggests that we see elements of a picture indiscriminately, that we just happen to see things. Such a view, of course, precludes the use of any controlled time pattern. If we design a picture from this viewpoint the result is usually a bull's-eye center of interest or utter chaos.

In our particular explanation of the entry we have explored a hypothesis that has been suggested by many artists over hundreds of years. We find that the best argument for the use of the entry is that it works. Whether or not it conforms to a particular theory, it is a positive way to control graphic space. It has been of utmost value to many artists and is a tangible factor in picture making, even though picture making is full of intangibles. Perhaps the greatest mystery is that the artist, in absentia, may direct the eye of the spectator, often a stranger, by using as a control a factor also unseen—graphic space.

# 28 Seeing Space in Nature

# VIII SPACE

**Atmospheric Space and Graphic Space**
As we have noted, it is possible for us to simulate atmospheric effects in a picture by the manipulation of light and dark or color. Although many painters have utilized atmospheric effects with great success, as Monet has in his *Westminster*, many more have been less successful.

Almost always when an atmospheric effect dominates the picture, the distance separating forms in nature, or volumes in a picture, is confused by the viewer with space. The impact of volumes and shapes usually is overwhelming. The surfaces become secondary to the images. So, as a rule, the relation of the surface of one volume to another becomes inconsequential. Tension between two or more volumes or shapes and their surfaces often is lost because of too much interest in subject matter.

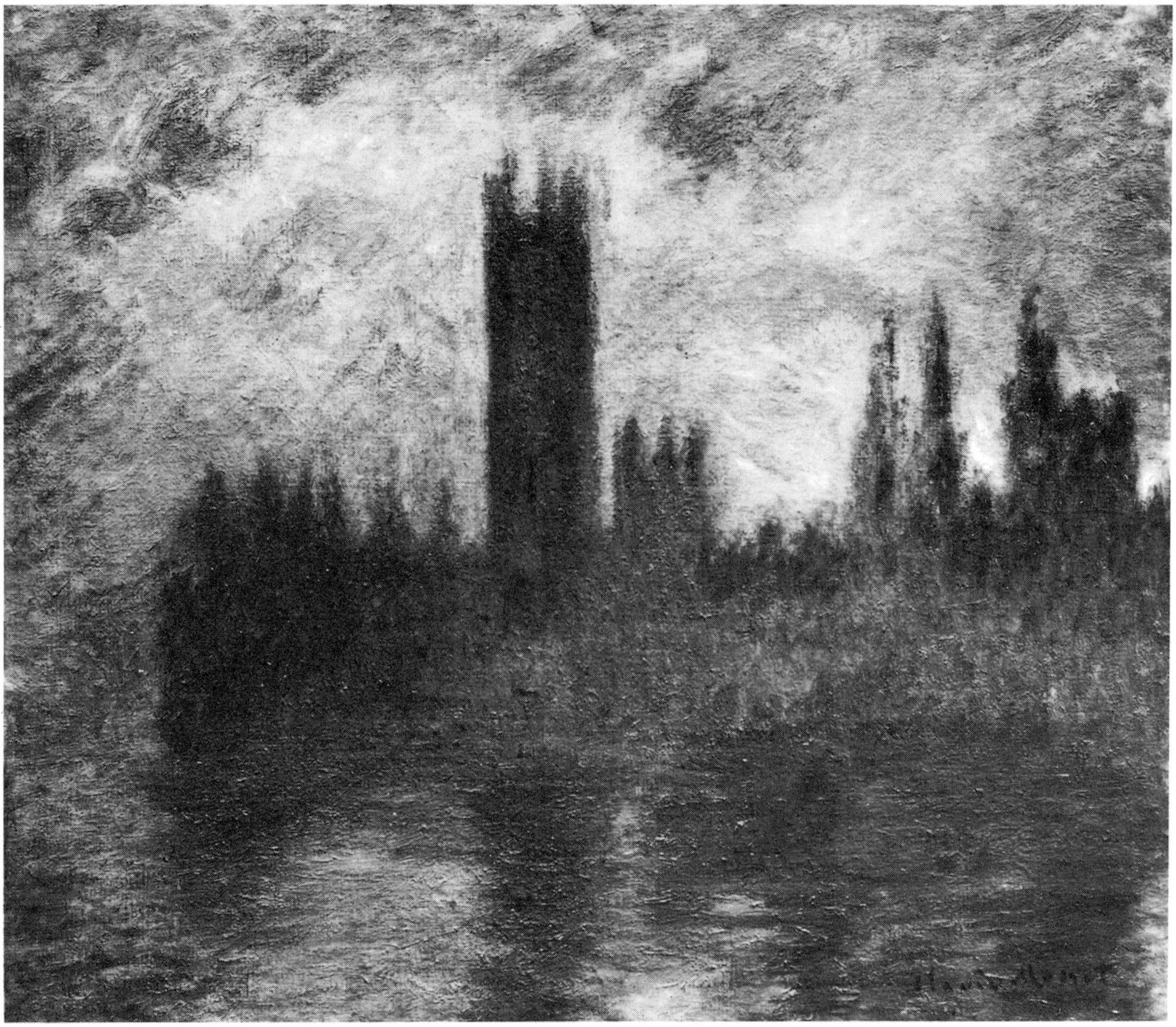

So we see that a picture of a form in an atmospheric environment in no way assures us of the reality of the space involved. A painted ship upon a painted ocean does not assure a spacious picture. A picture of an interior of a room does not guarantee us a feeling of looking into a space box.

The more factual the image, the more we tend, through association, to accept the space around it as we do space around a form in nature. We accept both form and image as normal occurrences. We ignore the surrounding space in both cases, for our reaction to space as an event has been dulled, made unimportant through familiarity.

Such factual association also blinds us to possible graphic excitement which may be generated in a picture. If we are satisfied simply with a representation of something existing in an atmospheric environment, we tend to ignore inherent graphic forces such as movement, shape impact, strong surface controls. Graphic space, contingent upon such forces, often suffers. So let us first learn to see space in nature as a dramatic event through performing a number of exercises. These will help us generate true graphic space in our pictures.

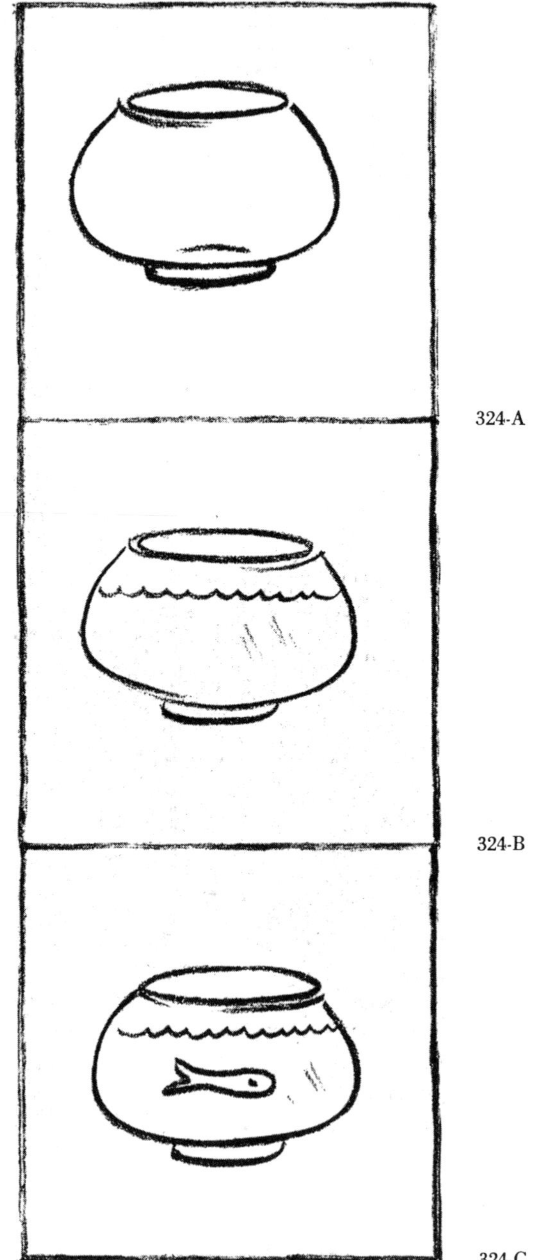



**324  Space as a Medium for Action**

The factor of space in nature, although seemingly so simple to understand that we take it for granted, has some baffling aspects. Let us explore the subject in this first of a series of mental exercises.

Suppose before us on a table is an empty goldfish bowl (*324-A*). Into the bowl we can thrust our hand and move it easily through the air enclosed by the bowl. Because our hand moves through the air, we refer to the air as space.

Now let us suppose the bowl filled with water (*324-B*). Our hand may still move through the water, but less easily than through the air. To our eyes the content of the bowl is a liquid, a mass of greater density than the air. To our hand the liquid is like space because our hand can still move about in it.

Let us drop a goldfish into the liquid (*324-C*). To the goldfish the liquid *is* space for he can swim in it. We witness the action of a mass within a mass. Although the fish and water are of different densities than our hand and air, we still are conscious of action being performed by a body in space.

Now let us imagine that the water has frozen. The liquid has now changed into a solid, a mass of great density. If the fish could survive the freezing, he would no longer be able to swim for the liquid has changed from space to solid.

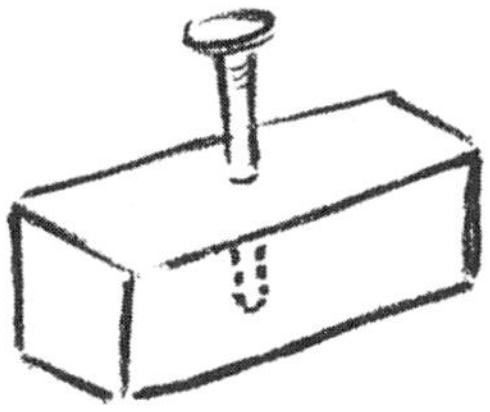

325-1

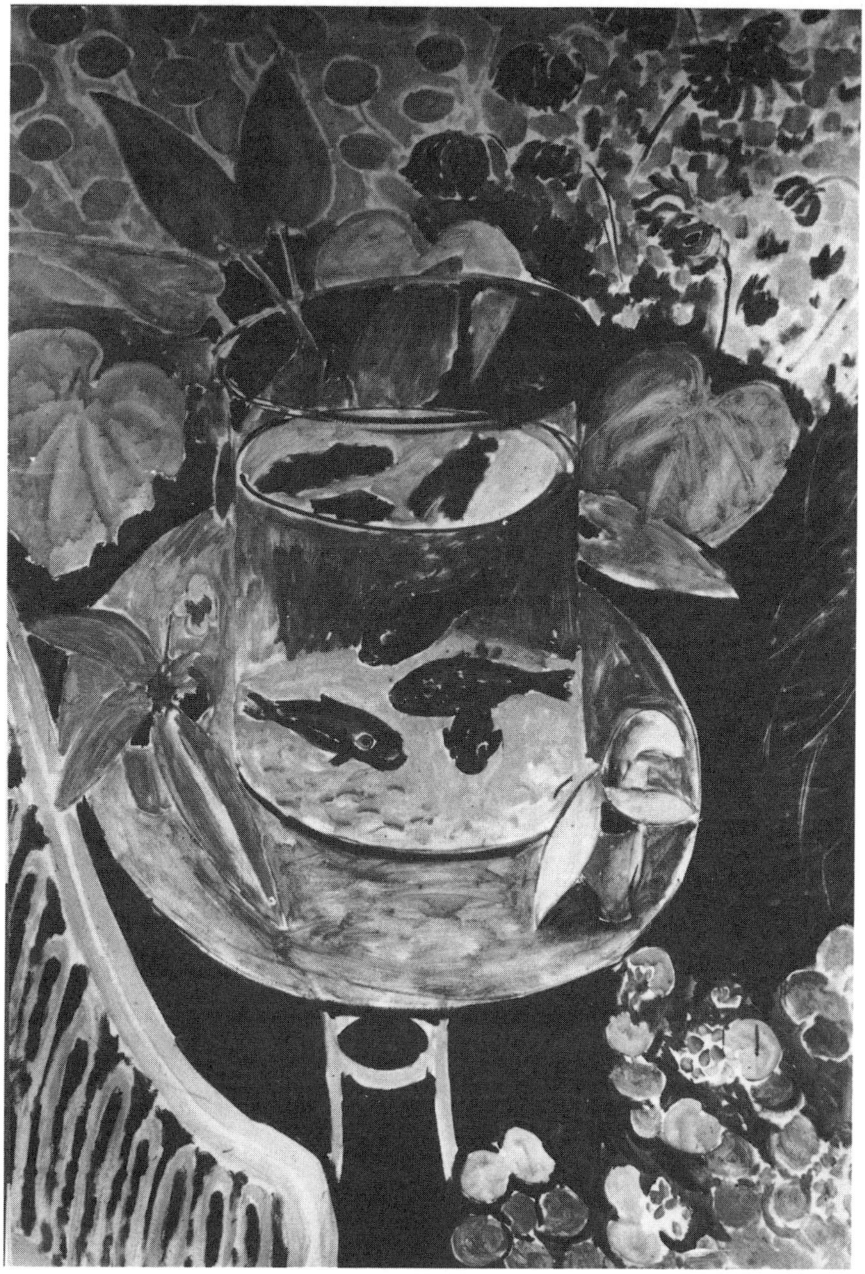

Henri Matisse (French, 1869-1954)
STILL LIFE WITH GOLDFISH, 1911
57⅞" x 38⅜"; oil on canvas
Pushkin Museum of Fine Arts, Moscow

Let us look at space another way. Suppose we observe a block of wood. The block is a mass of great density, a solid form. Now let us drive a nail into the block (*325*). To our eyes the nail and the block are both solid forms. To the nail, as it is driven in, the block is spacious. When the action stops, the block ceases to be spacious to the nail; the wood becomes an inert mass, much as the ice was an inert mass to the goldfish.

It seems reasonable to conclude that as long as action is possible a spacious condition exists. This space may or may not be visible. Only because of our acceptance of normal environments, which are usually enveloped in air, have we come to equate air with space. In so doing we often begin to think erroneously that since we cannot see air it follows that we cannot see space; therefore space does not exist.

## Distance versus Space



Our blindness to space often is due to our disregard for the very existence of space. We usually move through a familiar room avoiding the furniture quite unconsciously. But sometimes a chair is out of place, so we bump into it. We blame the chair for being in the wrong place, not the fact that our accustomed passage through space has been altered.

In other words, the existence of space becomes accepted through habit. We take space for granted, just as we do the air we breathe. As long as there is ample space to accommodate our actions, we accept its existence unthinkingly.

There are occasions, however, when we are well aware of space, as when we are in a tunnel, or if we are locked in a small closet. For now our actions are confined. This sense of confinement is also characteristic of certain aspects of space in a picture as we see here.

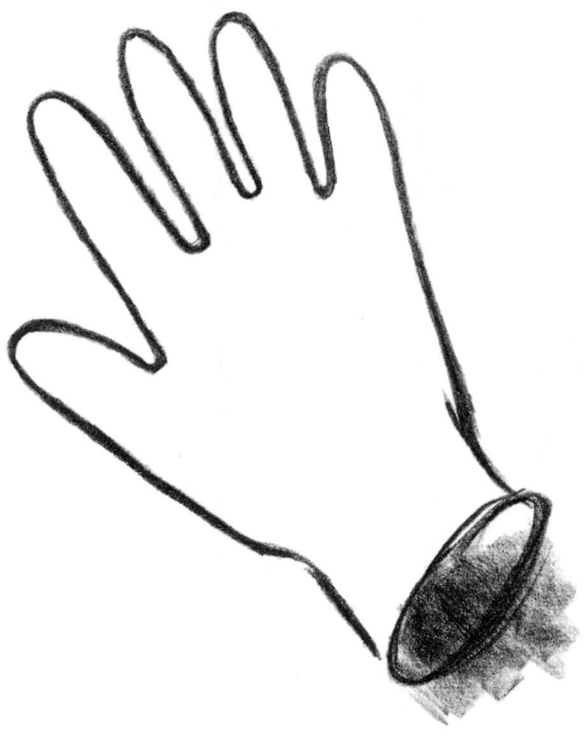

326



A factor contributing to our lack of awareness of space is confusion between space and distance. We often tend to think of the distance separating forms rather than of the space between them. For instance, we cross a street which is fifty feet wide. Our house is a block down the street. We think of a friend's farm as located ten miles down the road. We notice the mountains some twenty miles away. Seldom are we conscious that space between ourselves and these points even exists.

As distance between forms increases, our sense of space between them seems to diminish. Of course there are exceptions. On an unusually clear day when atmospheric conditions are ideal, as we often find in the desert, we may become startlingly aware of space. However, we may be unable to estimate distances even with approximate accuracy. But in most cases our ability to judge distance is no assurance of our being aware of space.

Another factor that contributes to our unawareness is actually determined by the way our eyes record. We have noted that as distance between us and a form in nature increases, binocular vision breaks down. Forms in the distance seem to flatten out. We tend to see a distant tree as a section, a shape, rather than as a three-dimensional form. In addition, such sections usually are modified by atmospheric effects which tend to diminish contrasts of color and value which otherwise might help to generate a sense of space. As a result space relations between us and distant forms weaken perceptibly.

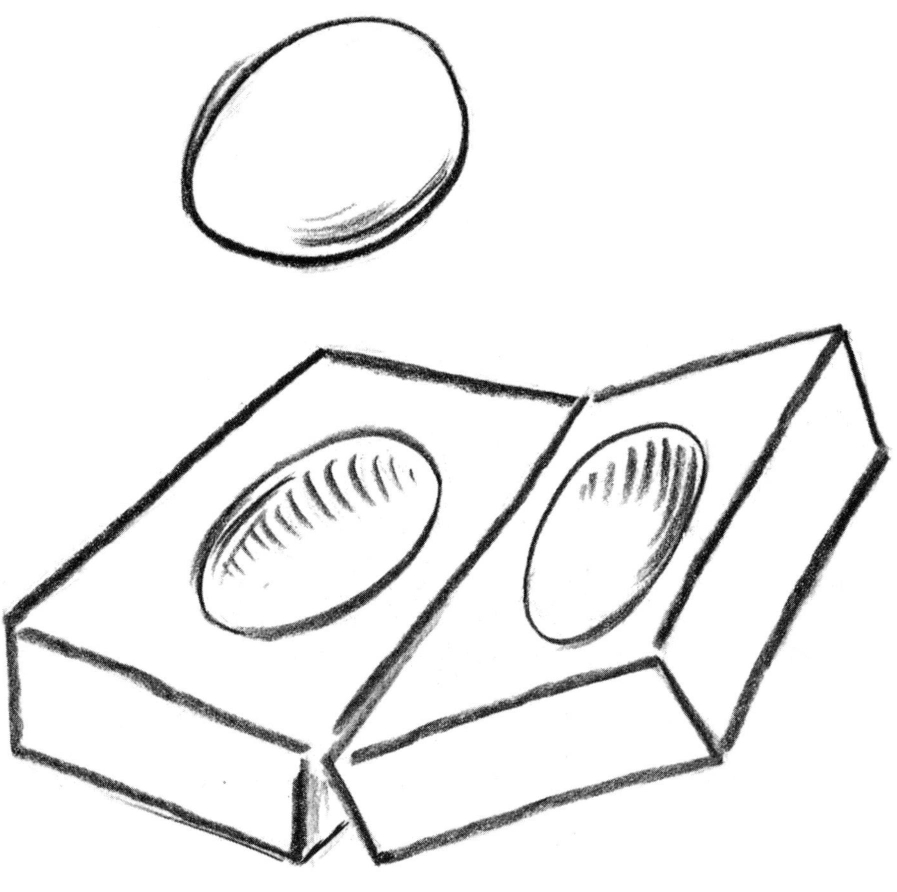



## The Reversibility of Form and Space

To see space we must condition ourselves to a slightly different way of seeing nature. For example, when we observe a hand we usually focus on its obvious properties: shape, color, physical structure. The form becomes the event.

But let us study the hand again. The visible surface of the hand is also the surface defining part of the adjacent space. The skin is common to both the form it contains and the space around the form. We may imagine an extremely thin glove as representing a surface common to both hand and space. When we remove the glove from the hand, we generate a space within the glove which is an exact duplicate of the hand (*326*). The glove is a surface of infinite thinness separating and defining two spaces of equal importance.

We find that it is possible to determine the shape of a space. The shape of a form is determined by the shape of its surfaces. The shape of an adjacent space is determined by the sum of such surfaces, in conjunction with other surfaces in close proximity.

To illustrate, let us imagine making a clay sculpture of a simple form, an egg, for example. Now let us make a plaster mold of this form. When the mold is opened and the form removed, the mold's concave surface is identical with the surface of the egg form but now defines a space (*327*). The longer we study this seemingly simple factor of surface, the more intriguing it becomes. We find that there are some unusual limits to both surface and space.

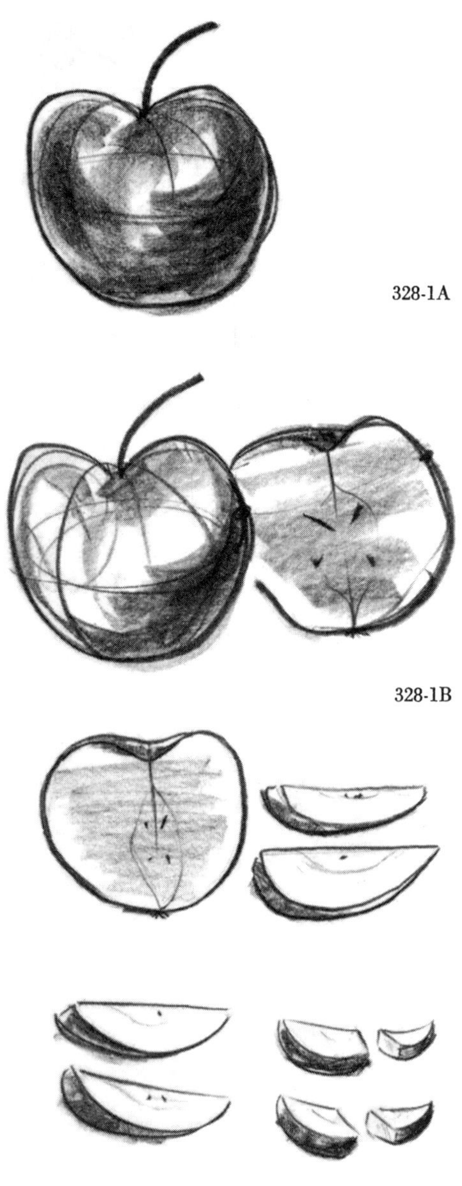

328-1A

328-1B

328-1C

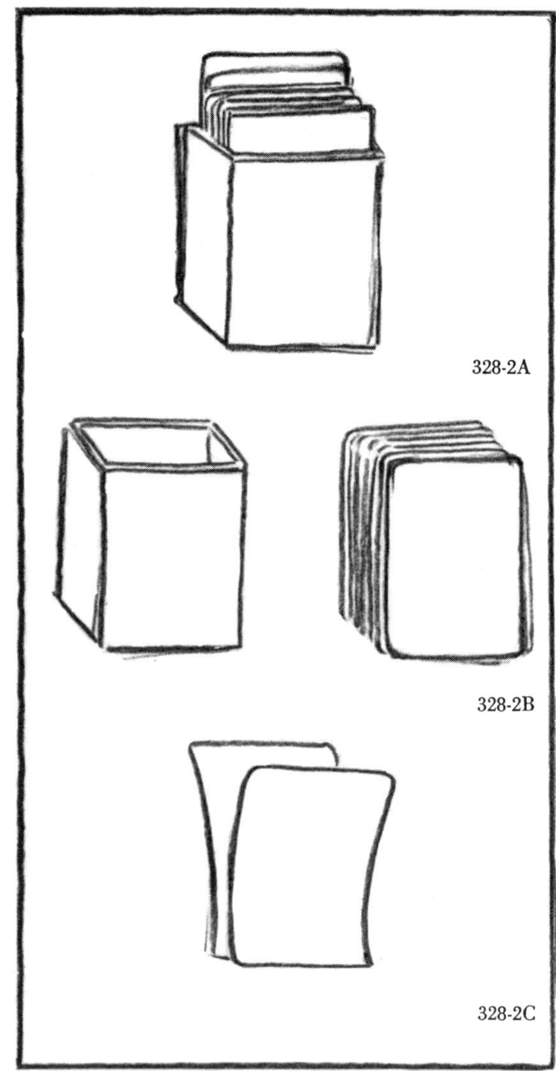

328-2A

328-2B

328-2C



As an example, suppose we examine an apple. Its surface is entirely red (*328-1A*). Now let us cut the apple into two parts (*328-1B*). There is still the same amount of red surface, but we have generated two new white surfaces. When we cut one half into two, we again generate new surfaces. As we continue to cut the apple into smaller and smaller parts, we continue to increase the area of the surfaces up to a point (*328-1C*). Eventually we arrive at not an infinite number of surfaces, but simply applesauce.

It is apparent that for surface to exist there must be a certain distance, a certain space between it and an adjacent surface, whether it be twenty miles or twenty millimeters. So we see that both form and space are dependent on our concept of surface.

## Space Through Surface Tension

Continuing our exploration of the relation of surface to space, again let us examine a box of playing cards, as we did in Chapter 4. (*328-2A*). The cards, taken from their box, are a replica of the box (*328-2B*). The box is a mold of the deck. The size of the box and the deck seem almost the same, for the sides of the box may be imagined as infinitely thin. But they are different, for the box is empty, while the deck made up of many cards seems solid.

Now again let us imagine the deck splitting into an infinite number of sections. If we imagine any two cards separated by a short interval we feel that they have a strong affinity for each other, almost as if they were magnetized, as if they would snap together if released (*328-2C*). This affinity is referred to as tension.

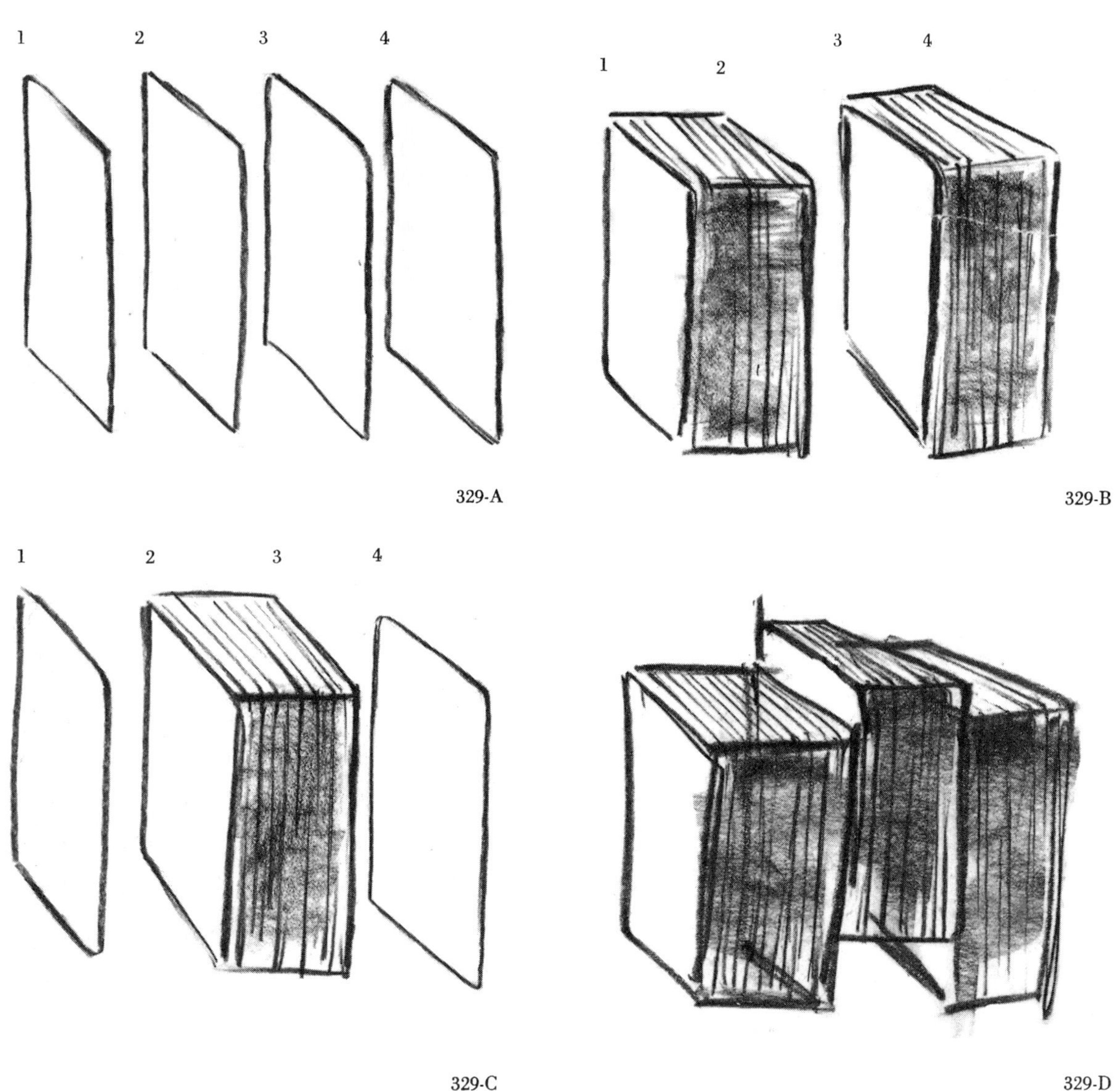



As we separate the two surfaces, they ultimately will arrive at the same positions as the outside cards of our deck. The intervening cards in the deck are but visual substitutes for the tension existing between the two outer surfaces.

By a few simple manipulations we may change the tension between surfaces. Let us arrange four cards parallel to each other, each the thickness of the deck apart (*329-A*). Between the two outer pairs let us substitute two decks, as indicated in *329-B*. A space is generated between the two adjacent surfaces of the decks. Each of these surfaces also partially defines a deck. In other words, the tension between 1-2 and 3-4, respectively, generates volumes; the tension between 2 and 3 generates space.

Now between 2 and 3 substitute a deck (*329-C*) and remove the other two decks, leaving only the outside card of each (1 and 4). The tension between 1-2 and 3-4 now generates two spaces; the tension between 2 and 3 generates a volume.

If we place three decks against each other, then slide the middle deck upward, we generate space above the outer decks and under the central deck (*329-D*). Looking back at *329-A*, we now realize how little we were concerned at that time with space. In looking at the arrangement in *329-D*, the surfaces take on a new significance in relation to the surrounding space. For as soon as we become aware of the tensions existing between surfaces we experience space.

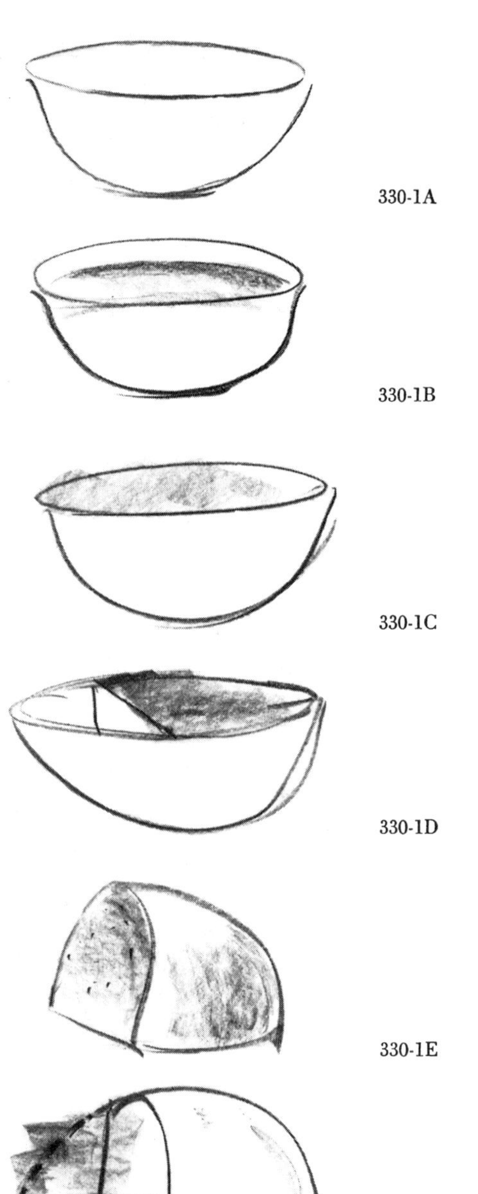

330-1A

330-1B

330-1C

330-1D

330-1E

330-1F

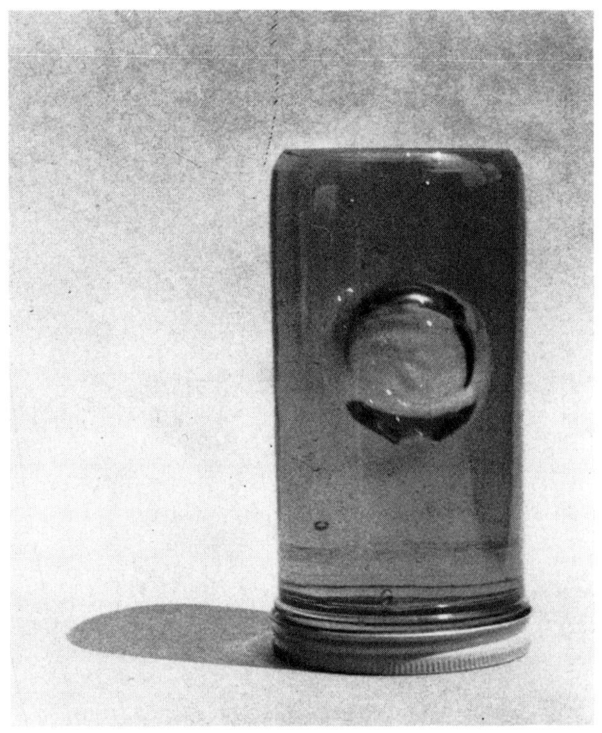

HONEY BUBBLE
(Photograph: Kenneth Graham)

## Seeing Space

330

Now when observing small objects in nature let us look at them intently not as forms but as surfaces. When we begin to relate one surface to another we actually "see" space.

So let us again examine an empty bowl, this time one of the kitchen variety (*330-1A*). Its inner surface clearly defines a space. Now partially fill the bowl with liquid gelatin which displaces some space and makes us even more aware of the space remaining in the bowl (*330-1B*). Completely fill the bowl with gelatin and allow it to set (*330-1C*). Now remove a portion of the gelatin (*330-1D*). The empty part of the bowl is a space event. When the gelatin is turned out upon a surface we have a partial cast of our original space, a form, equal to the space in the bowl, less the slice removed (*330-1E*). If we visualize the form completed, the space not actually defined will take on a quality in this specialized zone which we have not experienced elsewhere (*330-1F*).

As a final experiment in this series, let us purchase a tall thin jar of honey. Usually there is an air bubble at the top. If not, we can pour out a little honey and re-cap the jar. Now when the jar is turned upside down, the bubble of air rises slowly in the glass as a golden sphere. This is the honey bubble: it is space, but it will appear as a form. The light reflecting from the surface of the space, the bubble, or of the honey again demonstrates the importance of the surface factor.

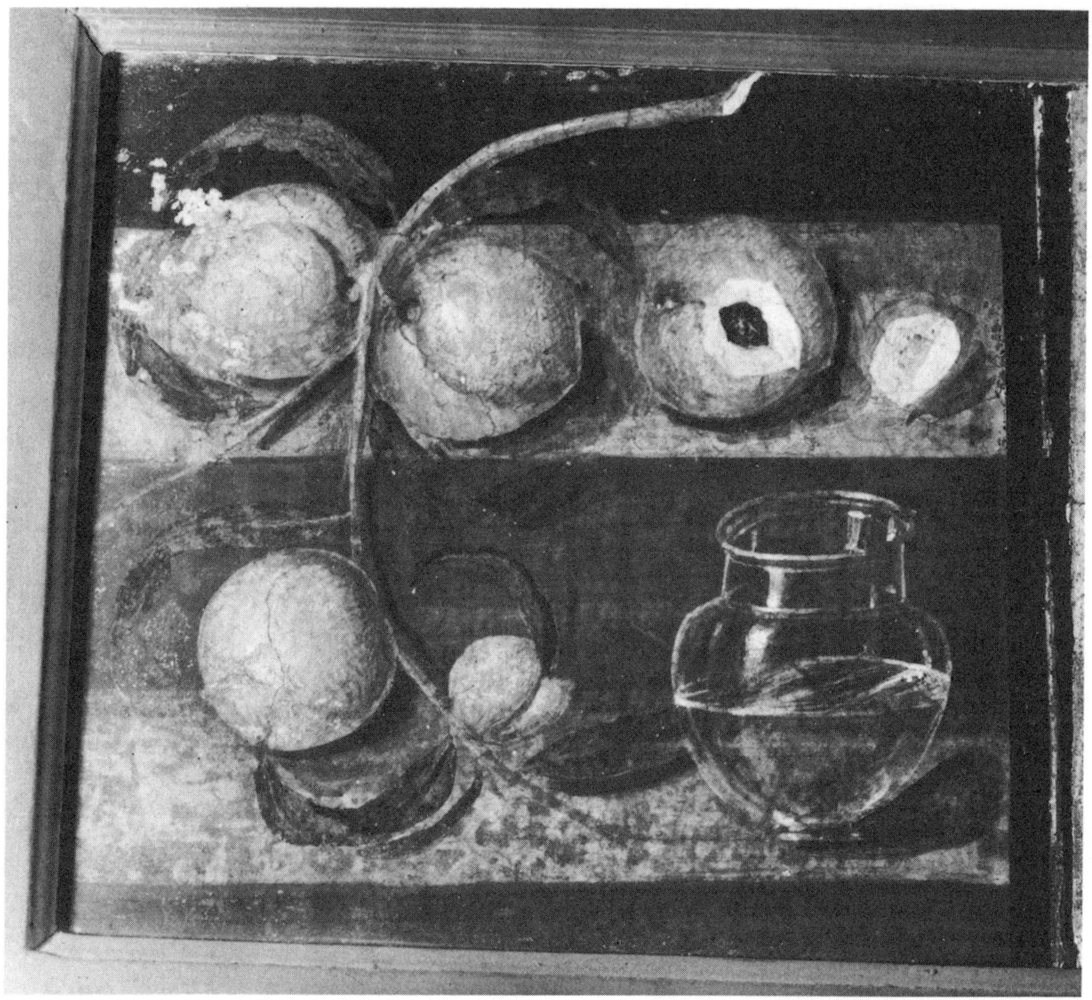

Artist unknown (Roman)
STILL LIFE, wall painting from Herculaneum
ca. 50 A.D.
National Museum, Naples
(Photograph: German Archaeological Institute
and Fototeca Union, Rome)

Once we begin to see space in nature, once we become aware of the tension between surfaces, our graphic world becomes more tangible This factor of space is not confined to any special school of painting. Here in this ancient Roman still life we see the artist's space concept revealed in a lucid exposition of familiar forms in a carefully controlled space environment. The way he explains the inside and outside surfaces of the peaches makes this commonplace subject into an unusual graphic statement.

So we find that as intangible as the subject of space may seem, it is possible to develop a real space sense. Now that we have begun to see space in nature, let us turn to the exploration of space in pictures.

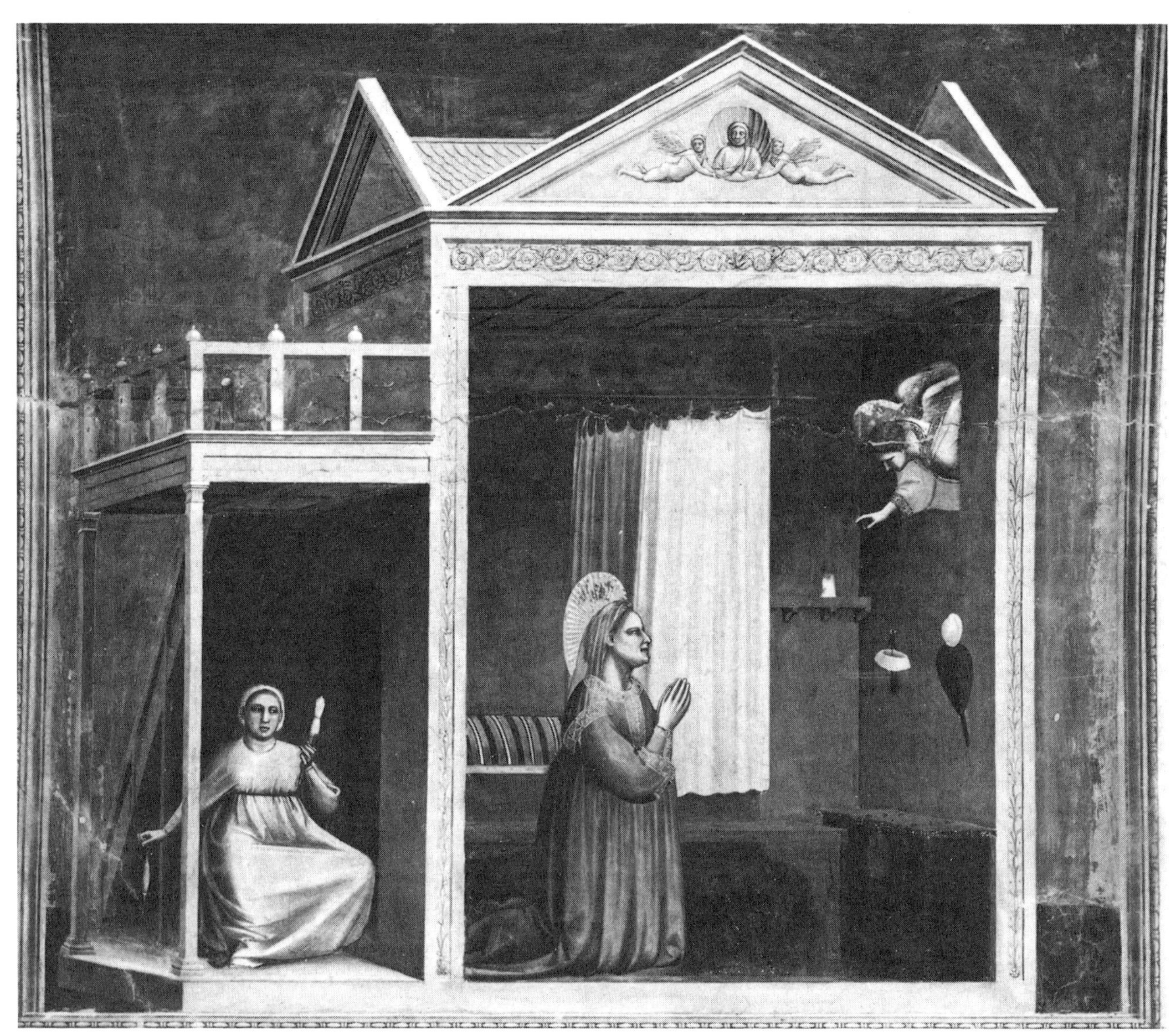

Giotto (Florentine 1266?-1337)
ANGEL APPEARING TO ST. ANNE, 1305-1306
fresco, Scrovegni Chapel, Padua
(Photograph: Alinari–Art Reference Bureau, Inc., N. Y.)



# 29 Generating Graphic Space

## Space and Surface Control

In our discussion of picture structure we have constantly emphasized the importance of maintaining strong surface control. This does not mean that our picture is contingent upon an organization of flat shapes. This is rarely the case. As we have seen, we constantly work with volumes suggesting three-dimensional forms, as Giotto's painting shows here. We also have seen how such volumes may be translated in terms of sectional perspective, rather than in terms of modeling and rendering. Strangely enough, it is usually through a true realization of volumes that the evolution of strong and original graphic shapes is possible.

For example, if a symbol of a figure is required in a picture, the artist skilled in abstracting the figure into strong graphic structures usually will arrive at a stronger, more exciting shape statement than will the artist with little or no understanding or experience in depicting the figure.

It also is very difficult to arrive at convincing abstractions of volumes without true understanding of graphic space. The following notes and series of exercises are aimed at developing control of deep graphic space. Those interested primarily in shallow space pictures may find this material helpful in developing control of surface by exploring this opposite problem.

## The Hidden Factors

Although graphic space is intangible and invisible, the picture maker must learn what it is, where it is, and how its presence is felt. In building a picture the artist is faced with problems involving other intangible factors as well. These factors such as tension, movement, shape impact, are truly abstract. None can be mastered easily, none can be realized in picture terms without constant and unending practice.

A factor such as space may be grasped mentally rather easily, but it is imperative that we practice with space in actual graphic terms. In other words, we actually must make hundreds of drawings and paintings, or shoot many feet of film, before we can control graphic space or any other hidden factors that make up a picture.

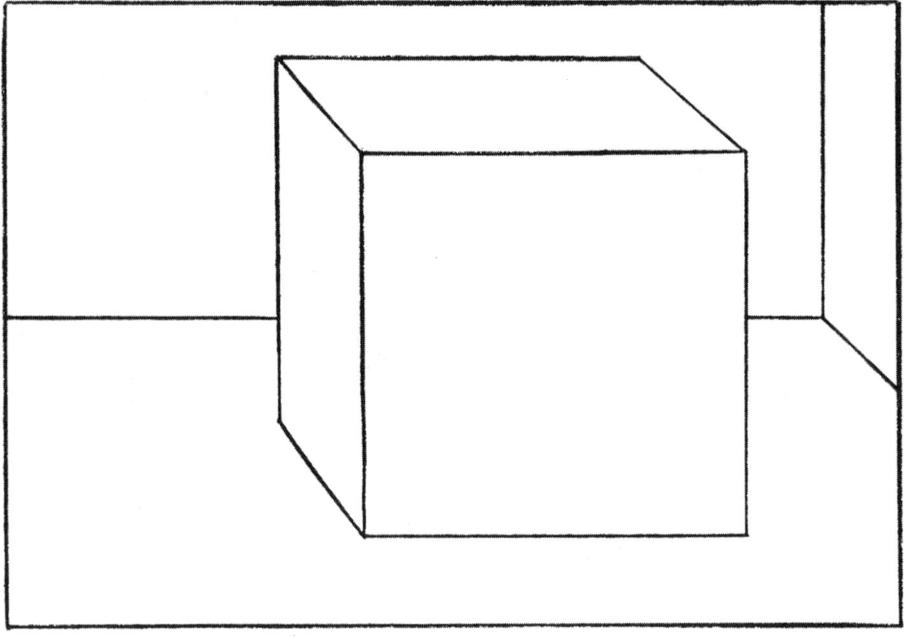

334

 **The Perspective Projection of a Cube**
To gain experience in generating graphic space,
let us first draw a simple cube within a cube
with a T-square and triangle (*334*). We are
aware of the exactness of the lines, the
correctness of the angles and the flatness of each
geometric shape. We now have a picture of a
form in depth, a volume. But as we examine
this "correct" drawing we are increasingly
conscious that something is missing. The
drawing seems sterile, cold, generating a
minimum of space.

As we study this projection, we begin to see
that there are reasons for the lack of space.
Some of the difficulty is caused by the generation
of graphic accents, since any two or more
intersecting lines create a strong graphic accent.
This is particularly noticeable where one line
impinges upon another at less than ninety
degrees.

Such an accent, a graphic star (*335-A*), may
occur in any drawing and results when two or
more lines intersect, especially if one or more
of them are diagonals (*335-B*). The more the
star is stressed, the more it tends to emphasize
picture surface rather than space.

When two lines intersect, they generate a
right angle, an acute angle, or an obtuse angle.
The acute angle generates violent graphic
activity (*335-B*); the obtuse angle is much more
recessive visually (*335-C*). The degree of angle
utilized in any drawing has great bearing on
the space structure of the picture, often causing
the difference between a tight and a generous or
"open" statement.

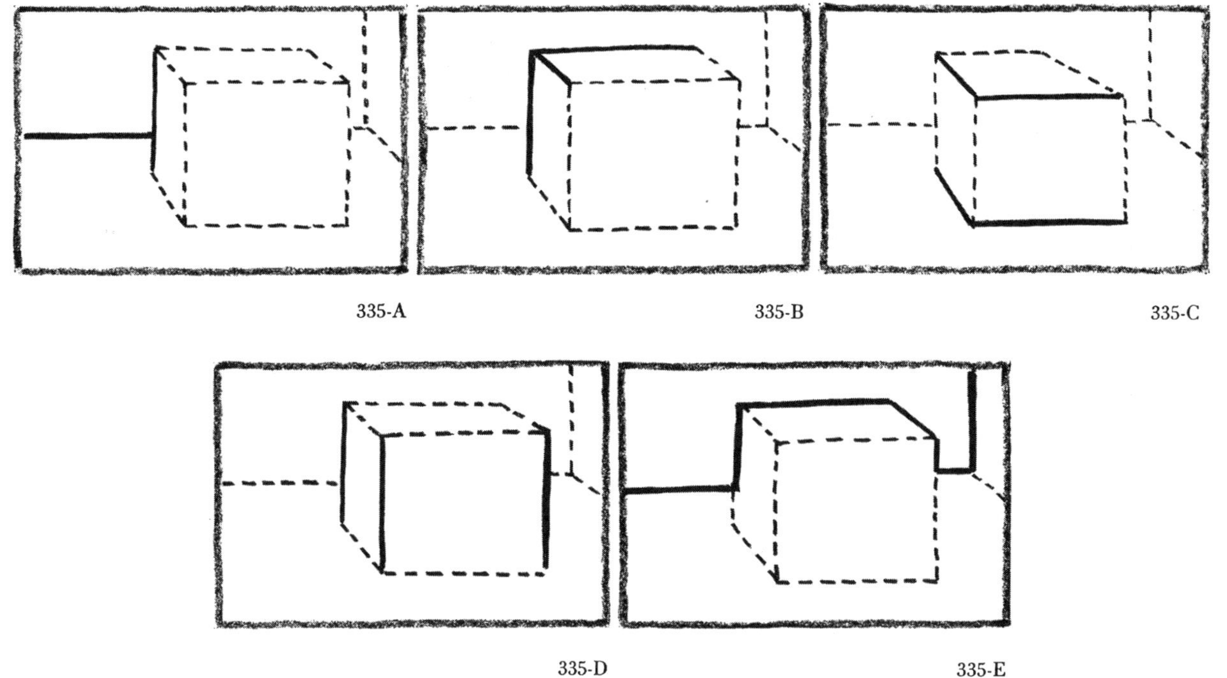

335-A        335-B        335-C

335-D        335-E

Parallel lines, no matter in what planes they lie, often tend to flatten the picture (*335-D*). However, parallel lines may at times be used to strengthen the surface impact of the picture, as we noted in our discussion of picture lines.

When a number of lines lying in different planes are connected consecutively, they often generate flat shapes. This device employed consciously may occasionally be useful, but unless carefully controlled it will destroy space (*335-E*).

## Graphic Adjustments



To overcome the rigidity of the perspective projection, or any drawing, many adjustments in the lines, shapes, and angles may be made.

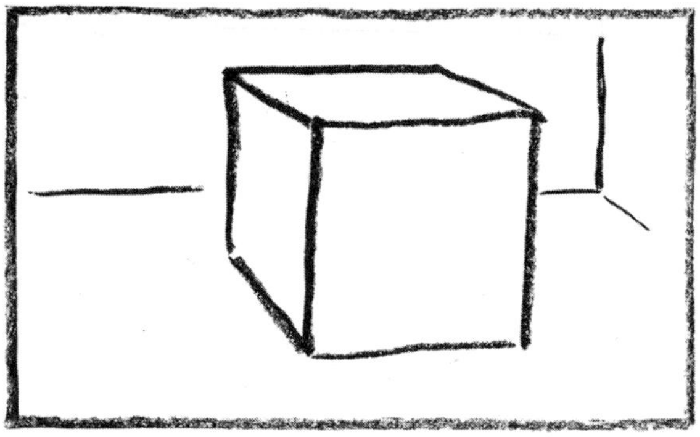

336-A

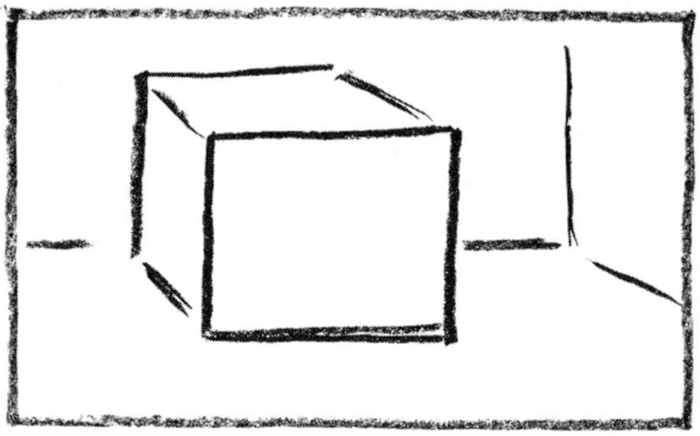

336-B

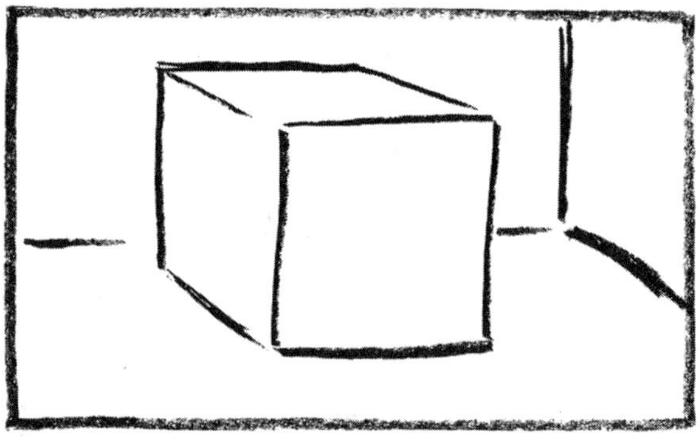

336-C

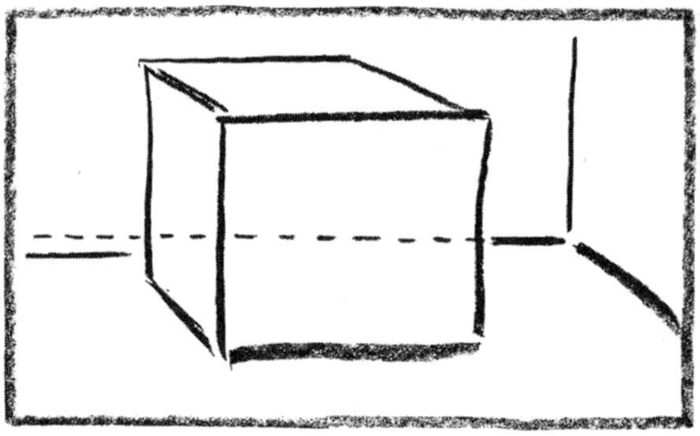

336-D

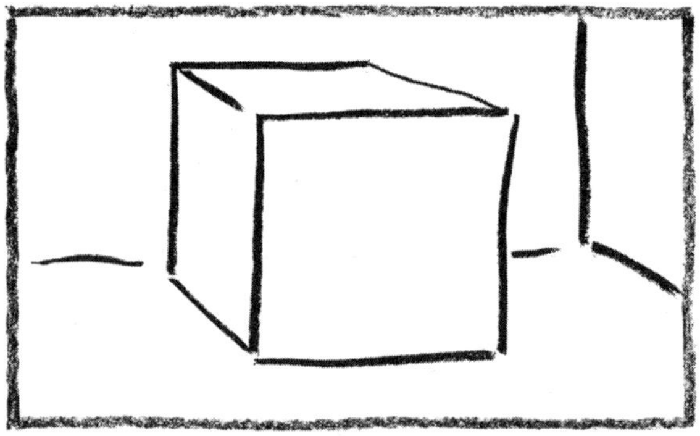

336-E

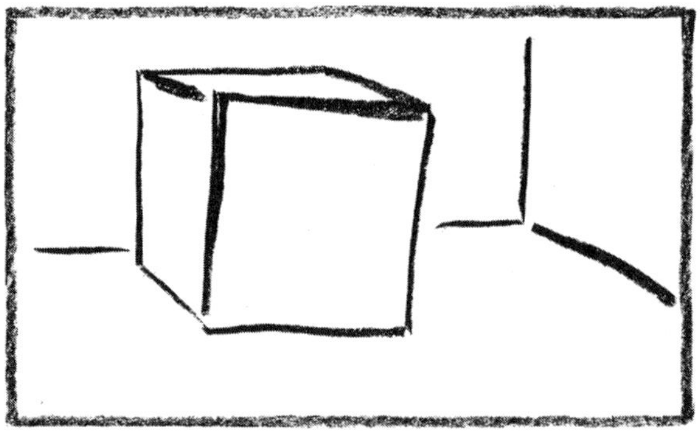

336-F



As a line approaches an intersection it may be feathered, or reduced in thickness, or separated from the second line by a passage, white, gray, black, or an appropriate color depending on the structure of the picture (*336-A*). The graphic star may be adjusted similarly, weakening the linear impact by changing the weight of the lines (*336-B*).

Straight lines within the picture may be adjusted slightly by bowing, instead of ruling them. The concavity or convexity of a line, or combination of both, may accommodate the direction of an adjacent line in this way. This is especially effective when a line is directed past a core (*336-C*).

A line continuing past a core and emerging on the other side of a volume may be offset, not aligned, thus generating a sense of movement and intensifying our sense of space (*336-D*).

We may accommodate the direction of the vertical corner of the enclosing cube to the inner cube, and generate more space (*336-E*).

An angle may be intensified or weakened to suit a picture problem. In so doing, the direction of a surface may be altered by tipping or rotating to generate space adjacent to a surface (*336-F*).

The accompanying diagrams have been purposely exaggerated to emphasize clearly each point under discussion. In most pictures slighter and more subtle adjustments may be all that is necessary to generate more space. An adjustment in a line, for instance, may be well within the actual width of a line.

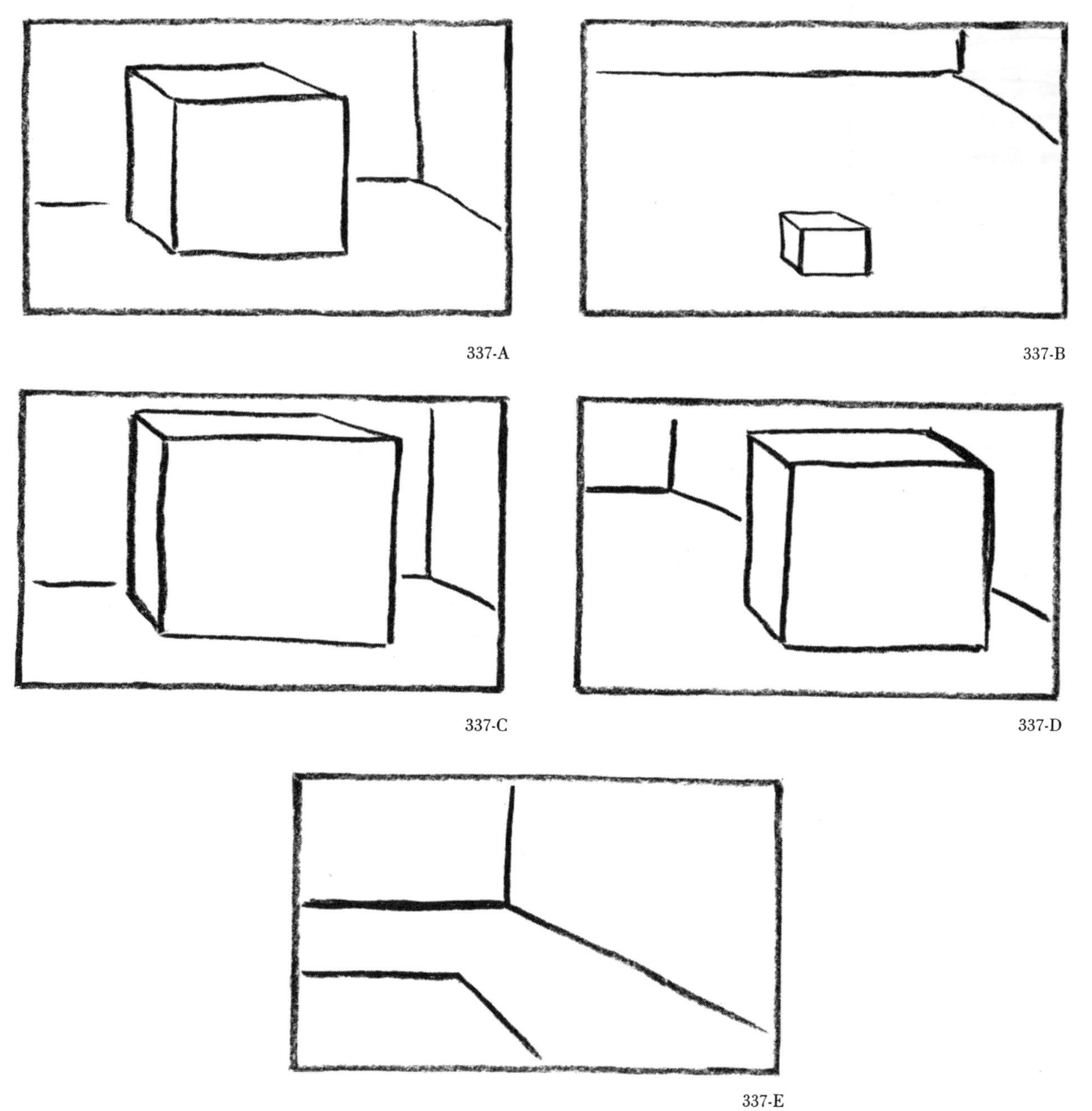

337-A

337-B

337-C

337-D

337-E

## Distribution of Space

As we continue to examine the perspective projection of our cube within a cube, we realize that the relation of the size and position of the internal cube to the external cube has great bearing on space distribution (*337-A*). As the size of the internal cube decreases we always experience greater extension of the surfaces of the enclosing cube, but not necessarily greater space (*337-B*).

As the size of our cube is increased, we often experience the space surrounding it more intensely *(337-C)*. But not always, for we can change the distribution of space visually by enlarging the enclosing cube. In *337-D* the internal cube is exactly the same size as in *337-C*, but the enclosing cube has been visually increased by pushing the back plane far into the picture.

We should note that by increasing the size of the internal cube in *337-D*, we mask out a great deal of the surface area of the enclosing cube, yet introduce more distance. Such a distribution of space often results in graphic holes which must be accounted for in designing the picture.

If the inner cube becomes too large its identity is lost. Instead of a cube we may read the partial shape as part of a flat rug (*337-E*).

By careful manipulation we may introduce a great deal of space in front of, to the side of, or above the cube.

To develop a real sense of graphic space we should draw a cube within a cube *every day* for a month. It is important that the exercise be performed *daily*. Making thirty drawings at one sitting is not at all the same as making one a day for thirty days.

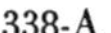

338-A

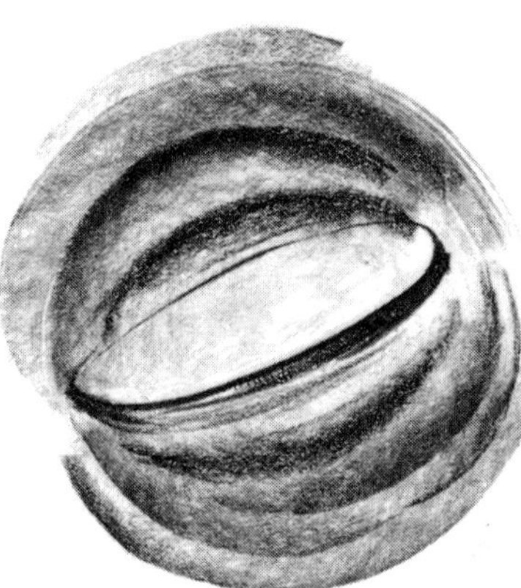

338-B

338 **Generating Space Through Action**

In Chapter 20 we noted how action transposed into graphic terms affects the energy emanating from our picture. Let us see how action affects graphic space. If we examine a coin we see that it has some depth, but primarily it is a flat disk. Let us flip it into the air. As we watch it spinning something magical occurs. The flat coin visually becomes a sphere. The action of the coin generates a convincing three-dimensional form in its own environment of space. When at rest the coin looks flat (*338-A*). When spinning, immediately around the sphere a new sense of space is felt (*338-B*).

In the same way a figure sitting on a park bench may seem almost flat, especially in a middle distant view. When the figure moves we become conscious of a new dimensional quality, an intensification of space in the immediate zone around the figure.

To further investigate this phenomenon, let us examine a simple gate in a wall. The function of a gate when open, is to allow us to pass through a barrier, when closed, to bar passage. Its basic action is to swing. Its extreme positions, where action no longer occurs, are reached when it is fully open or completely closed. Any one of the positions of the gate between these extreme positions is temporary, or an in-between position.

A drawing depicting either extreme position of the action represents a static condition and may be so drawn. Showing the gate in any one of the in-between positions it may temporarily occupy or pass through suggests a different graphic approach from that of a perspective projection.

If the angles and edges of the gate are projected as they are seen in nature when the gate is in an in-between position, the drawing

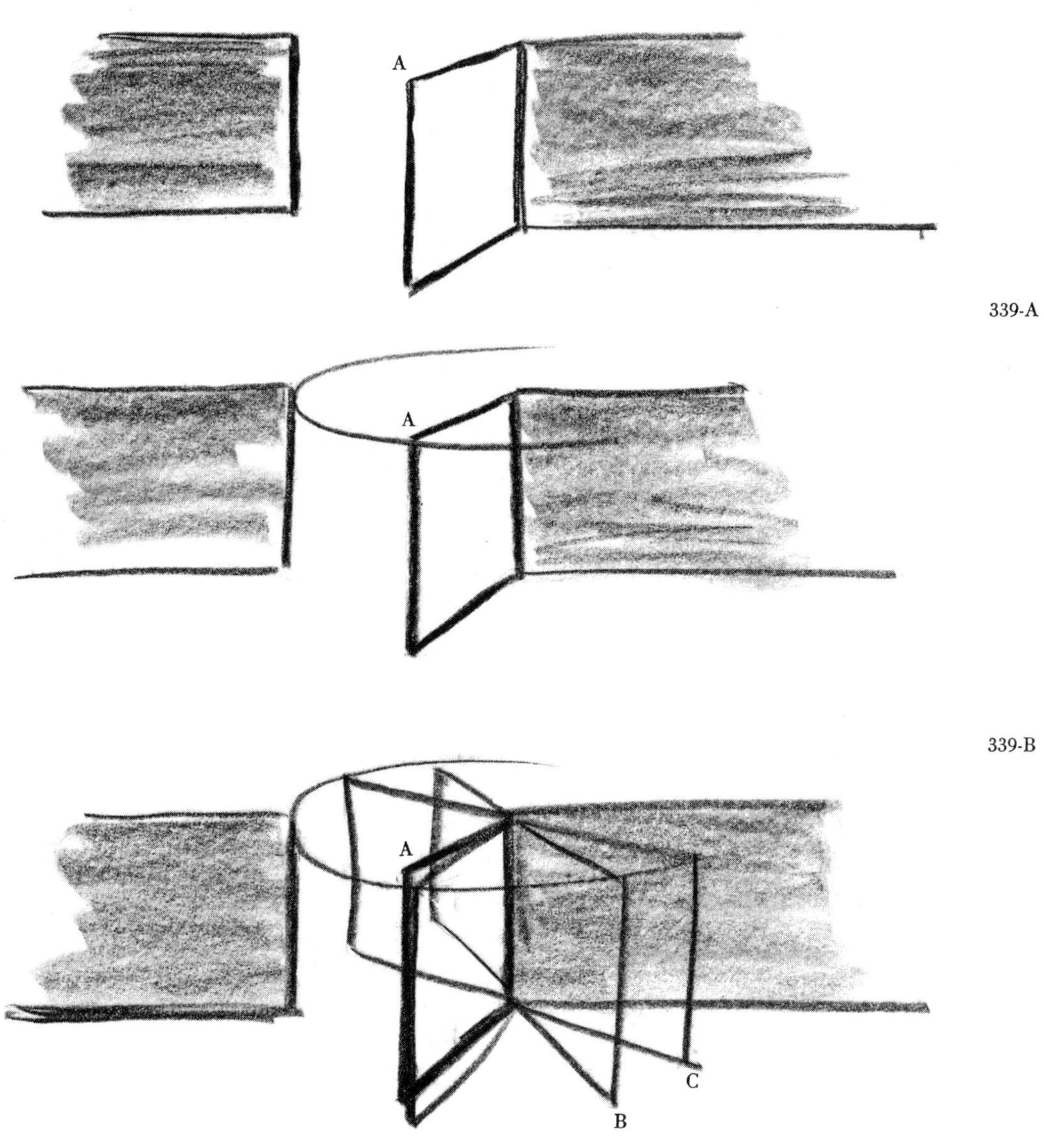

339-A

339-B

339-C

very likely will seem static and lifeless. Such a drawing is determined by carefully plotting the observed angles and lengths of the various elements (*339-A*). Because it is conceived as a picture of a motionless form, the drawn image of the gate will tend to lack space.

By visualizing the gate in action a new sense of life is given the picture. To demonstrate, let us indicate the arc described by the swinging gate (*339-B*). At one instant in the course of its swing the gate passes through point *A*. This point determines the position of the gate in time, and dictates the graphic structure of the gate (*339-C*). It is possible that point *A* accidentally may coincide with corner *A* in our perspective projection (*339-A*). In each drawing the gate may seem identical, open to the same degree. Yet something unusual has happened.

The similarity is purely coincidental. As the gate swings, it may be shown as having passed through not only *A*, but *B* and *C* (*339-C*), or any other position as it swings through its arc in time. Seen this way, the drawing takes on new meaning, a new vitality. And because the gate is visualized in action we become more aware of the space through which it moves. A new quality of space in the picture is almost inevitable.

The problem of indicating a symbol of the human figure in a picture suggests an approach similar to that of drawing the gate. We realize that a figure at rest in nature must have arrived at this position through action, although if the figure is reclining or dead we may tend to ignore this factor. Usually the figure in nature moves into various positions from some inert position which can be used as reference. This position is comparable to the extreme position of the gate, either open or closed.

339

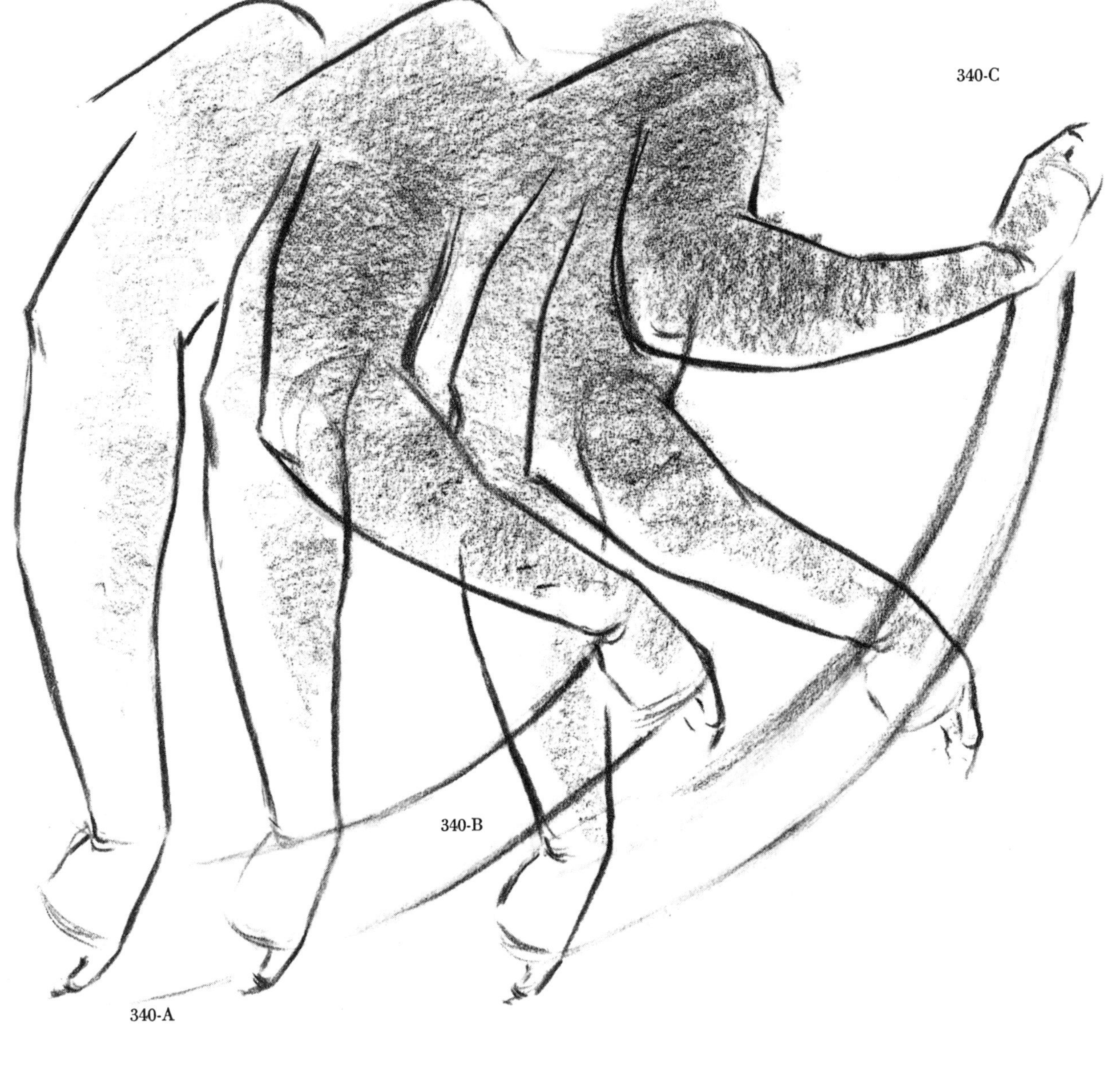





The positions through which the figure moves represents distinct intervals in a time sequence. In our drawing of the figure, as with the drawing of the gate, we first establish fixed references or extreme positions (*340-A*). We may then draw parts of the figure in any instant in time by moving them in arcs. For instance, the arm in position *340-A* is at rest, an extreme; when swung through arcs, the forearm and hand swing away from the body, *340-B*, and arrive at position *340-C*. The upper arm goes into perspective not as a projected angle, but as an image of the arm at an instant in time. Of course, in actual action in nature these arcs usually are generated simultaneously.

So we have a choice; to see the figure in a frozen pose and draw it as if it were a statue; or to see the pose as but an occurrence at a given instant of an action in time. If conceived as a projection, the edges and observed angles of the figure are drawn as if frozen in time and space. If conceived as an occurrence in a time sequence, a volume can be at a particular position in space only by arriving there through arcs representing phases of action. Instead of a copy of observed shapes, each volume will reflect what it is doing. Each volume or combination of volumes becomes a symbol which is a manifestation of forces. This concept of depicting a form moving in time has value in creating a dynamic still picture. As we shall see in Part IX, it is vital to making an animated picture.

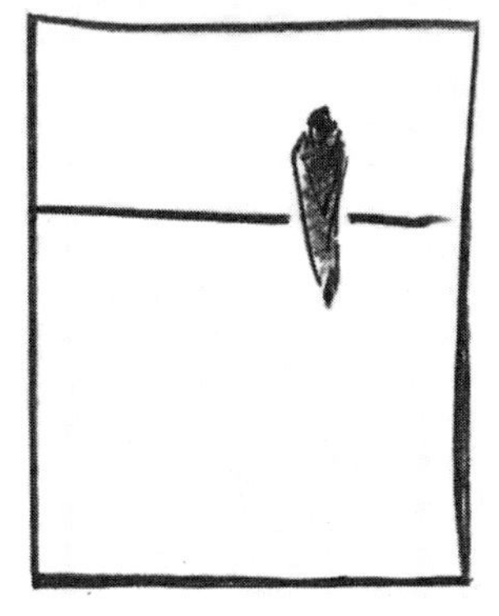

341-A

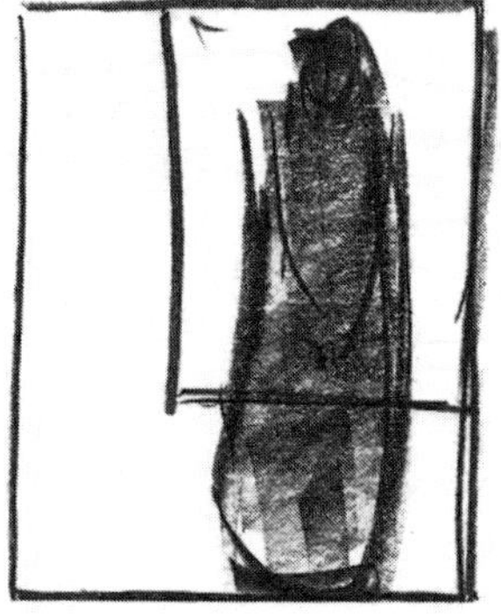

341-B

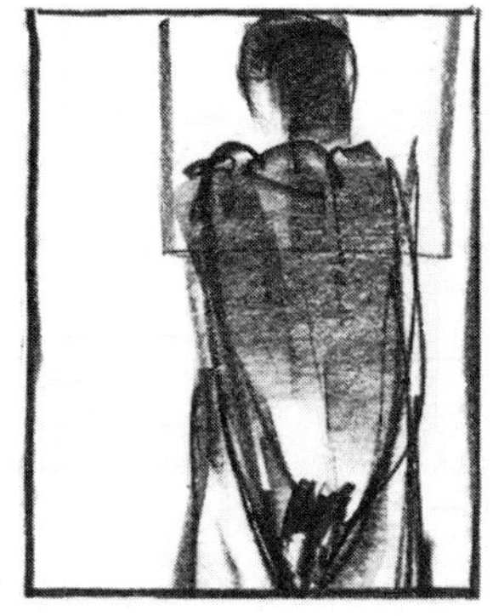

341-C

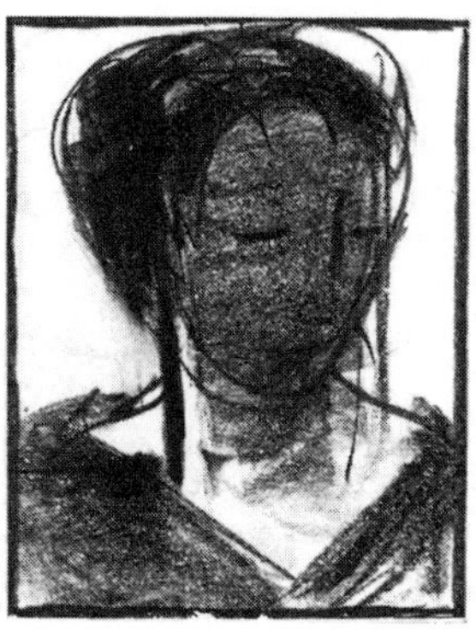

341-D

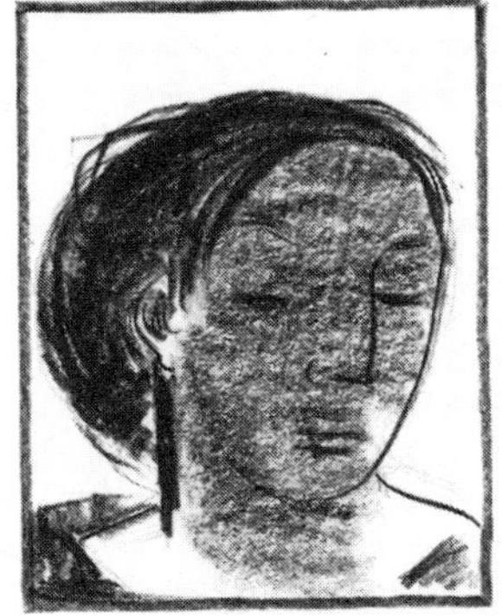

341-E

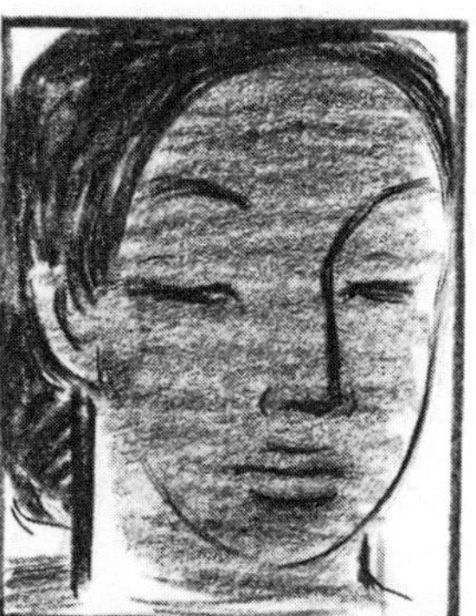

341-F

### Reducing Area to Intensify Space

In developing graphic space not only may the subject be conceived in action, but the artist also may be in action in relation to the subject, an adaptation of trucking as noted in Chapter 18. To illustrate, let us draw a figure symbol high in a field (*341-A*). As we approach the subject it seems larger (*341-B*). If we show only three-quarters of the subject the drawing begins to have intimacy (*341-C*).

As we draw the figure in close three-quarter view most area around it is eliminated, the rest now becomes spacious. The drawing takes on more reality (*341-D*).

When we draw the subject from a very close view almost all surrounding area disappears, we become more aware of the space generated by secondary forms making up the subject (*341-E*).

By staging the drawing from a station point even closer, it is possible to eliminate all background area, emphasizing only the internal space relations (*341-F*).

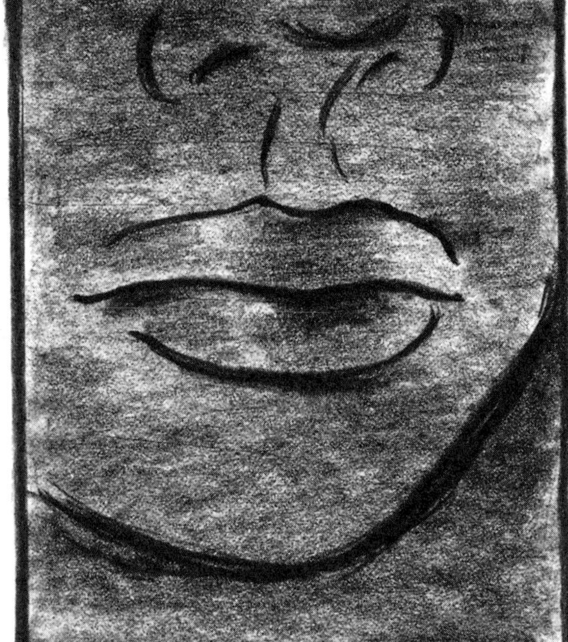

342



Ultimately our station point may be so close that the original external shape of the subject is lost. The picture must then be built around one or more significant parts (*342*). Such a drawing frequently is used in a series of drawings in which the subject previously has been identified. In a single drawing, such as a portrait, the lack of identification through loss of external silhouette shapes becomes a serious problem.

We see that as background areas of a picture are reduced our awareness of space often is enhanced. As we become more aware of space we begin to feel a new intimacy with the subject. Maximum intimacy is achieved when the space relations are generated entirely, or to a large extent, by the internal structures within a shape.

**Balancing Line and Area to Achieve Space**

In making drawings we often are confronted with a peculiar relation of line to area. The line creates a certain visual activity. It also generates area. An area, which in a drawing may be only the white paper, also creates a visual disturbance. A balance between the two factors must be achieved.

But in many line drawings the activity of the silhouette becomes excessive for various reasons. For instance, the line often becomes overactive because of emphasis on unimportant muscular outcrops or incidentals of hair or drapery, etc. Faulty line structure often results from too much importance being given to curved lines. Every volume given equal importance also overaccentuates line, thus destroying graphic space. This evenness often is aggravated by use of a mechanical line.

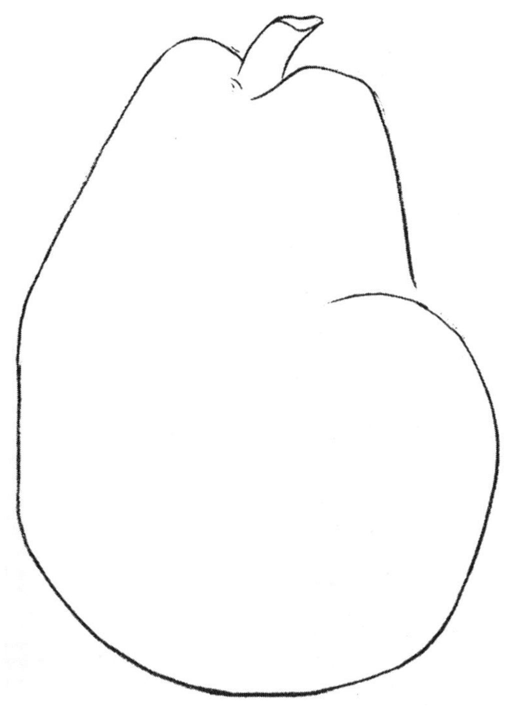

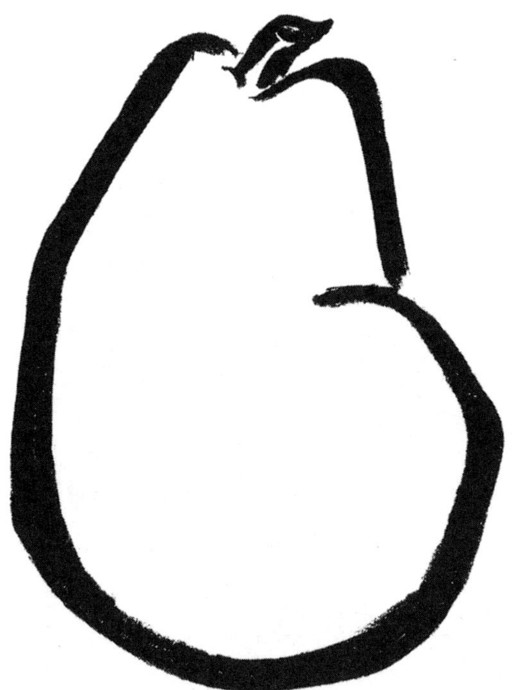

343-A

343-B

Unless artfully controlled, the unweighted line, one made with a stylus or inflexible point, can become quite noticeable. Also the so-called "sensitive line" too often becomes an affectation. It also may become mechanical, destroying picture space. As we noted in Chapter 7, if the spectator looking at our line drawing sees the line first, the line structure is faulty.

The degree of activity generated by an area can be equally troublesome. One of the most common difficulties occurs when area overpowers line. Usually this is due to a disproportion in the thickness of the line delineating the volume to the amount of area enclosed by the line.

To illustrate, let us make two drawings; the first with a very fine line enclosing a large area (*343-A*), the second with a heavy line defining the same volume and held to the same size (*343-B*). Overlooking the drawing as a symbol and observing it merely as a ratio of line width to area width, the line in *343-A* might be one-fiftieth the width of the area enclosed; a line in *343-B* might be but a tenth in width. As we decrease the ratio of line width to area width to one one-hundredth or one one-thousandth, it becomes more and more difficult for the line to control the area. Either the line becomes too fragile, or the area becomes too insistent. Such large areas seem to push us away from the picture. We begin to lose a sense of space. Such areas usually lack visual interest, thus further destroying our involvement in the picture.

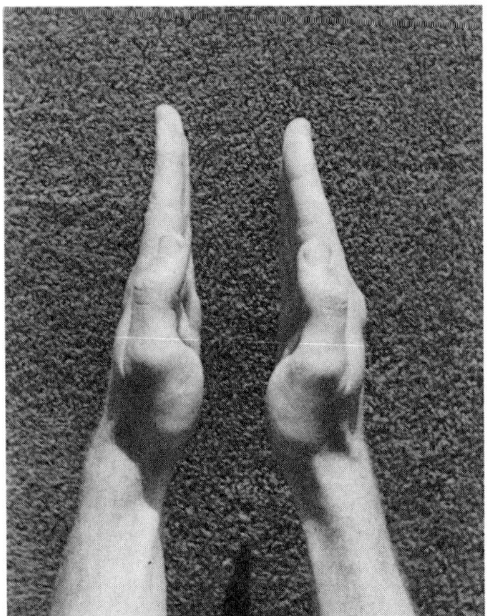

344-A

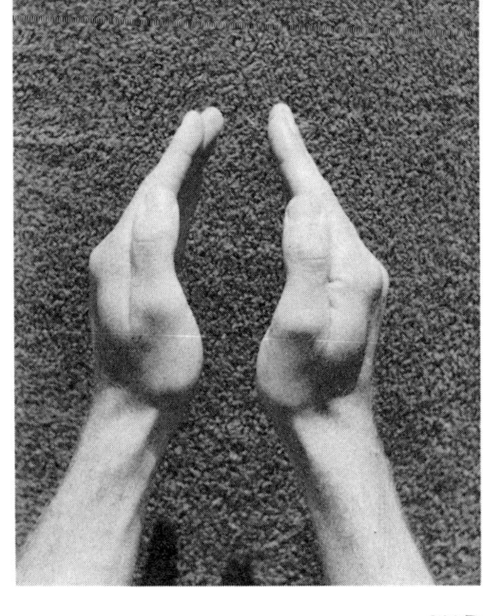

344-B

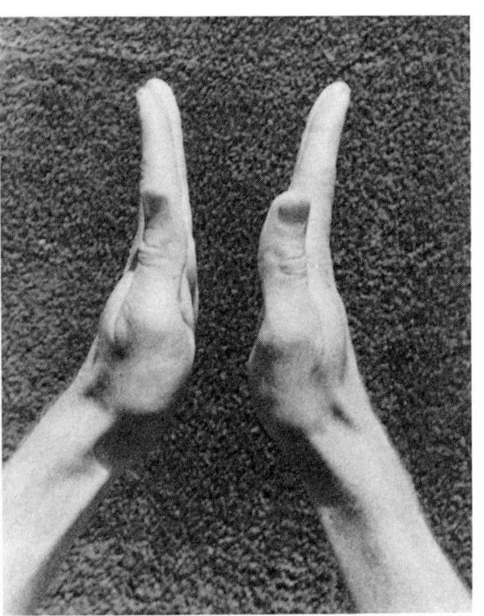

344-C

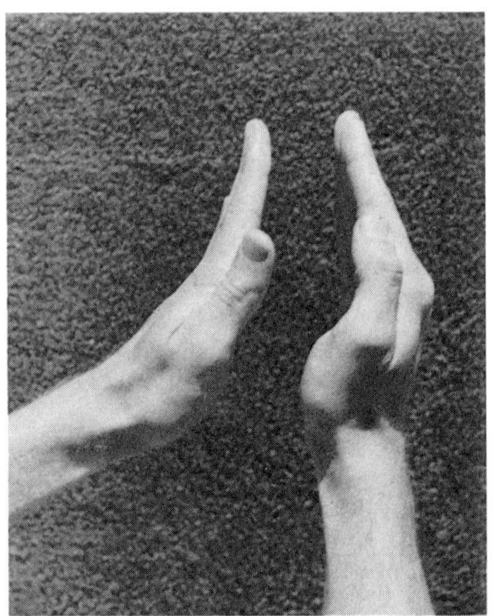

344-D



The over-insistent area often seems just to lie on the surface. It often ceases to have direction in relation to other shapes and lines. At times, by becoming so insistent, it loses its planal relation to the whole picture.

If we wish to develop picture space we find that too much line activity over-emphasizes the line as a design factor. It often is questionable as a design factor at all. Too much line activity usually forces us to see the line first, and as a result the drawing seems flat. The line overwhelms the space factor. On the other hand, too much insistence on area usually results in a sense of emptiness, remoteness, and often a sense of flatness. The space factor is reduced to a minimum.

When line and area are in balance a great sense of space is generated. This line-area balance is one of the keys to scale, which we shall discuss in the next chapter.

## Compression and Extension

To further develop control of graphic space let us try some simple exercises. First, let us hold the palms of our hands flat and parallel to each other about three inches apart. We probably will not notice the space between them unless it is brought to our attention (*344-A*).

Now if we slightly cup our hands we become aware of a stronger relation of one hand to the other. We feel the space between them is bounded, in a state of compression. The space becomes an event (*344-B*).

Now let us arch the hands away from each other. Physically we experience a strong tension between them. We seem to be pushing space out of the semi-enclosure. The space seems to be in a state of expansion or extension. Again the space between the hands becomes an event (*344-C*).

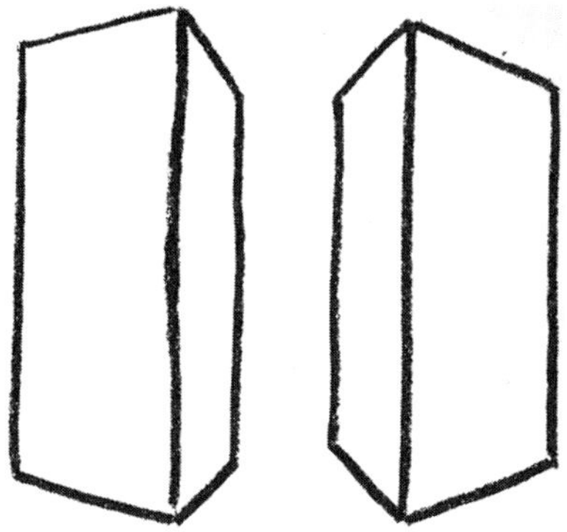

345-A

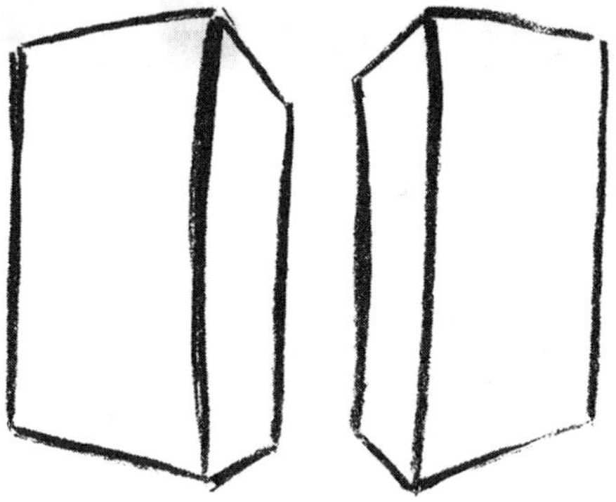

345-B

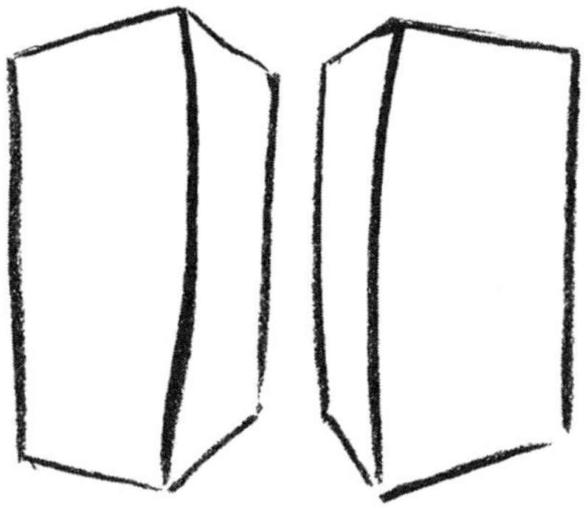

345-C

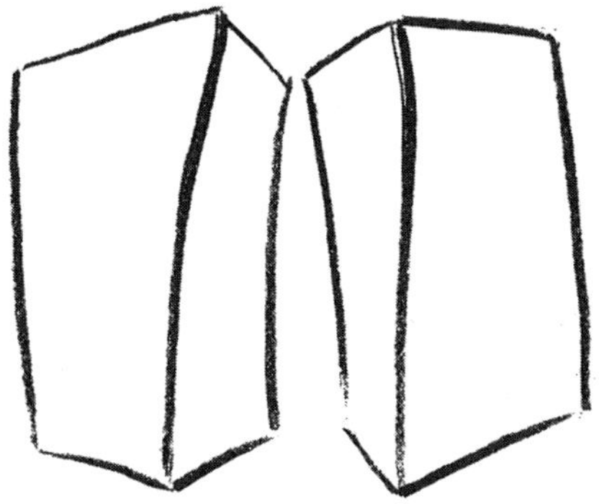

345-D

HANDS
(Photographs: Kenneth Graham)

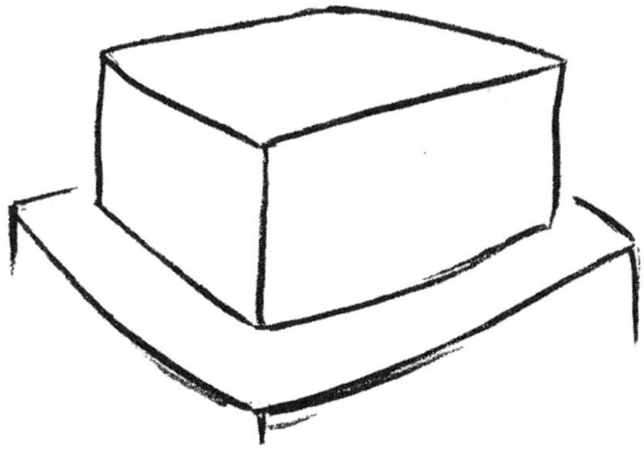

345-E

Now let us cup the palm of one hand and the back of the other as we would if stacking two spoons of the same size (*344-D*). When we separate the hands about three inches, their parallel condition becomes noticeable. The more we are aware of this paralleling, the less we are aware of intervening space. As we found when the hands were held flat and parallel, the space between them is not dramatized.

We have explored in some detail the construction of a perspective projection and found it characteristically rigid (*345-A*). To overcome this rigidity we found that great liberties could be taken in the actual structure of the lines and angles involved.

In the same way we find that the surfaces of a cubic structure may be manipulated to intensify our awareness of space in the picture.

We see in *345-B* that by cupping the related  surfaces and carefully weighing the importance of the various edges of the surfaces to each other, space seems to be captured or compressed. If we compare this diagram with *345-A*, the difference in the space realized should be apparent.

In *345-C* we have brought into play the factor of extension. By slightly arching the related surfaces, space seems to be pushed out of the semi-enclosure. And again we become aware of space as an event.

A surface may be warped or twisted, or both, to accommodate other such surfaces, as in *345-D*. The degree to which a surface is manipulated has direct bearing upon its graphic environment. Often the attributes of weight, lightness, and direction must be considered, *345-E*.

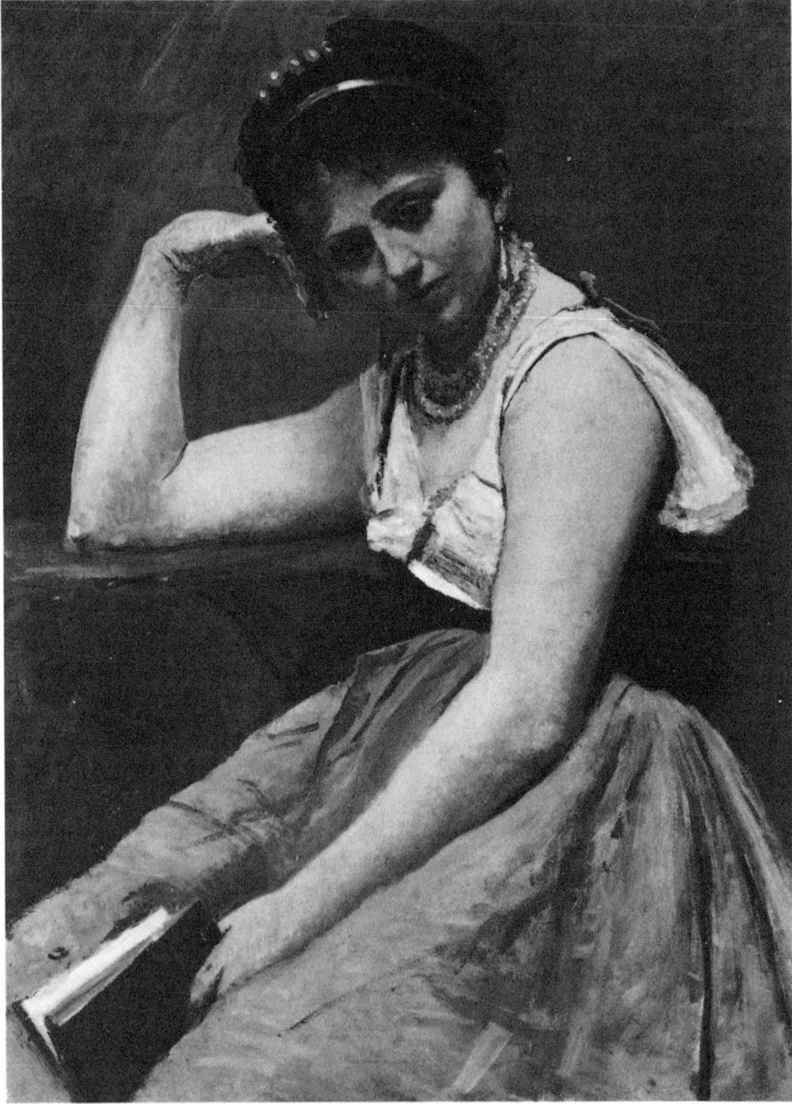

Jean Baptiste Camille Corot (French, 1796-1875)
INTERRUPTED READING, 1865 or 1870
36½" x 25¾"; oil on canvas
Courtesy of The Art Institute of Chicago
Potter Palmer Collection

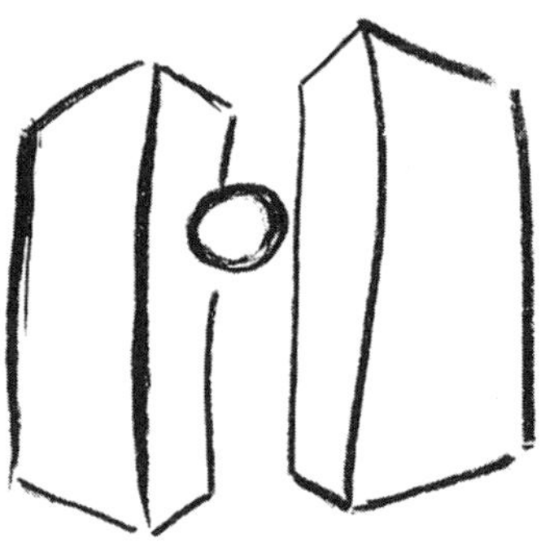

346-1A

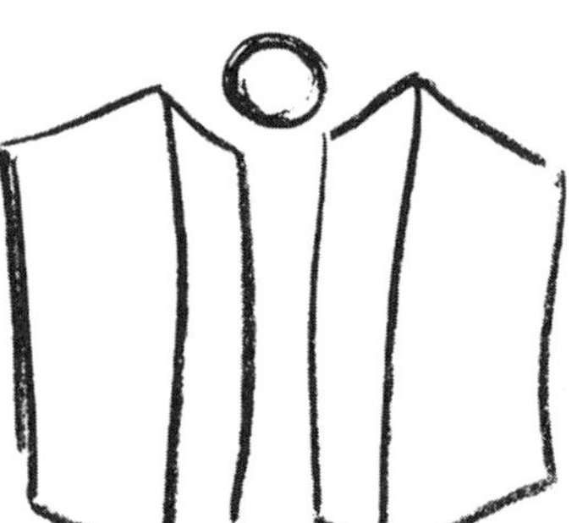

346-1B

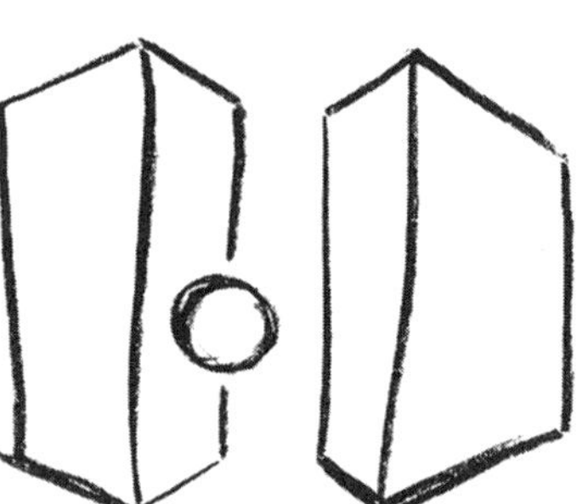

346-1C

346     A core between the two related surfaces intensifies space. By compressing the space the core takes on new weight. The space around the core in *(346-1A)* becomes an event.

By extension the core is made buoyant and seems to float or be pressed out of the space. Again we feel a great intensification of space *(346-1B)*.

By warping and twisting the surfaces, the space around the core may be concentrated even more *(346-1C)*.

In each case the linear structure involved, although important, is secondary to the surfaces generated by the lines. In all cases the linear structure has been transposed into a planal structure. We see again that either line or plane may generate a surface, but only through the tensions generated between surfaces is true graphic space experienced in full intensity.

The question now arises concerning the degree of manipulation of lines and surfaces permissible in a picture. Unless there is some manipulation of the surfaces, space in the picture usually is not fully exploited. This is especially true of line drawings. When color or modeling is admitted, of course there is much more scope. The in-and-out of color movement often makes the warping of planes unnecessary. A rendering in light and dark, or color, may be made so carefully that tension between surfaces is generated, yet the delineated volumes may be quite factual. We find this exemplified in the fine works of artists like Corot who prefer little or no distortion in their graphic subject matter.

So we discover that on one hand too little modification of surface may fail to generate graphic space. On the other hand, too much modification of surface may result in a

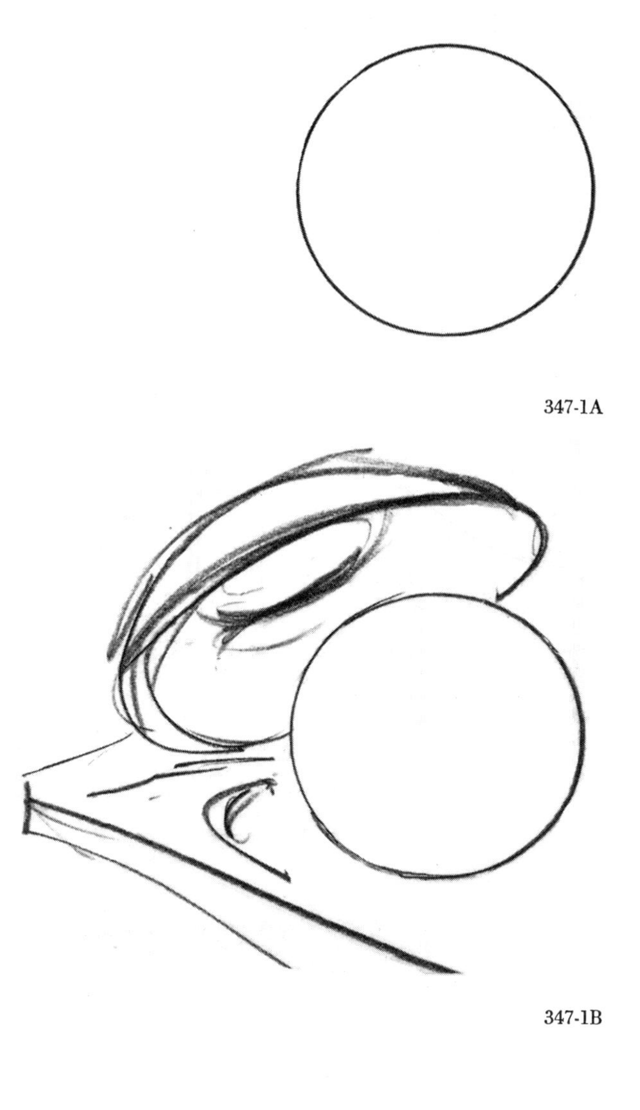

347-1A

347-1B

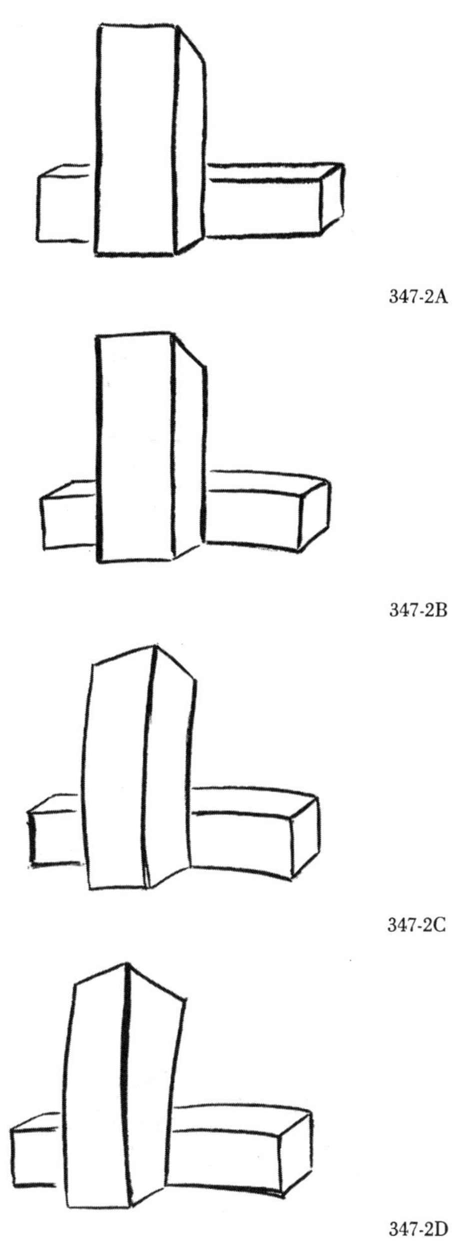

347-2A

347-2B

347-2C

347-2D

rubbery drawing. We should remember that if adjustments are noticeable, they are faulty.

## Space Through Movement

To explore graphic space through movement let us use some simple graphic volumes and shapes. First let us draw a perfect circle with a compass. It is absolutely flat, there is a minimum of space generated by the shape (*347-1A*).

Now let us draw the same circle again. This time around the lower part of the circle let us draw encircling drapery. Above the circle let us indicate the under side of a bowl (*347-1B*). The circle has now become a sphere. It has acquired the attributes of solidity and weight. By the direction of the secondary elements space is also generated by *wrapping* and *cupping*. It should be emphasized that the circles in both drawings are identical, they remain absolutely flat.

Two blocks drawn in perspective may be clearly read but not necessarily spacious (*347-2A*).

If the horizontal structure driving around the vertical core is slightly bowed, while the vertical remains rigid, more space is generated than in the first drawing (*347-2B*).

Now if the vertical structure accommodates itself to the horizontal structure (*347-2C*), more space is generated than in *347-2B*.

If, in addition, the drawings of both blocks are slightly twisted, a corkscrew movement results which generates even more space (*347-2D*).

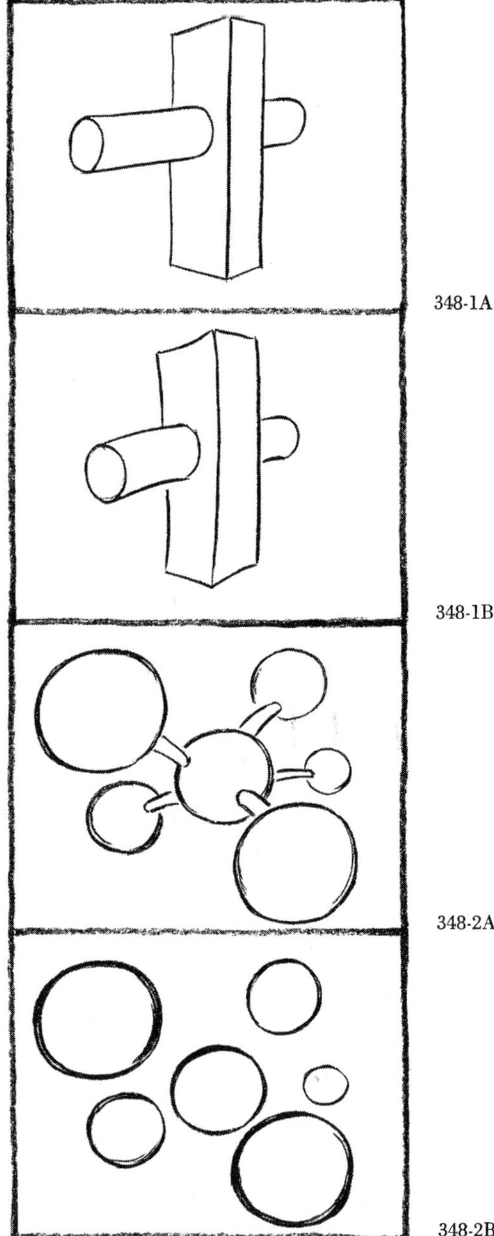

348-1A

348-1B

348-2A

348-2B



We may conclude from these observations that as the movements of elements in a drawing become stronger, space usually is enhanced.

When one element pierces another, the perspective projection of the occurrence is usually static (*348-1A*).

Now by visualizing the piercing element as driving through its target we realize that adjustments must be made in both elements (*348-1B*). Interrupted edges do not align. Surfaces are made to accommodate the forces exerted. When the movement is realized, space becomes dramatic.

## Bridging Between Tension Points

To demonstrate graphic space through tension let us draw a construction of rods and spheres similar to a child's building toy. Each sphere represents a position in space; the rods are bridges which hold these points in space. In drawing the construction, care must be taken to establish each sphere in its exact location in space. By emphasizing the size of the spheres, either large or small, by employing a certain amount of perspective in the rods, by overstating convergences, by manipulating the linear structures a remarkable sense of space can be achieved (*348-2A*).

Now let us imagine the rods removed and make a second drawing of the spheres. We now generate a stronger sense of space than if we had drawn the spheres alone, without imagining the rods connecting them (*348-2B*).

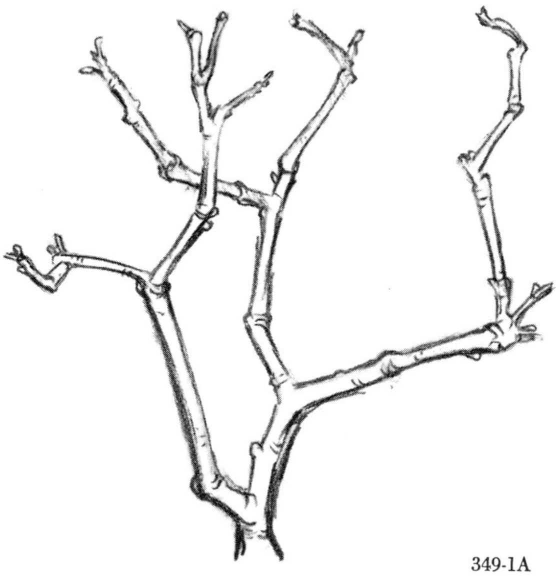

349-1A

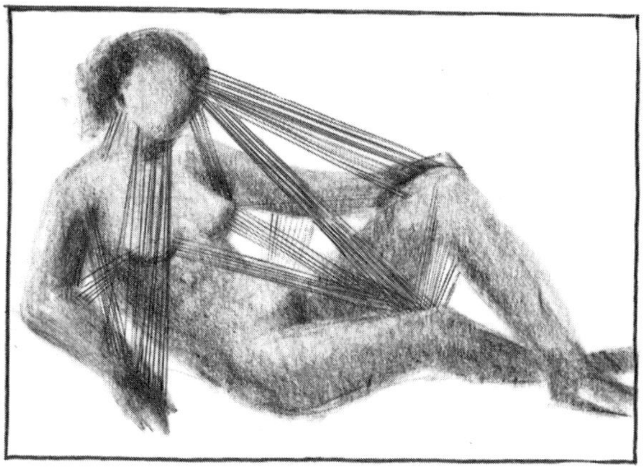

349-2A

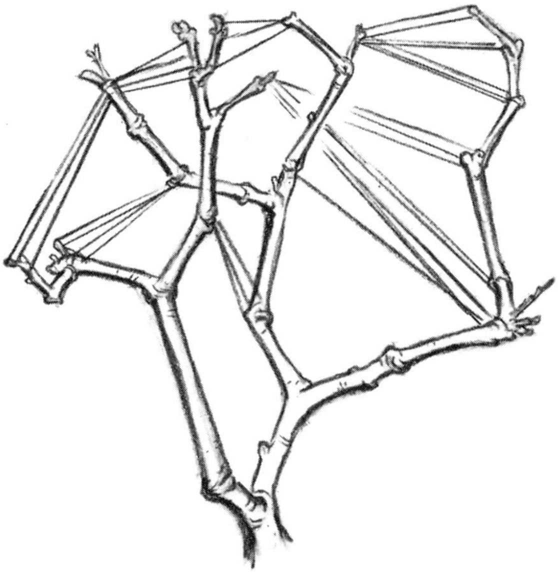

349-1B

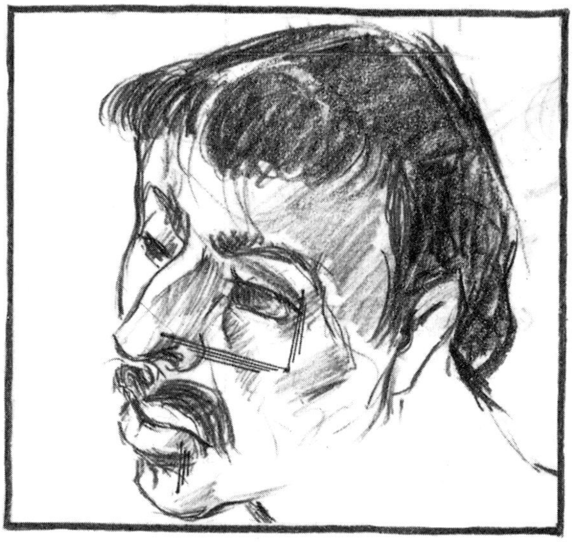

349-2B



This concept can be applied to drawing an object in nature. Suppose we draw a sprig of a fruit tree, one that is knobby and gnarled. By estimating the exact position of each joint of the sprig, by dramatizing the perspective of the connecting twigs we simulate, in effect, the construction of the rods and spheres (*349-1A*).

Now between the terminals of the sprig and between terminal and important joints of each twig, where the direction changes noticeably, let us imagine threads (*349-1B*). Let us draw this arrangement of twig and imaginary threads not once but many times.

Now let us draw the sprig without the threads. Soon a new sensation of space is realized. This procedure can be used with particular success in depicting the human figure. First look for important outcrops to use as tension points: head, hands, shoulders, knees, breasts (*349-2A*).

In closer views of the figure we may use outcrops of nose, lips, eyes, hair forms, knuckles (*349-2B*).

Between any two tension points separated by an interval, a thread can be imagined. In a head an imaginary thread can be visualized, for instance, from the brow to the nose. A bridge or thread can be visualized between a nearby tree and one in the distance. Once we have conditioned ourselves to visualize such bridges stretched taut between points we become aware of space existing between the points.

The ability to realize and control graphic space can be achieved through constant practice using these and similar exercises. This will help us control another mysterious picture factor interrelated with graphic space. This factor is scale.

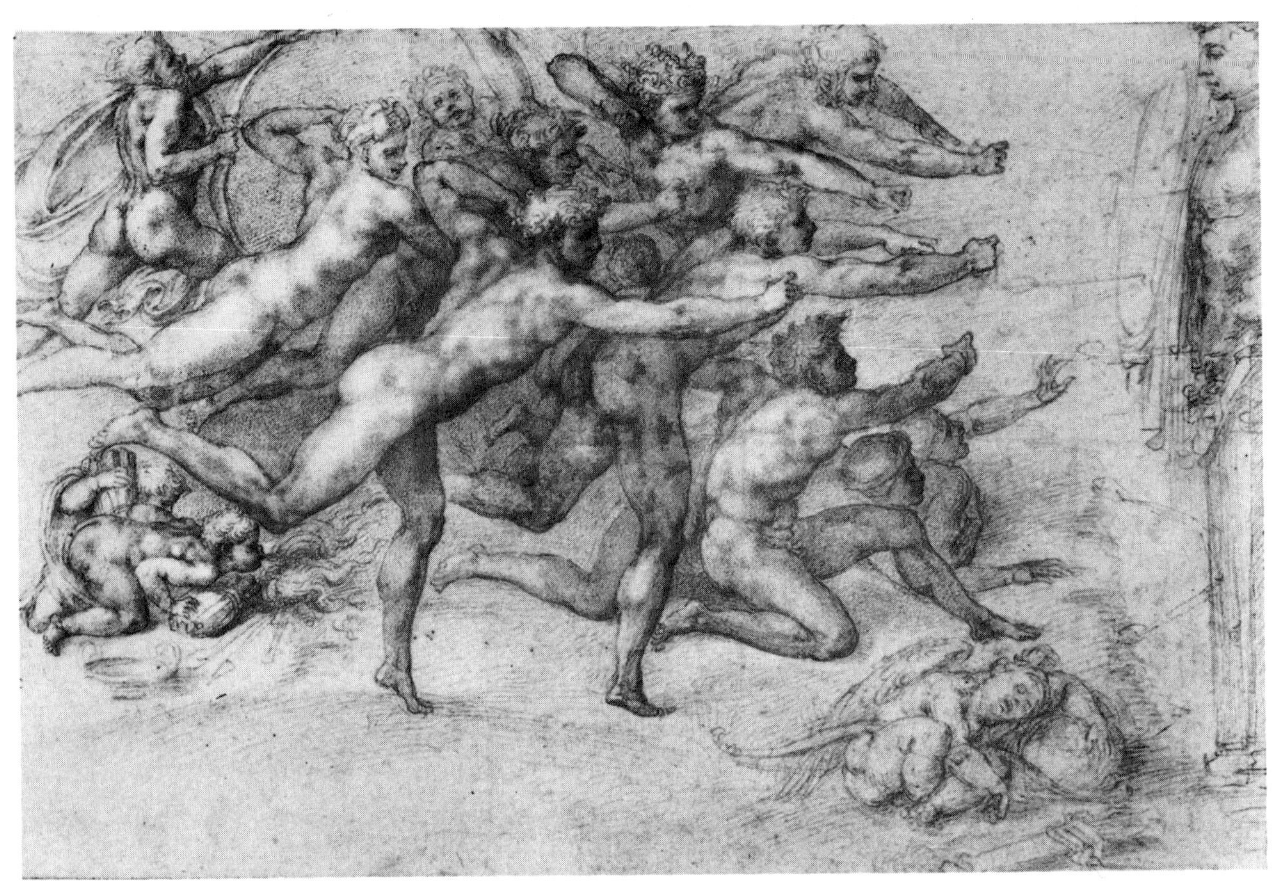

Michelangelo (Italian, 1475-1564)
THE GODS SHOOTING AT A HERM, 1530
8⅝″ x 12⅛; drawing
Reproduced by gracious permission of
Her Majesty Queen Elizabeth II
Royal Library, Windsor Castle



## 30  Scale

### The Intangible Subject

Scale, like space, is one of the hidden factors in drawing and picture making. At first it also seems baffling and intangible. Why does a certain drawing only a few inches in dimension seem huge? For example, this drawing by Michelangelo seems mural in scope, yet it is only about eight by twelve inches. Why does a drawing made by an experienced artist have a lucid, easy-to-read quality rarely experienced in the work of a beginner? Why do almost all professional artists have this control of scale in common, no matter to what time in history they belong?

There is only one answer. Each professional has a common understanding of all the factors contributing to a well-scaled picture. Not perceived by the uninitiated eye, scale becomes a tangible factor when once mastered.

Scale seems intangible because it is so complex. There are so many factors contributing to its control. But successful control of one factor in no way guarantees a solution to the entire problem. A sense of scale can be achieved, however, by constant effort to solve each problem encountered.

In a way we might say that scale is a matter of bringing a picture into focus, just as we bring a projection of a slide on a screen into focus simply by adjusting the lens. When we have accomplished this in our picture we have taken a major step in control of scale. But the task is by no means as simple as focusing a slide. In many instances an entirely new picture, or new groups of pictures must be made. Only rarely is an artist able to bring his picture statement into perfect focus on first attempt. Frequently a number of adjustments must be made, even by the professional artist.

Among the factors to which the problem of scale is intimately related are:

1. The relation of space to volume in a quantitative sense.
2. The relation of the sizes of parts to the whole picture.
3. The relation of sizes through association.

Only through an understanding, integration, and control of each of these factors can we master the problem of scale.

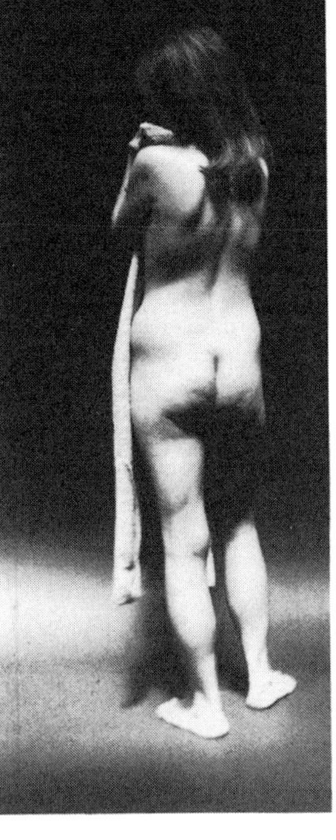

NUDE, BACK VIEW
(Photograph: Alexander Hovsepian)

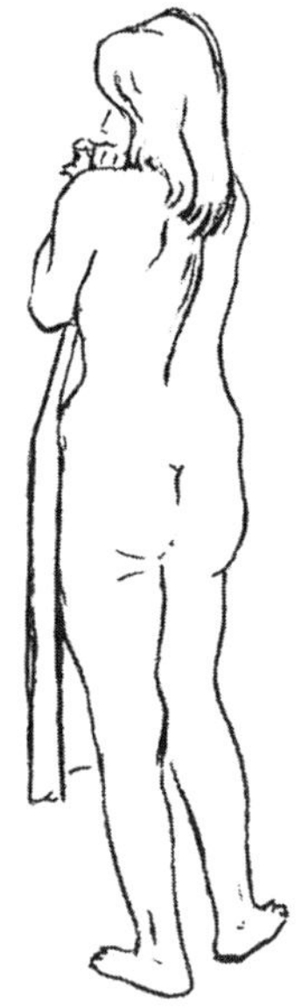

352-2

 **The Projection Trap**

There are various approaches to making a picture which most of us try at one time or another. If we are required to make a drawing of something, a head, a figure, an object, we may think it logical that if we project what we see in nature to our drawing surface, we will be assured of good results. The term "project" in this case means to copy, rather than to throw an image on a screen by means of a slide and a light source. But the effect is similar; we create an image which is simply a copy of the proportions of the shapes and forms in nature. But rather than achieving a good drawing we find that an exact projection is almost certain to be a faulty drawing, for it will be out of scale.

Another approach to drawing from nature, handed down through studios and art schools for years, has been that of drawing "sight size." This is accomplished by making a drawing conform in size to the apparent size of the subject matter. For instance, if the subject in nature appears ten inches high in relation to our drawing surface, the drawing will also be made ten inches high. In this way exact proportional relations of body to head, for example, will be the same in both subject and picture, corresponding parts will be visually the same size.

We note a strange phenomenon in studying such a picture. The projection, if successful, will seem to drift off into the distance. The subject may be only fifteen feet away from us in nature, but in the drawing the subject will seem thirty or more feet away from us. The drawing is again out of scale (*352-2*).

An even more serious difficulty with such a projection is that no matter how faithful it is to the subject, the picture fails to distinguish between important and unimportant parts. The importance of a large expanse of cheek may detract from the more interesting eye, for the cheek area usually is dominant and easily projected. Because of lack of emphasis of one volume over another, our interest in the picture lags. So the drawing becomes impersonal, remote. Almost always such evenness results in faulty scale.

We note that large, uninteresting, blank areas often dominate a drawing. These may occur in large body shapes or in areas of the cheeks, brow, and hair. They also occur frequently in large areas of drapery, props and architectural symbols. Such dull, empty shapes seem to drive us away from the picture, to make it less intimate.

In the same way, the overactive line or color separation often destroys space, as we saw in the previous chapter, and can result unintentionally in a flat, decorative picture. This, too, is the direct result of projection.

In any case we are pushed away from the picture by dull areas or overactive lines. In truth the drawing is out of focus.

354-1A

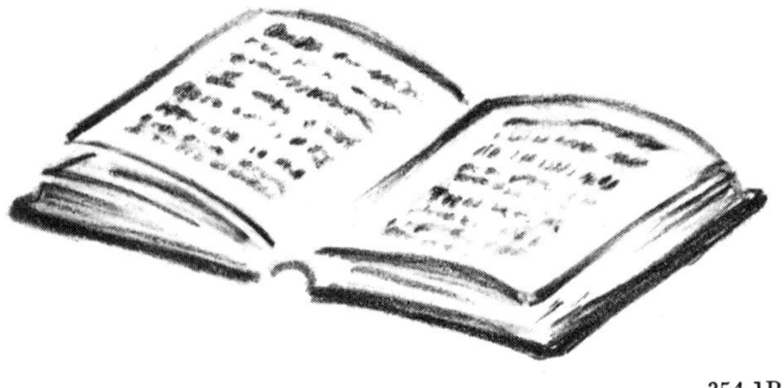

354-1B

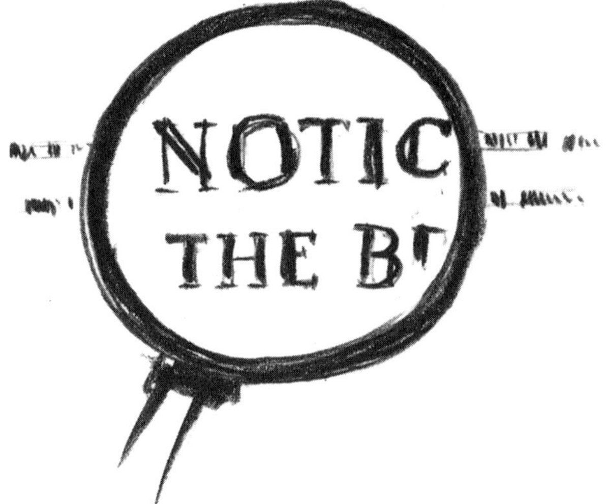


354-1C

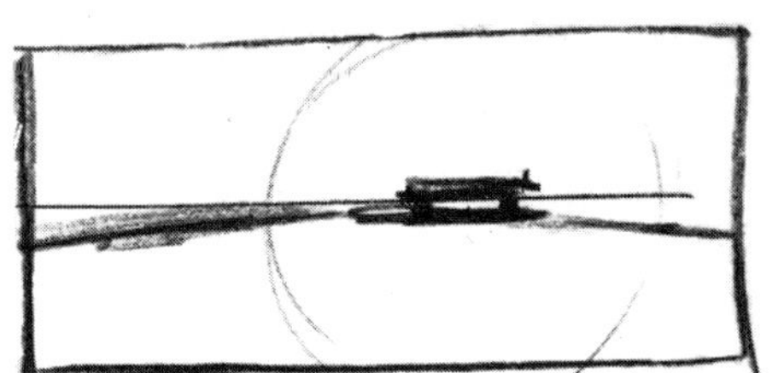

354-2A

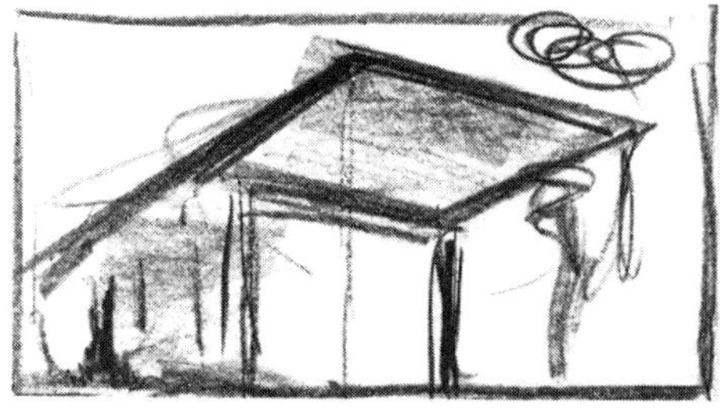

354-2B

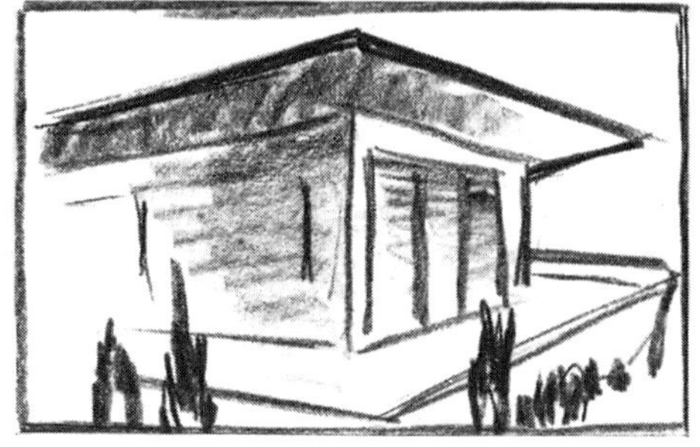

354-2C

354-2D

354    To examine the factor of focus in nature, let us look at a book from a distance of perhaps twenty feet. At this distance it is almost impossible to read the print (*354-1A*). Seen from a distance of fourteen inches, however, the print is easily read (*354-1B*). Now if we view the print through a reading glass we have no difficulty in examining the actual structure of each letter and the spacing between the letters (*354-1C*). It is important to note that the letters at no time change size or shape in relation to each other. The only change is in the way we view them.

In the same way, if we view a house on a distant hill, perspective convergences almost cease to exist (*354-2A*). If we observe the house through a telescope, the house seems closer, but the perspective convergences remain the same (*354-2B*). If we stroll closer to the house, the perspective convergences become more violent. We begin to experience a new depth in what we see.

A perspective drawing made from this close view seems far more three-dimensional than a similar drawing made from a telescopic view (*354-2C*). If now we assume an even more intimate view by looking up-down, down-up, and around, we introduce a new intimacy; the drawing begins to come into focus (*354-2D*). We see more aspects of the form than in any of the previous figures, yet at no time has the house itself changed. Only the way we see the house has changed.

As an exercise in scale, let us make a projection of a head from ten or fifteen feet. We immediately become conscious of large, blank, uninteresting areas, and an overactivity of silhouettes, either in line or color separations.

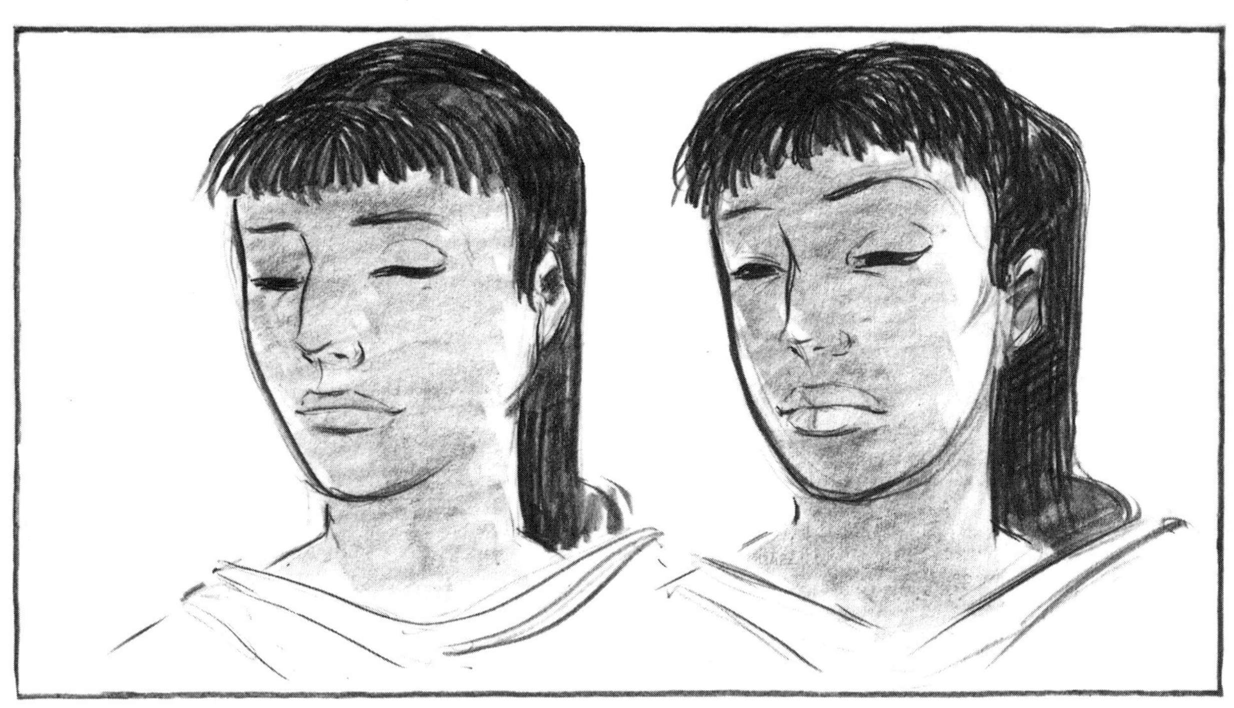

355-A            355-B

The projection is remote, impersonal. The drawing seems dull, unexciting (*355-A*).

Now let us make a drawing identical in size, but staged from a much closer distance (*355-B*). By bringing multiple station points into play, entirely new intimacy is achieved.

By looking up into the eyes and down on the chin, we assume and dramatize a close view. By looking at the upper part of the head from our left, we decrease the expanse of the rather uninteresting cheek and clarify the staging of the mouth. By looking up under the brow and down on the cheek, we clarify the structure around the eye and again reduce the area of the cheek. By looking up under the brow, we reduce the amount and insistence of the blank, dull forehead. By looking down on the chin, we reduce the area under the chin which, if too dominant, often detracts from the features.

When we compare this drawing with our projection we see that although they are actually the same size on our paper, drawing *335-B* seems much larger, more intimate, much closer to us. It seems much more spacious. The drawings are derived from the same subject in nature. They represent the same thing. Yet the second drawing certainly is different from the first, for it represents a different way of seeing a given object.

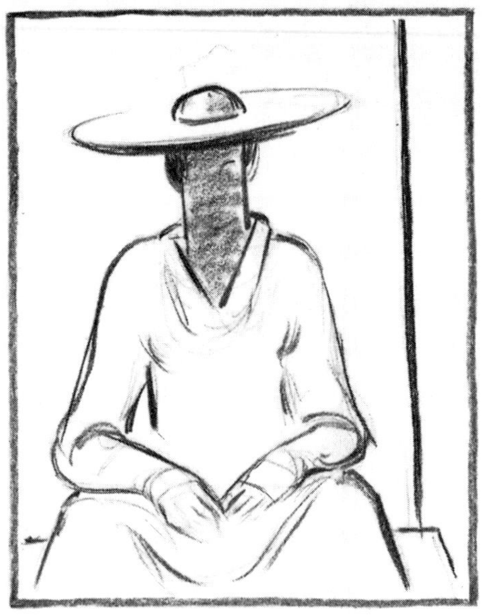

356-A

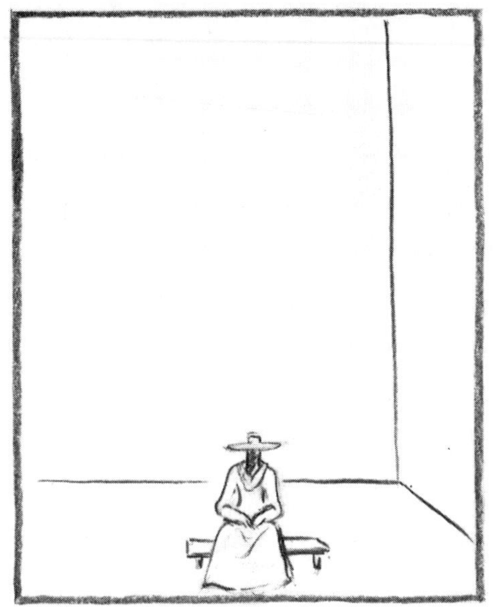

356-B

Ma Yüan (Chinese, late 12th- early 13th-century)
BARE WILLOWS AND DISTANT MOUNTAINS
Sung Dynasty
vertical diameter 9⅜″ approx.; ink, faint traces
of color, silk kakemono
Courtesy, Museum of Fine Arts, Boston
Chinese and Japanese Special Fund

## The Space Matrix

356

Upon examining a picture we find that the way we balance space to volumes has great significance. Two extremes are possible: a picture dominated by volumes, or a picture dominated by space. How we equate these factors determines the character of our picture.

In *356-A*, the space is a foil to the volumes; the surfaces of the volumes generate an intense awareness of space. This awareness makes us conscious of the volumes as an event. We are aware of volumes rather than space.

In a picture dominated by space, the volumes are foils to space. The impact of the volumes act as cores activating the space of the picture (*356-B*). Surfaces of the volumes are secondary to the shape impact of the volumes. The intimacy of the volumes is usually sacrificed to our awareness of space as the dominant factor of the picture.

This quantitative degree of space to volume, the *space matrix*, is the basis of various philosophies of painting.

In Renaissance pictures we usually are intimately aware of volumes; they are very important to the picture structure and to us as spectators. In fact the surfaces of the volumes become so dominant we often feel that they can be touched or stroked. Because of this intimacy the space around them is accepted but not noticed as a picture event by the spectator.

In much Oriental painting just the reverse is true. A twig, a solitary tree, may act as a foil to vast space. Although we are aware of the delicate shape structures of the bridge and willows in the Chinese landscape above, the space in the picture is the real event.

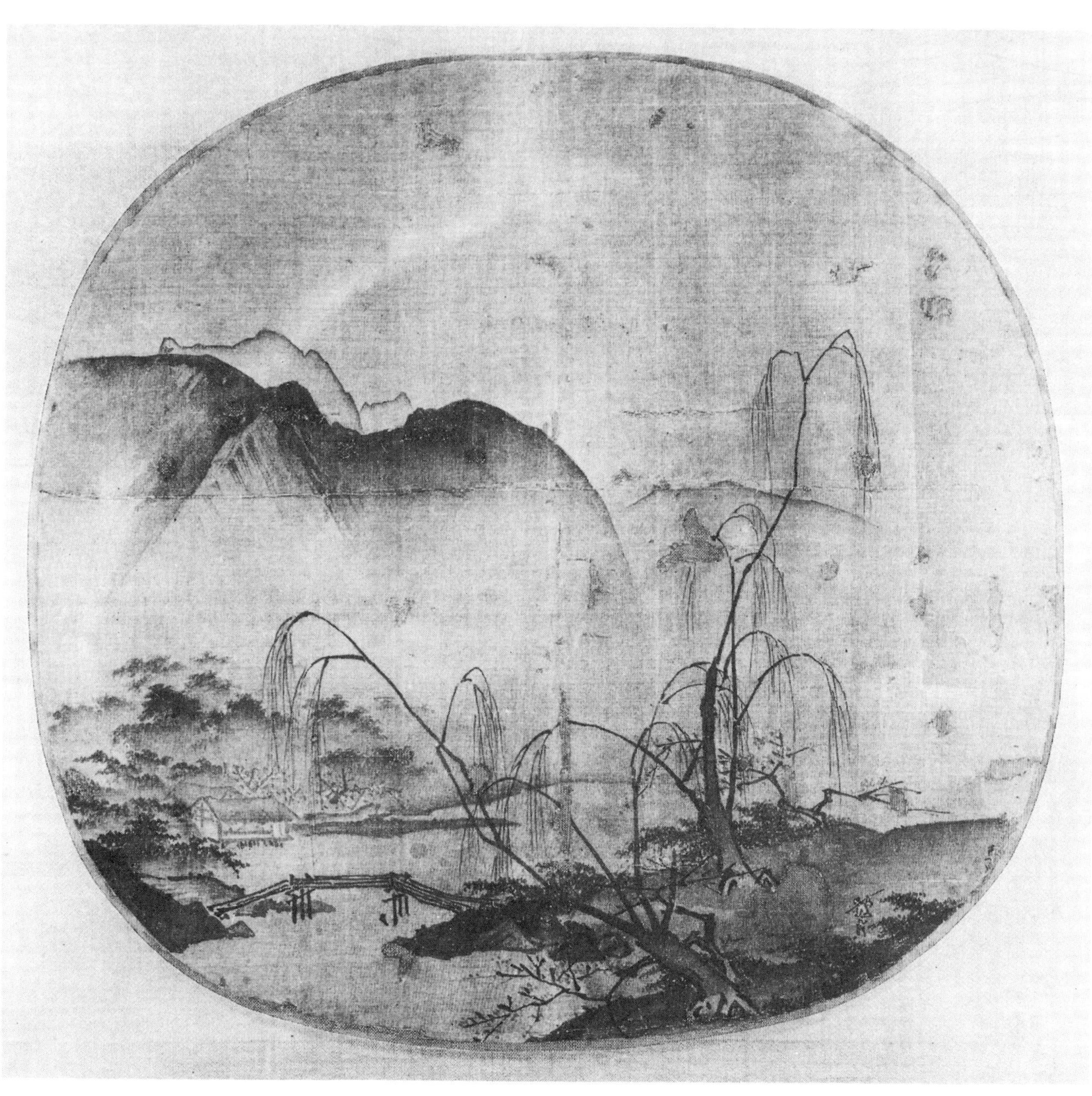

Because many non-representational pictures depend upon shape impact rather than intimacy with the surface of volumes, it is not surprising that the space matrix often is predicated upon vast space.

Although space and volume must be balanced quantitatively to achieve scale, if interest is divided equally between them there is risk of a cancellation. Usually if the emphasis on space is sacrificed it follows that there is too much attention placed on the volumes. This means that there is too much space in the picture to be controlled by the surface tensions of the volumes. In such instances much of the space becomes area, thus part of the picture becomes flat. How much of each to stress is a difficult decision. Yet our decision vitally affects the scale of the picture.

## The Balance of Space and Volume

In investigating the subject of scale there are great advantages in limiting our study to pictures dominated by volumes, because space-surface relations are more evident and thus are easier to discuss. Yet by limiting our study we should not infer that space generated by line or shape is not of equal importance. Once we have developed a true space awareness, scale becomes a tangible factor to be exploited in any type of picture.

As we have noted, scale in its finest sense results in a picture in which perfect quantitative balance between space and volume is achieved, but this does not necessarily mean equality. One approach to this problem of balancing something visible to something usually invisible is by working with space boxes.

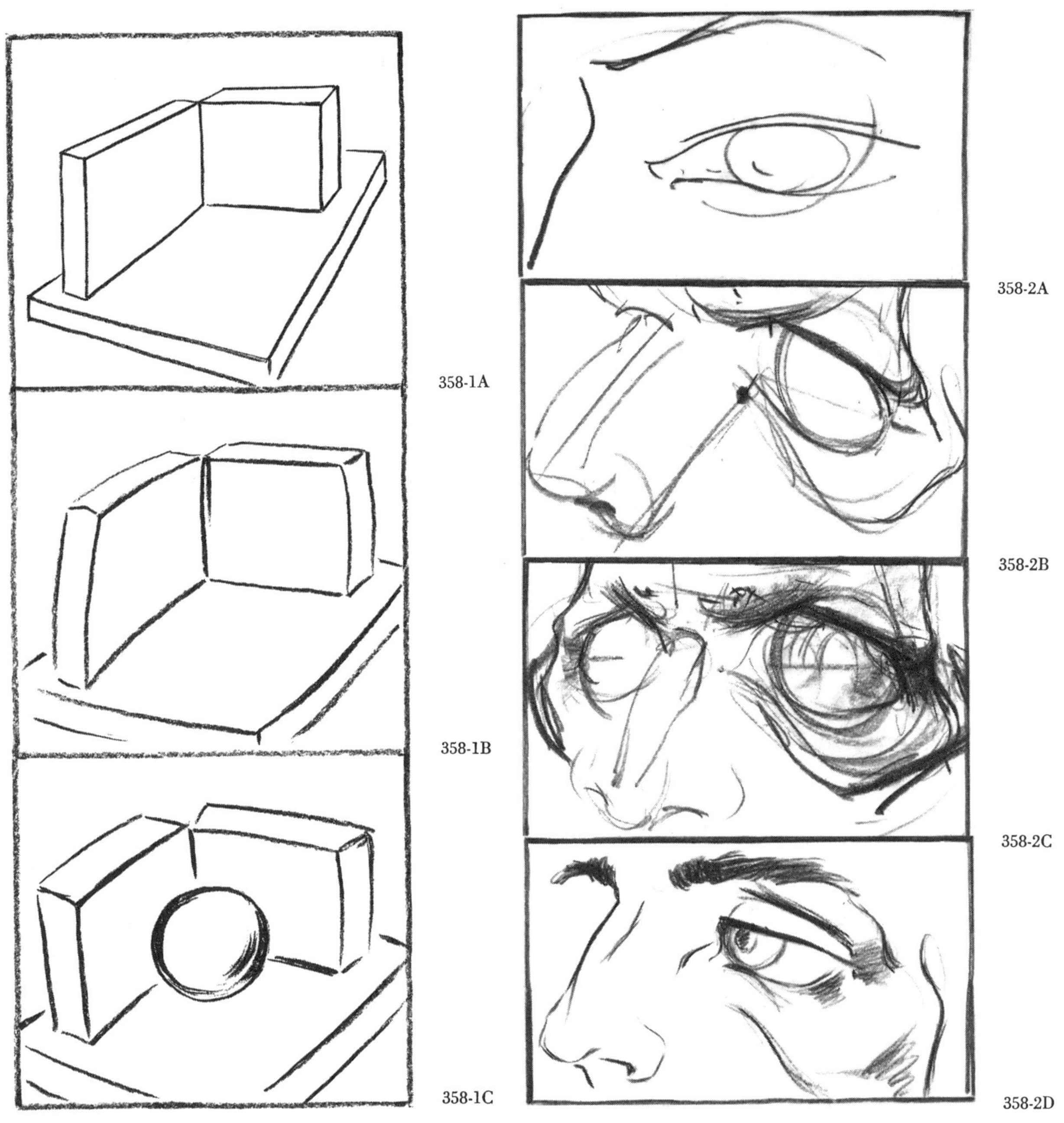





Let us define a space with three intersecting planes at right angles to each other. A perspective drawing may not allow us to achieve a true sense of space (*358-1A*). When we generate thrusts, and give direction to the elements, far more space may be realized (*358-1B*). By placing a core, a marble for instance, in the box we generate activity between the surfaces and movement around the core. The drawing begins to have scale (*358-1C*).

Another conflict between the position of a volume in graphic space and activity of the visual or graphic elements often occurs in depicting the eye. The human eye is a point of great interest in the figure, for it moves, it glistens, its pigment is different from its surrounding environment. So when we draw a head we are tempted to emphasize the eye by strong contrasts of light, dark, or line. But if we do we find a strange thing happening in our picture. The more contrast in the eye, the more it seems to pop forward away from the head (*358-2A*). Yet we know that the eye is set deep in the skull; that the brow and cheek bone protrude in front of the eyeball (*358-2B*). But in *358-2A* the eye seems closer to us than brow or cheek bone.

Suppose now we visualize the eye as a core in a space box. In *358-2C*, the nose, the superorbital structure around the eye, and the cheek correspond to the three sides of our box. If these are successfully indicated, the drawing of the eye becomes a rather simple operation (*358-2D*). Once we have realized the environment of the eye as a space box we experience a new intimacy. Surfaces, movements, space are dramatized. The drawing is in scale.

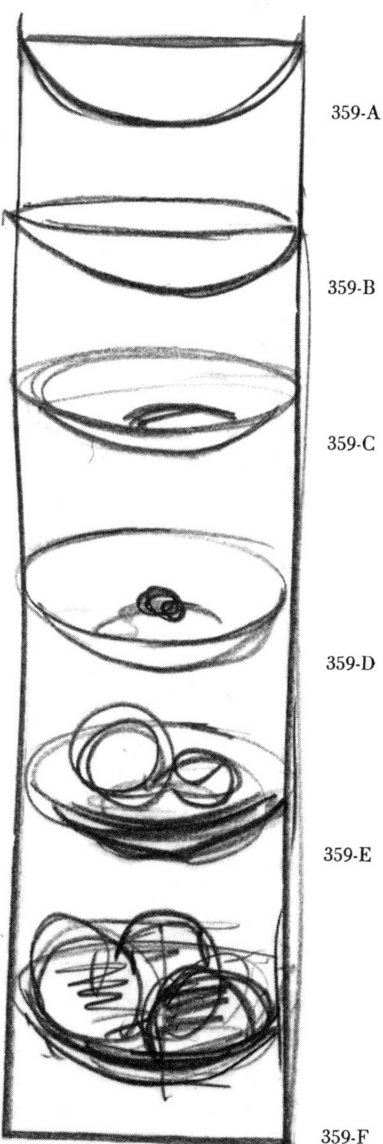



## Reducing Area to Achieve Scale

One of the magical factors in scaling a picture in which volume is the event is the relation of *sizes* of the volumes to the amount of space involved. When we first start to draw we may believe that the more area we generate the more we become conscious of space. Quite the contrary. As we reduce the amount of area in a drawing, we often become more deeply aware of space and less aware of the area which tends to negate space. As we reduced area to intensify space, so we may reduce area to achieve scale.

To demonstrate, let us make a series of drawings all the same width:

*359-A.* The bowl evidences a minimum of space.

*359-B.* The areas overwhelm the space.

*359-C.* The outside of the bowl is minimized, cutting down on area. The base within the bowl begins to generate movement in the enclosed space.

*359-D.* A small core within the bowl generates considerably more space.

*359-E.* Increasing the size of the core or additional cores pushes out space, reducing our awareness of areas.

*359-F.* By increasing the number and sizes of the cores, area has ceased to be a problem.

The drawing is now in scale. Drawings *359-A* and *359-F* are the same width although *359-F* takes up a little more room on the paper. Drawing *359-F* seems much closer to us, much more intimate, much larger.

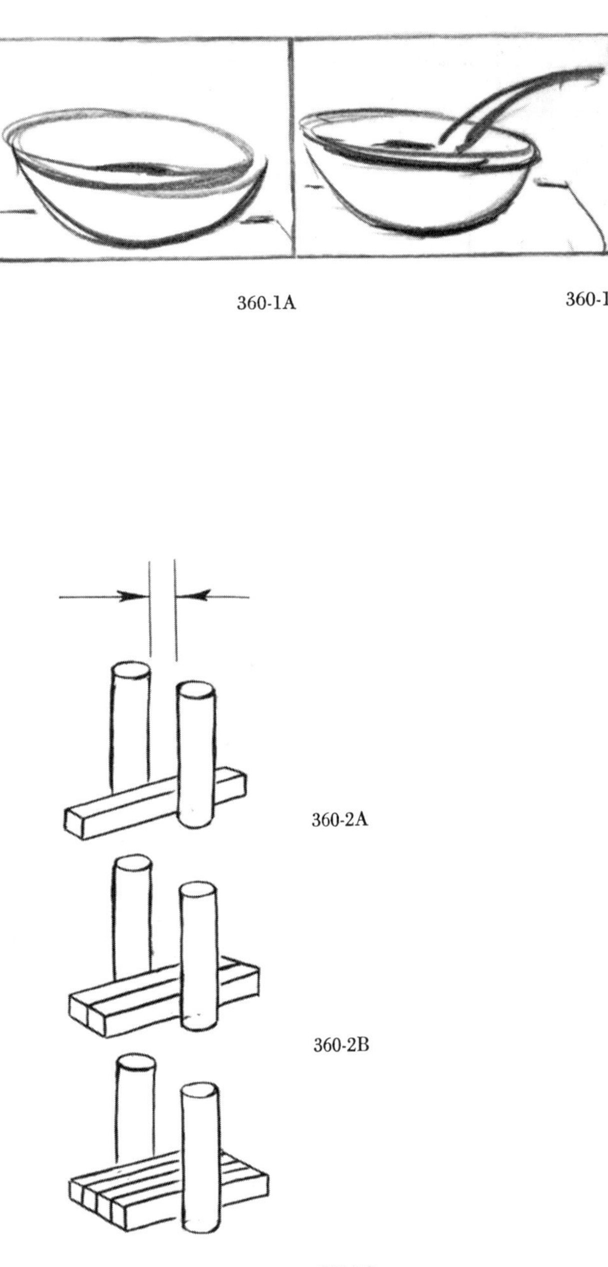

360-1A      360-1B

360-2A

360-2B

360-2C

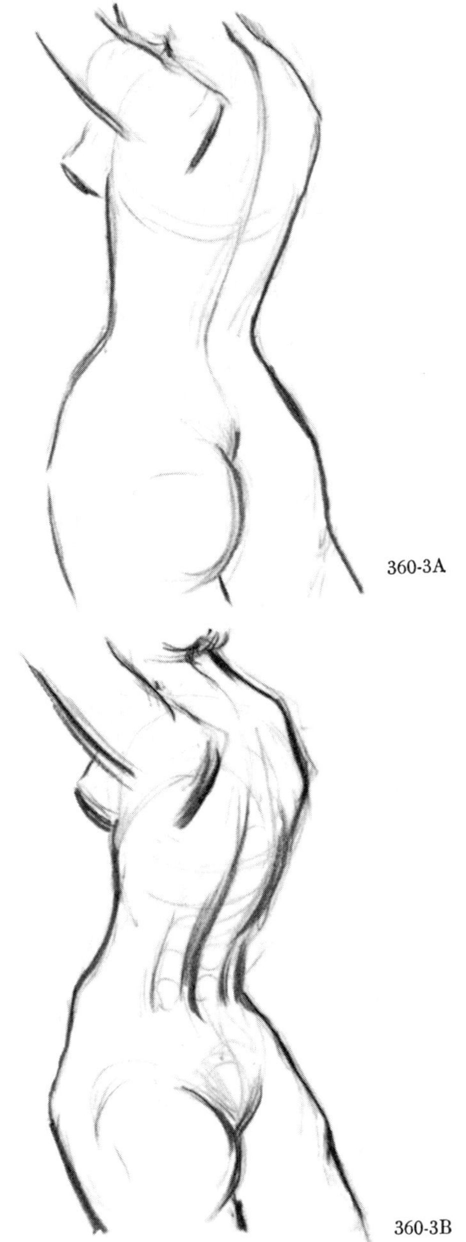

360-3A

360-3B



**Wedging**

A device long used by many artists to help achieve scale is that of wedging. A simple drawing of an empty bowl may seem flat, lacking space (*360-1A*). By depicting a spoon thrusting into the bowl the space is vastly intensified (*360-1B*).

A variation of this device is achieved by increasing the size of a wedge, but not increasing the size of the drawing. For instance, two posts of a given size are represented separated by the same interval. In *360-2A*, a wedge is shown driving between the posts. In *360-2B*, two wedges are shown driving through the same interval. In *360-2C*, we find four wedges driving through the identical interval.

In any involved structure such as tree forms, manufactured or constructed forms, and especially in the human figure we find innumerable examples of wedging. In drawing the human figure wedging is possible wherever one muscular structure drives between two similar structures.

For example, in *360-3A* we see a projection of a torso. The drawing is dominated by large blank areas. In *360-3B*, which is the same size as the first drawing, wedges have been dramatized. Excess area is pushed out of the drawing. We become more aware of the surfaces of the wedges and hence more aware of space. The movement of the wedges driving between other volumes generates a strong sense of space. Drawing *360-3A* is out of scale; drawing *360-3B* is in far better scale. It is more intimate, it seems larger, much closer to us.

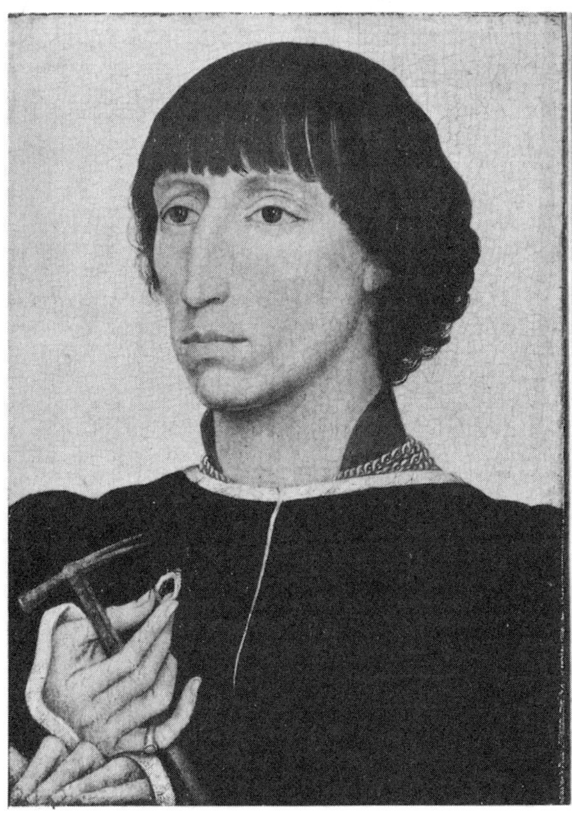

Rogier van der Weyden (Flemish, ca. 1400-1464)
FRANCESCO D'ESTE (about 1455?)
11¾" x 8"; tempera and oil on wood
The Metropolitan Museum of Art
The Michael Friedsam Collection, 1931

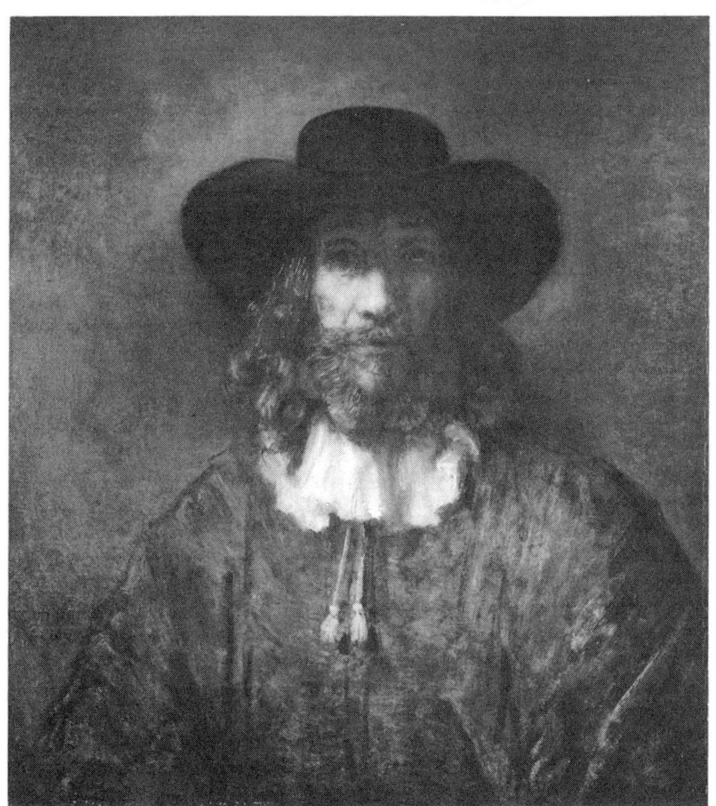

Rembrandt (Dutch, 1606-1669)
MAN WITH A BEARD, 1665
28⅞" x 25¼"; oil on canvas
The Metropolitan Museum of Art
Gift of Henry G. Marquand, 1889

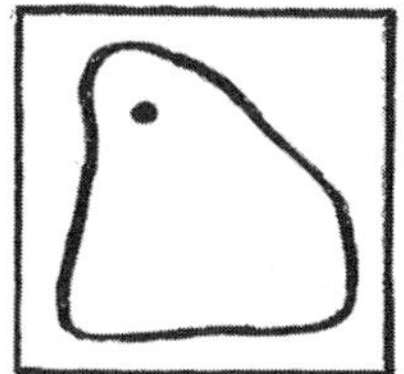

361-1

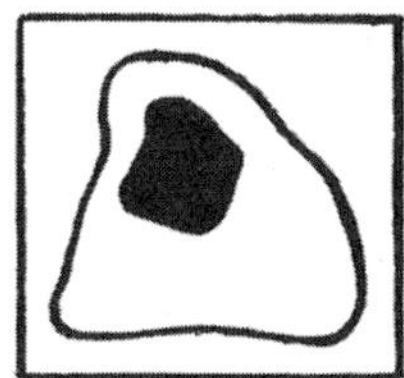

361-3

## Scale Through Emphasis of the Parts

If we find that our drawing is dull because unimportant areas are over-insistent, we may yet capitalize on this apparent graphic weakness. There are two approaches to the problem, each reflecting a different attitude or concept of design.

First, we can dramatize the areas by making them significant shapes. In a drawing of a head, for instance, if we treat the features as small disturbances in large shapes, their interest value is enhanced because a small spot in a large shape is noticeable (*361-1*). This van der Weyden portrait is an example; the features are made important by their relation to large handsome shapes. This approach is particularly appropriate in shallow space pictures, exemplified by most Japanese prints.

The second approach is to minimize blank areas in the picture by dramatizing the size and distribution of significant parts (*361-3*). Such an approach may also be demonstrated in the drawing of a head. Here the expressive parts of the head are considered more important than the impact of the internal shapes or areas. Important parts are usually staged in dramatic space boxes. Excess areas are reduced by utilizing multiple station points. By forcing the spectator close to the image, we make him more aware of the parts. In such a drawing the parts may seem larger than those of a projection, but in reality they are merely conceived and delineated in a new way. Rembrandt's *Man With a Beard* shows clearly such distribution of parts.

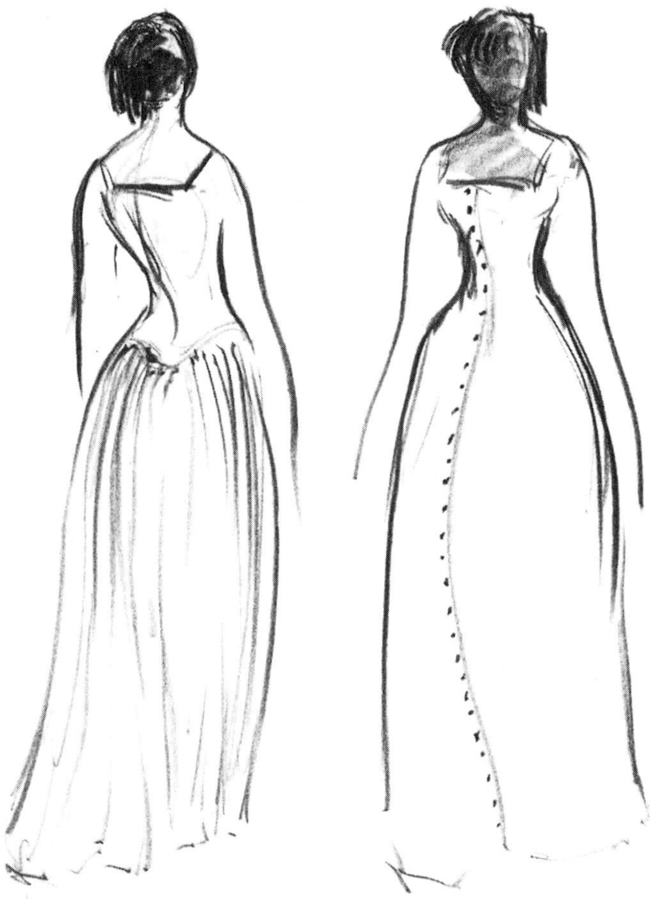

362-A               362-B

362     Either approach may be satisfactory. When large shapes are dramatized, the resulting space usually tends to be quite shallow, though not necessarily so. There are times when such a picture may generate almost infinite depth. When the parts of the shapes are dramatized, the resulting space is usually quite deep, as we see demonstrated in many paintings since the early Renaissance. In either type of structure as soon as we are aware of the surface relationships we begin to experience space and scale.

We found that we can enhance the scale of a picture by assuming multiple station points, that is, by viewing our subject from many points of view without actually changing the size of the parts. At times, however, it is advantageous to manipulate the size relations of the parts to the surrounding shapes. Again the character of the design determines whether the part should be made smaller or larger.

When strong shape impact is desired, a detail often may be reduced in size. For instance, drapery, buttons, cuffs, ornaments of various kinds, if reduced in size, become graphic accents to the surrounding shapes in a picture (*362-A*). Similarly, fine or narrow folds of drapery can emphasize the shape of a whole garment (*362-B*).

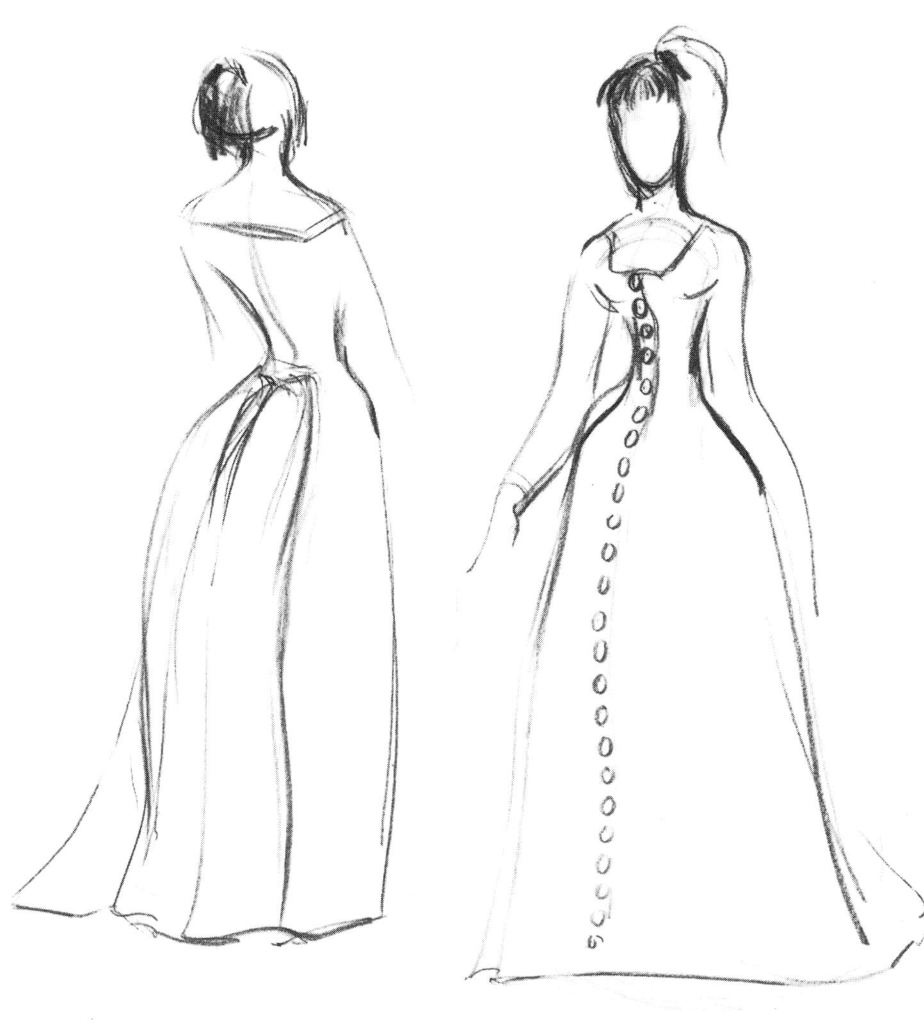

363-B                                         363-A

On the other hand, enlarging significant parts and reducing their number lessens the impact of the shape and forces us to view the picture in a more intimate way (*363-A*). Buttons, cuffs, ornaments, folds often may be enlarged in such pictures. A fold, for instance, may be enlarged to focus our attention upon its direction or structure as an event in the exposition of the whole shape. Secondary folds, or folds which duplicate the movement of the principal folds, then can be reduced in number or eliminated (*363-B*).

Strangely enough, a shape interrupted by many small details may seem much smaller and more remote than an identical shape with only a few large details. The latter will usually seem closer, larger, more intimate.

## Scale Through the Association of Sizes

Although we have investigated the subject of scaling a picture by various graphic means, the term *scale* in its conventional sense usually implies special relations of size of one object to another. For instance, we often remark that something is "in scale" or "out of scale" to something else. We say that a large fat man is out of scale to the small automobile in which he sits, or that the huge furniture is out of scale to the small room, or that the large hat worn by a tiny woman is out of scale. Our sense of appropriate size is disturbed.

Our awareness of correct scale is involved when we make mental comparisons to accepted standards of structure. We are awed by a giant space rocket or intrigued by a miniature golf-course or a doll's house.

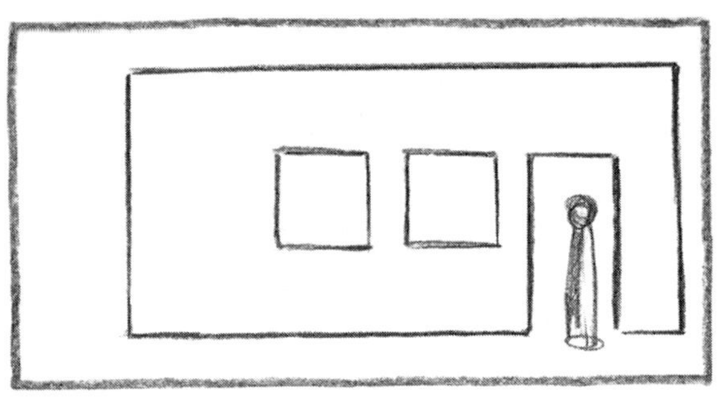

364-1A

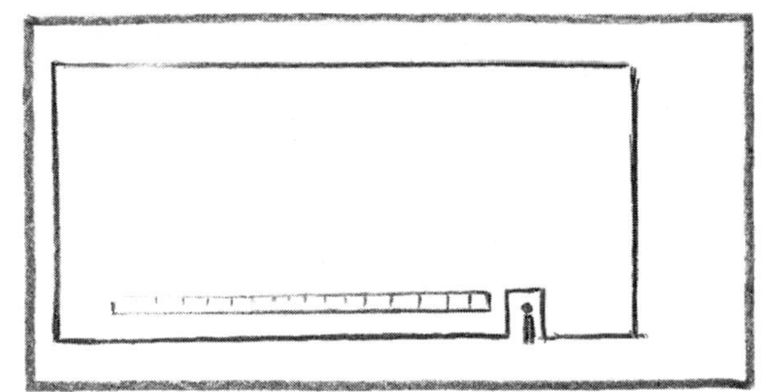

364-1B

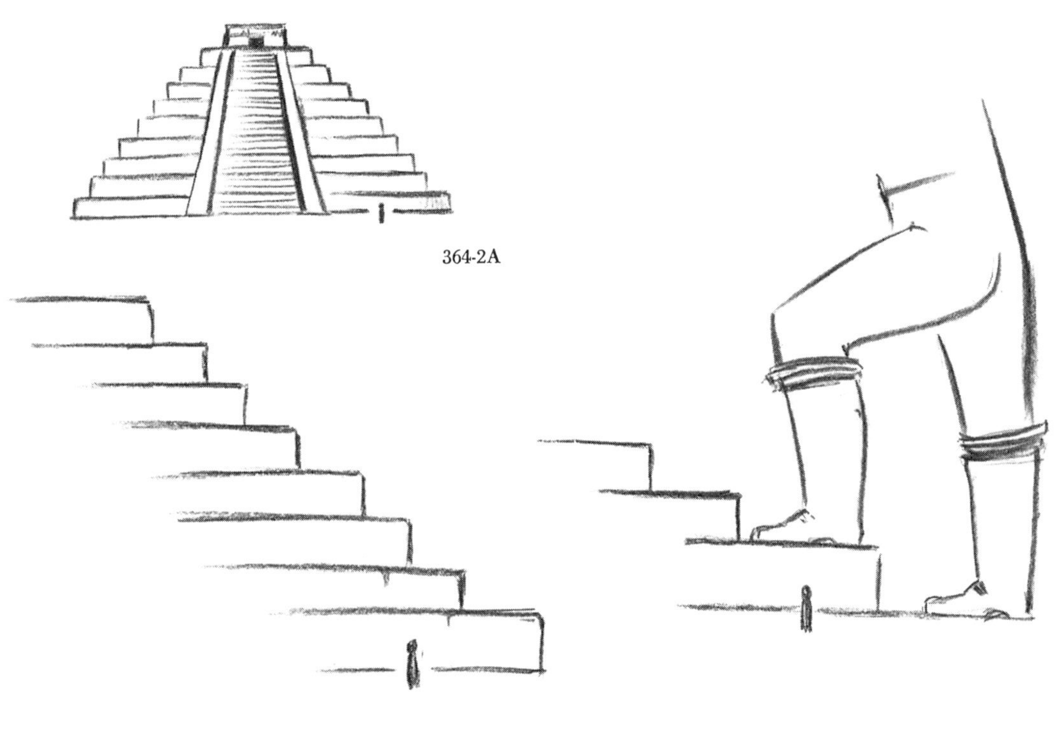

364-2A

364-2B

364-2C



Our standards of comparison may be rather vague in themselves, but they are generally accepted. For instance, people vary considerably in size and proportion, yet we may regard one man as a giant, another as a dwarf. We say that someone has huge eyes, that a small person has large hands, that a large person has tiny hands. In other words, we set standards of normal size even though few of us meet these standards.

We use this normal-sized human figure as a yardstick in judging the size of various objects in nature such as doors and windows. Two buildings drawn exactly the same size may be made to seem smaller or larger by relating a human figure to the openings. As we see in *364-1A*, the figure bears an expected relationship to the height of the door. The doors and windows, however, indicate that the structure must be small. In *364-1B*, the figure is in the same relationship to the doors and windows, but they now suggest a huge structure.

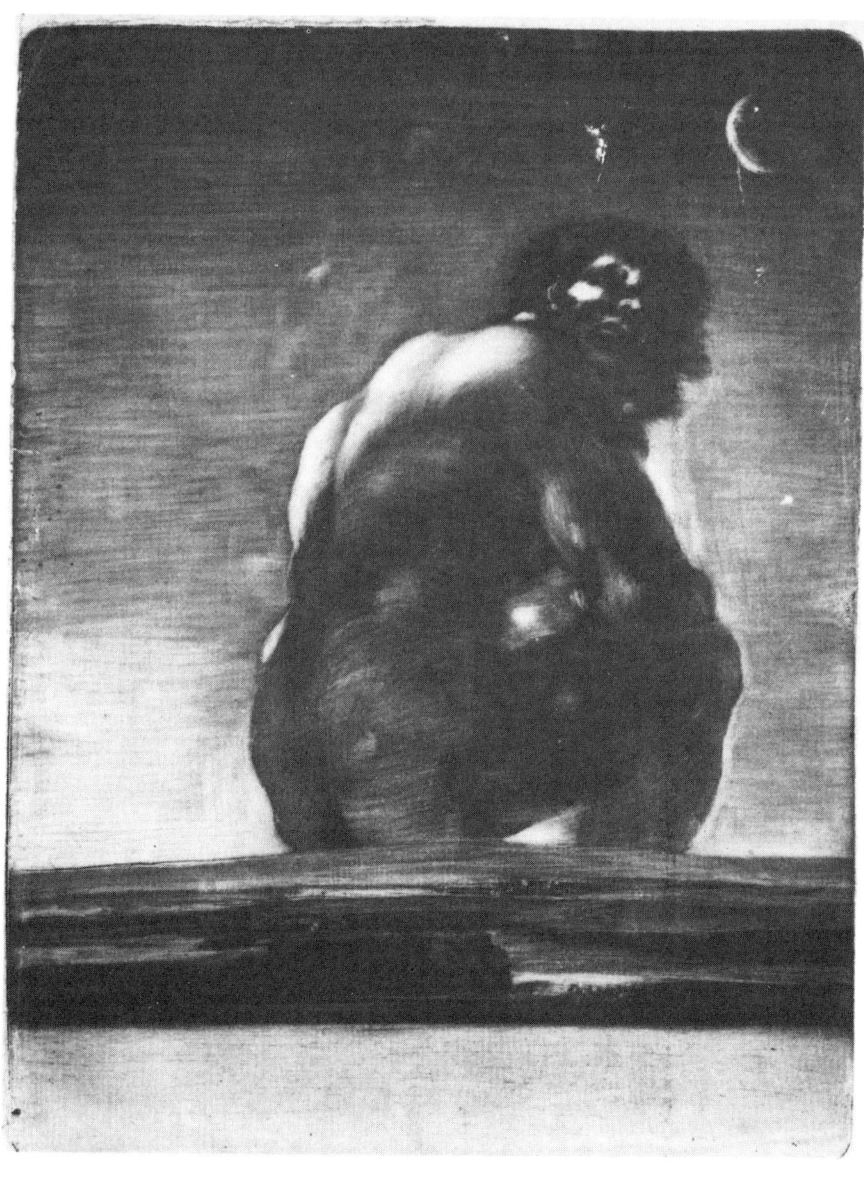

Francisco de Goya (Spanish, 1746-1828)
THE COLOSSUS, 11⁵⁄₃₂″ x 8⅛″; aquatint
The Metropolitan Museum of Art
Harris Brisbane Dick Fund, 1935

Stairs or steps in nature also are constructed to accommodate a normal human figure. A figure which seems comfortable in relation to such steps in a drawing will be in scale, but by increasing the size of the steps we change the scale of the relation of the figure. We either make the structure seem as monumental as a Mexican pyramid (*364-2A*) or the figure seems diminutive, doll-like (*364-2B*). By relating a figure mounting these huge stairs, we imply either that the figure is a giant (*364-2C*), or that it is normal size while the figure in the foreground is a toy.

Any structures in nature, such as houses, balconies, chairs, tables, which accommodate the human figure, can be used as scaling devices in a picture. Here Goya has utilized our association of the size of a landscape to his giant figure to help achieve scale. In the hands of a lesser artist the figure might have seemed of normal proportion sitting on a miniature stage set.

Any forms associated with our bodies, such as clothing, utensils, tools, also become scaling units in a picture. A picture of a person who appears tiny compared to a pair of pliers will seem small indeed since we associate pliers to a normal-sized human hand.

At times we may find it necessary to depict unusual or special proportional relationships within a human structure. The volumes we draw may not be distorted, yet they can signify strange categories of experience.

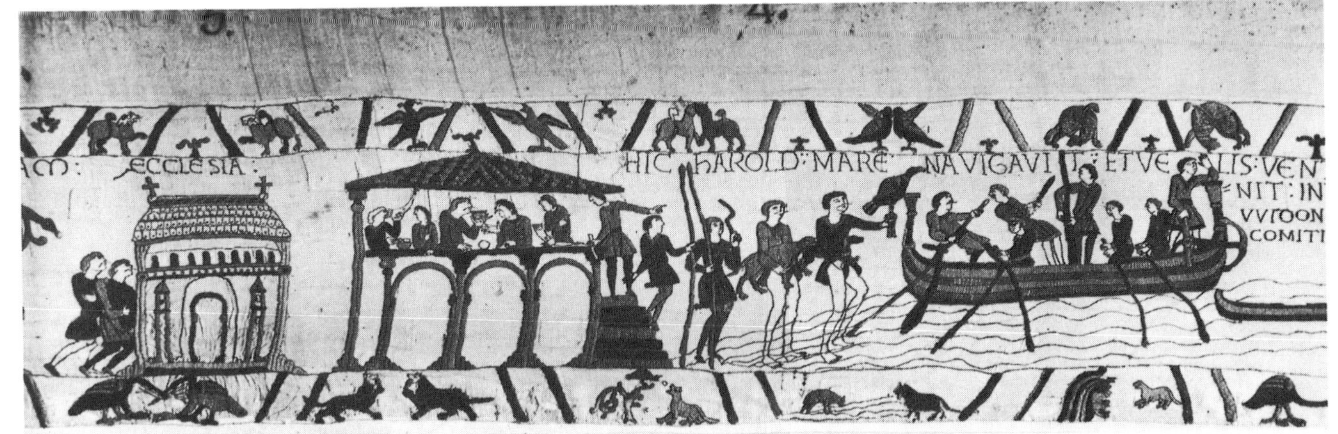

Queen Mathilde (Norman French, 11th century)
Portion of the BAYEUX TAPESTRY
"Harold sails the Channel in a fresh breeze,
disembarking on the lands of Count Guy.
Harold is apprehended by the Count."
ca. 1073-1083; 20″ x 200′ approx.
wool embroidery on linen
Archives Photographiques, Paris

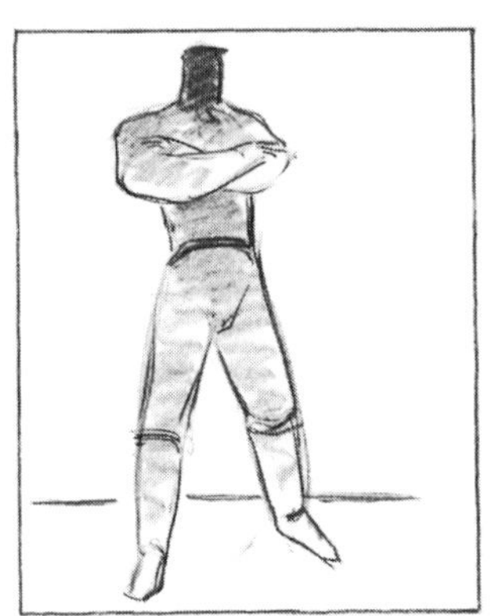

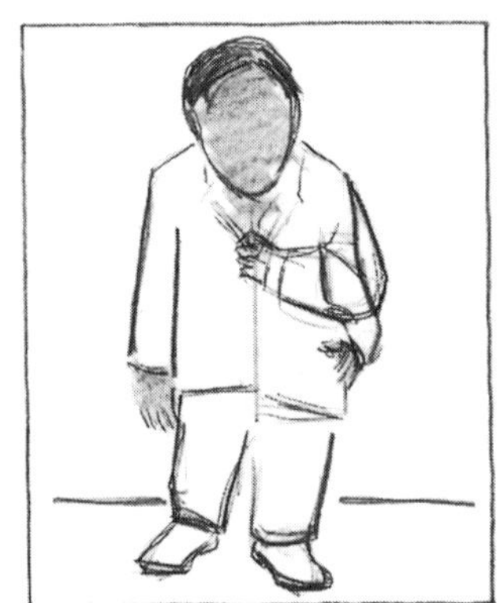

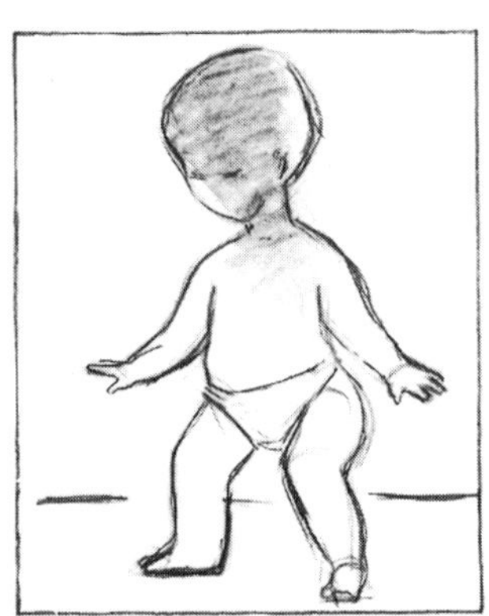

366-1A366-1B366-1C

366    For instance, an imaginary giant may be symmetrically formed, but in a picture his body may be proportionally huge in relation to his head, hands, and feet (*366-1A*). His gestures would be exaggerated because of the extreme leverage of his long arms and legs. His stride would be many yards long.

Conversely, a midget may be symmetrically formed, but his hands, feet, and head would be large in relation to his height (*366-1B*). His gestures would be limited because of the shortness of his arms and legs. He might have to make several strides to match one of a normal adult, or take many strides to keep up with a giant. We would have to account for such differences in depicting these characters.

In drawing children we also face a scaling problem. A very young child just beginning to walk is not proportioned like an adult. A child this age is mostly head and torso (*366-1C*). His arms, legs, feet, hands, and neck are still growing. His cranial structure seems huge compared to his facial structure. The nose and mouth are tiny in relation to his eyes. His shoulders have hardly begun to develop. Naturally his actions are limited and change as his structure changes.

Careful attention must be given to delineating such proportional differences. Often this is referred to as "scaling of the parts." Yet here we find another graphic trap: there is a real possibility of confusing scale through size relations with scale through surface and space relations. A picture may suggest great scale

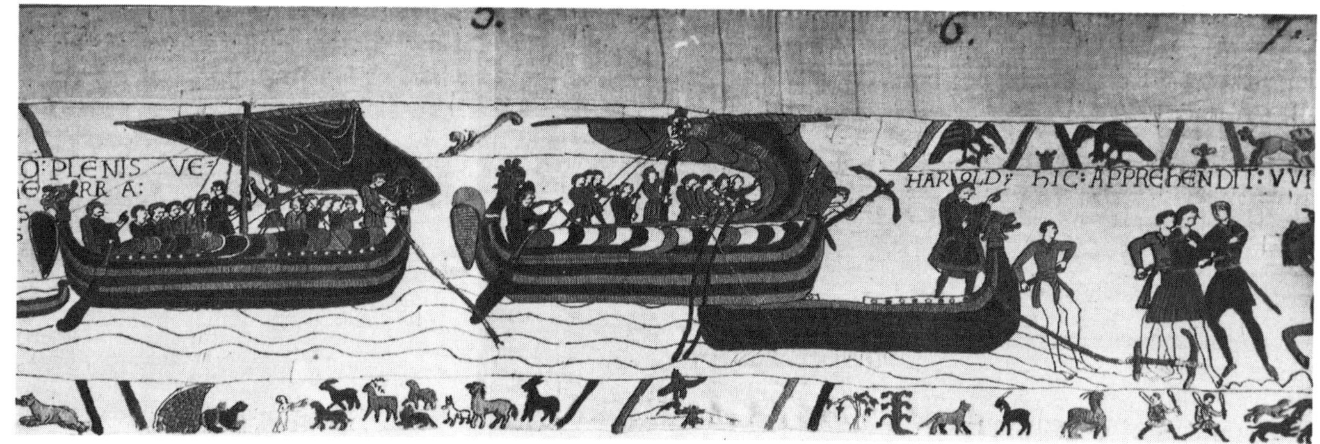



through size relations yet be faulty in space
structure. On the other hand, a picture may be
in perfect scale yet lack conviction as to relative
sizes. A figure may seem spacious yet not look
like a giant, midget, or child.

In certain types of design it is possible to
introduce a variety of elements reminiscent of
elements in nature but which may be manipulated in size to satisfy the demands of the
picture. In this portion of the Bayeux Tapestry
the relation of figures to buildings and boats
violates normal perspective and size standards
yet creates a clear statement of the various parts.

## The Legible Picture

So we find that the lucid quality so often
noted in the pictures of the great masters,
and which we so hope to achieve, stems from
control of scale. A fine picture can provide a
checklist against which to compare our own
work: there is subtle balance of volume to
space, careful proportioning and staging of
details and parts, careful attention to graphic
accents both on the surface and in picture depth.
At first trying to achieve all this we may feel
a bit like a juggler balancing sticks, plates,
chairs, hoops, and spheres while riding a
unicycle. But eventually, with constant practice,
the parts and pieces go where we wish. We
achieve order, clarity, and control of graphic
space.

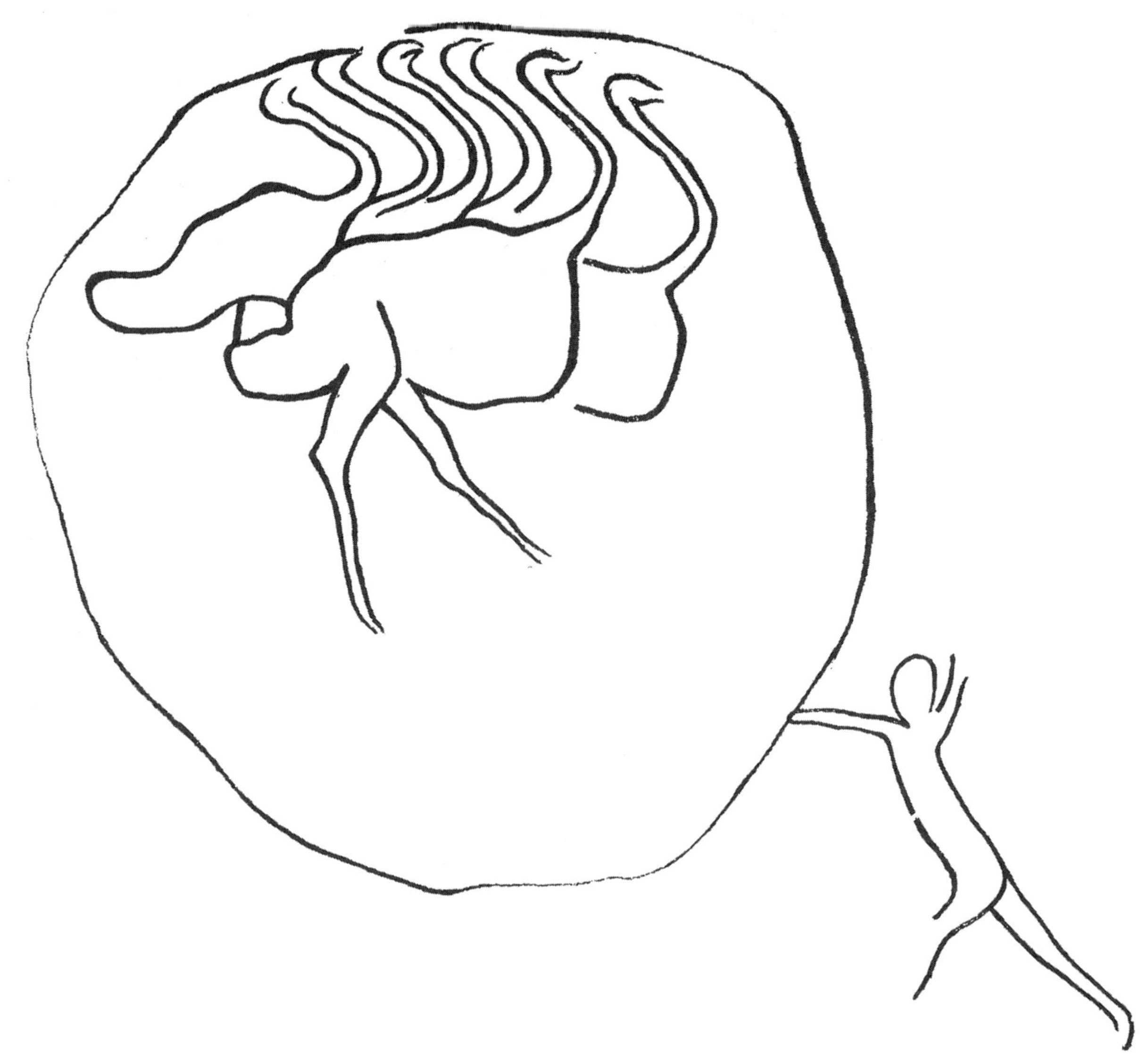

Prehistoric rock picture, Habeter, Fezzan
OSTRICH; copy by Cuno
Frobenius Institute, Frankfurt-am-Main



# 31 Action in Pictures

**Simulated Action in Pictures**
Making pictures which indicate the passage of time has been an assignment for the artist throughout art history. Ancient Egyptian murals depict incidents in the lives of people and gods, the Bayeux Tapestry seen in the previous chapter records the events of the Norman Conquest in a picture some two hundred feet long. These are only two examples of efforts to depict protracted action in a still picture.
But the illusion of action in pictures had never been a practical reality for the artist until the advent of film.

Long before motion pictures the idea of action in pictures was expressed by illustrating several phases of action in one still picture. This concept was explored by many artists, some even in prehistoric times.

# IX DESIGNING FOR FILM

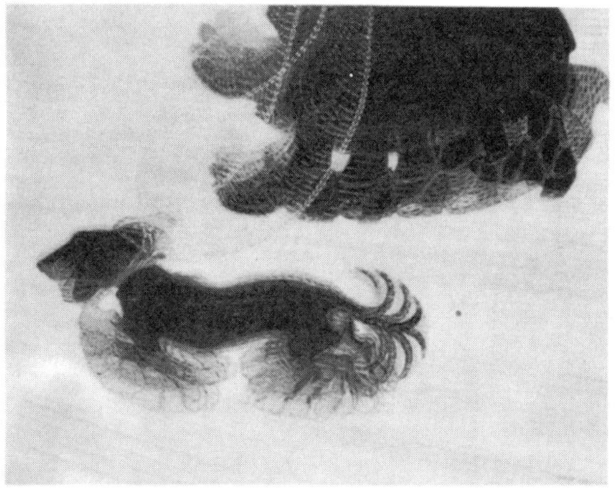

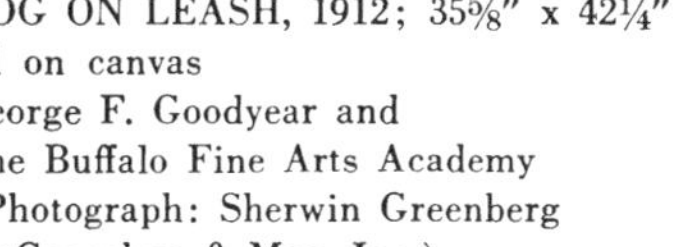

Giacomo Balla (Italian, 1871?-1958)
DOG ON LEASH, 1912; 35⅝″ x 42¼″
oil on canvas
George F. Goodyear and
The Buffalo Fine Arts Academy
(Photograph: Sherwin Greenberg
McGranahan & May, Inc.)

José Clemente Orozco (Mexican, 1883-1949)
THE MENACES, mural
Guadalajara, Jalisco, Mexico
Courtesy Sr. Jorge Hernandez Campos
Instituto Nacional de Bellas Artes, Mexico, D. F.

Pablo Picasso (Spanish, 1881-    )
WEEPING WOMAN WITH HANDKERCHIEF
Study for *Guernica*, 1937; 21″ x 17½″; oil on canvas
Los Angeles County Museum of Art
Gift of Thomas Mitchell

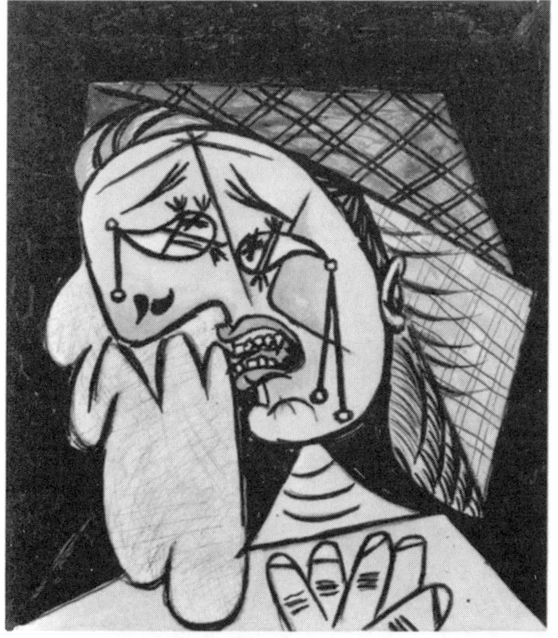

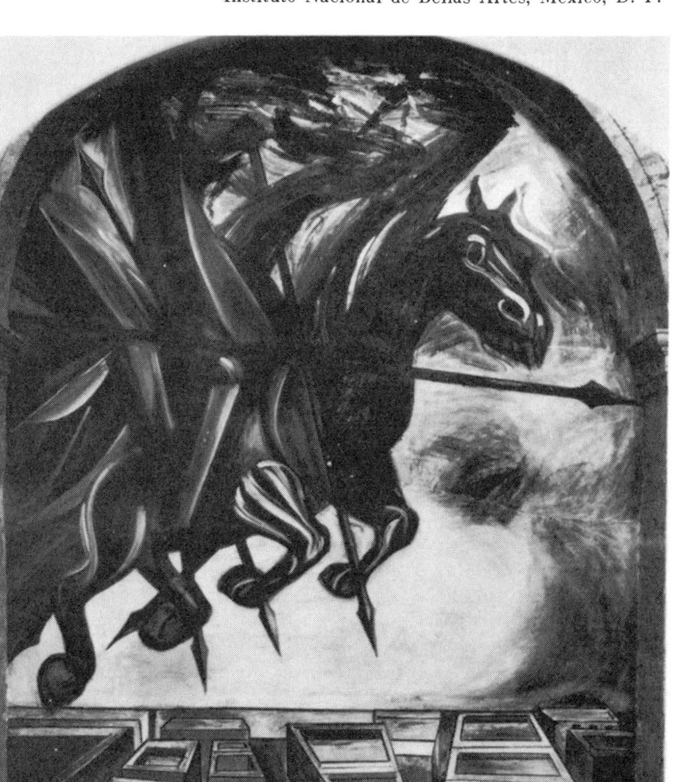

This copy of an ancient rock picture of an ostrich shows a skillful use of simultaneous views, phases of action displayed together. The picture may be read as one ostrich in action, or as a number of ostriches performing the same action.

In a more recent picture, Balla's *Dog On Leash*, the problem of simultaneous views is carried to a more extreme and complex solution. Other artists, particularly Picasso, have made simultaneous views quite commonplace in contemporary pictures.

## The Sensation of Action



At times a sensation of action may be depicted graphically other than by simply illustrating specific phases of an action. Lines of force, or the convergence of lines, and the impact of dynamic shapes may give us a feeling of speed or motion more intense than that which might be felt from a mere illustration of the form.

As the artist has tried to simulate action in the still picture he naturally has turned to other forces potential in picture making. In this picture, Orozco has skillfully combined the images of characters in action with graphic movements generated by images of inanimate objects and the architecture. The blending of simulated action and movement results in a powerful statement combining a picture of action and a sensation of action in a single picture.

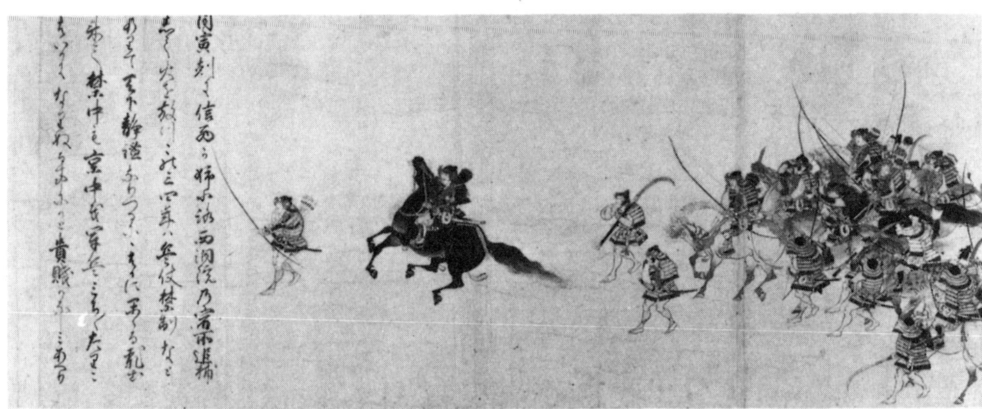

Heiji Monogatari (Japanese, 13th century)
THE BURNING OF THE SANJO PALACE
Kamakura Romantic, Middle 13th century
22′ x 10″ long, paper makimono
Courtesy, Museum of Fine Arts, Boston
Fenollosa-Weld Collection

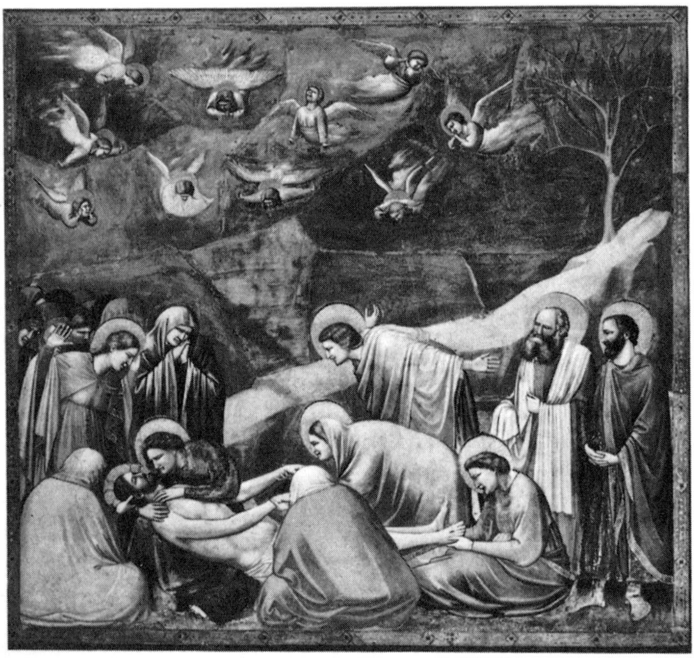

Giotto (Florentine, 1266?-1337)
THE LAMENTATION, 1305-1306; fresco
the Scrovegni Chapel, Padua
(Photograph: Alinari-Anderson-
Art Reference Bureau, Inc., N. Y.)

## Related Poses in One Picture

The particular arrangement of figures in
*The Lamentation*, by Giotto, gives us related
phases of an implied action in two or more
poses. The angels, compared one to another,
assume poses suggesting a number of positions
which one angel might assume during the
action of flight.

In like manner, the two standing figures
on the left assume two extreme positions of
a gesture. When we relate the two, we experience
an illusion of one figure performing the action.
Similarly, the two central figures represent
two phases of one action. The poses are
dependent upon each other. The true action
suggested lies somewhere between.

## Manipulating the Picture Surface

Artists have also tried manipulating the
picture surface itself. As an example, ancient
Japanese scroll paintings such as *The Burning
of the Sanjo Palace*, shown on consecutive
pages, generate a sense of progression as they
unroll, revealing only part of the picture at any
one time. These scrolls in many ways anticipated
the panorama background or *pan* used so
extensively in motion pictures. Illustrators have
tried folding pictures and pages of books to
indicated change of expression or scene.

Other artists have tried relating two or
more separate pictures in special ways to better
solve this problem of action. The idea of using
more than one picture to indicate action
developed into drawing in series.

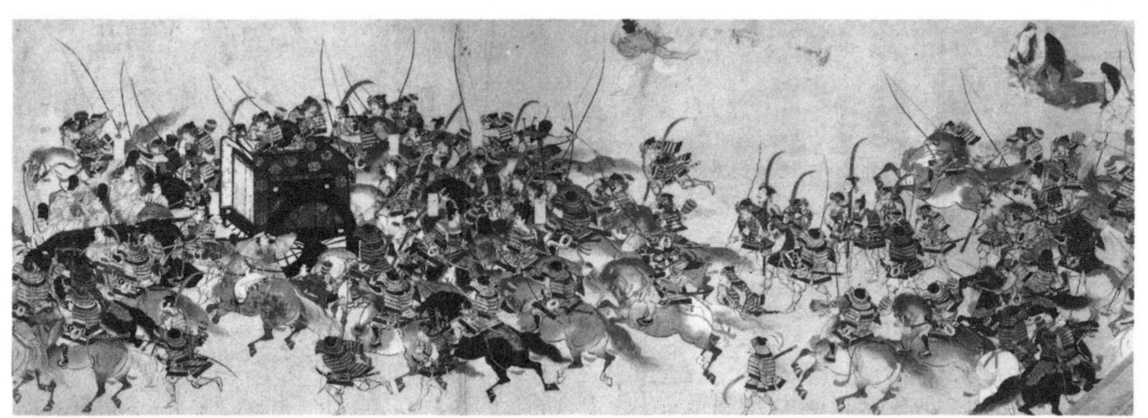

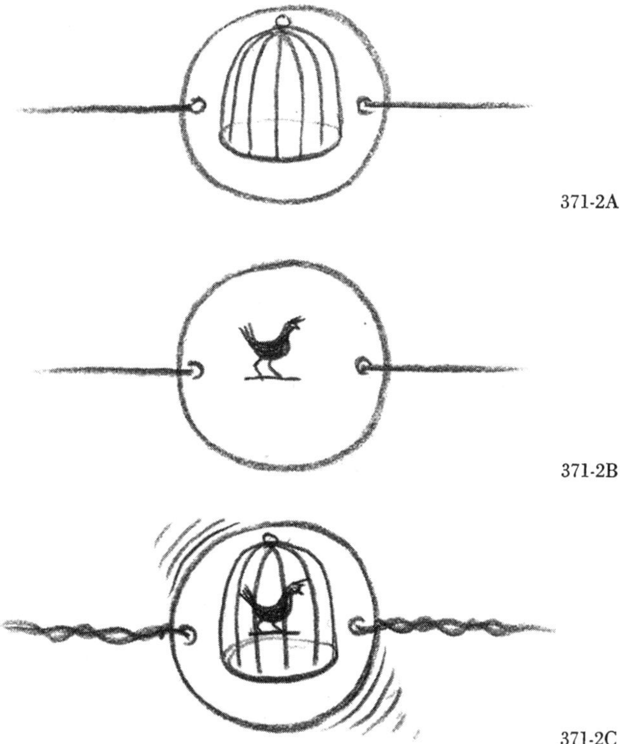

371-2A

371-2B

371-2C

## Multiple Pictures in Series

In the Giotto the two poses of the figures
on the left suggest one action. Much of this
effect is due to the fact that the two figures are
close together, of about the same size, and
draped in similar robes. We are made particularly aware of the related positions of each
pair of hands respective to the other.

From this observation we can derive some
conclusions: only two or more related pictures
placed together in series simulate action. The
parts to be compared must be similar; that is,
we can compare two similar arms, but not an
arm to a leg, or to a horse. The relative positions
of two or more such similar parts must be
different from each other, but this difference
must not be too great. We can compare two
closely related positions of a head turning, but
not a front view of a head to a back view.

## The Persistence of Vision



Early in the nineteenth century someone
devised a toy that proved to have great significance in the understanding of action in pictures.
For example, upon one side of a card let us
draw a birdcage (*371-2A*), on the other a bird
(*371-2B*). Spinning the card creates the illusion that the bird is actually in the cage. This
simple device demonstrates a principle which
made the motion picture possible. The
*persistence of vision,* as this effect is called, is
based on the fact that an image formed in our
eye lingers a certain time. If, under certain
controlled conditions, a new image is substituted while this first image still is in existence
the second seems to move in the first
(*371-2C*). We should note that by the time the
second image, the bird, is caught by the eye,
the first drawing, the cage, can no longer be seen.

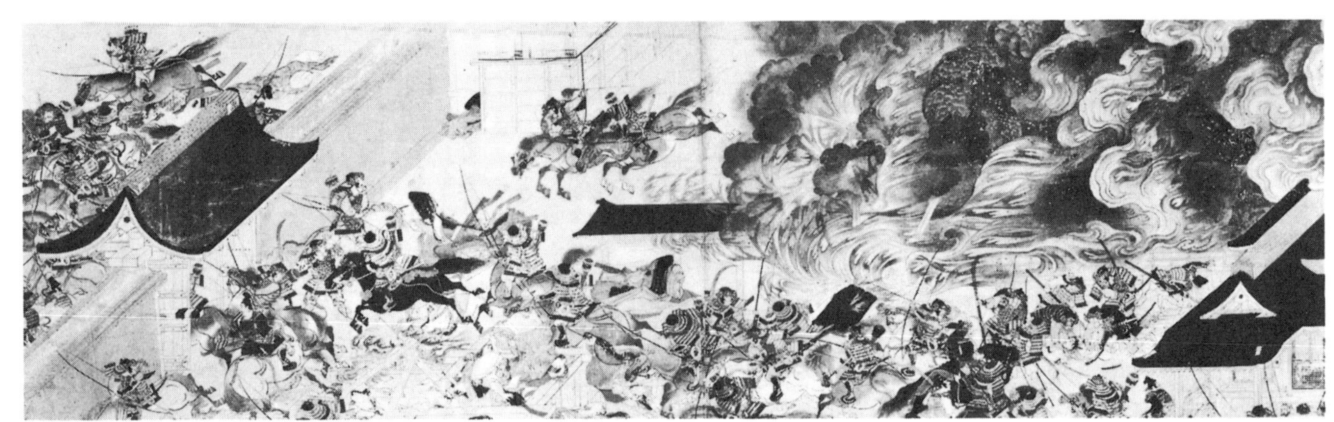

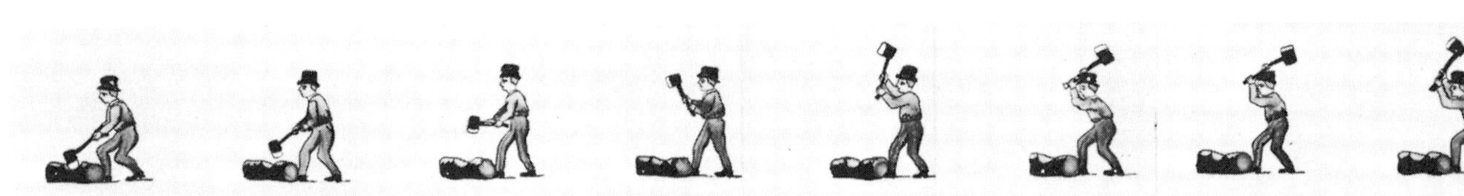


A zoetrope strip from the
Disney "Art of Animation" exhibit
© Walt Disney Productions

372 So we see that if a series of related pictures is viewed with a short intervening rest between each picture, the persistence of vision is sustained. But without this rest, the image is blurred.

As a development of this concept, a related series of action drawings can be made on separate cards which are then flipped or riffled. The rest or interval is preserved by the time lapse between cards and so a true illusion of action results. This is known as a kineograph or flip-book.

Another device to bring action to drawing is known as the zoetrope. Phases of action such as we see here are drawn on a paper strip, then observed through slots on a revolving drum. A version of this is the phenakistoscope showing phases of action on a disc. When the spinning disc is observed in a mirror through the revolving slots an illusion of action is achieved.

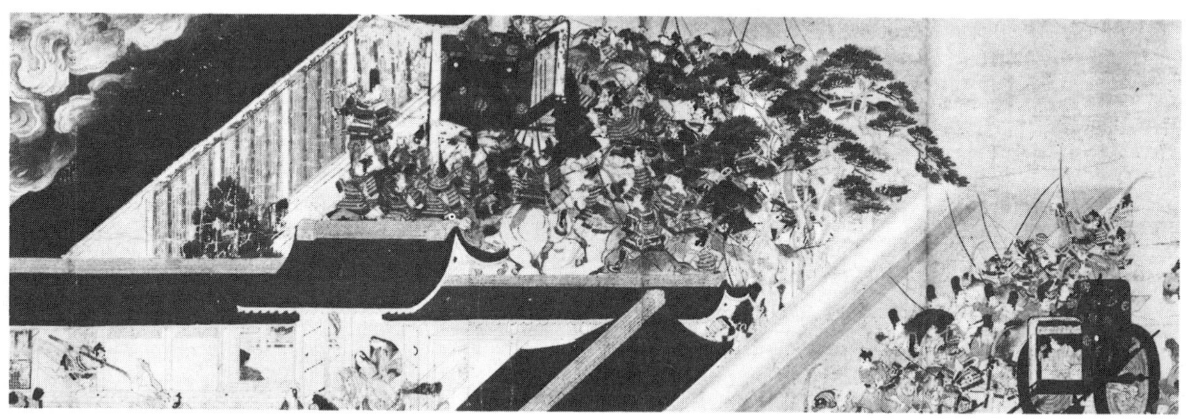

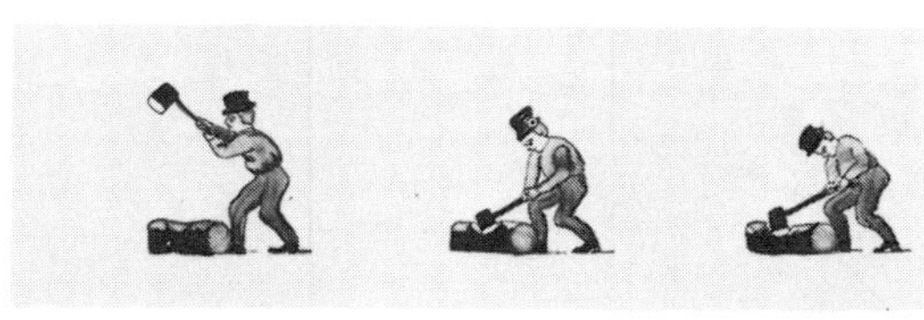



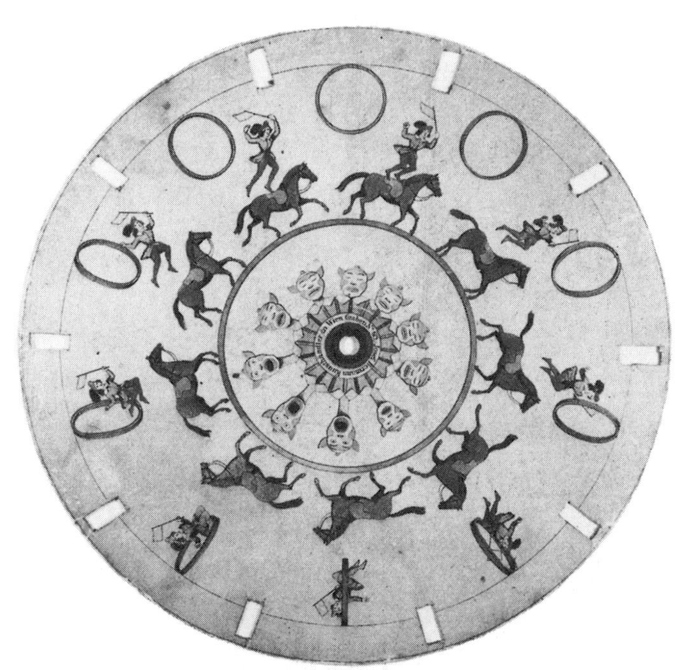

Phenakistoscope dial
from the collection of Earl Theisen
on indefinite loan to
The Academy of Motion Picture
Arts and Sciences, Hollywood

In the late nineteenth century the idea of projecting images upon a screen was made possible by the development of the "magic lantern." Many experiments were made in which pictures in series were projected by suitably modified types of magic lanterns. Often these pictures were painted on glass slides which were manipulated by hand.

With the advent of running film and the projector, real pictures in action became possible. The ancient problem had found an answer.

## Action and Vision



An understanding of how we see action in nature is prerequisite to creating believable action on the screen.

A form at rest may be scanned with the eye with a minimum of distortion. As the form moves into action a great number of changes take place. Muscles tense or relax, as one part of the form completes an action another part prepares for an ensuing action in a constantly unfolding series of overlapping actions. Visually the moving form is of a different order than when still.

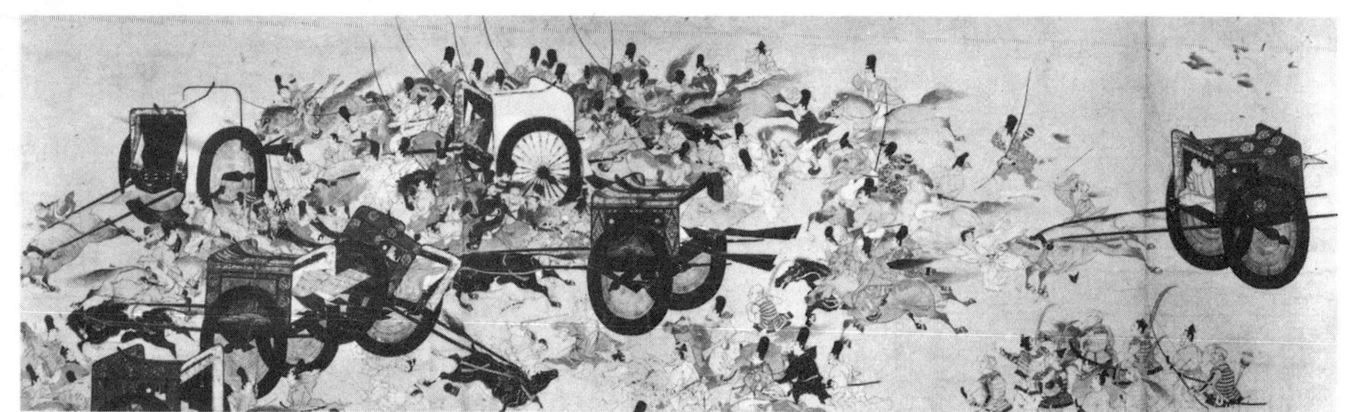

A page of studies of deer and frog
made by Rico Lebrun as research for BAMBI
© Walt Disney Productions

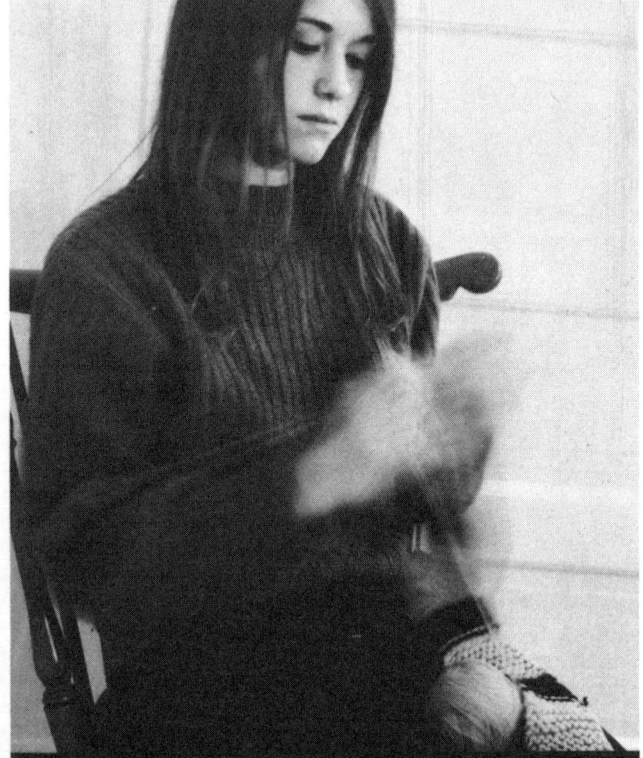

GIRL KNITTING
(Photograph: Sally Dunbar Andersen)

374    Now another phenomenon occurs. As the form increases speed, the eye is unable to record the shape in its entirety. Parts of the form blur. This can be easily demonstrated by moving our hand rapidly before our eyes. A figure in moderate to fast action can evidence both clarity in slow moving parts and distortion in fast moving parts, as we see in the photograph of a girl knitting. These effects are also modified by the distance separating the spectator from the moving form. His own speed also affects all that he sees.

**Action in Drawing**

In viewing motion pictures the brain seems to recognize not the exact image projected at any given instant but rather an imaginary image somewhere between two related and adjacent positions on the screen. Similarly, when we witness an actual action in nature, our brain seems to form composite images, new organizations that are imaginary but better express the action.

Since earliest times the graphic artist, whether making a still picture or an animated film, has searched for this evasive composite, this drawing between, this unseen but sensed image which suggests our sensation of action. This is the *action drawing*.

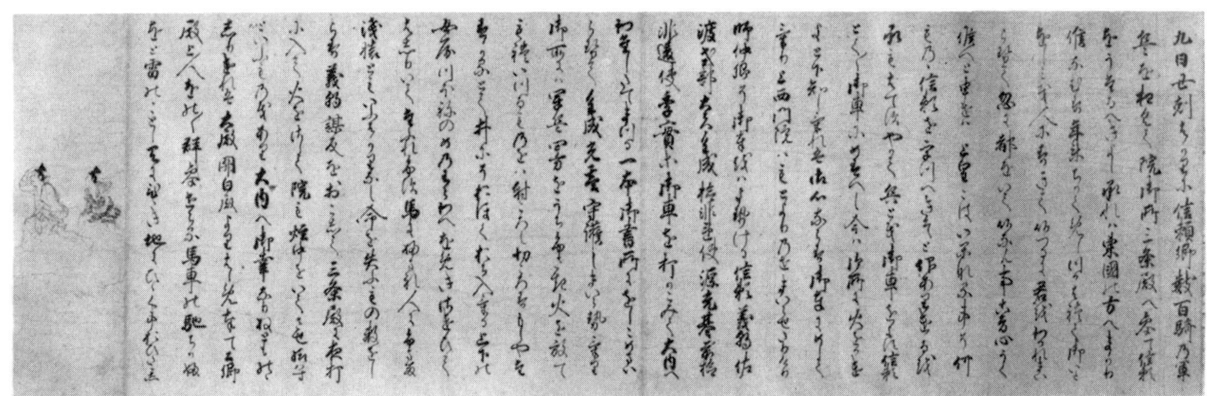

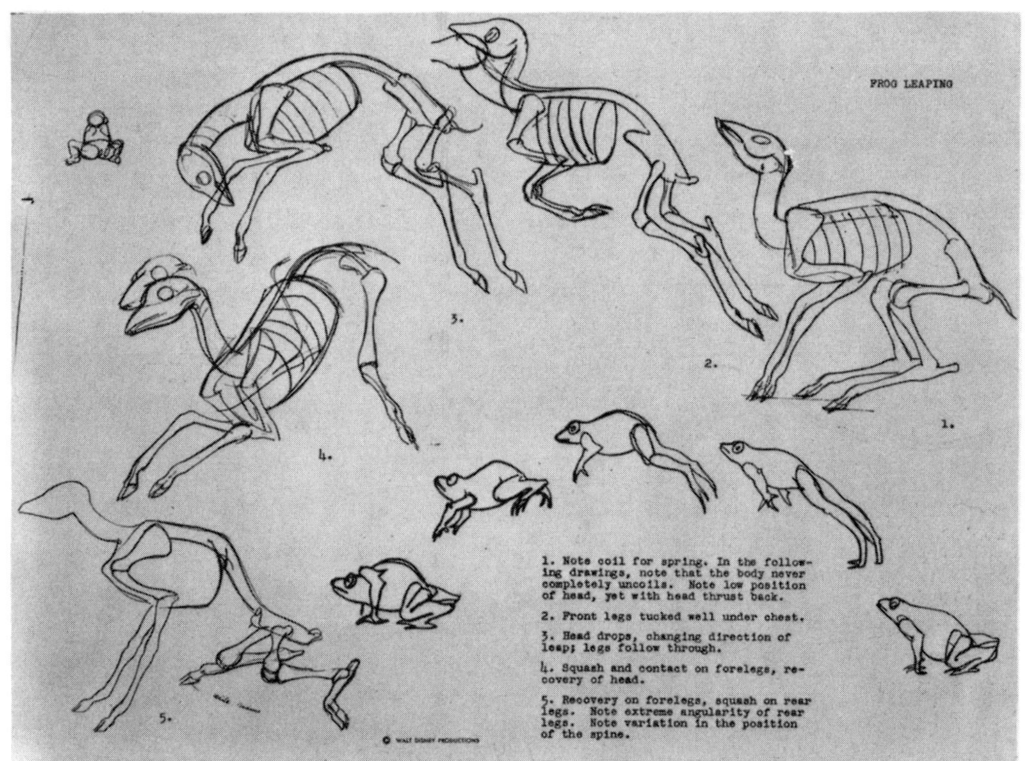


For instance, we have seen in Chapter 20 that a figure depicted seated comfortably in a chair is in a state of balance. If, now, he is shown at an instant just prior to this, as he is settling into the chair, he will be in a state of equilibrium. In the same way, if he is shown just about to rise he again is in a state of equilibrium. If either of these latter positions is used in a still picture a new dynamic is instilled into what might otherwise be an ordinary drawing.

An animation drawing showing a figure in a fast walk may fail to achieve a true sense of action because of the incorporation of minor details, exact delineation of local shapes, exact projection of the principal parts. In a more truthful action drawing many of these details would be blurred, many of the shapes modified.

A series of carefully related drawings projected correctly in time may not give a convincing sensation of action. In an action series careful delineation of each pose as an entity, a thing in itself, almost always results in stilted action. As we noted in Chapter 29, the volumes must be conceived as symbols of forms moving in time. Only if the drawings utilized are true action drawings, drawings that convey the idea of action, can convincing action be realized, as we see in these animal studies by Rico Lebrun. Whether the form is moving quickly or slowly, our drawing should express not what the form looks like, but what it is doing.

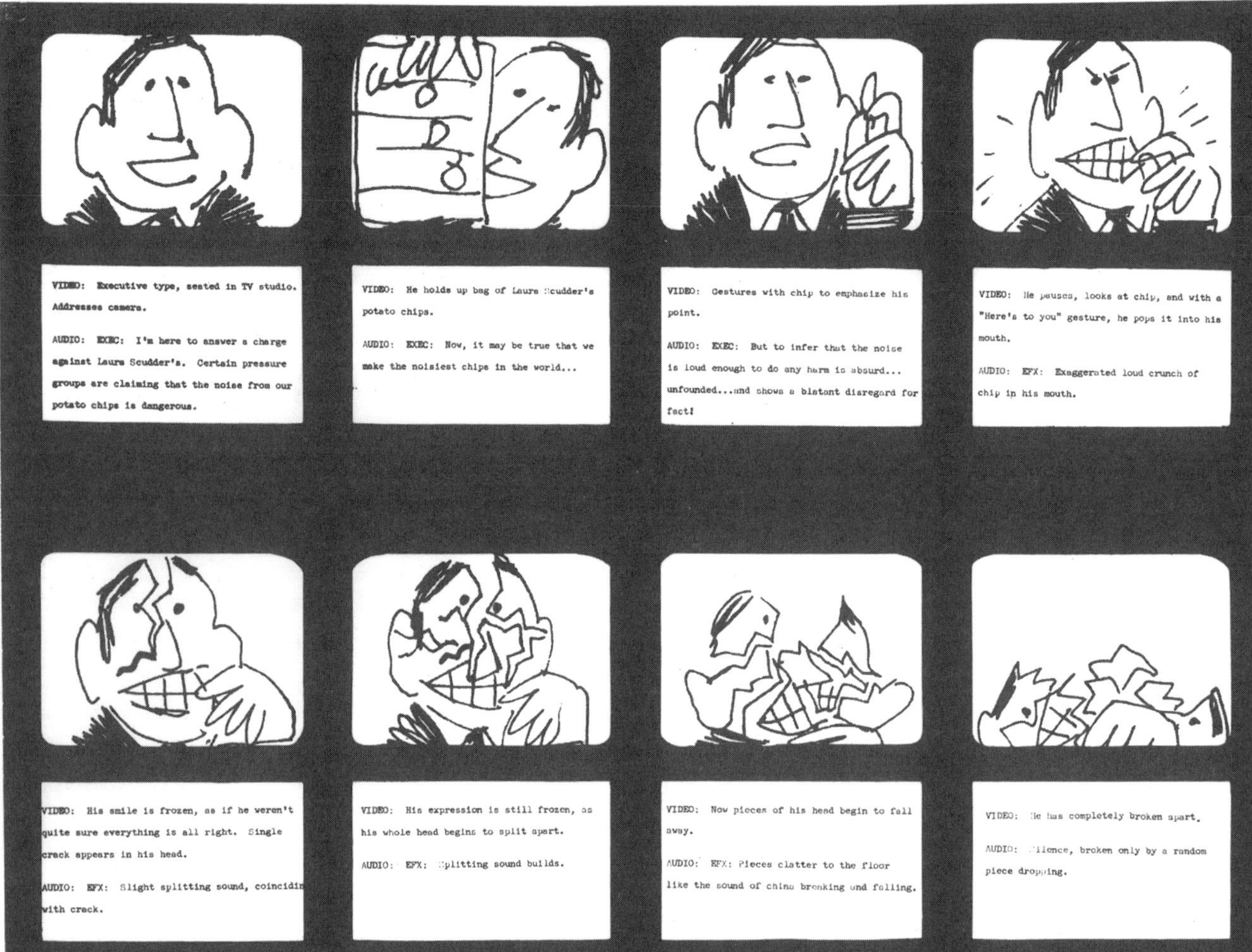


Television storyboard for commercial
"Rebuttal," retitled "Shattering Man"
Courtesy Laura Scudder's
Snack Foods Div., Pet Inc.
Agency: Doyle Dane Bernbach Inc.



# 32  The Storyboard

### Story Preparation for Film

Today many artists are faced with the problem of designing pictures or drawings which relate in some way either to motion pictures or to television, such as we see here, or to projected images involving some kind of time sequence.

A live action motion picture may be composed by a director or a camera man, or both; they often work with a written script, either complex or rudimentary. Even in motion pictures of a certain style involving no prior graphic planning, the trained eyes of the director and cameraman select and edit as action is filmed as well as later in the cutting room. Educational films, which often are live action, are usually based on very carefully prepared scripts.

Although a live action story may or may not be prepared graphically, an animated film, feature length or commercial, is developed

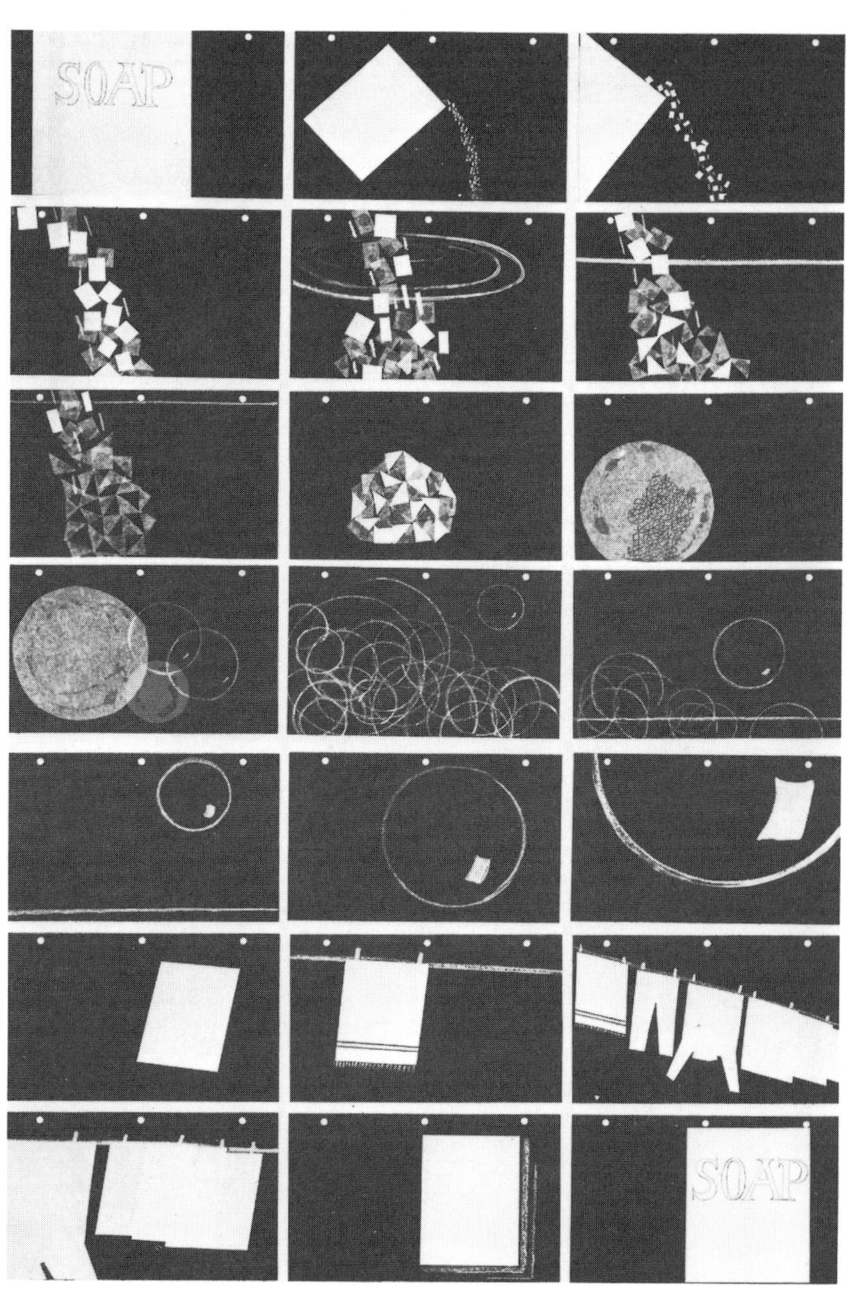

Proposed television commercial
in cut-paper animation
"The Shape of Washday"
Phyllis Graham

graphically in one form or another. An animation story may be first defined in some kind of written script ranging from a single page outline to an elaborate script. But the script has serious shortcomings simply because it is written, not drawn.

A writer is trained to think verbally, an artist to think visually. But to find a person skilled in both verbal and visual creativity is rare. So a compromise form has developed. This form has proved of such great value that it is practiced universally in the animation film industry and has been carried into related fields such as television and advertising. This compromise is the *storyboard*.

## Developing the Storyboard

All of us have found that a convenient way to view written notes, telephone numbers, photographs, drawings is to pin them on a convenient wall or board which we know as a pin-up board. From early days in animation, the pin-up board was used to present idea sketches, mood sketches, atmosphere sketches, any kind of illustration of a random idea. The pin-up board is not a storyboard but may be made one. When the order of the drawings constitutes a related series, a continuity to be read in time, the pin-up board becomes a storyboard, as in this example.

We have noted that when the artist begins to explore a story idea on the storyboard he already has some concept of the story. If it is to be a short film subject perhaps he has a written outline or script to guide him, but it is not necessarily confining. The storyboard in the beginning is very much in a state of flux. As story sketches are made, often suggested by accompanying music, new pictorial ways of expressing verbal ideas emerge.

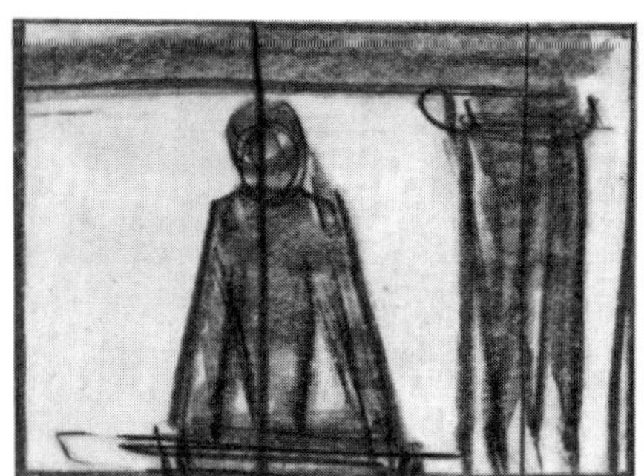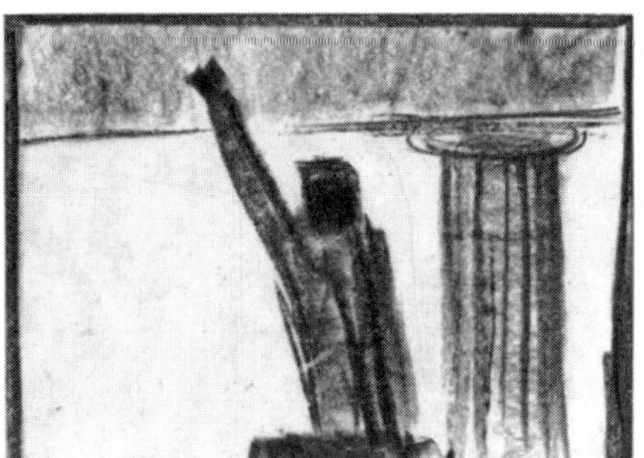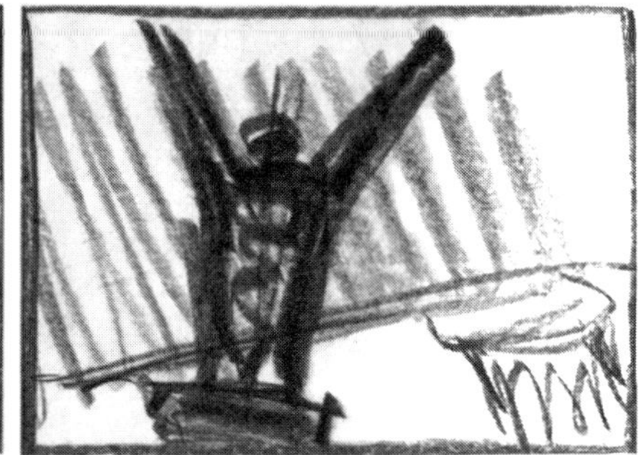



Model sheet of "Dopey"
copyright 1936 Walt Disney Productions

378     Unlike the illustrator who conceives and executes a single picture as his entire problem, the story artist must learn to think of his problem in terms of a series of pictures in time. Rarely is a single picture considered as an entity, it is significant only in relation to the picture preceding it and to the one following it. The single picture as a work of art ceases to be the concern of the story artist.

To explore the graphic possibilities of pictures in time, let us develop a simple continuity about a man giving a speech. In developing our story, and only as a discipline, let us limit the actual poses or actions of the speaker to three fixed poses. The symbol of the speaker is drawn in silhouette with no admittance of perspective changes at any time. He may be shown in close-up using only part of the silhouette, or in middle or long shots where he may be very small (*378*).

In any view the lectern behind which he stands should be revealed only near its top so there is no need to depict the audience. The background is a simple post-and-beam construction always in the plane of the picture, in the picture surface. At times we see little of the background, at other times considerable amounts.

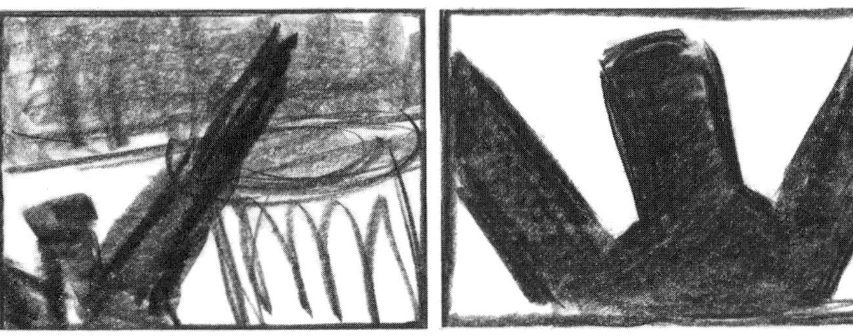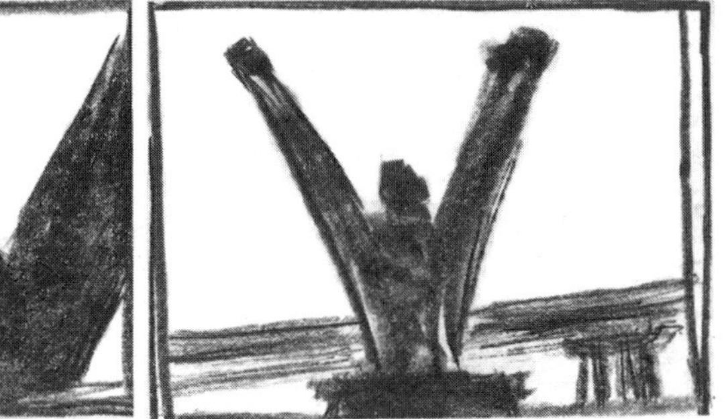



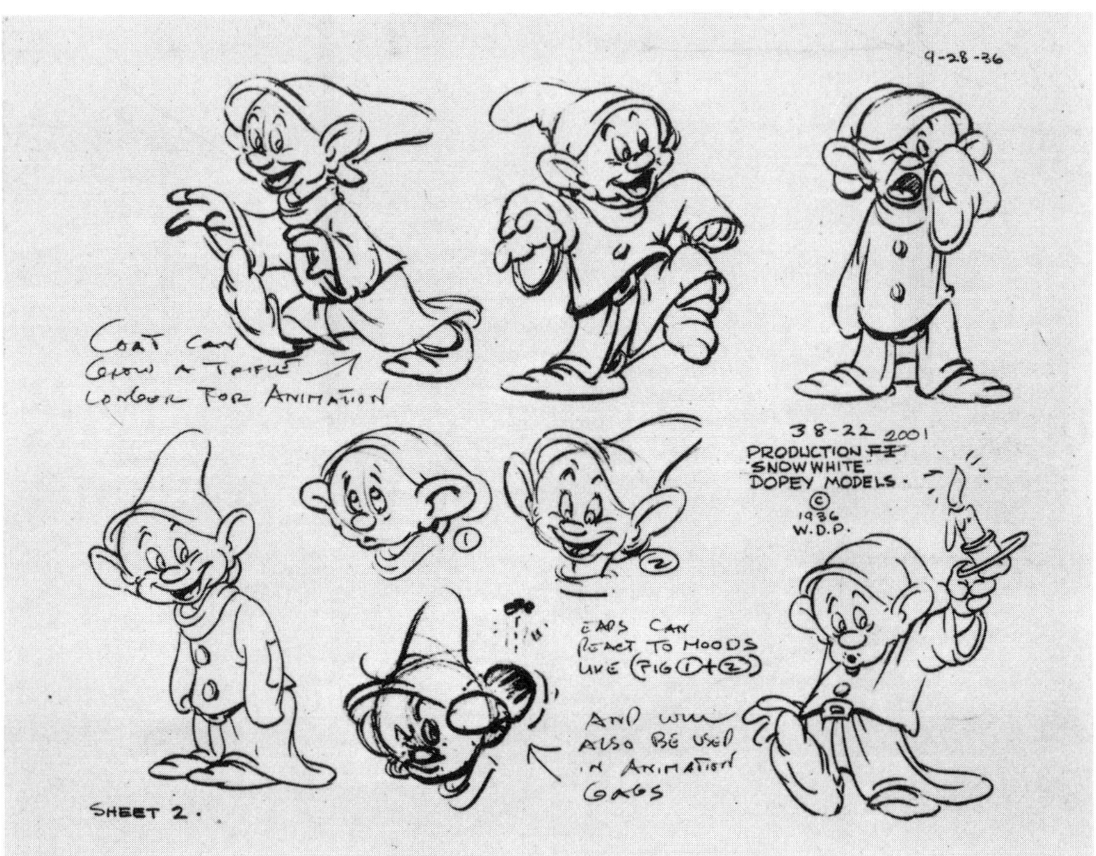


By varying the graphic activity of the pictures one to the next through shape impact, and the length of time each is seen on the screen, a change of tempo can be expressed. Some pictures may be calm, others more dramatic. Through such changes we build to a major climax or, if the continuity is longer, to a series of minor climaxes. In many stories the major climax is followed by a short finale or *top* which may be unexpected, amusing, thought-provoking, or dramatic, but is usually short (*379-1*).

The variety we discover in the use of only three simple poses, simple rotations, and elementary camera moves is only a hint of the vast potential variety in the combinations of graphic movement, camera action, and character action to be found in film, which can first be plotted on the storyboard.

Animated characters especially develop through visual exploration of a situation. The film designer first must conceive and draw such a character in various actions or situations to the best of his ability. Then the drawn character's potential as an actor is often explored in experimental footage. Model sheets, such as this of famous Dopey, are developed. The character begins to evolve and often may dictate certain changes on the storyboard. For example, a character may perform admirably in full-figure pantomime, but may not lend itself graphically to close-ups in which dialogue is involved.

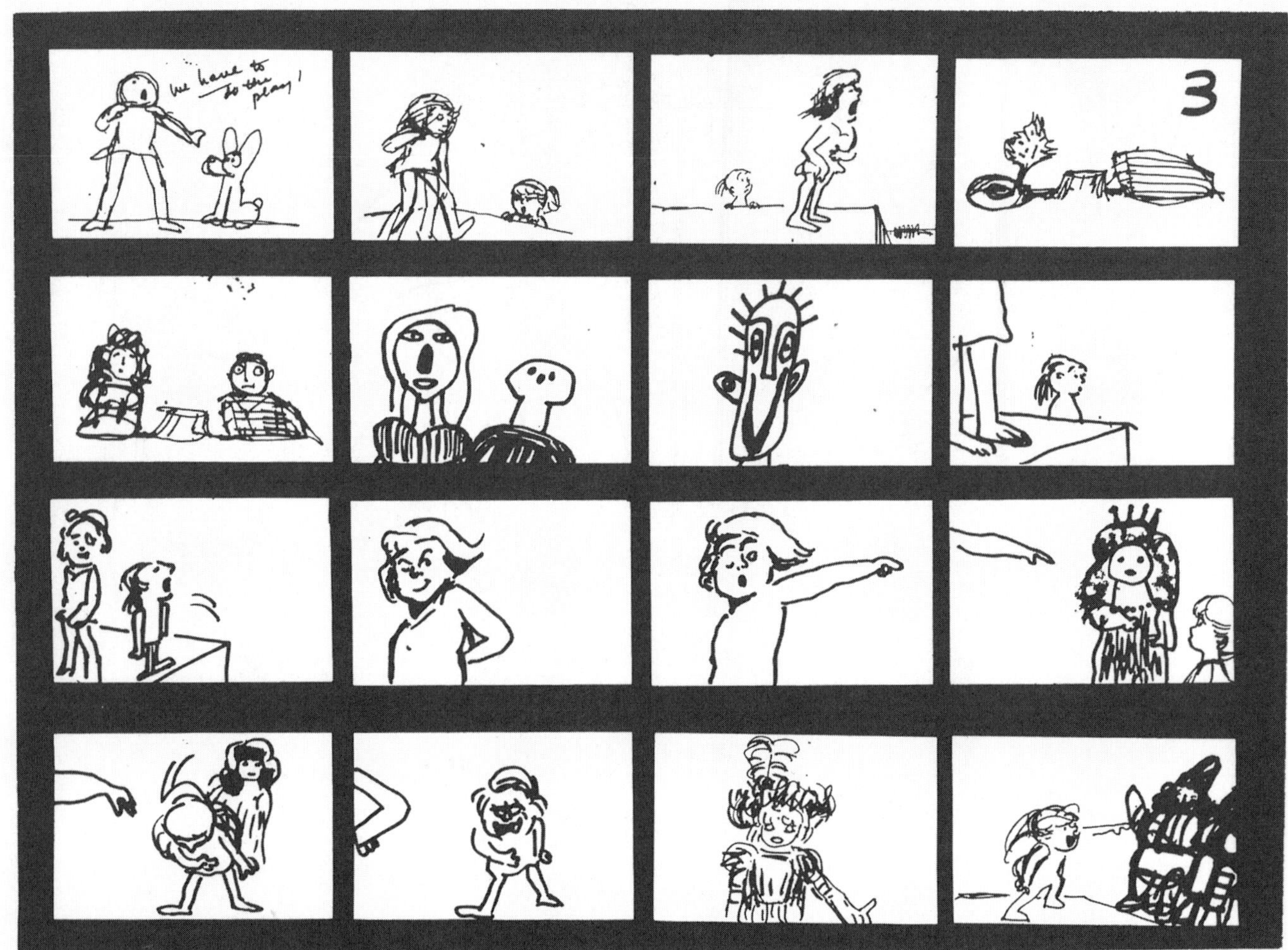




The storyboard has become an established way to preview a whole film. An error, a weakness revealed on the board can be corrected by remaking individual drawings, by eliminating them, or by moving them to more appropriate positions on the board. Whole sections can be rebuilt, moved from place to place in the continuity or simply eliminated. Glaring weakness in character construction, story development, film design can be discovered long before the film is shot, with consequent savings in time, effort, and expense. A change on the storyboard is relatively inexpensive. A change after the picture has been filmed can be a disaster.

A storyboard is often reviewed by a group of people. The problem of making a storyboard read quickly from a distance has resulted in methods of simplification that have a profound effect on the individual sketches. Only the very essentials are indicated. A background is usually indicated in one sketch and dispensed with in all other sketches in the particular scene. All detail is held to a minimum. The idea is suggested through gesture and a skillful use of meaningful poses, rather than through carefully rendered or polished pictures.

To make a picture four-by-five inches read from perhaps fifty feet implies a perfect control of space-volume relations. Every significant detail must be clearly presented. Unimportant areas supporting these details must be minimized. Expressions are dramatized not only

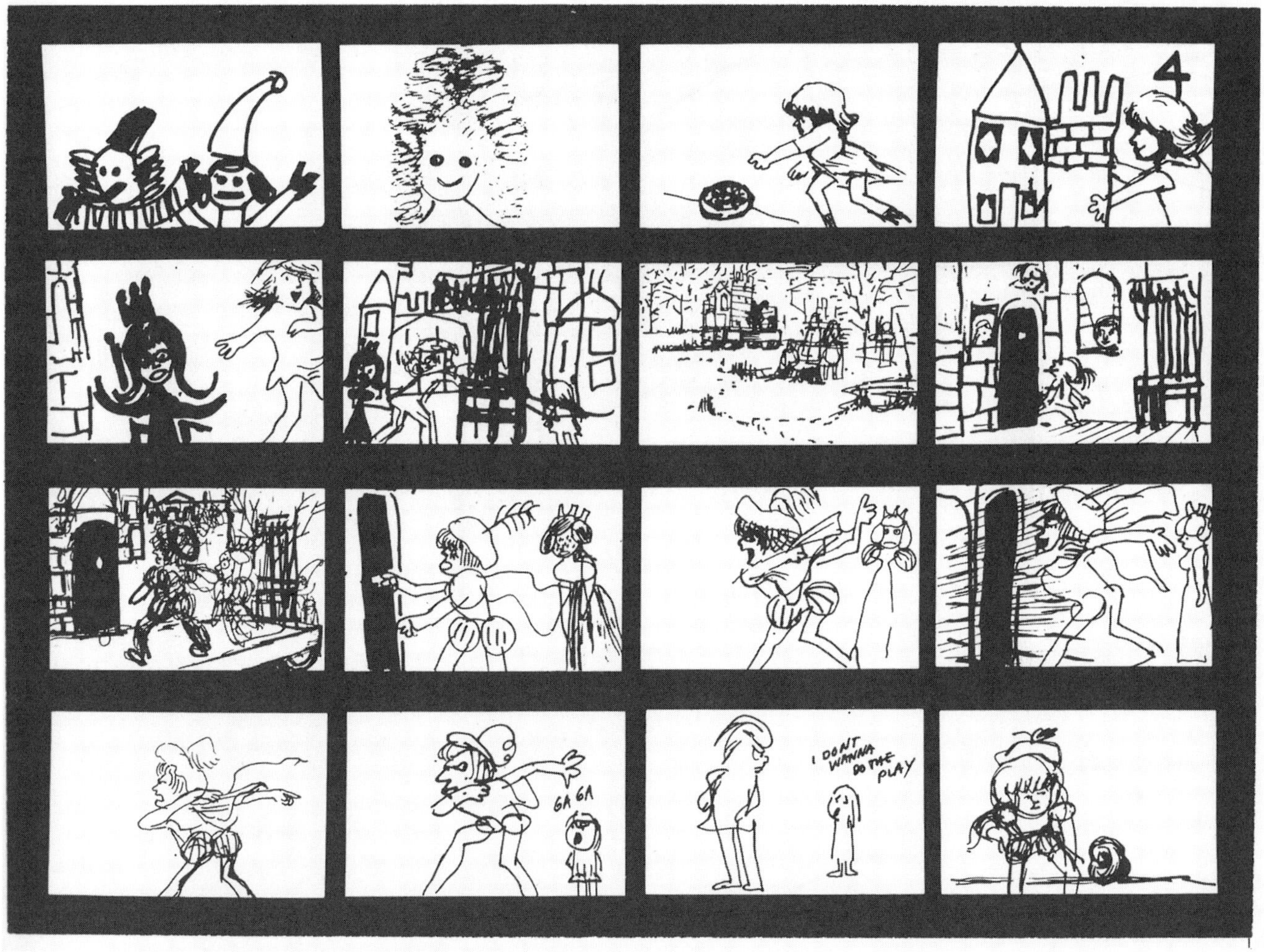

Portion of storyboard for WINDY DAY
John and Faith Hubley
The Hubley Studio, Inc., New York

through clear definition of the features, if shown, but also through the body gesture. The tempo and rhythm of the board is sustained through ingenious accenting of the individual pictures, which are made lighter or darker, or richer in detail, to act as accents in a series of closely related sketches.

One of the subtle devices used to clarify and pace a board is the sparing use of color. A board in full color, unless skillfully organized, is usually difficult to read. Some boards may have color indications occurring in every picture, but with great variety in the amount used in each. Often one colored picture will appear among several black and white pictures. The effect is that the whole board is colored. Such a board is usually more easily read than one in which color is used throughout.

Although the final timing or duration of a situation, a scene, or sequence involving many scenes is ultimately determined by the director, the story artist estimates roughly the timing of his boards. He spaces his scenes with long and short situations, he punctuates with appropriate close-ups or long shots. He paces the board roughly, working for variety, for accents, for possible rhythmic passages. It is by this pre-timing that graphic and dramatic interest is tested.

Every successful storyboard has a certain feeling of casualness or improvisation. But it is planned improvisation. Each picture, no matter how sketchy it seems, represents great understanding. The story must flow rhythmically; a tight, overworked picture brings the board to a jarring stop. Always it is the storyboard as a whole, never the beauty of a single picture, which matters.

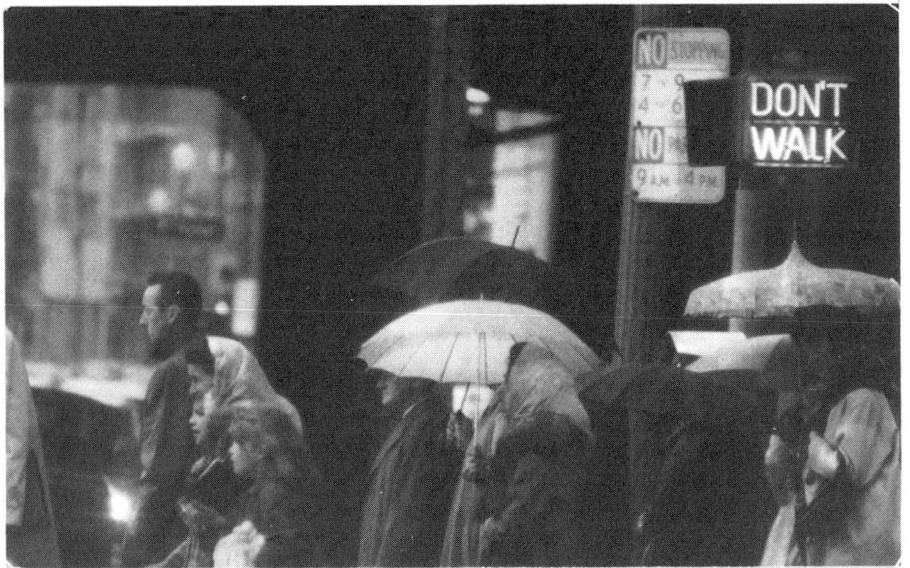

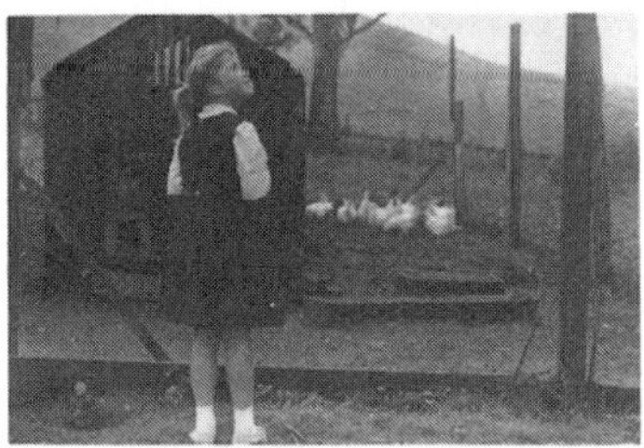

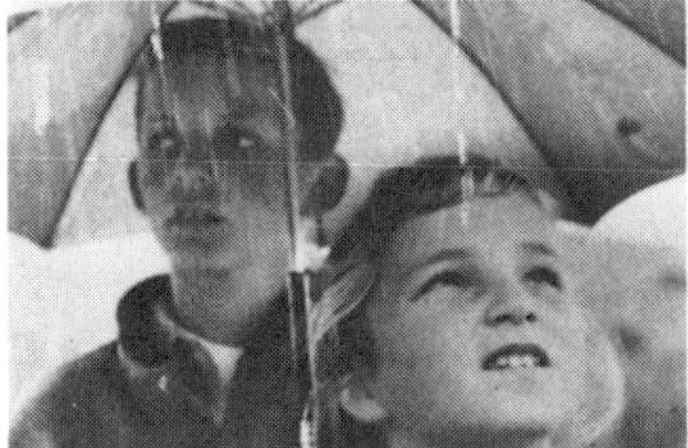

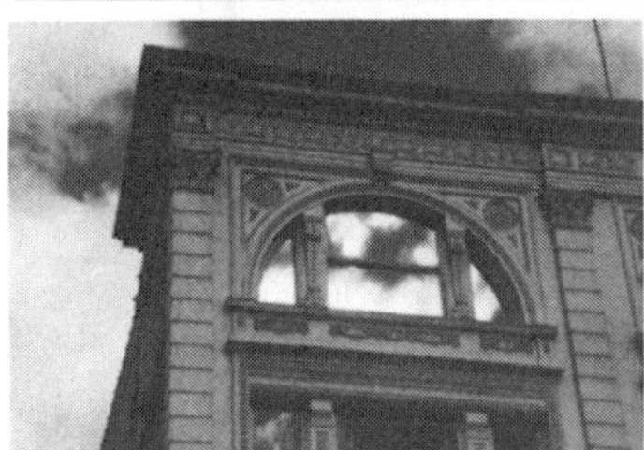

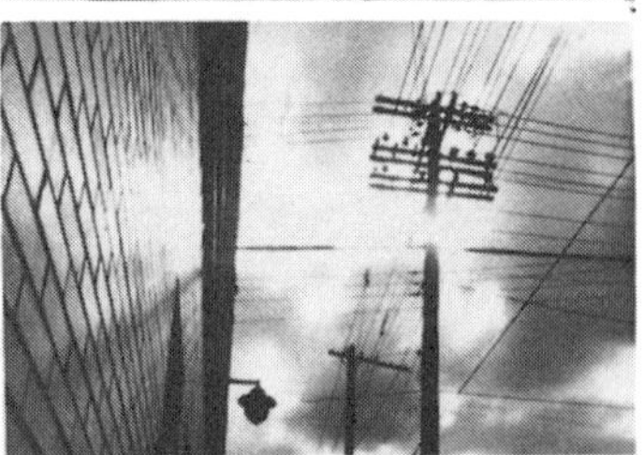

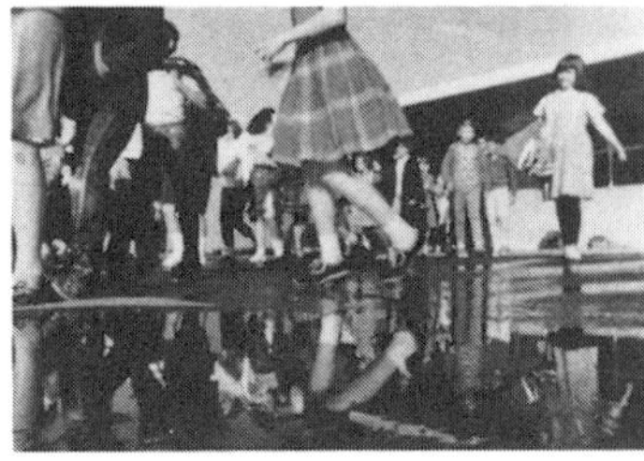

Stills from the film RAINSHOWER
Michael D. Murphy, Cinematographer
Edward Schuman, Producer
Produced by Dimension Films
Distributed by Churchill Films



## 33 Film Graphics

### The New Art Form

Film graphics is the only significant new art form of the twentieth century. It is so new in fact that its limits are constantly changing. In this short study we can only try to understand some things that have been done and anticipate some of the inevitable changes suggested by the medium itself.

Generally speaking, live action film deals with photographs of things in nature projected in time. Animation deals with photographs of drawings and paintings projected in time. The camera is the tool of the artist no less than the pencil or brush. But we should remember that no matter how the illusion of action is achieved, the images we see occur on the screen, a surface. The motion picture and the still picture have one thing in common, each is an image on a surface.

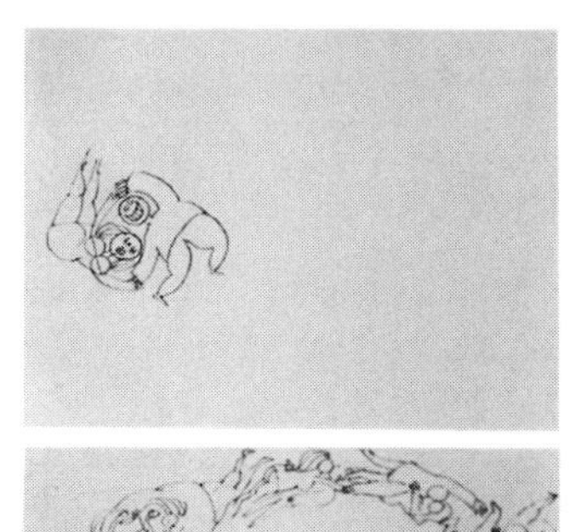
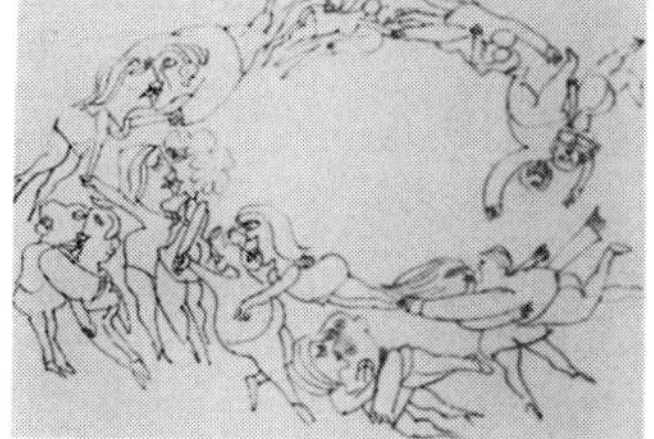
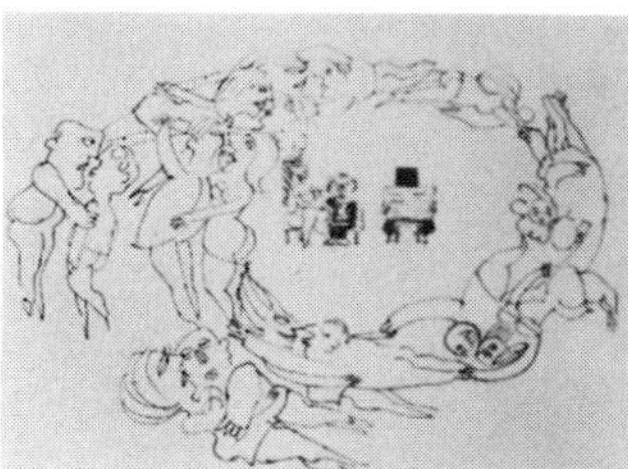
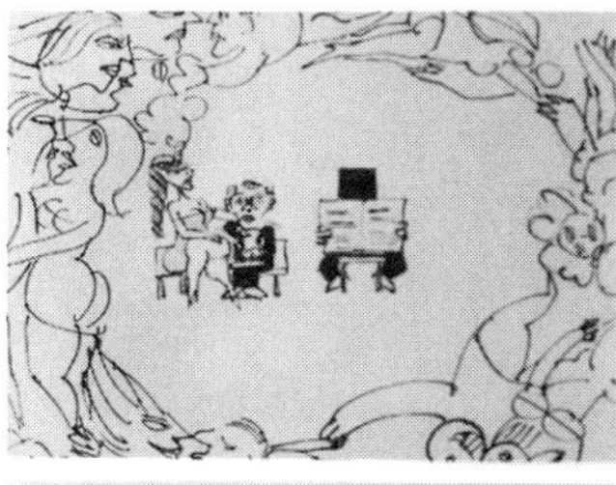
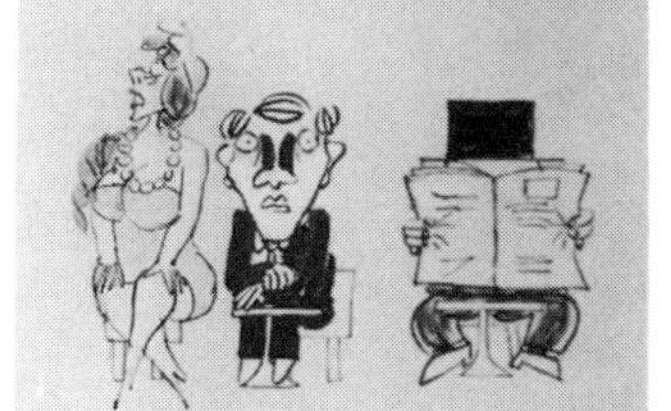

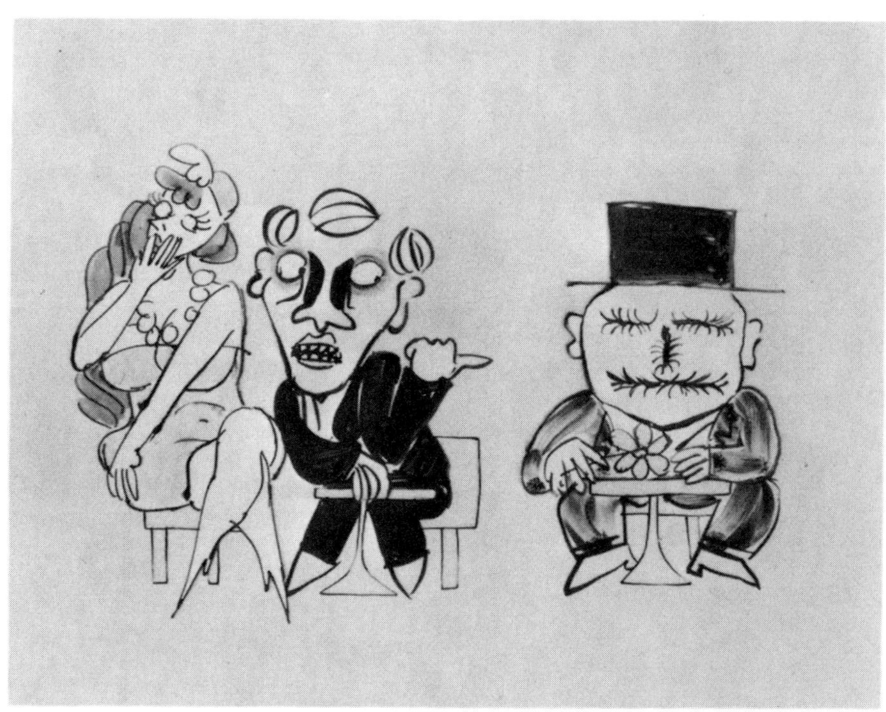
Still from the film THE GOOD FRIENDS
designed, animated, and produced by
Jimmy T. Murakami, Murakami-Wolf Films
under grant from The American Film Institute



As we have emphasized, it is the skillful organization of graphic elements on a surface rather than just subject matter that makes for maximum emotional impact. Although the motion picture gives us a moving pattern on the screen, it is the way this pattern is organized that eventually determines our visual emotional reaction to the picture. In animation the pattern is predetermined by the graphic film designer; in live action it is recorded by the camera controlled by a knowing eye, as these examples indicate. Too often in motion pictures, as in still pictures, the domination of subject matter weakens the visual impact. The visual problem in film is to develop exciting shapes or volumes in black and white, or color, in motion on the screen.

Few early film makers saw the screen as a surface, or film as a graphic medium. Everything was done to force the screen open like a window on reality. Film was used as a recording medium to capture realistic form. Gradually as the novelty of motion pictures and animation has worn off, film makers and audiences alike are more aware of the graphic potential of the screen.

**The Changing Pattern on the Screen**
There are four types of change inherent in this new graphics: change of size, change of position, change of shape, and change of color.

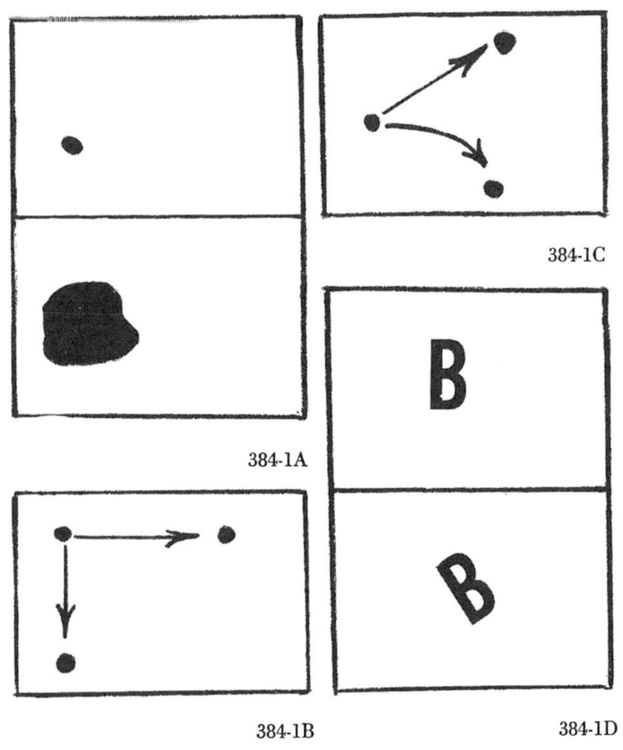

384-1C

384-1A

384-1B

384-1D

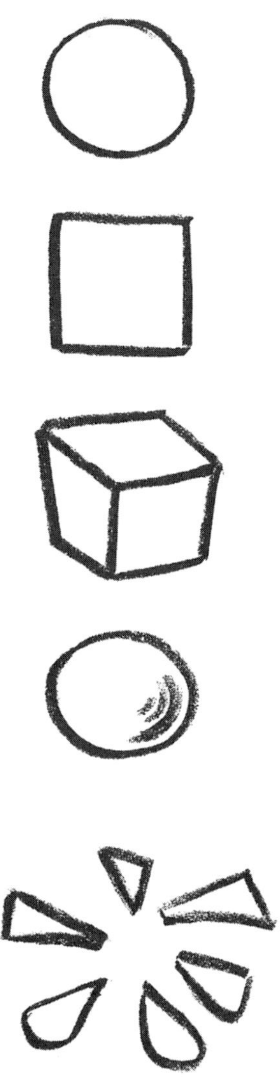

384-2

384 *Change of Size.* A point changes size as it visually moves away from or towards the spectator. It may seem to grow or shrink as it moves in space (*384-1A*).

*Change of Position.* A point may be shown moving from side to side or up or down on the screen (*384-1B*). Any combination of these actions results in a curve or diagonal action pattern (*384-1C*). These elemental actions on the screen are seldom witnessed as isolated actions. They are seen, however, when a flat shape, a letter, number, or object which seems flat is moved in the plane of the screen (*384-1D*). These are primarily two-dimensional actions.

The combination of change of size and change of position results in the illusion of action in deep space. Most animation made until the mid-twenties was primarily exploitation of these two fundamental types of change. For example, most of us have seen a cartoon character run from foreground to horizon and back in just a few frames.

*Change of Shape.* A shape may change from a circle to a square, or from a flat shape to a volume. In conjunction with change of position and change of size an almost infinite range of change of shape can be realized on the screen, especially in animation. Since a volume is always a shape, its limits of change are encompassed by those of shape. However, since a shape need not represent a volume many changes of shape go beyond those of volume. So we see that a volume may change into a shape having no bearing whatsoever upon the shape of the volume (*384-2*).

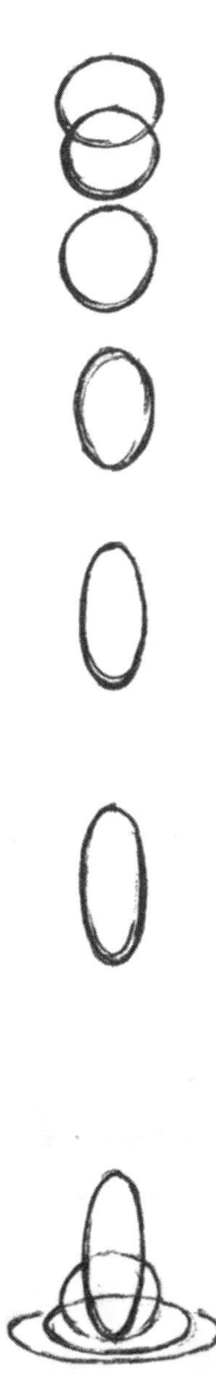

385-1

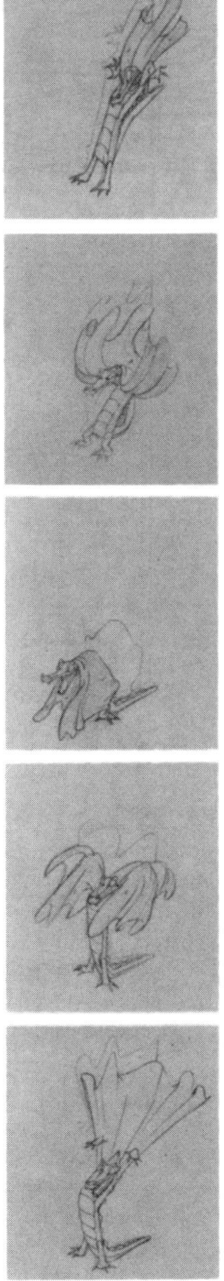

Five animation drawings of an alligator
used for FANTASIA
Copyright 1940 Walt Disney Productions

Although change of shape was utilized to a minor degree from the earliest days of animation, not until the mid-twenties was it fully accepted as an integral part of animation. Then the idea of stretching or squashing a volume to emphasize an action or gesture came to be incorporated into standard animation technique. At first arms and legs were stretched unmercifully, often as a gag. During the next twenty years the flexibility of an animation volume was finally understood and exploited. In live action the use of slow motion and time-lapse to accentuate change of shape has as yet been used sparingly.

Change of shape may be demonstrated in an elemental way by animating a bouncing ball (385-1). As it falls it is elongated, when it strikes a surface it squashes, then returns to its original spherical shape. Carried into involved character animation, as we see here, change of shape becomes a method of drawing that is unique in the history of art. A new flexibility, a new life quality is captured which goes far beyond the reality of much live action photography (385-2). It is through exploitation of this principle of stretch and squash that really believable dialogue, which is projected by the whole body, is achieved in relation to believable three-dimensional animated characters. Such animation is known as *full animation*.

Before discussing change of color we must first investigate some complex factors of film graphics.

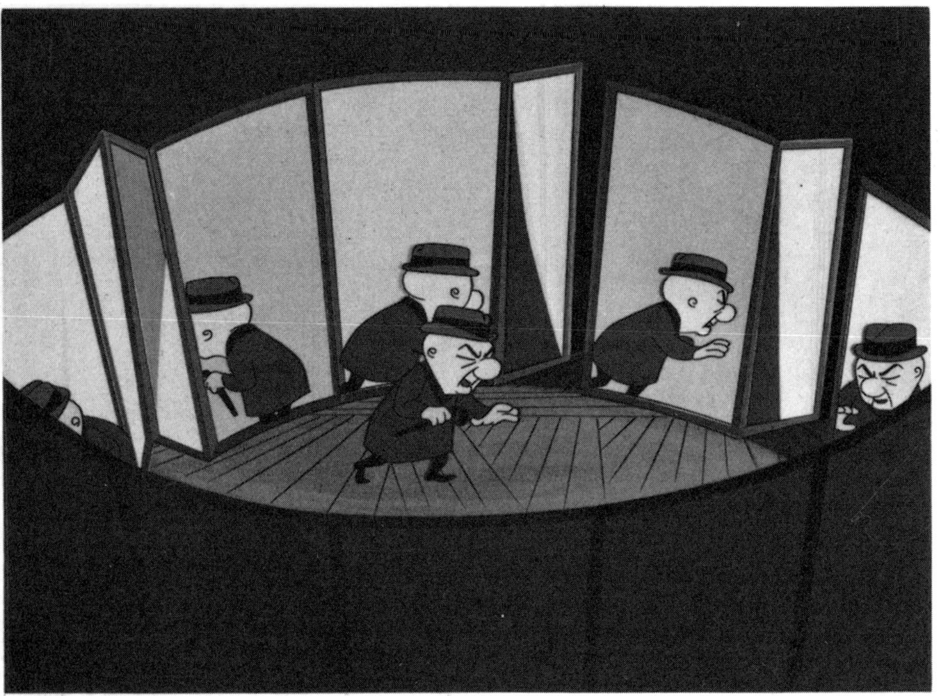

MR. MAGOO
UPA PICTURES, INC.

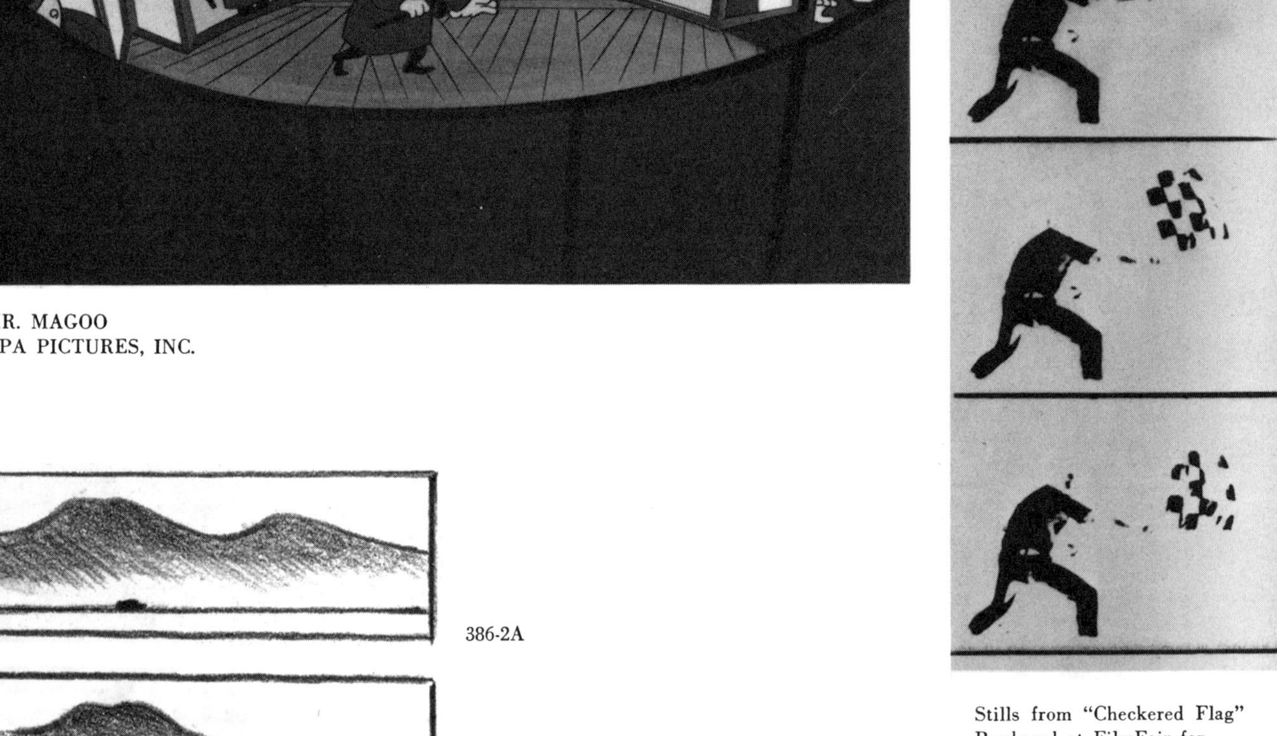

386-2A

386-2B

Stills from "Checkered Flag"
Produced at FilmFair for
Leo Burnett Co., Inc. on behalf of
Union Oil Co. of California

### Limited Animation

386

In the early forties the immense cost of full animation became prohibitive for the small producer. A new concept of animation evolved based upon change of shape. What started as an economic limitation soon proved to be stimulation to a revitalized form of animation.

We saw in Chapter 29 that a flat shape in action generates a space of its own, becoming a convincing volume. By conceiving a character as an organization of flat shapes without modeling or rendering, the idea of action, often stylized action, was achieved. In this type of animation, action in-and-out from the screen is held to a minimum, cuts and trucks are used whenever possible to indicate the character moving toward or away from the screen. Most action is performed in or parallel to the screen. Parts of a figure, such as the famous Mr. Magoo, often are moved without reaction indicated in the rest of the figure.

Fast or semi-fast actions are usually convincing with this technique, but slow action tends to create flat, unconvincing shapes. To circumvent this problem, for instance when a head turns slowly, a profile may animate into a front view by changing shape instead of by turning as a volume. An arm may bend by changing its angular and length relations. Lines and shapes are superimposed and moved independently of each other. Off-screen dialogue is used extensively.

The effect of limited animation upon film graphics has been profound. It helped establish the moving picture as a graphic as well as a dramatic structure.

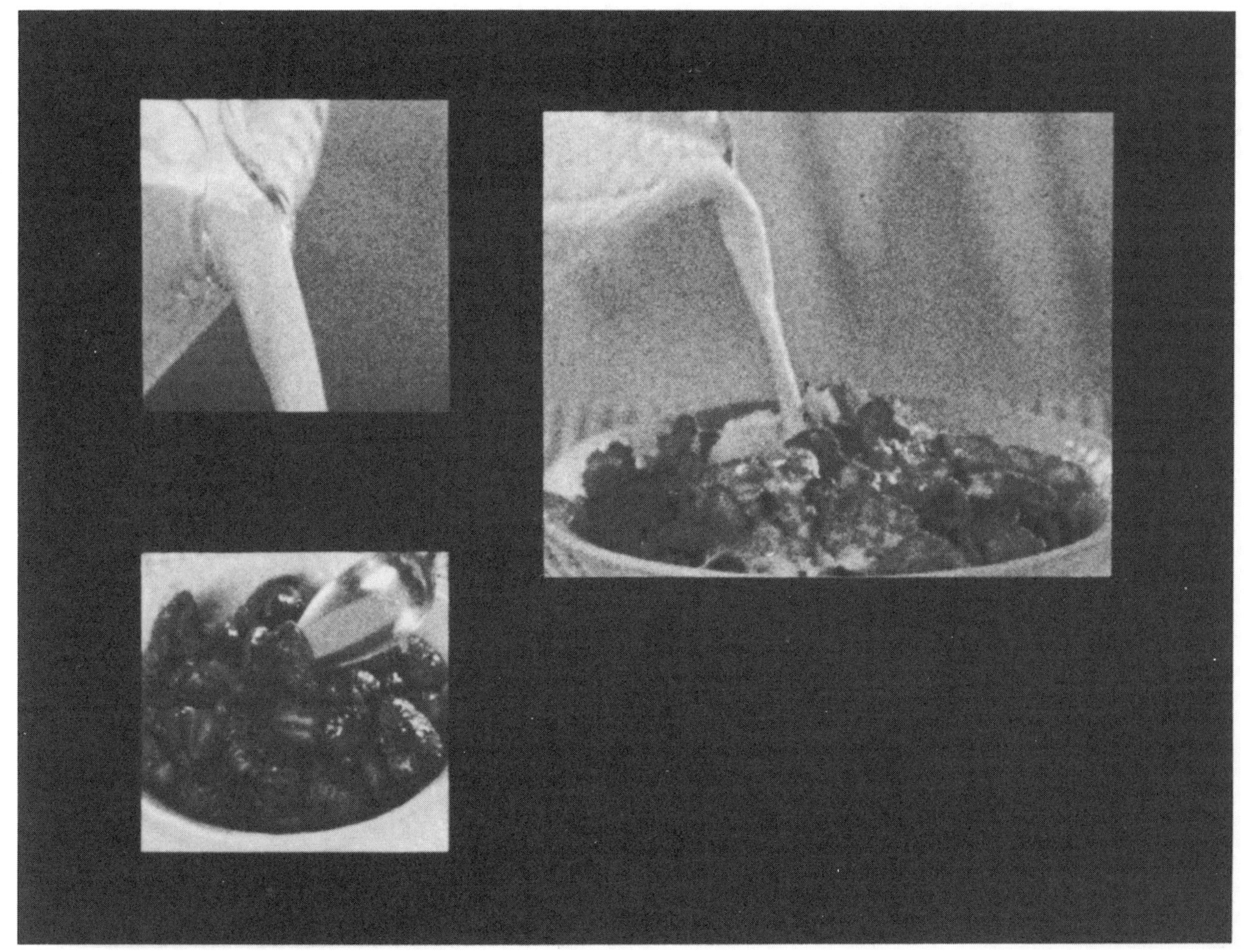

Still from "Midwest"
Produced at FilmFare
for Leo Burnett Co., Staff,
and the Kellogg Company

## The Moving Composition

At this point in our study of composition it might be helpful to review the content of these notes, to reexamine the various principles particularly in relation to film. Much that we have discussed has direct bearing upon the graphic aspects of film.

Certain still picture constructions, however, such as the use of fixed picture lines and proportional divisions of a fixed surface, are often destroyed when action is involved. The problem of scanning and finding the center of interest can be irrelevant to the motion picture. For instance, a tiny shape which might be overlooked in a still picture can become the center of interest in a wide-screen panorama, simply because the tiny shape moves while the large ones are still *(386-2A, -2B)*.

If we keep in mind that the shape impact of a still picture or the motion picture are both predicated upon a pattern, whether still or moving, we have a common point of discussion. A drawn animated shape, a character for instance, may be exaggerated as to shape and greatly simplified as to detail. Similar effects may be achieved in live action by the use of the telescopic lens or the zoom lens. Shape impact in live action can be exploited by back-lighting and dramatic use of stark overlays, as we see in the stills of the man with the flag.

The principle of multiple station points can be exploited in film by double exposure, and especially by the use of split screens where many views of one character, or views of objects or persons pertaining to his character are projected simultaneously, as we see here.

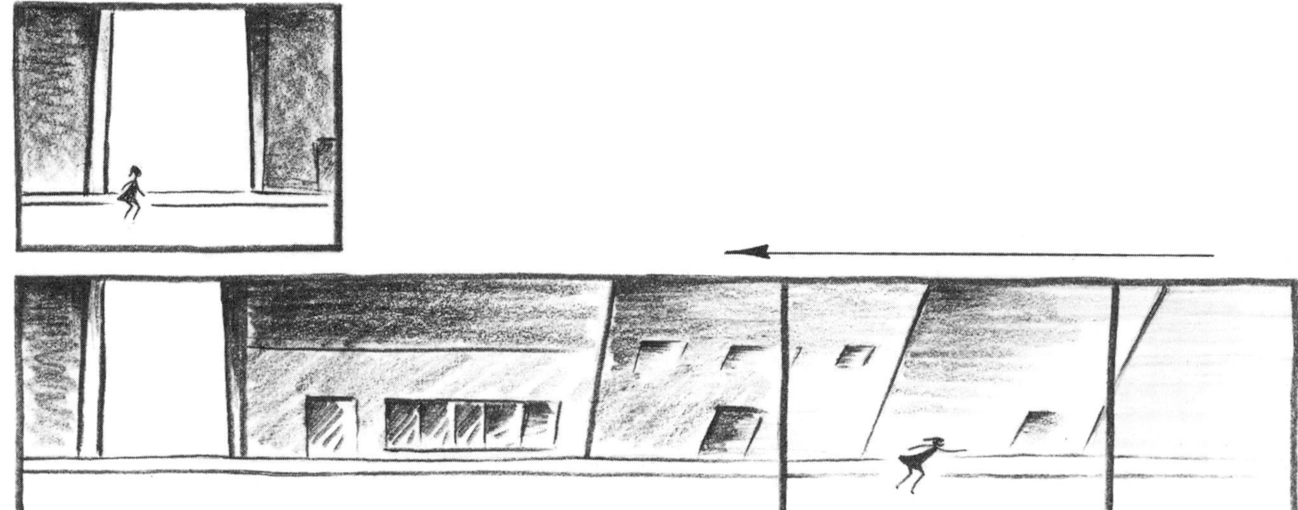

388

 With a still picture a viewer may scan at his leisure. If he desires he may spend hours studying any part of a picture which interests him. However, this leisurely perusal is not possible in viewing a motion picture. The screen image is recorded in the brain of the viewer in a predetermined time sequence and is seen only once as the film progresses. If this image on the screen is illegible in any way, the memory pattern of the viewer is broken and confusion results. When the film is over the viewer usually cannot request that it be rerun to study the confusing parts.

**Legibility and Staging**

Legibility, then, is the first concern of the film designer. The memory pattern of the whole picture must be preserved. This involves not only legible imagery, but clarity of sound, dialogue, music, and action. Yet legibility in no way guarantees a fine picture. A legible picture may be dull, uninteresting. But a confusing film which makes sense only to its designer can leave the audience feeling that the artist speaks a private language.

A factor allied to legibility is staging. Staging implies finding the best possible way to present a story point visually in relation to the scenes preceding and following it as well as to the entire sequence.

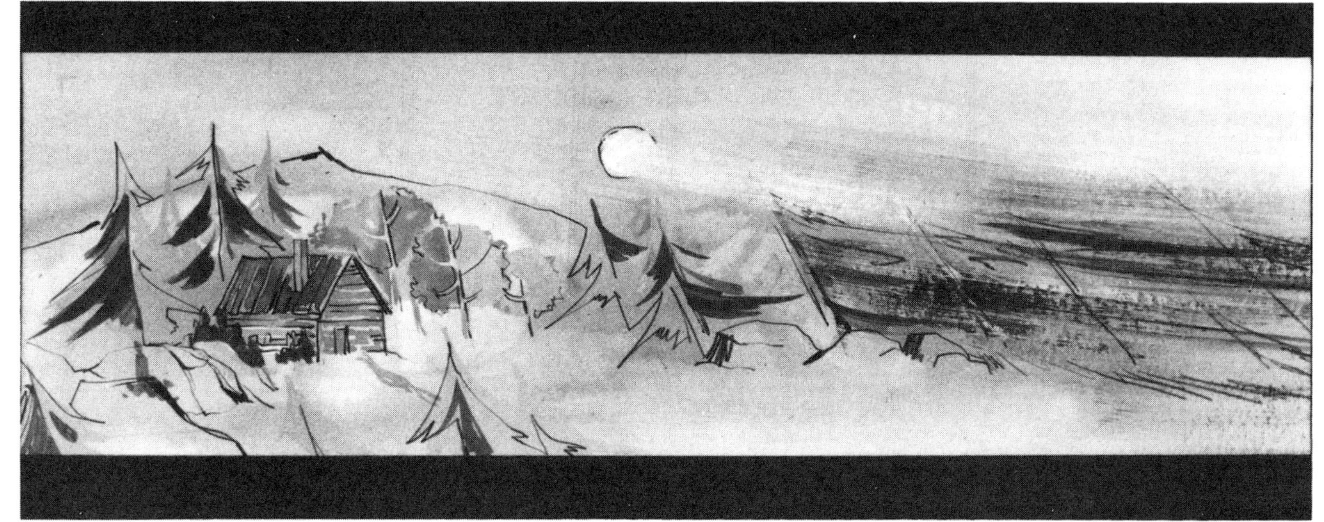

Example of "swishpan"
Courtesy FilmFair
Artist: Lee Storey

As an example, the film designer may be faced with showing at one moment an atmospheric long shot with little or no action, and next showing a medium shot of a character running which may be held on the screen but a few frames. In the first instance the film designer is faced with a compositional problem which might challenge an illustrator or painter. The shape impact of the held screen image may depend, for instance, upon an organization of large vertical shapes (*388*). But in fast action on a fast pan these same shapes suddenly may become diagonals.

Staging implies the use of still picture graphic structures understood by most artists and also the ingenious use of both live action and stop-motion camera. For example, in a moving composition on the screen what is about to happen may be as important as the action occurring.

The still picture painter may depend upon a limited number of compositional arrangements, since each picture is seen as an independent statement; however, the film artist must continually search for new and exciting ways to display his material. The same compositional arrangement used repeatedly in various scenes soon becomes monotonous. Fortunately for the film designer, a constantly evolving story in motion often suggests compositional solutions never imagined by most artists who design still pictures.

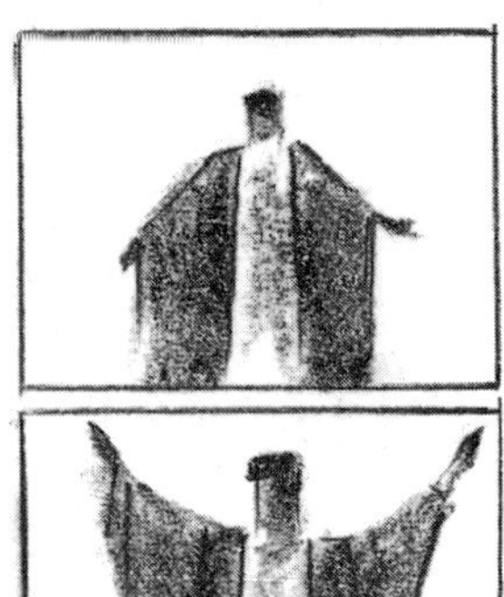
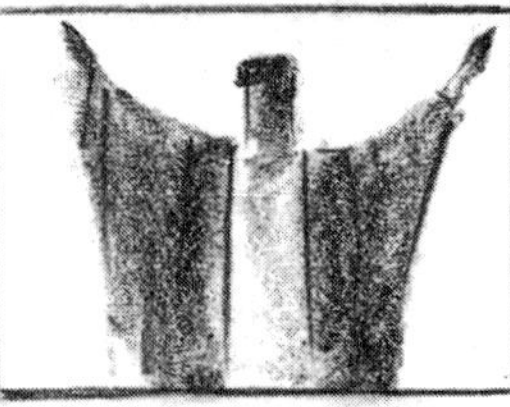

390-1A

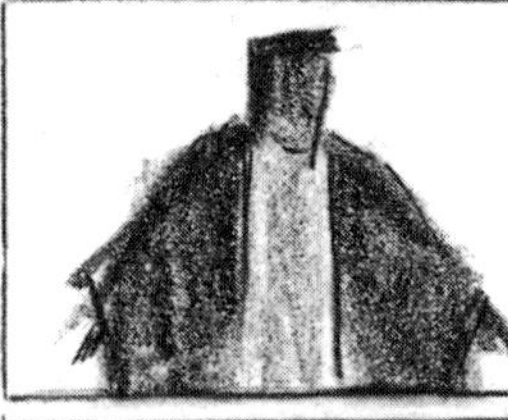
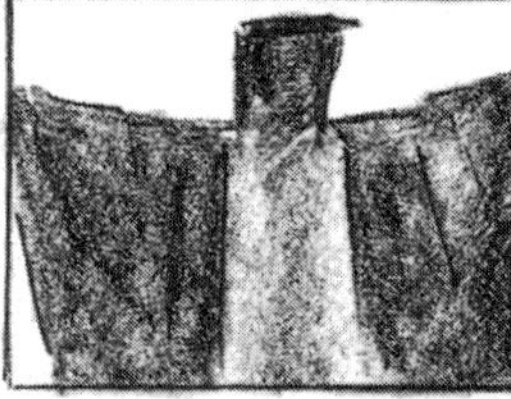

390-1B

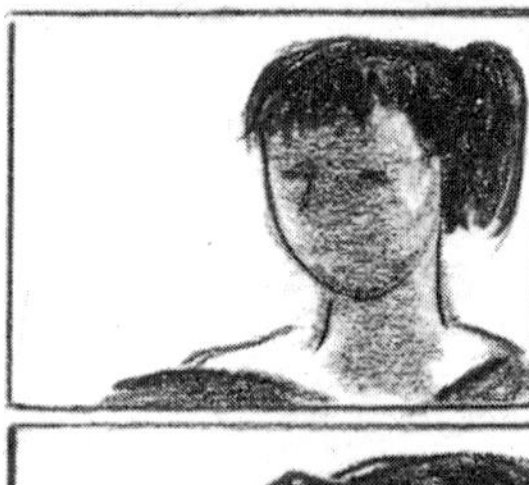
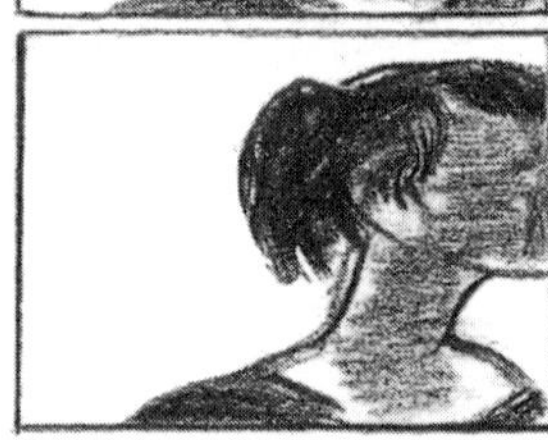

390-2

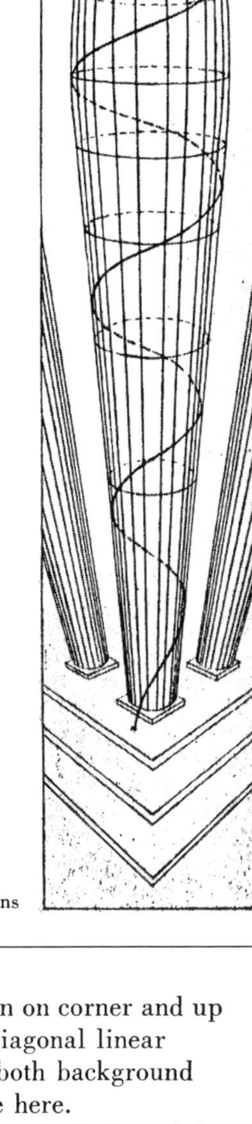

Vertical pan preliminary planning
sketch of column used for FANTASIA
Copyright 1942 Walt Disney Productions

390     A character may make a dramatic gesture, flinging his hands to both sides. In a medium long shot this presents no problem (*390-1A*). In a close middle shot as he makes his gesture both hands may leave the field. The gesture is ruined (*390-1B*). Or a character may turn as she delivers a line of dialogue and the film designer finds that her face is jammed against the edge of the field (*390-2*). The animation or the acting may be excellent, yet if it is badly staged or badly fielded the graphic results may be chaotic. By correct fielding or scene planning the action of the character will be clear, lucid.

At times the basic characteristics of a shape or volume not only may be echoed in background structures, as in still pictures, but also may be complemented by suitable camera moves. For instance, a camera move may echo the structure and action of a cubic form by lateral, up-down, and in-and-out moves.

In the same way a cube seen on corner and up or down resolves itself into diagonal linear structures which may affect both background and camera moves, as we see here.

With a knowledge of the manipulation of the stop-motion camera, the film designer can achieve many animation effects. Instead of animating an action, the camera and cell can be manipulated instead. With only simple movements of the cell startling effects may be achieved so simulating true animation that few in the audience are aware of the method employed. *Cell animation* as this procedure is known is used extensively in making commercials and educational films (*391-1*).

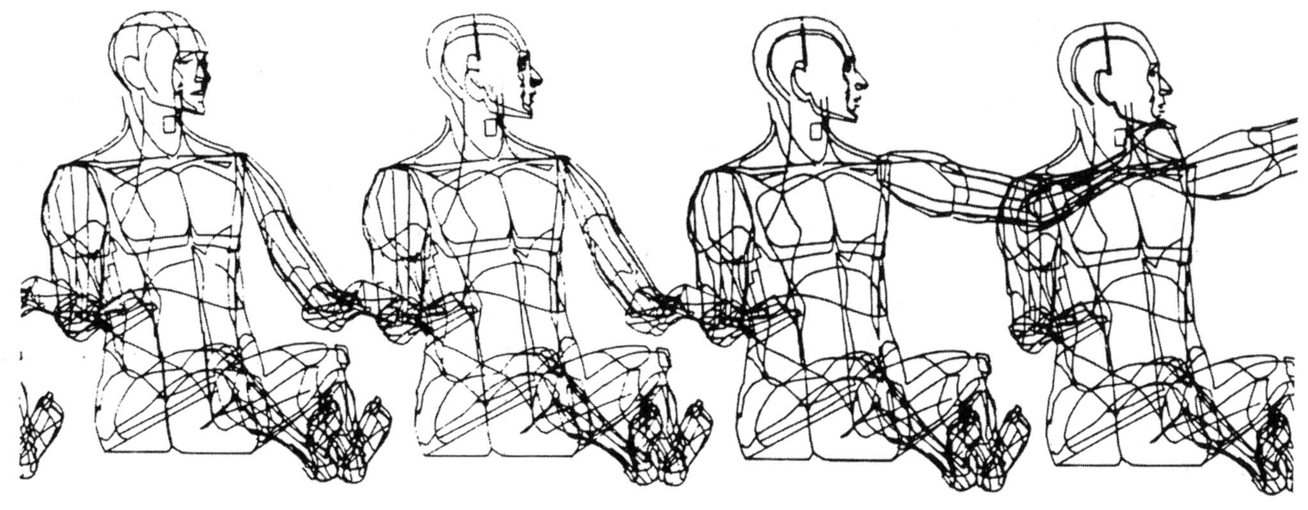

COMPUTER GRAPHICS, human figure base
Courtesy The Boeing Company

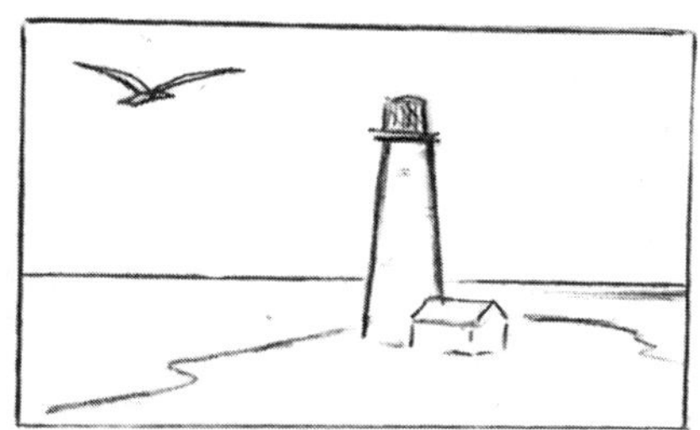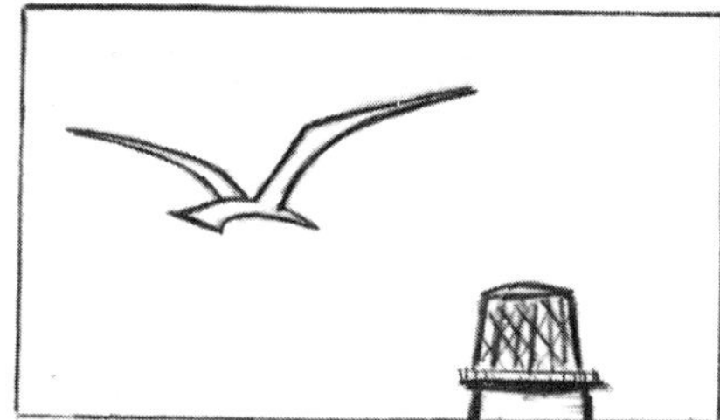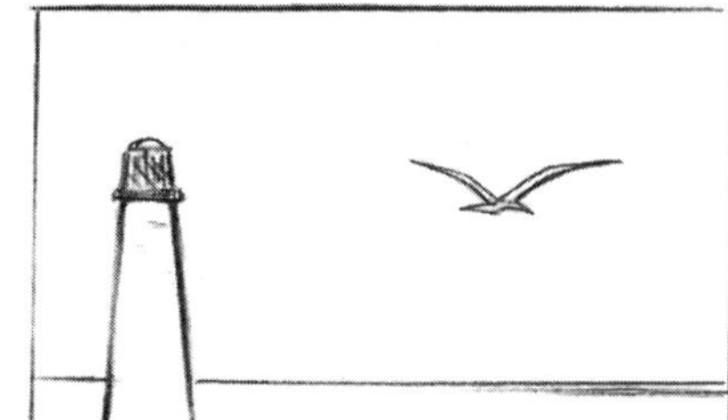

391-1

## Timing

The length of a film often suggests the appropriate graphics. Most short subjects lend themselves well to fast action, bright color, and short cuts from scene to scene. The longest scene may be only a few feet. As the tempo increases, scenes as short as three of four frames are not unusual. In many such films after the climax is reached the ending often is resolved in thirty feet or less. This fast pace, shape activity, camera activity, dialogue, music, and sound effects together create a new and bedazzling whole.

A feature film, on the other hand, makes possible the use of long scenes, slow development of a situation or a character, and slow action. But few pictures can be all fast or all slow without becoming monotonous. No matter what length the film, timing achieves variety and accenting.

Timing, especially in relation to a character,  implies the control of all the subtle actions which contribute to a gesture, the delivery of a line of dialogue or a song. Only through timing does the acting of a character become convincing. Subtlety of timing is an indication of the master of animation, acting, and direction.

## Film Graphics and Technology

The potential of film graphics is tied to changes in film technology. For example, television presents problems not encountered by the designer of theatrical film. Computer animation, divided screens, micro-photography, holograms, and other developments in film technique offer new scope for the artist.

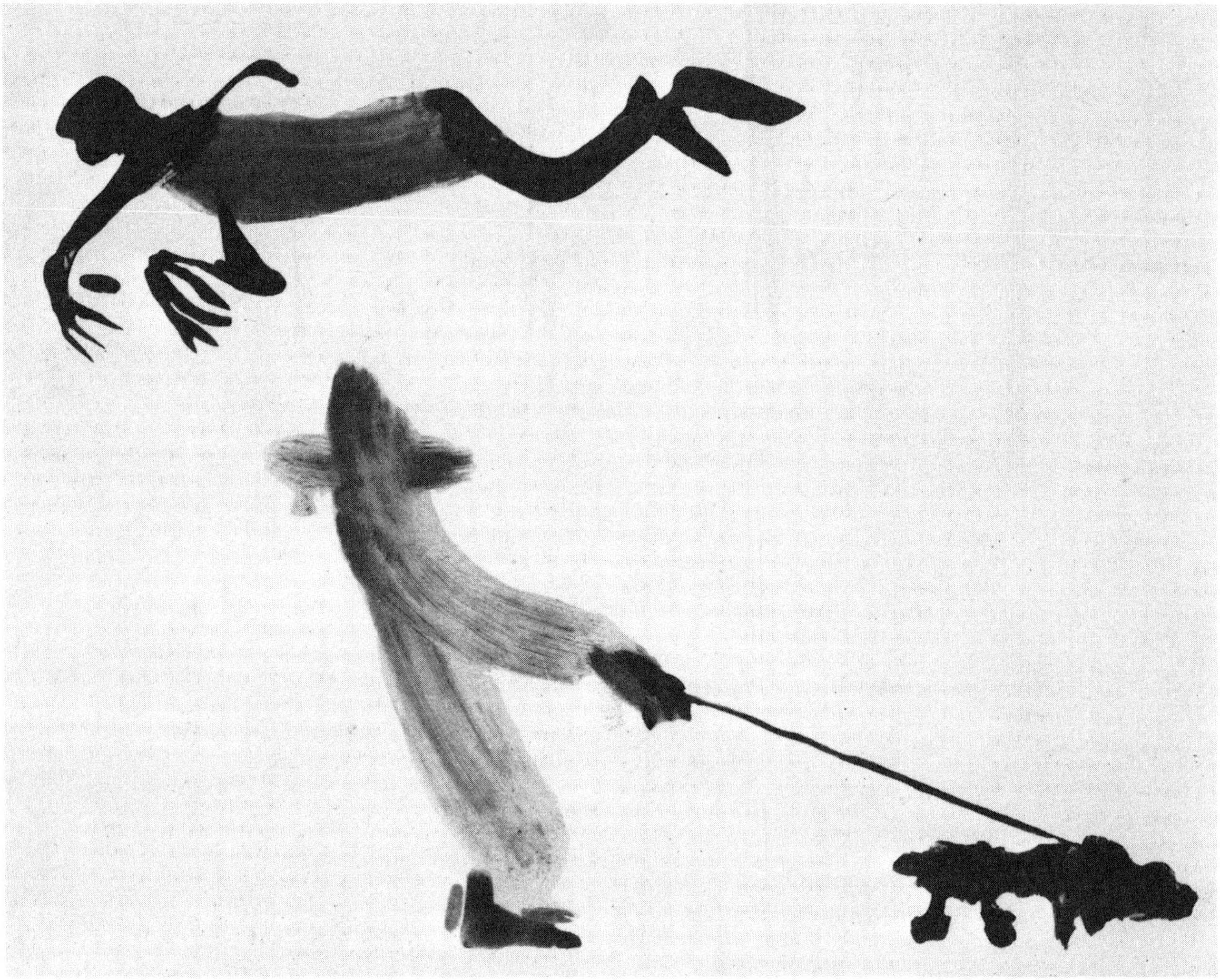

Still from THE FLYING MAN
Courtesy George Dunning
T. V. Cartoons, Ltd., London

392   Technological developments have consistently revolutionized film. For instance, in the early days of animation, backgrounds were copied onto each separate animation drawing. With the introduction of the cell each animation drawing was traced upon a transparent sheet, inked on one side, painted on the other. Now the film designer may paint or draw directly on the cell, as Dunning demonstrates here, photocopy his pictures onto the cell, or draw directly on the film itself, thus eliminating the inking and painting of cells.

The advent of sound recording made screen dialogue possible and revolutionized both live action and animation story structure. It became easier to describe an action than to show it on the screen. To say "I went to the store," is different from filming the journey.

Sound for many years was used in film simply as a recording medium tied to realistic form. As the camera developed from a recording device to a graphic tool of the artist, so the sound track and sound tape developed into a sonic tool to enrich the scope of film designer and musician. The use of multiple sources of sound in a theater was accomplished in the early forties. With the advent of multiple screens in conjunction with multiple sound sources, a new vocabulary of expression is available to the artist.

The development of stop-motion live photography made possible the animation of cutouts, three-dimensional forms, and puppets, such as these by Trnka. This type of animation, which is still developing, is a combination of live-action photography and animation, and each frame must be carefully designed and timed.

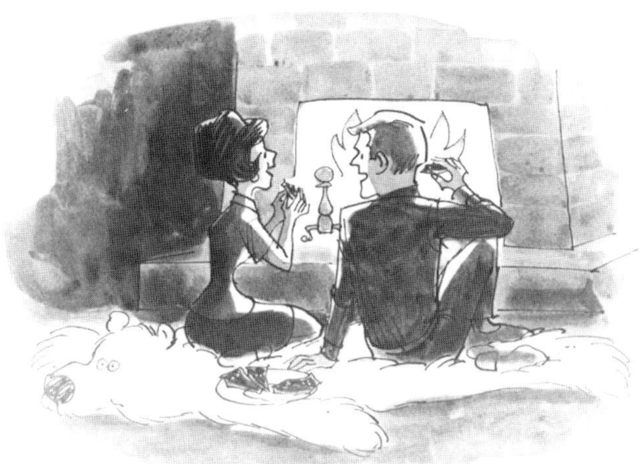

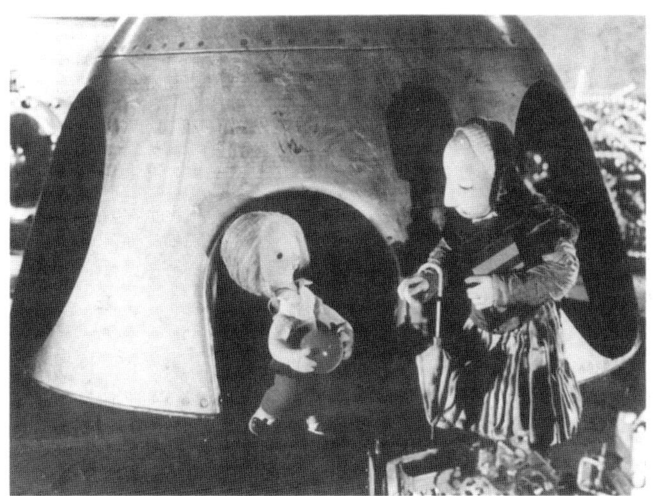



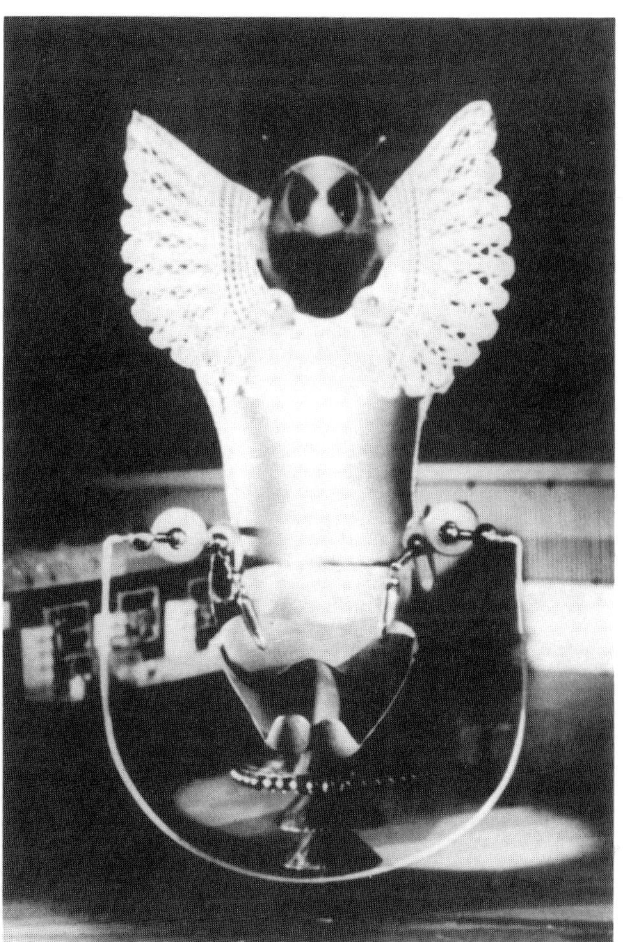

Puppets from CYBERNETIC GRANDMOTHER
Jiri Trnka
Courtesy Czech Filmexport
and Jiri Safar, Prague

The conventionally proportioned three-by-four screen developed into wide, curved, or circular screens. Film can be projected on the interior of a large dome with the audience seated or lying on the floor, upon the audience itself, or upon actors on a stage. These warped surfaces and erratic borders give great compositional scope, but create problems of legibility and surface control allied to those of the ceramist and painter of vignettes working with still pictures.

The development of large panel TV screens for the home and private film-tape libraries on closed-circuit TV offer new challenges to the artist rivaling the graphic scope and interest of serigraphs, lithographs, and other limited edition prints. Undoubtedly film graphics of tomorrow will no more resemble those of today than Renaissance painting does contemporary painting.

## Change of Color

Before the development of color film, black and white backgrounds were a form of abstraction which lent themselves rather well to animation action. In live action, striking black and white patterns are often seen in otherwise dull Westerns. With the introduction of color, backgrounds both in live action and animation present new problems. The very intensity of a colored shape becomes an event. Unfortunately there is often a temptation to mute color rather than to exploit its dynamic potential.

New techniques and concepts may solve old problems of film which have persisted since its inception. For example, one of the most trying problems in making an animated film has been to make a painted still background seem appropriate to the action of the characters as in this fireside scene.

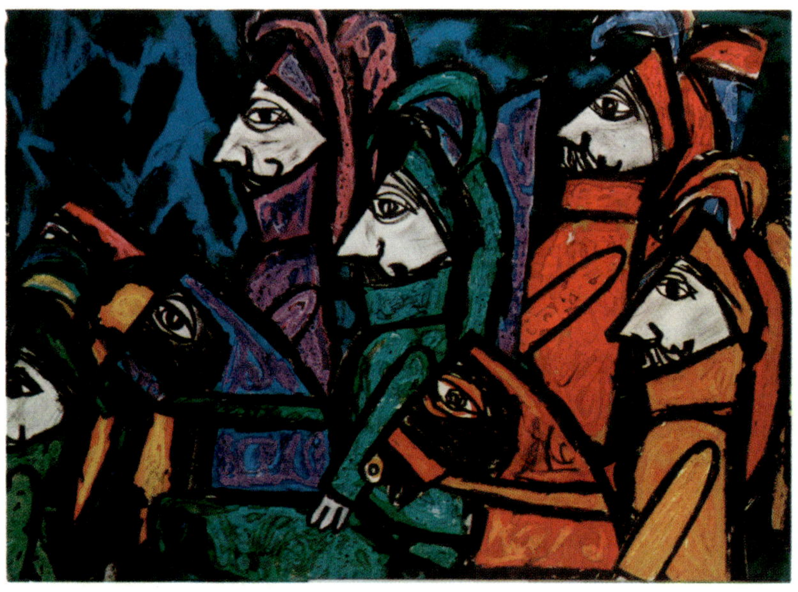

Still from THE THIEVING MAGPIE
Courtesy Emilio Luzzati,
Giulio Gianini, Rome

In spite of ingenious devices such as the multi-plane camera developed in the mid-thirties, the basic problem in animation still remains unsolved: that is how to relate the space generated by a moving shape or volume to a graphic space generated by non-moving painted shapes or volumes.

The introduction of limited animation with its accompanying emphasis upon flat shapes and highly styled action makes the use of bright color and flat backgrounds more acceptable. Even so, the discrepancy remains between still backgrounds and moving character.

There are clues to the problem. For instance, extended research into the function of color in motion may revolutionize film graphics just as other technological advances have in the past. Since color has been considered an attribute of shape or volume, color in film graphics usually has been considered less important than action.

For instance, a character wearing a red jacket normally moves on the screen as an actor moves on a stage. As he moves back and forth, fast or slow, the jacket maintains a constant red. Textured and patterned shapes also remain the same.

Change of color of a shape has been exploited in film to a limited degree since the early thirties, usually as a gag. For example, a character blushes or turns sickly green. Almost always, however, the change of color is confined to shapes involved.

With limited animation also came experiments in animating a character as a line drawing moving over areas of color. In this way background and character are integrated in color, but separated through action, as we see here.

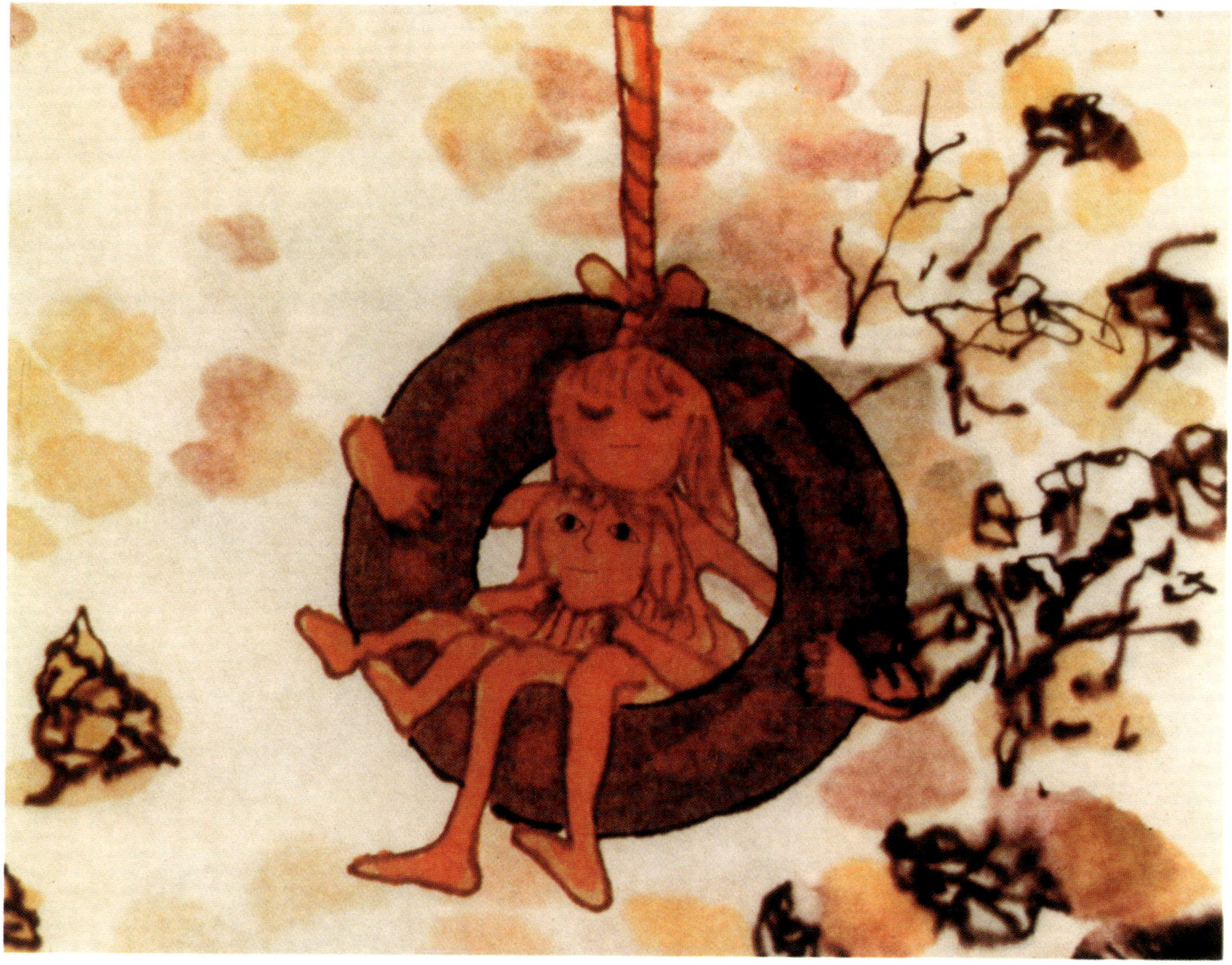

Still from WINDY DAY
John and Faith Hubley
The Hubley Studio, Inc., N. Y.

But color, as well as texture or pattern, need not be confined as an attribute of shape. Color may be conceived as having an independent existence, freeing itself of shape. The red of a jacket may be larger or smaller than the shape. In fact as an independent factor it need not even persist in remaining red.

Not only may color as an attribute of shape be liberated through action, but also its relation to a shape in action is yet to be explored. Little has been done to correlate speed to color especially in relation to characters. Backgrounds in animation often are made less intense as a character moves faster and faster across the screen on a fast pan, but change of color as an integral factor in character action has not been exploited in either live action or animation.

Can the red jacket change color, value, or intensity as the character intensifies or reduces speed? Should an arm in action change color or intensity from the rest of the body? Can change of color become a way to integrate background and action? Can change of mood or expression be sustained by a change of color, perhaps on a separate screen?

Here then in change of color may lie revolutionary developments in film graphics. We have seen that by accepting a new concept of color the still picture painter was forced to develop a new concept of drawing. By exploiting change of color on the screen new concepts of story, new concepts of shape, new concepts of picture making are inevitable. With the integration of color and action a whole new world of film graphics must evolve.

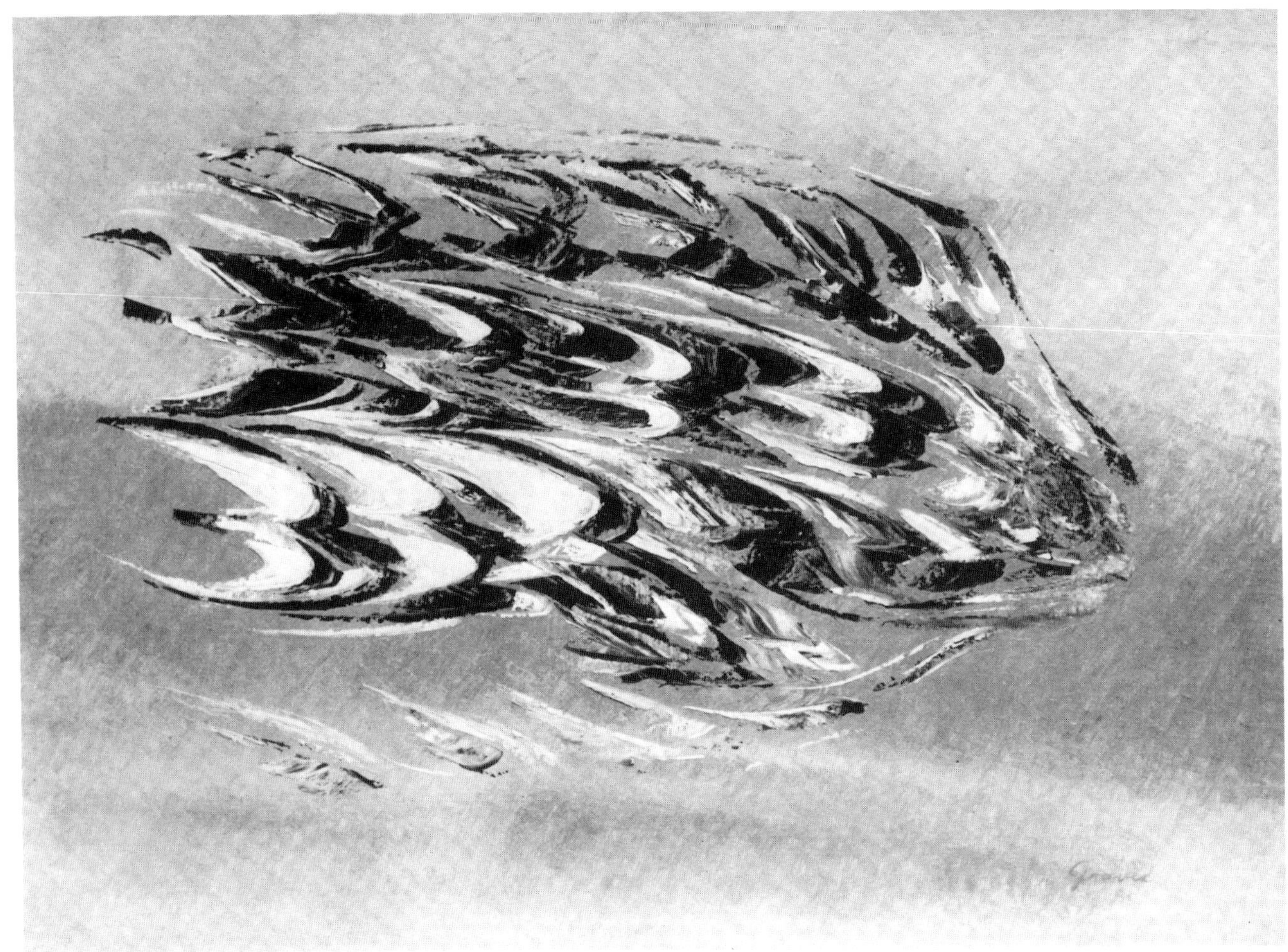

Morris Graves (American, 1910-  )
FLIGHT OF PLOVER, 1955; 36″ x 48″
oil on composition board
Collection of the Whitney Museum of American Art, N.Y.
(Photograph: Geoffrey Clements)



# 34  Conclusion

## The Limits of a Picture

To review, we have found that the overwhelming body of pictures produced to date have been organizations of graphic points, lines, or areas placed on, or projected on a flat surface, as in the Graves' painting above. Certain pictures may involve warped surfaces, but even collages and assemblages of three-dimensional forms usually relate to some kind of surface. Pictures now include constructions of all kinds, from the conventional painting on canvas to sculpture. Curiously enough, a picture of this latter nature is often an extension of bas-relief, exploited long ago by the Egyptians.

We also found that pictures as a rule fall into three categories: the illustrative, the abstract, the non-representational. Of course many pictures are almost impossible to consign to a particular category.

Artist unknown (Egyptian)
GEESE OF MEIDUM, frieze from the Mastaba of Itet
at Meidum, 2700; 9¾″ x 16½″
painting on stucco
Courtesy The Egyptian Museum, United Arab Republic

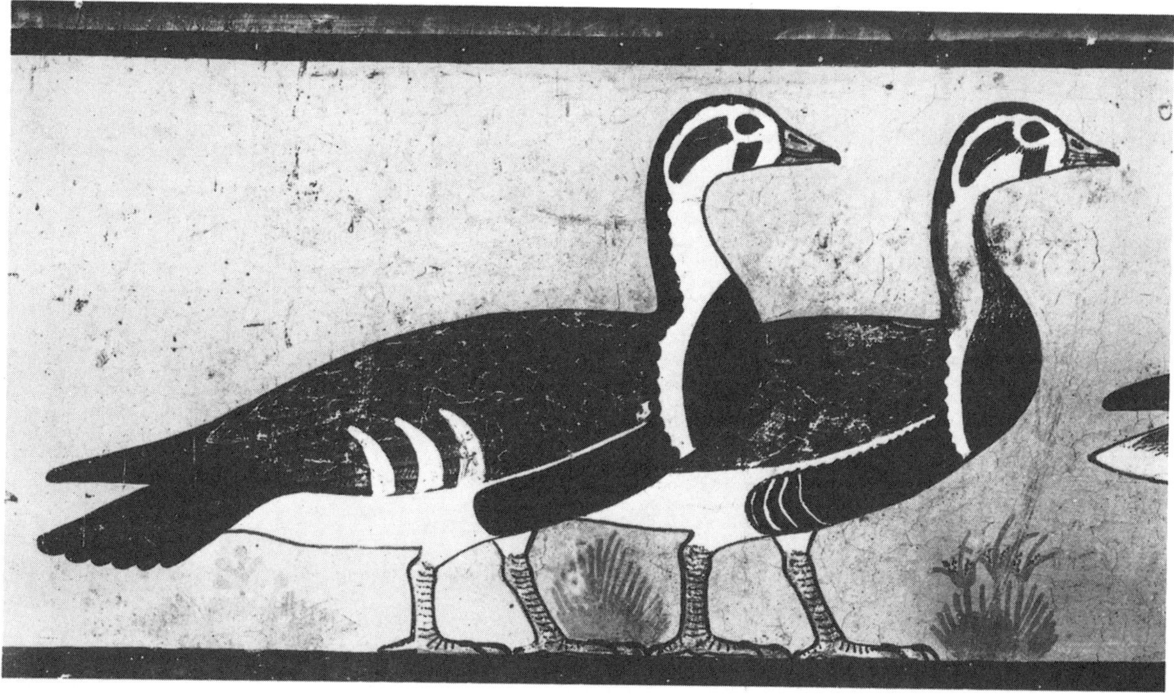

## Forces Manifested in Space

We have noted how a volume tends to overwhelm
space in a still picture. We also have found
that a volume is always a shape. By transposing
from rendering to sectional perspective, we
learn to see shape growing out of a section.
Consequently, we see that the control of section,
or shape, implies the generation of graphic
space.

However, as our awareness of shape becomes
more acute, we often become blind to graphic
space. We are tempted simply to design the
shapes and pay little or no attention to the space
factor. Frequently the picture then becomes flat,
overly decorative, or ornamental. A fine
decorative design, such as the geese in this
fresco, is based on a careful balance between
space and shape.

But shape is also a surface. When we draw a
volume we also draw a shape, and this shape is
a surface. It occupies a certain area of the
picture surface. This shape may, in turn, be
composed of more than one shape each
occupying part of the confined surface.

In the same way an abstract shape, one
suggesting no thickness, is still a surface for it
disturbs a certain area of the picture surface.
Since a line is one limit of an area, at times it
too may become a surface, either as part of a
volume or shape, or as an abstract element in
the picture.

And now we arrive at a critical point in the
structure of a picture, the space factor. Shape
and surface are synonymous. By controlling
shape, or surface, we generate space. Shape is a
manifestation of space.

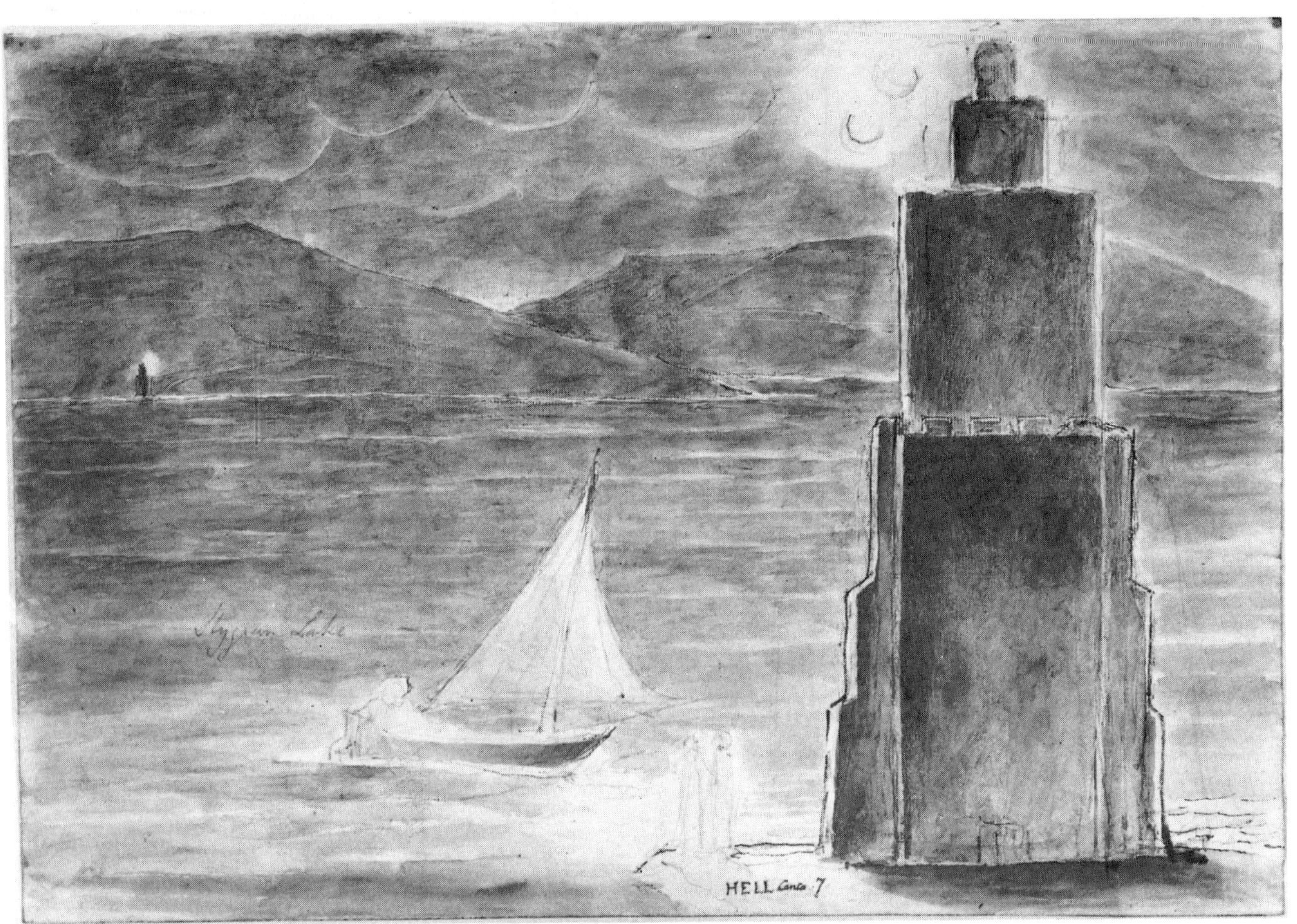



William Blake (English, 1757-1827)
DANTE AND VIRGIL ON THE EDGE OF THE
STYGIAN POOL AT FOOT OF A TOWER, from
Dante's *THE DIVINE COMEDY*
1824-1827; 14⅜" x 20½"; pencil and gray wash
Courtesy of the Fogg Art Museum, Harvard University
Bequest of Grenville L. Winthrop

Franz Kline (American, 1910-1962)
SIEGFRIED, 1958; 103" x 81"; oil on canvas
Collection of Museum of Art, Carnegie Institute, Pittsburgh

The surface of a volume is also the surface, or part of the surface, of space. As we have seen they are interchangeable. The color of a surface of a volume, or shape, is also an attribute of that portion of the space contacting either. As we saw in the exercise using the honey bubble, the golden globe is a manifestation of space, yet the color we see is associated directly to this space. The space is golden.

We discovered that primarily because of the way we use our eyes to observe nature, we consider a form more important than the surrounding space—the space matrix. This is partly because of the physical attributes of the form in nature (hardness, weight, etc.), partly because of the isolation of a form in its environment, and partly because of its action, real or apparent. Particularly in designing live action motion pictures may we tend to overemphasize aspects of form.

Much of our lack of awareness of the space matrix is due to its usual invisibility, its lack of local color. Unfortunately, we have learned to associate color to volume and shape, not to the enclosing space matrix. But with close observation we can train ourselves to see any color area or combination of black, grays, or white as a manifestation of space.

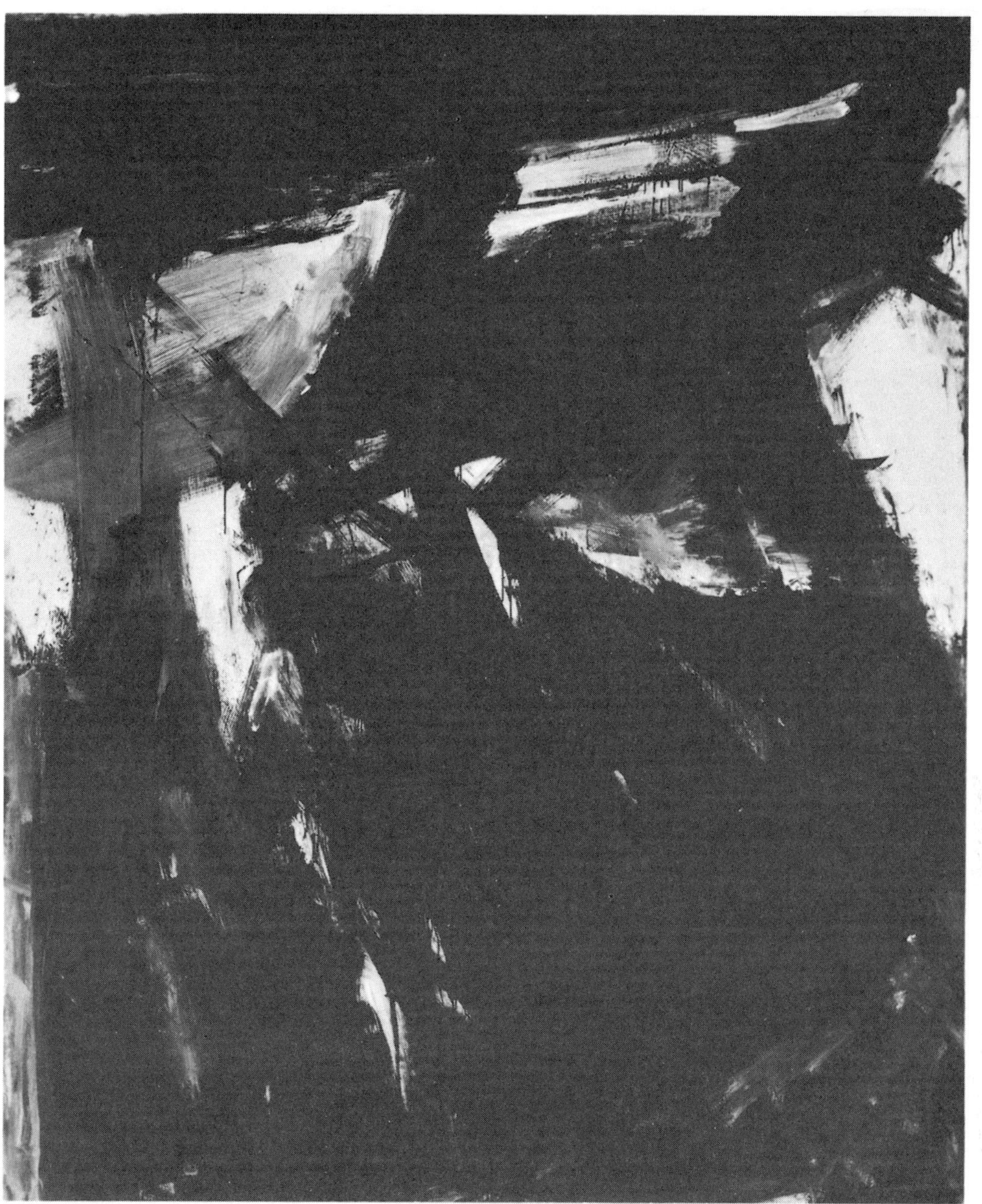

## Energy

We see now that all dynamic forces potential in
a picture must be translated into visual terms.
The intensity of color, the impact of shape, the
dramatic use of movement in a still picture, or
action in a motion picture must be expressed
first and last as an organization of graphic
surfaces. Tying all surfaces into a whole is the
space matrix which is manifested by these
surfaces.

How we organize these picture factors
determines the degree of energy, the intensity of
forces inherent in our graphic statement. Only
by exploitation of these forces can we move our
audience profoundly.

Whether this energy factor is restrained, as in
Blake's painting, or vibrant, as in Kline's
*Siegfried*, it seems to be the one link that makes
for universality of viewer response. It is the
energy factor which is common to all fine
pictures made by artists of all periods, in all
countries, through the whole history of art.
From primitive statements to the sophisticated
organization of a mural or a well-designed
motion picture, the amount of our emotional
response to such graphic organizations, such
manifestations of energy, is what determines the
successful picture. The degree of vitality of a
picture is an indication of its merits as a work
of art.

# ACKNOWLEDGMENTS

I wish to give special acknowledgment for assistance in obtaining rights and reproductions to the following individuals and organizations: Mrs. Barbara Adler, Head, Rights and Reproductions, Harry N. Abrams, Inc., New York City; Sam E. Brown, Asst. Exec. Director, Academy of Motion Picture Arts and Sciences, Hollywood, Calif.; Dr. E. Gunter Troche, Director, Achenbach Foundation for Graphic Arts, San Francisco, Calif.; Josef Albers, New Haven, Conn.; Marion B. Carr, The American Museum of Natural History, New York City; Robert G. Harper, Exec. Vice-President, American Republic Insurance Co., Des Moines, Iowa; E. Goeyvaerts, Treasurer, Antwerp Cathedral, Belgium; Dr. Harold Joachim, Curator of Prints, and Betty B. Saxon, Reproduction Rights and Contracts, The Art Institute of Chicago, Ill.; Aune Lindström, Director, The Art Museum of Ateneum, Helsinki, Finland; Dolores Fenn, Assoc. Editor, ART NEWS magazine, New York City; Janet L. Snow, Art Reference Bureau, Inc., Ancram, N. Y.; Prof. Dr. Kurt Badt, Uberlingen, Germany; David McIntyre, Asst. Director, The Baltimore Museum of Art, Md.; Mr. and Mrs. Edgar F. Berman, Lutherville, Md.; William Fetter and Rick Kiefer, The Boeing Company, Seattle, Wash.; Peter L. Macnair, Curator of Ethnology, British Columbia Provincial Museum, Victoria, B. C.; Henry Riad, Chief Curator, The Egyptian Museum, Cairo, United Arab Republic; Jiri Safár and Czechoslovakia Filmexport, Prague; Gene Deitch, Prague, Czechoslovakia; Mukul Chandra Dey (Deva), East Bengal, India; Gary Goldsmith, Producer, Dimension Films, Hollywood, Calif.; Ken Peterson, Andy Engman, and Esta Haight, Walt Disney Studio, Burbank, Calif.; H. E. Gagan, Doyle, Dane, & Bernbach, Los Angeles, Calif.; M. G. Rama Ram, Embassy of India, Washington, D. C.; Gus Jekel, Producer, FilmFair, Studio City, Calif.; Les Goldman, Producer, Film Sense, Hollywood, Calif.; Sr. Manuel Alvarez Bravo, Fondo Editorial de la Plastica Mexicana, Mexico, D. F.; Dr. Ernest Nash, Fototeca Unione, Presso Accademia Americana, Rome, Italy; Horace Marston, French Reproduction Rights, New York City; Dr. Hildegard Klein, Frobenius Institute, Frankfurt-am-Main, Germany; Prof. Italo Faldi, Galleria Nazionale d'Arte Antica, Rome, Italy; Elena Gianini, Giulio Gianini, Rome, Italy; Mrs. Maurice Gollub, Encino, Calif.; The Hispanic Society of America, New York City; John Hubley, The Hubley Studio, New York City; Sr. Jorge Hernandez Campos, Instituto Nacional de Bellas Artes, Mexico, D. F.; Sarah E. Freeman, Curator, Numismatics, The John Work Garrett Library of The Johns Hopkins University, Baltimore, Md.; Dr. Erwin N. Auer, Director, Kunsthistoriches Museum, Vienna; Georg Duthaler, Assistant, Kunstmuseum, Basel, Switzerland; Mrs. C. W. Wilson, Manager, Felix Landau Gallery, Los Angeles, Calif.; Gianni Mattioli, Milan, Italy; Mrs. Nada Saporiti, Photographic Services, The Metropolitan Museum of Art, New York City; Edward A. Foster, Curator of Prints & Drawings, The Minneapolis Institute of Arts, Minn.; Jimmy T. Murakami, Producer, Murakami-Wolf Films, Hollywood, Calif.; Michael D. Murphy, Malibu, Calif.; Richard L. Tooke, Supervisor of Rights and Reproductions, The Museum of Modern Art, New York City; Richard W. Lang, Curator, Museum of Navaho Ceremonial Art, Santa Fe, N. M.; Miss Ann Blyth, The National Gallery, London, England; R. H. Hubbard, Chief Curator, National Gallery of Canada, Ottowa; Rudolph G. Lorenz, The New York Graphic Society Ltd., Greenwich, Conn.; Mrs. Anna Horan, The Philadelphia Museum of Art, Penna.; Mowry Baden, Pomona College Art Dept., Claremont, Calif.; Irinia Antonova, Director, Pushkin Museum of Fine Arts, Moscow, USSR.; Gerald Nordland, Director, San Francisco Museum of Art, Calif.; Allessandro Bettagno, San Giorgio Maggiore, Venice, Italy; Daniel Potamio Dominguez Ponce, Curator, San Martin y San Tomás Apóstol, Toledo, Spain; Stanley W. Hess, Photographic Records, Seattle Art Museum, Wash.; Irene Gunther, Security-Pacific National Bank, Woodland Hills, Calif.; Earl Theisen, Sepulveda, Calif.; Gerald Ray, Director, Tompkins, Ray, Martel y Compania, S. A., Mexico, D. F.; George Dunning, T. V. Cartoons, London, England; Ryoji Ito, Secretary-General, Japanese National Commission for UNESCO, Tokyo, Japan; Prof. John Rewald, Art Department, University of Chicago, Ill.; Henry G. Saperstein, President, UPA Pictures, Inc., Burbank, Calif.; Mrs. Denny Judson, Whitney Museum of American Art, New York City.

# BIBLIOGRAPHY


Barr, Alfred H. Jr., ed. *Cubism and Abstract Art*. New York: The Museum of Modern Art. 1936.

————. *Picasso-Fifty Years of His Art*. New York: The Museum of Modern Art, 1946.

Bouleau, Charles. *The Painter's Secret Geometry*. New York: Harcourt, Brace & World, Inc., 1936.

Charlot, Jean. *Art from the Mayans to Disney*. New York: Sheed & Ward, 1939.

————. *Charlot Murals in Georgia*. Athens: University of Georgia Press, 1945.

Christensen, Erwin O. *A Pictorial History of Western Art*. New York: Mentor Books, 1964.

Dey, Mukul Chandra. *My Pilgrimages to Ajanta and Bagh*. New York: Geo. H. Doran Co., 1925.

Douglas, Frederick H., and d'Harnoncourt, René. *Indian Art of the United States*. New York: The Museum of Modern Art, 1941.

Eisenstein, Sergei M. *The Film Sense*. New York: Harcourt, Brace & Co., Inc., 1942.

Frobenius, Prof. Leo, and Fox, Douglas C. *Prehistoric Rock Pictures in Europe and Africa*. New York: The Museum of Modern Art, 1937.

Gardner, Helen. *Art Through the Ages*. New York: Harcourt, Brace & Co., Inc., 1936.

Janson, H. W. *History of Art*. New York: Harry N. Abrams, 1962.

————. *The Picture History of Painting*. New York: Harry N. Abrams, Inc., 1957.

Kepes, Gyorgy. *Language of Vision*. Chicago: Paul Theobald, 1945.

Klee, Paul. *Pedagogical Sketchbook*. New York: Nierendorf Gallery, 1944.

Loran, Erle. *Cézanne's Composition*. Berkeley and Los Angeles: University of California Press, 1944.

Maholy-Nagy, L. *Vision In Motion*. Chicago: Paul Theobald, 1947.

Power, J. W. *Eléments de la Construction Picturale*. Paris: Antoine Roche, 1932.

Read, Herbert. *A Concise History of Modern Painting*. New York: Frederick Praeger, 1959.

Rich, Daniel Catton. *Seurat and the Evolution of "La Grande Jatte"*. Chicago: The University of Chicago Press, 1935.

# INDEX

410

413